Limits
of
Justice

Limits
of
Justice

The Courts' Role in
School Desegregation

Edited by
Howard I. Kalodner and James J. Fishman
with an introduction by
Howard I. Kalodner

Ballinger Publishing Company • Cambridge, Massachusetts
A Subsidiary of J.B. Lippincott Company

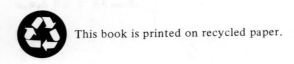

 This book is printed on recycled paper.

International Standard Book Number: 0–88410–226–2

Library of Congress Catalog Card Number: 77-1848

Printed in the United States of America

Library of Congress Cataloging in Publication Data
Main entry under title:

Limits of justice.

Includes index.
1. Segregation in education—Law and legislation—United States—Cases. 2. School integration—United States—Case studies. I. Kalodner, Howard I. II. Fishman, James J.
KF4154.L5   344'.73'0798   77-1848
ISBN 0-88410-226-2

Contents

v

Preface

The essays in this volume were prepared as part of a project of the Institute of Judicial Administration. Funds for the project were provided by the Ford Foundation. The purpose of the project was to study the role of courts in the adjudication of school desegregation cases. The work was conducted over an eighteen-month period from the fall of 1974 until the spring of 1976. The project consisted of the preparation of essays, primarily case studies, and the conducting of conferences. The conferences, held in the fall and winter of 1975, included judges, lawyers, and educators. The conferences were not recorded and the views expressed by the participants are confidential, but they served to inform me, and I hope are reflected in the essay that introduces this volume.

I am grateful to IJA, to the Ford Foundation, and to those who contributed, both in writing and orally, to this study. The views expressed throughout the book are those of the respective authors and not necessarily those of IJA or the Ford Foundation.

Several of the case studies and essays prepared under the auspices of this project have already been published elsewhere. One fine essay, on Richmond, Virginia, by Professors Leedes and O'Fallon, was published in the *University of Richmond Law Review.* Leedes and O'Fallon, "School Desegregation in Richmond: A Case History," 10 *University of Richmond Law Review* 1 (1975). Because of the age of the case and limits on the length of this volume, it has, regretfully, been omitted here. The essay on Indianapolis, in somewhat differet form, is being published by the *Indianapolis Law Review.* Professor Bell's essay has been published in 85 *Yale Law Journal* 470 (1976).

My personal gratitude is expressed to Mrs. Gerry Hansen at IJA who served as the administrative genius behind both our conferences and our extensive communications with our authors; to Cynthia Philip who aided our literary style; and to Jim Fishman, co-editor of this volume, who worked tirelessly as author and editor on this effort.

HOWARD I. KALODNER

Limits
of
Justice

 *INTRODUCTION*

Howard I. Kalodner

Twenty-two years have passed since the Supreme Court of the
United States decided in *Brown v. Board of Education* that the
Constitution of the United States prohibited segregation by race in
the public school systems. The twenty-two years have been marked by the
gradual disappearance of the "dual school system" that existed throughout the
southeastern United States, but an increase in the degree to which school systems
in metropolitan areas throughout the United States have become predominantly
characterized by one race schools has also occurred. Most school board members
contend that this pattern simply and sadly reflects the segregated housing patterns of the United States coupled with the neighborhood school attendance-
zone practice, which antedates any issue of race and which is based on sound
educational psychological theory. In many cases, however, including cases involving major cities in the United States, the federal courts have been persuaded
by evidence adduced by plaintiffs that the segregation of the races has, in these
instances, been in part at least the product of manipulations of the attendance
zones and of new school construction programs. These findings have required
the courts to design and implement remedies that will eliminate any vestige of
unconstitutional segregation in the schools of the offending school board.

In recent years public consciousness of school desegregation litigation and of
judicial orders affecting the school systems has grown as an increasing number
of nonsouthern cases are decided. Increases in public consciousness are not
necessarily accompanied by increases in public understanding. This volume is

A co-editor of this book, Professor Kalodner was project director of the project of the
Institute of Judicial Administration pursuant to which this essay, and the others in the
volume, was prepared. He was then a professor of law at New York University School
of Law and director of the Institute of Judicial Administration. He is presently Dean of
Western New England College School of Law.

1

intended to serve as a basis upon which an interested lay person, lawyer, professional educator, government functionary, or judge can become informed about one important aspect of school desegregation—the role of the courts as revealed by several important desegregation cases.

There have been forty or fifty cases in the federal and state courts in the 1970–1975 period that have reached at least the stage of trial. More than one-half have arisen in the North and West in jurisdictions that never maintained a dual school system. We have selected case studies of seven legal cases for inclusion in this volume. In addition to these studies of individual litigation, there are essays on the role of the professional educator in desegregation cases and the plaintiff client-counsel relationship. The authors are, in general, experts, and come to their studies with both expertise and a point of view. We believe that the diversity of authors represented here provides a multiplicity of perspectives which, in totality, generates—if not an unbiased product—at least one that is multi- and not uni-biased.

It is not the primary purpose of this introductory essay to describe in detail the studies; they must essentially speak for themselves. The function of this essay is to provide a structure and a context for analysis. In doing so the emphasis is placed on issues other than constitutional interpretation. None of these constitutional questions differs in character from hundreds of other constitutional law issues that can be listed as pressing for decision in any given year.

But the problems of the role of the courts in desegregation cases may raise problems which, if not unique, are at least unusual. And many, if not all, are not likely to be resolved by appellate decisions.

ISOLATION OF THE COURTS

The power of the courts to order compliance with the U.S. Constitution distinguishes our system as one whose devotion to democracy is qualified by the realization that justice and fair treatment may not in some instances be generated by majority decision-making. But the power thus vested in the courts carries with it serious burdens; relevant here is the burden borne by one whose obligation is to tell the majority or a controlling minority that it is wrong, and more than that, to order it to do right. This is not, of course, a situation unique to school desegregation cases. These cases, however, more than any other, combine two characteristics—first, that the courts have been virtually entirely abandoned by every other actor in our array of governmental institutions; and second, that masses of persons are limited in their individual initiative by the order of the courts.

Flight from issues of school desegregation has characterized the federal government in recent years. Virtually the only question remaining in Washington is whether the Congress and President will attempt to limit more stringently the scope and duration of remedies to which resort has been made by the courts in their effort to procure for all public school students their constitutional rights.

Virtually every case study contained herein shows a school board in similar flight. I do not refer to the stage at which a particular school board contests the issue of whether it has in fact violated the Constitution, at least in those cases in which the school board is in good faith of the opinion that it has not violated the Constitution. But I do refer to the variety of delaying tactics school boards have resorted to after a judicial decision that their past conduct has violated constitutional rights.

If it is possible to generalize from desegregation cases at all, and if it is not unreasonable to judge motive from conduct, many school boards pursue from the outset a course designed to shift the entire political burden of desegregation on the courts. This may seem to be a politically rational path. It also appears to be one which claims some justification for noncompliance with the Constitution. But there is none. Democracy may not long be able to afford civil disobedience in the form of citizen noncompliance with penal or civil laws; it is certain that democracy cannot long survive governmental noncompliance with constitutional rights.

Nor are the school boards alone in this behavior. Mayors, governors, city councils, and state legislatures all turn their backs on the issue. Indeed, at least one view would have it that in Boston the police turned their backs, as well.

Since the institution most directly affected by a school desegregation case is the school system itself, one would expect to find the professional school staff in each city working to desegregate—even absent litigation—if only to avoid the disruptive impact of litigation. It may be that much of such planning has been done but has not been implemented because of opposition of the school board. But in many cases it has not been proposed for adoption by the professional and then refused by the board; rather, it has not been proposed at all. The professional school person's position seems to be that it is not wise to move one-quarter inch in front of the perceived position of the school board. One can speculate about the reasons for this view. First, the superintendent is subject to and may realistically fear dismissal by the board. Superintendents apparently move about more than baseball players, except that departure from one employer is not automatically accompanied by assignment to another. Second, school staffs as a whole seem to operate, throughout the structure, on the principle that advancement through the ranks goes to persons who most ably preserve the status quo. Third, the complex bureaucracy which typifies the large urban school is resistant to and discourages innovation.

None of these phenomena would quickly bring the professional school person to raise in public the existence of segregation and propose plans for ending it. And yet in many cities and towns, school boards and superintendents—or the latter alone—have moved their systems toward desegregation, sometimes without litigation, sometimes immediately upon a holding that the system has operated in violation of the Constitution. It would be useful to know what the cultural, intellectual, and political components are that have characterized these latter situations. The present study is one of litigation, and all too frequently the case studies reflect quite different behavior on the part of the school boards and school personnel involved.

And so, with rare exceptions, the school staffs, school boards, state commissioners of education, state legislators, governors, and federal agencies and officials have left to the courts the job not only of defining the scope of constitutional rights but of implementing those rights.

CONFLICT RESOLUTION WITHOUT
A JUDGMENT ORDER

Every litigator knows that, quite aside from a formal resolution of a dispute through final adjudication, dispute resolution is facilitated by the knowledge that there is about to be imposed upon the client a judge-made resolution. This leverage toward a negotiated settlement between the parties grows larger as one moves progressively through the stages of litigation, from the filing of a complaint until the closing arguments of counsel. These pressures produce settlements. The consequences of agreed-upon resolutions are several. On the most mundane level, settlements relieve the courts of the time that would be occupied with the balance of the adjudication. Jurisprudential significance is far greater, however. Even if negotiated under pressure, the stipulated settlement represents a commitment by each party; thus compliance with the resolution is anticipated not alone on the basis of the principle of obedience to authority but also on the principle of compliance with one's own word—a principle of private rather than public morality.

In cases involving the more general public interest, settlement might be perceived as a way of relieving the courts of at least a portion of the burden of responsibility and, in the public eye, the blame of decisions opposed by the general public. Whether that decision is one requiring more money to be spent on prisons or mental treatment facilities, or one that orders desegregation of the schools, stipulated settlements would relieve conflict resolution from a part of its autocratic posture. At the same time it permits the parties to exert some control over the result.

There may, in fact, be settlements in some desegregation cases that look as though they were decided by final judicial adjudication. Persons serving as "masters" or "experts" in some cases may well, in fact, be serving as mediators between parties prepared to negotiate an agreement—provided the agreed-upon resolution is not presented to the public as such but rather as the plan of the court or of the master or expert. Such "settlements" do relieve the court of a part of the burden of creating a resolution, but the public nevertheless perceives the responsibility for the decision as one resting solely on the court. Settlements remain, however, the exceptions in major desegregation cases. The posture of defendant school and governmental bodies precludes settlement largely on political grounds. Once in litigation, a school board will seldom be prepared to accept the political onus of desegregation, particularly if the solution lies in some attendance re-zoning that necessitates busing. There are, however, also inhibitions to settlement on the plaintiffs' side.

The plaintiffs' litigative posture has in general been as unyielding as that of the defendant school board. One explanation may lie in the fact that what is at stake is no ordinary point of law—it is rather the alleged violation of a constitutional right. Arguably, compromise is not an acceptable course of action when dealing with this specie of right. On the other hand, other explanations may at times be more aptly descriptive of the adamant position of plaintiffs' lawyers.

These actions are class actions, and they are class actions in which the class is so large (and sometimes ill-defined) that discussion of compromise settlements— and indeed discussion of proposed remedial requests—can never be undertaken with all the members of the class. If such discussion were undertaken, there can be little doubt that a variety of views would be expressed by the class members, some, perhaps, at variance with the plaintiff class's view (or the courts' view) of the scope of the constitutional right; or, rather, that irrespective of entitlement under the Constitution, some members of the class might prefer other solutions. Professor Bell's essay explores some of these, although perhaps without adequate sympathy for the position of plaintiff class's lawyers who, faced with what they regard as the safe touchstone of the Constitution, are reluctant to step into the mire of conflicting individual class members' preferences. It is not surprising, then, that plaintiffs' lawyers seldom move from the remedy they believe implements the constitutional right to nonsegregated educational opportunities. There can be little doubt that in so doing the lawyers deviate from what some (whether most is unknown and perhaps unknowable) class members would want if they were fully informed of alternatives.

One alternative resolution of the situation described here might follow the route of declaration of constitutional right followed by some sampling of the plaintiff class; if followed then by a division of the plaintiff class into subclasses for remedial purposes it might be possible to achieve some areas of negotiated settlement for those subclasses whose prefereed resolution is more acceptable to defendants, leaving for the courts' remedial powers the implementation of rights for a smaller group. In desegregation of schools, numbers mean a great deal in the public consciousness.

There is probably another inhibition to settlement that must be noted. Reluctance to settle may reflect certain areas of doubt about both the substantive constitutional principles involved in desegregation cases and the scope of the remedial power of the courts. In the former category rest the questions of whether it is necessary to prove that the school board "intended" to segregate (see the *Johnson* case in San Francisco) and what the word "intent" means in this context. Specifically, does nonaction by the school board in the face of residential patterns that produce segregated school patterns constitute unconstitutional behavior by the school board? Or is it unconstitutional only when the residential patterns are the product in whole or in part of governmental policies (of other governmental bodies)? (See the *Hart* case in Coney Island.)

Other questions concern the remedial powers of the courts. In this category reside not only the very large question of the power of the court to order interdistrict remedies (compare *Milliken* in Detroit with *United States v. Board of Commissioners*, Indianapolis), but also such questions as the power of the court to establish student disciplinary codes, to order the creation of magnet schools, to establish various kinds of citizen monitoring bodies, to modify rules on teacher selection, promotion, and transfer, and a variety of other educational matters with which the courts have, in recent years, concerned themselves in remedial orders.

In many instances these areas of doubt are the inescapable product of case-by-case adjudication certainly appropriate within our system. In other instances they may simply reflect too little care on the part of appellate tribunals (see the Winston-Salem case study).

Finally, some plaintiffs' attorneys argue that only by system-wide compliance with the Constitution can any one plaintiff's constitutional rights be implemented. If this is so, the class-action form has no impact on the remedy, and any one plaintiff unwilling to settle on less than constitutional entitlement could require a system-wide order.

To the extent that unwillingness to settle is the product of doubt about the requirements of the law, more settlements should be possible as case-by-case adjudication produces clarity in the law. But to the extent that settlements have been avoided because they require taking on the political burden of responsibility, or because they are deemed constitutionally unacceptable by all, some, or one of the plaintiffs with power to frustrate the settlement, the present patterns will continue into the future.

PROCEDURAL INGENUITY AND PROBLEMS OF PROPRIETY

With adamancy on the part of plaintiffs' and defendants' lawyers, passivity and withdrawal of political leaders, and political cowardice or principled hostility on the part of school boards, the federal court confronts the desegregation case with few, if any, friends in the courtroom. As the years go on and violence or strife is reported in the media as the by-products of school desegregation cases, the judges feel themselves the objects of fear and, often, hate. Individual judges have reacted differently to this position. Careful reading of the case studies in this volume will assist the reader in understanding some of these responses. In this introductory essay a number of the major objectively demonstrable judicial responses will be noted.

Public Acceptance of Decree

Rare is the litigation in which the judge will hold a press conference before, at the moment of, or after issuing the court's mandate. But in school desegregation cases press conferences or other off-the-bench statements have become common. The explanation for this phenomenon should be clear, though it may not justify the practice. The court knows that if its order is to be accepted it is the general public that must accept it. It knows that if the decision is one that finds violations of the Constitution and orders structural changes in the school system to end such violations, the general public must somehow be persuaded to accept it. Failure of the public to understand and accept it (if not necessarily agree with it) will provide the basis for the defendants or for others opposed to the remedial orders to organize opposition in the form of election of a new, more hostile school board, boycotts, or even violence. But willingness of a substantial part of the public to accept the authority if not correctness of the judicial order will facilitate an orderly compliance. Both forms of public behavior are observable in these essays; it is doubtful that the courts' efforts through press conferences have had much impact.

One particularly moving example of this judicial recognition of the persons to be communicated with is to be found in Chief Judge Noel Fox's opinion in *NAACP v. Lansing Board of Education* issued in December 1975:

> The court recognizes that the issues involved are of particular interest and vital significance to all Lansing area citizens. Therefore, this opinion is aimed at communicating the factual and legal bases for the court's decision, not only to the parties and reviewing courts, but also to the community. For it is the hope of the court that a sincere civic involvement in implementing the terms of this decision will help improve the school system and strengthen the community, for citizens of all races, and their children.

Other devices utilized by the courts to achieve public understanding are also unique to school desegregation cases. Some courts have made extensive use of the Department of Justice's Community Relations Service in a variety of roles— one being to keep the judge attuned to public reaction. Some courts have used masters as much to reach out to the public as to conduct hearings and make recommendations on remedy. Finally, various organizations of citizens have been included in remedial orders (or formed at the private request of the court) to influence the public to accept a judicial decree.

Cities differ, however. A device that works in one place may do less, or fail totally, in others. The reader should compare the use of the citizen committee device in Denver with the committee patterned after it in Boston.

In sum, the courts in desegregation cases have adopted patterns of conduct beyond normal judicial practice in an effort to mobilize public support for the courts' orders. That they do so is a reflection of the breakdown of the three otherwise prevailing modes of obtaining compliance: an automatic willingness to abide by the rule of law; a mobilization of public support by political leadership which accepts the legal and moral obligation to support the effectuation of constitutional rights as declared by the courts; and sanctions imposed by the court for noncompliance.

The unavailability of the first two sources of compliance has already been noted. The third needs perhaps additional explanation. Noncompliance with an equitable decree has historically been treated by the exercise of the judicial contempt power. A noncomplying defendant was simply put in jail until he or she agreed to comply. The court in the desegregation case has two obstacles that effectively block the use of the contempt power. First a technical problem: where noncompliance is on the part of the general public (boycott or violence), the conduct is that of a nonparty. The equitable decree is addressed only to those who are party defendants. Second, and perhaps more importantly, use of the power to jail is more likely to lead to the enhancement of the leadership potential of the jailed person (martyrdom if the punishment is not too severe is an important route to leadership) than to compliance. An analogous problem confronted the court in Boston in its attempt to use the contempt power to force the Boston School Committee to produce a workable and constitutionally acceptable remedy to terminate the existing violation of constitutional rights in the Boston public school system. The Boston case study permits the reader to observe the contempt threat at work in that litigation.

Remedy Formulation: Masters and Experts

Preparation of a proposed remedial decree in conventional equity litigation is the obligation of the plaintiff. In school desegregation cases that burden is placed upon the defendant school board. In more recent litigation, however, the court has found it necessary to turn to other sources for assistance in the preparation of the decree. While the nomenclature is sometimes baffling in use, these assistants can be divided into "masters" and "experts." The master is one (or a panel) serving in lieu of the judge, presumably circumscribed by the rules of judicial conduct, but with the assignment of devoting substantial time to the preparation of a remedy to be recommended to the court in the master's report. The court's expert, on the other hand, is not one who is expected to serve as a substitute for the judge but rather as the judge's advisor. The technical nature of the remedy problem, together with the presumed bias on the part of both plaintiffs' and defendants' experts, are thought to make necessary the appointment by many courts of a court's expert (whose biases are either those of the court or at least whose fidelity runs primarily to the court rather than to the parties).

In fact masters and experts have not always served in roles this narrowly defined. In a number of cases described in this volume, and in others as well, the masters have, as has already been noted, served a kind of public information role, trying to provide more two-way communication between the court and the public than would otherwise exist in desegregation cases. In other cases the masters have assumed the role of mediators, attempting to find some solution acceptable to all parties. As prior analysis suggests, a public statement of agreement by the parties is not to be expected, but some masters hope to find a compromise solution to which all will take some, but not much, exception.

Masters have seldom if ever been effective in the effort to find a solution that is both acceptable and constitutional. It may be that the involvement of persons of substantial reputation in the community in the search for solutions may have important long-term impact on social acceptance of remedial decrees, but such an impact is purely speculative and unsupported by our studies.

More difficult problems have arisen from the use of court experts; it is not surprising that this should be so since the courts experts have played a more significant role in the formulation of the remedial decree than have masters. It should be noted that a decade ago, courts regularly looked for expert help to the Department of Health, Education and Welfare. In recent years HEW has been reluctant to carry out its mandated supervision of the use of federal funds to assure compliance with the Constitution by recipient school boards, let alone to function as an expert assistant to the federal courts. This, of course, reflects the political realities of the 1970s, and can be altered by a strong-willed President and secretary of HEW, or by a determined congress.

In the meantime, courts have turned to a small number of experts for help. In some desegregation cases in the 1960s experts attempted to impose favored universal remedies on a particular school system without detailed knowledge of that system. Such attempts were bound to be vulnerable to attack as insensitive to local factors (such as lack of available transportation from some residential area to the school designated as theirs). The persons who have served as court experts both then and now say they are aware of such early errors and currently strive to learn in detail about each school system in which they serve as court expert.

There is only one place such detailed knowledge can be found. That is within the files and expertise of the local education professional staff (in the larger cities, the planning staff). Staff members thus relied upon must cope with conflicting pulls. As professionals, aware of the influence of the expert with the court, they wish to provide the expert with information and ideas that will serve as the basis for an intelligent, efficient, and workable remedy for the school district they must administer long after the experts, plaintiffs, and court are gone from the scene. However, they do not wish to prejudice their careers by appearing to the defendant school board to be behaving in a traiterous manner.

One judge, in a case not reported in this volume, learned of a staff person in the local education department who was particularly knowledgeable and imaginative in the matter of attendance re-zoning to avoid continued segregation. The judge asked that individual for help and then privately informed the school board members, in strong language, that they had better not attempt to impose sanctions against that individual. Fortunately the influence of the judge over the board members made it unnecessary to discover how the court would have gone about protecting the individual if the school board had fired or demoted him as punishment for his cooperation with the court.

If the courts' experts are indeed now working with the professional school staffs, it may be that their most important function is not, as originally conceived, aiding the court in understanding technical matters; instead they work as a conduit for professional planners—normally controlled by the defendant school board—to carry out their professional task of designing the school system in accordance with the court's finding of constitutional right, free of fear for their jobs. The expert becomes the nominal expert; the work of the expert is "ghosted" by the defendant's employees. This is, of course, an overstatement of the state of the art now, but is correctly descriptive of the trend of one use of experts. To the extent an expert and the court so function, the claim that the court is taking over the school professionals' function must be tempered by an understanding that appearance and reality are not identical.

There are other instances, however, of the expert operating principally on the basis of his or her own perceptions of the needs of the educational structure that is the subject of the litigation. Coupled with a judge who interprets broadly the scope of equity jurisdiction, this can result in sweeping decrees covering a multiplicity of educational functions; these decrees may reflect the views of the expert and the court and be only indirectly tied to the prior unconstitutional conduct of defendant. By definition, they do not derive from the internal operation of the school system's staff. Here the charge that the court, and its expert, are displacing ordinary educational processes may be justified. When this circumstance occurs—and it is rare—it usually takes place in the context of a hostile, recalcitrant school board with a staff that is either uncooperative or of dubious competence.

From the point of view of judicial administration of litigation, use of experts has sometimes raised other issues. Most serious of these are the matters of access to the expert and opportunity to oppose the views of the expert. While masters tend to function as courts do, with equal opportunity of access for all parties in each others' presence and formal opportunities to rebut on the record assertions of fact, conclusions of law, and remedial recommendations, experts tend to function privately, outside the confining bonds of the rules of judicial conduct. There have been reports of the court's expert meeting privately with one party, or its attorney, outside the hearing, and indeed without the knowledge of the other. For a judge to do so would clearly be a breach of the rules of judicial conduct. It is quite impossible for a lawyer to assure a client of unbiased treatment when there is no opportunity to hear and rebut presentations of the opposing party. Equally serious for the lawyers, but less yielding to a reasonable solution, are the instances of private audiences between the court and expert in which decisions are made without the opportunity for public presentation of all sides by opposing lawyers. Devising a rule that balances the need of the court for a research tool in the shape of an expert against the entitlement of the parties to a full and open hearing is a difficult task.

Remedy Supervision

Historically, a court of equity approached with great reluctance a request by plaintiff for an order compelling defendant to engage in affirmative conduct. Thus the negative injunction—do *not* do such-and-such—was far more common than an order to perform a particular function. In effectuating the constitutional right to an education free of intentional segregation by race, the courts, under the leadership of the Supreme Court, have determined that the negative injunction—do not unconstitutionally segregate—is an insufficient order to assure plaintiffs that their constitutional rights will no longer be abridged.

It was not largely concern with formulation of the remedy that led courts of equity to eschew affirmative decrees, but concern over supervision of the remedy. If the court ordered the defaulting contractor to complete the building, was the court not then going, inescapably, to be thrust into supervising the construction itself?

An elegant articulation of the problem is to be found in a recent decision of Judge Marvin E. Frankel in the case of *ASPIRA of New York v. Board of Education of the City of New York,* 432 F.Supp. 647 (S.D.N.Y. 1976). In that case, Judge Frankel found the New York City Board of Education in contempt of court for failing to comply with an equitable consent decree designed to vindicate the rights of plaintiffs to a bilingual education. He wrote:

> The extensive steps required for compliance have placed this court in an increasingly common, bur unvaryingly delicate and difficult, role for federal trial courts—the role of supervising faithful performance of tasks that are in their nature primarily administrative rather than judicial. Cf. Chayes, The Role of the Judge in Public Law Litigation, 89 *Harv. L. Rev.* 1281 (1976). The court's assignment in such cases calls for a nice mixture of humility and resolve. On the one hand, seeking to superintend and rule upon intricate and technical programs like the ones in this case, an appointed judge is, or certainly should be, forcefully reminded that "[c]ourts are not the only agency of government that must be assumed to have the capacity to govern." Stone, J., dissenting in *United States v. Butler,* 297 U.S. 1, 87 (1936). On the other hand, the rights of the people under the law, when they are duly brought to issue before the court, must be forthrightly declared and enforced. *Id.* at 648.

In desegregation cases, the federal courts have undertaken that "delicate and difficult" role. The courts have recognized that issuance of an affirmative decree imposes on the court the obligation to monitor and assure its implementation. In the first instance, monitoring a decree is the obligation of the plaintiff; if the plaintiff perceives a violation of the decree, exercise of the court's power to compel compliance is sought by plaintiff. In large city school systems that are the subject of decrees compelling reassignment of faculty, reassignment of substantial numbers of students, busing, curricular revisions, and the like, however, monitoring requires substantial staff work, frequently involving cost and man-power beyond the capability of the plaintiff. This is particularly a problem if the plaintiff attorneys are, for the most part, from outside the school district.

Federal courts establishing monitoring systems have sought more than a substitute for an augmentation of the plaintiff's capacity to identify and report violations. These courts have clearly attempted to use broadly based citizen monitoring committees to perform three other functions: first, to increase the base not only of public support but public effort to implement the decree; second, to alert the court, without the bias of the parties, to inadequacies in the decree; third, to supply a kind of interstitial adjudicatory or mediating function, resolving minor disputes between parents and principals, for example, without invoking the jurisdiction (and taking the time) of the court.

There is too little evidence to generalize about the circumstances under which monitoring committees will accomplish any of these tasks. It is increasingly clear, however, that there are post-remedy-order functions to be performed that require structures and procedures not yet formalized in our adjudicatory process. Perhaps, in a theoretical world, the functions assigned to monitoring committees should be designed by—and the committees themselves be created by—executive action (probably at the state level since education in most states is regarded as a state function). Unfortunately, reliance on executive action in the post-remedy stage is at present as useless as reliance on the executive at earlier stages of the litigation. In the relatively few cases in which a state commissioner of education has attempted strong executive action in this area, higher executive officers have impeded the commissioner's course.

Summary
The federal courts in desegregation cases have adopted behavioral patterns, have employed personnel, and have utilized procedures that are unprecedented or at least unusual. They have done so in response to perceived needs of this branch of adjudication which would otherwise have remained unsatisfied. Some of these—perhaps many—are inappropriate to our traditional adjudicatory process, but without them it would not otherwise be possible to implement constitutional rights. And thus we have a dilemma too little recognized and entirely unresolved. The apparent lack of limited duration of equitable supervision exacerbates these problems. Recent decisions appear to define that duration more narrowly. They are discussed at the end of the next part of this essay.

CURRENT TRENDS

Very recent decisions suggest that school desegregation cases, particularly in the North and West, have begun to resemble each other more and more. It is not surprising that such a formalization is taking place. Adjudication is, after all, the business of the legal profession which, even at its most radical, prefers order and redundancy to continual change. Thus one can now confidently anticipate that a plaintiff will attempt to persuade the court that its prima facie case—that is, its evidence of defendant school board conduct with respect to some sectors of the school system—is sufficiently probative of unconstitutional behavior as to shift to the defendant the burden of demonstrating that racially imbalanced student bodies or faculties are the result of something other than unconstitutional action. That prima facie case will draw from among the following: discriminatory hiring of faculty; discriminatory assignment of faculty; redrawing of attendance zones for one or more schools in a way that maintained their one-race structure as neighborhoods changed residentially; patterns of school closings and school construction that created one-race school situations; use of temporary school rooms to relieve overcrowding where reassignment to another school with available space would have been less racially segregatory; withdrawal by a newly elected school board of actions taken by the prior board to ameliorate segregation; student voluntary transfer plans which have operated to permit white students to leave schools in which they are in the minority in favor of schools in which white students are in the majority. Defendant school board will defend by introducing evidence that it has historically pursued a neighborhood school system and that such one-race schools as do exist reflect racial segregation of neighborhoods over which they have no control. And there, in virtually every case, the battle lines are drawn. Plaintiffs, their experts, and indeed courts themselves have become skillful in distinguishing between faithful uses of the neighborhood school and what, unfortunately, our school systems more frequently evidence: a neighborhood school structure manipulated so as to contain blacks, particularly poor blacks, within segregated schools.

Similarly, the judicial process, after a finding that the defendant has violated the constitutional rights of the plaintiff class, is also becoming routine. The appointment of a master in one recent case, *Amos v. Board of School Directors of City of Milwaukee,* 408 F.Supp. 765 (E.D.Wisc. 1976), was made immediately upon the rendering of the substantive decision, departing from the practice in earlier cases of awaiting submission of plans or proposals by one or both parties (as in the Detroit and Boston litigation, infra). This should be viewed as a further acceptance by the courts of the master's role. Unfortunately, there is no evidence that the earlier appointment time made the master more effective in the Milwaukee litigation than in others. The court's appointment of a court expert has also become rather common. While by no means universal, these appointments of masters and experts in recent desegregation cases suggests an acceptance by the courts—if by no one else—that they are in need of assistance.

Less common, but increasingly to be found, are attempts by the courts to restructure the educational system so as to make it more likely that the result of the remedial decree will assure the plaintiff class that the litigation will move in a significant affirmative way toward assuring it of its constitutional right. To the extent that the courts do so, there are bound to be debates over the appropriate scope of the equitable power of the court.

A close reading of the studies of the Detroit and Boston remedial orders in this volume is necessary to all concerned with desegregation litigation. In these and other cases courts have found themselves bound by a dilemma. It is evident from the trial records, in the northern and western cases particularly, that the white core-city population is leaving the public school system. Much of that movement is movement to the suburbs by white families with school-age children, usually referred to herein as white flight. Some is due to movement from public to private schools. Even if one assumes that a desegregation decree will be neutral in its impact on this population movement, a continuation of the movement will leave very little white school population with which to integrate.

This dire prognosis unquestionably underlies Judge Garrity's elaborate educational restructuring of the Boston educational system—if the system is good enough, perhaps whites will stay. It probably also underlies Judge DeMascio's refusal in Detroit to take that city's white school population and distribute it among all of the schools in that majority-black districts as well as his orders calling for educational change. The court of appeals and Supreme Court have left the Boston remedial order intact. The Detroit order was modified on appeal, and Judge DeMascio will have to cope with three of Detroit's black districts again. Both decisions reflect a single concern: whether the court is compromising on the degree of desegregation, or rebuilding a school system to make it more attractive, these are but two responses to a common concern about white flight.

The propriety of ordering educational improvements as a remedy to past segregatory acts or to avoid future resegregation was the subject of Supreme Court deliberation in a review of a portion of the district court's Detroit order affirmed by the Sixth Circuit. The state of Michigan argued to the Supreme Court during the 1976/77 term that the district court was without power to order educational programs such as reading and career guidance but was, rather, limited to reassignment of students. Any narrowing of the remedy in this way by the Supreme Court would have simplified the role of district court judges at the cost of removing from them one tool, a tool which some believe can both help remove the effects of past segregation and serve to create a school system that has at least some chance of maintaining an indispensable resource for desegregated education—some white students. The Supreme Court refused to accept Michigan's position in *Milliken* v. *Bradley,* 45 U.S.L.W. 4873 (1977).

One alternative to the Detroit or Boston orders is to approach the remedial order in the context of entire metropolitan areas. The availability of that alternative was greatly narrowed, if not eliminated, by the Supreme Court in *Milliken v. Bradley* and by the Supreme Court's remand of the Indianapolis case, a study of which is contained in this volume. The Wilmington, Delaware case, *Evans v. Buchanan,* which involves a remedial order extending beyond a single city school district, must be regarded as an exception to the Supreme Court ruling in *Milliken,* which imposed on plaintiffs a burden that will be difficult to meet—evidence that each of the suburban school districts sought to be included in the remedial order had violated the constitutional rights of the plaintiff class. In *Dayton Bd. of Educ.* v. *Brinkman,* 45 U.S.L.W. 4910 (1977) the Supreme Court, making reference to *Washington* v. *Davis,* 426 U.S. 229 (1976), insisted on limiting desegregation orders to redressing intentional segregatory acts, a holding with significant substantive and remedial aspects.

The long-term impact on federal adjudication of desegregation cases of the combined concern of judges about white flight on the one hand and the *Milliken* decision on the other is speculative. The most recent round of district court decision-making in Detroit and Boston may, however, serve as the basis for predicting that controversy over reassignment of pupils to other than the nearest school (inappropriately called "forced busing") may be matched by controversy over activism by the courts in ordering educational changes. This development will, of course, be accelerated by litigation over bi-cultural education and tracking (or ability grouping).

Thus, to the political isolation of the court in desegregation litigation and to the animosity toward court remedial orders of increasing numbers of white parents will be added the negative response of persons who believe the courts are wrongly attempting to supplant the professional educator, and bring on the anger of militant desegregationists who perceive the courts as retreating from the full thrust toward desegregation of *Brown v. Board of Education, Swann, Green,* and other leading decisions of the Supreme Court.

An additional source of irritation to the state and local government of desegregation orders—particularly those ordering educational change—is to be found in the fiscal burdens implicit in them. Busing sometimes requires the purchase of more buses. But even more substantial may be the cost of educational enrichment programs. The formulation of a remedial order thus frequently involves, though seldom do the opinions reveal it, resource allocation decisions affecting both the state and the board of education. The Supreme Court's review during the 1976/77 term of the Detroit order included affirmance of that part of the order which imposed certain costs on the state, requiring it to reimburse the Detroit School Board for certain of its compliance costs.

In four recent cases, three involving action by the Supreme Court, some evidence may be found that the limits on equitable jurisdiction in school desegregation cases are narrower than many believe. First, in October 1975 the fifth circuit court decided *Calhoun v. Cook.* The case arose in Atlanta in 1958 and a remedial order had been entered in 1973 which was designed to achieve a minimum of a 30 percent black enrollment in every majority white school. The terms of that decree had been agreed to by some plaintiffs, who represented by local counsel, and the school board. Other plaintiffs, represented principally by the NAACP Legal Defense and Education Fund, Inc. (LDF) objected at that time to the narrowness of the order, asserting it fell far short of remedying the constitutional violation since it did not make use of the full range of techniques for terminating segregation. In a recent renewal of that objection, attorneys for LDF argued that the school district had never achieved unitary status, had never "purged itself of all vestiges of the formerly state-imposed dual system." As evidence of this failure, the plaintiffs rested on the failure of the district ever to use noncontinguous pairing or to bus white children to black schools, and on the fact that over 60 percent of the schools in the district had a pupil enrollment which was all, or substantially all, black.

The court of appeals found the system to be "free of racial discrimination" and that it "wears no proscribed badge of the past." Between the plaintiffs' constitutional argument and the court's conclusion lay the following analysis, which apparently led the court to its result:

> The district court found that the black citizens who occupy the majority of the posts on the school board, in two-thirds of the posts in the school administration and staff and in over 60 percent of the faculty, as well as the numerous nonappealing black plaintiffs who agreed to and support the present plan attest the district's lack of discrimination against black students as well as its freedom from the effects of past race-based practices. The district court also found that Atlanta's remaining one-race schools are the product of its preponderant majority of black pupils rather than a vestige of past segregation. These findings are not clearly erroneous. The aim of the Fourteenth Amendment guarantee of equal protection on which this litigation is based is to assure that state supported educational opportunity is afforded without regard to race; it is not to achieve racial integration in public schools. [Citations omitted.] Conditions in most school districts have frequently caused courts to treat these aims as identical. In Atlanta, where white students now comprise a small minority and black citizens can control school policy, administration and staffing, they no longer are.

Calhoun v. Cook thus appears to be based on two different theses, both of which suggest time limits on desegregation cases. First, that once the initial remedial order is complied with, evidence of discriminatory conduct by the board after the remedial order (and not simply inaction in the face of demographic changes) must be shown before the court can or will issue a further remedial order. Second, that an inference of nondiscriminatory conduct can be derived from a school structure in which blacks comprise the majority of school board, school personnel, and students.

The first of these theses was reviewed by the U.S. Supreme Court in *Pasadena City Board of Education v. Spangler,* 427 U.S. 424 (1976). In an opinion by Justice Rehnquist, with only Marshall and Brennan dissenting (Justice Stevens did not participate in this case), the Court described the situation in Pasadena, first in the initial litigation phase (remedial order in 1970), and then in the instant case initiated by the school board in 1974:

> In this case the District Court approved a plan designed to obtain racial neutrality in the attendance of students at Pasadena's public schools. No one disputes that the initial implementation of this plan accomplished this objective. That being the case, the District Court was not entitled to require the School District to rearrange its attendance zones each year so as to ensure that the racial mix desired by the court was maintained in perpetuity. For having once implemented a racially neutral attendance pattern in order to remedy the perceived constitutional violation on the part of the defendants, the District Court had fully performed its function of providing the appropriate remedy for previous racially discriminatory attendance patterns.

The Court therefore reversed the order of the district court which had been affirmed by the Court of Appeals for the Ninth Circuit; the Supreme Court construed that order as requiring readjustment of attendance zones; such readjustment, as the Court saw the matter, could be ordered only if racial discrimination after the implementation of the remedial order and not demographic changes could be shown to have been the cause of the increased segregation of the schools. The Court so held even though other parts of the original remedial order (dealing with desegregating school system personnel) had not yet been complied with by the school board.

In combination, these cases suggest that the courts may be at the initial point of developing limits on the continuous and indefinite supervision of defendant school boards by the district courts. Such a development will undoubtedly influence significantly the course of future desegregation litigation.

On December 6, 1976, the Supreme Court vacated a ruling by the Court of Appeals for the Fifth Circuit in a school desegregation case arising out of Austin, Texas. The Supreme Court ordered the reconsideration of the Austin decision in the light of *Washington v. Davis,,* 426 U.S. 229 (1976), in which the Court held that the fact that blacks failed an examination for the District of Columbia police force in higher proportion than whites did not demonstrate a violation of the legal rights of black applicants. The opinions of the lower courts may have been sufficiently unclear to justify reading the Supreme Court's Austin order narrowly, though at a minimum it signaled the Supreme Court's intention to apply a more rigorous discriminatory intent test to school desegregation cases as well as to employment-testing cases. On January 25, 1977, the Supreme Court, in vacating the Indianapolis metropolitan order discussed later in this volume, again cited *Washington v. Davis* and also *M.H.D.C. v. Village of Arlington Heights,* which it had decided in the interim (upholding local zoning laws although their effect was to exclude blacks). In view of the clarity of the lower court opinions in the Indianapolis litigation concerning the basis of that decision, one can only conclude that the Supreme Court has determined to insist on proof of intent going beyond proof that segregation was the reasonably foreseeable conse- quence of state action. Such a conclusion would be supported also by the Court's decision in the *Dayton* case, discussed above, decided in June 1977. This test goes of course to the substantive question of violation of constitutional rights. It is, however, also closely related to a scope-of-remedy question: that is, does the judicial remedial power extend beyond individual schools as to which intentional segregation can be shown to reach other one-race schools in the same school system. A negative response to this question, perhaps implicit in the *Austin, Indianapolis* and *Dayton* remands, would overturn the Supreme Court's Denver decision (*Keyes v. School District No. 1, Denver, Colorado*), dicussed later in this volume and substantially impede efforts to induce the federal courts to end the racial segregation of America's schools.

Such a reading of the *Austin* case may not be inappropriate. Justice Powell, speaking for himself, Chief Justice Burger and Justice Rehnquist, wrote:

> Whether the Austin school authorities intentionally discriminated against minorities or simply failed to fulfill affirmative obligations to eliminate segregation, . . . the remedy ordered appears to exceed that necessary to eliminate the effect of any official acts or omissions.

RECOMMENDATIONS

Reflection upon the case studies in this volume, other desegregation cases, and conversations with judges, educators, and lawyers have persuaded me that the following recommendations on judicial administration of school desegregation cases would improve the quality of the litigation by approaching more nearly a proper combination of traditional adjudicative rules and the demands of desegre- gation litigation. They are not by any means offered as a solution to the appar- ent distress of a sizable portion of white urban America at the prospect of transportation past the nearest school building, or as a solution to the frustration of many black Americans at the largely unrelieved burden of inadequate and mostly segregated public education. Nor will these recommendations relieve the courts of their political isolation, the school boards of the political pressures generated by the desegregation issue, or school staffs of the interference with their function by school boards and the courts alike once desegregation litigation is instituted. The aim of the recommendations is, therefore, far more modest than a restructuring of our society; they are intended only to improve the opera- tion of the courts as they stand, virtually alone among government institutions, to assure to minority Americans that no state will be permitted to deny them the equal protection of the laws by requiring their attendance at schools segregated by state action.

Experts and Masters

Time of Appointment. Experience has demonstrated that federal judges presiding over desegregation cases have generally felt the need, at some point in the litigation, for expert advice independent of plaintiffs' and defendants' experts. For a number of reasons it seems most appropriate that the court appoint an expert early in the litigation, indeed just after assignment of the case to the judge, before pretrial discovery procedures are initiated. This will ensure that the judge has continuous expert help in interpreting the evidence before the court and thus assist the court in its sometimes difficult task of maintaining an orderly and reasonably efficient trial. The early appointment will also provide a proper period of education of the expert in the school system so that the expert will be informed (as well as, presumably, wise) if the court should later need help in remedy formulation.

Masters, on the other hand, should probably not be appointed until after defendants are found to have violated the constitutional rights of the plaintiff class and have submitted, upon order of the court, a proposed plan of action to remedy that violation. At that point a master may be superfluous. Or the court might wish a master to conduct hearings on the defendants' plan, and on any other plan that others, parties or not, may wish to submit.

Function. In theory, the function of a master is akin to that of a judge, the difference measured only in that the master's "decision" is in the form of a recommendation to the presiding judge. It is apparent that in carrying out this role the conduct expected of a judge should likewise be demanded of a master. This means that he or she must be ruled only by the evidence adduced at a public hearing and must be governed by applicable principles of law both in procedural and substantive matters. In fact, in desegregation cases the masters have often played roles besides this one, ranging from that of a communications medium for the judge to that of a mediator. In performing these less judge-like roles, the ethics and law based on the judicial model is applied only with grave difficulties. For example, if the master is trying to sound out local parental response to some ideas for a remedial order, must that investigation be carried out in the form of a public hearing with opportunity for cross-examination? If the answer is affirmative to this question, then what of the master's occasional role of trying to explain to a group of parents the reasons for the court's decision about the existence of constitutional violations? What is needed is a clear delineation of what functions the appointing court intends the master to perform, together with appropriate instructions to the master about such matters as right of examination and cross-examination in public hearing of persons to appear before the master.

While solution to potential problems involving the master in a desegregation case is difficult, more serious problems have arisen in connection with the court's expert. The source of the problem lies in the understandable desire of the court, in pursuing its required tasks in such cases, to have a confidential relationship to a professional educator whose allegiance lies solely with the court. I will pass by, without comment, the matter of whether any expert approaches matters involving race and education without prejudgment or bias which may or may not prove ultimately to be the same as those the court reaches after considered judgment.

A less philosophical, more mundane, and more troubling (to day-to-day lawyers) matter arises from the fact that the expert in these cases does not function as a repository of knowledge tapped by the court when needed. The expert is not always, therefore, like a book or a law review article. The expert often obtains the information the court needs by interviewing school personnel and others familiar with the school system. In some cases the expert has spoken separately with parties or counsel out of the hearing and without the knowledge of opposing party or counsel. Whether this conduct is or is not seriously prejudicial is a matter of conjecture. It is contrary to rules erected for the purpose of maintaining both the fairness and appearance of fairness of adjudication. I suggest that at the point that the expert begins functioning for the court outside the judge's chambers, strict rules of judicial ethics should apply. This will make the expert's role more public and will to some extent reduce the intimacy the expert and the judge may share. But that is a price which fairness requires.

Still another problem created by the expert-court relationship has been found in the tendency for decisions to be made prior to a reasonable opportunity for the parties to be heard. Nowhere is this more a danger than where the expert-court consultation develops remedial ideas that are beyond the recommendations of the parties and which have, therefore, not received the benefit of examination and advocacy afforded by traditional adjudicative procedures.

Monitors and Implementors

The solution of courts of chancery, in their development of equitable jurisprudence, to the problem of implementation of their decrees was, in large part, to avoid decrees that would require judicial supervision. Many orders were negative and the burdens of supervision were thus minimized. It is far easier to determine compliance with an order not to act than compliance with an order compelling a course of conduct. Other orders could if necessary be fulfilled by the court itself. Thus an order to convey real property was a common affirmative remedy. But if the party so ordered refused to comply, the court could itself execute the deed. Rare, however, was the affirmative order which could not be fulfilled by the court iself. The judges of the chancery courts knew that supervision of a detailed affirmative decree involved difficult ministerial problems better left unassumed.

In constitutional adjudication of students' rights to nonsegregated education, the court must order affirmative action to undo past wrongs as well as order that no future segregative acts be committed. Having so ordered, the court is confronted by implementation.

It is apparent that the system used in Denver, as described in this volume by the Pearsons, worked. But a similar system in Boston, described by Smith, did not do as well. In large part the reason may lie in the type of personnel willing to serve in Denver, but unwilling to serve in Boston, on an implementation committee. That experience, in turn, reflects the political attitude of each city.

The more basic question is whether the job of implementation should be that of court-created committees of citizens or parents. If the court is confronted by apparent recalcitrance on the part of the defendant to abide strictly by the court's order, the court should be able to order appropriate levels of the state or federal executive to monitor the implementation of its order. Such a judicial order to the state or federal executive should be free of legislative interference—it is an order to carry out constitutionally required acts. To bring this suggestion within the framework of conventional adjudication, the state and federal executive should be made parties at the remedial stage. This recommendation may itself raise constitutional or jurisdictional questions, but they should be resolved in favor of the suggested procedure.

If this model is not feasible, then Congress should provide personnel to the courts to carry out the burdensome task of monitoring implementation. It may be that the expansion of equitable jurisdiction in cases involving desegregation, other education issues, mental hospitals, and prisons may require such additional staffing of our courts. But it would be far more in keeping with our adjudicative process, and more compatible with separation of powers, for the executive branches of the federal and state governments to take charge of monitoring the implementation of such orders.

It must be noted that school boards may pay a high price when their conduct necessitates the creation of any agency other than itself to implement the desegregation decree. This compromise of function is grave indeed where the judicial order goes beyond student attendance, coming to such matters as student discipline, quality of education, and bilingual education. Where the court chooses a citizen monitoring panel, there is generated a transfer of power from the school board to parents or other interested citizens. While such a shift may be politically justifiable, the role of the court in producing it is of doubtful validity.

Counsel's Role

Lawyers are frequently political beings. It is not accidental that so high a proportion of legislators, mayors, and governors are lawyers. In desegregation litigation there have been too many incidents of lawyers for the parties, and particularly for the defendants, manipulating adjudication to increase their personal reputations. When faced with a recalcitrant client in private litigation, counsel will advise the client that compliance is required and will resign representation if the client will not yield. Happily, there have been some instances of such behavior by defendants' lawyers in desegregation cases. Sadly, more often lawyers for school boards have themselves been influenced as much or more by personal political concerns as by traditional notions of the lawyer as an officer of the court. Such conduct is not only a violation of professional ideals, but is ultimately a disservice to the client. The bar owes an obligation to the public to remind lawyers regularly of basic principles of professional obligation. Finally, one must question whether a school board attorney ought not to include within advice to client such matters as public costs of litigation and the polarization of the community.

On the plaintiffs' counsel side the problem has hardly been one of personal aggrandizement. With virtually no exception, attorneys in desegregation cases persist in their work with selfless idealism. Unfortunately there are aspects of selfless idealism that are also sometimes inconsistent with an attorney's professional obligations. The problem here, as Professor Bell describes it, is in no small part a function of the difficulties of class-action representation. Lawyers representing both a local chapter of the NAACP *and* all other black parents with children of school age sometimes neglect to make a careful inquiry into the view of the latter part of the class. They excuse this occasional failure by stating that what they are demanding in court is simply what the Constitution requires. Such a stance ignores the infinite varieties of bargain and compromise in which what law requires can become more significant as leverage than as result. I have elsewhere in this essay suggested that the device of subclass delineation may be of some use in dealing with this problem. Making such a suggestion practical would require plaintiffs' attorneys to be more active than they now are in discovering what the views are of the parents and pupils who, in totality, they represent. Litigation necessitates simplification, but not, I hope, at the cost of attempting to meet the desires ot those in whose behalf adjudication is sought.

How Long the Chancellor's Arm?

It was sometimes sarcastically said that the chancellor, largely ungoverned by precedent, determined justice by the length of his foot. In desegregation cases the issue may well be the length of the chancellor's arm. In reviewing the case studies in this volume a reader may consider the degree of the court's sensitivity to the limits of the judicial power. The source of the limits is to be found in the nature of adjudication and court structure, detailed below.

Adjudication is basically a negative response to a phenomenon. A court may chafe at the limiting implications of this concept, but it cannot alter it. The court's function is to determine whether there have been constitutional violations and, if so, to order them ended and undone. The limits of the court's reach are defined by what the defendant has done wrong.

And so adjudication of school desegregation must necessarily leave unchanged the departure of whites (particularly middle- and upper-economic-class white families with school-age children) from the cities of America, residential segregation within our cities, and the racial and cultural biases of the teaching profession (white and, sometimes, black). In some instances courts have, basing their jurisdiction on past constitutional violations, attempted to improve the quality of schools, attempted to shift toward or away from vocational education, attempted to affect teachers' values and biases, but it is unlikely that these efforts will prove more than that there are real limits to the judicial function.

Any effort to deal with racial bias, housing, schooling, income, and other such broad social problems must come from the legislative and executive branches of government. The further the attempted judicial reach in desegregation cases, the less likely the executive and legislative branches will be pressed into action. In that sense the ever-lengthening judicial reach may be deceiving the most those people the courts wish to help the most—those who have been on the receiving end of racial discrimination and poverty. The courts may ultimately find that their finest and furthest efforts in desegregation cases are, in the words in another context of Mr. Justice Jackson, "a munificient bequest in a pauper's will."

The structure of courts limits their capacity to enforce their decrees. This point has already been made sufficiently in this essay.

The power of courts is based upon public acceptance of their exercise of power. While there are, of course, threats of contempt citations to recalcitrant parties, police action against violent protesters, and threats of federal action for conspiracy to obstruct persons in the exercise of their civil rights, the court's most effective weapon in seeking obedience to its authority lies in the willingness of those who lose to accept the exercise of judicial authority. The more the court's action is within the perceived appropriate judicial role, the greater the ultimate power it wields. As it extends its role into, for example, day-by-day educational administration, public acceptance will become less general. At the point that acceptance is limited to those who have won, adjudication as an effective device for dispute resolution has been seriously impaired.

CONCLUSION

It is neither for pity nor tolerance that I argue, but for understanding of the difficult—sometimes unbearably difficult—position of the courts in formulating and implementing remedial decrees in desegregation cases. But for all of the faults that have characterized adjudication, it is not possible to conceive of a constitutional system in which no institution of government is prepared to declare and enforce constitutional rights.

In the short run the adjudication process could be improved in its functioning as I have suggested. Let me not, however, be misunderstood. None of these changes would alter the essential character of the role of courts in school desegregation litigation. It is when the court is able to define the constitutional right to an education free of discriminatory school board action—and then confidently to expect the school board, the state commissoner of education, or other state or federal officials or agencies to formulate and implement the requisite changes to implement that right—that the role of courts can be reduced to more traditional dimensions. The failure of political leadership to play that proper role has led to the expansion of equity jurisdiction; only a reversal of that failure will lead to the contraction of equity jurisdiction.

There is probably a price that our society will pay for its decison to rest upon the federal courts the entire burden of protecting this right of the black minority. No political institution can long withstand the punishment of political isolation without an impact on its conduct. A plea to political leadership to accept its constitutional responsibilities is therefore much more than a plea in behalf of the constitutional rights of a minority; it is, rather, a plea in behalf of the survival of our governmental structure as established in Articles I, II, and III of the Constitution of the United States.

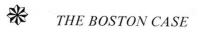

THE BOSTON CASE

Two Centuries and Twenty-Four Months: A Chronicle of the Struggle to Desegregate the Boston Public Schools

Ralph R. Smith

Boston schools have for the past few years been the focus of nation-wide attention following the determination of the U.S. district court that the Boston School Committee had engaged in unconstitutional segregatory practices. The litigation has been characterized by events of unusual notoriety. Tracing the complex events of this litigation has occupied the author of this essay for at least two years, and his effort provides a useful basis for analysis of the possibilities and limitations of adjudication as a tool to vindicate the constitutional rights of all children to nonsegregated education.

Professor Ralph R. Smith is an Assistant Professor of Law at the University of Pennsylvania School of Law.—Eds.

On June 21, 1974, Federal District Court Judge W. Arthur Garrity filed an order that set in motion a chain of events that in succeeding months would permanently affect the city of Boston. In a lengthy, well-reasoned, meticulously drafted opinion, Judge Garrity concluded that the black plaintiffs in the case before him had "proved beyond question" that the Boston School Committee "knowingly carried out a systematic program of segregation affecting all of the city's stu-

This paper owes a large measure of credit to the students who not only assisted in the research (among others, Peggy Massey, Boston College J.D. 1976, and Henry Woo, University of Pennsylvania J.D. 1978) but also helped make what could very well have been a frustrating endeavor into a first-rate teaching and learning experience. Helen P. Brown, Boston College J.D. 1976, who has at various times been my research assistant, administrative assistant, and editor, while at all times being valued friend, contributed immensely. Atty. Robert Pressman of the Harvard Center for Law and Education generously lent his time, his thoughts, and his files to this effort. I am also indebted to the many people in the city of Boston who shared their particular perspective of this most singular event.

dents, teachers and school facilities and have intentionally brought about and maintained a dual school system."

The words had a now-familiar ring. In the two decades since the Supreme Court of the United States outlawed segregation in public education, federal district courts throughout the South had been called upon to vindicate the rights of black school children. As of late, even some northern school districts were found to be engaging in conduct constituting unlawful discrimination.

But the focus of this opprobrium was not the South, nor was it just any city in the North. Judge Garrity was referring to the proud city which Daniel Webster had enshrined as "the cradle of liberty." Still sharing his vision, much of the country revered Boston, remembering that this is where the American Revolution started, where Paul Revere commenced his now legendary ride. This is the city regarded as the Mecca of higher education (even though the most prestigious of its institutions, Harvard and M.I.T., lie across the river in Cambridge). Boston is known as the home of the Adamses and the Kennedys. It exemplifies and epitomizes new-world charm and sophistication.

There has always been another side to Boston—one not so glamorous, not so romantic, and therefore not as well publicized. Few outside Boston realized the extent to which the city is an archipelago of isolated, ghettoized ethnic communities sharing at best an uneasy truce.

Avid students of American history may realize that Judge Garrity's decision merely began another skirmish in a battle that began in this city almost two centuries ago. The year was 1787, a decade after Bostonians John Hancock and Samuel Adams signed the Declaration of Independence, proclaiming to the world that "all men are created equal," and one year before representatives of the city of Boston joined Massachusetts in "securing the blessings of liberty" by approving the U.S. Constitution. In that year, black parents in Boston—"free," taxpaying citizens of Massachusetts—petitioned the commonwealth legislators. "We must," they declared, "fear for our rising offspring to see them in ignorance in a land of gospel light. . . ."[1]

Three-quarters of a century later, Benjamin Roberts, another black Bostonian, refused to send his daughter past five schools reserved for whites to the one set aside for blacks. No less eminent counsel than Charles Sumner and Robert Morris argued to no avail that the school committee could not legally or reasonably assume "that an entire race possess certain moral or intellectual qualities, which render it proper to place them all in a class by themselves." Perhaps intuitively perceiving the essence of the issue, Chief Justice Shaw saw this as "a question of power." But he then went on to find "no grounds of doubt" that this segregation was "the honest result of [the school committee's] experience and judgement."[2]

---

1. Petition to the State Legislature, dated October 17, 1787. The text of the petition appears in A Documentary History of the Negro People in the United States 19–20 (H. Aptheker ed. 1963).
2. Sarah C. Roberts v. City of Boston, 59 Mass. 198, 209 (1849).

It is with the bittersweet irony which so characterizes the history of injustice that we realize that *Morgan v. Hennigan*[3] told the Boston School Committee in 1974 that they could not do what Justice Shaw in 1850 said they could.

Though over a century apart, both had far-reaching consequence. "By ruling against little Sarah Roberts, the Massachusetts court set a precedent by which the United States Supreme Court could formulate its pervasive exclusionary doctrine as expressed most odiously in . . . 1896."[4] Coming some forty years before *Plessy*,[5] Justice Shaw laid the foundation for the "separate but equal" doctrine that was to become the law of the land. Not civil war, civil rights acts, or constitutional amendments would remove what appeared to be the indelible stamp of separatist policies from official dogma. It was not until 1954 that the U.S. Supreme Court, having to that point successfully avoided the issue, declared for all to hear that segregation in public education was unconstitutional.[6] In effect, it was Benjamin Roberts and not the Boston School Committee who eventually prevailed. *Morgan v. Hennigan* set off shock waves. It exposed the Boston that

3. The lawsuit was originally entitled Morgan v. Hennigan, 379 F. Supp. 410 (D. Mass. 1974). After Judge Garrity's opinion came down in June 1974, James W. Hennigan, then chairman of the Boston School Committee, was replaced on the committee by Kathleen Sullivan, and John J. McDonough became chairman. The suit has from this time been called Morgan v. Kerrigan, after another committee member, John J. Kerrigan.

4. Leonard, *De Funis v. Odegaard: An Invitation to Look Backward,* 3 Black L.J. 224 (1974).

5. Plessy v. Ferguson, 163 U.S. 537, 16 S. Ct. 1138, 41 L. Ed. 256 (1896).

6. Following *Plessy,* the Supreme Court has given education cases a treatment distinct from other discrimination cases. In Sweatt v. Painter, 339 U.S. 629, 70 S. Ct. 848, 94 L. Ed. 1114 (1950), and McLaurin v. Okla. State Regents, 339 U.S. 637, 70 S. Ct. 851, 94 L. Ed. 1149 (1950), the Court developed its own concept of the process of education, above and beyond mere tangible factors such as physical facilities, instruction, and allocation of resources. *Plessy* distinguished between social and political equality, and cited *Roberts v. Boston* as its prime authority for refusing to enforce the former in the area of education. But *Sweatt* and *McLaurin* gave education a unique status and responsibility in the country, and declared that inequality of educational opportunity was to be measured by intangible factors as well:

> In terms of number of faculty, variety of courses and opportunity for specialization, size of the student body, scope of the library, availability of law review and similar activities, the University of Texas Law School possesses to a far greater degree those qualities which are incapable of objective measurement but which make for greatness in a law school. [Sweatt v. Painter, 339 U.S. at 633-34.]

In *McLaurin* the Court amplified by holding that a black graduate student while in the same school, if separated from fellow white students, was "handicapped in his pursuit of effective graduate instruction: such restrictions impair and inhibit his ability to study, to engage in discussions and exchange views with other students, and, in general, to learn his profession." (339 U.S. at 641.) Brown v. Board of Education, 347 U.S. 483, 74 S. Ct. 686, 98 L. Ed. 873 (1954), took the next obvious step—to apply those findings in *Sweatt* and *McLaurin* "with added force to children in grade and high schools." *Brown,* however, based this finding on social science data: "To separate them [black students] from others of similar age and qualification solely because of their race generates a feeling of inferiority as to their status in the community that may affect their hearts and minds in a way unlikely ever to be undone." (347 U.S. at 494.) The Court declared: "We conclude that in the field of public education the doctrine of 'separate but equal' has no place. Separate educational facilities are inherently unequal." (*Id.* at 495.)

lay behind the carefully cultivated facade. The nation was transfixed as the electronic media brought home white mobs who rained stones upon and into yellow buses carrying black children, viciously attacked and clubbed an innocent passerby whose only involvement was the hue of his skin, pelted a favorite son and U.S. Senator with eggs and tomatoes as he appealed for calm and decency, and applauded dilatory tactics and demagoguery by the officials charged with implementing the court order.

But the impact of Judge Garrity's decision was not confined to Boston or to the tarnishing of its image. As with *Roberts,* this case had national implications and ramifications. Local antibusing groups rallied to the cause and joined forces with their counterparts throughout the country to establish a national pressure group to bring an end to "forced busing." Their efforts have produced immediate results. For the next several years there was to be renewed interest in constitutional amendments that would prohibit the transporting of school children to achieve racial balance. President Ford would later play election politics with Boston by publicly deliberating on whether to seek reconsideration of Judge Garrity's order by the U.S. Supreme Court.

This paper will discuss the litigation and the order that precipitated the current crisis in the city of Boston. It examines the setting of the case and presents an historical and political overview. It will focus on the pretrial, trial, and judgment stages. It will explore some of the problems in implementing the decree. It will, in a very general way, seek to distill from the Boston experience those lessons that can be of value to others. The considerable time spent on the setting is justified not only by the aphorism that the past informs the present, but because the unique confluence of circumstance and events constituting the setting significantly affected the manner in which the parties viewed the court, the source and nature of the constitutional violation, and the content and scope of the remedy ordered.

After nearly two centuries of struggle through the state courts and legislature, plaintiffs perceived the federal court as a last resort and invoked its processes to seek the redress which had been denied them in fact if not in theory. Defendant, on the other hand, having successfully prevailed against the constant pressure to effect a change in policy, saw the federal court as an officious intermeddler with little real concern for the city of Boston and the majority of its population. The school system is statutorily designed and operated in a manner that effectively frustrates meaningful change not supported by the majority of the city's electorate. This fact suggests that, even without whatever malevolence suggested above, a voluntary curing of the constitutional violation alleged was unlikely, and litigation inevitable.

Not since Little Rock have the events surrounding the desegregation of a public school system so transfixed the nation. "Busing in Boston" has more than mere alliterative appeal. It is a phrase loaded with the irony and hypocrisy that permeates America north of the Mason-Dixon line. It is a concept that juxtaposes with the repository of American refinement and culture the necessity of judicial fiat to undo invidious discrimination.

Boston seems once again a watershed. National attention is again focused on segregation in public schools and the judicial branch's twenty-year struggle to bring it to an end. The support that militant anti-busing organizations have received seems to indicate that it is the struggle which might very well be forcibly terminated, not the segregation. While southern cities acquiesced to the inevitable, whites in Boston are apparently prepared to continue to fight. They have the ear of national and local political leaders. They have the support of people across the country. And they have the historical blend of revolutionary determination and prolonged discrimination to make Boston as likely a northern city as any to test the viability of desegregation in education. It is for that reason if for no other that a closer look at Boston is desirable.

PRELUDE TO FEDERAL INTERVENTION

The City and the School System

Despite its unique place in American history and folklore, the city of Boston has not been immune from the pressures and problems plaguing American cities. Major shifts in political power, ethnic isolation, exodus to the suburbs, and deteriorating public services are problems Bostonians share with the rest of the country.

From colonial times and throughout the nineteenth century, the city was dominated by the Yankee descendants of the Puritans. As the potato famine in Ireland sent wave after wave of immigrants to Massachusetts shores,[7] the Yankees battled to maintain this dominance. The struggle was in vain. The

---

7. The 1846 potato harvest in Ireland was almost entirely rotten, and the winter of 1846/47 was severe. There was at the same time an outbreak of typhus fever in Ireland. Wholesale evictions, lack of food and employment, sickness, religious and political oppression, and cheap passage by sea combined to cause dramatic numbers of Irish people to look to America for relief. Before the potato famine, between 1837 and 1845, an average of 5,500 Irish emigrated to Boston every year. In the single year of 1847, however, 25,000 landed, with 12,500 more arriving either by land or illegally. In 1845, Boston's recorded population had been 114,366, and in 1847, over 37,000 Irish immigrants arrived; by early summer 1847, the city was overrun by starving, sick, and impoverished Irish immigrants. They did not all settle in Boston, but those who did, along with immigrants from other European countries, swelled the city's population between 1845 and 1855 by one-third. Although the Irish emigration fell off in the late 1850s, it was not until after the potato famine had subsided in the mid-sixties that there was a substantial decrease in the numbers of Irish emigrants. For an excellent historical account of the events and the consequences of the potato famine, *see* C. Woodham-Smith, The Great Hunger (1962). Other works on the subject include: C. Wittke, The Irish in America (1956); and R.D. Edwards & T.D. Williams, The Great Famine (1957). Perhaps the best-known work on the subject of immigration in Boston is O. Handlin, Boston's Immigrants (1959). F. Levy, Northern Schools and Civil Rights (1971), and P. Shrag, Village School Downtown (1967), provide some insight into the expectations, goals, and political accomplishments of the Irish in Boston in the twentieth century.

Yankees lost, abandoned the city, and retreated to the suburbs. By the 1920s political control of the city was consolidated in the hands of the Irish, even as it is today.

The retreat of the politically defeated but still affluent Yankees, a stagnant economy, and the traditional lure of green suburbia combined to assure a 13 percent population decline in Boston during the three decades from 1940 to 1970. This net loss of 100,000 residents is all the more dramatic when one realizes that during this same period the black population increased sixfold. Migration from the South swelled the number of blacks in Boston from 20,000 in 1940 to 127,000 in 1970.[8] (Ironically, much of Boston's attraction was its reputation for racial tolerance and excellent public education.) Unlike whites, blacks have not found it easy to escape to the suburbs. Restrictive covenants, snob zoning, and the general unavailability of moderate- and low-income housing combine to trap Boston blacks in Boston.[9] Boston is characterized by ethnic isolation. The Irish, the Portugese, the Italians, and the blacks came to Boston at different times for different reasons and settled in different areas of the city.[10]

8. Center for Law and Education, Harvard University, A Study of the Massachusetts Racial Imbalance Act 11 (1972) [hereinafter cited as the Harvard Study]. This study is an excellent detailed account of the history and operation of the Massachusetts Racial Imbalance Act (RIA). Attorney Robert Pressman, one of plaintiffs' counsel, is presently director of the center, and was involved in the preparation of the Harvard Study. Chapters include: *The Evolution of the RIA: Requirements and Procedures of the Act; State-Level Implementation; Implementation of the Act in Boston; Springfield; New Bedford; Cambridge; Medford; the Racial Imbalance Act and Its Broader Purposes; Achieving Integration; and Appendixes.* Another valuable work on the subject is J. Bolner & R. Shanley, Civil Rights in the Political Process: An Analysis of the Massachusetts Racial Imbalance Law of 1965 (1967) [hereinafter cited as Bolner & Shanley, Civil Rights]. It contains an excellent summary of social, economic, and educational factors relating to racial imbalance in Boston, a political and legislative history of the RIA, and a summary of the racial imbalance situation in Springfield, Mass.

9. For an excellent historical survey of suburban segregation in Boston, see Joint Report of the Massachusetts Advisory Committee to the United States Commission on Civil Rights and the Massachusetts Commission Against Discrimination, Route 128: Boston's Road to Segregation (January 1975) [hereinafter cited as Route 128: Boston's Road to Segregation].

10. For Irish immigration, see *supra* note 7; For Italian immigration, see Handlin, *supra* note 7. The causes of Portuguese immigration to the United States have been cited as largely economic: harmful political and economic policies of the government, overpopulation at home, and the prospect of industrial employment or independent farming in the United States. D. Taft, Two Portuguese Communities in New England 95–99 (1923). A majority of Portuguese immigrants settled in Fall River and New Bedford, but in 1910 the Massachusetts Census showed 1,125 in Boston and 1,857 in Cambridge. C. Bannick, Portuguese Immigration to the United States: Its Distribution and Status 29–30 (1917). At the turn of the century, substantial numbers of Black West Indians emigrated. Between 1900 and 1930, well over 100,000 immigrants entered, and many more came both legally and illegally after 1945. They settled in eastern port cities, especially New York and Boston. M. Jones, American Immigration 243–44 (1960). Haitians often came to escape a politically repressive regime and overpopulation, and to seek educational opportunities. I. Reid, The Negro Immigrant: His Background, Characteristics and Social Adjustment, 1899–1937 54 (1939). Southern blacks first came to Boston in numbers during World War I in response to both the need for industrial and domestic workers and Boston's liberal reputation. The migra-

Both manmade and natural barriers tend to aggravate the normal tendency toward group affiliation. South Boston, populated almost exclusively by the Irish and a few Lithuanians, is almost completely surrounded by water. Only two bridges provide access to and from the rest of the city. The North End, Boston's Italian section, is bounded by waterfront and cut off on other sides by arterial highways. Other highways demark Roxbury and North Dorchester where the black population is concentrated. A turnpike and expressway confine the Chinatown section. Even where these barriers do not exist the casual observer can easily tell whose neighborhood ends where.

This geographic isolation, when coupled with a neighborhood school policy, assures a fairly homogeneous racial and ethnic student body in most schools. As with other cities, the flight of wealthy white residents and industrial firms to the suburbs, with the resulting erosion of the tax base, are reflected in deteriorating services. In no area is this more apparent than in the public school system. Boston's school system was founded in colonial times almost a century before public education became an American phenomenon. In the nineteenth century while other cities were making their first feeble attempts to provide education for the masses, Boston was expanding its system and building it into what Horace Mann would praise as a model of efficiency.[11]

Much has changed. The pride and joy of the system was the Latin school (Boston Latin), which was established in 1635 and at one time sent three-fourths of its graduates to Harvard College. No more. Though Boston Latin maintains its relative status within Boston, it is clear that by the 1960s this once excellent school had descended to mediocrity and was saved from oblivion only because the rest of the system by comparison seemed even worse. This once proud and

tion north changed the whole fabric of black society in the country. In 1910, only 11 percent of black Americans lived in the North, while by 1960, 40 percent did. In 1910, 73 percent of black Americans lived in rural areas; and in 1960, 73 percent lived in urban areas. R. Coles, The South Goes North 653 (1972). Boston blacks generally live in Roxbury, North Dorchester, and the South End; while South Boston, Hyde Park, Charlestown, East Boston, and West Roxbury are customarily "white neighborhoods." For a breakdown of housing trends in Boston, see *Boston Redevelopment Authority Working Paper, Housing in Boston: Background Analysis and Program Directions* (1974); and Route 128: Boston's Road to Segregation, *supra* note 9.

11. Born in Massachusetts, educated at Brown University, and an accomplished lawyer, Horace Mann in 1837 became secretary of the Massachusetts Board of Education. At that time the conditions of the state public school system were atrocious. Mann reformed and reorganized the system, stressing the importance of good teaching, moral and physical education, and discipline; he revamped the textbooks and library facilities then in use, and disapproved of corporal punishment. Although his interest in "quality education" had a slightly puritanical flavor, he was concerned foremost with inspiring in students the desire to learn. In 1848 he became a member of Congress, where he became known for his speeches against slavery. As a result of many of his reform efforts, a century ago the Boston school system was a model for many other states. R. Downs, Horace Mann: Champion of Public Schools (1974); and J. Messerli, Horace Mann: A Biography (1971). For a shortened version of Mann's writings on education, see Horace Mann on the Crisis in Education (Antioch ed. 1965).

efficient system is today characterized by outdated texts, unimaginative teaching methods, old, dilapidated and overcrowded facilites, patronage, politics, and corruption. Not surprisingly, the end product has been affected. The average Boston school child is now far below national averages in reading and arithmetic skills.[12] As could be expected, this situation accelerated the exodus to suburbia of those who could afford it. However, there were and are other alternatives. Many parents placed their children in private schools; some sought out the parochial schools. It has been estimated that up to one-third of Boston's school-age children are not in the public schools. In 1974 enrollment in Boston public schools hovered around 96,000. At that time it was estimated that almost 30,000 students attended the city's private and parochial schools.[13]

As a consequence, the students remaining in Boston's public school system were disproportionately black. In 1964, when blacks constituted 12 percent of the city's population, black students comprised 23 percent of the total public school enrollment. In 1974, blacks were 19 percent of the city's population, while over 30 percent of the student population was black.[14] The net effect is that white enrollment in the public schools has declined both proportionately and in absolute numbers, while black enrollment has increased substantially. These trends give every indication of continuing. The Boston public school system gets progressively worse and its clients are increasingly black. And yet it seems impervious to change.

An examination of the way the system is set up and operated may suggest a rationale. In theory it works this way: the Commonwealth of Massachusetts has a school department which is supervised by a state board. The state board has far-ranging powers over local schools. However, by statute, primary responsibility for the public school system in the city of Boston is vested in the Boston School Committee, a five-member body elected at large by the voters for four-

---

12. In 1967, Peter Shrag wrote:

Each year the children who attend Boston's schools fall further behind national norms in reading and arithmetic. In the second grade Boston children read about five months above grade. By the sixth grade they are four months behind and Negro children are almost a year behind (by contrast, the average sixth grader in New York is four months ahead); by the time they are in the tenth grade they rank in the bottom third in the national tests (that is, the average Boston pupil falls into the 35th percentile in reading: the 50th percentile is "average.") Concurrently, the Boston mean in arithmetic falls in the 37th percentile. Until recently there were no remedial reading programs in the junior high schools.

P. Shrag, Village School Downtown 74–75 (1967) [hereinafter cited as Shrag]. This book makes up for what it may lack in scholarship in bringing the Boston school system, teachers, and officials to life. It is especially good in describing such public figures as Louise Day Hicks, and members of the Boston School Committee and the Boston School Department. It is good background reading for anyone interested in the Boston school crisis.

13. Massachusetts School Directory, 1973/74 at 93–96.

14. Morgan v. Hennigan, 379 F. Supp. 410, 424 (1974). Attached to the Memorandum of the Boston Home and School Association Relating to "White Flight," filed April 18, 1975, is a copy of a chart of white-nonwhite student enrollment for 1964 through 1973.

year terms. (Under the applicable statute the committee "shall have general charge of all the public schools . . . when not otherwise provided for. . . ." One such proviso concerns the selecting of sites and contracting for the construction of new schools. This responsibility lies with the Public Facilities Commission, an independent city agency.)[15] The Boston School Committee then appoints a superintendent of education to administer the system. The system is funded through a complex statutory formula (applicable only to Boston), which at various times may involve the school committee, the mayor, the Boston City Council and the state board.[16] In fact the state department and board have little direct influence on education policy within the city. The state concerns itself primarily with the disbursement of federal and state aid and the promulgation of minimum educational, nutritional, and safety standards.[17] The school committee has consistently been populated by would-be politicians rather than by educators; these school committee members with some justification view the highly visible body as a natural stepping stone to higher office. And the superintendent,

It provides figures for 1974/75 also:
According to the Boston Globe, March 15, 1975 at 1, Boston has lost 10,000 pupils since busing, most of them white. According to the Boston School Department's Department of Statistics, the October 1974 figure for enrollment was 85,826. It has since declined as students are transferring out of the system.

Year	Total Enrollment	White	Nonwhite	Percent
1964/65	91,800	70,703	21,097	23%
1965/66	93,055	69,136	23,919	25.7
1966/67	92,127	68,050	24,077	26.1
1968/69	93,815	66,366	27,449	29.3
1969/70	94,885	65,627	29,258	30.8
1970/71	96,432	65,108	31,328	32.5
1971/72	97,227	63,775	33,452	34.4
1972/73	95,615	60,556	35,059	36.7
1973/74	93,647	57,623	35,024	38.5
1974/75*	87,169	50,088	36,481	41.9

*Source cited as Boston Public Schools, 1974.

15. City of Boston Code, Ordinances, Title 8 §§1–4 (1975). *See also,* Morgan v. Hennigan, *supra* note 3, at 422.

16. Morgan v. Hennigan, *supra* note 3, at 422. Appropriations were to be made directly to the Boston School Committee up to the statutory limit. In 1898 the statutory limit was expressed in terms of dollars per thousand dollars of the assesed valuation of the city, to be certified by the assessors (Stat. 1898. Ch. 400). In 1936, the legislature set fixed dollar amounts as the limit, and any additional funding might be appropriated by the city council at the recommendation of the mayor following a request by the school committee (Stat. 1936. Ch. 224). In 1963 a new statute was enacted to enable the school committee to appropriate of its own accord a sum equal to that of the previous year, plus salary increases effective during that preceding year (Stat. 1963. Ch. 786, §3). The history of the school committee's funding appropriations authority is traced in the illuminating opinion Pironne v. City of Boston, 305 N.E. 2d 96 (Supreme Judicial Court 1973). It is also well summarized in the City of Boston's Report on School Finances in Boston, filed in July 1974 in Morgan v. Kerrigan.

17. Morgan v. Hennigan, *supra* note 3, at 422, and Mass. Gen. Laws, Ch. 15, §1G.

while having authority over personnel and related matters, if forced to administer the system with a board of superintendents consisting of the business manager, the chief custodian, and the chief structural engineer, all of whom are appointed by and report directly to the school committee, not the superintendent.

In addition to problems inherent in having educational policy made and promulagated by a body composed of politicians, the Boston School Committee brings another affliction to the public school system. It has never been at all representative of the multi-ethnic population. Ironically enough, the same at-large system devised by the Yankees to keep the Irish off the school committee now serves to perpetuate Irish domination of that body. In the past decade only one person on the school committee has not been Irish.[18] And as the school committee has become a bastion for the preservation and perpetuation of political power, the deterioration of the system proceeds unchecked.

The Battle of the Sixties

The battle to desegregate the Boston schools, begun in the eighteenth century, flared up again in the nineteenth and continued, if at a somewhat lower pitch, during the twentieth.[19] The immediate antecedents to the present controversy occurred in the early 1960s, an apparent by-product of the national civil rights movement. In 1961 the Boston chapter of the National Association for the Advancement of Colored People (NAACP) asked the Massachusetts Commission Against Discrimination (MCAD) to conduct a study of discrimination in school assignments in the Boston system and the effect of racial isolation on the educational process.[20] The MCAD concluded that there was no discrimination in the distribution of students and that there was no difference educationally between white and black schools.[21]

18. Joseph Lee, first elected in the early forties, Yankee.
John McMorrow, first elected 1955.

John Tierney,	"	1957.
Thomas Eisenstadt,	"	1961, Irish mother, Jewish father.
Arthur Gartland,	"	1961.
Louise Day Hicks,	"	1961.
William O'Connor,	"	1961.
John McDonough,	"	1965.
Paul Tierney,	"	1967.
John Kerrigan,	"	1967.
John Craven,	"	1969.
James Hennigan,	"	1969.
Paul Ellison,	"	1971.
Kathleen Sullivan,	"	1973.

Unpublished manuscript, 1. DiCara and F. Levy, Northern Schools and Civil Rights, at 36–37 (1971).

19. See text and notes, *supra* pp. 26–27.

20. Bolner & Shanley, Civil Rights, *supra* note 8, at 29.

21. The Annual Report of the Massachusetts Commission Against Discrimination, January 1, 1961 to December 31, 1961. The MCAD conducted a study of six Massachusetts cities: Boston, Cambridge, New Bedford, Pittsfield, Springfield, and Worcester. "In Boston," the report stated, "schools had a preponderance of Negro children in their enrollments. It appears that the bulk of the Negro enrollment is in the section of the city

However, the members of the Boston NAACP continued to meet with school officials attempting to get them to recognize what was then called "de facto segregation" and to seek remedies for it. After a disappointing session with Superintendent Frederick J. Gillis in March 1962, the NAACP decided to take its case directly to the school committee. The school committee at this time (1961-1965) consisted of Thomas Eisenstadt, son of a Boston political family; Joseph Lee, the committee's perennial Yankee member: William O'Connor, a retired teacher; Arthur Gartland, a Harvard-educated businessman; and the now well-known Louise Day Hicks. Of these, only Gartland was demonstrably sympathetic with NAACP concerns.[22]

On May 22, 1963, the Education Committee of the Boston NAACP released a report charging that there were 13 predominantly black schools in the city; that expenditures per child at these schools were less than the citywide average; that the facilities were older; and the classrooms more crowded. The report also pointed out the desirability of adjusting intelligence tests to reflect the rural upbringing of many of the city's black students, and stressed the need to make curriculum changes to reflect the needs of black students.[23] A week later, on

where the Negro population is most heavily centered. From the trip it was professionally deduced that there is a good feeling of comradeship in the classrooms, corridors and playgrounds and the same standards of teaching and professional backgrounds seem to prevail in schools regardless of color membership. . . ." *Id.* at 24. The study emphasized that the concentration of blacks in schools in Boston resulted from residential concentration and the neighborhood school policy, though it conceded that the situation might amount to "*de facto segregation.*" *Id.* at 25. Defendants in *Morgan v. Hennigan* would some twelve years later make the same arguments in their defense. The report concluded as follows:

> The Commission has emphasized its belief that the high standards of educational procedure in Massachusetts should provide equal learning opportunities for ALL children. This should include both the quality of trained teachers and the housing and equipment for all sections of a city. In the sections visited it seemed that an effort is being made to maintain these qualities. The printed rules and regulations on such matters as transfer, selection and promotion of teachers are clear and the authorities state that no discrimination is involved. . . ."

Id.
22. For the political inclinations of past members of the school committee, see Shrag, *supra* note 12, at 6-10, 61. Arthur Gartland, an insurance executive, was first elected to the school committee in 1961. Although Irish, he has often been accused by his fellow Irish of "Yankee leanings." Educated at Harvard (he has often been called "the Harvard Irishman"), he has also been a professor of economics at Notre Dame. He was supported for his election to the school committee by a reform group called Citizens for the Boston Schools. Although resented by many Irish elements, he is known to have established good communication lines in the Italian sections of the city, especially in East Boston. Shrag, *supra* note 12, at 7, 9, 11, 14, 17, 24, 41. F. Levy, Northern Schools and Civil Rights, *supra* note 7, at 36. For an example of Gartland's stand on education for black children, see his "Letter to the Editor from Gartland" in the Boston Sunday Globe, January 17, 1965, at 2A. In May 1975, Judge Garrity appointed Gartland to chair the Citizens Coordinating Council for Phase Two, composed of forty-two prominent Boston citizens, white and black. Boston Globe, May 31, 1975, at 3. The school committee voted 3-2 for his removal from this position on the grounds of conflict of interest. Boston Globe, June 5, 1975, at 9.
23. Bolner & Shanley, Civil Rights, *supra* note 8, at 30-31. The Boston Globe, May 24, 1963, at 1, 2. The two most outspoken advocates of quality education for black students

May 29, 1963, the Congress on Racial Equality (CORE) issued a similar report charging that the Boston public schools were segregated and provided unequal educational facilities for black students.[24]

At a public hearing before the school committee on June 15, 1963, black leaders presented a fourteen-point program to remedy the complaints made against the system. The program called for: (1) recognition of de facto segregation; (2) review of open-enrollment procedures; (3) faculty training in human relations; (4) training programs for prospective teachers; (5) permanent teachers in grades 1–3, and smaller classes; (6) visual aids having all the races represented; (7) a developmental reading program for grades 1–8; (8) expansion of counseling programs; (9) expansion of vocational guidance programs; (10) elimination of discrimination in the hiring and assignment of black teachers; (11) investigation into why Boston has no black principal; (12) review of intelligence testing; (13) adoption of the Sargent report with reference to the programs of building construction for the system; and (14) the right to discuss the selection of a new superintendent.[25]

The school committee agreed to study points 2, 3, 6, 7, and 8, and was conciliatory on others.[26] It also asked for suggestion with regard to multi-ethnic tests. However, it balked on two points. The committee refused to recognize the existence of de facto segregation in the school system (point 1) or discrimination in the hiring and assignment of teachers (point 10).

Convinced that the school committee's refusal to recognize de facto segregation suggested that the fourteen-point program was not accorded the consideration it deserved, leaders of the black community announced that Tuesday, June 18, 1963, would be Stay Out for Freedom Day and called for black students to boycott the schools on that day.[27] On the appointed day, 8,260 secondary school students, including some whites, stayed away from regular classes and attended "freedom schools." The normal 10 percent rate of absenteeism increased to 30 percent.[28]

have been Ruth Batson and Paul Parks. Both have been active members of the NAACP's Education Committee and the Attorney General's Advisory Committee on Civil Rights. Back in 1950, Batson had told Dennis Haley, superintendent of Boston's schools, that the city's black children were getting an inferior education. She was elected to the Massachusetts Democratic Committee, and chaired the Massachusetts Commission Against Discrimination. She became executive director of the Metropolitan Council for Educational Opportunity (METCO). Paul Parks has been vice president of the reform group Citizens for the Boston Public Schools, and a member of the Massachusetts Advisory Committee to the U.S. Civil Rights Commission. He has also been involved with the management of METCO, and has been executive e director of the Boston Model Cities Administration. Harvard Study, *supra* 8, at 13–14. At present Parks is Massachusetts State Secretary of Education.

24. Boston Globe (P.M.), May 29, 1963, at 4.

25. Boston Sunday Globe, June 16, 1963, at 1, 22.

26. Harvard Study, *supra* note 8, at 21. Boston Globe, June 16, 1963, at 1, 22.

27. Harvard Study, *supra* note 8, at 23. Boston Globe, June 18, 1963, at 4.

28. Boston Globe, June 19, 1963, at 1. In all, 8,260 secondary school students stayed away from classes, whereas normally only about 2,800 would have stayed away. Harvard Study, *supra* note 8, at 23.

On August 15, 1963, during the summer recess, leaders of the black community met again with the school committee, which again denied that the Boston schools were segregated except as the result of housing patterns.

A second boycott was organized for February 26, 1974, and 20,571 students (about 22 percent), stayed away from the schools on that day.[29] The boycotting students again attended the "freedom schools." One day later, the State Board of Education announced that it would undertake a study of racial imbalance in the public schools of Massachusetts. In March the 21-member blue ribbon Advisory Committee on Racial Imbalance and Education was established under the chairmanship of Owen Kiernan, the commissioner of education. Members included four university presidents and various civic, business, labor, and religious leaders.

The final report of the Kiernan Commission was issued a year later, on April 15, 1965. The report, entitled *Because It is Right—Educationally,* concluded that racial imbalance was harmful educationally because: it impairs the confidence of black children, destroying their self-image and lowering motivation; it encourages prejudice in children regardless of color; it presents an inaccurate picture of life in a multi-racial community; it produces inferior educational facilities; and it impairs opportunities of blacks to prepare for professional and vocational careers.

Because It Is Right—Educationally defined racial imbalance as any school with over 50 percent enrollment of black students. Among other things it recommended legislation that would bring about the elimination of such schools by means including but not limited to the withholding of state aid. The short text of the report was followed by lengthy appendixes recommending redistricting and busing as the means of eliminating racially imbalanced schools. Of imimportance to Boston was a suggestion for the two-way busing of 2,500 blacks and 2,500 whites in fairly close districts.[30] The Boston School Committee voted to reject the report by a margin of 3 to 2.[31]

The report nonetheless had its impact. Shortly after the report's release, the school committee was served notice by Governor Volpe that if it failed to act to lessen imbalance, he would propose legislation to that end.

Many black parents refused to wait for legislative change. In September 1965 a group of parents from North Dorchester formed Operation Exodus, a private organization to bus black children into white areas whose schools had available seats. At the cost of about $1,200 per week, 400 black children were bused throughout the city.[32]

29. Harvard Study, *supra* note 8, at 27. Boston Herald, February 27, 1964, at 1.
30. Report of the Massachusetts Advisory Committee on Racial Imbalance and Education, Because It Is Right—Educationally 2 (1965).
31. Boston Globe, April 16, 1965, at 1, 3. Harvard Study, *supra* note 8, at 36.
32. Operation Exodus was first organized by parents of black public school students in Roxbury. They established an office on Blue Hill Avenue to raise funds for busing, and for an after-school tutorial program. At first the children were bused to schools that had vacant

A year later a similar program was undertaken by the interracial suburban-urban Metropolitan Council for Education Opportunity (METCO). Financed by a $239,000 grant from the U.S. Office of Education and a smaller grant from the Carnegie Corporation, METCO bused 200 black students to seven participating suburban school systems.[33] By 1974 the state had undertaken the funding of METCO and the organization was busing 2,300 students to an expanding number of suburban schools systems.[34] While originally regarded with disdain, METCO now enjoys support of a large cross-section of the Boston community. Many see it as a regional solution to Boston's desegregation problem. They feel that white suburbs which drain the inner city of its resources are being asked to contribute something in return. One current proponent, John Kerrigan, currently a member of the Boston School Committee, has sought to have METCO expanded to include 19,000 black students—one-half of the number of blacks in the Boston system—thereby bringing the suburbs into fuller participation in solving the city's problem.[35]

The Racial Imbalance Act

Just prior to the release of the Kiernan Commission's report, a Massachusetts civil rights worker was murdered in Selma, Alabama.[36] This prompted an outpouring of sentiment in favor of civil rights. Many felt that this was the appro-

---

seats in white Dorchester and Hyde Park, but later the buses reached a greater variety of locations. Although the funding efforts started out privately, later on churches, civil rights organizations at university campuses, and others joined to raise funds. Eartha Kitt and Odetta gave benefit concerts. Convinced that their children benefited educationally from the program—from smaller classes, updated textbooks, and individual attention—parents running the program sought to expand it. Shrag, *supra* note 12, at 13, 41, 119–25. Harvard Study, *supra* note 8, at 31. But Exodus has run into funding problems. According to Judge Garrity in *Morgan v. Hennigan,* at its peak in 1969 Exodus bused 1,100 black students, but in 1972 the number was down to 170. Morgan v. Hennigan, *supra* note 3, at 424.

For a sociological study of Operation Exodus, *see* J.E. Teele, Evaluating School Busing: Case Study of Boston's Operation Exodus (1973).

33. Shrag, *supra* note 12, at 134–38.

34. Boston Globe, October 28, 1974, at 1, 18.

35. In a public statement delivered January 2, 1975 (the last day of his chairmanship), Kerrigan spelled out his expanded METCO plan. "Instead of busing 2,000 students to 34 suburbs, transport 19,000 to 85 towns and cities in the Boston SMSA [Standard Metropolitan Statistical Area]. The result would be an average of 45 non-white students per school, hardly a takeover. . . ." Kerrigan, The Hub at the Bicentennial, at 2 (speech delivered January 2, 1975). He went on to say, ". . . Suburban children would have the opportunity of going to school with children of a race other than their own, and inner city children would reap the benefits of a better financed suburban education. Busing within the City of Boston would be substantially reduced, tension would be relieved, and the rising tide of white flight might abate. . . ." (*Id.* at 3.)

36. Reverend James Reeb, 38, a Massachusetts resident and father of four, was violently attacked in the streets of Selma in March, 1965. He died two days later. The incident was widely publicized; it was on the front page of the *Boston Globe* both March 11 and 12, 1965, and there were many letters to the editor and editorials. Massachusetts Lieutenant Governor Elliott Richardson flew to Selma in response. Boston Globe, March 11, 1965, at 1; March 12, 1965, at 1; March 13, 1965, at 1; March 15, 1965, at 1, 6. Harvard Study, *supra* note 8, at 8.

priate time to confront the racial imbalance problem that had been festering for years.

An effort was begun to implement the Kiernan Commission's recommendation for state legislation. After several months of intense drafting, redrafting, and politicing,[37] the legislature passed and the governor signed the Massachusetts Imbalance Act (hereinafter called the Racial Imbalance Act).[38]

As enacted in 1965, the Racial Imbalance Act operated as follows: local school committees were to submit an annual racial census of their student population to the State Board of Education. If any district had a school that was imbalanced (over 50 percent black student enrollment), that school committee would be required: (1) to prepare a plan designed to eliminate such racial imbalance; (2) to file the plan with the state board; and (3) to make reports on the progress and implementation of the plan. The state board could invoke the aid of the state courts to compel compliance by reluctant school committees. Moreover, if a local school committee did not show "compliance within a reasonable time" in eliminating racial imbalance, the commissioner of education was required to order a suspension in future state aid, in previously certified state aid, and in state assistance in school building construction projects.

In response to the requirements of the Racial Imbalance Act, the Boston School Committee filed a number of plans that were subsequently rejected by the state board. Staff from the state board were then assigned to advise the school committee and to make recommendations for a satisfactory plan. Although many of these recommendations were ignored, no sanctions other than the withholding of state funds were imposed.

Four plans submitted by the Boston School Committee were approved by the state board. These include: (1) the 1966/67 plan approved on March 15, 1967; (2) the Second Stage plan, approved June 25, 1968; (3) the Third Stage plan, approved July 22, 1969; and (4) the Fourth Stage plan, approved August 31, 1971. In none of these was the means of redistricting and busing seriously utilized. Meanwhile, the number of imbalanced schools in Boston increased from 58 in 1965 to over 70 in 1972.[39]

The Boston School Committee and its supporters in the legislature sought to

37. At first, Republicans and Democrats produced separate bills. But Republican Lieutenant Governor Elliott Richardson and Democratic House Speaker F.X. Davoren decided to join forces for one strong bill. NAACP leaders and state department of education officials lent their support. It was mostly Democratic legislators who opposed the bill and attempted to cripple it with antibusing amendments which nearly passed. Senator Beryl Cohen sponsored the bill. She gathered a group of NAACP officials and attorneys to consult with her on the detailed drafting. When the bill finally passed August 5, 1965, it contained a modified antibusing provision over the objections of Ruth Batson and Paul Parks, in order to placate earlier opponents of the bill. *See* Harvard Study, *supra* note 8, at 38–47, which though not legislative history, does offer a guide to analysis of the Racial Imbalance Act. *See also* Bolner and Shanley, Civil Rights, *supra* note 8, at 49–74, for a more detailed account of the above.

38. Boston Globe (P.M.), August 18, 1965, at 1.

39. Harvard Study, *supra* note 8, at 1.

avoid the Racial Imbalance Act by annual attempts to repeal it or to amend it into extinction. Thus there were petitions to further define the term "racial imbalance" so as to make the act harmless, and petitions to make the Racial Imbalance Act inapplicable to state aid for new school construction.[40] It was proposed that whenever children were transported 1.5 miles or more in order to eliminate racial imbalance the state would pick up 100 percent of the cost. This amendment was passed in 1969.[41]

A second amendment to the Racial Imbalance Act was passed by the legislature in 1971. It required a public hearing before a school committee could redistrict under a plan to racially balance its schools. Notice of the hearing had to be given in a newspaper or by posting notice in a public place. A school committee was also required to mail a notice to the parent of each child who would have been affected.[42]

Anti-busing forces finally gathered enough strength in the Massachusetts legislature to pass legislation repealing the Racial Imbalance Act in May 1974. However, on May 10, 1974, Governor Francis Sargent vetoed the bill.[43]

On May 21, 1974, eleven days after his veto, the governor submitted proposed legislation for a new racial imbalance law. The governor's plan abandoned mandatory busing, seeking instead to achieve voluntary integration. Under his plan, minority children in a city school where they were a majority would have an "absolute right" to transfer to another city school in which they comprised less than a 30 percent minority. If no places were available in the school which a minority child wished to attend, the local school committee would be required to implement plans to provide a place within the same school year in which they were notified of the child's choice. The State Board of Education was given the power to approve a local committee's plan and to implement a plan of its own if one was not forthcoming from the city.[44]

The success of the Sargent plan depended on a series of incentives and penalties to get a school committee to comply. Thus, the state would pay 75 percent of the school expansion cost needed to provide a place for a minority student. In addition, there would be a $500 bonus per student to each school receiving minority children. The latter incentive would also apply to suburban systems receiving minority students from the inner city. Finally, the state board could cut

40. H. 2612 in 1967, and H. 3648 in 1968.

41. H. 88 became Ch. 643 of the 1969 Acts.

42. H. 6273 was signed by the governor on October 20, 1971 to become Ch. 958 of the 1971 Acts.

43. Boston Globe, May 14, 1974, at 12, and Christian Science Monitor, May 13, 1974, at 4A. In 1973 the governor had sought a declaratory judgment on the constitutionality of House Bill 6657, an act amending the Racial Imbalance Act to prohibit forced busing. In an Opinion of the Justices, 298 N.E.2d 840 (1973), the Supreme Judicial Court denied the constitutionality of the amendment. Again, in 1974, the state sought a declaratory judgment on the repeal of the Racial Imbalance Act. In an Opinion of the Justices, 1974 Mass. Adv. Sh. 545, the court condemned the repeal legislation.

44. Boston Globe, May 21, 1974, at 1, 14; *id.,* May 25, 1974, at 3; Stat. 1974, Ch. 636, §1 *et seq.*; Christian Science Monitor, May 21, 1974, at 4A.

off state aid to a school committee that failed to come up with an acceptable plan to place minority children who desired to transfer from schools in which they were a majority.[45]

This proposal was generally welcomed by anti-busing forces and condemned by black leaders. In the latter's view the plan put the burden of transferring on the minorities. They were also critical of the $500 subsidy which would allow the suburbs to make money out of the integration effort.[46] In spite of these criticisms the proposal passed in the legislature and was signed by Governor Sargent on July 26, 1974.

In addition to attempts to repeal the Racial Imbalance Act in the legislature, the Boston School Committee sought to avoid compliance with the act by taking its case to the courts. In 1966 the school committee sought to have the act declared unconstitutional by the Massachusetts Supreme Judicial Court. The effort was unsuccessful.[47]

In 1972 the state board was withholding $52 million in state aid to the Boston schools in connection with the Fourth Stage Racial Imbalance Plan. The Boston School Committee challenged the withholding of the funds by a suit in superior court.[48] The superior court found the school committee to be in minimal compliance with the Racial Imbalance Act and ordered the funds released. On February 2, 1973 the Massachusetts Supreme Judicial Court upheld the superior court's determination.[49] The rationale was that the state board's action had been arbitrary because it was based upon a single school committee vote rather than all the circumstances of imbalance in Boston.

Although the funds had been released, the state board had again voted to reject the latest plan submitted by the Boston School Committee.

The board then adopted the Revised Short Term Plan to Reduce Racial Imbalance in the Boston Public Schools, which was drafted by the Task Force on Racial Imbalance. In addition to its obvious concern for racial balance,[50] the

45. *Id.*

46. Boston Globe (P.M.), May 21, 1974, at 1, 9; Christian Science Monitor, May 21, 1974, at 4A; *id.*, May 22, 1974, at 4B.

47. School Committee of Boston v. Board of Education, 352 Mass. 693, 698, 227 N.E.2d 729, 733 (1967); *appeal dismissed*; 389 U.S. 572 (1968). The constitutionality of the Racial Imbalance Act was affirmed. The school committee had raised the due process clause of the Fourteenth Amendment, arguing vagueness, the equal protection clause, and Article I of the Declaration of Rights. The court stated, "It would be the height of irony if the racial imbalance act, enacted as it was with the laudable purpose of achieving equal educational opportunities, should, by proscribing school pupil allocations based on race, founder on unsuspected shoals of the Fourteenth Amendment." But the court went on to say, "The Committee seems bent on stifling the act before it has a fair chance to become fully operative."

48. School Committee of Boston v. Board of Education, Equity 94524 (Suffolk Superior Court, filed October 26, 1971).

49. School Committee of Boston v. Board of Education, 363 Mass. 20, 292 N.E.2d 338 (1973).

50. This document contained an "emergency preamble:"

The Board of Education hereby issues *Emergency Regulations Pertaining to the*

plan stressed "safety" considerations. Kindergartens were excepted and travel time was limited for younger children. Where maximum desegregation would necessitate overcrowding certain facilities, the plan allowed for less. Insofar as possible, crossing of major thoroughfares was eschewed, and when such was necessary detailed precautionary measures were outlined. Where children walked, extensive recommendations were made to assure their safety. Whenever walking would be hazardous, it was mandated that transportation be provided in a manner consistent with ongoing transportation and safety practices within the city.

In addition to the safety aspect, the plan sought to prevent substantial impairment of the educational process or unnecessary fragmentation of neighborhoods, districts, and communities. Under "racial balance considerations," the plan assured that districts would bear a reasonable (though not necessarily fixed) proximity to recognized neighborhoods; that even though clustering of several schools within a district could be utilized, enlarged districts would be limited in size; and that precautions would be taken to protect against gerrymandering of districts.

Despite all this, the plan's provision for busing over 2,000 additional elementary and intermediate public school students was unacceptable to the Boston School Committee. They invoked the statutory right to have the plan reviewed. The Massachusetts Supreme Judicial Court decided that the review should be made upon the basis of an administrative record. Professor Louis Jaffe of Harvard Law School was appointed to conduct the hearings.[51]

The Jaffe hearings resulted in a finding that the state board's plan was consistent with the Racial Imbalance Act. On June 25, 1973, the state board ordered the Boston School Committee to racially balance Boston schools by September 1974. On the following day it overruled a proposal by Jaffe to eliminate South Boston from its plan because of hostility to blacks in that neighborhood. In yet another case, the court rejected the school committee's challenge to the state board order.[52]

Preparation of Racial Balance Plans which Involve Redistricting. These regulations are issued in accordance with the provisions of General Laws Chapter 30A, under the authority of General Laws Chapter 15, Section 1G, and in accordance with the decision of the Supreme Judicial Court of the Commonwealth in *Springfield v. Board of Education,* 362 Mass. 417, 287 N.E.2d 438, 455–56 (1972). The Board hereby finds that due to the press of litigation, the fact that one major city in the Commonwealth is under a court ordered deadline, and the urgency of planning deadlines for all those engaged in racial balance planning, the observance of the requirements of notice and public hearings is unnecessary, impracticable, and contrary to the public interest.

Revised Short-Term Plan to Reduce Racial Imbalance in Boston Public Schools Commonwealth of Massachusetts Task Force on Racial Imbalance, December 12, 1973.

51. The hearings were held between March 20 and May 3, 1973. Jaffe submitted his Report and Recommendations to the state board on May 29, 1973. The state board issued their Opinion and Order, substantially adopting Professor Jaffe's report, on June 25, 1973. It again rejected the committee's plan and called for implementation of the state board plan. For an account of these proceedings, see School Committee of Boston v. Board of Education, 364 Mass. 199, 302 N.E.2d 916 (1973).

52. *Id.*

However, the Boston School Committee and the state board continued to battle in the Massachusetts courts over whose plan for desegregation was better. On March 22, 1974, the Massachusetts Supreme Judicial Court again found that the Boston School Committee had not complied with the state board's order or with the court's own order. On April 17 a single justice of the Massachusetts court ordered that staff assignments with respect to balancing the schools be made by May 1, 1974, and that plans for the safety and transportation of students be completed by May 15, 1974.[53]

THE LAWSUIT

The Parties and the Trial

By 1971, leaders in the black community had become disenchanted with prospects for meaningful implementation of the state's Racial Imbalance Act. Taking their cue from communities across the country, they decided to turn to the federal courts for relief. The community groups, headed by the local chapter of the NAACP, enlisted the aid of the Harvard Center for Law and Education[54] and the Boston chapter of the Lawyers' Committee for Civil Rights under Law.[55]

Both responded promptly and positively. The Harvard group expanded its ongoing involvement in the area and assigned attorneys Robert Pressman and Eric Van Loon to work on the case. The Lawyers' Committee, which had been serving as a local clearing-house for *pro bono* work by the private bar, obtained a major commitment from the prestigious Boston law firm of Foley, Hoag & Eliot. Attorneys Laurence Fordham, John Leubsdorf, and Roger Abrams were assigned to the case.[56]

On March 15, 1972 the complaint was filed in United States District Court for the District of Massachusetts. The named plaintiffs were fourteen black parents and their children who attended Boston public schools.[57] As in many

53. Interlocutory Decree, entered April 17, 1974 in Board of Education v. School Committee of Boston, Equity 73–190 (Supreme Judicial Court, filed September 26, 1973).

54. The Harvard Center for Law and Education is funded by the Community Services Agency (formerly OEO) as a backup agency on education issues for local legal services throughout the country. The center does research, distributes materials, and participates in training and litigation. Attention has focused on issues of students' rights, federally funded programs (such as Title I of ESEA), special education, student fees, testing, tracking, classification, desegregation, bilingual and bicultural education, and Indian education. The center staff includes attorneys, researchers, a director of publications, and clerical and administrative personnel. Center for Law and Education, Harvard University, descriptive sheet entitled About the Center.

55. Interview with Attorney Robert Pressman at the Harvard Center for Law and Education, May 21, 1975.

56. Interview with Attorney John Leubsdorf at Foley, Hoag & Eliot, April 9, 1975.

57. Plaintiffs named in the complaint filed March 15, 1972 were: Tallulah Morgan, Petri Morgan, Kimberly Morgan, and Kirsten Morgan; Sandra Purcelle, Dee Anna Purcelle, and Michael Purcelle; Richard N. Yarde, Leslie R. Yarde and Richard N. Yarde II; Lorraine Wheaton and Teddy Wheaton; Joann Reed, Aaron Thomas Reed and Leigh Ann Reed; Addell Vaughn, Raymond Joseph Vaughn and Kevin Arthur Vaughn; Arthur Eskew, Kemya

other desegregation cases, the NAACP was the principal, if unnamed, plaintiff.

The complaint listed as defendants the Boston School Committee, its individual members, the superintendent of the Boston public schools, and the state commissioner of education.[58] At that time the Boston School Committee was composed of James W. Hennigan (chairman), Paul J. Ellison, John J. Kerrigan, John J. McDonough, and Paul R. Tierney. William H. Ohrenberger was superintendent of Boston public schools. Cecilia Kipp (chairwoman), Richard Banks, Walter Borg, Romona Correveau, William Densmore, J. Richard Early, Allan Finlay, Mrs. David Hardenberth, Joseph Saleino, John Sullivan, Janet Tobey, and Joseph Weisberg were members of the State Board of Education, and Neil Sullivan was commissioner of education.

The state defendants were represented by attorneys from the state attorney general's office and from the legal department of the Massachusetts Department of Education. The city defendants decided to employ outside counsel on the ground that the case was much too complex and time-consuming for the city's corporation counsel. The long battle in the state courts demonstrated that the interests of the Boston School Committee were not the same as those of their state co-defendants.

The school committee selected the Boston firm of Dimento and Sullivan to represent them.[59] However, Mayor White refused to grant the required approval of the contract. He preferred to have the city defended by Hale and Dorr, one of Boston's oldest and most respected law firms. More specifically, he wanted attorney James St. Clair, a senior partner of Hale and Dorr.[60] Neither the mayor nor the school committee would abandon their first choice, so a compromise was effected and both firms were retained.

Federal District Court Judge W. Arthur Garrity was assigned to the case.[61]

Eskew, Tashia Eskew, and Toure Eskew; Carrie Phillips, Norman Arthur Phillips, Tyrone Phillips and Robert Phillips; Earline Pruitts, Lynette Pruitts, Betty Jean Pruitts, Valeria Pruitts, Robert Edward Pruitts, James Neal Pruitts, Denise Pruitts and Kevin Pruitts; Diane Bassett and Celeste Bassett; Fern Burdette, Pamela Burdette and Yvonne Burdette; Mary Crockett and Beverly Crockett; Mary Murphy, Anthony Murphy, Arnold Murphy and Ricky Murphy; Grace Means, Hudis Means, Karen Means, Donna Means, Michael Means, Bryan Means, Kevin Means and Corey Means.

58. Plaintiffs' Complaint, filed March 15, 1972, in Morgan v. Hennigan, *supra* note 12, at 1.

59. Interview with Boston School Committeeman John J. Kerrigan, at 15 Beacon Street, Boston, May 21, 1975.

60. James St. Clair would later become nationally renowned as the last in a succession of attorneys representing then President Richard M. Nixon as he sought to avoid impeachment and removal from office.

61. Wendell Arthur Garrity, Jr. was born in Worcester, Mass. on June 20, 1920. He graduated from Holy Cross College in 1941, and attended Harvard Law School for two years. He interrupted his legal education to enlist in the U.S. Army, and finally received his law degree in 1946. He then spent a year as law clerk to U.S. District Court Judge Francis J.W. Ford, and two years as an assistant U.S. attorney. In 1950 he entered private practice with friends Richard Maguire and J. Joseph Maloney. In 1961, President Kennedy appointed

None of the parties objected, and counsel for both sides indicated that they were pleased with his selection. He was well regarded. He had a reputation as a fair and conscientious judge. And even though he had liberal leanings, defendants seemed satisfied at the outset.[62]

Before the case could get underway, efforts were made to join other parties, and still others sought to intervene. The Boston Teachers' Union sought to be heard on issues of liability. Its motion was supported by the city defendants and opposed by plaintiffs, who successfully argued that at the violation stage the interests of the teachers' union and the school committee were identical and that therefore intervention would cause unnecessary complication.[63]

The defendants made an early motion to join 65 suburban communities as defendants. In support of the motion the defendants argued that the racial problems were metropolitan in scope and thus any remedy that might be forthcoming would have to be a metropolitan one. Plaintiffs opposed this motion arguing that to join the suburbs would cause unnecessary delay and confusion. Moreover, they contended that no suburban violation need be proved to effect a metropolitan remedy.[64]

---

him U.S. attorney. For five years he was the chief federal prosecutor in Boston. In 1966, President Johnson named Garrity to the federal bench. Boston Globe, June 22, 1974, at 3. 34 Who's Who in America (1966-1967).

62. Judge Garrity had become associated with fairly controversial "liberal" cases. When this suit went to trial he was still involved in a case challenging the conditions of Boston's Charles Street Jail, Inmates of Suffolk County Jail v. Thomas Eisenstadt, No. 71-162-6 (U.S.D.C., filed January 1, 1971). He was also handling Aaron D. Hazard v. Eugene Rida (U.S.D.C., filed July 17, 1969), a case involving allegations of police brutality.

63. The joinder of many parties whose interests were substantially the same was not in the plaintiffs' interests strategically, for it would have meant responses to numerous additional pleadings and the needless complexity of issues. Interview with Attorney Robert Pressman, *supra* note 55. Interview with Attorney John Leubsdorf, *supra* note 56.

64. This particular contention would shortly thereafter be discredited by the Supreme Court's decision in *Milliken v. Bradley,* 418 U.S. 717, 94 S. Ct. 3112. The court declared that in order for there to be an interdistrict (or metropolitan) remedy, there must first be evidence of an interdistrict constitutional violation. The theory was set out in the opinion as follows:

The controlling principle consistently expounded in our holdings is that the scope of the remedy is determined by the nature and extent of the constitutional violation. *Swann* [citation omitted]. Before the boundaries of separate and autonomous school districts may be set aside by consolidating the separate units for remedial purposes or by imposing a cross-district remedy, it must first be shown that there has been a constitutional violation withon one district that produces a significant segregative effect in another district. Specifically it must be shown that racially discriminatory acts of the state or local school districts, or of a single school district have been a substantial cause of inter-district segregation. . . . Conversely, without an inter-district violation and inter-district effect, there is no constitutional wrong calling for an inter-district remedy.

418 U.S. at 744-45.

Again the court agreed with plaintiffs, and the case went to trial in much the same alignment as outlined in the complaint.

In the complaint, plaintiffs charged that defendants engaged in conduct that was in violation of rights secured to plaintiffs by the Thirteenth and Fourteenth Amendments to the U.S. Constitution and 42 U.S.C. 1981, 1983, and 2000d. Plaintiff alleged as follows:

9. The [city] defendants . . . have effected racial segregation and discrimination in the Boston public schools and have otherwise denied equality of educational opportunity to black children by acts and practices including, but not limited to:
   (a) adopting and maintaining parent-pupil school selection policies and practices, including open enrollment transfers and optional school attendance zones, which have contributed to pupil racial segregation;
   (b) establishing and manipulating district lines, attendance areas for schools and classes, assignments within and among attendance areas, and school feeder pattern in ways promoting racial segregation of students;
   (c) transporting pupils to schools in ways promoting racial segregation of students;
   (d) establishing and manipulating the organization of schools and grade structures in ways promoting racial segregation of pupils;
   (e) adopting and maintaining pupil assignment policies and practices which have built upon and reflected residential racial segregation resulting from public and private discrimination in housing;
   (f) administering school capacity, enlargement, and policies in ways promoting racial segregation of students;
   (g) failing and refusing without justification to adopt, implement, or continue policies reasonably available to remedy pupil racial segregation;
   (h) adopting and implementing pupil classification practices which discriminate against some children in their admission to certain schools, classes, and courses of study, on the basis of their race and color, and which deny to such children, on the basis of their race and color, educational opportunities afforded other children in the system;
   (i) denying equal educational opportunities to black children by adopting and maintaining a pattern of lower instructional expenditures, including

---

In applying this theory to the Detroit situation, the Court held:

With no showing of significant violation by the 53 outlying school districts and no evidence of any inter-district violation or effect, the court went beyond the original theory of the case as framed by the pleadings and mandated a metropolitan area remedy. To approve the remedy ordered by the court would impose on the outlying districts, not shown to have committed by constitutional violation, a wholly impermissible remedy based on a standing not hinted at in *Brown I* and *II* or any holding of this Court. [*Id.* at 745.]

Nonetheless, subsequently the metropolitan issue was raised by the mayor. His counsel argued that the case should be reopened to consider a metropolitan remedy. On June 11, 1975, Judge Garrity heard arguments by Professor Leonard P. Strickman of Boston College Law School in support of the mayor's metropolitan plan. The next day the court denied the motion. Boston Globe, June 12, 1975, at 4.

expenditures for teacher services, in schools attended disproportionately by such children.

10. The Boston defendants and their predecessors have engaged in racial discrimination with respect to the recruitment, hiring, assignment and reassignment of faculty and staff.

11. The Boston defendants and their predecessors have engaged in racial discrimination in the operation of the programs in the public schools, including with respect to curricula, instructional materials, and resources.

12. Policies, acts, and practices of the [state defendants] . . . have contributed to causing and perpetuating the racial segregation and denials of equal educational opportunity alleged. . . .

13. The acts and practices of the defendants alleged in this Complaint deny to plaintiffs their rights to equality of public educational opportunity without regard to race and their right to be free from racial segregation and discrimination in the operation of the public schools, in violation of rights secured to plaintiffs by the 13th and 14th Amendments to the United States Constitution and 42 U.S.C. 1981, 1983 and 2000d.[65]

Unlike other suits wherein counsel would have to develop plaintiffs' case from sparse information, in *Morgan v. Hennigan* plaintiffs had available at the outset much of the documentation they would need. Under the state's Racial Imbalance Act the school department had been required to compile racial data since 1965. During the interim between the filing of the complaint and the trial, a federal administrative hearing had produced a considerable amount of data on Boston School Committee policies and practices on hiring, student assignment, and utilization of facilities.[66] For their own purposes, the Boston Housing Authority and the Massachusetts Commission Against Discrimination had also compiled voluminous amounts of relevant information.[67] All this information was

65. Plaintiffs' Complaint, filed March 15, 1972 in Morgan v. Hennigan *supra* note 3, at 5–6.

66. The opinion in *Morgan v. Hennigan* describes the federal administrative proceedings. 379 F. Supp. at 420–21 (D. Mass. 1974). For full details, see *In the Matter of Boston Public Schools, Massachusetts and State Department of Education of Massachusetts,* Administrative Proceedings in the Department of Health, Education and Welfare National Science Foundation Department of Housing and Urban Development, initial decision of Laurence M. Ring, Administrative Law Judge, March 2, 1973 (affirmed April 19, 1974).

67. Plaintiffs' Exhibit List appears in Volume II of the Appendixes to the City Defendants' Appellate Brief in Morgan v. Kerrigan in the U.S. Court of Appeals for the First Circuit. Data from the BHA and the MCAD were used to document the issues of open enrollment—controlled transfer, housing, and special enrollment schools. A partial listing of those documents used includes: Decision MCAD *ex rel.* Underwood v. Boston School Committee, E.D. XIV-1-c Docket and Complaint; Report and Evaluation of Activities, Nov. 15, 1963–Nov. 15, 1964 from Advisory Committee to the Boston Housing Authority; Commonwealth of Massachusetts MCAD Complaint, Boston Branch NAACP v. Boston Housing Authority, PHxii-2-c, 10/17/64; 1965 Report and Recommendations of the Advisory Committee to the Boston Housing Authority, 10/6/65; Third Ann. Rep. and Recommendations of the Advisory Committee to the Boston Housing Authority, 11/10/66; Fourth Ann. Rep. of the Advisory Committee to the Boston Housing Authority, 11/67; Ann. Reps. of the MCAD 1950/51, 1955/56, 1957/58, 1959/60, 1961, 1965–1970; Minutes of the

obtained in pretrial proceedings. Added to that which the Harvard Center for Law and Education had as a result of its two-year continuing study of the Boston public school system, plaintiffs had as impressive an array of documentary evidence as had been seen in this type of litigation.[68]

In addition to the obvious advantage afforded plaintiffs in terms of trial preparation, the availability of this data allowed extensive stipulation; as a consequence, the trail lasted only 15 days.[69]

Plaintiffs' trial strategy was designed to rely heavily on the documentary evidence to establish the constitutional violation they had alleged. They planned to put all this evidence before the court, explaining its content and significance as the trial progressed. They believed that this would allow them to build a persuasive case without the confusion and credibility problems usually attending oral testimony by witnesses.[70]

Much to their dismay, Judge Garrity expressed some impatience with the strategy and urged live testimony. Counsel then called several expert witnesses whose testimony dealt with the issues of teacher hiring practices, school facility utilization, and residential segregation.[71]

Counsel for city defendants had a multifaceted strategy. *First,* they would rely on live testimony to oppose plaintiffs' dry statistical data. *Second,* despite the fact that it was their motivations, words, and action that were at issue, the members of the Boston School Committee would *not* be called to the stand. *Third,* only the high-ranking administrators and the professionals would be asked to testify.[72]

Advisory Committee to the Boston Housing Authority, 11/15/65, 12/9/65, 2/10/66; Chart *re.* BHA Housing Projects—Occupancy by Race, 1956–1972; Boston Redevelopment Authority Map *re:* Public Housing Projects—1960, 1966; Boston Housing Authority Reports on Non-white Occupancy, 1965–72; MCAD v. BSC, 71-ED-1-c/No. 71-EU-2-c/No., Transcript pages, Complaint and Settlement Correspondence. Two recent publications helpful in understanding the setting of *Morgan v. Kerrigan* are the *Boston Redevelopment Authority's Working Paper, Housing in Boston, supra* note 10 and Route 128: Boston's Road to Segregation, *supra* note 9.

68. Attorney Robert Pressman was also involved in the preparation of the Harvard Study, *supra* note 8. In his interview, *supra* note 55, he listed the following as the main sources of plaintiffs' documentary evidence: records of the Boston school system; MCAD proceedings on the exam schools and open enrollment; state department of education records; statistical data from the Boston Redevelopment Authority and from the city government; files from HEW proceedings and studies; transcripts from HEW and state court proceedings; and depositions. Defendants' attorney John Mirick in his interview, *infra* note 72, praised plaintiffs' attorneys' preparation of their documentary evidence in charts, maps, graphs and other statistical preparations.

69. Trial commenced February 5, 1973, and closing arguments were heard on March 22, 1973. In all there were 15 days of trial testimony.

70. Interview with Attorney John Leubsdorf, *supra* note 56.

71. *Id.* Four of plaintiffs' expert witnesses were: Richard Scobie, expert in housing; Stefan Michelson, research associate at the Harvard Center for Law and Education, expert on teacher exams; Richard Majetic, program director for the National Teacher Exams of Educational Testing Service in Princeton, New Jersey; and Michael J. Stolee, school desegregation expert.

72. Interview with attorney John Mirick at Hale and Dorr, April 7, 1975.

This strategy was designed to bolster defendants' contention that neither the statistics nor the recorded remarks and attitudes of individual school committee members should be dispositive. Rather, they consistently argued that the school committee acted on the informed recommendations of administrators and professionals who were not racially motivated.[73]

The Opinion and Orders

On June 21, 1974, fifteen months after final argument, Judge Garrity filed his opinion, a partial judgement, and an interlocutory order.

The Opinion. The opinion was 150 pages long, well reasoned and well drafted. There was little doubt that Judge Garrity expected an appeal and had meticulously sought to avoid either reversal or remand.[74]

In the opinion Judge Garrity first set out the background and significance of the Racial Imbalance Act.[75] He chronicled the prior litigation in the state courts.[76] And he discussed the nature and substance of the federal administrative proceedings.[77] Turning to the plaintiffs' contention, the opinion articulated the constitutional test that would be employed and examined the evidence addressed at trial to ascertain whether defendants' conduct passed constitutional muster.

State Defendants. The court could find no constitutional violation on the part of state defendants. On the contrary, the court found that "the evidence established that [the state defendants] did everything within their limited authority under the law to compel the city defendants to obey the state law and

---

73. *Id.* The school administrator was Paul A. Kennedy, an associate superintendent of schools in charge of personnel.

74. On June 26, 1974, the school committee voted 3–1, against the advice of their attorneys, to appeal Judge Garrity's decision (Tierney, Ellison, and McDonough for the appeal; Sullivan against it). Boston Globe, June 27, 1974, at 1, 10. On September 22, 1974, the appeal was filed, and on December 19 the U.S. Court of Appeals for the First Circuit affirmed the Garrity decision. Chief Judge Frank Coffin wrote the opinion:

> It is beyond dispute that the defendants took every opportunity to maintain segregation where it existed and to foster segregation where it did not. To use the Supreme Court's language "the 'neighborhood school' concept has not been maintained free of manipulation." [Morgan v. Kerrigan, 509 F.2d 580, 592 (1st Cir. 1974).]

On March 19, 1975 the school committee appealed to the U.S. Supreme Court. Boston Globe, March 19, 1975, at 5. On May 12, 1975, the Supreme Court denied *certiorari*. *Sub. nom.* Kerrigan v. Morgan, 421 U.S. 963, 95 S. Ct. 1950.

The school committee then filed a motion for a stay of Garrity's May 10 (Phase II) order. This was denied by the court of appeals on June 17, 1975 (523 F.2d 917). Nevertheless the school committee appealed the order. The appeal was heard on September 12, 1975. On January 14, 1976 the court of appeals again affirmed Judge Garrity (530 F.2d 401). Defendants then sought Supreme Court review and were once again rebuffed.

75. Morgan v. Hennigan, *supra* note 3, at 417–18.

76. *Id.* at 418–20.

77. *Id.* at 420–21.

the federal constitution. . . . [Their] efforts to reverse the increasing segregation in Boston's schools was considerably hampered by the limited authority conferred upon them by statute."[78]

Despite this finding, the court declined to sever state defendants from the case. Noting *Griffin v. County School Board*[79] and Rule 19(a) of the Federal Rules, the court retained state defendants as parties defendant so that they could assist in the formulation and implementation of whatever remedies the court ordered.[80]

City Defendants.   In considering the liability of city defendants, the court outlined and considered conduct in six principal areas: (1) facilities utilization and new structures; (2) districting and redistricting; (3) feeder patterns; (4) open enrollment and controlled transfers; (5) facility and staff; and (6) vocational and examination schools.[81]

After discussing each of the areas the court concluded "that the [city] defendants . . . knowingly carried out a systematic program of segregation affecting all of the city's students, teachers and school facilities and [thus] have intentionally brought about and maintained a dual school system. . . . [T]he entire school system of Boston is unconstitutionally segregated."[82]

The Orders.   The court attempted to provide both immediate and long-term relief. It entered a partial judgment which enjoined the city defendants from "discriminating upon the basis of race in the operation of the public schools of the city of Boston and from creating, promoting or maintaining racial segregation in any school or other facility in the Boston school system."[83] The court further ordered the city defendants "to begin forthwith the formulation and implementation of plans which shall eliminate every form of racial segregation in the public schools of Boston, including all consequences and vestiges of segregation previously practiced by [city] defendants."[84]

The court also outlined Remedial Guidelines which would assist compliance with its order.[85] These guidelines imposed the primary responsibility for desegregation on the Boston School Committee, and charged its members with the affirmative duty to take all steps necessary to implement the court's order regardless of public or parental opposition. Moreover, conscious of the history

---

78. *Id.* at 476.
79. 377 U.S. 218, 234, 84 S. Ct. 1226, 12 L. Ed.2d 256 (1964).
80. Morgan v. Hennigan, *supra* note 3, at 477.
81. *Id.* at 425.
82. *Id.* at 482.
83. *Id.* at 484.
84. *Id.*
85. *Id.* at 482–83.

of delay, the court ordered that defendants proceed *now,* taking only that time necessary to design, evaluate, and implement plans.

Since there was less than three months between the opinion and the scheduled reopening of schools, it was clear that the comprehensive desegregation plan ordered by the partial judgment and Remedial Guidelines could not possibly be implemented for the 1974/75 academic year. Thus, in its final order, on October 31, the court sought to establish a time-table for implementation as of September 1975.[86] The defendants were given until December 16, 1974 to file an acceptable plan for student desegregation. To be acceptable, the plan would have to "set forth the basis for assigning students to each school" in a manner which, "taking into account the safety of students and the practicalities of the situation," would "provide for the greatest possible degree of actual desegregation of all grades in all schools in all parts of the city."

Of more immediate impact was the court's interlocutory order which enjoined city defendants from aggravating the situation. The order specifically forbade: (1) beginning the construction of any new school or the placement of any new portable ones; (2) granting teacher transfers that would further the current staff imbalance; and (3) granting student transfers under exceptions to the controlled transfer policy.[87]

The interlocutory order offered a federal sanction to the Racial Imbalance Act by enjoining city defendants from failing to comply with the plan which had been devised by the state board and ordered implemented by the Massa-

86. The order provided as follows:

The defendants Boston School Committee and Superintendent (hereinafter called the defendants) shall file with the court and serve upon other parties on or before December 16, 1974 a plan for student desegregation, for implementation in September, 1975.

. . . .

It is further ordered that the commissioners of the public facilities department designate a specialist in planning to work with the school committee and superintendent on a full-time basis from November 1 through December 16 in the development of the student desegregation plan.

The defendants shall file with the court and serve upon the other parties on November 18 and December 2, 1974, brief written reports generally describing their progress in preparation of a student desegregation plan. The plan shall be approved by vote of the defendant school committee before submission to the court. On or before December 14, 1974, all parties shall submit to John O. Mirick, Esquire, counsel for the defendants, lists of the names and addresses of persons and community groups who they believe should receive copies of the plan, including maps, and copies shall be sent to those persons and community groups as soon as possible after December 16.

Until January 20, 1975, the plaintiffs, state defendants, intervenors consistent with the conditions of their intervention, and other interested community groups shall have the right to submit to the court alternative plans to all or any portion of the defendants' student desegregation plan.

87. *Id.*

chusetts Supreme Judicial Court.[88] It is this unique federal adoption and enforcement of the state agency and state court order that would be the nucleus of what has become known as Phase I. The state plan which Judge Garrity endorsed has been discussed earlier. However, one aspect should be noted here since it was this particular feature that provided the elements for the ethnic confrontation. Ignoring the advice of Professor Jaffe, the state board had provided in its plan for the pairing of the white South Boston community with predominantly black Roxbury.

IMPLEMENTATION OF PHASE I

In the months that followed his decision, Judge Garrity learned that desegregation was much more easily ordered than implemented. If anything at all can be deduced from the complex series of events following the decision, it is that Judge Garrity was quite unprepared for what was to come. He had not anticipated the variety and complexity of devices that public officials and bureaucrats would employ in their all-out attempt to undermine and frustrate the desegregation order. Moreover, he seemed unprepared for the degree of public opposition and polarization.

Official Recalcitrance
While the terminology "dismantling of a dual school system" may imply certain economies, desegregation has generally been a fairly expensive process.[89] With the advent of busing as an appropriate remedy, costs have skyrocketed to amounts which in some cases would have been prohibitive for local school boards without various federal assistance programs.[90] However, despite the pro-

88. The language in the order was:

It is further ordered that, pending further order or unless specific leave of this court is obtained, said defendants be preliminarily enjoined from: (a) failing to comply in any respect with the Racial Imbalance Act plan ordered by the Supreme Judicial Court of Massachusetts to be implemented on or before the opening day of school in September, 1974...."

Morgan v. Hennigan, *supra* note 3, at 484.
89. See generally U.S. Commission on Civil Rights Desegregation of the Nation's Public Schools, included in the staff report of the subcommittee on Constitutional Rights of the Senate Judiciary Committee, 94th Cong. 2d Sess. 1976, p. 167 *et seq.*
90. The two main sources of federal desegregation funding have been the Emergency

90. The two main sources of federal desegregation funding have been the Emergency School Aid Act (ESAA), 20 U.S.C. 1601 (1972), and Title IV of the 1964 Civil Rights Act, 42 U.S.C. 2000(c) (1964). The purpose of ESAA is to provide financial assistance in the form of basic grants to school districts in the process of desegregation. In the case of Boston, the school system became eligible for ESAA funds when it began implementation of a court-ordered desegregation plan. Title IV of the Civil Rights Act of 1964, on the other hand, was designed to give technical rather than financial assistance to desegregating school systems. Although there is a provision for grants, Title IV is designed primarily for technical and training assistance equivalent to funding, but not the funding itself. In New England,

grams a federal court ordering desegregation is in the anomalous position of ordering a financially strapped school system to raise and spend a significant amount of money to remedy a situation it created or at least did not find objectionable.

Boston public officials were almost unanimous in the condemnation of the court order.[91] For many of them, the cost far outweighted whatever benefit could possibly be derived.

On June 26 the Boston School Committee voted to request Mayor White to submit an order to the city counsel requesting the sum of $8,846,207.[92] The school committee had concluded that this amount represented the as yet unbudgeted costs of implementing the racial balance plan.[93] (The school committee in that motion also requested that the governor of Massachusetts be requested to furnish an unspecified amount for the same purpose.)

Mayor White forwarded his request to the city council on July 11. However, his figures differed substantially from those of the school committee. Instead of the $8.8 million the school committee requested for desegregation purposes, the mayor sought $4.9 million. Of that amount, $700,000 had been previously requested and eliminated from the city's budget. Thus only $4.2 million was actually requested for desegregation.

In a letter to the school committee on the following day the mayor indicated that he had honored its request for $4.2 million for transportation in full.

He went on to state:

As for the other terms in the Committee's Racial Balance request, we believe they are all extremely important, especially the funds for human rela-

---

the General Assistance Center of the University of Hartford provides personnel and services for the preparation and training of desegregating school system administrators, teachers, and staff. Telephone interview with Fred J. Wilkinson, U.S. Department of Health, Education, and Welfare, Office of Education, Bureau of Equal Educational Opportunities, Assistant Regional Commissioner of the Division of School Systems, August 27, 1975. For figures for ESAA and Title IV awards to Boston for Phase I, see *infra* note 95.

91. School Committeeman John Kerrigan called Garrity "the man who's going to destroy the Boston schools." He called the court order "idiotic." Boston Globe, June 24, 1974, at 12. City Councilwoman Louise Day Hicks called for the school committee to appeal the decision. Mayor White was characteristically vague and evasive. He said: "It is time for us as a city to live up to and face the reality that one issue now is the safety and well-being of our children. . . . I intend to uphold the law." On the other hand, he also said, "The Mayor is powerless to implement the decision. . . . The School Committee will both take the lead role and will have final power and control in implementation. The Mayor's role is to provide the resources to appropriate officials and to do everything in my power to preserve the public safety." Boston Globe, June 24, 1974, at 1, 8; *id.*, May 25, 1975, at A6.

92. Boston School Committee order, dated June 26, 1974, Attachments, School Committee Motion for Relief, filed July 25, 1974, in Board of Education v. School Committee of the City of Boston. Equity 73–190 (Supreme Judicial Court, filed September 26, 1973).

93. Attached to the order was the following breakdown of the proposed budget:

tions training and community information, but these are costs which must be borne by Federal and State grants. The School Committee is being ordered by a Federal court to carry out a State-developed desegregation plan, and equity demands that a substantial part of the financial burden be shared by Federal and State governments.

. . . I hope the Committee will join with me in bringing all possible pressure on Federal and State officials in meeting their responsibilities to assist the overburdened taxpayers of Boston in sharing the costs of carrying out the Court's desegregation order.[94]

Despite the mayor's appeal, neither federal nor state assistance was immediately forthcoming.[95] And the ensuing weeks witnessed a political battle to obtain even the transportation funds from the Boston City Council.

Transportation	$4,262,000
*Safety	
Facility Needs	1,300,000
Renovations	
Reallocation of Equipment	
Redistribution of Material and Supplies	75,000
Orientation for Integration (Human Relations Programs)	151,300
Interaction Workshops (stipends)	638,000
Community Relations and Informational Services including printing and visual materials	305,000
Planning and Implementation Activities	125,307
Consultants	25,000
Multi-Ethnic Educational Materials	500,000
Transitional Aides	1,425,600
Data Processing	10,000
Total	$8,817,207

*Police Crossing Guards—Financial Responsibility through Police Department.

See attached sheets to School committee Motion for Relief, *supra* note 92.

94. Letter from Mayor White to Edward Winter, dated July 12, 1974, attachment to School Committee Motion for Relief, *supra* note 92.

95. As of mid-summer 1975, there had been some funding from state and federal sources with more expected in the near future. In November 1974, Boston was provided with the first installment of $1.8 million promised in federal funds; $2.7 million had been requested. Until 1974, Boston was not eligible for Title VI of the 1964 Civil Rights Act monies, available to school districts in the process of desegregation on a competitive basis. It was expected that there would be another month of negotiations in the competitive process for further federal funding. Contracts under the Emergency School Aid Act, which also provided discretionary funding for numerous federal programs, were also in the process of negotiation. Telephone interview with Ken Franks, Boston HEW Office, Grants and Contracts, July 16, 1975. As for state funding, there had been little so far, though more was expected in the near future. The state hoped to reimburse the School Department nearly $4 million for the cost of transportation last year; $5.7 million was asked for. In May 1975 the state paid an advance of $1.3 million on this amount. The balance was to be paid out of fiscal 1976 funds, but still considered a reimbursement. There were two other state sources of funding: the Equal Education Improvement Fund, and the Magnet School Program. Neither applies exclusively to Boston, nor exclusively to desegregation programs. Under the Equal Education Improvement Fund (Mass. Gen. Laws, Ch. 636, §1), $4.7 million was to

As luck or fate would have it, ardent busing foe Councilwoman Louise Day Hicks chaired the Boston City Council's Ways and Means Committee. No revenue measure can pass the Boston City Council without first going to the Ways and Means Committee. This was no exception. Councilwoman Hicks sat on the appropriation for weeks.[96]

With the beginning of school fast approaching, Judge Garrity requested a recommended course of action. Plaintiffs responded on July 25 in a memo out-lining their views about the role of a federal court in financing desegregation.[97] Plaintiffs argued that a federal court has the power to order school authorities to use funds already in their budget to accomplish desegregation, regardless of how the funds were designated to be used.[98] Similarly, a federal court may require that additional funds be made available to finance implementation of a desegregation plan.[99] However, plaintiffs encouraged restraint by the federal court.

> In the unusual circumstances of this case, and at this time, plaintiffs submit that the decision whether the City Council of Boston should be required to appropriate additional funds is one which should be made in the first instance by the Massachusetts Supreme Judicial Court.
>   . . . While there is no jurisdictional bar to federal court action, a solution

---

be made available to Boston. Of that, one-third was to be used for special programs in the schools for improving the quality of education, and two-thirds to be used as the School Department saw fit. Thus, close to $3 million was used for direct costs of desegregation. Under the Magnet School Program (Mass. Gen. Laws, Ch. 636 §8), $1.96 million was made available to state school systems; out of that, $432,645 was to go to Boston for urban-suburban programs, many of which were desegregation-related. But $900,000 of these funds have been designated for summer planning for Boston-area universities, an activity that is in preparation for Phase II. Telephone interviews with Ramona Helgencamp, director of the Mass. Department of Education's Bureau of Budget Management, and Carl Fuller, senior supervisor of the Mass. Department of Education's Bureau of Educational Opportunity, June 21, 1975. Helgencamp stated that the School Department was claiming that the total cost of desegregation in Boston for the first year was in excess of $18 million.

96. Ostensibly, her reason for holding up the money was because the required item-by-item breakdown of how the money was to be spent had not been provided. But some said that she was actually waiting for the outcome of an aid-to-education bill still needing Nixon's signature (the bill contained an amendment banning forced busing). Boston Globe, July 31, 1974, at 32; August 1, 1974, at 1, 13; August 5, 1974, at 4.

97. Morgan v. Kerrigan, Plaintiffs' Memorandum Concerning Integration Financing, failed July 25, 1974.

98. Plaintiffs cite the following cases for this proposition: Goss v. Bd. of Educ. of Knoxville, 482 F.2d 1044, 1046 (6th Cir. 1973); Brewer v. School Bd. of the City of Norfolk, 456 F.2d 943, 947 (4th Cir. 1972), *cert. denied,* 409 U.S. 892; Davis v. Bd. of Educ. of North Little Rock, 449 F.2d 500 (8th Cir. 1971). See Plaintiffs' Memorandum Concerning Integration Financing, *supra* note 97, at 1.

99. Plaintiffs cite Griffin v. School Board of Prince Edward County, 377 U.S. 218, 232–34 (1964); Plaquemines Parish School Bd. v. United States, 415 F.2d 817, 820–34 (5th Cir. 1969); United States v. School Dist. 151, 301 F. Supp. 201, 232 (N.D. Ill. 1969), *aff'd* 432 F.2d 1147 (7th Cir. 1970), *cert. denied* 402 U.S. 943. *See* Plaintiffs' Memorandum Concerning Integration Financing, *supra* note 97, at 2. At the time of the filing of the memo, the Supreme Court's decision in Bradley v. Milliken was unknown. For an analysis of the difference it has made, see *supra* note 64.

within the framework of the Massachusetts school financing statutes would, if possible, be preferable to immediate invocation of the federal court's powers.[100]

On July 23 and 26 respectively, both the Massachusetts State Board of Education and the Boston School Committee filed motions for supplemental relief in state supreme court.[101]

For its part, the state board outlined the events leading to the funding impasse and requested:

1. The members of the City Council of Boston be added as parties defendant in the state action since "complete relief cannot be accorded among those already parties" unless they were joined.
2. They forthwith approve the mayor's recommendation of July 11, 1974 for an additional appropriation for the school committee.
3. They grant such other and further relief as may be appropriate.[102]

The school committee sought joinder of relief against the mayor contending that relief against the city council was inadequate.

Even if the City Council . . . grants the full amount of the Mayor's recommendation . . . the School Committee will lack approximately $4.6 million . . . [which is] absolutely necessary in order to comply with outstanding orders of the [State] Board . . . and this court.

. . . .

Orderly implementation of the . . . [State Board's] Racial Balance Plan in the City of Boston requires that . . . [all of the monies] requested by the School Committee on June 26, 1974 be recommended forthwith by the Mayor so that the City Council may consider and approve this amount.[103]

In an accompanying memorandum the Boston School Committee contended that without the action on the part of the mayor it could not expend funds for the desegregation effort.[104]

The state court, disagreeing with the school committee's rather modest view of its fiscal autonomy, denied the motions and in effect ordered the school com-

---

100. Plaintiffs' Memorandum Concerning Integration Financing, *supra* note 97, at 2–3.

101. For a description of prior proceedings in the state court litigation, see text and notes, *supra* pp. 41–42.

102. See State Board of Education Motion for Supplemental Relief filed July 23, 1974 in Board of Education v. School Committee of the City of Boston, *supra* note 53.

103. School Committee Motion for Relief, filed on July 25, 1974, *supra* note 53, at 4.

104. Defendants first argue that the school committee does not have the independent authority to increase the amount of money spent on education. They quote Pirrone v. City of Boston, 1973 Adv. Sh. 1565, 1571 as holding: "If the School Committee determines that additional funds are necessary, it must resort to the usual municipal finance system and re-

mittee to reallocate the necessary funds from other categories of the budget already approved.[105] The school committee complied and what could have been a rather untidy confrontation was averted. Moreover, resolution of the issue at the state court level obviated the necessity for Judge Garrity to issue a ruling which would almost certainly have been appealed.

Public Opposition

Most of the public opposition to the desegregation order was concerned with the student assignment and transportation issue. The Boston community was uniquely prepared to oppose the federal court order. Recent events had resulted in a highly politicized community, sensitive to the busing issue and polarized around it.

Anti-busing groups had been meeting regularly for several months to oppose implementation of the state board's plan.[106] In an exercise of sheer political power, the busing foes had engineered a state-sponsored citywide referendum on busing.[107] Despite the low turnout, the referendum clearly demonstrated that

---

quest an appropriation by the city council subject to the Mayor's absolute vote." Second, defendants argue that the Committee is limited by statute in its power to incur liabilities: Chapter 486 of the Acts of 1909, as amended by Stat. 1941, Ch. 604, and Stat. 1947, Ch. 120 state: ". . . that the total liabilities incurred during said interval do not exceed in any one month the sums spent for similar purposes during any one month of the preceding fiscal year. . . ." Thus, defendants argue that even if the committee did have $8.8 million in funds available for reallocation, they could not touch anywhere near the entire amount. *See* Memorandum of Law of the Boston School Committee, filed August 5, 1974, in Board of Education v. School Committee of the City of Boston, *supra* note 53.

105. *In the matter of Board of Education v. Boston School Committee,* Supreme Judicial Court, Equity 73–190 (hearing before Justice Kaplan, July 31, 1974).

106. These meetings had been held on Friday afternoons to accommodate state representatives Ray Flynn and Michael Flaherty, and Senator Bulger. They were held at the Boston City Council's executive hearing room on the fifth floor in City Hall. At first only proven antibusing activists were invited—the legislators above, and community organizers against busing such as Rita Graul—Hick's new administrative assistant, Virginia Sheehy of the South Boston Home and School Association (see note 143 *infra*), Pat Ranese, Fran Johnnene from Hyde Park, and Elvira (Pixie) Palladino from East Boston. After Judge Garrity's decision, the group expanded its members by the already successful "block captain system" of telephoning potential supporters, and from the membership lists of the Boston Home and School Association. After schools opened in September, regular meetings would include 400 members, and the meeting time was rescheduled for Wednesday nights. Meetings concentrated on the plans for the school boycott, marches, demonstrations, and efforts to promote a federal constitutional amendment prohibiting forced busing. Shortly thereafter the group decided to call itself ROAR, the acronym for Restore Our Alienated Rights. Once an easily identifiable name was selected the group then organized itself on a citywide basis with two representatives from each section of the city. Interview with Fran Johnnene, July 21, 1975; interview with Virginia Sheehy, president, South Boston Information Center, July 28, 1975.

107. State Representative Raymond Flynn from South Boston persuaded legislators to approve a home-rule petition for Boston which would permit a busing referendum to be held in June 1974. Boston Globe, May 25, 1975, at A3. In an Opinion of the Justices, 310 N.E.2d 348 (1974), the Mass. Supreme Judicial Court declared the referendum nonbinding. The referendum was paid for by the state, and it cost an estimated $136,000. Black state representative William Owens called it "a waste of taxpayers' money." Boston Globe (P.M.), May 21, 1974, at 1, 8; *id.,* May 22, 1974, at 1, 24.

white Bostonians were overwhelmingly opposed to busing.[108] However, since the referendum was not binding the euphoria experienced by opponents of desegregation was short-lived, and the group dug in to do their political homework.

Just two weeks after the busing referendum, Boston voters again went to the polls. This time it was the Boston School Committee that was the bone of contention. The perennial efforts to change its structure had been highlighted by the ongoing battle with the state board. There had appeared to be a growing consensus that the present structure and composition of the school committee contributed to the problems of deteriorating education and racial isolation rather than to the solutions. A multiplicity of alternatives were suggested by community groups and public officials. Four were eventually put before the voters on June 4, less than three weeks before Judge Garrity's opinion.[109]

Having two electoral contests immediately preceding the federal court order assured that education was foremost in the minds of Boston voters. But more importantly the invocation of the political process resulted in the identifying of a hard-core cadre firmly committed to a point of view unlikely to be shared by the court.

108. The referendum was held on May 21, 1974. Voter turnout was low, estimated at 12 percent, but 30,798 voted against busing, 2,282 for. Boston Globe, May 22, 1974, at 1, 24.

109. The first plan, sponsored by School Committeeman Paul Tierney, left the present structure largely intact except that membership on the school committee was expanded to eight members elected at large. The mayor was to serve on the committee ex officio and to have a tiebreaking role in committee votes. *See generally,* Boston Globe, October 29, 1974, at 13; *id.,* October 30, 1974, at 4; *id.,* October 31, 1974, at 19.

Plan II was sponsored by the Parents' League for Better Education, and called for an 11-member committee elected by zones. In addition, there was to be a 22-member school congress acting as an advisory body. Boston Sunday Globe, June 2, 1974, at 2.

Plan III was the most radical; it had been drafted by a group of professional people who had organized themselves into the Coalition for School System Reform. It would have abolished the school committee and replaced it with 36 neighborhood school councils which would send representatives to area and citywide advisory committees. Powers to be given to the local councils would have included the discretionary expenditure of 8 percent of the system's budget and the right to determine elementary school attendance patterns. The School Department itself would have been brought under the mayor's office. The mayor would appoint the superintendent subject to approval by the citywide advisory committee; he would also get control over the budget and personnel. The School Department itself would have been restructured so that matters affecting personnel and curriculum development would have been in the hands of six area superintendents rather than directly under the superintendent's control. A proposal similar to Plan III had emerged from the mayor's office in August 1973 and the mayor supported Plan III in the referendum runoff. Boston Globe, October 29, 1974, at 1.

Plan IV was sponsored by City Councillor Gerald F. O'Leary. It left the present system largely intact except that committee membership was to be expanded to eleven members, five elected at large and six by districts. O'Leary's plan was not given much of a chance because it had no organizational support. Boston Sunday Globe, June 2, 1974, at 2. On the eve of the April 2 runoff, the referendum was cancelled by a member of the Mass. Supreme Judicial Court because of an error in the enabling leglislation. The election was finally held on June 4, 1974, but campaigns for the various plans had lost momentum. Plan III won the election, but with only 9 percent voter turnout. It was defeated in the November election which followed.

On the very evening of Judge Garrity's decision, the Save Boston Committee met and adopted a program for defiance. The group decided to express their opposition to the federal court order through demonstrations and protest marches, to resist the order by boycotting during the opening weeks of school, and to evade the order by establishing alternative schools to take their children out of the Boston public school system entirely.

The Search for Alternatives. Some white parents in Boston responded to the desegregation order by deciding they would attempt to abandon the public school system. They perceived three options: suburban, parochial, and alternative schools.

Much to their dismay, Cardinal Medeiros adhered to his publicly announced policy and refused to permit the enrollment of children whose families were merely seeking to avoid desegregation.[110] So adamant was he that many Catholic schools opened with empty seats in September despite the long lines clamoring for admission.

Of course there were those within and outside the religious community who disagreed with the Cardinal's policy and who sought to subvert it. There is evidence that some schools ignored the policy while still more schools merely looked the other way as parents employed one subterfuge after another to get their children into school. However, while enrollment in some parochial schools did increase somewhat, it is clear that the forthright stance of the Cardinal precluded the parochial school as a viable alternative to desegregation. Total enrollment actually declined in 1974/75.[111]

Despite much fanfare,[112] lack of time and capital made it impossible for the heralded "alternative freedom schools" to get off the ground. And these same

110. Humberto Cardinal Madeiros first made these statements in February 1974 and they were to be repeated in September. Boston Globe, February 18, 1974, at 1, 10; *id.*, February 28, 1974, at 48; *id.*, September 1, 1974, at 12; *id.*, September 29, 1974, at 15. For a good summary article on Cardinal Madeiros's stand on desegregation, see the Boston Globe, July 10, 1974, at 14.

111. Enrollment in parochial schools in Boston for the years 1971/72 through 1974/75 was as follows:

1971/72	25,280
1972/73	27,837
1973/74	24,385
1974/75	23,498

Data supplied by the Massachusetts Department of Education, Division of Research, Planning and Evaluation, September 3, 1975. These figures show an actual decrease in Boston parochial school enrollment during 1974/75 from the previous year. But interpretation is made difficult by the fact that there was also a decrease in 1973/74 from the previous year.

112. After *Brown* v. *Board of Education,* white parents in the South established so-called "freedom schools" and private "academies." These schools served to circumvent desegregation orders for over two decades. After the Boston desegregation order, several white

factors, along with the strongly held belief that desegregation was not really going to occur, precluded significant white flight to suburban school districts in time for the September 1974 academic year.

The Boycott and Civil Disobedience. Thus, with no place to go, a substantial number of white parents in Boston decided to support a two-week boycott co-ordinated by the South Boston Information Center and the various home and school associations.[113] The boycott strategy was vigorously promoted at several rallies held just before the school year began. On the first day of the semester, over 30 percent of the 70,000 students the school department had predicted would attend failed to show up.[114] This was double the normal opening day absentee rate and was attributable primarily to those schools and districts involved in the desegregation effort.[115] While the attendance figures steadily improved, it was clear that the boycott had taken its toll and that a substantial number of students were not being educated.[116] Plaintiffs sought the assistance of the court. In an order of September 19, however, Judge Garrity found that parents who kept their children out of school because of a genuine concern about their safety were not fostering truancy.[117] Nevertheless, State Education Commissioner Anrig announced that state school attendance laws required the school department to investigate when any student between the age of 7 and 16 was absent seven or more days within a six-week period.[118] Those statutes, he pointed out, provided for the imposition of fines on anyone inducing a child to stay out of school, including parents.[119] Urging an end to the boycott, he announced that he would launch a crackdown on absenteeism beginning Monday, September 30.[120] On that day 80 percent of the students attended classes. And except where specific circumstances arose, attendance returned to near normal throughout the city with the salient exception of South Boston High. That this was due to the fact that the two weeks designated for the boycott had expired and not out of deference to Commissoner Anrig's warnings was under-

---

parents visited some of these southern schools with the idea of developing Boston analogs. July 21 Interview with Fran Johnnene of the South Boston Information Center.

113. Coordinators of the boycott emphasize that the decision to join the boycott was an independent one made by individual parents according to each parent's view of what would best benefit their children. Interviews with Johnnene and Sheehy, *supra* note 106.

114. Boston Globe, September 13, 1974.

115. At the South Boston High School Annex, less than 1/6 of the 600 pupils enrolled attended. At Roxbury High, only 20 white students showed up. At Dorchester High, of a projected enrollment of 2265, only 561 attended. At the King School in Roxbury, less than half of the expected students arrived. At the Gaven School, the figures were less than a quarter. *Id.*

116. Although the South Boston Information Center arranged for several groups of students to meet in various locations during the period, even the most liberal estimates suggest that these programs reached only a small fraction of the boycotting students.

117. Boston Globe, September 18, 1974.

118. Boston Globe, September 27, 1974.

119. Mass. Gen. L., Ch. 76 § § 1, 2, 4.

120. Boston Globe, September 27, 1974.

scored by National Boycott Day when only 13,000 of the school system's 43,000 whites showed up for classes.[121]

Public Protest vs. Public Safety. There were spontaneous demonstrations on and off during the summer. However, September 9 was the target date for official public protest. On that day thousands of white parents gathered to confront the federal judge who had ordered desegregation of "their" schools and the two U.S. senators who supported him.

Senator Edward Kennedy attended the rally but was prevented from addressing the crowd by shouts, jeers, and epithets. As he attempted to leave, members of the crowd tossed eggs, tomatoes, and insults at him. What had started out as a rally ended as a near riot, lending credence to those who feared the worst when the schools opened.

From the outset, many had feared that widespread public opposition posed a threat of violence. The safety of the school children was a factor people thought about and talked about often as the summer progressed.[122] Plans were quickly made to implement the safety recommendations outlined by the state board.[123]

Meanwhile, the ominous overtones and stridency of opponents to his busing order had not gone unnoticed by Judge Garrity. On August 19 he announced that he had requested assistance from the Community Relations Service of the

121. Boston Globe, October 8, 1974.
122. After the June order and during the summer, concern was expressed in the press over the safety of school children in the fall. There was debate over whether raising the issue would inflame anti-busing forces to acts of violence or whether safety was an issue that needed to be aired. As September approached, Mayor White, Thomas Atkins of the NAACP, and Superintendent Leary all made appeals to Boston citizens to keep the safety of the children uppermost in their minds. *See* Boston Globe, August 26, 1974, at 1; Christian Science Monitor, June 24, 1974, at 4A; *id.,* August 2, 1974, at 4D. Black leaders were not satisfied with the way safety was being handled by the mayor's neighborhood teams, and they began to organize their own safety effort in the black community. Two black southerners, Percy Wilson and Patrick Jones, formed a coalition among Freedom House, the Roxbury Multi-Service Center, Lena Park, and Model Cities to focus on the safety of black children bused into the white community. Their strategy included making sure that white children bused into the black community were not hurt so as to avoid white backlash against black children. *See* Boston Globe, May 25, 1975, at A7. State Senator Joseph Timilty, though a foe of busing, agreed to appear with black State Representative Mel King on TV to stress that the real issue was the safety of the children. Other public figures were also to make public-service spot TV announcements to "cool it." Boston Globe, September 1, 1974, at 12.
123. In the State Plan, the safety issue is linked more to transportation hazards than to the danger of racial violence. The plan quotes Mass. Gen. Laws, Ch. 71 §37D to state: "Any plan to detail changes in existing school attendance districts . . . with the intention of reducing or eliminating racial imbalance must take into consideration on an equal basis with the above mentioned intention the safety of the children involved in travelling from home to school and school to home." The plan mentions ways to avoid the problems of busing the very young, overcrowding facilities, crossing of major thoroughfares by children walking to school, etc. The only real indication in the plan that racial violence might be expected was the provision for bus monitors for each bus. *See* Commonwealth of Massachusetts Board of Education Short Term Plan to Reduce Racial Imbalance in the Boston Public Schools, February 1, 1974, at 49 (also known as the State Plan or the Phase I Plan).

U.S. Department of Justice.[124] This agency had had considerable experience in school desegregation matters and was well regarded by federal judges. During the decade since it had been established, the agency had resolved many potentially violent situations through conciliation and mediation.

Clearly Judge Garrity hoped for similar success in Boston. In his words, the agency would be his "eyes and ears" for the implementation process.[125]

At the court's direction the Community Relations Service assigned a larger-than-usual team to Boston and immediately attempted to get involved with the various groups in the community in a vain attempt to preclude the possibility of violence when school opened. In addition to checking and rechecking the contingency plans of the school and police departments, the Community Relations Service team sought to contact the leaders of ROAR and offered to assist in training demonstration marshals to assure orderly and peaceful protest. ROAR regarded them with suspicion and excluded the team from all meetings, activities, and planning sessions. Despite their efforts, it became increasingly clear that there was little the Community Relations Service could do but sit and watch the bitterness brew and explode.

For awhile it appeared that the safety aspect could be handled by effectively using the command structure of the Boston Police Department. A series of events brought even that notion into question.

On August 30, legal counsel for the Boston Police Patrolmen's Association, Inc., the collective bargaining unit for Boston's police force, wrote a letter to Judge Garrity expressing the association's concern over the "lack of information, direction and guidance" it had been provided. The association also requested the court to "provide answers to certain questions" so that it could properly "advise" its members.[126]

The questions were ominous in their implications. There was the clear suggestion that the association was not at all enthusiastic about the federal court order

124. The Justice Department's Community Relations Service (CRS) was created by Congress under Title X of the 1964 Civil Rights Act to provide technical assistance to communities involved in racial or ethnic conflicts in communications, housing, or education. Boston Globe, May 25, 1975, at A8. There are now ten regional offices, and the Boston office supervises activities in the New England states. CRS has no enforcement power and it is not an undercover organization. Telephone interview with Lawrence Turner, Community Relations Service, June 5, 1975. In the preceding spring of 1974, Judge Garrity, along with other Massachusetts federal judges at a judicial conference in Lynnfield, Mass., first explored the capabilities of CRS with the service's general counsel, Hayden Gregory. Gregory outlined to the judges what the purposes and functions of the service were, and what its experience and success had been. Its main goal had been to substitute the use of mediation and conciliation skills for court litigation and police enforcement of court orders. After the meeting in Lynnfield, CRS sent Garrity additional materials informing him of its methods. Even without Garrity's request, it is highly likely that CRS would have monitored the Boston desegregation situation for the Justice Department, but with Garrity's request, the service more readily received cooperation from city and school officials. Boston Globe, May 25, 1975, at A8; telephone interview with Lawrence Turner, *supra.*

125. Boston Globe, August 28, 1974, at 3.

126. Letter to Judge Garrity from Frank J. McGee, Jr., attorney for the Boston Police Patrolmen's Association, Inc., dated August 30, 1974.

and would not gratuitously enforce any part of it not made explicit.[127] In the days which followed, the implication crystalized into policy. In a September 5 press release, the association announced that it would tell its members that there were circumstances in which they were not compelled to obey their superiors.[128] Disturbed by this turn of events, Plaintiffs requested the court to clarify the situation and moved for entry of an order concerning peaceful integration.[129]

The court responded promptly. Judge Garrity met in closed session with the attorney serving as legal counsel to the police association on September 6 and "clarified" the legal and ethical issues.[130] Then, after two hearings, he issued the

127. The ethnic composition of the Boston police force was the basis for suspicion that police officers were not happy with the federal court order. As many as 60 percent of Boston's 2,100-member force had strong ties to South Boston, either by birth, marriage, or residence, and most were sympathetic to the anti-busing forces in the white community. Mayor White, Deputy Mayor Kiley, and Police Commissioner DiGrazia were all concerned about the conflict in officers' minds between their professional duties and their sympathies, and DiGrazia composed a training film to be shown to all officers assigned to desegregation duty a week before schools opened. DiGrazia asked Louise Day Hicks to appear on film in an appeal for police discipline also to be shown to the officers, but she refused. Boston Globe, May 25, 1975, at A6.

128. Attorney Frank McGee said that the state statute dealing with trespassing in a school building was not mandatory but discretionary in that it said that an officer "may" arrest trespassers, not that one must do so. He said further that before arrests would be made against trespassers, district court complaints would have to be filed against the offenders. The implication of the press release was that anti-busing forces could do anything to express their opposition, including trespass and other interference and law-breaking, and that police would not only not arrest the law-breakers, but would stand by and look the other way. Boston Globe, May 25, 1975, at A8.

129. Plaintiffs filed, on September 9, 1974, a Motion for Entry of Order Concerning Peaceful Integration, a Memorandum Supporting Motion for Entry of Order Concerning Peaceful Integration, and Plaintiffs' Requested Findings of Fact Supporting Order Concerning Peaceful Integration. The Motion for Entry of Order joined the Boston Patrolmen's Association for purposes of the safety issue, and declared that police officers are legally required to protect students, teachers, and staff, and make arrests of persons interfering with school functions as instructed by their superior officers. The association was also to be ordered to communicate the contents of the order to the other police officers. The association was to be ordered not to incite or advise members of the association to disobey orders of their superior officers. Also, any future press releases were to be filed in advance and approved by the court. Plaintiffs' Memorandum Supporting the Motion outlined safety reasons for the order and plaintiffs' awareness of possible conflict with First Amendment rights of peaceful demonstration. Finally, plaintiffs requested the court to make the following findings of fact supporting the order concerning peaceful integration: (1) possibility of widespread demonstrations near school buildings; (2) the Boston Patrolman's Association officers and counsel have made widely reported statements that patrolmen are not under duty to obey orders of superior police officers to make arrests; (3) these statements will hamper the efforts of superior police officers to protect the public and will intimidate children, parents and teachers from attending schools; and (4) the Order Concerning Peaceful Integration will prevent irreparable injury to the patrolmen's association since it simply restates the already existing duties of police officers.

130. According to the Boston Globe, on September 6, 1974, Judge Garrity met with Frank McGee in chambers and gave him a short lecture on the real meaning of interference with a federal court order, and what the sanctions were for a lawyer. Boston Globe, May 25, 1975, at A8. This report appears to be in error. There is no evidence that any such meeting took place. Rather, it appears that Judge Garrity dealt with this matter in the presence of all the attorneys.

order requested by plaintiffs. He did not join the association as a defendant. However, he did respond to the specific question raised on its behalf:

1. *"If a person or persons attempt to block the entrance to a school, would the activity be in violation of the federal court order?"* Yes. Teachers and students assigned to particular schools must be able to enter and leave freely if the schools are to be desegregated. . . .
2. *"If so, what powers of arrest would a Boston patrolman possess?"* He would possess the powers conferred by Massachusetts Laws § 98, which provide, "The chief and other police officers of all cities and towns shall have all the powers and duties of constables except serving and executing civil process. They shall suppress and prevent all disturbances and disorder"; and "Whoever wilfully interrupts or disturbs a school . . . shall be punished by imprisonment for not more than one month or by a fine of not more than fifty dollars."
3. *"Whether a person may be arrested for an alleged trespass in a school building or whether a district court complaint must be sought against the person alleged to be trespassing?"* Such an arrest may be made in a school building and there is no need to obtain beforehand a district court complaint. Massachusetts Laws, provide, "Whoever without right, enters or remains in or upon the . . . buildings . . . of another, after having been forbidden to do so by the person who has the lawful control of said premises . . . shall be punished by a fine of not more than one hundred dollars or by imprisonment for not more than thirty days, or both." The word "buildings" includes schools and other buildings of the State and its municipalities. . . .
4. *"If, for instance, a parent brings a child to school 'X' and under the desegregation plan the child is supposed to attend school 'Y' the question arises as to what point in time the parent and child are trespassing in school 'Y'?"* Under the hypothesis stated, the trespass would be committed (a) when the parent and the child enter school "X" after having been forbidden to do so by the school principal or his agent. This ruling applies to all parts of school buildings, auditoriums and cafeterias and meeting and reception rooms as well as to classrooms. . . .[131]

Nonetheless, the first day of school was marred by violence. Black students were attacked and abused. And in the eyes of some observers, the police did very little about it.[132]

131. Declaratory Memorandum (Order) Concerning Peaceful Desegregation, filed September 10, 1974, in Morgan v. Kerrigan, at 2–4.
132. There was rock-throwing at buses at South Boston High, obscenities shouted at black students by 200–300 protestors, eight black students and a black woman monitor were cut and bruised in the stoned buses, and ten out of twenty buses were damaged. Only five South Boston youths were arrested, on charges of disorderly conduct. Boston Globe, May 25, 1975, at A10. In Plaintiffs' Report to the Court filed September 13, 1974, several affidavits by news reporters and black students were attached citing police officers' observing but ignoring lawless activity of angry white mobs and individuals. One news reporter stated: "This officer observed the angry whites surrounding the school bus but made no move to operate the traffic light manually, direct the school bus traffic through the intersection, or to calm the crowd. Instead he turned his back and began walking away. . . ." (Affidavit of Pamela Bullard, at 2.)

As the situation continued to deteriorate, the school committee renewed an earlier motion to join the mayor as a party defendant.[133] It was argued that in his position as chief executive officer of the city of Boston he controls the supporting services and departments, including the police and fire departments, and as such is an indispensable party to assure peaceful desegregation. The major ground put forward in the motion, however, was that the mayor was a "leading political and community figure" whose statements and actions are accorded widespread attention. The school committee argued that the mayor had become increasingly vocal in his criticism and had moved from constructive criticism to obstruction of the federal court order. "The appropriate vehicle for such criticism is the court," counsel contended.[134] The court granted the motion, and the mayor, after having sought to avoid the entire issue, was now a named defendant.[135]

These in-court maneuvers did not resolve the basic problem or end the violence. The situation worsened. On October 8, after a particularly volatile week, both plaintiffs and the mayor urged the court to take additional steps to assure the safety of the children.

The mayor sought an order requesting the court to assign not less than one hundred twenty-five U.S. marshals to South Boston.[136] Accompanying the motion was a letter from the mayor and affidavits from the commissioner and superintendent of the Boston Police Department which outlined in detail the safety measures the city had taken. The letter and the affidavits strongly contended that the city had done all that it could and that it could no longer guarantee public order and safety in relation to the desegregation effort without a substantial federal presence.

Plaintiffs agreed with the mayor that further assistance was needed. However, they did not support his request for federal marshals.

> . . . [P]laintiffs do not believe that it [the request] is adequate. The basic and continuing responsibility of maintaining order falls on local authorities (first City and then State), and there has been no showing that local resources (including police officers from other cities and towns, State Police, and the National Guard) have been exhausted, or that those who control them refuse to make them available.[137]

133. The earlier motion was entitled "City Defendants' Motion to Join Additional Parties Defendant," and was filed July 2, 1974. The new motion was entitled "City Defendants' Renewed Motion to Join Kevin H. White, As He Is Mayor, as a Party Defendant," and was filed September 26, 1974.

134. *See id.* at 4, filed September 26, 1974, in Morgan v. Kerrigan.

135. Order Joining Kevin H. White, as He Is Mayor, as a Party Defendant, filed September 30, 1974, in Morgan v. Kerrigan.

136. Motion of Kevin H. White, as He Is Mayor of Boston, for an Immediate Hearing and for an Order of the Court Requiring the Presence and Assistance of United States Marshals, filed October 8, 1974, in Morgan v. Kerrigan.

137. Plaintiffs' Motion for Relief Concerning Law Enforcement, filed October 8, 1974, in Morgan v. Kerrigan, at 2.

The court granted the hearing sought. At its conclusion Garrity ordered the mayor: "(a) to use his powers under existing agreements to secure additional law enforcement officers from other cities and towns in Massachusetts and from the state police; (b) upon a showing that exercise of such powers would not suffice to restore and maintain order, to call on the Governor of Massachusetts for further assistance, including the use of the National Guard."[138]

Further disturbances prompted the court to reaffirm its October 9 order on December 17.[139] This order followed plaintiffs' recommendations and set out other explicit guidelines to assure effective compliance: (1) the mayor was ordered to inform the court and the parties on a daily basis of the number and source of law enforcement personnel stationed inside South Boston High School; (2) the school committee, superintendent, and the mayor were directed to ban all unauthorized persons from school premises; (3) the school committee, superintendent, and mayor were ordered to prevent three or more persons from gathering near the schools or along bus routes; (4) the school committee and superintendent were ordered to proscribe racial epithets and to insure enforcement of the ban by appropriate sanctions and rules; (5) all parties were directed to cooperate with the Community Relations Service in preparing a draft plan for use by the monitors in troubled schools.

In the same order the court directed the city and state defendants and the Public Facility Commission to design methods of permanently closing several schools if the safety of the children could not be otherwise assured.[140] This alternative was seriously considered on several occasions but was never in fact implemented.[141]

A major disturbance outside South Boston High School on May 8 added a new wrinkle.[142] Plaintiffs responded by moving to depose two officers of the

138. The contents of the judge's October 9 order are summarized in his Order on Motion for Relief Concerning Security, filed December 17, 1974, at 1.

139. *Id.*

140. *Id.* at 1–4.

141. The only time that schools were closed for an extended period of time was in December, following the stabbing incident at South Boston High on December 11. Although many South Boston parents, the mayor, Police Commissioner DiGrazia, and several black leaders—including State Secretary of Education Paul Parks—urged that South Boston High be closed for the year and students moved to a neutral site, Judge Garrity refused to make such an order. Eight South Boston and Roxbury schools were closed between December 11 and January 8; they reopened several days after other Boston schools following the Christmas break. Boston Globe, December 12, 1974, at 1; *id.,* January 2, 1975, at 1, 30; *id.,* January 8, 1975, at 1, 14; *id.,* January 9, 1975, at 1, 11; *id.,* May 25, 1975, at A21–22. Later in the school year, in early May, there were several incidents at Hyde Park High and South Boston High where students were injured. At Hyde Park High, classes were dismissed an hour early. New York Times, May 10, 1975, at 23. At that time, Judge Garrity reiterated that in order to avoid an explosive situation, he would support a decision by Superintendent Leary to close either of the schools. Boston Globe, May 12, 1975, at 1, 3. Leary was, however, known for his "no-close policy," and the schools were not closed. Boston Globe, May 25, 1975, at A12.

142. On Wednesday, May 7, 1975, two South Boston white students and one Dorchester black student were arrested for two fighting incidents inside South Boston High School.

South Boston Information Center.[143] In support of this motion plaintiffs alleged that this and other incidents had been precipitated by the South Boston Information Center and its officers in violation of the December 17 order of the court.[144] This tactic by plaintiffs raised a host of issues, not the least of which concerned First Amendment rights to protest. Both individuals admitted they were opposed to "forced busing," but they denied having any personal knowledge of the planning of the demonstration or advocating violence at any time. In separate affidavits, each contended she had "exercised [her] first amendment right to free speech and voiced opposition on Constitutional [sic], philosophical, and moral grounds," and indicated an intent "to continue to vocalize opposition to the arbitrary, unconstitutional, and irrational program of forced busing."[145]

After hearings, Judge Garrity granted plaintiffs' motion and the depositions were scheduled.[146] However, while they presented themselves at the appointed time and place, each claimed the Fifth Amendment protection against self-incrimination and refused to answer counsel's questions about the incident.[147] Expressing the hope that the point had been made, plaintiffs did not pursue the matter.[148]

When the final bell rang on June 20, 1975, at the end of Phase I, the Boston public school system ended a year that had to be the most tumultuous in its long history. Disturbances were recorded on 130 of 174 school days.[149] As a conse-

Early in the afternoon about 1:00, South Boston residents gathered outside the school to protest. Leaflets were circulated publicizing a 7:00 A.M. protest meeting on Thursday, May 8. Before school opened the next day, about 600 protestors had gathered. White adults encouraged white students not to enter the building, Police dispersed the crowd after classes began. The next day at Hyde Park High School's Rogers Annex four incidents occurred where white and black students fought each other. Boston Globe, May 8, 1975, at 11; *id.,* May 9, 1975, at 5; *id.,* May 10, 1975, at 4; *id.,* May 11, 1975, at 3.

143. Plaintiffs' Motion for Leave to Take Depositions and for an Order to Show Cause, filed May 10, 1975. Plaintiffs moved to depose Rita Graul and Virginia Sheehy. Rita Graul in plaintiffs' motion is represented as the regional representative of the South Boston Home and School Association, and an officer in the South Boston Information Center. She is also, according to the Globe, considered the informal chairman of ROAR's executive board and an assistant to City Councilwoman Louise Day Hicks. Virginia Sheehy is a member of the Executive Board of ROAR, and employed as an information specialist for the South Boston Information Center. She is represented by the *Globe* as vice president of the South Boston Home and School Association. Boston Globe, May 12, 1975, at 3.

144. In their motion, plaintiffs allege that on Wednesday, May 7, 1975, persons were urged to gather outside South Boston High School on May 8 by leaflets and persons using a sound truck. Plaintiffs allege that a person working for the South Boston Information Center encouraged these people to gather outside the school on that day. *See* Plaintiffs' Motion for Leave to Take Depositions and for an Order to Show Cause, filed May 10, 1975, at 2. Plaintiffs included with their motion exhibits of the leaflets and affidavits linking the South Boston Information Center and the gathering outside South Boston High on May 8.

145. Affidavit of Virginia Sheehy, attached to Motion to Quash on Behalf of Rita Graul and Virginia Sheehy, filed by their attorney on May 19, 1975.

146. On May 14, 1975, Judge Garrity filed his Order on Plaintiffs' Motion for Leave to Take Depositions. The Graul-Sheehy Motion to Quash, *supra* note 145, was denied.

147. Morgan v. Kerrigan, Transcript on May 20 hearing; Boston Globe, May 21, 1975.

148. Interview with Attorney Robert Pressman, October 10, 1975 *supra* note 55.

149. The 174 school days to the 1974/75 school year figure was given out by the superintendent's office of the Boston School Department.

quence, classes were suspended in at least one school on 17 of those days.[150] A record 8,158 students were suspended and dismissed and thousands of others disciplined for minor infractions.[151] There were 40 complaints of students assault-

---

During Phase I, the deputy superintendent's office kept daily logs of happenings at Boston schools, called "Communications Logs." The Harvard Center for Law and Education, *supra* note 54, received logs for 139 out of the 174 schools days. Of the 139 school days covered by the logs, there were only 9 days in which no disturbances were reported in any of the schools. In September, October, November, and December 1974, there was a rough average of 10 incidents a day in the Boston schools, 5 in January and February, and 2–3 in March, April, May, and June.

There were a great variety of school desegregation-connected disturbances: bomb scares; arson and fires; buses and students stoned; students and/or parents demonstrating inside and outside schools; food-throwing in the cafeterias; students fighting in bathrooms, classrooms, at busstops, in buses; stonings and beatings by gangs and by individuals; weapons such as knives, files, hair picks, etc. taken from students are some examples.

A sample excerpt from a Communications Log (for Monday, December 9, 1974) included some of the following incidents:

9:30   Area II—at 8:10 there was a fight in the girls locker room at South Boston High School–G Street. The following girls were involved and injured. Alice McDonough received a gash on the head and is in City Hospital, Susan Foster, a bruise with some swelling on the face, Donna Nilan, a lump on the head. The injuries were inflicted by a girl who was using a padlock as a weapon. More information to follow. Building is tense.

9:32   Area VI—a bus going from the Whittier to Trade was stoned at Franklin Park. A student, William Gallagher was cut by flying glass. He was taken home because his mother wanted him examined at the hospital. The police have been alerted.

. . . .

12:20   Area II—some white students brought whistles to school to sound danger signals and were blowing them in protest. They were escorted from the building. There was a walk out by white students at the Hart-Dean at 11:10. These students are now at G Street building. David McDonough a South Boston High School student is at Carney Hospital with a broken bone in his hand. Three black females have been injured—one with a bruised eye has been taken home by her parents. The other two were engaged in fights one in the cafeteria—the other was thrown down and beaten by a group of white students.

. . . .

3:15   John Doherty—BTU reports that the building representative of the Lewis reports that a large group of black girls had stoned the building.

3:40   Information Center reports that the police informed them that the incident at the Lewis occurred at the close of school (2:40) when about 25 black girls entered the building and overturned furniture in two rooms and set fire to a poster in a corridor and this set off the fire alarm summoning the apparatus. Apparently there is no damage to the building.

The purpose of the School Department in keeping the logs was to keep the deputy superintendent's office in touch with all incidents that might be taking place in the system. Area superintendents were expected to pick up the "hotline" to call in any disturbances. The logs were for daily administrative purposes, then, not for statistical purposes; therefore, they are often sketchy in character, with little follow-up. As a result, one gets the feeling that disturbances, suspensions, arrests and hospitalizations are underreported rather than accurately portrayed. For example, the logs mention only some 146 student suspensions, while actual suspensions numbered in the thousands. Arrest and hospital figures are also inadequate. But the logs do provide some School Department figures, and the plaintiffs have used them several times to show the disparity between discipline of black students and white students.

150. The Communications Logs, *supra* note 149, indicated that schools were closed or classes suspended early as follows: South Boston High, October 2; English High, October 8; Curley, October 9; O'Reilly, October 9; Andrew, October 9; Hyde Park High, October 15; Hyde Park High, December 11; South Boston/Roxbury High, December 11, 12, 13, 16, 17, 18, 19, 20; January 2, 3, 6, 7; Hyde Park High, May 10. For the reasons cited in *supra* note 149, these figures are probably underestimates.

151. Affidavit of Paul V. Smith, Appendix N to Memorandum in Support of Plaintiffs' Proposed Code of Discipline, filed February 6, 1976 in Morgan v. Kerrigan. Plaintiffs contended that the present code of discipline was used discriminately against black students, with the result that disproportionate numbers of black students were suspended from school. Paul Smith, an educational data analyst employed by the Children's Defense Fund of the Washington Research Project, Inc., 24 Thorndike Street, Cambridge, analyzed data taken from Monthly Suspension Summaries supplied by the Boston Public Schools to the Children's Defense Fund, giving the number of students by school and by race for the year 1974/75. He warned that certain factors undercut the reliability of the figures, such as some tendency to underreport and the fact that suspensions given to previously suspended students were reported inadequately. Smith combined the suspension summaries with the Daily Attendance Summaries to determine a "suspension rate" by race; that is, the number of suspensions given per 100 students in average daily attendance in the high and middle schools in Boston, 1974/75. He found that the rate for black students was much higher than that for whites.

Smith checked the Monthly Suspension Summaries with special suspension lists, area superintendents' End of the Day Reports, and incident reports, and found small but insubstantial differences.

Charts giving Smith's figures on suspensions given during 1974/75 in the high schools and in the middle schools follow:

Boston High Schools Affected by Phase I	*Suspensions Given During 1974/75, by Race*			
	White	*Black*	*Other*	*Total*
G Street	338	271	5	614
L Street	50	204	4	258
Hart-Dean	61	275	6	342
Roxbury	3	18	0	21
Burke	32	342	14	388
Dorchester	115	256	5	376
Hyde Park (Main)	247	426	0	673
Hyde Park Annex	30	235	0	265
Jamaica Plain	41	87	16	144
Roslindale	249	186	3	438
Brighton	146	225	24	395
English	107	324	66	497
1974/75 Totals, Phase I Highs	1,419	2,849	143	4,411
Middle Schools				
All Boston Middle Schools, Grades 6–8, 1974/75	1,103	2,451	193	3,747
Total, Middle and High Schools:				8,158

According to the *Globe,* the number of suspensions during the preceding school year (1973/74) was 4,827, and there were 200 more white students suspended than black students that year. Boston Sunday Globe, May 25, 1975, at A24. A comparison of these figures with the Phase I school year figures is dramatic. There were just under twice as

ing teachers and school personnel and numerous allegations of the reverse.[152] More seriously, 459 students had been arrested.[153] Hundreds of persons were

---

many total suspensions during Phase I as compared with the preceding year. During Phase I, there were 2,522 white students suspended as compared with 5,300 black students, over twice as many black students suspended as white. The preceding year there were 200 more white students suspended than black students. The figures speak for themselves and exemplify the reasonableness of plaintiffs' concern that the school code of discipline is being used to discriminate against black students.

152. This figure, also taken from the Boston School Department Communications Logs, is probably low because of incomplete recording and little follow-up. An example of an entry recording a student assaulting a teacher appears on Monday, June 9, 1975:

12:10 Area II—Edward Cheng—student, South Boston High punched teacher (Robert Donovan) teacher treated at hospital (4 stitches below eye). Student taken home by police—teacher presently filing complaint in South Boston District Court.

There were incidents recorded of students assaulting aides, bus monitors, and bus drivers in addition to teachers.

153. The arrest figures provided by the Communications Logs, *supra* note 149, provide a case in point on the unreliability of Boston School Department figures for statistical purposes: the logs cite arrests of 146 students and 20 others. On the other hand, the Boston Police Department Office of Informational Services kept track of Boston Police Department arrests related to Phase I between September 12, 1974 and May 15, 1975. Officer Al Knupis related these figures in a telephone interview on March 9, 1976, quoting from an Informational Services' document entitled "Busing-related incidents, arrests and injuries." He noted that he is keeping monthly records of arrests for Phase II, and is making distinctions between MDC and state police and city police arrests. He stated that arrests made for Phase I can be assumed to have been by the Boston Police Department exclusively. He also stated that no teachers were arrested for Phase I.

He quoted the following figures for arrests of blacks and whites, juveniles and adults:

Arrests: Phase I (9/12/74–5/15/75)

Blacks	Juveniles 172	Adults 103	Total: 275	
Whites	Juveniles 58	Adults 126	Total: 184	Combined: 459

He stated that although Phase II was being broken down to distinguish student arrests from nonstudent (i.e., parents or others), Phase I had not been broken down that way. Juveniles are those up to 17 years of age, and adults those 17 and over, students and nonstudents alike.

Phase I arrests were, however, broken down by the numbers of blacks and whites arrested for each crime. Figures for the following crimes were reported:

	Black		White	
Crime	*Juveniles*	*Adults*	*Juveniles*	*Adults*
Armed Robbery				1
Vandalism				1
Rape		2		
Unarmed Robbery	4	1	2	
Attempted Armed Robbery	5			
Attempted Unarmed Robbery	1			
Stoning MBTA Bus	1			
Stoning Police Vehicle	1			
Stoning School Bus	3		2	
Threats to do Bodily Harm	1			
Trespassing	19	2		1

treated at Boston hospitals for assorted injuries and at least four were hospitalized for more serious injuries.[154]

These statistics clearly underscore the fact that the educational process had been severely disrupted. To a large extent, normality became simply the absence of anarchy.

While fewer apparent disruptions characterized the initial year of Phase II, this experience lends itself to a series of questions. What, if anything, was accomplished? Was it worth the admittedly awesome costs? What does it forebode

According to Officer Knupis, these figures were taken from the official Boston Police Department arrest reports. It is to be noted, however, that they too are not exact when compared with the totals first given, but they are very close. According to the Boston *Globe,* no such figures were kept the preceding year, but the police have stated that they are certain that there has been an increase in arrests. Boston Sunday Globe, May 25, 1975, at A24.

Crime	Black		White	
	Juveniles	*Adults*	*Juveniles*	*Adults*
Aiding Prisoner to Escape	1			
Affray (2 or more persons fighting together)	3	3	1	1
Assault	3	1		1
Assault and Battery	13	8	2	2
Assault by Means of a Dangerous Weapon	10	1	4	2
Assault and Battery with a Dangerous Weapon	19	9	6	4
Assault and Battery on a Police Officer	4	7		16
Disturbing a Public Assembly	15	9	8	7
Unlawful Assembly	2	1	10	9
B&E Daytime, School Building	4			
B&E nighttime	8		1	
Possession of Controlled Substances	6	7		3
Possession of a Dangerous Weapon	3	1	3	1
Kidnapping		1		
Larceny	1	18		
Attempted Larceny		1		
Disorderly Person	47	31	15	75
Mayhem			2	1
False Fire Alarm Pulled in School				1
Incapacitated Person				1
Malicious Destruction of Property			1	

154. The Communications Logs, *supra* note 149, mention only 96 persons connected with hospital treatment, including students, police officers, bus monitors, MTA employees, and bus drivers. They also indicate that 4 persons were hospitalized for more than a day, including Michael Faith—a white student at South Boston High School stabbed on December 11, 1974, but not including Andre Yvon Jean-Louis, a black man on his way through South Boston to pick up his wife at work, viciously beaten by a crowd of whites on October 7, 1974.

The Boston Police Department Office of Informational Services also kept figures of

for the future of desegregation? These questions are fundamental. And the inability to articular ready answers is disturbing. As noted at the outset of this paper, Boston may indeed be a watershed in the struggle to desegregate America's schools and its society.

THE ROAD TO PHASE II

Pursuant to the court's order, Phase II of the desegregation of Boston's public schools was being planned even as Phase I was being implemented. As a consequence, the planning of Phase II was substantially affected by the implementation of Phase I, and vice versa. This fact presents a substantial problem in discussing either phase. This section will focus on the planning and implementation of Phase II, and will not dwell on the interaction between the two phases.

The Boston School Committee and the superintendent had been directed to prepare a comprehensive student desegregation plan providing for the "greatest possible degree of actual desegregation of all grades in all schools in all parts of the city" as of September 1975. In his October 31 order, Judge Garrity detailed just how this was to be accomplished and mandated inclusion of a detailed implementation schedule. When filed, the plan was to show the proposed completion dates for a number of events including: (1) notifying faculty, staff, and students about their assignments; (2) arranging for necessary transportation; (3) planning for orientation of students and parents; (4) recruiting, hiring, and training additional personnel; and (5) preparing an implementation budget. This plan was to be filed on or before December 16, 1974, and was to be preceded by interim progress reports. As these interim reports were issued, many people in Boston breathed a sigh of relief, hoping that despite the ongoing agony of Phase I, the tensions would be eased by the clarity of the orders, the additional time, and the specificity with which the conduct required of defendants was spelled

---

injuries. Officer Knupis cited the following figures from his document entitled "Busing-related incidents, arrests and injuries," *supra* note 153:

Injuries: Phase I (9/12/74–5/15/75)

Students	91
Police	57
Other	58
Total	206

Officer Knupis said that these figures probably were a very inadequate measure of how many injuries were actually sustained. He stated that he believed that many went untreated. The reason for this was that Boston hospitals had been alerted to report any school-related injuries to the Boston Police Department, so that the police could arrest any suspects for misconduct. Since this procedure became common knowledge, one may assume that many persons who were injured avoided hospital treatment out of fear of being reported and arrested. Actual injuries were more likely several times higher than those figures reported above.

out. A review of the events immediately preceding and following the December 16 deadline will demonstrate that this relief was premature and the hope largely unfulfilled. Rather than an easing of tension, a crisis of gargantuan dimensions would develop.

The Education Planning Center[155] had been assigned the task of coming up with the plan. Working furiously, marshalling all their resources, they did. On November 14 they presented the fruits of their labor to the Boston School Committee. The many innovative features of the options they proposed reflected the tremendous amount of work the staff had done.[156] The primary plan was particularly interesting. That plan provided for the introduction of substantial changes in the instructional program. It established geographic school zones. It sought in numerous ways to maximize parental options. However, to assure accomplishment of the court's desegregation order it provided for mandatory assignment in the event that the racial composition of the schools within the system was not within the range set by the court. In a word, the plan devised by the Education Planning Center for school committee approval called for busing.

The case seemed on the verge of a conceptual breakthrough. Thus far busing had been imposed only over the opposition of the school committee. To a large extent this fact added to the tensions. School committee adoption of the Educatinal Planning Center's plan even in a modified form would substantially change the nature of the debate. The difference would become one of degree and not of specie. The question would no longer be *whether* busing, but how much. Realizing this, observers braced themselves while the battle that had raged over two centuries, decades, years, and months became a drama to be played out in weeks, days, and hours.

At center stage once again were the five members of the school committee playing to their respective audiences. Sullivan, the newly elected member who was education reform-minded, voiced her objection to some elements of the plan but indicated that she would vote to approve it and submit it to the court.[157] Tierney assumed the role of the reluctant law-abider compelled by law to resolve his

---

155. The Educational Planning Center (EPC) is part of the Boston School Department. EPC originally had broad responsibilities for dealing with new school plannings and organizational renewals. However, in the last few years it has dealt primarily with racial balance and desegregation problems. The EPC is headed by Joseph Carey, director, and John Coakley, associate director.

156. The report contained several options. One was the December 16 plan (Boston Globe, November 14, 1974, at 1). The other options were the zonal approach, which requires twice as much busing as Phase I (Boston Globe, November 23, 1974, at 6), and the Minneapolis plan, which provides alternative, magnet schools to attract white students to black schools (Boston Globe, November 11, 1974, at 3).

157. Kathleen Sullivan was one of the dissenters when the Boston School Committee on December 16 voted against the submission of the plan developed by the EPC. On December 16, Sullivan urged that the plan be endorsed and forwarded to the judge, though she expressed strong reservation about the proposed pairing of the elementary schools. Boston Globe, December 17, 1974, at 1.

substantial doubts in the court's favor.[158] Ellison, Kerrigan, and McDonough jockeyed for the position of conscience-bound servant of the community who would stand with his constituency regardless of personal cost. It seems, in retrospect, that Ellison, Kerrigan, and McDonough each hoped that at least one, and preferably both, of the other two would vote with Sullivan and Tierney. This would assure submission of the plan and yet afford the lone dissenter the popular position of community advocate. This was not to be. All three so thoroughly committed themselves publicly that there remained no politically feasible way to recant. And so, at 12:20 P.M. on December 16 the Boston School Committee, by a 3-2 vote, rejected the plan presented them and implicitly refused to make the required submission to the court.

The issue was now joined. The Boston School Committee had crossed the line from tactical delay to outright disobedience of a lawful order of the federal district court. However inadvertantly, they had in effect challenged the court.

Among other things, the refusal to obey the court would result in the resignation of the school committee's legal counsel. Attorney Mirich, representing Hale and Dorr, had warned repeatedly of the risks to which members of the school committee would be exposed should they refuse to comply with the court's order. He had opined that such refusal would amount to contempt of court. When the school committee ignored this advice and voted not to submit a plan, the law firm announced that it would not be party to conduct constituting contempt of court. Consequently, Attorney Mirich filed the Educational Planning Center's plan (henceforth referred to as the December 16 Plan) with an accompanying letter which stated that while the school committee had neither approved nor submitted the plan, it was being submitted by Attorney Mirich on his authority as a lawyer and an officer of the court. Hale and Dorr then announced that it wished to resign as counsel to the school committee and filed a motion for leave to do so. In granting the motion, Judge Garrity displayed his confidence in and admiration for young Mirich by stating that he would accede "however reluctantly" to his wishes.

After the school committee's vote, plaintiffs' counsel saw themselves with three options. First, plaintiff could file the desegregation plan which had been developed for the NAACP by Florida desegregation expert Michael J. Stolee.[159]

---

158. On December 16, Tierney said: "I see nothing to be gained by disapproval. The Judge could remove the Committee and appoint substitutes who have never held office." *Id.* at 5. Four days after the voting, Tierney also said:

> There is nothing we can do in terms of changing the Garrity order on forced busing for September, 1975, but we can help him refine the plan to reduce busing as much as possible. Further rallies, boycotts or marches will be of no value for September. People have to realize that the busing aspect of the plan is going to happen in September and work to improve the situation.

Boston Globe, December 20, 1974, at 19.

159. Michael J. Stolee is a professor of education and associate dean of the School of Education at the University of Miami. Stolee received his master of arts degree in education administration from the University of Minnesota. He had prepared close to 50 desegregation

The absence of an opposing comprehensive plan made this seem like a particularly attractive course of action. However, the filing deadline for parties other than defendants was still a month away. Moreover, this plan had been developed as an opposition plan and thus was not as comprehensive as it would otherwise have been.[160] Perhaps for these reasons this course of action was not chosen. Nor did plaintiff choose what they saw as a second option—supporting the December 16 Plan. Rather, on December 17, plaintiffs' counsel asked the court to initiate proceedings to find Ellison, Kerrigan, and McDonough in both criminal and civil contempt.[161] The motion urged that the court impose sanction of fines and imprisonment for the contempt. Even before plaintiffs' motion, Judge Garrity had ordered the school committee to appear in court on December 18.[162] After sternly lecturing the three dissenters he noted that they had cited issues of conscience to justify their conduct. As a consequence, he summarily dismissed the criminal contempt charge. However, he distinguished civil contempt.

A civil contempt order is remedial, not punitive. The purpose of it is to aid the party in whose favor the order has run.[163] The three were ordered to appear

---

plans implemented in Dade County, Florida; Tampa, Florida; Tallahasee, Florida; Lynchburg, Virginia; Chattanooga, Tennessee; Minneapolis, Minnesota; Kalamazoo, Michigan; Denver, Colorado; and San Francisco, California.

In preparing for the Boston plan—to wit: the NAACP Plan—he had seen and photographed all the schools that were in existence in Boston in the fall of 1972. In total, he made twelve trips to Boston dealing with this case. The shortest was one day and the longest was four days Transcripts of the Hearings before the Masters [hereinafter Transcript], at 874. During these trips, he met with Joseph Carey, John Coakley, Dr. Leftwich and Jack Halloran; representatives from BET, Citywide Educational Coalition, Inc.; Massachusetts Chinese Association; Blackstone Community Council; Curley Parent-Teacher Advisory Council; and Parkman Parent Council (*id.* at 879). However, he did not meet with community people from South Boston, East Boston, Charlestown, and West Roxbury (*id.* at 857–80).

160. See discussion, *infra*, p. 87.

161. Plaintiff's Motion for an Order Holding Certain City Defendants in Civil Contempt and Other Relief, R-349; and Morgan v. Kerrigan, Plaintiff's Motion for Initiation of Criminal Proceedings, R-348 on December 18, 1974.

162. Order issued on December 16, 1974: Morgan v. Kerrigan, Order, that Five Members of Boston School Committee Attend a Hearing on 12/18/74, R-340.

163. Morgan v. Kerrigan Transcript of the December 18, 1974 Hearing, at 28–29.

Again, preliminarily, it probably would be helpful, not necessarily for counsel but for persons not lawyers, to briefly draw the distinction between criminal contempt and civil contempt. Criminal contempt is punishment for an offense to the Court, or an offense against the Court's dignity and authority and responsibility. When a spectator stands up in the back of the room and starts shouting curse words and obscenities to the judge on the bench, that is criminal contempt. . . . Civil contempt is different. Civil contempt usually arises in the context of parties against whom an injunction has been issued or an order entered requiring the payment of money who refuses to pay. . . . In cases of civil contempt, when it is determined to exist, this Court's order is remedial, it is not punitive. The purpose of it is to aid the party in whose favor the order has run, so that if a plaintiff in a case has an order entitling him to enter on a certain piece of real estate and the man on the other side of the case decides to put up a barrier or a fence, well, then the Court as a remedy for the contempt of the other party will order that the fence be removed, or make some order that is remedial in its purpose.

in court on December 27 to show cause why they should not be held in civil contempt as requested by plaintiff's motion.[164] Explaining that he wished to clearly examine their motives, Judge Garrity requested that each provide written answers to specific questions.[165] He found the answers to be unsatisfactory in

164. The judge orally notified the three members of the school committee to appear at a hearing on the plaintiff's motion and that they must appear on the date which he will work out with Sullivan and others. The written order was issued on December 23, "Confirming oral orders of the court at the preliminary hearing December 18, 1974 on Plaintiff's motion filed December 17, 1974 for civil contempt and other relief, which will be heard December 27, 1974 at 10:00 A.M." Morgan v. Kerrigan, Orders in Preparation for Civil Contempt Hearing, at 1.

165. Garrity questioned the motives of the defendants at the December 18 hearing:

If you cannot bring yourself to approve a desegregation plan of your own design, how can you bring yourself to carry out a plan not of your own design and one which you believe is unconstitutional and a threat to the safety of the children? . . . [A]long the same line, is your opposition in principle only; or is it opposition which you feel obliged to act upon? It's the difference between feeling that a law is bad but you will obey it nevertheless, or feeling that it is bad and therefore undertaking to obstruct it by acts. . . . [H]ere are the three questions that I drafted; and they will be addressed to each of you three gentlemen, because the answers to these questions will determine the remedy that the Court must adopt.

Transcript of the October 18 Hearing, at 37–39.
The three questions became five, and they were listed in the written order of December 23, 1974. The questions are:

1. What affirmative steps, if any, will you take to promote the peaceful implementation of the state court plan currently in effect?
2. Will you vote to take the steps necessary to implement a citywide desegregation plan, as outlined in the eleven timetables included in section VII of the plan submitted December 16, 1974, such as approval of contracts for transportation of students and for changes in and repairs of facilities?
3. Will you obey and carry out future orders of the court concerning implementation of a citywide student and faculty desegregation plan, such orders as are now being formulated or may in the future be approved by the court?
4. To what extent, if at all, has your commitment made in the letter of November 11, 1974 from Secretary Winter of the School Committee to the Department of Health, Education and Welfare that

    "The Boston public schools presently are, and will continued to be, in full compliance with these orders of the Federal Court for the desegregation of the Boston public schools. The Boston public schools will comply with all future modifications of the order."

    been changed and abandoned?
    And to the following further question:
5. In view of the decision and opinion of the Court of Appeals dated December 19, have you changed your position regarding approval of the December 16 desegregation plan, and if so, in what way?

Orders in Preparation for Civil Contempt Hearing, December 23, 1974 at 1–3.
The answers of the three defendants are as follows:
Kerrigan:

1. I will continue to obey lawful orders of the court, but I will take no initiative or affirmative action to advocate or supplement this plan, which in conscience and principle I oppose, based on my belief that the plan increases racial hatred in Boston, endangers the safety of school children in Boston and leads to white

flight from Boston to the suburbs, where one can live free of forced busing.
2. If and when a citywide desegregation plan is enacted by the court, I will obey lawful orders issued by the court with respect to the plan, but I will take no initiative or affirmative action to advocate or supplement such a plan unless it reduces racial hatred in Boston, provides adequate safety for the school children in Boston and reduces the white flight from Boston to the suburbs.
3. I will obey and carry out lawful orders of the court as may in the future be formulated, but I will take no initiative or affirmative action to advocate or supplement any such plan unless in my belief it reduces racial hatred in Boston, provides adequate safety for the school children in Boston and reduces white flight from Boston to the suburbs.
4. The letter of November 11, 1974, recites my intention to obey all lawful orders of the court. I have not changed that intention, but I will take no initiative or affirmative action to advocate or supplement the plan, which in conscience and principle I oppose, based on my belief that the plan increases racial hatred in Boston, endangers the safety of school children in Boston and leads to white flight from Boston to the suburbs, where one can live free from forced busing.
5. No.

McDonough:

1. I will continue to obey lawful orders of the court, but I will take no initiative or affirmative action to advocate or supplement this plan, which in conscience and principle I oppose on my belief that the plan increases racial antagonism and endangers the safety of school children.
2. If and when a citywide desegregation plan is enacted by the court, I will obey lawful orders issued by the court with respect to the plan, but I will take no initiative or affirmative action to advocate or supplement such a plan unless it reduces racial antagonism and provides adequate safety for the school children.
3. I will obey and carry out lawful orders of the court and as may in the future be formulated, but I will take no initiative or affirmative action to avocate or supplement any such plan unless in my belief it reduces racial antagonism and provides adequate safety for school children.
4. The letter of Nov. 11, 1974, recites my intention to obey all lawful orders of the court. I have not changed that intention, but I will take no initiative or affirmative action to advocate or supplement a plan which in conscience and principle I oppose, based on my belief that the plan increases racial antagonism and endangers the safety of school children, nor will I take any initiative or affirmative action to advocate or supplement any future plan unless in my belief it reduces racial antagonism and provides adequate safety for the school children.
5. No.

Ellison:

1. I will take only those steps which the court by lawful order directs. In principle and conscience I oppose this plan. As an elected public official, I am required to vote my conscience and cannot therefore endorse or advocate this plan,
2. If and when such a plan is enacted by the court, I will obey lawful orders for implementation, but in conscience and principle I do not intend by vote in my official capacity to endorse or advocate a plan unless it reduces racial hatred and provides adequate safety for the school children. Program preference in the form of alternative magnet learning style choices such as in effect in Minneapolis to be preferred over no-choice forced busing.
3. I intend to obey the lawful orders of the court, but in conscience and principle I do not intend by vote in my official capacity to endorse or advocate a plan unless it reduces racial hatred and provides adequate safety for the school children.
4. The letter of November 11, 1974, recites my intention to obey all lawful orders of the court. That is still my intention, but I cannot endorse or advocate a plan which in conscience and principle I oppose.
5. No.

light of the circumstances. He pointed out that defendants could have challenged the October 31 order, but had not. They could have asked the court to modify it to remove the term "approve" if that was in fact the core of their objection, but they did not. They could have indicated their objection to the order by refusing to submit the progress reports in November and early December. Rather, they chose to submit these reports, and despite public posturing to the contrary, misled the court into thinking that its order would be obeyed. Having simply disobeyed the order, they now sought to construct reasons to protect themselves. Holding that the explanation proffered was inadequate, Judge Garrity found the three guilty of civil contempt.

The issue had matured into a full-fledged *cause celebre*. It was widely reported in the local media. The courtroom had been packed on both occasions with supporters of the three contemnors. There was even talk of setting up a defense fund the the Boston Three.[166] The popularity of the contemnors was of such magnitude that they seemed destined to martyrdom should they lose the confrontation with the court.

The legal issues were also far from clearcut. As a popularly elected body, the school committee claimed immunity from judicial scrutiny of their votes on behalf of their constituents. The location of the line where such a vote merits judicial intervention and coercive reversal cannot be pinpointed with any exactitude. Legal precedents in this area are fraught with ambiguity and it seemed quite possible that the inevitable appeals would further confuse the principal objective—accomplishing the desegregation of Boston's schools.

As judge of the federal district court, Garrity could not capitulate. Nor did it seem likely that defendants could abandon their position and their constituency and recant. Judge Garrity repeatedly searched for that middle ground which would provide a graceful way out for all concerned. He had dropped the criminal charge from the outset. He had given them an opportunity to reflect upon and answer written questions. They failed to seize the opportunity. He then asked them to take the stand at the December 27 hearing. Rather than improving upon their answers, which the judge had just found unacceptable, they used the witness stand to expound further on their opposition to the court, and to engage in additional public posturing.[167] Seeking even to use the period be-

---

166. On January 1, 1975, Louise Day Hicks announced the formation of a committee to "coordinate the financial support of the Boston School Committeemen under Court-imposed sanctions. . . ." She said the committee is called Boston S.O.S. for Boston Save Our Schools, and that it was seeking nationwide support. Boston Globe, January 3, 1975, at 3.

167. The Boston Globe reported on the hearing:

Kerrigan: "The burden of desegregation is too much on the core cities." Then he read figures showing that more blacks had assaulted teachers than whites, that more black than white students were suspended this year under the temporary desegregation plan.

"If you point out a thing like that, you are a 'racist,'" he said, repeating his familiar charge that the press doesn't report such comments for that reason. Then in response

tween his finding of contempt and issuance of the written order, Judge Garrity urged the contemnors to meet with counsel over the intervening weekend to work out a compromise. No meeting was held.

The written order was issued on December 30.[168] After outlining the proceedings and the basis of his finding of civil contempt. Judge Garrity provided that "each contemnor may purge himself of civil contempt by voting at a meeting of the Boston School Committee to 'authorize' the prompt submission to the court of a citywide student desegregation plan." The order went on to impose a coercive fine (the amount of which would be fixed after examining each contemnors' individual financial status) and to remove the contemnors from participation in any school discussion, decision, or function pertaining to desegregation. Moreover, since both Kerrigan and McDonough were attorneys, the order directed the United States Attorney to commence proceedings to suspend them from the bar so long as they remained in contempt. Stern as this order appeared, Judge Garrity had provided defendants another opportunity to avoid confrontation. Holding that "plaintiffs' constitutional rights and racial harmony must not founder on the ambiguity of a word," he allowed the opportunity for the contemnors to purge themselves without having to "approve" a plan. According to this order, they now had merely to "authorize" the submission of a plan. Moreover, the sanctions would not begin until some ten days later.

---

to the question concerning the dialogue between the black and the white community, he shifted his gaze to the five NAACP lawyers only a few feet in front of him: ". . . I feel what we have done, your Honor, is to have a lack of honesty on the black community in the city, in particular the NAACP. You know, there has been an awful lot of talk about the violence that occurred a few weeks ago on Wednesday when South Boston High was cut down and it was caused—the plaintiffs would like you to believe—by the School Committee. I was 2,500 miles away at that time." When he was asked by the judge if there is any sort of desegregation plan he could support, he responded: "I can't support a plan that involves the forced busing of school children, but there is no vote I can make to prevent the court from ordering forced busing."

McDonough: "To begin with, I have always complied with the orders of this Court. I intend to do so in the future, but if you ask me to go one step beyond where you direct me, I will not take that step." He continued, in an even tone, ". . . I thought it was clear to the court that it was not a good plan, the plan is wrong, because you are throwing people from different cultures at each other in such a way that they cannot back off from each other, and we are going to have violence, injury, and possible death to the school children and perhaps other people in this city as a result of this plan."

Ellison: Responding to the question ". . . if the Court approves a plan, will you vote to carry it out even though you don't approve of it?" Ellison said: "I will vote as I did before, but I respect the rights given to me by the electorate of having to make a— If my conscience tells me to approve of something that I disapprove, I cannot do, and I want to make that clear, and I think that you have made mention of that when we were here before. You found no fault with that. If we don't have that, if we are elected by the people and we can't vote our conscience and we have principles and we know and we gave reasons for not voting, I think that should be sufficient."

Boston Globe, Dec. 28, 1974, at 3.

168. Morgan v. Kerrigan, Memorandum and Order as to Sanctions on Civil Contempt, R-374, December 30, 1974.

The contemnors unsuccessfully sought to have Judge Garrity stay the December 30 order pending appeal.[169] Pointing to the ten-day period before the order would take effect, Judge Garrity said a stay had already in effect been granted.[170] He outlined three further reasons for denying the stay. (1) To grant it would further delay the school committee's affirmative obligation to come forth with and implement a desegregation plan; (2) as a consequence of defendant's conduct some $1.9 million in federal financial assistance was being withheld by HEW; and (3) plaintiffs not only had substantial interests here but those interests were of general public importance.

On January 7, after the U.S. Court of Appeals also refused to stay the contempt sanction,[171] and with less than one hour left before it would go into effect, the contemnors joined the other members of the school committee in voting to direct the Educational Planning Center to amend the December 16 Plan so that it complied with the court's October 31 order and yet would not entail compulsory busing.[172]

Defendant's counsel then informed the court that the school committee was in "literal compliance" with his order and ought to be found to have purged themselves.[173] Plaintiffs' counsel, on the other hand, argued that this was a transparent attempt to violate the spirit of the order by literal compliance with its spirit. Recalling an earlier statement by Kerrigan that desegregation was impossible without busing, counsel dismissed the vote as a frivolous and absurd decision to do the impossible.

Having sought so long for a way to resolve this issue, Judge Garrity was not prepared to let opportunity slip away from him. After a mere fifteen minutes of argument, he retired to his chambers. Later that day, in a written order,[174] he

169. Morgan v. Kerrigan Motion for Stay of Order of December 30, 1974, Pending Appeal, R-382, January 2, 1975.

170. Morgan v. Kerrigan Order on Motion for Stay of Order Pending Appeal, Entered (Denied—further stay must be sought in Court of Appeals), R-386, January 3, 1975.

171. Morgan v. Kerrigan, 509 F.2d 618 (1975).

172. Boston Globe, (p.m.) January 7, 1975, at 1. *See also* Morgan v. Kerrigan, Letter to Judge Garrity from Attorney Sullivan, re: Vote of School Committee on 1/7/75, R-401, January 7, 1975.

173. Morgan v. Kerrigan, Transcript of Hearing on 1/8/75, R-407, January 8, 1975.

174. The text of that order is as follows:

January 8, 1975

GARRITY, J. At a meeting of the Boston School Committee yesterday the defendant school committee members Kerrigan, McDonough and Ellison endeavored to purge themselves of civil contempt found by the court at a hearing on December 27, 1974, as to which sanctions were ordered by memorandum and order dated December 30, 1974. The question now is whether they succeeded. After hearing counsel earlier today, the court finds that they did, on condition that they follow up their vote to submit an amended citywide student desegregation plan on or before January 20, 1975.

In so finding the court relies upon (a) the contemnors' position before the Court of Appeals, as stated at page 3 of its decision entered January 7, 1975, as follows: "They point to the facts that counsel for the Committee filed a plan with the court, that this action was not disavowed by the Committee, and that copies of the plan

admitted that the "special circumstances of widespread public controversy and tensions" had persuaded him that doubts be resolved in favor of the contemnors. He found the vote adequate to purge them of civil contempt providing they in fact submitted the proposed amended plan by January 20.

Defendants viewed this development as a victory. They had purged themselves without seeming to change position at all. They had avoided the proposed sanctions, kept control of the school committee and retained the confidence of their constituency. After still another seven-day extension, on January 17 the school committee submitted a plan. A major crisis had been averted.

The preliminaries were now out of the way. The opposing parties had done as they were instructed. The court now had before it the task of formulating for a final order a comprehensive plan that would be implemented in the fall. In addition to the school committee's plan (the Authorized School Committee Plan), four others were submitted to the court. The earliest, of course, was the December 16 Plan, submitted by Attorney Mirich. The other three were plans of the

---

were printed for distribution, and assert that there has been a 'ratification by silence'"; (b) defendants' first vote yesterday which further ratified the December 16 plan by directing the Educational Planning Center to amend it; and (c) defendants' literal compliance with the provision of the December 30, 1974 order, which stated at page 4 that they might purge themselves "by voting at a meeting of the Boston School Committee to 'authorize' the prompt submission to the court of a citywide student desegregation plan." True, as argued by plaintiffs' counsel, the court's order contemplated authorization of an existing plan. On the other hand, as argued by counsel for the contemnors, they relied upon the specific terms of the court's order and, under the special circumstances of widespread public controversy and tension here presented, doubts should be resolved in their favor.

The court's finding is conditioned upon the defendants' submission of the amended plan after reviewing it and voting to authorize its submission to the court. Otherwise it cannot constitute, in the words of the Court of Appeals, "a representation, made under the court-imposed limitations and restraints of the order of October 31, that a plan as developed by school department staff and reviewed by School Committee members is their best effort to respond to the objectives and guidelines of the court." The time within which the defendants' amended plan must be filed is January 20, 1975, the date fixed in the court's order of October 31, 1974.

The prospects of the school committee's submitting an amended plan which meets the requirements of the court's order dated October 31, 1974 but does not employ forced busing, that is, the assignment of students to schools beyond walking distance, are remote in the extreme. The defendant Kerrigan, at the hearing on December 27, 1974, himself testified, at pages 112–113, "the only way you are going to desegregate city schools is through forced busing." As for attracting volunteers to so-called magnet schools, the court's opinion dated June 21, 1974, at page 35 and elsewhere, described the failure of this device when attempted in connection with the opening of the Hennigan and Lee schools. However, in the preamble to their vote on January 7 the defendants asserted their belief that submission of a citywide student desegregation plan without forced busing should be at least tried. The court will not today deprive them of that opportunity. During the entire period of the operation of the city's schools covered by the evidence received at the trial, students were assigned to schools beyond walking distance. After the defendants have filed the amended plan which they have in mind, the question whether citywide desegregation may be achieved without such assignments can then be settled once and for all.

Morgan v. Kerrigan, Memorandum and Conditional Order as to Three Defendants' Civil Contempt, January 8, 1975.

NAACP and the Boston Home and School Association (BHSA) and Massachusetts State Representative Melvin H. King.[175]

The BHSA plan was dropped from consideration very early in the process. The plan and supporting memoranda had sought primarily to limit the scope of the desegregation remedy pending a final word from the U.S. Supreme Court.

175. Melvin H. King is a well-known activist leader in the black community. He had unsuccessfully sought a seat on the Boston School Committee. Nevertheless, he has remained involved in education matters. In his letter of submittal to Judge Garrity he defined the components and objectives of his plan.

Briefly, this plan does the following things:
—redefines "integration" to mean the distribution of power to all groups in Boston's population by providing decision-making control to parents and representatives in an equitable way. Integration in this sense means that all of Boston's children have access to the assets of the public school system, and that the system is accountable to their needs;
—reinforces the uniform grade program built along the K–5–6–7–8, and 9–10–11–12 model to eliminate the tracking that was effectively segregating Boston's public schools. At the same time,
—recognizes the reality that the Boston School Committee has failed to provide quality education to *all* of Boston's school patrons except for the very few in the technical and Latin schools. All schools should provide the quality of education available at these exam schools. At the heart of the conflict over the schools and the lack of quality education are the issues of governance—who makes the decisions about hiring and the use of resources? The Judge has initiated a plan to increase the number of Black, Puerto Rican, and Chinese staff, but the plan does not go far enough. The value placed on providing role models for students of their own ethnic group must similarly be placed on the power of representatives to have direct and effective input into the design and operation of curriculum and learning programs. The mandate for this kind of input is implicit in the Bilingual Act and in the Special Needs Act. But neither of these acts fills the glaring gap of power for the groups who have been collectively oppressed and denied by the operation of the Boston School system through the years;
—recognized the precedent that other court decisions have allowed all-Black schools to exist so long as those parents and parties involved do not feel they are being denied. This plan suggests that only those districts which have a majority of Black students should have access to seats in metropolitan or other school systems and continues the present policy that any student may move into a school where such a move would increase racial balance;
—stresses the importance of demonstrating that all the schools in Boston belong to all the people of Boston. The school system must not be exclusionary in any way;
—deals with the role of the State in supporting public education and eliminating the disparity between the rich and poor communities;
—eliminates the stigma which even today accompanies the students who participate in such programs as Metco. These students are never fully part of the school community; their problems and needs are always handled separately because they are "different" or "special" in the eyes of the administration, the teachers, and the other students;
—emphasizes the educational issues of content, programming and experience, which are so often left undiscussed during the concern over busing, districts, and classroom seats. The content of education available in Boston schools must be radically revised to meet the vastly different needs of students today and the changing needs of the students of tomorrow.

Morgan v. Kerrigan, An Alternative Plan for the Integration of Boston's Public Schools, January 20, 1975.

BHSA argued that the remedy should be limited only to those schools in the system as to which specific instances of segregative action could be shown. The plan sought to exclude from the remedy all other schools. Judge Garrity considered this a substantive assult at the remedy stage, and decided to construe the BHSA plan as a motion to modify this October 31 order. After a separate hearing on February 5, he denied the motion and refused to allow further consideration of the BHSA plan.

Even so, there remained three very different plans offered by the parties, around none of which there could be said to be concensus. Plaintiffs objected to the Authorized Committee Plan. Defendants objected to the NAACP plan. Plaintiff and Defendants both objected to the Educational Planning Center's December 16 Plan. While some of the objections were superficial and inconsequential, many reached important substantive issues and served to highlight the very wide gulf between the expectations and perceived interests of the parties involved.

Whether those differing expectations and interests could in fact be reconciled in any one plan remain unclear. What is clear, however, was that the plan that finally emerged from the weeks and months following January 27 did not do so.

The apparent complexity of the three plans submitted in January and the necessity to decide quickly which if any of the three would be adopted by the final order underscored a decision reached by Judge Garrity at least a month earlier: the time had come to seek the advice and input of experts in the development of a viable desegregation plan.

In mid-December, after consulting with Gregory and Walsh of the Community Relations Service, Judge Garrity met with Robert Dentler, the Dean of the School of Education at Boston University. Dentler was a desegregation expert who had worked on desegregation plans in eleven other cities. The judge and the dean shared views on the case and explored some tentative solutions to the ongoing problems. At the judge's request, Dean Dentler submitted to the court a memorandum expanding upon his earlier remarks and outlining how he thought Phase II should proceed. This was the first in a series of communications which would become known as the Dentler Memos.

Although Judge Garrity did not directly respond to the Dentler Memos for almost a month, it seemed to have aided him immensely in refining his conception on how to proceed. In the intervening weeks he moved from seeking a single reputable middle-of-the-road type expert to a broader search for several people. He remained interested in assuring that the technical expertise needed would be available. However, he now seemed much more attuned to the politics of the situation. The fact that public acceptance of the process and the plan would require some demonstrated sensitivity to the city's various ethnic groups argued for a balanced panel. Thus Dentler, soon to become a pivotal figure in the desegregation process, had an impact even before Judge Garrity's January 31 order naming him and his associate dean, Marvin Scott, to be the two court-appointed experts.[176]

By this time the Garrity-Walsh process had narrowed a long list of possibles down to about seven, four of whom would agree to serve as masters. On February 4, the order was issued:

> The Court designates Hon. Frances Keppel, Hon. Edward J. McCormack, Jr., Hon. Jacob. J. Spiegel . . . and Dr. Charles V. Willie as a panel of Masters to begin hearing on or about February 16, 1975 on various student desegregation plans and proposals which have been filed and to request their recommendations to the Court.[177]

The composition of the panel reflected the time and thought which had gone into selecting its members. Francis Keppel, then director of education of the Aspen Institute Program, had served on the U.S. Education Commission of the Kennedy administration. Prior to that, he had been dean of Harvard's School of Education for twenty-seven years. Just as important as this impressive array of credentials were both his reputation for being knowledgeable about the federal bureaucracy and his skill at obtaining federal funds.

Edward T. McCormack was a successful Boston lawyer and nephew of John McCormack, the former Speaker of the U.S. House of Representatives. Although he was now in private practice, this had not always been the case. In 1975 he was elected to the Boston City Council. The following hear he served as its president. In 1960 he succeeded Edward Brooke as Attorney General for the Commonwealth and was elected with the largest majority ever recorded. In 1962 he sought the Democratic nomination for the U.S. Senate seat vacated by John Kennedy. After he failed to achieve that nomination (his successful rival was Edward Kennedy), McCormack, the "golden boy" of Massachusetts politics, returned to private practice. No doubt his name identification, his political connections, and his reputation as a law-and-order man made him an attractive candidate for master. More relevant to any of these, however, was the fact that McCormack was born and raised in South Boston, attended its public schools, and graduated from South Boston High. His was clearly the appointment Judge Garrity thought was needed to legitimate a plan to the dominant ethnic population.

Hon. Jacob J. Spiegel was asked to preside over the panel of masters. He had served with distinction on the bench of the Supreme Judicial Court of the Commonwealth of Massachusetts. He retired in 1972 and had since served as a member of the State Judicial Council and chairman of the Commission on Corrupt Practices. He would bring legal expertise to the panel.

176. Morgan v. Kerrigan, Order Appointing Masters, R-516, January 31, 1975.
177. Morgan v. Kerrigan, Designation of Masters and Notice of Hearing on the Draft Order, R-535, February 4, 1975.

Charles V. Willie was then a professor of education and urban studies at Harvard's Graduate School of Education. A nationally acclaimed scholar, Willie had just joined the faculty at Harvard after being sought after by several other schools. He was the educator-sociologist and the only black person on the panel.

Defendants immediately challenged both Keppel and Willie, claiming they should be disqualified because of their associations with Harvard Univeristy. Counsel pointed to the ongoing role of the Harvard Center for Law and Education in the preparation and conduct of plaintiffs' case. They noted the the center was located at Harvard, that it was jointly sponsored by the Harvard School of Law and the School of Education, and that three of plaintiffs' counsel (Flannery, Pressman, and Van Loon) were either presently or formerly employed by the center. On February 7 Judge Garrity refused to withdraw either name. In the written memorandum he concluded that "there is no existing or foreseeable conflict of interest in Dean Keppel's or Dr. Willie's serving as Master in these proceedings and no basis for their disqualifications."

With its membership now formally appointed, the panel held its first working session. They had met with Judge Garrity several days earlier to set out the ground rules. Generally they would operate independently of the court, but within his guidelines. The February 7 order outlined what was expected of the masters. They were directed to consider first the adequacy of the Authorized Committee Plan in light of the remedial guidelines established by the court in earlier proceedings, and the general constitutional and legal standards developed in applicable cases or promulgated by statute. The objective was stated to be a report recommending "a plan meeting constitutional standards" and assuring "prompt systematic desegregation". By implication, the masters had to find the Authorized Committee Plan inadequate before they could proceed to any others. Once they so found, however, they could consider all other plans and could develop their own plan using magnet schools, metropolitanization, mandatory busing, and any other options "to the extent they are compatible with the essential objective. . . ."

The February 7 order also detailed how the masters should proceed:

5. The masters will hold evidentiary hearings subject to applicable rules of evidence and procedure commending on February 10, 1975, in the Court of Appeals' courtroom on the fifteenth floor. Hearings generally will be on the day-to-day basis, from 10:00 A.M. to 4:00 P.M. unless otherwise ordered by the masters. The masters may order that hearings be held on Saturdays. Three masters shall be sufficient to constitute a quorum. The masters may regulate the proceedings before them, including (a) whether to hear proposals of counsel with respect to procedural matters before receiving any evidence; (b) the order of witnesses' testimony and the early filing of lists of witnesses to be called by the parties; (c) acceptance of plans and reports in lieu of the testimony of any witness; and (e) whether to postpone consideration of issues pertaining to the examination schools until after hearing evidence as to most

or all other issues. The masters may decide whether or not to hear oral presentations by community groups and others who have filed written proposals and comments on plans previous to the commencement of the hearing before the masters; and may within their discretion permit such groups and persons to appear without counsel. The masters shall call upon the court-appointed expert(s) to testify and may also call other witnesses as they may determine. The masters may consult with the court-appointed experts as they deem necessary.

8. After the hearings, the masters shall file a draft report setting forth the plan they recommend and the reasons for recommending it, and shall schedule the reasons for recommending it, and shall schedule on short notice oral argument on the draft report. The masters shall then file their final report with the court and notify the parties. Within 5 days after being served with notice of the filing of the masters' report, any party may serve written objections thereto upon the other parties. Within 5 days after the filing of objections and applications to the court for action upon the report, the court will hold a hearing on such objections and applications.

After three days of reviewing the file and eleven days of evidentiary hearing, the masters entered the deliberative stage of the process. For three weeks they worked behind closed doors. By the time their preliminary report emerged, they had rejected all three plans and developed still another. This new plan, the Masters' Plan, borrowed many of its important features from its predecessors. However, it was not solely a composite. These borrowed features were combined with new ones to produce a plan which in retrospect may best have served to reconcile the conflicting interests in the Boston community. The Masters' Plan reflected not only the diversity of the panel, but also the way the panel came to view its role.

Throughout the litigation certain words and phrases had become symbolic handles for the various parties. Black parents sought "equality of educational opportunity" for their children and had been convinced that only "racial balance" could assure attainment of that objective. The Boston School Committee, representing a large portion of the whole community, had vociferously opposed "forced busing" and argued instead for "quality education." The masters reduced their multiple objectives to one simple but descriptive phrase—"desegregate and defuse." Translated, "desegregate and defuse" said that the Boston public school system would not achieve "racial balance" if purely voluntary measures were employed. Some "forced busing" would severely disrupt the educational process unless it was part of a plan which promised "quality education" and recognized traditional neighborhoods and communities. In fact and effect, the masters realized that while Boston—having been found guilty of unconstitutionally segregating its public schools—could not avoid desegregation, if the pressures of desegregation went unchecked the resulting explosion would at best assure a pyrrhic victory.

The panel adopted the language of *Green v. County School Board*[178] and sought a plan that "promises realistically to work and promises realistically to work now." None of the three plans could meet the test—the Authorized School Committee Plan, with it almost exclusive reliance on voluntary parental action, held no such promise. It was conceded that the "home" schools would probably remain primary one-race schools. The masters found that the integrated experience to which the students would be exposed at the "third-site resource centers" could not be substituted for ongoing desegregated eduation. The NAACP plan fell short of the *Green* standard for other reasons. It was a comprehensive student assignment plan that would require the busing of some 30,000 students. If implemented, the NAACP plan could guarantee a far greater racial mix than either of the others. But it could also guarantee and escalation of the tensions then still afflicting Phase I. Since there was no educational component to the NAACP plan, it promoted desegregation without defusing the situation. The masters noted that aside from mentioning the importance of a nondiscriminatory curriculum, the NAACP plan failed to detail what should be done to meet the needs of the students it had asserted had been victimized by segregation. It failed to deal adequately with the special needs of bilingual students. Several of its provisions would significantly disrupt continuity in school. Moreover, the districts set out in the plan appeared to be arbitrarily designed and did not reflect any consideration for traditional neighborhood boundaries.[179] The December 16 Plan came closest to meeting the masters' "desegregate and defuse" objective. Yet it, too, was found to be inadequate when measured against the *Green* standard.

Having disposed of the three plans presented to them, the masters had to develop their own plan. Even had they been so inclined, it is unlikely that time would have allowed the development of a completely new plan. Although the February 7 order had not set forth a required reporting date, it had stated as the *raison d'etre* for the panel "the need for speedy determination of a plan to go into effect in September 1975." This was early March. If a plan was to be ready, the masters had no choice but to rely upon some of the work that went into the earlier plans.

To some extent what they did could be described as reassembling parts of three jigsaw puzzles to create a fourth. Portions of all three plans were retained. All three had provided for the creation of identifiable attendance districts to replace a situation the court had aptly described as a "complex maze of single school and multi-school districts." The Masters' Plan provided for ten districts. It also

---

178. Green v. County School Board of New Kent County, 391 U.S. 430 (1965).
179.

. . . [T]he plaintiff's plan, although assuring thorough desegregation, does not reflect a sufficient concern either for the city's peculiar characteristics or for the educational complications of plan design.

Draft Report of the Masters in Tallulah Morgan, *et al.* versus John Kerrigan, *et al.* (hereinafter cited as *Draft Report*), submitted to the parties on March 21, 1975, at 7.

provided for the various educational innovations proposed by the December 16 Plan. It incorporated the concept of parental options that was an important feature of both the December 16 and the Authorized Committee plans. And it retained among other things the transfer option proposed by the NAACP plan.

The task remained to take these pieces of the puzzle and fit them into a single coherent concept that would not dissolve into chaos when implemented. That synthesis occurred sometime during the deliberations. As a result, the masters emerged with a plan they hoped would desegregate by requiring limited use of the bus and defuse by providing for substantial improvements at the end of the ride.

This plan may be considered in terms of its proposed administrative impact, educational content, and desegregation potential. How would it affect the organization and operation of the school system? What new education programs wold be forthcoming? Did it propose a sufficient enough racial mix to in fact work realistically in the dismantling the dual school system? To a large extent the court answered "No" to the last question. But to an even greater extent the administrative and educational aspects of the Masters' Plan would eventually prevail.

The Masters' Plan proposed to reorganize Boston's public school system into ten school districts.[180] Nine of the districts would be geographically determined areas designated "community school districts." The tenth would be a citywide school district composed of those schools "offering distinctive programs of instruction that may serve the needs and interests of students residing anywhere within Boston." Each of the ten districts would have a district superintendent who would serve as chief school officer. Each would have a council of principals which would be composed of all the principals and headmasters in the district. This council of principals would be responsible for internal monitoring of the district and would be chaired by the district superintendent.

The masters also envisioned a much greater degree of formal citizen participation than had previously existed. Their plan called for the establishment of a Citywide Educational Council and of a community council in each of the ten districts.[181] The Citywide Education Council would be composed of not more than fifteen "distinguished and broadly representative citizens of Boston who can deliberate and act regularly and vigorously as the eyes and ears of the court." Its basic function would be to monitor the implementation of the various phases of whatever plan was eventually ordered by the court. The community councils' function would be "to advise and co-plan with the Community Superintendent and the Council of Principals, and to *guide* the planful [*sic*] achievement of quality desegregated public instruction inside each district." Each community council would consist of: (1) five parents of children attending schools in the district, to be elected by district parents; (2) two students attending the district

180. *Id.* at 32.
181. *Id.* at 38.

high school, elected by district high school students; (3) a representative of the district teachers; (4) a representative of a business organization working with the district high school; (5) a representative of a college or university paired with a district school; (6) a representative of a labor union paired with a district school (or with the nearest district or citywide school if there is no union pairing in the district; (7) a representative of the Boston Police Department of the district, or of any police department having jurisdiction in the district or assigned responsibility for a school in the district; (8) the superintendent of schools for the district.[182]

The Masters' Plan placed considerable emphasis upon the quality of education the students would receive. The three main features of this aspect of the plan were: (1) its demonstrable concern for the special needs of different groups of students: (2) the rearranging of ongoing educational programs and the adoption of new ones; and (3) the involvement of institutions of higher education, business, and labor in the educational programs of the public schools.

The masters took particular pains not to compound the already existing disadvantages of students who were poor, non-Anglo, or handicapped by depriving them of the opportunity to participate in available special programs. This has been a particularly troublesome aspect of desegregation. Poor black students are often "desegregated" into a white middle-class milieu. While the debate still rages as to whether this is educationally productive, there is no question that if this change is accompanied by the loss of special funding for previously existing remedial programs, the result will in all probability be educationally catastrophic. This is precisely what often happens as a consequence of a desegregation decree. A good example of this is the federal Title I program.[183]

> Title I provides compensatory funds for a range of classroom, diagnostic and supportive services to educationally deprived children who live in poverty areas. Under Title I, each local educational agency receiving funds must designate "target schools" (i.e. schools with substantial numbers of poor children) which will be the schools conducting the Title I program.
>
> When poor black children are transported to new schools as a part of a court order to dismantle a dual school system, the issue of their continued eligibility for Title I service is placed in doubt. ESFA Title I Program Guide #64 governs this situation and provides that school districts must make a redetermination of the eligible target areas based on incidence of poverty. Only those schools which are "poverty schools" under the new, post-desegregation determination may receive Title I services. HEW has expressly recognized that this will occur: Unfortunately in some instances children who have participated in Title I programs under previous determi-

---

182. Community councils were proposed at 38 of the *Draft Report, supra* note 179, but the exact composition of the councils—to wit, 5 parents, 2 students, and representatives from business, universities etc.—was included only in the final report presented to the court on March 31, 1975. *See* Boston Globe, April 1, 1975, at 8.

183. Elementary and Secondary School Act of 1965.

nations of eligibility will be ineligible for Title I services: (Program Guide #64). Program Guide #64 does provide an exception in instances where there is a voluntary transfer from the poverty school to a non-target school: "Children who reside in eligible attendance areas but by specific arrangements attend schools serving ineligible areas may be considered for participation in the Title I program."

Thus, the clear effect of Program Guide #64 is to penalize the very children whose constitutional rights were violated by the local educational agency. Indeed, it is only when black children successfully challenge unconstitutional segregation that they run the risk of losing Title I funds.[184]

The Masters' Plan provided that the programs would still operate in the city-wide district and explicitly suggested that eligible students be "guided into the City-Wide District Schools." Students for whom English was not the first language presented much the same problem and were handled in a similar fashion.

Physically handicapped and mentally retarded children also posed special problem for desegregation in Boston. After a protracted legislative struggle, the Commonwealth of Massachusetts had recently enacted a special statute mandating schools to develop programs for educating these special students. Requiring these students to be bused could destroy their programs. After initially imposing upon each school the primary obligation to provide for the special needs of those students, the masters effectively exempted them from the desegregation effort. The rationale was simple and straightforward. "Special needs transcend ethnic definitions. Children of all groups have disabling and handicapping conditions. Assignment . . . on the primary basis of special needs should have no adverse effect upon desegregation. Assignment to specific schools and programs will inevitably involve children of ethnic backgrounds and should in most instances result in special programs which are themselves desegregated."[185]

Three other groups of students received special attention from the masters. Students in kindergarten, seniors in high school, and students who had just been reassigned as a consequence of Phase I would all be excluded from the plan insofar as mandatory assignment or busing was concerned.

Throughout their plan, the masters stressed that quality education was of major importance. To facilitate this, they proposed that the community districts abandon the multiple-grade structures in favor of a uniform tripartite structure which would have grades 1-5 as elementary level, 6-8 as the middle leve, and 9-12 as the high school level.[186] They envisioned that the educational program at all levels would be "planned to reinforce the quality of learning with the [community district] high school . . . [and] each high school shall be a four year comprehensive institution which serves with equal and uniform excellence of

---

184. *Draft Report, supra* note 179, at 62.
185. *Id.* at 64.
186. *Id.* at 41.

instruction, students seeking general culminating education, those seeking vocational training or experience, and those seeking preparation for post-secondary study."[187] Quality education was also fostered by requiring the establishment of district offices which would be staffed and equipped to provide a range of supportive services to the schools in their respective districts.

The most innovative educational component of the plan was its provision dealing with the area colleges, universities, and businesses. The educational institutions and the businesses were paired with specific high schools and districts and invited to involve themselves in the education programs and activities of their partners.[188] This marked the first time that a comprehensive formal effort had been made to draw upon the resources of these institutions.

In its report, the panel of masters candidly admitted that they "constantly have kept in mind that compulsory busing of students should be kept at a minimum, yet managed so that it will achieve the desegregation which the law requires."[189] The extent to which the former factor outweighed the latter is still being debated. The Masters' Plan would have required the busing of between 10,000 and 15,000 students in Phase II, compared to 17,000 in Phase I.[190] The racial ratios would vary considerably from district to district.

The racial mix at each community district school would be required to approximate that racial composition of its particular district. The effect of this would be to leave many schools predominately black or white. The plan proposed that by September 1976 the student body of every school in the citywide school district would have neither more than 60 percent nor less than 40 percent white students; neither more than 50 percent nor less than 30 percent black students; neither more than 25 percent nor less than 5 percent other minority students.[191]

There is no question that, except for in the citywide school districts, the Masters' Plan did not promise to remedy significantly the racial imbalance in Boston's public schools. Whether that fact was enough to find that the dual school system was not dismantled is another question. As it turned out, no higher court had to rule on the issue. Judge Garrity himself severely modifed that aspect of the plan.[192]

The masters may not have been quite prepared for the reaction to their plan. It was immediately branded as a "compromise" and subjected to criticism from all sides almost as soon as the preliminary report was released on March 21. The NAACP strenuously objected to the wide variations in racial percentages and

187. *Id.* at 40.
188. *Id.* at 43–49. Also see discussion *infra*, pp. 101.
189. *Id.* at 8.
190. *Id.* at 51.
191. *Id.* at 43.
192. See discussion *infra*, pp. 95–96.

questioned the constitutionality of the plan. Busing foes expressed continued opposition to mandatory busing even on the reduced scale the plan proposed.[193] The Educational Planning Center disagreed with their calculations of how many students would be bused and inquired about the legal and administrative responsibilities of the community councils.[194] The Boston Teachers Union said that it would not support the involvement of colleges and universities because the precise roles were not adequately defined.[195] A similar concern was voiced by Committeeman Ellison who saw the involvement of the colleges and universities as "a disgrace and an insult."[196] Counsel for the school committee expressed his clients' concern over the seemingly enlarged role of the experts. He said that the Masters' Plan seemed "to give almost absolute discretion to the experts to run the school department." Moreover, the school committee was "very unhappy with the plan" and pledged to "do everythin in our power to reduce the number bused from 10,000 to zero."

Not all the reaction was as negative, however. Rose Marie Ruggerio, leader of an anti-busing group in East Boston, ventured that the plan was "certainly not as drastic as what my people had expected."[197] Thayer Fremont Smith, attorney

193.

. . .[T]he Masters seem to have realized that forced busing is a bad trip . . . it's too bad that they have not been blessed with enough vision to see that the cancer of forced busing can not be treated piecemeal, but could only be cured by total elimination.

Representative Raymond Flynn, as quoted in Boston Sunday Globe, March 23, 1975, at A4.

194. The Educational Planning Center estimated that 22,570 children would have to be bused if the proposed desegregation plan was implemented without modifications. The center also expressed concern over: (1) will the students be forcibly assigned to citywide magnet schools?; (2) will there be any blacks at Charlestown High or any whites at Roxbury High?; and (3) what will the legal and administrative responsibilities of the ten Community Councils be? Boston Globe, (P.M.), March 24, 1975, at 1.

195. John P. Doherty, Jr., the president of the Boston Teachers Union, said: "It is clear to us that the precise role of colleges and universities must be more clearly defined than it has been by the experts." He said the union would "support and cooperate" if the colleges and universities would place their resources at the School Department's disposal but "if, however, the local colleges and universities enter the public schools with the attitude that they are the experts who will solve all of the problems of an urban school system undergoing a difficult desegregation order, then the Boston Teachers Union views their role as an unnecessary burdensome intrusion that will further complicate an already difficult situation." He also stressed that the following issues needed clarifications:

1. The number of teaching positions.
2. The number of students involved in Phase II.
3. The role of Community District Councils.
4. The change in examination schools.
5. The time table proposed by the experts.

Boston Evening Globe, March 24, 1975, at 8 (*Teachers' Union warns it may not back college role in plan*).

196. Boston Globe, March 22, 1975, at 3 (*Many applaud new plan while busing foes attack it*).

197. Boston Sunday Globe, March 23, 1975, at 1 (*Reaction mixed as leaders assess new plan*).

for the Home and School Association, agreed, saying "It's better than I'd expected or hoped for."[198] Bill Owens, the single black state senator, expressed the thought that parents would accept the plan because of its emphasis on equality education and parental options. "I've never been hung up on 50–50 balances or anything like that".

The various objections were formally presented on March 25. The masters duly recorded them. Although the final report filed on March 31 was substantially the same plan, it reflected an attempt to deal with many of the prior criticisms. Despite the changes, all parties filed objections to the revised plan.[199]

198. Boston Globe, March 24, 1975, at 7 (*NAACP gives Qualified Approval of Masters' Phase II Plan*).
    199.

Date	Objections	Docket number
April 7	Plaintiff-Intervenor El Comite's Objections to the Report of the Masters	R-716
"	Objections to the Masters' Report by Intervenor Boston Association of School Administrator and Supervisor	R-719
"	Objection of the Boston Home and School Association to the Masters Final Report	R-720
"	School Committee of the City of Boston's Objection to Masters Report	R-721
"	Dorchester United Neighborhood Association's Written Objections	R-722
"	Plaintiff's Statement of Objections to the Masters' Phase I Desegregation Plan and Request for Additional Relief	R-723
"	Teacher Union's Objections to Masters' Relief	R-724
"	Mayor of Boston, Public Facilities Commissioner and Director of the Public Facilities of Boston Objection to the Masters' Report	R-725
April 8	State Defendent's Critique of Masters' Plan	R-731

The NAACP objected to the plan, contending that it failed to provide the degree of actual student desegregation required; that it required the closing of schools and would place a disproportionate busing burden on black children; and that planned community role in monitoring the plan was very weak.

The school committee's objections centered around the district and citywide councils, the role of colleges and universities in upgrading curriculum, and the abolition of the 7th and 8th grades of the Latin Schools.

Mayor White objected to the dropping of the 7th and 8th grades of the Latin Schools, the mandatory racial ratio for "citywide" magnet schools, the moratorium imposed on school construction by Garrity, and the fact that the community school superintendent's seat on the District Council reduced the spots for the parents.

El Comite objected because East Boston would remain virtually white, there were no provisions for Spanish-speaking kindergarten students, and the plan threatened existing bilingual programs.

As during the contempt crisis in December, attention was now focused directly on Judge Garrity. The masters had acted much more independently than most people had expected. As a consequence they had come up with a plan which made Judge Garrity obviously uncomfortable. While he did not savor the continuing confrontations with the school committee, he was not inclined to endorse a compromise remedy for the clear constitutional violation he had found. Despite (maybe even because of) the continuing opposition to Phase I, Garrity seemed resolved to avoid either capitulation or the appearance of capitulation. He had eagerly seized defendants' minimal "curing" of contempt in December only because he wanted to get on with framing the remedy.

Judge Garrity had three options. He could adopt the Masters' Plan with some slight technical modifications. He could reject the masters efforts in favor of one of the plans submitted to the masters. Or he could disect the plans and accept those parts he approved and add whatever new aspects he thought necessary.

There were some very good reasons to adopt the Masters' Plan. By now it had become common knowledge that he had spent a great deal of time selecting the individual members of the panel. They in turn had approached their task with an admirable seriousness of purpose and had carefully followed the guidelines he had set out. The plan the panel submitted was the product of their combined wisdom informed by thoughts and testimony of people and organizations from all facets of the Boston community. Moreover, the plan also reflected the input of the two court-appointed experts. To a large extent, the court was already implicated in the plan. By adopting it, he need only go a single step further. Moreover, the court could assure substantive changes later on by ordering a Phase III.

There were also factors that argued against this course. The defendant Boston School Committee had made it clear that an appeal would be taken from any plan that included mandatory busing. In effect, they would appeal no matter which course the court chose. Plaintiff, on the other hand, while having no outstanding promise to appeal, would most certainly do so if the racial ratios of the

---

The Home and School Association objected to those proposals which would truncate the Latin Schools, eliminate advanced work classes which centralized students from several parts of the city in the Arlington-Sawyer complex, and require the closing of some Roxbury schools.

The Boston Teachers Union objected to the fact that the role of teachers on the District Council was not clearly specified; that unlike the biracial councils modeled after the racial-ethnic councils, the Community District Councils were not necessarily integrated; that the role of colleges and universities in curricula matters was not clearly spelled out; that the presence of college and university personnel might cause problems because of contractual obligations between the city and the union; that the masters' assessment of space needs for various programs steering of Title I funds into the citywide districts could result in more economic and social isolation.

The state board of education objected to the plans since it offered no justification for the ten districts and the racial composition of each district; promised seats in Community District schools to students, even at the high school level, where there is a shortage of seats citywide. Boston Globe, April 8, 1975, at 19 (*NAACP, City Says Plan Unconstitutional*).

Masters' Plan were adopted.[200] So the plan would be appealed to the circuit court by all parties. This would place the court in the position of having to defend a plan to which both sides objected. While it is far from clear that this fact would have had much impact on the outcome of an appeal, it was clearly not the best of all possible worlds.

Also arguing against the Masters' Plan was the fact that it could be interpreted to suggest that the court was relenting in the face of continuing white opposition and violence. Ray Bulger said that "the first plan [Phase I] was horrendous and this is an attempt to retreat from it. Implicit in that attempt is an admission that the original approach is wrong."[201] John Kerrigan announced that he felt vindicated by the plan despite its insistence on mandatory busing. In his opinion the December defiance of Garrity had served notice on the masters and accounted for the reduced busing and the inclusion of many aspects of the Authorized School Committee Plan.[202]

Whether Kerrigan's view was true or not, Garrity was not inclined to give the appearance of giving in to mob rule. He did not accept the Masters' Plan. Neither adoption of one of the original plans nor creation of a totally new one was a viable option. The observations of the masters were substantially correct. None of the plans submitted "promised realistically to work and realistically to work now." Moreover, as the masters had found, it was much too close to the fall to begin development of a totally original plan.

So Garrity was left only one option. He had to accept the basic framework established by the masters and modify those aspects to which he objected. For the most part he liked the plan. He was particularly encouraged by its involving business, labor, and higher education. He found the concept of a citywide school district to be a promising one. In his words, this was "the most magnificent feature of the plan." However, the student assignment arrangements and the permissable racial ratios were not to his liking. And it was this aspect that he would completely redesign, thus causing revisions throughout the rest of the Masters' Plan.

The final desegregation order with the Garrity Plan was issued on May 10. None of the revisions contained therein really surprised anyone. In a series of hearings, the judge had telegraphed his changes well. He had announced that the district lines should be redrawn so that, with the exception of East Boston, no district would have more than 60 percent and less than 40 percent of either black or white students. It was his feeling that by reducing the wide disparity between the community school district and the citywide district, more students would elect to attend the magnet schools. Since both types of districts would

200. Boston Globe, April 5, 1975, at 3 (*Masters' Phase II Plan falls short, NAACP says*).
201. Boston Sunday Globe, March 23, 1975, at A4 (*Reaction Mixes as Leaders Assess new school plan*).
202. Boston Globe, March 22, 1975, at 3 (*Many applaud new plan while foes attack it*).

have approximately the same racial composition, there would be a greater incentive for making a purely educational decision. For this same reason he proposed reducing the number of magnet schools from 32 to 28. He also suggested that the 7th and 8th grades of the Latin School be abolished.

Basically the plan contained the changes Garrity had telegraphed. The district lines were redrawn. New racial ratios were required. Fewer schools would be closed. There would be fewer magnet schools. And, most important of all, over 20,000 students would be bused. With the exception of the NAACP, the various vocal elements in Boston expressed vehement opposition to the plan.

Despite the protest, the final order remained unchanged. Eleven months, countless hours, and hundreds of thousands of transcript pages after the "Garrity decision" furor, there was now a "Garrity Plan" to effect the permanent desegregation of the Boston public school. The test was now the plan's workability.

ASSESSING PHASE II

Before the Boston public schools began class in September 1975 there appeared to be some degree of optimism. Despite the continually articulated concern about the safety of the children there was some feeling that the national embarrassment of the preceding year, the planned educational innovations, the months of planning, and the broader-based community involvement would all combine to produce a normal school year. The alchemy was not to be.

The process of implementing Phase II proved to be as eventful as Phase I. The anger of the anti-busing forces in the white community did not subside. Public protest continued, spread, and often erupted into violent opposition. The political polarization of the community continued and was accompanied by an increasing number of racial incidents. The feared white flight from the school system occurred, even if not in as great a proportion as some had predicted. Increasing pressure was put on the parochial schools to accept transferees. The "alternative schools," patterned after southern "academies," were developed into a viable option. The year would begin with a teachers' strike and a police "sickout." South Boston High would be placed in federal receivership by Judge Garrity. More people would be arrested for desegregation-related offenses and injured during racial confrontation incidents. Vandalism would increase, and explosive devices would be detonated in protest against the desegregation effort.

These statistics ought not to overshadow the instances which were not characterized by violence and which many participants felt made the year a success. In their view Judge Garrity's Phase II plan worked and worked well. On balance, that may be an accurrate assessment. However, it is by no means one about which there is likely to be concensus. Indeed, there is no concensus on the standard to be applied. Perhaps the best approach is to utilize the criteria outlined by Dean Dentler in a memorandum to the masters.

1. *Educational Improvement:* A plan should manifest the ways in which its im-

plementation would *improve* the teaching and learning conditions characteristic of the system.

2. *Ethnic Balance:* The plan should show any reader how the redistribution of students will result in a mix that is roughly reflective of the overall mix inside the system at present. If the proportion of black students in the total public school system in City X is 32%, the mix in any one school should fall between 16% and 64% black, with desirability going toward 32%.

3. *Educational Equity:* The plan should affect each local school especially at the elementary level in roughly similar ways. Hence, one school should not go unchanged while others are used for one-way out-busing of black students, for instance.

4. *Fiscal Soundness:* The plan should propose changes within realistic fiscal parameters. For example, existing plant must be used optimally. Program and staff costs cannot increase markedly overall, and transport and safety costs must prove reasonable. New plant cannot be projected if the State announces a moratorium of school plant construction monies.

5. *Clarity:* The plan should be able to infer accurately from it where pupils would be assigned; what the grade structures, feeder patterns, and sub-districts of the system are to be; and how the system will change both educationally and demographically. The plan should reduce, not increase, the confusion of taxpayers, parents, teachers, and students.

6. *Durability:* The plan should stabilize the system for at least five and preferably ten years ahead. Professionals and the public should be able to infer easily how the plan, once implemented, would give City X a fairly steady state public school system for the years ahead.[203]

And although he did not specifically describe it as such, Dean Dentler set out as a seventh criterion, *public support:*

> As the U.S. Court of Appeals . . . said in *Morgan v. Kerrigan,* "*. . . public clamor has been deemed beyond the pale as justification for racial segregation.*" Legally sound as this is, it has been my experience that a plan for City X could meet my criteria and fail for lack of public acceptance. Moreover, a plan could meet none of the criteria and be widely accepted. For these reasons, the character of public concerns and expectations unique to City X must be studied in the course of appraising the effectiveness of any planning proposal.[204]

To these an eighth consideration should be added—administrative normalization. Local school authorities have primary responsibility for running local schools. That is as it ought to be. While the courts must necessarily play an uncharacteristically activist role in implementing any desegregation plan imposed upon recalcitrant school officials, that ought not to be a permanent state of

203. February 4, 1975 Memorandum to the Masters from Robert Dentler re: Tentative Outline of Criteria for Gauging Effectiveness of Planning Proposals.
204. *Id.* at 3.

affairs. No desegregation plan can be said to be effective if its effect is to require the federal district court to administer local schools for a prolonged period.

Because of the care and planning that went into Phase II, the ethnic balance, educational equity, fiscal soundness, and clarity factors were all pre-programmed. It is yet unclear whether the school system will be sufficiently stabilized to satisfy Dentler's "durability" test. Thus five of the eight criteria can be disposed of rather summarily. The remaining three (educational improvement, public support, and administrative normalization) must be considered in greater detail.

Public Support

Part of the challenge that Phase II raised for the city of Boston was to improve upon what the U.S. Commission on Civil Rights had accurately described as "the crisis of civic responsibility" during Phase I. Despite the heroic efforts of individual people, groups, and organizations, the absence of meaningful political leadership and effective support from the religious, intellectual, and business leaders undermined positive community support for the desegregation efforts in 1974/75.

To a large extent the Boston community rose to the challenge of Phase II in both the public and private sectors. On the public side, election-year politics provided the excuse for the mayor to maintain his low-profile, ambivalent position. However, unlike a year earlier, this time other public officials filled the vacuum. State Attorney General Bellotti emerged as an outspoken and ardent advocate of vigorous prosecution of anyone interfering with the desegregation programs. Assistant U.S. Attorney General Stanley Pottinger spent a considerable amount of time in the city lending a federal enforcement presence to the federally imposed plan. Governor Michael Dukakis lent the weight of his office to the effort.

Despite the initial misgivings so many had about her, the new superintendent proved to be willing to cooperate with the court. As could be expected, this did not sit well with many of those who had supported her at the outset. When she publicly admitted her frustration with the recalcitrant school committee members and so-called "radical anti-busing group," her new opponents immediately demanded her resignation. She refused, saying, "I am [the] superintendent. . . . I ask only that I be allowed to do my job. . . . I call on everyone in the city to understand we are under a court order and we have to abide by it."[205]

There were also heartening signs in the private sector. The most comprehensive voluntary mechanism for community involvement was provided by the Freedom House, a black community-based organization. During Phase I, Freedom House served as an information and rumor control center. The group developed a whole range of activities designed to encourage constructive discussion

---

205. These comments were made during a school committee meeting on February 4 when the antibusing group ROAR (Restore Our Alienated Rights) demanded Superintendent Fahey's resignation. They were upset over earlier comments by Fahey in which she criticized the more radical anti-busing elements.

about and input into the desegregation process. They sponsored weekly seminars, circulated pamphlets and flyers, and in general became a focal point for the interaction of civic and community leaders. During Phase II, Freedom House expanded its activities. It initiated an educational counseling service specially tailored to the needs of juniors and seniors wishing to consider higher education. It developed "socio-legal teams" composed of lawyers and social workers. These teams would represent students involved in desegregation-related incidents and would provide support services to these students and their families. Freedom House sponsored Saturday Morning Conference Sessions at which various aspects of school desegregation were discussed throughout the school year.

While neither the city nor state bar associations issued any public statements, the Boston Bar Association did publish and distribute a very good booklet explaining the legal aspects of desegregation.[206] Moreover, the Boston Bar Task Force was established to provide ongoing assistance on a variety of issues relating to the desegregation process. As demanded by the plan, colleges and universities and businesses became involved as "partners" to designated schools. In addition to the various activities this role demanded of individual businesses, the business community by way of the Chamber of Commerce sponsored various scholarships and job programs.

The religious community assumed a more active role in Phase II. According to the U.S. Commission on Civil Rights, "active personal involvement of some clergy from all religions had been a positive factor during the opening weeks of Phase I."[207] Commitment and effectiveness are very different things, however. The Civil Rights Commission also found that "the leadership . . . of the religious community . . . was not as effective as it could have been in identifying and supporting [the] moral issues confronting Boston during Phase I.[208] This was an assessment shared by many of the religious leaders themselves.[209] The commis-

206. J. Adkins, J. McHugh & K. Seay, Desegregation: The Boston Orders and Their Origin, (Boston Bar Association Committee on Desegregation, August 1975).
The preface of the publication reads:

The Boston Bar Association Committee on Desegregation was organized with the intention that its members would act as a source of information for individuals and groups involved in and affected by the desegregation orders. Its members have familiarized themselves with all of the orders and the background law, and are available, upon request, to meet with anyone interested in an objective commentary on the law as well as our understanding of the Phase II plan. As lawyers, we are committed to the Rule of Law as we are committed to this community which must live under the Rule of Law
We believe that this document carefully presents in layman's language what the orders and our constitution are all about. Our hope is that it will make a contribution to a better understanding of the background and of the orders, for we believe that with understanding will come greater support for the Rule of Law.

207. Desegregating the Boston Public Schools: A Crisis in Civil Responsibility—A Report of the United States Commission on Civil Rights, at 171 [hereinafter cited as Crisis in Civil Responsibility].
208. *Id.*
209. *Id.* at 173, 461.

sion recommended a series of steps to be taken during Phase II. The clergy was to be better informed. The local churches and synagogues were to disseminate accurate information, noting the positive aspects of Phase I. They were also to serve as "models of interracial activity in their respective communities." Finally, interfaith committees were to be established to plan programs that would articulate the "moral principles inherent in racial desegregation."[210]

The churches and synagogues did not become exemplars of integrated activity. Except for their participation in the Consolidated Service Council of the Freedom House, there were relatively few discernible interfaith efforts at joint programs. Nevertheless there was a considerable increase in vocal and visible support for the desegregation effort. The Black Ecumenical Commission (BEC) was among the more active religious groups. BEC assigned several ministers to assist in the desegregation process. These ministers monitored bus stops, escorted students going home for health and other reasons, and even went to courts with students. BEC also compiled a directory of religious institutions and paired them with contiguous public sschools so that whenever difficulties arose, there would be an easily accessible church or pastor.

Because so many of the busing foes were Catholic, special attention was paid to the activities of the Catholic Archdiocese. On August 27 Humberto Cardinal Medeiros announced the creation of the Cardinal's Coordinating Council. In the letter establishing the council, the Cardinal described the challenge facing it as "not merely to keep the peace [but] to . . . actively, earnestly and courageously strive to insure justice, quality education and human dignity."[211] He directed the council to coordinate the work of the city's clergy and gather information which would subsequently be provided to the court, the City-wide Coordinating Council, and the local religious communities. Despite this broad mandate, it appears that the council's primary task during the school year was to advise the Cardinal on what to say about the desegregation issue. This in and of itself was important, since the Cardinal, in one of the few times he spoke extemporaneously, created a furor within the Catholic community. During an exclusive wide-ranging interview with the Boston Sunday *Herald Advertiser* he was reported to have said: "I am not going into South Boston to speak, to exhort as many think I should . . . why should I go? To get stoned? Is that what they'd like to see?" Despite his subsequent apology to the South Boston community for these remarks the Cardinal had accurately conveyed the frustration of a religious community preaching morality over a cacaphony of emotion.[212]

210. *Id.* at 174.
211. Boston Globe, August 8, 1975.
212. The Cardinal's initial remarks were made during an exclusive interview with Eleanor Roberts and reprinted in a copyrighted story, *Cardinal Rejects Leadership Role,* Boston Sunday Herald Advertiser, May 2, 1976.

Educational Improvement

The Phase II desegregation plan had publicly committed itself to improving the quality of education in the city of Boston. The professionals at the Educational Planning Center, the politicians on the Boston School Committee, the four masters, the two experts and the court all agreed that the deterioration of the school system had to be arrested if the system was to survive with or without desegregation. They thought it equally clear that without an education component, implementation of the desegregation plan would be exponentially more difficult. So what remained was a queston: Could Phase II deliver a demonstrably better education to the public school students of Boston? The answer seems to be a fairly unequivocal "yes."

The lynchpin of effecting educational improvement in the city's education process was the involvement of the city's colleges, universities, cultural institutions, and businesses. In his May 10 order, Judge Garrity adopted the concept as proposed by the masters:

Institutions of higher education and culture, business corporations, labor unions and other organizations in the Greater Boston area have committed themselves to support, assist, and participate in the development of educational excellence within and among the public schools of Boston. These institutions shall not be asked or required to make grants of their funds, or to be responsible for administration. There is no wish or intention on the part of the court or of these institutions to usurp or replace the proper role of the School Department or any of its employees; their sole purpose is to benefit the public school children of the city.

The court has matched colleges and universities with particular high schools, both community and city-wide, and with selected other schools and programs, in ways that fit the capabilities and needs of the partners. Other colleges and universities may be added as this Plan is implemented. In addition, businesses have been explicitly paired and associated with schools. The leadership of the Boston Trilateral Task Force , composed of business and other concerned institutions, has pledged itself to continue and enlarge this kind of support in order to supplement academic theory with business practicability.

Labor organizations have expressed a readiness to support and assist in occupational vocational, technical, and trade education, and planning for some programs has already begun. The court will foster paired relationships in similar detail at a later stage in the planning. A committee of the Boston Bar Association has assisted the court in developing institutional support and will continue to do so.

The Metropolitan Cultural Alliance, a membership organization of 110 cultural institutions, has also renewed its commitment to continue its support and assistance to schools in the City-Wide district as well as in several community school districts. The Alliance made a major contribution to the implementation of the state plan in 1975–75 by working with thousands of students and hundreds of teachers. This work will continue to expand and improve. Its major impact will be upon City-wide magnet programs.

The pairing shall enable participating institutions of higher learning to share in the direction and development of curriculum and instruction with the School Department.[213]

Despite its potential, the involvement of the colleges and universities was not always universally acclaimed. At the outset, school system bureaucrats worried about overinvolvement of the institutions of higher learning. Even the black community had its reservations. To the black community it was "a case of the blind leading the blind." According to a Freedom House report, "The community experience is that the very colleges and universities [involved] . . . in Phase II of the Desegregation Plan are in fact the trainers of those teachers and administrators who currently run ineffective schools." The report continues:

1. In recognizing that the universities have historically been plagued with the same patterns of discrimination, ineffectiveness and bureaucrats that they are now being called upon to exorcise from others, we are concerned that without significant monitoring their role will simply be that of the blind leading the blind, and the further legitimization of miseducation. In line with this concern, we strongly urge that *all* decisions made and programs implemented be supervised by a wide spectrum of participants who reflect the community to be served, and that universities undertake internally to rectify their problems so that they may be better prepared to educate all of those who are there now, and who may come to them in the future.
2. We recommend that:
   A. University representative[s] identify and draw together appropriate individuals *within* the university who have expressed interest and/or have experience in working cooperatively with urban schools, so that planning within the university community can begin;
   B. University representative[s] initiate meetings with school personnel, the Boston Teachers Union, and local community groups in order to launch the planning process.
3. We recommend that:
   A. The required needs assessment be initiated within each school zone;
   B. That a resource assessment be conducted within each university;
   C. That both of the above be completed by July 1, 1975;
   D. That final decisions regarding pairing be delayed until the needs and resource assessments are completed. We feel that the rationale for some pairing under the Masters' Plan is unclear and that it is important to make certain that school/university partners are appropriate for each other.
4. We suggest that each university, in conducting its resource assessment, con-

213. May 10 Student Desegregation Plan, Morgan v. Kerrigan, 401 F. Supp. at 216, 259.

sider total institutional resources. In the past only certain departments, principally Education, Psychology and Sociology, have been involved in local schools, We think, however, that many other university departments and individuals have resources to offer and that these resources should be utilized as well.

5. We recommend that each university appoint a full-time coordinator to coordinate university involvement. This individual would participate in the needs and resources assessments and would work with community councils to maintain lines of communication.

6. We recommend that the universities and colleges demonstrate their commitment to Boston students by guaranteeing admission to designated numbers of Boston students, including in particular, Black and minority students. These students should be provided with full support services, including financial aid, counseling, and tutoring if necessary, to ensure that they can compete on an equal footing with other students in the school. They should also be allowed to participate in university courses while they are seniors in high school.

7. Concerning specific programs, we recommend that universities institute work/study programs for their students in the community following minority college action program models. We think that professors as well as students should be actively involved in such programs.

8. In these particularly troubled times . . . , with respect to a lack of understanding among the cultures represented in the Boston School District, highly informed, multi-cultural leadership at the administrative and teacher levels is required. We recommend that the Boston Area Black Studies Consortium be commissioned to develop and implement a teacher and administrator training program for use in the Boston Public High Schools, in order to provide the perspective and specific instruction through tests and multi-media teaching packages, which our administrators and teachers need. . . .

9. Finally, we recommend that colleges and universities "get their feet wet" now by assisting in after-school programs, such as those offered in the Community Schools, or in summer programs, such as career counseling for college-bound juniors and seniors.

At all stages of this process, genuine community participation is essential if university involvement in our schools is to be relevant and useful. Official channels for community input (i.e. community councils) have yet to be established, although there is an immediate need for community involvement as plans develop in the next weeks and through the summer.[214]

Although several of these recommendations were never implemented, the component worked well enough so that one year later another group commissioned by Freedom House would find that the "partnerships are working satisfactorily, that some progress has been made toward the goals established for

214. A Response to the University Component of the Masters' Plan, Freedom House Institute on Schools and Education, May 1975.

them by the Court, and that they clearly merit strong continued support from the state, city, the school system and the community.[215]

This seemed a generally accepted conclusion. In the initial installment of a series assessing the impact of desegregation on the Boston community, the Pulitzer Prize-winning Boston *Globe* agreed.

> The ambitious pairings of schools with colleges, universities, businesses and cultural institutions [are] beginning to pay off in more and better services to the individual children. For instance, Boston University ran diagnostic reading tests in one elementary school; Boston College has supplied guidance in another. New England Merchants National Bank is among a score of private sponsors that have paid for field trips and have opened job opportunities in larger numbers than ever before.[216]

Phase II saw the establishment of a multi-tiered system for judicial monitoring and implementation of the desegregation plan. Judge Garrity accepted the masters' proposal and established the Citywide Coordinating Council (CCC). CCC was designated as "the monitoring body for the Court." It was authorized to hold public meetings, conduct hearings, make written reports, and inspect school facilities. CCC would not, however, supplant the Citywide Parents Advisory Council (CPAC). CPAC would remain a parents-only body which would concern itself with the resolution of racial problems within the schools. One step down the line were the nine Community District Advisory Councils (CDAC). Each CDAC would serve in an advisory capacity to school personnel in that district. They would also monitor the progress in implementing the desegregation plan in their particular district. To accomplish this, they were assured of "reasonable access" to any information they desired. Racial-Ethnic Parent Councils (RPCs) established during Phase I would also continue. RPCs were organized on a school-by-school basis and charged with the responsibility of providing a "mechanism for concerned parents to address racial problems in their children's school."

Fully implemented, the CCC, CPACs, CDACs, and RPCs would involve hundreds of parents, teachers, students, and community people in helping to implement the desegregation plan. This was clearly a major educational reform for Boston. It assured a greater degree of community involvement in the educational process than ever before. Though not "community control" in the classic sense, these bodies did afford a significant degree of community influence.

215.The University/Boston School Pairing, Preliminary findings and recommendations of the University/Community Special Resources Subcommittee. Freedom House Institute on Schools and Educations, May 1976, at 5.

216. Boston Globe, June 26, 1976, at 1.

Administrative Normalization

Judge Garrity intended to use the time between his final order and the beginning of the school year to finalize the detail of Phase II. His orders established a timetable specifying the dates by which the following were to be completed: Student assignments, faculty and staff assignments, orientation process, transportation arrangements, safety and police-utilization planning, and contractual agreements with the college and university partners.

The chances for the summer to be as productive as Judge Garrity hoped were seriously diminished when the school committee refused to reappoint Superintendent Leary. After several weeks of posturing and politicking, the school committee voted in April to appoint Marion Fahey, a careerist in the Boston School Department, to succeed William Leary. Although his three-year contract had expired and thus there was no obligation to reappoint him, it was clear that Leary was a casualty of the desegregation battle. The fact that he had cooperated with the court during Phase I virtually assured his early retirement.

The age-old admonition against changing horses in midstream suggests that the mere naming of a new superintendent would cause some problems. This was particularly so in this situation. Much of the planning for Phase II would have to be done over the summer. Since Leary's term did not expire until the end of August, he was the senior administrator responsible for implementing the court's order. However, once Fahey's appointment was announced, his lame-duck status severely hampered his effort to do so . The resulting confusion and uncertainty seemed perfectly consistent with the Boston School Committee's strategy. Consultation with the incoming superintendent became another reason for delaying the implementation of every aspect of the plan to which the school committee objected. Moreover, the extensive reshuffling of positions and responsibility and the promotions and demotions of key personnel which accompanied the transition served to severely retard the implementation process.

The school committee's recalcitrance affected virtually every aspect of the planning. Judge Garrity had set June 20 as the submission date for student assignments, enrollment totals, and racial ratios for each school. "Technical problems" arose, and the submissions were delayed. This problem persisted until the judge considered calling in a computer expert. The assignments were finally forthcoming and were eventually mailed—two weeks behind schedule. As a direct consequence it was impossible to meet the court's June 30 deadline for making faculty and staff assignments. Nor could the deadlines for the comprehensive transportation plan and safety arrangements be met. Planning for the court-ordered orientation programs was delayed beyond the set date. Colleges and universities assigned to work with various schools were subjected to a bureaucratic maze which prevented most of them from getting their contracts until the following spring.

As the confusion and delay continued, Judge Garrity's orders became more numerous and specific. Long before the end of the summer it seemed that the court was in fact "running the school system," as some had already charged. Needless to say, when he decided to place South Boston High in federal receivership in December the charges rose to a crescendo.[217] To many, this seemed the inevitable consequence of judicial involvement in the administration of local schools. An examination of the facts reveal no particular zeal for federal receivership by Judge Garrity. Nor does it appear that the step was an inevitable consequence of judicial involvement or due to some defect in the design of the Phase II plan. Rather, the placing of South Boston High in federal receivership was an extraordinary measure reluctantly undertaken by an embattled judge who had no choice.[218]

217. Morgan v. Kerrigan, Order of December 15, 1975 placing South Boston High School in federal receivership.

218. On November 17, 1975, plaintiffs asked the court to consider *inter alia* the closing of South Boston High School In support of this position they made several serious allegations:

. . . .

(2) The severity of the ongoing mistreatment of black students at South Boston High School is demonstrated by recent events. The affidavits and other attachments show, for example:

(a) Black students in South Boston High School are presently being subjected to discriminatory treatment, abuse, and other lack of support by the predominantly-white faculty and staff of that school. One teacher, James Scalese, has climbed upon his desk and made gestures and sounds like a monkey in ridicule of black students. On a separate occasion he made similar monkey sounds and gestures in the doorway of his classroom at several black students outside.

(b) Another teacher, Arthur Perdigao, who is the school football coach, initially thwarted all attempts by black students to go out for the school's football team. On one occasion, he disregarded a note from the school's headmaster directing him to allow a black student to practice with the team. After a black assistant football coach was added to the coaching staff and six black students were allowed to come out for the team, the black players were made to ride to practice on separate buses, and were directed to practice, for the most part, separate from the white members of the team. After the team's October 23 game at White Stadium, Coach Perdigao told the white players to "get them [the black players] at school the next day." Later he removed the black players from the team for asserted offenses such as "smoking," although at least one of the black players is a total nonsmoker.

(c) Other offensive, racially discriminatory actions by other individual faculty members are described in the attached affidavits and in subsequent evidence and testimony plaintiffs intend to present at the evidentiary hearing.

(d) Other actions by South Boston High School faculty have undercut the smooth implementation of this Court's desegregation orders. After the South Boston Black Student Caucus met on October 8, 1975, and issued a list of grievances, the City-wide Coordinating Council (CCC) established a mediation panel to attempt to work out some of the problems in the school. On or about Thursday, October 16, 1975, after meeting with members of the panel, the South Boston High School faculty voted 26–24 not to cooperate with the work of this group. On information and belief, the faculty voted subsequently not to cooperate with a separate task force established by Superintendent Fahey.

(e) Despite this Court's ban on the use of racial epithets within the schools, black students in South Boston High School continue to be subjected to daily verbal abuse.

The Commission on Civil Rights had recommended federal receivership for the entire school system:

There is a point at which *de minimus* compliance with Court orders, when viewed as a whole, becomes intentional obstruction of those orders. There may also be a point at which the Court is required to order so many specific actions that the Court itself is operating the school system. Should

---

In addition to familiar racial slurs, white students this year have employed the chant "2, 4, 6, 8, assassinate the nigger apes."

During the changing of classes, groups of white students frequently sing "bye, bye, blackbird" and "jump down, turn around, pick a bale of cotton." The white student caucus of South Boston High School also issued a list of demands which included the demand that music be played over the school's public address system during the changing of classes for the express reason that "music soothes the savage beasts." The attached affidavits detail a number of instances in which school staff and police authorities stationed inside the building have heard such remarks and chants but have failed to take any corrective or disciplinary action.

(f) Black students in South Boston High School continue to be subject to frequent physical attacks by groups of white students. Many such incidents are described in the attached affidavits, and other examples of such incidents can be presented at an evidentiary hearing. Frequently, one or two black students have been attacked by a much larger group of white students, without provocation. More often than not, school and police authorities detain and suspend all the black students involved in the incident, but only one or two white students. The black students are disciplined for defending themselves from an unprovoked attack while numbers of the white attackers escape any disciplinary measures.

(g) The police force stationed within the building has not been a neutral disciplinary force. The attached affidavits, and other testimony to be presented at an evidentiary hearing, reveal incidents in which police officials responsible for breaking up an interracial fight have held black students while white students continued to hit or kick them. One black female aide, wearing a clearly identifiable jacket with the word "aide" on it, was hit, clubbed with a nightstick, and handcuffed by a state trooper, who later apologized to the aide and asked that charges not be pressed against him, when he learned that his actions were in error. On another occasion, several police officers physically carried a non-resisting black student down to the basement of the school, dropped him onto the floor, and threatened to "break his arms."

(h) During recent weeks, persons presently unknown to plaintiffs' counsel have promoted racial tension within the school through the distribution of inflammatory handbills to white students. Black students have observed the distribution of such handouts inside a small sandwich shop near the school, and at other places. One such handbill, distributed in late October, 1975, reads in part:

TO ALL THE WHITE KIDS IN ALL THE SOUTHIE SCHOOLS . . . IF YOU THINK ITS JUST BUSING YOURE WRONG. ITS TOTAL TAKE OVER AND YOURE JUST SITTING ON YOUR ASS LETTING THEM . . . WAKE UP AND START FIGHTING FOR YOUR SCHOOL AND TOWN. ITS TIME YOU BECOME THE AGGRESSORS . . . DONT BE SCARED BY THE FEDERAL OFFENSE THREATS. A FIGHT IN A SCHOOL ISNT A FEDERAL OFFENSE . . . BE PROUD YOU ARE *WHITE* AND FROM SOUTHIE AND SHOW EVERYONE THAT THIS IS HOW YOU ARE GOING TO KEEP IT NO MATTER WHAT.

Morgan v. Kerrigan, Plaintiffs' Motion for Further Relief, November 17, 1975.
At subsequent hearings these and other allegations were substantially proved.

the school committee continue its present course of opposition, the best interest of the public school students of Boston may be served by removing the school committee from the governance of the Boston public school system and replacing it with persons who can and will devote their time to the administration of the school system in accordance with the 14th amendment.[219]

This recommendation was not implemented. When federal receivership did come to Boston, it came in a limited fashion involving only South Boston High, and not the entire system.

Judge Garrity considered the appointment of the Citywide Coordinating Council to be a major step toward normalization and away from ongoing direct judicial intervention in the school system. Court-appointed citizens' committees had proved successful in other cities subject to desegregation orders. All parties hoped that this model would be successful in Boston. CCC was given herculean tasks.

> The CCC will foster public awareness of an involvement in the process of implementation of the court's desegregation orders. It will be the primary body monitoring implementation on behalf of the court. It will in this connection file monthly reports with the parties and the court covering its activities. It will attempt to avoid the difficulties caused by lack of preparation and community education associated with the state plan currently in effect. It will work to develop the cooperative efforts of universities and colleges, cultural institutions and business and labor organizations with the Boston schools. The CCC will attempt to identify and resolve problems by mediation and conciliation. In its actions, it will act with awareness of the needs of non-English-speaking groups and communities in the city. It may bring unresolved problems to the attention of the parties, the court or other appropriate persons. It may communicate and publicize its views and recommendations to the public, the parties and court. The CCC will not co-manage or make policy for the Boston schools. Neither will it assume the responsibility of the Boston school committee and superintendent and other defendants to carry out the court's orders.[220]

The court sought to ensure the success of CCC by taking special pains with its composition and structure. Believing that the group should "reflect the richness of Boston's human and community resources," Judge Garrity appointed as broadly representative a group as he possibly could. The 42 members did indeed represent the many factions in the Boston community. And conscious of the unwieldiness of so large a group, the judge explicitly provided for separate subcommittees to deal with the various identified areas: public information, moni-

219. Crisis in Civil Responsibility, *supra* note 207 at 64.
220. May 10 Student Desegregation Plan, Morgan v. Kerrigan, at 87. 401 F. Supp. at 265.

toring, community liaison, CDAC liaison, education programs, and public safety and transportation. He also provided for an executive committee of the various subcommittee chairpersons, a member of the Citywide Parents' Advisory Council and the CCC chairperson.

The CCC never quite worked as hoped. It was supposed to be the eyes and ears of the court. However, as one reporter would note, "the eyes didn't see and the ears didn't hear what the court wanted to know."[221] At the end of its term, Garrity would drastically alter its size, structure, and mandate. The advantages of diversity sought at the outset proved to be far outweighed by the disadvantages. Throughout the year CCC members brought to its deliberations the hardened perspectives and positions of their constituencies. They "fought among themselves over internal organization, over strategy, over personnel, over big issues as well as small."[222] The subcommittees churned out report after report. Many merely reiterated those that had preceded them. Others said little if anything and made even less of a contribution to furthering desegregation in Boston.

Broadly interpreting CCC's mandate, CCC members involved themselves in so many aspects of the desegregation program as to at times blur the jurisdictional lines between it and the other groups and even the school committee. All the while members privately complained that despite assurances to the contrary, they lacked access to the man who had appointed them and had promised to meet with them.[223]

Recognizing the problems they had confronted, members of CCC recommended that Judge Garrity reduce the size and budget of the group and simplify its committee structure. The court complied.[224] The 42-member panel was reduced to 15. Despite indications that many on the larger body wished to continue on for at least another year, 14 of the 15 were brand-new appointees. Only the new chairman, Robert Wood, president of the University of Massachusetts, stayed on. He would head a vastly streamlined panel into Phase III and a new era in the desegregation of Boston's public schools. In his order, Garrity gave a clear signal of his desire for normalization.

> The decision to reduce the size of the CCC and the scope of its concerns rests mainly on the desire of the court and the parties to move gradually toward termination of this litigation, or at least to its deactivation with the court reserving a merely dormant or standby jurisdiction.[225]

Garrity thus signaled the beginning of the end. How long the process will take

221. Boston Globe, August 8, 1976, at 12.
222. *Id.*
223. *Id.* This particular point was corroborated in an interview with 1975 CCC member Hogan.
224. Boston Globe, August 25, 1976, at 13.
225. Order Appointing New Citywide Coordinating Council, Morgan v. Kerrigan, August 24, 1976, p. 2.

will depend upon the citizens of Boston and whether they finally accept what has become a reality—the forced desegregation of the Boston public schools.

CONCLUSION

It would be a pleasure to be able to conclude this paper by stating that the battle to desegregate the Boston public school system had come to an end. However, after two years of studying the struggle that has been fought in the city for two centuries, the best we can muster is a very cautious optimism.

There is certainly ample evidence to support the optimism. There are black children in previously all-white schools and vice versa. The resources of the system are more equitably distributed. Teachers may have fewer options, but white children have more black teachers and black children more white teachers. Because of the various citizens' committees and councils, more parents are involved in the schools than ever before. The colleges, universities, businesses, and cultural institutions have all added very special dimensions to public school education in Boston. In sum, the overall quality of education in Boston has been vastly improved as a direct consequence of the infusion of attention, talent, resources, and energy due to the desegregation attempt.

There are, however, some very good reasons for caution. School desegregation cases present a federal court with a unique situation deserving of special consideration. Legally and factually, the issues are framed around *educational opportunity for children*. The perceived fundamental nature of education and the instinctive protective attitude toward children assure that even were it not for the racial overtones, the problem would be a volatile one. This volatility is measurably increased when the issue arises in an adversary context with the opposing parties racially different and unsympathetically viewed and caricatured.

Unlike commercial litigation, there is no strong incentive to settle the dispute. This fight-to-the-finish posture is partly a function of the fact that the very invocation of the judicial process suggests the failure of the political process and the exhaustion of whatever good will and good faith that may have previously existed. By the time the parties get to court, they have probably entrenched themselves in what may be the only position they feel they can politically or constitutionally accept. From plaintiffs' point of view, to compromise would be tantamount to accepting segregation in principle and in fact. For a defendant school committee, compromise may be viewed by an aroused electorate as cowardly concession. So from neither standpoint is settlement attractive.

The normal implied cost-benefit analysis which would require the party appealing to assess the probability of success on appeal in light of the resource drain that prolongation of the process would necessarily entail is not operative in these instances. There is no erosion of good will in the traditional sense of the word. Nor is there the same level of concern about the financial burden of attorney fees, transcripts, and the like. Even if such a balancing were attempted, political pressure from a heavily politicized community would seem to clearly outweigh the other considerations. Because of the nature of the injury, the remedy is not clearly ascertainable money damages. Nor is the remedy generally limited to proscribing certain ongoing patterns of conduct by specified officials. Rather, the remedy is in the form of injunctive relief requiring affirmative action to undo the effects of past misdeeds and can be implemented only with the involvement and cooperation of large numbers of people, most of whom feel they played no part in the past misdeeds and ought not to be dislocated to remedy them. As a consequence, the remedy ordered is seen as inherently objectionable by a significant number of "ordinary nonofficial" people. In a sense, remedy without violation is seen as a taxation-without-representation, punishment-without-crime type issue.

This heightens the affected community's awareness of the anti-majoritarian quality that is the essence of the judicial institution. This awareness turns to frustration as the community realizes that the court is not subject to the political processes of recall or rejection by ballot. And the frustration turns to bitterness when it is a branch of the *federal government* (a presumptive outsider) which engenders the dislocation and frustrated expectations.

The situation in Boston followed the script to the letter. Boston was and still is a highly politicized and polarized community. The litigation in federal court reflected the inability of the political process to assure black parents that their children would have an equal opportunity to quality education. Since neither plaintiffs nor defendants expressed any real interest in settling, the case wound its way through trial to the inevitable finding of a constitutional violation. The corrective remedy proposed was seen as a punitive measure imposed. An angry, hurt, and frustrated community responded violently to what they clearly considered to be outside interference.

In its 1975 report the Commission on Civil Rights said that the federal district court in *Morgan v. Hennigan* provided the leadership essential to Boston's coming to grips with the unconstitutional practices that characterized the operations of its public school system. That statement is only half right. Judge Garrity did perform with distinction under circumstances that were difficult in the best of times. However, many white Bostonians have yet to "come to grips" with desegregation. They still feel that it is *their* constitutional right which has been infringed upon. Despite losing all appeals, they seem determined to continue their resistance.

Boston public schools may have been desegregated. But the Boston public school system has not been. School committee members are still selected in at-large elections. This assures that the black community will continue not to be represented in the body where the critical decisions on educational policy are made. This exclusion precludes the normal functioning of the political processes and virtually assures that black parents will once again feel compelled to seek judicial protection for their children.[226]

The court having intervened has temporarily created a balance of power in the political sphere. As it withdraws, a vacuum will be created. Hopefully, inertia will assure that the equilibrium be maintained. Unfortunately it seems

226. This at-large system has been twice challenged in court by the black community. The first complaint was filed in September of 1969: Owens v. School Committee of Boston, CA 69-934-F. Plaintiffs alleged that the Boston City Charter, insofar as it provided for the at-large election of school committee members, violated their constitutional rights. Plaintiffs' motion for a preliminary injunction was denied. Owens v. School Committee of Boston, 304 F. Supp. 1327 (D. Mass. 1969) Two and a half years later, in an unreported one-sentence order, Judge Ford allowed the defendant school committee's motion to dismiss for failure to state a claim.

The second complaint was filed in March 1975: Black Voters, Rose Jolley *et al.* v. John McDonough, *et al.,* CA 75-812-T. Plaintiffs alleged that the at-large system operated to dilute the vote of black voters and thus violated the rights of black voters as defined previously by the Supreme Court in White v. Regester, 412 U.S. 755 (1973); Whitcomb v. Chavis, 403 U.S. 124 (1971).

Plaintiffs successfully contended that this second action was not barred by the doctrines of *res judicata* or collateral estoppel since there had been substantial changes in the factual and legal developments since the *Owens* decision and because the failure to bring a class action in *Owens* precluded the requisite finding of privity or identity of the parties. Black Voters v. McDonough, 421 F. Supp. 165 (D. Mass. 1976).

However, while being courteous and responsive to plaintiffs' counsel during trial, Judge Tauro was clearly not moved by their arguments or their evidence. He ruled in favor of the defendants on the merits. In doing so he committed the ultimate irony by concluding that the pervasive supervision presently being exercised by Judge Garrity as a result of the Boston School Committee's failure to voluntarily comply with the *Morgan* desegregation order was a factor which favored the school committee:

. . . [T]his court must point out the difference between this case, involving the School Committee, and the *White* and *Whitcomb* decisions, which focused on elections to the Texas and Indiana Legislatures. The problem of an unresponsive legislative delegation, as a practical matter, can only be solved through some restructuring of the election process. The responsibilities of legislators are so varied, their discretion so great, and the problems of separation of powers so enormous, that it is hard to conceive of a court supervising, except in relation to very specific issues, the performance of a state legislature.

Court supervision of an elected body having a much narrower function, such as a school committee, is a more manageable operation. The unresponsiveness of Boston School Committees, about which plaintiff complains in this case, is already being dealt with under the close supervision of Judge Garrity. A five-member School Committee having two blacks might still be deemed unresponsive so as to require the same supervision provided for in *Morgan.* The point is that School Committee unresponsiveness is being dealt with by this federal court without the necessity of restructuring underlying electoral procedures. [Black Voters v. McDonough, *supra.*]

For the black community, this was not half as objectionable as the political science lecture with which he ended his decision:

The political history of blacks in Massachusetts has had its success stories as well as its failures. It is discouraging to lose an election, whether one is white or black. But survivors learn from defeat. They come to realize that visibility, credibility and organization are absolute musts for success. An impressive biographical sketch alone has never been enough to insure election for any candidate, white or black. There is an inherent subjectivity in the process by which the majority selects its leaders that

just as likely that the situation may deteriorate. The two centuries of struggle to desegregate Boston's public school system have taken their toll. The community's reservoir of good faith and good will had long been exhausted by the time the federal court joined the fray. It is not likely that any judicial decree, no matter how carefully considered or thoughtfully framed, could change that in just twenty-four months.

---

defies any computer-like approach to assessing qualifications. [Black Voters v. Mc-Donough, *supra*.]

This particular passage convinced counsel that Judge Tauro had listened but had not heard and did not understand the allegations and arguments.

The Limits of Remedial Power: Hart v. Community School Board 21

James J. Fishman

Hart v. Community School Board 21 *was the first New York City desegregation case to reach a federal court. In his initial decision the district judge found widespread constitutional violations on the part of Community School Board 21 and city, state, and federal housing authorities that resulted in the segregation of a junior high school. The judge suggested a wide-reaching approach to integrate the school and housing patterns in the community. The final decision, which came after the appointment of a special master and extensive hearings, was more modest in scope.* Hart v. Community School Board 21 *demonstrates the complexities and interfacing variables in litigation of this type.*

James J. Fishman is the associate director of the Courts' Role in Desegregation of Education Litigation Project and a member of the New York Bar. —Eds.

Hart v. Community School Board 21[1] was the first New York City school desegregation case to reach a federal court. It began as a class-action suit against a single junior high school in Brooklyn, New York. The plaintiffs alleged that the school board maintained the Mark Twain Junior High School as a racially segregated and underutilized school. The initial decision by Federal District Court Judge Jack B. Weinstein found extensive constitutional violations and ordered a

The author wishes to thank Richard Fries, A.B. Brooklyn College (1974), J.D. New York University School of Law (1977), for his assistance in the preparation of this paper. Mr. Fries wrote the section dealing with the special master's housing report. He provided invaluable assistance in this project.
Copyright © 1975 James J. Fishman.
1. Hart v. Community School Board of Brooklyn, New York, School District #21, 383 F. Supp. 699 (1974) [hereinafter cited as Hart I].

wide-ranging remedy involving school and housing authorities. The final judgment,[2] more modest in scope, ordered the conversion of Mark Twain into a magnet school. *Hart v. Community School Board 21* illustrates the limited remedial powers of courts in the desegregation of education.

THE SETTING

The Structure of Education in New York State

Education in New York is a state function delegated to local municipalities.[3] In 1969 the New York State Legislature passed and the governor signed a school decentralization law for New York City.[4] Prior to the enactment of the decentralization legislation, the school system had been completely governed by a centralized citywide board of education. The decentralization law provided for no less than 30 or more than 33 community school districts.[5] Districts were not to cross county lines and no district was to contain less than 20,000 pupils in average daily attendance.[6]

Authors have ascribed the impetus for school decentralization and for community control of the schools to several origins. There was a widespread belief that the quality of education provided by New York City's schools was declining. This was evidenced in part by a decrease in pupil reading scores during the 1960s. An influx of black and Hispanic pupils and the subsequent failure of the citywide board of education to integrate the school system led to an alienation from the school system by minority sectors of the population. Furthermore, the rigidity of the board of education in resisting all suggestions of change and its unresponsiveness to minority demands offered the image and reality of a lack of accountability.[7]

Community School District 21

At present there are 32 school districts in New York City, of varying pupil populations. Community School District 21, which administered the Mark Twain School, comprises the southern part of Brooklyn, one of the five boroughs of New York City.[8] The district fronts on the Atlantic Ocean approximately three miles from east to west and three and a third miles north to south. It is an

---

2. Hart v. Community School Board of Brooklyn, New York, School District #21, 383 F. Supp. 769 (1974) [hereinafter cited as Hart II].
3. N.Y. Education Law, Art. 52-A, §2590-b[2(a)] (McKinney, 1970).
4. N.Y. Education Law, Art. 52-A (McKinney, 1970).
5. *Id. See* §2590-b[2(b)]. The citywide board of education retained many powers. For the best discussion of the decentralization law, *see* Laverne, Gordon & Landers, Impact of School Decentralization in New York City on Municipal Decentralization (1975).
6. N.Y. Education Law, Art. 52-A, §2590-b[2(b)] (McKinney, 1970).
7. *See generally* D. Ravitch, The Great School Wars (1974); D. Rogers, 110 Livingston Street: Politics and Bureaucracy in the New York City Schools (1968); M. Gittel, Crisis at Ocean Hill-Brownsville (1971).
8. *See* Hart I, *supra* note 1 at 708 for a map of District 21.

area populated by nearly 290,000, most of whom are white, lower middle class.[9] Much of District 21 consists of one- and two-family houses and small apartment houses constructed during the period between the world wars. After World War II, a number of large housing projects were built by private developers with the assistance of federally insured loans, state and city taxes, and other aid.

Coney Island

The Mark Twain Junior High School lies in the extreme southern boundary of the district. Coney Island is a peninsula; it faces the Atlantic Ocean on the south, lower New York Bay on the west and northwest, and Coney Island Creek on the north. Once best known for its broad public bathing beaches, a boardwalk, and an amusement park, much of Coney Island is now one of the city's worst neighborhoods.

The western nose of Coney Island is known as Sea Gate. Physically and socially isolated, Sea Gate is segregated from the rest of the peninsula by a high fence with access controlled by private guards. On the inside, Sea Gate is a community of white, middle-class, one-family homes along privately owned streets. Unlike the remainder of the peninsula, there has been no deterioration. Only 30 percent of Sea Gate children of junior high school age attend public schools; these children go to Mark Twain.

In the middle of the peninsula is an amusement park near a boardwalk. Prior to World War II there were two principal types of housing here. Some brick two- and four-family homes and small apartment houses were occupied year round by families of workers and owners of small businesses in the area. There were also wooden summer bungalows.[10] The severe housing shortage of the late 1940s and early 1950s led to the winterization of the summer bungalows. They were occupied by veterans and others with backgrounds similar to the permanent residents.

Later, the availability of housing in the suburbs and completion of newer apartment houses to the east left vacancies. Housing deteriorated. Speculators rented to welfare recipients and to other poor families, many of whom had been displaced by the new developments. An increase in crime and the physical destruction of abandoned buildings—familiar problems of urban decay—led to an exodus by white residents.[11]

The eastern portion of Coney Island is a middle-class area with modern apartment houses, built in the 1940s and 1950s near Ocean Parkway.[12] This exten-

9. Demographics are taken from the 1970 Census and the court's decision, at 708–10. School district lines are not coterminous with census tracts, so analysis is sometimes difficult.

10. Hart I, *supra* note 1, at 709.

11. The court noted that the physical deterioration of Coney Island was a factor in the decline of the white population. *Id.*

12. *See* Hart v. Community School Board of Brooklyn, New York School District #21, no. 76-C-1041, at 7 (unreported portion of opinion, E.D.N.Y. January 28, 1974), for illustrative map.

sive area was once utilized by Luna Park, an amusement park. Large areas were claimed from wetlands by earlier city dumping and land fill.[13]

A total of 8,157 units of middle-income non-federally funded housing projects were built in the 1960s in the eastern part of Coney Island—Luna Park in 1961, Trump in 1964, and Warbasse in 1965. The projects were occupied by the white lower-middle class. Rents excluded all but a few middle-class backs and Hispanics. The children in these housing developments went went to P.S. 303, an elementary school which opened its doors in September of 1965. When children from the Warbasse houses and Luna Park houses graduated from the sixth grade, they went to Mark Twain Junior High School.

Public Housing and Urban Renewal in Coney Island

In 1968 a 60-square-block area in central Coney Island was selected by the city and federal government for complete reconstruction under the Neighborhood Development Program, a species of urban renewal.

The central Coney Island urban renewal area involved the cooperation of city, state, and federal agencies in building, sponsoring, and managing several publically assisted housing developments. These projects covered much of the feeder area to the Mark Twain Junior High School.

Under New York City Housing Authority regulations, site and former site residents receive first priority for new public housing.[14] Priority is also given to residents relocated from the Coney Island urban renewal area from the Neighborhood Development Program area and to persons in emergency need of housing in the greater Coney Island area. When dislocated by urban renewal, white families fare better than nonwhite. Remaining in the urban renewal area tend to be a disproportionate number of non-white former site residents. Under the Housing Authority's priority policy, these former site residents, usually more minority than the original site's population, get first choice.

The new units of housing opening in the early 1970s in central Coney Island were overwhelmingly minority, with a higher proportion of welfare and problem families.[15] This stilled any in-migration of middle-class white families with children. The white population in the newer housing projects was aged. Furthermore, the demand for public housing was so great that many apartments were converted into larger units for sizable families. Virtually all of the large families moving into the new projects were minority. And in the older public housing in Coney Island, with the exception of one all-elderly project, all had lost between 20 and 30 percent of their initial white populations by the early 1970s.

The Demographics of District 21

Compared to the rest of District 21, blacks and Hispanics are in high concentration in central Coney Island. The total District 21 population in 1970 was

---

13. Hart I, *supra* note 1, at 699.
14. N.Y.C. Housing Authority Text Regulation, GM 1810. *See* discussion *infra* at 1154.
15. Hart I, *supra* note 1, at 722.

288,694. The black population was 79,300. In 1970 only 17.6 percent of the district's population lived in Coney Island, but 71.9 percent of the district's black population lived there. In the area comprising the feeder patterns of Mark Twain, of a total population of 50,776, blacks and Hispanics totaled 10,123.

In central Coney Island, the median family income is much lower than in the rest of District 21. The number of families with incomes of less than $4,000 is high.[16] The percentage of the population between fourteen and twenty-one and over sixty-five years of age is high. The homicide and robbery rates are high.[17] The unemployed nonstudent male population, 16–21, is high.

The percentage of families on welfare is high. As of 1969, a New York City Planning Commission study found that the welfare rate in central Coney Island was three times the city average; the juvenile delinquency rate was two and one-half times the city average; 45 percent of the population lived below the federal poverty standards. Central Coney Island is a sea of urban misery.

The Mark Twain School

The Mark Twain School is situated at the northern edge of the middle part of Coney Island.[18] The school is a well-constructed, three-story brick building approximately forty years old, but thoroughly rebuilt and recently refurbished. It is fully equipped with a rare advantage for an urban school—it is adjacent to a sizable city park with tennis and handball courts, grass, ballfields, and track facilities.[19]

Utilization. Despite its sound physical structure, Mark Twain was under-utilized and racially segregated. Qualitatively, the performance of its pupils was declining. Mark Twain's utilization rate was almost 50 percent below the district average (see Table 1).

By 1972 its utilization had declined to 41 percent. It remained at that level in the fall of 1973. The next lowest junior high school utilization rate in the district was 80 percent. The district court found that the drop in utilization[20] was due to the attrition of white students during the past ten years. The other junior high and intermediate schools in the district did not show a similar decline.

Combined with its low utilization rate, Mark Twain had the highest absentee rate in the district. Average daily percentage of attendance from September 1972 to June 1973 was 72.26 percent. The next lowest school in the district's attendance percentage was 85.15 percent. The New York City average was 83.41 percent.[21] Compared to the rest of the district, reading scores for Mark Twain

16. In the whole district, less than 5 percent of the families have annual incomes over $25,000.

17. Hart I, *supra* note 1, at 710.

18. To be precise, it is where Coney Island enters Gravesend Bay, an arm of New York's lower harbor. *See* Hart, unreported opinion, *supra* note 12, at 9.

19. Hart I, *supra* note 1, at 710.

20. *Id.* at 713.

21. *Id.* at 710.

remained low and were getting worse. In 1971 the eighth-grade median grade score was 5.8. In 1972 it had dropped to 5.7. The percentage of all Twain students reading on or above grade level was only 13.8 percent.[22]

Racial Imbalance. In the past ten years, Mark Twain had become increasingly racially imbalanced. In 1962 the school was 81 percent white, 7.4 percent black, and 11.6 percent Hispanic. In each of the last ten years, the percentage of nonwhite students had increased. By 1973, blacks constituted about 43.3 percent and Hispanics 38.6 percent of total enrollment.[23]

Table 2 indicates the increasing racial imbalance in Twain, while Figure 1 compares the number of students, black, minority, and others in the years 1963-1972.

The district court determined that the drastic change in the racial balance at the school was due more to the attrition of white students than to any influx of minority students.[24] Table 3 illustrates that the other junior high schools in District 21 were predominantly white.

In October 1972 the total intermediate and junior high school population of

22. New York Times, September 26, 1973, at 51, col. 1; *id.,* March 18, 1973, at 1, col. 1. The percentage indicates the portion of people in each school at or above their grade school level. According to national standards, a school should have one-half of its pupils at or above their grade level and one-half of its pupils at or below grade level.

Reading Scores, District 21

	Grade 8 Median Grade Score		Percentage of Students Reading At or Above Grade Level		Ranking of City Junior High Schools
	1971	1972	1972	1973	1973
J.H.S. 43	9.3	8.7	48.3	53.4	23
I.S. 96	8.0	8.2	36.6	38.2	56
J.H.S. 99	9.3	9.3	*	50.5	*
J.H.S. 228	8.4	8.0	39.7	41.6	46
J.H.S. 238	8.4	8.4	*	53.7	*
J.H.S. 239	5.3	5.7	13.8	13.9	108
J.H.S. 281	8.2	7.8	42.7	42.4	43
I.S. 303	9.8	9.0	45.9	47.2	38

*Not published.

23. Hart I, *supra* note 1, at 711.
24. *Id.* In 1962, whites numbered 1,566 out of a total of 1,933 students. By 1973, only 129 out of a total of 713 students were Anglo. In contrast to these figures, in 1962, blacks numbered 143 and Hispanics 224 out of a total of 1,933 students. By 1973, blacks still numbered only 309 and Hispanics 275 out of 713. The percentage of black students at Mark Twain increased even during the 1969/70 and 1971/72 school years when there was a slight decrease in the actual number of black students.

The percentage of Hispanic students increased during the 1968-1972 period even when the actual number of Hispanics at Mark Twain declined.

Table 1. Utilization Rates, District 21 Junior High Schools–Intermediate Schools

School[a]	Utilization Rate		
	1970–71	*1971–72*	*1973–74*
J.H.S.239 (Mark Twain)	57%	43 %	41%
J.H.S.228	108%	116.8%	100%
J.H.S.43	96%	96.7%	80%
J.H.S.281	113%	116 %	108%
I.S.96	111%	107.6%	106%
I.S.303	114%	105.7%	80%

Utilization, Mark Twain 1962–1973

Year	Percent Utilization
1962	88%
1963	91%
1964	98%
1965	95%
1966	81%
1967	82%
1968	75%
1969	66%
1970	57%
1971	43%
1972	41%

[a]J.H.S. refers to junior high schools (grades 7–9); I.S. refers to intermediate schools (grades 5–8); P.S. as used in this essay refers to public schools (grades 1–6).
Source: 383 F. Supp. 713; Vol I, Record on Appeal.

Table 2. Racial Imbalance in Mark Twain School

Year	Percent Black and Puerto Rican Students
1962	19.0%
1963	23.4
1964	25.2
1965	26.6
1966	32.3
1967	38.9
1968	42.9
1969	48.0
1970	60.7
1971	69.8
1972	76.1
1973	81.9

Source: Vol. I, Record on Appeal.

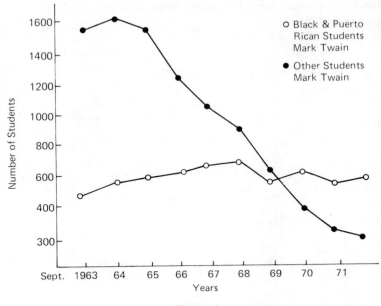

Figure 1
Source: 383 F. Supp. 712.

District 21 numbered 8,752, of which 7,833 were resident students.[25] About 17 percent of the resident enrollment at the intermediate and junior high schools in the district were nonwhites.[26] But 41 percent of the total resident non-white students enrolled in District 21 intermediate and junior high schools attended Mark Twain. In 1973, 30.4 percent of all students—resident and nonresident —attending all schools at any level in the district were minority; 17.43% were black, 11.54 percent were Puerto Rican, and 1.41 percent were other Spanish surnamed. Yet, at the same time, 81.9 percent of the student enrollment at Mark Twain was nonwhite.

The increase in minority enrollment and corresponding decrease in utilization at Mark Twain was not accidental. To a great extent these changes were due to alteration in the feeder patterns of elementary schools whose graduates were fed into the district's junior high schools. Over an eight-year period, school officials changed the feeder patterns to Mark Twain so that graduates of pre-dominantly white elementary schools were re-zoned away from Mark Twain. In addition, elementary schools were converted into intermediate schools and

25. Of the total school population, 919 were "open-enrollment students"—students who did not reside in the district but who attended school there in order to find a school which was more racially balanced than one in their home district. These open-enrollment students came from the heavily minority area of Bedford-Stuyvesant.
26. The figures are 1,337 of 7,833.

Table 3. Racial Composition of District 21 Junior High and
Intermediate Schools, 1973–1974

School	Black	Puerto Rican	Other	Total
J.H.S.239 (Mark Twain)	309 43.3%	275 38.6%	129 18.1%	713
J.H.S.228	246 14.7%	34 2.0%	1394 83.3%	1674
J.H.S.281	253 15.2%	86 5.1%	1331 79.7%	1670
J.H.S.43	236 17.9%	133 10.0%	956 72.0%	1327
I.S.96	185 11.5%	68 4.2%	1558 84.3%	1611
I.S.303	187 14.4%	371 28.5%	743 57.1%	1301

Source: Hart v. Community School Board, 72C 1041, Advance Opinion at 23.

new junior high schools were opened, which had the foreseeable effect of draining white children from Mark Twain. Table 4 illustrates these changes in feeder patterns.

The record of the *Hart* trial revealed a considerable amount of segregation within the school based upon ability grouping. There were seven classifications of students ranging from special students with high reading scores who accomplished the three-year course of study in two years, to children so disinterested in academic matters (usually older boys with substantial emotional or physical problems) that they did not attend school regularly and required some sort of work-study program.[27]

27. Hart I, *supra* note 1, at 713. The most recent figures, for the incoming class, show some improvement in internal desegregation:

J.H.S. 239: Ethnic Distribution by Section, Seventh Grade—September 1973

Section	Register	Puerto Rican	Negro	Others
7 SP[1]	22	2	6	14
7[1]	33	14	14	5
7[2]	30	10	14	6
7[3]	24	8	13	3
7[4]	31	5	20	6
7[5]	27	14	12	1
7[6]	24	8	11	5
7[7]	19	11	7	1
7[8]	28	15	13	0
7[9] CRMD	14	6	8	0

The court noted (Hart I, *supra* note 1, at 713) that the first two tracks had been almost entirely white, and the sixth and seventh tracks had been almost entirely nonwhite.

Table 4.   Changes in Feeder Patterns at Mark Twain

1965	1966	1969	1970	1972–73
	J.H.S.281 (opens doors) P.S.212 →			
P.S.212 (1973–74) white 60.8 blk & Hisp. 39.2				
P.S.188 (1973–74) white 38.8 blk 40.3 Hisp. 30.9	P.S.188 → Mark Twain	P.S.188 → Twain	P.S.188 → Twain	P.S.188 white 28.8 blk 40.3 Hisp. 30.9 → Twain
P.S.288 (1973–74) white 8.1 blk 50.4 Hisp. 41.5 → Mark Twain	P.S.288 →	P.S.288 → 8th and 9th grade from P.S.303 area → Twain	P.S.288 → 9th grade from I.S.303 area only → Twain	P.S.288 white 8.1 blk 50.4 Hisp. 41.5 → Twain
P.S.303 (middle class white) 50%	P.S.303 →	P.S.303*– I.S.303 (adds 7th grade)	P.S.303– I.S.303 (adds 8th grade)	
P.S.216 (1973–74) white 90.4 blk & Hisp. 9.6 → 50% → J.H.S. 228	P.S.216 100% → J.H.S.228			

*Conversion to intermediate school from elementary school meant dropping grades K–4, retaining grades 5 and 6, and gradually adding 7 and 8.
Source: Derived from *Hart v. Community School Board of Brooklyn, New York School District #21*, 383 F. Supp. 715–17.

THE ORIGINS OF THE LAWSUIT

In July of 1970, Community School Board 21 first took office. One of the first items on its agenda was the severe racial imbalance at Mark Twain, brought to the board's attention by Acting Superintendent Doris Chitraro. The school board had been requested by the parents' association of Mark Twain to correct conditions in the school. In September 1970 the Coney Island Community Council, a coalition of 61 community organizations, adopted a resolution urging Community School Board 21 to take steps to correct the severe racial imbalance at the school. At that time Mark Twain was 57 percent utilized and 38 percent white.

Ms. Chitraro, the Office of School Zoning of the Central Board of Education, and Community School Board 21 developed a plan to re-zone Elementary School 216 so that it would again feed into Mark Twain.[28] Community School Board 21 met with representatives of the parents' associations of all the schools in District 21 and with other members of the community to discuss the possibility of implementing the plan.

On March 25, 1971, the board issued notice of a public hearing to be held on March 31 with regard to the proposal to re-zone P.S. 216. At the meeting were representatives from various sides and schools in the district. Some spoke in favor of the re-zoning plan. Others, particularly those who resided in the P.S. 212 and 216 areas, were overwhelmingly opposed. These latter speakers argued that the educational facilities at Mark Twain were inferior to those of the other junior high schools. They also feared for the safety of their children. On April 7, 1971, Community School Board 21 announced that it had decided to make no changes in the status quo.

Two weeks later the Mark Twain Parents Association appealed the board's decision to Harvey Scribner, the chancellor of the board of education. Scribner failed to act until the parents association filed a petition with New York State Commissioner of Education Ewald Nyquist. Then Scribner sent a letter dated September 7, 1971 to the president of Community School Board 21, directing the board to formulate and approve a plan to eliminate "racial imbalance and improved building utilization" at Mark Twain by no later than December 31, 1971.[29]

Throughout the case, the central board of education's principal desire was noninvolvement. If that was not possible, the board wanted to avoid controversy by doing the minimum acceptable.[30]

At the time of Scribner's September 1971 letter, Mark Twain's utilization had dropped to 43 percent and was only 33 percent white. One week before the year-

28. *See* text Table 4 *supra,* which shows re-zoning of feeder schools.

29. These actions are described in Hart I, *supra* note 1, at 716–17.

30. No doubt this was due to the intraorganizational pressures upon the board of education resulting from the new decentralization law as well as the natural bureaucratic propensity to resist conflict and change.

end deadline, the president of Community School Board 21 advised the chancellor that the plan he requested would be submitted in January of 1972.

Community School Board 21 offered a freedom-of-choice plan which included increased educational expenditures for Mark Twain in the hope that white parents would voluntarily send their children there.[31] At the board meeting at which the plan was adopted, Allen Zelon, a board member, proposed an amendment to re-zone Elementary Schools 212 and 216 into Mark Twain, thereby increasing the student enrollment and utilization. Zelon's plan involved busing. The amendment was voted down 7–2.

There was no publicity given to Community School Board 21's education improvement program for Twain. Not one white student enrolled at the school pursuant to the board's free-choice plan. On April 7, 1972, Chancellor Scribner rejected the free-choice plan. The board was ordered to take action, including the adoption of a plan, no later than May 17, 1972, to insure that by September 1 of that year the percentage of minority-group students would not vary from the district-wide average for intermediate and junior high schools by more than 30 percent and the building utilization would not vary by more than 35 percent.[32] The chancellor directed that by September of 1973, Mark Twain could not differ by more than 20 percent in racial composition and 25 percent in utilization from the rest of the district. By September 1, 1973, the percentages had to drop to approximately a 10 percent variance from the rest of the district in both racial composition and utilization. The only way these percentages could have been achieved would be through re-zoning, which clearly Community School Board 21 would refuse to approve.

On May 17, Community School Board 21 said that it would not comply with the chancellor's directive. Five days later the chancellor told James Meyerson, assistant general counsel of the NAACP, that he had no intention in the near future of compelling the community board to implement its April 7 directive. On June 30 Scribner met with Acting Superintendent Chitraro. They reached a decision whereby in September of 1972 there would be some re-zoning and increase in utilization as well as a limitation to the increase in racial imbalance. Also on June 30, Scribner met with the community board, which refused to modify their own plan of January 5. One week later, on July 5, 1972, the chancellor modified his April 7 directive and specifically requested that:

1. A sixth grade be added to Mark Twain for September 1972.
2. Normal feeder patterns be reintroduced to terminate all options for students who would normally attend schools that would feed into Twain.
3. To move forward with the board's plan for special financing to improve the Mark Twain School.[33]

31. Apparently the additional funds for Twain were diverted from the elementary schools feeding into the school. The court suggested that this probably caused a further deterioration of Twain's entering class the following year. Hart I, *supra* note 1, at 716.
32. *Id.* at 717.
33. *Id.* at 719–20.

At the trial, counsel to the chancellor, Elliot Hoffman, said that the chancellor modified his April 7 directives because he felt that forced integration of Twain would lead to white flight in the district. Irving Anker (later Scribner's successor) confirmed the white-flight argument and added an explanation for the failure to desegregate: the opposition of the parents in the district.

On August 8 Community School Board 21 informed the chancellor that they did not intend to implement either the April 7 order or suggestions 1 and 2 of the July 5 letter. Thereafter, the chancellor did little.

THE SUIT

The Complaint

On August 4, 1972, lawyers of the National Association for the Advancement of Colored People began a class action on behalf of the children attending Mark Twain. The suit alleged that Community School Board 21 and the chancellor of the citywide board of education were maintaining Mark Twain as an unconstitutionally racially segregated and underutilized school. The plaintiffs prayed for declaratory and injunctive relief, including a direction to defendants to formulate and implement immediately a comprehensive plan that would eliminate the racially segregated and underutilized nature of Mark Twain, and which would provide for equal educational opportunities for plaintiff children.

The defendant school board denied any segregative acts and charged other governmental agencies with the full responsibility for the racial imbalance in the school. Impleaded as third-party defendants were city, state, and federal authorities.[34] The defendants maintained that if segregation existed, it was due to the housing patterns fostered and maintained by the third-party defendants,[35] who were engaged in a policy of affirmative action designed to perpetuate racial imbalance in public and publically aided housing. Further, this policy was the basic cause for racial imbalance and segregation in the public school system. Approval of public housing project construction sites in Coney Island in particular perpetuated the segregated living patterns; and New York City had established a policy of separate-but-equal housing and education facilities.

Specific relief requested was an order that city authorities desegregate existing public housing and the court direct the federal and state defendants not to

34. The impleader was on the basis of FRCP 14:

(a) When Defendant May Bring in Third Party. At any time after commencement of the action a defending party, as a third party plaintiff, may cause a summons and complaint to be served upon a person not a party to the action who is or may be liable to him for all or part of the plaintiff's claim against him.

35. Impleaded as defendants were: (a) New York City—the mayor, the Housing and Development Administration and its administrator, the New York City Housing Authority and its chairman; (b) New York State—the Urban Development Corporation and its president, the Division of Housing and Community Renewal, the executive department, and its commissioner; (c) the United States—the secretary and the New York area regional administrator of the Department of Housing and Urban Development.

approve new loans and new grants to the city until its discriminatory practices were eliminated.

One party missing from the proceedings who could be expected to play a major role in any education matter in New York City was the United Federation of Teachers. Hyman Bravin, counsel for Community School Board 21, had known Albert Shanker, the UFT's leader, from Liberal Party politics years ago.[36] The UFT never became involved in the case, and Shanker, who has a weekly column in the Sunday *New York Times* (in an advertisement paid for by the UFT), never wrote an article on the *Hart* case. The UFT probably felt that as Bravin thought the way they did, he would argue their position in representing the community school board.

The Cast

The *Hart* suit was instigated by several residents from Sea Gate, the nearly all-white enclave. Some close to the case have uncharitably suggested that these residents were less interested in the education of the deprived plaintiffs than in the threat that a blighted Coney Island posed to the value of their property. An integrated Mark Twain and Coney Island would provide a helpful buffer for Sea Gate. But Sea Gate residents whose children attended public schools had an interest in getting more white classmates for their children.[37]

Leo Shapiro, a former local school board member, went to the NAACP to inform them of the situation at Mark Twain and to obtain their participation.[38] Shapiro's law firm, Kestenbaum & Shapiro, became local counsel. At the NAACP, the case was assigned to James Meyerson, a 1969 graduate of Syracuse University Law School, and a former VISTA volunteer. Meyerson was concurrently engaged in a number of education cases around the country. Although under the supervision of Nathaniel Jones, NAACP general counsel, he operated with a free hand. Throughout the case Meyerson had difficulty keeping his emotions and ideology under control. Others close to the case felt that he needed guidance he never properly received.

Normally the Corporation Counsel's Office, the city attorney for New York, would represent the defendant community school board. Since the complaint had also named the chancellor of the central board of education, and since there were existing disputes between the chancellor and the community school board, the local board retained its own counsel. The central board and the city housing agencies were represented by Elliot Hoffman, a senior attorney in the Corporation Counsel's Office.

The then head of the community board, Evelyn Aquila, selected Hyman Bravin as counsel. An individual practitioner, Bravin was a well-known criminal de-

36. Bravin also knew Eugene Kaufman, the UFT's counsel. Interview with Hyman Bravin, June 25, 1975 [hereinafter cited as Bravin Interview].

37. Interview with Allen Zelon, president of Community School Board 21, August 11, 1975 [hereinafter cited as Zelon Interview].

38. Shapiro has previously appealed to the state commissioner of education to protest the school board's failure to integrate Twain.

fense lawyer. He was the most inexpensive lawyer who offered to serve as counsel. He said he would charge $50 per hour and estimated a $5,000 maximum, a figure quickly exceeded.[39] Bravin had defended Nathan Voloshen when he was accused of improprieties as an assistant to the then Speaker of the House, John McCormick. Bravin had close ties to Roy Cohn. An Orthodox Jew who had represented the Jewish Defense League, Bravin was also a lifetime member of the NAACP. Bravin was the chairman of the Bronx Liberal Party and had political contacts around the city. One attorney involved in the case said of Bravin, "If Nixon had Bravin as his lawyer, he would still be President."

The life of the individual practitioner concentrating on criminal law in New York City is a difficult one.[40] For Bravin, this regular source of income must have been most gratifying.

Lawyers representing the other government agencies included Jean Hollingsworth for the New York City Housing Authority; Steven Lefkowitz for the Urban Development Corp. (UDC), a state agency; Robert Hammer, an assistant attorney general in the New York State Law Department; and Assistant U.S. Attorney for the Eastern District of New York Cyril Hyman. Elliot Hoffman represented the chancellor, the mayor, and the city's Housing and Development Administration. Counsel for the third-party defendants played a relatively passive role in the proceedings until the judge's decision indicated their agencies were part of the problem and of the solution. Lefkowitz, the UDC lawyer, was generally credited with being the most able counsel in the case.

The three leading powers on the community school board were Evelyn Aquila, president during the period prior to 1974; Vincent Fonti, a local lawyer; and Allen Zelon. Aquila in 1972 was a 39-year-old woman who had been active in many community affairs. She was head of a Brooklyn coalition to keep neighborhood schools, and had stated that any school that had black, white, and Puerto Rican pupils in it, regardless of the ratio, was an integrated school and did not need any change.[41] She was against attempts to integrate Twain. Fonti was publicly and privately the board's most outspoken opponent of busing. "I won't permit a kid on a bus" was his slogan.[42] Zelon, a 43-year-old biology teacher, was one of the two pro-integrationists on the board, and testified for the plaintiffs.[43] There were no blacks or Hispanics on the board. The black and Puerto Rican communities could not agree on a single candidate or slate, and their members did not vote in proportion to their numbers. When Zelon became

39. Zelon Interview, *supra* note 37.

40. *See* J. Carlin, Lawyer's Ethics (1966); A. Wood, The Criminal Lawyer (1967).

41. Trial Testimony of Allen Zelon, Record on Appeal, Vol. 2, at 14. Aquila never saw a contradiction between the development of a magnet school and her support for neighborhood schools.

42. Zelon Interview, *supra* note 37. *See also,* Zelon testimony, *supra* note 41, at 113.

43. The board had usually divided 7-2 against motions to improve integration. Beside Zelon, the only other pro-integrationist was Virginia Freedman, a housewife and mother long active in school affairs. It should be pointed out that Zelon did not send his younger child to a District 21 Junior High School. Hearings, January 4, 1973, at 328.

president of the board, ironically he unified it. Zelon was practical, articulate, and played a major role in formulating the ultimate plan.

The board frequently misunderstood the legal process and the use of counsel. Many had never used an attorney other than for house closings, so were uncertain of their relationship to their lawyer, to the judge, and to the media. For many members the community school board elections were their first attempt at public office. As one participant said, "They all thought they had charisma." If the board had a problem, its first reaction was to call a press conference. Or the members wanted to sit down directly with the judge, for they believed that he was basically a politician, too. Only over a period of time was Bravin able to build up credibility and respect from the board, and to educate them about their proper role and his in the lawsuit.

The judge assigned to the case was Jack B. Weinstein. If a good government group were to draw up the qualifications of an ideal jurist, they could begin with Judge Weinstein's. A professor at Columbia Law School before he ascended the bench, Weinstein was best known in legal circles as the author of the standard treatise on the rules of evidence in New York State.[44] Possessing prodigious work habits, the judge was well organized and tremendously energetic. Weinstein still teaches part-time at Columbia, and while on the bench, had managed to produce a new treatise, *Weinstein's Evidence,* a commentary on the *Federal Rules of Evidence.*[45] One lawyer who likes him very much said, by way of criticism, that he thinks others should have his capacity for work.

Weinstein is a liberal, activist, result-oriented judge, whose critics call him political. His decisions tend to be innovative and long. In December of 1972 he began a campaign for chief judge of the New York State Court of Appeals.[46]

Trial Strategies

In November of 1972 the plaintiffs moved for preliminary relief to integrate the schools because of the delay caused by an extensive trial. The motion was withdrawn because of assurances by the court that the trial would proceed without delay. The trial began in January 1973.

Plaintiffs rested at the end of July. The defendants rested their case in March. The delay was caused in part by additional time granted to the defendants because of the testimony of plaintiffs' expert witness, Dan Dodson. In May the plaintiffs unsuccessfully sought preliminary relief in view of the delays incurred as a consequence of postponements given to the defendants.[47]

44. Weinstein, Korn, & Miller, New York Civil Practice (8 Vol. 1974).

45. Weinstein & Berger, Weinstein's Evidence (5 Vol. 1975).

46. He lost the Democratic primary by a few hundred votes. All attorneys associated with the case felt his campaign had no impact whatsoever on the trial. Whether an image of the judge as a "political animal" was created in the minds of the school board and of the residents of District 21 is hard to say. Zelon worked on the local Weinstein for Chief Judge Committee. *See* Zelon Interview, *supra* note 37.

47. Plaintiffs appealed from Judge Weinstein's denial of their motion for a preliminary injunction. (Apparently, the plaintiffs were upset at the length of time the defendants were being allowed for briefs.)

The plaintiffs' basic tactic was to prove that Mark Twain was a consciously segregated school, and to get an order desegregating the school. Proof of segregation in fact and that the segregation was caused by school board action and inaction was relatively easy. The demographics spoke for themselves. The dreary record of community board inaction was not contradicted. Plaintiffs' expert witness, the well-traveled Dan Dodson of New York University, who had ridden circuit for the NAACP in its cases around the country, testified to the segregation in the school.

Particularly telling to Judge Weinstein was the perception of Mark Twain as a segregated and poor school by members of the community and by the school administration itself. Then Deputy Chancellor Irving Anker, and the principal

---

The appellate court found that the district court (Weinstein) failed to make the necessary findings of fact and conclusions of law as required by FRCP 52(a) when a temporary injunction is denied. The appellate court remanded for the purpose.

The court noted that its opinion should not encourage delay in the case or prevent a consolidation under Fed. R. Civ. P. 65(a)(2) of all or part of the hearing on preliminary relief (the subject of the appeal) with the trial on the merits for permanent relief. In a footnote, the court added, "should the trial on the merits occur within the time limit set forth above, [by the end of 1973], it might then be unnecessary [for Judge Weinstein] to proceed with findings of fact and conclusions of law on the motion for preliminary relief." 487 F.2d 223 (*decided* Nov. 2, 1973).

The plaintiffs moved for reconsideration. The city defendants and the third-party defendants made a cross-motion for dismissal or in the alternative the city defendants asked for summary affirmance of Weinstein's denials below. The court noted that the defendants did not believe Weinstein's April 1 decision was appealable at this time, since he only found that the segregation practiced by the board was unconstitutional, and directed a plan be submitted to him.

The court agreed with this analysis and said were it to hold the postponement order appealable it would then feel compelled to allow the defendants to contend postponement was proper and that desegregation should not have been ordered at all. This would have forced the court to consider "a most serious constitutional question" on an expedited basis; this the appellate court deemed unwise in a situation in which the judge, the master, and the adversary parties' cooperation on a plan might make it unnecessary for the appellate court to decide any question. 497 F.2d 1027 (2d Cir. 1974).

Taylor v. Board of Education of New Rochelle, 288 F.2d 600 (2d Cir. 1961) results in a conclusion of inapplicability since the judge entered no final judgment, issued no injunction or any legally effective order which he could modify or stay. When viewed in this light, Weinstein did not, in his January 28, 1974 decision, direct desegregation by September 1974, but simply directed that plans submitted by March 1, 1974 should provide for it. (When he examined the plans, he saw none was suitable for implementation and ordered the postponement.) Plaintiffs argued that Weinstein said a plan could be drawn in a matter of weeks so there was no need for a one-year postponement—this argument was rejected by the court.

The court said that it didn't disagree with plaintiffs that there might be circumstances where failure to order a long-overdue desegregation could constitute a denial of an injunction, even though no words are uttered (and therefore be appealable) as in Kelly v. Board of Education of Nashville, 436 F.2d 856, where the case had begun in 1955 and the judge stayed indefinitely all proceedings and hearings on the desegregation plan or alternatives until the Supreme Court had decided pending school cases. In *Hart,* the district court was "laboring" and hoping to finish just three years from the date of the complaint. "No one could properly characterize this vigorous conduct as a *de facto* denial of an injunction."

The court held that the action taken by Judge Weinstein on April 1, 1974 was not appealable, thereby dismissing the plaintiffs' appeal and mooting the preference. The court added that even if the order were appealable it would have granted the city defendants' motion for summary affirmance.

of Mark Twain, testified that they had such a perception. The court visited the school. Combined with the statistics relating to reading scores, feeder patterns, utilization, indicators of intraschool segregation, the fact of segregation was irrefutable.

Nathan Glazer, a witness for the defense, acknowledged that segregation "is the perception and the reality there,"[48] but testified that there was no intent to segregate on the part of the school board. The defendants generally denied unlawful segregation existed and predicated their defense on two arguments. The first was the central board's claim that they had not been more forceful in urging the desegregation of Mark Twain because of opposition by white parents and fears of white flight from the district if a widespread integration plan were introduced. Alternatively, the defense claimed that if segregation existed it was due to the housing patterns fostered and maintained by various governmental agencies. The school board also argued that the utilization of Twain would increase with the addition of new public housing. It was apparent, however, that such an increase in utilization would still be insufficient. The new school children would be overwhelmingly minority.[49]

As to the relationship between housing and segregated schools, and its converse—that racially imbalanced educational facilities caused segregated neighborhoods—housing witnesses claimed that racially imbalanced schools would make it more difficult to induce white families with school-age children to rent or purchase housing in the area served by Twain. Not surprisingly, school officials suggested that housing influenced the school makeup and there was a need for the fertilization of the housing project with new (that is, white) families. Professor Dodson said that in his estimation, "Schools come nearer to determining the housing of the neighborhood than vice versa."[50]

Given the complexity of the relationship between residential and school segregation, the quality of evidence was rather poor and incomplete.[51] Bravin had wanted to introduce more testimony on the relationship of imbalanced neighborhoods upon schools, but found that he could not get people to testify. Once potential expert witnesses found that the NAACP was on the other side of the case, they would not get involved.[52]

The third-party defendants presented two procedural defenses. The first was that under Rule 14 of the Federal Rules of Civil Procedure, their impleader was improper.[53] Second, administrative remedies to correct governmental segregative housing practices, if they existed, had not been exhausted.

48. Hart I, *supra* note 1, at 715, quoting Nathan Glazer.

49. *See* text summarizing Part I of the Special Master's report, *infra* at 147–51.

50. Hart I, *supra* note 1, at 725 quoting Dan Dodson.

51. *See* E. Wolf, Social Science Testimony in the Detroit Desegregation Case, paper presented at the Institute of Policy Sciences and Public Affairs, Duke University Conference, August 20, 1974, and discussed *infra*.

52. *See* Bravin Interview, *supra* note 36. The only exception was Nathan Glazer, who testified that his perception of Twain was that it was segregated.

53. The third-party defendants suggested that they were not liable to the community

Presenting evidence proving school board liability was relatively easy. The proof of the housing agencies' liability was less clear, both in terms of the facts in the case and in the relation between housing and segregation and racially imbalanced schools.

THE INITIAL DECISION

School Board and Housing Agency Liability

On January 28, 1974, Judge Weinstein issued his decision. The 152-page opinion said that the school board and the chancellor were liable for conducting a segregated school, in violation of the Constitution, and that the court would require a plan, effective in September 1974, which would integrate the Mark Twain School. The court ordered the cooperation of school authorities, city, state, and federal housing bodies, and other government agencies in developing an acceptable plan. Although the school authorities did not have the racial motivation or desire that Twain be segregated, the court determined that the segregated nature of the school was the result of de jure as distinguished from de facto segregation.

Judge Weinstein found that the various actions of Community School Board 21 and predecessor local school boards, including the rejection of re-zoning plans, refusal to follow orders of the chancellor, adverse racial impact resulting from re-zoning of various elementary schools, a conversion of an elementary school into a junior high school, taken "individually and together, had the foreseeable and inevitable effect of decreasing the white student enrollment at Mark Twain and bringing about the severe racial imbalance."[54]

The Court found:

Demographic trends have been accentuated by government choices. Decisions have been made knowing that they would encourage segregation, and failure to take available steps to reverse segregative tendencies have made a bad situation worse. [*Id.* at 707.]

School authorities acted and failed to act knowing segregation would be the result of their decisions. [*Id.* at 741.]

An interesting part of the decision was the treatment of the impleaded third-party housing defendants. The judge concluded that racially imbalanced housing was a contributing cause of racial segregation in the schools.[55] Illegal activities in

school board for plaintiffs' claim against the board, since the defendant could not assert an entirely separate claim against the third party under Fed. R. Civ. P. 14, even though it arose out of the same general set of facts as the main claim. (There must be an attempt to pass on to the third party all or part of the liability asserted to the defendant.) *See* Hart I, *supra* note 1, at 752.

54. *Id.* at 716, 721.

55. *Id.* at 748. To reach this conclusion, the court cited footnotes to two law reviews which in turn were citations to cases in which housing culpability was found.

the way of segregation in public housing leading to segregation in the schools were chargeable to all three levels of government.[56]

The judge turned down the procedural defenses of the third-party defendants, but mooted the third-party claim by deciding that the plaintiffs were constitutionally entitled to a comprehensive remedy. To the first defense, that impleader was improper, the judge said that while in a literal sense the housing authorities were not liable to the defendant school authorities "for all or part of the plaintiff's claim against the defendants, they were partly liable for the harm since their actions helped to maintain segregated schools."[57]

While admitting that impleader was not a device for bringing into an action any controversy which may happen to have some relation to it, the court relied upon the sixth circuit court decision in *Bradley v. Milliken*.[58] He said that the housing aspects of the controversy were inextricably intertwined with the school dispute. Therefore, a dismissal on the grounds of improper impleader was denied.

The argument that the defendants had failed to exhaust their administrative remedies was turned aside on the grounds that the housing authorities had to remain in the case because without them no effective remedy could be granted.[59]

The parties were to submit by March 1, 1974 a detailed plan to be placed in operation by September of that year.[60] The educational plan had to integrate Mark Twain so that it would not deviate by more than 10 percent from the district-wide average of minority pupils in junior high and intermediate schools. Housing officials of the city, state, and federal government were ordered to provide a joint plan to undo the racial imbalance in the publicly supported housing in Coney Island. The corporation counsel would coordinate the planning efforts by other government agencies.[61]

---

56. *Id.* at 751, 749.

57. *Id.* at 752. The federal housing authority was also in privity with state and city agencies and bound by the decree (*id.* at 753).

58. 484 F.2d 215, 254 (6th Cir. 1973), *cert. granted* 414 U.S. 1038 (1973). The *Milliken* court recognized that a district court's equitable powers to remedy past wrongs is broad and that the court has not merely the power but the duty to render a decree which will eliminate the discriminatory effects of the past. The court further acknowledged the power of the district court "to disregard such artificial barriers." *Id.* at 249.

59. Hart I, *supra* note 1, at 754. The court cited *Otero v. New York City Housing Authority* for the proposition that no administrative rule could afford an excuse for violating the Constitution. The court also ordered any entity not already a party should be made a party either by plaintiffs or defendants. Additional parties would include the Metropolitan Transit Authority, the New York City Parks Department, and the police commissioner.

60. In devising the education plans, the parties were to take into account "six basic elements in successful school integration: (1) Community Participation; (2) Socio-Economic Diversity; (3) Early Integration; (4) Integrated Classroom; (5) Excess of Language Minorities to Bilingual Programs; and (6) Mutual Understanding and Respect."

61. The police commissioner was to present a plan for adequate protection of the children in the city and the schools. The Metropolitan Transit Authority was to cooperate in arranging bus schedules; and the Parks Department was to assist in this planning as the children in Twain make heavy use of Park Department facilities.

The Analysis of Hart I

The De Jure-De Facto Distinction. "The *de jure-de facto* distinction is not helpful in a situation such as the one before us," said Judge Weinstein.[62] Although he went on to note the rule in the district for ten years had been that de facto segregation which could be avoided was unconstitutional,[63] he did maintain the de jure-de facto distinction. He found a de jure segregated system without racial motivation on the part of the school board.[64] Weinstein used a foreseeable-consequences test in reading a proof of de jure segregation. Although he relied on the test used by the Supreme Court in *Keyes v. Community School District 1,*[65] his *Hart I* decision further blurred the de facto-de jure distinction the Supreme Court confusingly retained in *Keyes.*[66] While *Keyes* spoke of the deliberate racial segregation in the context of Denver schools, the Court did not decide whether intentional action leading foreseeably to discrimination but without racial motivation was also de jure segregation. So, at least in the majority's opinion, there is still a distinction, albeit unclear, between de jure and de facto segregation.

The circuit courts have split over whether a plaintiff must prove (1) that the school authorities had intentionally discriminated against minority students by practicing a deliberate policy of racial segregation (that is, a discriminating motive),[67] or (2) whether sufficient evidence of segregative purpose may be found in the foreseeability-of-segregative result of state action.[68] In the second, proof of motivation is not required. In review of *Hart,* the second circuit court said:

> The question is simply by what standards state action is to be judged, whether on the foreseeable consequences of acts or on an indispensable finding that the act or omission was racially motivated. We believe that the question has not been settled authoritatively by the Supreme Court.[69]

62. Hart I, *supra* note 1, at 728.

63. Branche v. Board of Education of Town of Hempstead, 204 F. Supp. 150, 153 (E.D.N.Y. 1962).

64. Judge Weinstein said that since the school authorities did not have "any intent or desire that Mark Twain be segregated . . . the school officials cannot be charged with racial prejudice."

65. 413 U.S. 189 (1973).

66. In maintaining the de jure-de facto distinction, Justice Brennan in *Keyes* noted that "petitioners apparently concede for the purposes of this case that in the case of a school system like Denver's, when no statutory dual system has ever existed, plaintiffs must prove not only that segregated schooling exists, but also that it was brought about or maintained by intentional state action." 413 U.S. at 198.

67. Johnson v. San Francisco Unified School District, 500 F.2d 349 (9th Cir. 1974); Soria v. Oxnard School District Board of Trustees, 488 F.2d 579 (9th Cir. 1973); *cert. denied* 416 U.S. 951-52 (1974).

68. Oliver v. Michigan State Board of Education, 368 F. Supp 143 (W.D. Mich. 1973); *aff'd.* 508 F.2d 178 (6th Cir. 1974); Morgan v. Kerrigan, 509 F.2d (1st Cir. 1974).

69. 512 F.2d 37 (2nd Cir. 1974). In late 1976 and early 1977 the Supreme Court began to authoritatively settle the issue by requiring intent on the part of the government bodies

But the second circuit court upheld the use of the foreseeable consequence test to find de jure segregation in *Hart*.[70]

The Interactive Theory of State Action. In finding state complicity in actions relating to the segregated school, Judge Weinstein used an interactive theory of state action in which the state as a whole is seen as the responsible party due to the activities of its discreet agencies and organs. This approach has been used in other desegregation of education cases.[71]

Though the interactive theory is an innovative and useful approach for determining liability, it creates tremendous difficulties at the remedial stage. The interactive approach raises the spectre of an overwhelming supervisory task when the court grants equitable relief. Not only is the court responsible for dealing with the school system and its bureaucracies, but it thrusts itself into the politics of other administrative agencies and brings upon itself a burdensome amount of additional freight. In such sociological and political areas, the more expansive remedial role a court takes, the more legislative in effect its decisions become. Also, the court's orders are perceived by the public as political rather than judicial judgments.

Judge Weinstein based his powers to restructure Coney Island on the inherent equitable powers of a court to remedy constitutional wrongs and upon his expansive view of state action, which brought into his decretal power any and all state bodies.

The Relationship Between Housing and School Segregation. The relationship between housing and school segregation is a difficult matter of proof and harder still in implementation of a remedy. Judge Weinstein quoted general inclusions of government agencies' actions in the 1930s to 1950s which promoted segregated neighborhoods. These references demonstrated that at one time federal practices did locate public housing and federal mortgage guarantees in certain areas and deny them in others, with a knowledge of foreseeable racial consequences.[72] However, the court combined former federal housing policies with recent state and city actions and found the foreseeable consequences of which would increase the minority populations in central Coney Island.

---

accused of segregative actions. *See e.g., Indiana Board of School Commissioners v. Buckley,* New York Times, January 26, 1977, at 1, col. 5; Austin Independent School District v. United States, 45 U.S.L.W. 3413 (December 7, 1976); Pasadena City Board of Education v. Spangler, 427 U.S. 424 (1976). *See also* Washington v. Davis, 426 U.S. 229 (1976).

70. *See* Hart II, *supra* note 2, at 752.

71. U.S. v. Texas Education Agency, 467 F.2d 848, 863 (5th Cir. 1972); Swann v. Charlotte-Mecklenburg Board of Education, 379 F. Supp. 1102, 1107 (W.D.N.C. 1974); Bradley v. Milliken, 484 F.2d 215, 222 (6th Cir. 1973).

72. *De Facto School Segregation and the "State Action" Requirement: A Suggested New Approach,* 48 Ind. L.J. 304 (1973); Goodman, *De Facto School Segregation: A Constitutional and Empirical Analysis,* 60 Cal. L. Rev. 275, 320 (1972).

But the causes of segregated housing may be more complex than Judge Weinstein or others are willing to admit. As Justice Stewart said in *Bradley v. Milliken:*

> It is this essential fact of a predominantly Negro school population in Detroit—caused by unknown and perhaps unknowable factors such as in-migration, birth rates, economic changes, or cumulative acts of private racial fears—that accounts for the "growing core of Negro schools." A "core" that has grown to include virtually the entire city. The constitution simply does not allow federal courts to attempt to change that situation, unless and until it is shown that the state, or its political subdivisions, have contributed to cause the situation to exist.[73]

One problem with Weinstein's initial decree is that the factors mentioned above are still unknown as they relate to Coney Island. They were not introduced into evidence by counsel. The court proceeded upon a series of assumptions based on other case conclusions about other cities, and more general nonacademic studies that implied that racially imbalanced housing is a contributing cause of racial segregation in the schools.[74]

Hart I may have overestimated the demographic permanence of communities once they achieved a certain ethnic or racial mix. Public and private housing create a long-term physical imprint on the community landscape. Yet it is less certain that the composition of communities themselves remain the same even if they become predominantly minority. As Justice Burger said, "It does not follow that communities served by such systems will remain demographically stable, for in a growing mobile society, few will do so."[75] One-time federal and state housing practices may have had foreseeable segregative effects and channeled minorities into certain communities and away from others. The foreseeable effect of present construction and neutral policies of housing authorities may cause a disproportionate number of minorities to reside in the new public housing. But will this minority concentration be permanent? In contrast to other cities, New York's communities have changed greater and integrated more.[76]

73. 418 U.S. 717, at 756 n.2.

74. Aside from cases mentioned *supra* note 71, the court cited United States Commission on Civil Rights, Racial Isolation in the Public Schools; the Coleman Report, Equality of Educational Opportunity (1966); and the lower court's decision in *Milliken v. Bradley,* which has been criticized for its assumptions of the relationship between housing and school segregation. *See* Wolf, Social Science Testimony, *supra* note 51.

75. Milliken v. Bradley, 418 U.S. at 731-32.

76. Reynolds Farley has used an "index of dissimilarity" to measure the extent of racial segregation. The numerical value of the index represents the proportion of either whites or blacks who would have to shift from one area to another to effect complete integration of the residential areas of a city. If a city were completely integrated so that all neighborhoods or subareas has an identical racial composition, the value of the index would be zero. If residential segregation were so pervasive that all blacks lived in exclusively black areas and all whites in exclusively white neighborhoods, the index would assume its maximum value,

The New York metropolitan area physically developed later than other cities. Queens and the suburbs, particularly those on Long Island, are post–World War II developments.[77] After World War II, the already extensive intra–New York City migration was extended to the suburbs. Migration patterns for immigrant groups in New York City have been from Manhattan to the outer boroughs to the suburbs.[78] While the post–World War II in-migration of blacks and Hispanics from the South and from Puerto Rico may have ended, one cannot with assurance say the same about the intra–New York City migration of these minority groups. They may soon follow the migration patterns of other New York City ethnic groups.[79] What is certain is that New York City has been a transient city. Communities have been changing, and to assume that Coney Island will remain as it has if it becomes overwhelmed by minorities ignores the trends of the past. In any case there was no introduction of testimony in *Hart* as to New York City's residential mobility.

Judge Weinstein based the affirmative responsibility of the housing authority to promote integration on *Otero v. New York City Housing Authority*, which was cited for the proposition that the housing authority had an affirmative duty to integrate, constitutional and statutory in origin, which took precedence over the housing authority's own administrative priority policy and procedures.[80]

---

100. Reynolds Farley, *Residential Segregation and Its Implications for School Integration*, 39 Law and Contemporary Problems 164–65 (1975).

Of the thirty cities surveyed, New York had the fifth lowest segregation index (54). Only Fort Lauderdale (43); Norfolk (16); Oklahoma City (25); and San Francisco (20)—all following court-ordered desegregation plans—had lower indexes of segregation. Cities with higher indexes included Boston (74); Chicago (93); Dallas (89); Detroit (78); Los Angeles (87); Minneapolis (71); Philadelphia (81); St. Louis (92); Seattle (62); and Washington (81). Five years previously New York's segregation index was 52. Several other cities had lowered their segregation indexes or kept them constant in that period. *See* Farley, *Residential Segregation, supra.*

77. Glazer & Moynihan, Beyond the Melting Pot (1963).

78. *Id.*

79. A difference with the minority group migration into Coney Island compared to other groups' moves to the outer boroughs and to suburbs was that they were not the socially mobile, but welfare, families. Central Coney Island became a dumping ground for welfare and problem families. A second distinction was that the in-migration into Coney Island was through direct government assistance rather than the result of private action.

80. The issue in *Otero v. New York City Housing Authority* was whether the housing authority, in selecting tenants for a public housing project, was required to adhere to its regulation which would give first priority to present and former occupants of the urban renewal site upon which the project was constructed despite its contention that the effect of adherence to its regulation would be to create a nonwhite "pocket ghetto" that would operate as a racial tipping factor causing white residents to take flight. The court disagreed with the district court's interpretation of the housing authority's duty to integrate. Integration is not viewed as a "one-way street" limited to introduction of nonwhite persons into a predominantly white community. The authority is obligated to take affirmative steps to promote racial integration even though this may in some instances not operate to the immediate advantage of some nonwhite persons. The housing authority was entitled to show that adherence to its regulation would conflict with this duty. 484 F.2d at 1125.

The court also held that the fact that the primary intention of the Fair Housing Act of 1968 was to benefit minority groups does not mean that the affirmative duty to integrate

Otero is useful for analyzing *Hart*. One issue was left unresolved in *Otero* when the case was remanded back to the district court—a determination of what was the size of "the community" affected.[81]

A similar question in *Hart* is: How do you delimit the boundaries of "community" when District 21 and even Coney Island itself is overwhelmingly white? Only in certain sections do minorities predominate. How large a concentration of a particular ethnic group in how large an area can be allowed to develop as a result of an effect of government policies to renew housing?[82] Judge Weinstein initially felt that central Coney Island needed to be refertilized with white middle-income families. However, as plaintiffs' attorney suggested in January of 1974 and the intervenors later argued, white areas of District 21 could be "refertilized" with minority families.[83] The courts have clearly stressed the moral and legal imperative of integration as a national policy. But a question remains. How does the responsibility to integrate balance with other responsibilities of government, such as urban renewal and providing decent housing for the poor? These are broad social, political, and moral questions that need careful consideration by the legislative or executive branches, which are best suited to institute and execute such policies.

The Use of Social Science Evidence. Perhaps the major difficulty in proving the relationship between housing and school segregation is the type and quality of evidence needed to be introduced. Factual information about the case in hand, the traditional type of evidence introduced in desegregation of education cases, is particularly useful for the liability stage, for specific actions and inactions with obvious results can be documented in the case study leading to the court's decision.

A second type of social science evidence, more applicable to the housing situation—but more difficult to fit within the customary framework of evidence—is that which examines the causes of residential segregation and the linkages between housing and school segregation.[84] While in education it may be possible to develop valid cause-and-effect conclusions by considering evidence only for the case at hand, the approach is less valuable in the housing

public housing should not be given effect where it would deprive such groups of available and desirous housing. *Id.* at 1134.

To the extent that the housing authority regulation conflicted with the duty to integrate, the regulation would have to yield, but on the other hand, absent a showing of such conflict, the authority could not disregard its regulation where the effect would be to violate the due process rights of former site residents who relied upon it. *Id.* at 1135.

81. *Otero* was settled out of court before the district judge held a hearing and ruled on the issue of community.

82. *See* Swann v. Charlotte-Mecklenburg Board of Education, 402 U.S. 1, 23–24 (1971).

83. *See* letter of James Meyerson to Hyman Bravin, January 1974, on file, national office of the NAACP.

84. Karl E. Taeuber, a demographer, has differentiated between these two types of evidence. *Demographic Perspectives on Housing and School Segregation,* 21 Wayne L. Rev. 833 at 846 (1975). Of the second type he says:

area where there are limits to the conclusions of evidence drawn from a single historical case. This second type of evidence, appropriate to the housing situation, attempts to draw a number of probabilistic consequences and conclusions from a series of hypotheses.

In *Hart,* neither counsel introduced this more sophisticated method of proof. Even if counsel were willing and such proof were at hand, the adversary process is not the most appropriate forum for the introduction of this sort of evidence. Eleanor Wolf in analyzing the introduction of social science testimony and demographic changes in residential patterns, in *Bradley v. Milliken,* on which Judge Weinstein relied, noted that the presentation of evidence was by the plaintiffs only, and dealt with a selective presentation of issues and narrow perspective offered in the testimony.[85] The weakness of evidence became more telling, says Wolf, during the remedy stage when the plans for desegregation were developed to some extent on the basis of inadequately verified hypotheses:

> Since legal advantage, rather than sociological relevance, governed the choice of material to be presented, there was no testimony which reflected the studies of scholars who attribute much greater importance to the economic ability of blacks, or who attach great significance to black social class distribution in accounting for the residential preference of whites. There was no testimony which emphasized the similarities, rather than the differences, between blacks' residential behavior and that of other ethnic groups; indeed, no expert who testified appeared to define black Americans in these terms.[86]

Similar criticisms could be made about the evidence introduced in *Hart.* There was no reference to research, or to a review of the continuing trends of social relationships among ethnic groups despite cultural assimilation. Nor was there in-depth analysis on the causes of racial transition in urban neighborhoods. In the housing situation, where there are so many more individual transactions and subtle relationships, there is a need for the second type of empirical evidence to analyze the complexities of these questions.

The initial decision assumed that the continuing high degree of racial separation in residential patterns was due principally to individual acts reinforced by

---

Here the factual content includes material outside the nominal domain of the case, such as data on other cities, and on race relations in the United States. The interpretation of these data has the distinct character of empirical social science—not simply deductive logic, but a complex interplay of hypotheses and evidence. One of the dividing lines between the traditional historian and the comparative social scientist is that the social scientist wants to study a universe of events that vary among themselves in several dimensions; while the historian prefers to accumulate additional knowledge about the case at hand, in as many dimensions as contribute to human understanding.

Id. at 847.

85. *See* E. Wolf, *supra* note 51.

86. *Id.* at 3–4.

government actions and private discrimination as opposed to other factors, such as sources of employment, quality of education sources, relations between the two, or economic factors. For instance, the Warbasse and Luna Houses in eastern Coney Island are overwhelming white private housing virtually excluding minority families because of financial reasons. The Sea Gate community is similar.

If we are correct in assuming that proof of relationship between housing and school segregation required a different kind of evidence, more attuned to the methodological rigors of modern social science, we believe that the adversary method offends the most fundamental characteristics of scientific inquiry.[87] The difference between intellectual inquiry and the adversary method is summed up by Barrington Moore:

> If a defense lawyer is suddenly surprised by a piece of evidence as an argument turned up by the prosecution, he is never supposed to say: "My, I had never thought of that! It's a good point and my client must be guilty." On the other hand, that is exactly what an intellectually honest scholar is supposed to do under the circumstances.[88]

If any judge could pierce the complexities of the housing issue, it would be Jack B. Weinstein. Yet such technical social science studies are beyond the ken of the normal trial judge. At one point Judge Weinstein remarked he would spend the summer reading works on education. But the sheer volume of educational studies, not including the sociological and demographic work relating to the housing area, resulted in Judge Weinstein eventually citing the more popular studies of integration, education, and equality of educational opportunity. Judge Weinstein also rejected the appointment of a master, prior to the finding of liability, to assist in uncovering the facts or to evaluate the evidence.

IMPLEMENTING THE DECISION

The Appointment of a Special Master

Judge Weinstein had ordered all the parties and third-party defendants to submit plans by March 1, 1974. The decision created great consternation for the community school board. Until the decree, the majority of the school board had refused to allow black pupils from central Coney Island to attend schools in the overwhelmingly white Bensonhurst and Gravesend communities.[89]

87. *Id.* at 15.

88. Quoted by Michael Katz in *The Unmasking of Dishonest Pretensions: Toward an Interpretation of the Role of Social Science in Constitutional Litigation,* American Sociologist, June 1971, at 55–56.

89. One month prior to the initial decree, the closing of Mark Twain and the distribution of its student body to other District 21 schools was voted down at a board meeting. *See* Zelon Interview, *supra* note 37.

The *Hart* decision raised a spectre of widespread forced busing with unfore-seen consequences that threatened the board members personally and politically. Allen Zelon first conceived of the idea of converting Mark Twain into a special school, which would centralize all District 21. The plan offered the beauty of integrating Mark Twain without disrupting other district school patterns, and without causing the turmoil expected from widespread busing.

Zelon then had to convince Bravin, his fellow board members, and the dis-trict superintendent of schools, Bartelo Peluso. Bravin immediately recognized the attractiveness of the plan and became an ally. The district superintendent was initially neutral. He had been a junior high school principal and feared the plan's impact upon the district's other junior high schools. The most important battle was convincing the school board. To the board, the attractiveness was that the magnet concept was a plan of least disruption. And for board members, it was politically the least damaging. The board agreed surprisingly quickly. Zelon convinced Vincent Fonti, the most outspoken anti-integrationist, and Mrs. Aquila.[90]

Zelon pushed for board unanimity because he felt without it the plan could not succeed. The board did give unanimous support, and throughout the im-plementation process, unwaveringly supported the magnet school concept.[91]

The plan as submitted to Judge Weinstein on March 1, 1974 would make Mark Twain an integrated but somewhat underutilized school for gifted and talented students drawn from throughout the district. Only one class would occupy the school in 1974 and full utilization of Twain would not begin until 1975.[92]

The plaintiffs submitted six possible educational models designed by Pro-fessor Dodson, which outlined in broad terms, methods of desegregating the school. They expressed preference for the Model II plan, which focused on the use of busing to equalize utilization of all the middle schools in the district and would bring the ratio of white-to-minority students within each school into general alignment with the ratio within the district as a whole. Under the Model II plan, the burden of busing would be allocated more evenly between white and minority schools than under the school board's plan, although minority students would still be bused more than whites. The Model II plan provided for nearly equal minority percentages and utilization in each junior and intermediate school in the district.[93]

The submissions by the other parties to the action were less detailed. The chancellor supplied two "feeder patterns" which met the literal terms of the

90. *Id.*
91. When the board was to vote on the question of supporting the magnet school, one member was ready to back down, but the others leaned on her and got the unanimous support. The board gave continuous unanimous support to the idea of the magnet school. For Zelon, most of the implementation battle was then won. *Id.*
92. The school board resolution relating to the magnet plan can be found at 383 F. Supp. at 771.
93. The Model II plan is described in 383 F. Supp. at 772.

court's orders. However, he disavowed the patterns as "fraught with educationally unsound practices."[94] The chancellor's plan was so unimaginative that children living across the street from I.S. 303 would be bused to Mark Twain and children living across the street from Mark Twain would be transported to I.S. 303.[95]

The police department submitted a plan to protect children on their way to and from school against intruders in the schools during school hours. The Metropolitan Transportation Authority offered a schedule of their available transportation and the Department of Parks said they would fix the showers and comfort stations in the park next to the school.

From the housing authorities no definite proposals were received beyond an expression by the housing officials at each level that they would cooperate.[96] The housing agencies had met with each other but were unable to reach a consensus. New York State Commissioner of Housing and Community Renewal Lee Goodwin claimed an inability to deal with the housing problems in the Mark Twain area. She said that the present tenants' population was stable, and that a busing plan would undermine that stability. White tenants would move out. Other white families would refuse to move into the area.[97]

The New York City Housing and Development Administration submitted descriptions of a variety of programs, none of them prepared specifically for the lawsuit. Edward Logue, president of the Urban Development Corporation, a state agency, declared that to achieve housing integration in such form as to provide stable integration of the public schools

> would be necessary to make housing competitively attractive to white families as compared to other options available to them and *equally important* [emphasis in original] provide a community setting for such housing which offers the level of municipal services, shopping areas, and plain safety in the streets that will make young white families, not only willing, but eager to move into such a community.[98]

Logue added that no one entity of government had the resources to accomplish the "refertilization" of Coney Island. Thus the court through the aid of a master

94. Hart I, *supra* note 1 at 759.
95. Nor did the central board's submission solve problems such as the imminent tipping of I.S. 303 and the overcrowding of other District 21 junior high schools.
96. Nancy LeBlanc, attorney for intervenor residents of Coney Island, believes that the housing authorities were cooperative because they did not realize the financial impact of *Hart I.* When they realized that *Hart* would cost them money and force a shift in their priorities and policies, they opposed the suggested remedy. Interview with Nancy LeBlanc, June 2, 1975.
97. The commissioner spoke of the crippling inflation and lack of essential funds that would forbid that agency from moving into a leadership position. Judge Weinstein acidly noted that removal and displacement of problem families was due to the state's action in building projects in eastern Coney Island. *See* Hart II, *supra* note 2 at 762.
98. Hart I, *supra* note 1 at 760.

should undertake the burden of devising a joint plan and in the process examine the multitude of laws, regulations, and practices needed.[99]

S. William Green, regional administrator of the Department of Housing and Urban Development, testified that hundreds of millions of dollars of federal housing monies had been impounded by the U.S. Office of Management and the Budget, making it impossible without court intervention to use federal funds to improve housing and integrate the community.[100] Green also pinpointed a problem area on which the special master would later focus—the city's right-to-return regulation.[101]

Green said that the federal requirements only mandated that relocation be provided within the municipality, but not necessarily to the particular renewal site.[102] He expressed concern at the number of problem-ridden families on welfare placed in publicly aided buildings in Coney Island. He also felt that it was difficult to integrate in such a way for housing to affect the school population.

During the March hearings, Weinstein had decided to appoint a court master to consider the various plans and to evaluate them.[103] The judge asked for a

99. *Id.* at 768.
100. *Id.* at 761.
101. Discussed *infra* p. 000. The right-to-return regulation accentuated the integration problems because it restrained the housing authority's latitude in selection of tenants.
102. *Id.*
103. *See* Record on Appeal, Vol. 6, at 1434.

My conception of a Master here would be a Master to consider the various plans presented and their interreaction, because, as you recognize that has to be considered, with the hope that very promptly, based upon what the parties have so effectively put together, a report will be available which would permit the Court to make a general order providing for specific plans in fairly general terms, of course, and a final judgment which can be appealed from if anybody wants to appeal from it.

I don't conceive of the Master having any powers to supervise day-to-day operations at all, or to make any detailed orders. There is ample authority for a Master of this kind, Rule 53 of the *Rules of Civil Procedure* furnish explicit authority. Rule 706 of the *Proposed Rules of Evidence* on Court-appointed experts expresses both common law and other authority.

The power of the Chancellor in Equity, whose powers the Federal District Court Judges have inherited, includes the power to appoint Masters. Masters have been appointed in many instances. One, for example, is *Swann v. Charlotte-Mecklenburg Board of Education*, 343 F. Supp. 667 (W.D.N.C. 1965); *affirmed* 369 F.2d 29 (Fourth Circuit, 1966).

I do not think that there is any question of power. I do not think there is any question that it would be undesirable for this Court to become heavily involved in examining records of individual departments and divisions of the City, State, and Federal Government. A Master would have the advantage of being able to proceed informally by interviewing people and looking at records and perhaps meeting with people so that the various proposals can be measured and integrated so they work.

Part of our problem is that we have so many different units which want to do the job properly and want to be helpful, that they cannot.

I think a Master would be quite useful in further developing these plans and in reporting to the Court—and that is all the Master could do—proposals for handling it expeditiously.

If counsel object, I will provide that he may not hold hearings and issue subpoenas without the Court's consent, because I do not think that that is necessary. I think we

submission of names. Only Elliot Hoffman, the corporation counsel, objected to the appointment of a master on the grounds that "this does not lend itself to the judicial solution."[104] In a supplemental opinion issued April 2, 1974, Judge Weinstein announced the appointment of Curtis J. Berger, professor of real property at Columbia Law School.[105] He ordered the special master to formulate a "joint plan" and to consult informally with the various parties, with and without the presence of counsel. The master's report should include a comprehensive plan dealing not only with the elimination of segregation of Mark Twain, but also with housing, nonresidential development, community, social welfare, recreational, transportation, and protective facilities near the Coney Island neighborhood.[106] The special master was directed to furnish a final report no later than July 1, 1974. A hearing on that report was scheduled for July 15, 1974.

Although Berger was acceptable to all parties once the judge had determined to appoint a master, the community school board had preferred a Brooklyn resident, someone with more in-depth knowledge of the community. Berger is Lawrence A. Wein Professor of Real Estate Law at Columbia and an expert in the relationship between law and real property. His most analogous position was as chairman of the redevelopment agency in Englewood, New Jersey at a time when that city was divided over the construction of low-income housing in middle-income areas. At the time of appointment, Judge Weinstein said:

> I asked Curt to take the job because I was impressed by his grasp of the whole real estate problem as it relates to society. . . . He's a person who can work with people as well as ideas.[107]

In the next four months, Berger expended a tremendous amount of time and energy in Coney Island. Endless hours were spent, talking to almost anyone who wanted a hearing, walking the streets, visiting the school and housing projects, reassuring parents.

On a personal level, Berger was described as gentle, decent, likeable, and various other encomia. But after his report came out, he was described by many as naive, without a sense of politics, and a typical academic liberal.

As Berger plunged into Coney Island, the community began to react to the initial decision. Letters in support of and against the decision began to pour

---

have enough materials available and I think whatever else is needed can be obtained informally, since counsel have been extremely cooperative.

Id. at 1862.

104. *Id.* at 1865.

105. Reprinted, 383 F. Supp. 758.

106. *Id.* at 767–68. Defendant school board and other government bodies were ordered to cooperate with the master and to provide him with office space, information, and other assistance. The Central Board of Education would assume the master's expenses.

107. New York Times, Biographical Edition, April 1974, at 478.

into Judge Weinstein from residents and parents. What is striking about this correspondence is the sincerity of the letters and a style and tone usually reserved for petitions to elected legislators.

Opposition to the initial decision also began to unfold in District 21. Senator James Buckley conveniently held hearings at P.S. 97 in Bensonhurst. The purpose of his hearings was to give the senator guidance on anti-busing proposals before the Congress. Encouraged by Buckley, twenty speakers assailed the initial Weinstein decree.[108] The senator said:

> I do not believe it is the job of the courts to define social goals. The parents of children in this district must not be deprived by judicial adventurism of their God-given rights as parents for the ultimate responsibility for the education and welfare of their children.[109]

Fortunately, the school board was uninvolved in this incitement against the decision. The principal pro-integration speaker was Zelon, whose comments were interrupted by boos, hisses, and shouts of "sit down." But even Evelyn Aquila, then president of the board, said that while she was opposed to forced busing, "it's not an easy problem with an easy solution." She also told Buckley that she wished his voting record on federal aid to education was better.

Intervention by Affected Site Residents

The most surprising voices of protest were not from the white middle class, but from minority residents, a class of nearly 1,000 low-income black and Puerto Rican families. They were occupants in the Coney Island Development Program Project area who might be displaced by urban renewal and who had relocation rights under federal and local law. These protesters were threatened with relocation out of the Coney Island area if the neighborhood was "refertilized" with white families. These residents would be unwelcome in another community.

An application for intervention by this class of residents was made on June 4, in the middle of the master's deliberations. The applicants, represented by Nancy LeBlanc, an experienced housing attorney for Mobilization for Youth, argued that their rights might be impaired as a result of a court decision ordering a "reseeding" of public housing with white families. They feared that they would lose their right of return to housing within the urban renewal area. Without intervention, the applicants argued, they might be removed from Coney Island. Besides, no one in the lawsuit was representing their interests.

There were two groups represented in the intervening class: those adversely affected residents who had children in public schools; and a second group—site residents without children in school. In an interesting intellectual construction,

108. New York Times, April 16, 1974.
109. *Id.*

Judge Weinstein allowed as intervenors those with school children who might be affected by the housing report and also were affected by the court order involving schooling. The judge allowed as *amicus curiae* those members of the class who could be affected by the housing report alone.[110]

In his earlier functions as master, Berger had developed a good informal working relationship with all attorneys. However, when Nancy LeBlanc entered the case, she adopted a much more adversary role toward him. This in turn affected Berger's relations with the other attorneys, particularly Meyerson.

Berger's relationship to Weinstein was always formal. He was assigned to gather information for a report and to submit it upon completion to the judge. There was no communication with the court in developing the plan or after the plan was submitted. Once Berger received his charge from the court, he was on his own.[111]

Report of the Special Master: Part I—The School Plan

This is Brooklyn in 1974, where ethnic surgery of the most delicate order is needed to preserve a fragile social order. The recommendations herein do not shirk the responsibilities of integration; they do provide a reasonable framework within which it can function.

On July 1, 1974, Berger submitted his report on the school plan. He adopted and expanded upon the community school board's proposal for a magnet school, which would be attractive to white parents who would send their children because of the special courses offered there. Mark Twain would become a school for gifted and talented children, modeled after a magnet high school in the district.[112] The advanced instruction courses, the SP and SPE programs, would be phased out of other middle schools in the district.[113]

110. *Amicus curiae* (friend of the court) is a bystander who interposes during a trial and volunteers information upon some matter of law in regard to which the judge is doubtful or mistaken; he may also remind the court that a legal matter has escaped its notice. The *amicus curiae* is neither a party to the action nor interested in or bound by the decision. In contrast, an *intervenor* has an interest in the outcome of the case and specifically applies to be made a party to the action. The intervenor voluntarily interposes in an action to protest an interest of his or her own, which neither the plaintiff nor the defendant is interested in protecting.

111. He never met with the judge *in camera,* but only in open court. This formal procedure was quickly made apparent to Berger. Shortly after his appointment, the special master discovered that the housing authority was attempting to fill one of the housing projects with blacks who were neither former nor present residents of Coney Island. He contacted Judge Weinstein, who told him to seek a restraining order in open court, which he did. Interview with Curtis Berger, June 30, 1975.

112. The John Dewey High School.

113.

"SP is a program in which qualified children are able to complete the normal three-year middle school program in two years. Eligible children are those who in the sixth grade have achieved a reading score of 8.9 and a math score of 8.0 on the City-wide

The basic difference between the school board's plan and the master's was that the latter would admit children talented in areas such as wood and metal skills, typing, shorthand, athletics, music, and art. Only 10 percent of the children in the district's SP and SPE programs were minority.[114] Admitting talented as well as gifted children would draw many neighborhood children into Twain and meet the integration guidelines set by the court.[115]

Berger was sensitive to intraschool tracking. To allow tracking to develop, he felt, would be violative of desegregation. He suggested that students of all abilities attend basic courses together. Tracking would be eliminated through flexible programming.[116] Combined with the attempts to eliminate tracking would be a program of individualized instruction, tailoring instruction to fit a particular student's needs.[117]

The special master agreed with the school board's proposal of building up the student body to full utilization over a three-year period, rather than opening the school at its maximum utilization in September of 1975. Because of the experimental nature of a magnet type school, Berger suggested that the full utilization rate should be only 60 percent of capacity or a total number of students of 1,050.[118] A second reason for a staggered schedule of utilization was to allow the school to gain acceptance in the community and to work out problems. Under the staggered schedule, as of September 1975, 350 students of seventh-grade age would attend the school. At least 250 students would be majority and 100 would be minority. In each entering class, the percentage of minority students would equal the district average. In the second and third years,

---

aptitude tests, and whose maturity for an accelerated course has been confirmed by teachers and guidance counselors. SPE is an enriched three-year middle school program, in which the children take Earth Science, normally a high school course, in the ninth grade, receive advanced foreign language credit and are eligible for certain art and music courses. The qualifications for SPE are generally the same as those for SP. The decision between SP and SPE is made by parents of eligible children, upon consultation with school officials. Occasionally, the school will override a parent's decision to opt for the SP on the grounds that a child is not mature enough for a two-year program. Both programs carry considerable prestige for both parents and children.

Report of the Special Master: Part I—The School Plan, at 8 [hereinafter cited as S.M., Part I].

114. *Id.* at 19.

115. *See* Zelon Interview, *supra* note 37.

116. S.M., Part I, *supra* note 113, at 17–18. Children admitted to Mark Twain for their talents would still have most of their basic courses with the gifted children. They would have separate classes in areas of their particular skills. *See* Zelon Interview, *supra* note 37.

117. Individualized instruction is the attempt to get learning theory in harmony with the individual differences of each student. It is based on the two major premises that students learn at different rates, and that learning is incremental and sequential. It attempts to custom-tailor instruction to fit a particular student at a particular point in time. *See* S.M., Part I, *supra* note 113, at 19.

118. *Id.* at 39. The experimental nature would require a lower integration rate than normal because of the flexible programs requiring smaller class size and a need for more classrooms due to the variety of courses offered.

the school would add a new seventh grade of not fewer than 400 students so that by 1977/78, the school would be a three-year junior high school with its maximum student body of 1,050.

Under Berger's plan, the other middle schools in the district would be integrated as Coney Island children who did not qualify as either gifted or talented would be bused to them.

In the school portion of the report, Berger also elaborated upon funding sources, funding problems, the need for excellent guidance counselors and a qualified staff, physical needs in the area, and the need to secure the environment and the role of parents and the board.[119]

Berger was most sensitive to the politics of the community and to the limits within which integration was possible without provoking a widespread withdrawal of white children from the public school system. The key problem was encouraging white parents to send their children to Mark Twain. Berger offered a carrot and two stick approach. The carrot was the educational attractiveness of the magnet school. The first stick was the phasing out of all SP and SPE programs in the district's other intermediate schools. The second and more forceful stick was the recommendation for a back-up plan, Dodson's Model II, which called for widespread busing throughout the district to equalize the majority-minority proportions at all schools. Berger recommended that if the magnet school concept was unsuccessful in integrating Mark Twain, then the Model II plan would be introduced.[120]

Berger approached the school plan with political and social sophistication. Politically he knew that he needed the support of the school board, and their pressure against the central board of education. More importantly, he wanted to allay the fears of the community. In implementing any plan, Berger knew that the community board would be the primary force in making the plan a success or failure.

Sociologically, the master was aware of the social fragility of this part of

119. Berger urged that public and private sources be utilized to obtain extra funding. He suggested that admission be extended to children who did not necessarily reside in District 21, which would extend the sources of available funding. One result of this policy is that several of the eligible minority students do not come from the district. *Id.* at 41.

120. The Dodson proposal (Model II plan) as to Mark Twain is described as follows:

Raise utilization to 30 percent which would require 1,396 students. "Other" enrollment at present of 135 would be augmented by 791 if minimum percentage were achieved. 577 of these would be sent from the lower end of the P.S. 281 zone. One hundred-ten would be transferred from the 228 zone. This would leave the arrangement short of the guidelines standard by only 114 students.

Present black enrollment of 309 is 57 above the guideline requirement. The Puerto Rican enrollment of 239 is 51 above the guideline specification.

These three imbalances with regard to the guidelines are the result of not compensating for fuller utilization of the schools in the "Others" areas. These could be handled administratively. If "CR" class were removed from the building it would reduce the black by 27, the Puerto Rican by 26 and the "Others" by 8.

See Hart II, *supra* note 2, at 772.

Brooklyn. Berger said that "the desegregation of Mark Twain must be considered within the context of demographics."[121] He knew that too rapid a change in the ethnic composition of the district's schools would not be the only factor to cause an acceleration of white flight, but it would be an important one.

> It is inescapable that both the number and the percentage of minority students will increase within the foreseeable future, not impossibly, to to some irretrievable "tipping point" beyond which the ethnic composition of the District schools will cause the trends evident elsewhere in the City to become irresistible.[122]

Plans such as Model II would add to otherwise avoidable tensions, increase white flight, and make segregation harder, if not impossible. The master felt that he not only had to recommend a short-term plan, but had a responsibility for the long term. He also developed a plan for the stabilization of I.S. 303 which also was reaching the "tipping point," and would jeopardize racial balance in the district.

The plaintiffs' reactions to the school plan were quick and strident. In written submissions, in testimony, and in a press release, the NAACP and Dan Dodson called Berger's plan "racist." It was a cruel, cheap shot. The charge also seemed a ploy to move evaluation of the plan from an educational to a political level.

Dodson felt that there was little experience to indicate that magnet schools were innovative educational programs that had ever drawn white students into minority areas. In testimony, he said that the plan was a blatantly racist solution because it forced half of the complainants to transfer out of neighborhood schools; it did nothing for minority children in terms of remedial programs, and was voluntary—a modified freedom-of-choice plan for majority students.[123] Minorities, he said, were all bused out in 1975, but white students were allowed to come into the school voluntarily over a three-year period. Furthermore, Dodson argued that the basic burden was on blacks. Nor did the plan meet the future problems of declining white enrollment, because it had exempted whites from involuntary assignments. The magnet program, said Dodson, was a glorified tracking system.[124]

Kenneth Clark's objection was basically that the solution was improper in that it was elitist and did not go to the issue of desegregation.[125] Clark felt that

---

121. *Id.* at 51.
122. *Id.* at 53. The "tipping point" is an unspecified percentage of concentration of minority residents in a given area that will cause white residents to flee. It has been legally recognized as a factor to be considered where avoidance of segregation is at issue. *See, e.g., Otero v. New York City Housing Authority,* 484 F.2d 1122 (2d Cir. 1973).
123. Trial Testimony of Dan Dodson, Record on Appeal, Vol. 2 at 470.
124. *Id.* at 473.
125. Trial Testimony of Kenneth Clark, *id.* at 469f–g.

the plan would really lead to a desegregated school with totally segregated mini-schools within it composed of elitist special classes.

In his testimony and in his report, Berger met Dodson's objections. He felt that widespread busing had to be the solution of last resort in today's emotional climate.[126] The Model II plan was too general, for it was devised without data on attendance loads, without plans for residential changes, and without data on long-term trends.

Under the magnet school plan, there was a marginal increase in the burden on blacks. Furthermore, whites would perceive a burden on them by having to go into Mark Twain special courses.[127] The Model II plan made absolutely no provision for educational benefits or for qualitative improvement.

It is ironic that Berger, the housing expert, was more successful in his school plan than in his housing proposals. His school plan was based on a pragmatic political reality, if perhaps an uncertain educational philosophy.[128] His housing plan was a skillful, creative technical proposal with little relationship to the political and economic atmosphere of the city.

Report of the Special Master: Part II—Housing and Physical Renewal. No one controverted that public housing in Coney Island had become increasingly imbalanced racially. Short of some drastic change of policy or conditions, the percentage of white children in housing authority projects would continue to decline. Reciprocally, the absolute and relative number of minority children attending public schools will rise sharply.[129] The special master's report, "Housing and Physical Renewal," predicted that "if existing housing, physical development, and human services policies continue unchanged, central Coney Island [could not] escape further segregation."[130]

Berger felt that the occupancy of *new* units with expected completion dates in April 1975 would determine whether racial balance was possible in Coney Island.[131] The housing authority, on its new and turnover rentals, achieved only 5 to 6 percent white tenancy.[132] One alternative Berger would not con-

126. S.M., Part I, *supra* note 113, at 3.

127. Trial Testimony of Curtis Berger, Record on Appeal, at 298.

128. Berger's plan was not involved with remedial and adjustment efforts for the very large number of minority students in the Coney Island area who would be bused to other district schools where students would be in need of remedial assistance. In achievement, they would be a numerical minority in these new schools. At Twain, even the court admitted that the school had initiated several good remedial programs for students. With the district's extra money going to the magnet school, one wonders what will be in store for minority students who need such assistance.

129. *See* Report of the Special Master: Part II—Housing and Physical Renewal, at 1 [hereinafter cited as S.M., Part II].

130. *Id.* at 5.

131. *Id.* at 7.

132. *Id.* at 11. Of the total number of children in Central Coney Island City housing projects, 771 (18 percent) were majority; 2105 (49 percent) were black; and 1406 (33 percent) were Puerto Rican. S.M., Part II, Table 2, at 4. And the percentage of white children occupying UDC state-funded projects was only 19.5 percent.

sider was a moratorium on renting to black families until enough white families could be found to desegregate the units.[133]

While the public housing in question was designed for all low-income families, the number of nonwhite families with qualifying incomes greatly exceeded the number of white families. Also, the citywide pool of eligible families who applied for public housing was not more than 10 percent white.

Berger's housing report presented a wide-ranging plan for the revitalization of Coney Island. The key to attracting white families to the area was the creation of a housing bargain to attract large numbers of middle-class (that is, whites) to move in. Other basic recommendations were: a speeding of urban renewal plans to create owner-occupied dwelling units, a relocation plan that meets the needs of an integrated community and the interests of site residents, and a vigorous code enforcement program directed against the tremendous amount of substandard housing in the area. This would lead to renovation or renewal of the property if it remained unsafe and dangerous.

He also suggested: early and continuous planning for all of Coney Island, the launching of an energetic promotion of Coney Island which would assist in marketing the area and improving its image, an expansion and coordination of social services programs to meet the area's human needs, the opening of an Office of Coney Island Planning and Development, and introduction of new shopping and transportation facilities.[134]

The Housing Bargain. Berger argued that segregation in central Coney Island housing could best be reduced by providing incentives for white middle-class families to move in. One technique would be to create a "housing bargain." This would enable middle-income families to rent apartments that they could not otherwise afford. Berger suggested two techniques: (1) lowering rents; and (2) raising maximum income-eligibility requirements. These could be facilitated by increasing housing subsidies.

By lowering the rental of a three-bedroom apartment, currently ranging from $265-$316 per month, to $220 per month, this housing bargain would induce families who were free to settle elsewhere into entering Coney Island.[135] Berger calculated that the cost of this rent subsidy would be as little as a total of $643,104 or $673.53 per unit.[136]

As an alternative to direct subsidy, Berger suggested raising the income-level eligibility while absorbing the corresponding increase in rent. Higher-income families would then be able to rent apartments in Coney Island. For example, under present housing authority guidelines, a family paying $250 per month

133. Aside from social objections to this policy, a moratorium would cause a substantial revenue loss while empty apartments were awaiting white tenants. Empty apartments in projects do not fare well physically as vandalism usually occurs.

134. *See* S.M., Part II, *supra* note 129 at iii-iv.

135. *Id.* at 22.

136. *Id. See also id.,* Table 10, at 26.

rent for public housing could not earn more than $12,000 annually (one-fourth of their salary for rent). Berger proposed to maintain the same rental of $250 per month, but allow a family earning up to $21,000 to rent the apartment. The family would only pay one-seventh of its salary for rent. The housing authority would absorb any increased costs. Thus the marketing program could reach well into the city's own employees, who otherwise had little incentive to reside within Coney Island.

Home Ownership. Berger also suggested that home ownership should be encouraged by the city because a financial and emotional commitment to the neighborhood makes for stability and the seeds of group activity. Home ownership would further the goal of bringing middle-income, child-bearing families into Coney Island. The master concluded that plans for the various housing projects would add at least 1,200 units of middle-income ownership housing and at least 500 new units of elderly housing to the Coney Island total.[137]

Physical Renewal. The remainder of Berger's report dealt with physical renewal and redevelopment of the Coney Island community itself. The master suggested the development of convenient commercial centers with the creation of a major shopping complex with a pedestrian mall. He recommended relocation of those tenants residing in unfit premises. The housing authority discouraged such hasty relocation. Such a plan, that required the housing authority to accept unlimited numbers of site families into Coney Island projects, forced them to relax their screening procedures aimed at limiting the number of problem families within a new project. Also, relocation, unless delicately undertaken, was a very political matter. With the site residents already in the case and mobilized to protest any change in housing policy, it was an invitation to disaster.

The Reaction of Housing Officials. Berger was ambushed by the city housing authorities. During his deliberations, the city officials often gave private assurances of their support to much of this thinking. Yet when his report was submitted to the court, they opposed it *in toto*. While much of the housing officials' disagreement was of a technical nature, their objections were overlaid with political and administrative reluctance as well. Generally, the housing authority rejected the housing solutions as unrealistic. They argued that merely raising the income base for those allowed to rent apartments was an insufficient incentive for attracting white middle-class families. White families with $30,000 incomes and small children who have to grow up in at least what is perceived as a racially segregated area would simply not move in. The implication behind the city's position was that most families would prefer to move into more expen-

137. *Id.* at 46.

sive housing elsewhere and permit their children to remain in predominantly white areas.

The housing authority pointed out that if income eligibility were raised to $17,000-$18,000, only middle-class blacks would move into Coney Island. Berger's incentive of no more than a 25 percent discount on rent, according to them, was clearly insufficient. Those who would be eligible under Berger's plan would prefer to obtain mortgages for small homes.[138]

The Housing and Development Administration was also disturbed by Berger's motion that the city should use its money to create a special housing bargain unavailable to the people already living in the involved area. This would be a complete about-face of the city's right-of-return policy.[139] Furthermore, there was a dispute between the city's position on right of return and the federal government's, hardly a propitious disagreement when cooperation between housing officials was needed.[140] It was also questionable that the federal government would allow a wider eligibility band to be stretched for Coney Island but retain former regulations intact elsewhere in the country. This was a political and administrative nightmare.

The housing authority accurately criticized the monetary incentives Berger offered, noting that they were not sufficient to induce people to live where they did not want to live. Berger's meticulous financial calculations were a poor substitute for correcting an area perceived as both racially segregated and physically debilitated. Basically, housing officials thought that changing perceptions of a community were more difficult than merely increasing the financial attractiveness. Perhaps they were the product of an academician's attempt to grope with implementation. One participant in the case said bitterly: "Berger was a typical academic liberal engaged in social engineering; he forgot that there were people at the end of the line."[141]

The cooperation of the housing agencies ended when they were faced with the financial implications of the special master's housing reports. The administrative and financial complications caused by the master's proposed restructuring of Coney Island led housing officials to suggest a shifting of the burden to levels of government other than their own.

Roger Starr said that the UDC projects should be turned into cooperatives to attract the middle class. The state would assume this financial burden.[142] Starr felt that the master's reports understated the full financial costs to the city. Even if they did not, there would be tremendous political pressures to offer

138. Interview with Elliot Hoffman, July 18, 1975.

139. Trial Testimony of Roger Starr, administrator of the New York City Housing and Development Administration. Record on Appeal, Vol. 6, at 563-69 [hereinafter cited as Starr Testimony].

140. *See* Trial Testimony of S. William Green, Record on Appeal.

141. LeBlanc Interview, *supra* note 96.

142. *See* Starr Testimony, *supra* note 139, at 613-33.

the same benefits in other areas of the city. The master's proposals could not be contained to Coney Island.

State and federal officials pleaded poverty and a need to allocate their resources for larger areas. There were $18.9 million in federal funds available for land acquisition in all of New York City. The master expected nearly $12 million to be spent in Coney Island, a politically impossible skewing of resources.[143]

There was a fear that the master's proposals would be treated as precedent by other courts with jurisdiction over other sections of the city or state and order similar rehabilitation to that area of the city. The potential financial costs to the city were limitless.[144] Also, while the UDC's and city's financial crises were in the distance, even in July 1974 it was clear that all government bodies were in need of fiscal retrenchment. Berger's plans seemed more appropriate to the Great Society programs of the 1960s than to the financial realities of 1974.

The housing report also presented administrative difficulties. Government housing agencies move only one way—slowly. Berger's goal of relocating more than 850 households in one year (2.5 families a day for 365 days) could not be reasonably attained given the bureaucratic sluggishness of housing authorities. Berger did not face the practical problem of mobilizing a large number of families that have lived in substandard housing for generations.

The element of time was a major factor. Berger minimized the time-consuming procedures that had to be followed before relocation and revitalization could be undertaken. City agencies had to approve the plans and authorize the appropriations of funds, municipal services, and developers for the projects. A proposal for a major clean-up often could not be quickly instituted, or even if it was, it could not serve to alter the perception of a slum once that perception had been created.[145] Physical renewal in Coney Island was not the quick, smooth procedure Berger presented.

143. Statement of S. William Green, New York Times, July 18, 1974.

144. Starr & Zuccotti, Response of Third-Party Defendant City of New York to Part II of the Report of the Special Master in *Hart v. Community School Board 21*, Record on Appeal, Vol. 2, 535, 539.

145. While Berger recognized that major urban renewal projects take many years (S.M., Part II, *supra* note 129, at 72), he dismissed this time-frame by declaring that Coney Island is no ordinary project. Yet he failed to acknowledge that necessary time-consuming procedures must be adhered to before efforts could be "immediately" undertaken. The City Planning Commission must approve of his plan; at least one month must elapse between the City Planning Commission's approval and the start of Board of Estimate public hearings on the plan. Then the Corporation Counsel must approve the resolutions. The Bureau of the Budget must authorize the charging of the condemnation to the city's capital budget.

Before this is done, HUD would have to approve the city's application for $12 million in NDP (urban renewal) funds needed to carry out the plan. Additionally, the city must obtain two appraisals of each property to be acquired; these must be approved by the Housing and Development Administration, the Corporation Counsel, and the Department of Real Estate. The Corporation Counsel must publish notice of the condemnation, notify each property-owner, and undertake the mechanics of title vesting. Following acquisition, HDA must complete relocation, obtain any requisite zoning changes, demolish buildings and prepare the

Glossing over the technical, administrative, and financial objectives, the political problems were insurmountable. Berger's notion that middle-income families from outside the community should get first preference would probably politically mobilize the minority community in central Coney Island for the first time. A major difficulty was limiting the proposal to Coney Island. As Housing Administrator Starr testified, there would be tremendous pressures to replicate in other poverty areas any programs introduced in Coney Island. The Coney Island redevelopment program would have a tremendous impact socially and politically in other communities. To expect that other neighborhoods would quietly accept the relocation of former site residents from Coney Island, all minority and many problem families, was unrealistic.

Housing officials justifiably feared the ripple effect of housing bargains and other redevelopment plans in other areas of the state and city. Other communities with more political muscle would demand to have their areas similarly benefited.

Even if the court ordered the housing remedy, there were no people in the local power structure in the community or in the housing agencies who would pressure for implementation. Thus the court would be completely isolated and forced to maintain a day-by-day supervision. In sensitive areas where courts are implementing a broad remedy, decisions which have great political and social ramifications need political and social support by those affected. This was missing in the housing report.

The Intervenor's Response. If the housing officials' response was hostile, the intervenors' could be termed vicious. Their objections were political and moral. The intervenors allied themselves with the plaintiffs' objections to the school plan, going so far as to call it "inherently racist."[146] More specifically objecting to Part II of the master's report, the intervenors claimed:

—Only 450 units of the new housing units would be set aside for site area families awaiting new housing in the Coney Island area.
—The people in Coney Island were presumed by the master to be "part of the problem."
—The master felt it appropriate for a court simply to order that a substantial number of families living and a part of that community be uprooted and moved to accommodate the beliefs of other members of the community that their presence is a threat.
—It was particularly objectionable that this position be put forth in regard to

---

sites. It must also find redevelopers and enter into land disposition agreements, which require City Planning Commission and Board of Estimate approval. It becomes clear that physical renewal in Coney Island is not a quick, smooth procedure.

146. Objections to Report of the Special Master Parts I and II Pursuant to Rule 53(e)(2) Fed.R.Civ.P.: The Intervenors' Response, Vol. II, Record on Appeal, at 479h.

minorities living in an area which is heavily white without regard to the fact that parts of the area are over 95 percent white.
—The special master made no suggestion of how to order integration of the areas which were 95 percent or more white.
—There was a denial of equal protection of blacks and Puerto Ricans who are treated as inferior, but a community of people who were predominantly black and Puerto Rican was prohibited.
—The special master failed to reorganize the policies underlying all the renewal and development in Coney Island.
—If one considered people ultimately more important than buildings, seawalls, and so on, then it might be appropriate before denying families the right to remain in Coney Island because they are "problems" to put some of the money to be spent on buildings into providing supportive services for these families.
—The problems would not disappear because the families are forced out of Coney Island. While Coney Island would be relieved of the problems, some other community will have to cope with them, "unless, of course, the Special Master intends that these people be sent to a desert island."[147]

These were heavy charges. There were overlaid with the threat, in a harsh tone, of endless litigation. The intervenors also suggested that the court lacked jurisdiction to enter an order requiring the implementation of such a proposal and that even if it had jurisdiction, the broad and sweeping nature of the proposal required submission to the political process for discussion, decision, and implementation and ought not to be ordered by a court.[148]

The intervenors pointed out that the issues raised in the housing report were so broad that they defied judicial competence to deal with them. The written submission was phrased in an emotional manner which, combined with well-prepared community representatives in the courtroom, raised a threat of disruption and even violence in the community if an attempt were made to implement the master's recommendations. Most importantly, the intervenors pointed out the broad, perhaps unanswerable, social policy questions raised in the report and the impossibility of containing its impact to Coney Island alone.

THE FINAL ORDER AND AFTERMATH

The Court as Institution with Limited Power

On July 26, 1974, four days after *Bradley v. Milliken* was handed down, Judge Weinstein issued his final order. He completely adopted the special master's magnet school plan, but ignored the housing proposals. Most striking about

147. *Id.* at 482–89.
148. *Id.* at 491, 493.

the final decision is its tone. The judge defined his own role in much more modest and limited terms:

> As institutions with limited powers, courts are mandated by law and tradition to interfere as little as possible in the work of other branches of government. So long as the Constitution and laws are not violated, state school officials must be afforded the broadest latitude to meet their educational responsibilities.[149]

After quoting the Supreme Court in *Bradley* for the deference to local school board judgment,[150] the judge cited a number of cases which held that local authorities retain wide discretion to choose among acceptable programs of desegregation.

Then, reviewing the proposed plans and objections to them, the court said that it was bound to accept the judgment of school authorities even though the burdens of desegregation were not exactly equalized.[151] The court's stipulation of its remedial responsibilities was greatly narrowed in the final order.

> . . . this Court's jurisdiction is narrowly confined to the issue of whether the plans will in fact desegregate Mark Twain Junior High School—i.e., provide a racial and ethnic mix reflective of that in the district.[152]

Turning to the housing issue, Judge Weinstein said that housing authorities had begun to take action to meet the goals of the special master's housing report—a statement one can call exaggeration out of respect for the court—and that in view of this cooperative spirit and the complexity of the matter, a rigid decree was undesirable.[153] The court requested monthly reports from all parties and did not grant a stay during the pendency of any decree.

The plaintiffs and the community school board appealed. Plaintiffs protested the selection of the magnet school plan and the pushing of desegregation forward to September of 1975 rather than 1974. The community school board appealed that part of the order which mooted the third-party complaint, the decision holding it liable for the segregated condition at Mark Twain, and the use of the Dodson Plan as a back-up.

The second circuit court, Judge Gurfein writing for a unanimous bench, upheld the district court's conclusions about the school as well as the test for find-

---

149. *See* Hart II, *supra* note 2, at 770.
150. *Id.* "Local control over the educational process affords citizens an opportunity to participate in decision-making, permits the structuring of school programs to fit local needs and encourages 'experimentation, innovation, and a healthy competition for educational excellence.'" Bradley v. Milliken, 418 U.S. at 737 (1974).
151. Hart II, *supra* note 2, at 770-71.
152. *Id.* at 773.
153. *Id.* at 775.

ing Twain a segregated school.[154] It also affirmed the use of the magnet plan, the mooting of the third-party complaint, and the delay in the desegregation time-table. However, the court was critical of the district court judge's handling of the case:

> [The community school board] succeeded initially in getting the district judge to convert a narrow issue, involving a single junior high school with a capacity of about 1,000 students into what could only become an issue so broad as to defy judicial competence, a matter which would require action by three governments, federal, state, and city, for a solution.[155]

Since the housing authorities did not appeal, Court of Appeals for the second circuit never considered whether the district court was in error when it found the housing authorities not literally liable to the school authorities but partly liable for the harm in the sense that their action helped maintain segregated schools. They felt, however, that Judge Weinstein should formally dismiss the third-party action since he mooted it:

> [W]e find it hard to see why a federal district judge should superintend so vast a series of continuing enterprises and be in a position to interpose a remedy whenever he does not agree with the voluntary action undertaken by appropriate public bodies.[156]

Creating the Magnet School

The community board began implementing Weinstein's final order at the end of August 1974. By then the special master stepped out of the case. With the exception of a hearing at which he requested the state and federal governments to seek financial assistance, Judge Weinstein was not directly involved. Yet the court's resolve to integrate Twain and the back-up threat of the Dodson Plan was a powerful impetus to make the magnet plan work.[157]

The community board sought outside assistance from Brooklyn College. They also retained Jacob Landers, an integration expert formerly with the board of education. Landers proposed a detailed committee structure which involved professionals and broad ethnic and geographical distribution in the community.[158]

A majority of the members of the subcommittees consisted of parents of

154. Hart v. Community School Board of Education, New York School District 21, 512 F.2d 37, at 44 (2d Cir. 1975) [hereinafter cited as Hart III].
155. *Id.* at 41.
156. *See id.* at 54. A petition for *certiorari* was denied, 417 U.S. 943 (1974).
157. *See* Zelon Interview, *supra* note 37.
158. This section is drawn from the monthly reports submitted by the community board. The planning group was headed by a steering committee and broken into subcommittees on: safety, curriculum, community relations and information, selection of pupils, organization, pupil personnel and other supportive services, personnel selection, human relations.

children eligible to attend Twain. Landers made the committee system work by creating a feeling of participation in the community and with education professionals.[159]

The board then held a series of meetings with the district's staff to inform them of the plan and to obtain their cooperation. One problem was how to promote the virtues of the magnet concept without seeming to downgrade the other schools in the district. Another was a fear of plummeting morale of staff at the other schools. In the summer of 1975, a federal grant of $500,000 was received for community liaison efforts in the other intermediate schools. This could ease the transition in the other junior high schools and aid in the acceptance of the increased numbers of minority students.

An early decision of the planning committee was that pupils leaving the Coney Island area to attend other schools in the district (minority students) would have the same claims upon transportation as the majority students to be bused into the magnet school. A key element in the implementation was gaining the central board's commitment to provide the money for buses. On October 7, four board members and the community superintendent met with Chancellor Anker who gave a verbal commitment for busing funds. The board pressed for a written statement to that effect, which was obtained. Those extra buses proved crucial in assuaging fears of white parents.

The central educational administration cooperated to a degree. Anker understood that the school board's solution was the only one possible, yet he was faced with severe financial pressures throughout the system and would commit funds only reluctantly and after delay.[160] The cost of converting Twain to a magnet school was estimated at $450,000, exclusive of busing and safety. This perhaps explains why Anker had ignored requests to send representatives from the central board as consultants, observers, or advisors. Peluso, the community superintendent, was a key person in making the board of education responsive to the district's needs. The state education department, which had not played a major role in the implementation process, did provide a $70,000 grant for curriculum development.[161]

In devising curriculum and educational requests, the various committees wanted to ensure a sufficient minority participation.[162] The areas of talent eligible for admission were increased to include athletics and foreign languages. Talented children would be auditioned to demonstrate their talent; gifted children would be tested. But their skills in language and mathematics were not

159. *See* Zelon Interview, *supra* note 37.

160. *Id.* Zelon said that "Once we got the commitment for busing, we knew the plan would succeed."

161. One hundred thousand dollars was spent on physical refurbishing of the structure. *Community School Board 21 Monthly Reports,* December 1974 [hereinafter cited separately as *Monthly Report*].

162. After students were admitted, the board wanted to make certain they would perform, so no children with a record of disruption or poor attendance were accepted.

more than one year behind their natural grade average.[163] In January 1975, a new principal was selected for the school.

An extensive public relations campaign involving widespread press, radio, and television coverage, personal appearances by members of the board, the superintendent, and new principal, was set up to inform parents of the magnet school concept and to encourage them to send their children. Mailings to families with eligible sixth-grade children began in November.[164]

By the end of March, over 650 applications had been received. The 70-30 majority-minority ratio ahd been attained.[165] Six hundred and two acceptances were sent out in April for September of 1975. In the entering class were 180 minority pupils. The number of Coney Island residents in that figure is uncertain. Zelon claims that 160 or more have gone to elementary school in the district and would be zoned into District 21 intermediate schools.[166] This does not mean all 160 reside in the district. Twain opened in September. The uncertainties ahead include a fear that the Coney Island black community will protest the loss of a neighborhood school.

It was feared also that the morale in the other schools among teachers, parents, and students would decline. The scarce resources of District 21 were all poured into Mark Twain. All special programs were to be phased out, and for the first time large numbers of black students were attending the other schools. The best students in the district were going to Mark Twain, leaving the rest to the other schools. But the biggest problem ahead is a new lawsuit filed by the NAACP, *Jiminez v. Community School Board 21,* a complaint alleging widespread racial imbalance in the district's elementary schools. A decision in favor of the plaintiffs is expected to bring with it widespread busing, which would lead to an undermining of the magnet school. There can be no magnet solution for the elementary schools. The case is a rematch of *Hart.* It is before Judge Weinstein. Plaintiffs are represented by Meyerson, the school board by Bravin.

The demolition of buildings in the urban renewal area has not proceeded as fast as expected. There are still no white tenants in the new projects, which are vertical ghettos.

CONCLUSION

If Judge Weinstein's first decision made the court a super-legislature, his final order showed judicial restraint. Between the two decisions, the court learned the

163. Zelon said, "They may be here because they are fantastic tenors, but not because they are fantastic black tenors." Zelon Interview, *supra,* note 37.

164. *See Monthly Report,* February 1975.

165. *See Monthly Report,* March 1975.

166. *See* Zelon Interview, *supra* note 37. This does not mean that they reside in the district, let alone Coney Island. The open-enrollment program has enabled out-of-district minority students to attend district schools. Other minority students attending Twain include a few children of school staff and former pupils at private schools.

limits of judicial remedial power. Perhaps Judge Weinstein initially felt that once he found the liability, he could give an impetus to various governmental agencies to take action and to initiate new polices in line with his finding of liability. In retrospect, he underestimated the difficulty of the housing problem and of instigating bureaucratic change.

Yet he did successfully integrate Mark Twain with minimum community upheaval. Implementing a decree ordering school desegregation is complex and trying. But it is easier than exercising judicial remedial powers in the housing area.

Success and Failure in Overseeing Integration

When courts assume a more active role in the implementation of institutional change involving important social issues, they become involved in the political and administrative process in a judicially atypical way.[167] Courts are in the difficult situation of finding bureaucracies or agencies of government constitutionally liable for a wrong, and then in supervising the correction of that wrong, they must rely on that same agency to correct it.[168] Even with exceptional judges like Jack B. Weinstein, and a fair and knowledgeable special master as Curtis Berger, courts must rely upon the professionals in the bureaucracies to implement the needed remedy. They need the support of some of those professionals, of the political elite to which particular bureaucracy is responsible, or of politically powerful voices in the community. While courts can be catalysts for social change, without the assistance of political and bureaucratic forces, the process is much more difficult.[169] Most important is the court's display of firm resolve that the implementation will occur. This was the key to the success of the school plan.

The success of the school plan was based in large part on its support from the community school board which had conceived it, convinced the community of its advantages, and later implemented it. Here the court had local proponents in the power structure to reduce community tension. The court also used the community board as its agent vis-à-vis the central board and the education bureaucracy. The local board oversaw the work of the district superintendent.

It knew the political parameters of the community and could use the threat of the back-up plan to its fullest advantage. The board became a buffer between

167. *See* The Wyatt Case: Implementation of a Judicial Decree Ordering Institutional Change, 84 Yale L.J. 1338, 1340–43 (1975).

168. Baratz, in review of Hopson v. Hanson, 269 F. Supp. 401 (D.D.C. 1967), says: "Thus we have an anomalous situation in which to expect change to flourish: Those who resisted the change are the ones responsible for rectifying it. Unless the penalties for noncompliance are great or the rewards for implementation greater [than] the risks involved, it is unlikely that old resisters will charitably give up their policies and objectively seek to make the plaintiff's ideas work." *Court Decisions and Educational Change: A Case History of the D.C. Public Schools, 1954–1974,* 4 J. Law-Educ. 63, 79 (1975).

169. As R. Mandel has suggested: "The probability [is] that most social changes occur as the incremental of multi-institutional and societal forces rather than as a direct result of a Supreme Court decision or set of decisions." Mandel *Judicial Decisions and Organizational Change in Public Schools,* 82 School Review 327–46, 329 (1974).

court and community. Furthermore, the magnet school was a localized plan with no immediate impact on other districts and marginal impact over the other intermediate schools. For the majority community, it presented no involuntary action against them. The remedy could be financially, politically, and socially contained. Unlike the housing proposal, the magnet plan involved one school, one school board, one bureaucracy.

The housing proposals, on the other hand, involved many governmental agencies, at three levels, plus thousands of private actions by individual renters and homeowners. For the housing plan to be successful, there was a need for affirmative action on the part of private individuals to move into Coney Island. This was a greater and more permanent commitment than in the school situation. To make the school plan successful, a negative or passive action was required on the part of individuals not to withdraw their children from school.

Politically, the people who would benefit from housing renewal did not yet live within the district and were unidentifiable. There was no community leadership at all in favor of the housing plan. Combined with a lack of interest of state housing agencies in implementing it, there were no community residents who would argue strongly for the plan. The housing authorities' reaction was one of passive cooperation until they realized their participation would require additional financing, bureaucratic change, reallocation of resources and priority, and intense activity of their own.

But the ultimate failure of the housing remedy was that the judge could not isolate the impact of his decision to Coney Island. With finite financial resources and with unlimited political pressures able to be exerted upon housing authorities, any plan that changed policies in Coney Island would be subject to similar demands in other areas of the city, state, and federal government. In addition to the impossibility of isolating the impact of the decision, the time frame before change could be instituted was a much longer process than the court initially imagined. Housing itself is a long-run proposition. To change housing policies is a much more difficult and time-consuming process than to alter school lines or to restructure a school system. The litigative process in school desegregation cases normally takes many years. For a court to supervise housing change, the time could be even longer.

Education is a state function delegated to local bodies, but housing in New York is a local, state, and federal responsibility. With such interlapping and overlapping functions, conflicting interests and bureaucracies become too much for any one court to handle. As the Supreme Court said in *Swann,* "one vehicle can carry only a limited amount of baggage."[170]

The Lessons of *Hart*

An important question is judicial strategy in these cases. If a broad constitutional liability is found, what should be a court's remedial approach? Desegregation cases overlaid with such complex social and political issues as *Hart*

170. Swann v. Charlotte-Mecklenburg Board of Education, 402 U.S. 1, 22 (1971).

threaten to become so broad as to defy solution. *Hart* shows the dangers of courts' expansion of remedial powers into new areas to achieve desegregation. People directly affected by the court's decree had no representation except after the finding of liability. Nor is the class-action device helpful, for not all plaintiffs or defendants are in the same priority to the cause of action. Nor will all plaintiffs or defendants in the class be similarly affected by a favorable decision.

In cases like *Hart,* where the finding of broad liability creates an atmosphere of fear, making it more difficult to implement a remedy, or if there is a danger of broadening the scope of the case so much that supervision becomes impossible, courts should make the greatest effort to achieve an out-of-court settlement.

Judge Weinstein unsuccessfully attempted to induce the parties to settle out of court. *Hart* seems to be a case that should have been settled long before it was. The plaintiffs felt they had nothing to offer to promote an out-of-court settlement.[171] As a result, they won a pyrrhic constitutional victory, but lost the remedy. One wonders if the court could have leaned harder to force the parties to settle.

Another question is, When did the court change its mind? Was the use of the special master merely a facade? The final order was written before *Bradley v. Milliken* was handed down. Probably doubts arose at the March 1974 hearings when it was apparent that the housing authorities really had planned nothing except verbal offers of cooperation. The intervention led by Nancy LeBlanc had no doubt an effect on the final order, as did the increasing complexity of the housing aspects.

The site residents' intervention raised the possibility of additional legal proceedings that would have delayed any housing resolution and only inflamed passions in the community. In a revealing passage in the final order, Judge Weinstein noted:

[T]he hostility in the courtroom mirrored in the faces of some black and white spectators, and some of the mail and other communications received by the court during the pendency of this proceeding, suggest that the road ahead will be extremely difficult if individuals and groups do not refrain from stirring up unnecessary racial division and hostility.[172]

Site residents were the leaders of that courtroom hostility.

In addition, Judge Weinstein apparently was affected by his own tours of the central Coney Island area. In riding the elevators in the housing projects, and looking at the rapid deterioration in the buildings and the sullen despair on the faces of the tenants, the difficulty of the task must have hit home.

171. Interview with James Meyerson, April 29, 1975.
172. 383 F. Supp. 769, 775.

One option that Judge Weinstein would not countenance was the closing of Mark Twain. However, the magnet school achieved indirectly what the court said it would not do. Mark Twain is no longer a neighborhood school. Within District 21, only blacks and Hispanics do not have a community-based intermediate school. There is little doubt that the burden, at least in 1975, is most heavily upon the black residents in the Coney Island area, most of whom are bused to other district schools.

Nor is there great concern in the final order over the education that blacks will receive in the other schools. The court admitted that attempts had been made at racially imbalanced Mark Twain to provide a strong remedial program. Will those programs, expensive to run, be available in the same degree at other interracial schools where students in need of remedial programs are a small minority? Extra resources will go into Mark Twain to ensure the success of the magnet. But in a financially deprived school system, are there funds to go around for all kinds of students?

There are also valid educational questions as to the wisdom of the magnet school concept at the junior high level. The magnet school assumes that varying and enriching the inputs into an education experience will lead to a qualitative and quantitative improvement in achievement, that is, in outputs. Recent educational studies dispute that the educational achievement is directly related to resource allocation.[173]

The magnet concept can also be a short-run integration solution. While the special master may have corrected the danger of I.S. 303's tipping, if the district's demographic trends continue, as most people predict, there will be more and more minority students. If another school begins to tip, will it be able to be turned into another magnet? Probably not. Zoning and restructuring can only go so far. After a certain point, perhaps when another school in the district will get the image that Mark Twain had, the danger of white flight may set in again. There will be neither the resources nor the individuals to create another magnet school.

A lesson of *Hart* is that while a court may be a proper forum for the airing of grievances reaching a constitutional magnitude, it is less suitable in using its full remedial powers to decree social reform that must be instituted by several agencies, and borne in different ways by many individuals, many of whom have no relation to the initial cause of a constitutional violation.[174]

One of the lessons of the last ten years has been that we must expect less from legislative and political branches of government. And we should also expect less from our court system. Courts cannot remedy social ills that have accumulated because of failure of political, legislative, and popular will. They are not the institutional mechanisms to engineer and to oversee broad social change.

173. *See* Jencks, et al., Inequality: A Reassessment of the Effect of Family and Schooling in America (1972), at 93, and his citations at 126.
174. *See* Baratz, *supra* note 168, at 79-80.

Keyes v. School District No. 1

Jessica Pearson and Jeffrey Pearson

Keyes v. School District No. 1, *involving the city of Denver, was the first nonsouthern desegregation case to reach the Supreme Court. Denver's school system was charged with de facto as opposed to de jure segregation. The city was one of the few municipalities to successfully implement a desegregation decree. This study examines why Denver succeeded: the steps taken by the district judge; the nature of the school system; Denver's class and social structure; and the political mobilization in support of the decree.*

Jeffrey Pearson is a member of the Colorado Bar. Jessica Pearson is a visiting assistant professor in the Department of Sociology at the University of Denver. They are presently writing a book about rural America.

—*Eds.*

INTRODUCTION AND METHODOLOGY

This is a descriptive study of the conduct and setting of a desegregation lawsuit in Denver, Colorado. The suit began in the summer of 1969; it produced one final order and decree in 1970; it was then in the appeals process for two years; it produced a second final order and decree in 1974; as of January 1976, the appeals process had come to an end.

The study is also a history in miniature of the functioning of the judical process. The Denver case is one of many in the last twenty years which have faced the courts with an intractable dilemma: A clear constitutional violation is proved; a legislative body refuses to take remedial action. The courts, equipped with limited equitable powers, must wheedle and cajole, threaten and coerce, and, on occasion, assume for all practical purposes a plenary legislative role. In the Denver case, the courts may be seen as having walked the full distance, wheedling in the beginning, threatening along the way, and by the end, virtually legislating a remedy.

Faced with such a dilemma, the judicial process reveals its weaknesses. In the Denver case, the judicial process proved slow, sometimes lacking in real-world sophistication and reluctant to take initiatives. It also proved, as time went on, that it could gain sophistication, sometimes move cautiously without tarrying and, if confronted by a vacuum, act decisively.

Denver is a city in which the city and county are coterminous. In 1970 the U.S. Census reported Denver's population as 514,678. Surrounding Denver is an all too typical ring of predominately suburban, metropolitan sprawl. The 1970 population of "Metropolitan Denver" was 1,227,529. Only the 122 public schools in the city and county of Denver proper were involved in the desegregation lawsuit.

In rough numbers, and the numbers change each year, the city and county of Denver is 73 percent white (referred to herein as Anglos), 10 percent black, and 17 percent Chicano (Hispanos). The school population is 51 percent white, 19 percent black, and 27 percent Chicano.

The study utilizes demographic data, court testimony, open-ended interview data, court decisions, journalism, legal documents, and secondary studies. It reconstructs the historical and sociological development of a controversy which started in the streets, went to the courts, and, to date, has not been conclusively resolved in either.

GENERAL DEMOGRAPHIC HISTORY
OF DENVER

The city of Denver was established in 1858 subsequent to the discovery of placer gold in the nearby mountains. During the mining boom lasting from 1880–1910, it grew rapidly as a distribution center. After 1910, however, population growth in Denver slowed to an average annual increase of between 1 and 3 percent. It was not until World War II that Denver's isolated location and limited water resources ceased to pose obstacles to industrial development and population growth. In addition to a great number of government and military employment centers, Denver attracted airlines, railroad, and trucking companies. Research and light manufacturing industries also developed. In recent years, many firms have made Denver a location for their national headquarters. In 1940 the population of Denver was 322,412. In the next decade the population increased 29 percent to 415,786. The population of the city of Denver during 1950–1960 increased by 18.8 percent to 493,887. Between 1960 and 1970, the rate of increase tapered considerably to 4.2 percent, and Denver actually experienced a large net out-migration of 28,960 while metropolitan areas surrounding Denver surged ahead.

Nonetheless, Denver's population increased absolutely as a result of natural increase and in 1970 it stood at 514,678.[1]

Since World War II the area of Denver has increased about 40 square miles by annexation of undeveloped lands to the east and south of the historical city. Currently, the boundaries of Denver comprise approximately 100 square miles.[2] Population density in Denver in 1970 was about 5,417 persons per square mile. As a result of annexation, this was lower than the 7,493 persons per square mile recorded in 1960.[3]

Denver Minority Groups: Hispanos

Numerically, Hispanos make up the most significant minority group in Denver. In 1960, however, the census identified 60,294 Hispanos in Denver, 12.2 percent of the total population.[4] By 1970 the number of Hispanos had risen to 86,345, 16.8 percent of the total population of Denver.[5]

The Hispano population first came to southern Colorado and New Mexico as miners and agricultural workers. With the closing of the mines and the mechanization of farm work many moved to Denver.[6]

The Hispano population of Denver has always been a highly disadvantaged group. In 1970, median school years completed by Hispanos totalled 10.0. This was far below the citywide median of 12.1 for both blacks and whites. The 1970 median family income for Denver Hispanos was $7,323; the percent employed in white-collar occupations was 33.6. Both measures were far below those reported for Denver city whites in 1970: $9,654 and 58.3 percent, respectively. They were, however, comparable to levels for blacks as a whole ($7,287 and 38.7 percent), although far below levels reported for the blacks of Park Hill, a neighborhood of middle-class blacks to be discussed shortly. The Hispano population of Denver has the weakest professional class of all ethnic groups in the city. In 1970, only 8.4 percent of the Hispano population were classified professionals, while 12.3 percent and 18.4 percent of blacks and whites, respectively, were classified professionals.[7] Additionally, in geographic terms the Hispano

1. The preceding paragraph was based on Charles P. Rahe, The Economic Base of Denver Ch. 2 (1974).

2. On writ of *certiorari* to the United States Court of Appeals for the Tenth Circuit, Brief for Respondents, at 9.

3. Rahe, *supra* note 1, at 11.

4. U.S. Bureau of the Census, Census of Population and Housing: 1960—Census Tracts, Final Report, Denver, Colorado SMSA.

5. *Id.,* 1970—Census Tracts, Final Report PHC (1)-56, Denver, Colorado SMSA.

6. Appendix, Volume 5, Supreme Court of the United States, October Term, 1971, No. 71-507 (Wilfred Keyes, *et al.*), at 2002a.

7. The preceding paragraph was based on material from the U.S. Bureau of the Census, *supra* note 5.

population of Denver is spread over a larger and less well-defined area than that occupied by the black population.[8]

Denver Minority Groups: Blacks

The black population of Denver in 1970 comprised 9.1 percent of the total city population. Black population growth in Denver has been a post–World War II phenomenon. In 1940, blacks accounted for only 2.4 percent of the city's population; in 1960, 6.1 percent.[9]

In part the recent increase in the percentage of the black population is due to the movement of whites out of the central city into suburban areas. However, another large part of the increase in blacks may be safely attributed to in-migration in recent years. The actual number of Denver blacks during the 1940–1970 period increased tremendously, from 7,836 in 1940 to 47,011 in 1970, an increase of 499.9 percent.[10]

Historically the black population in the city of Denver was situated in a small area immediately north of the center of the city, commonly called Five Points. It is an area meeting the classical sociological definition of a zone of transition, replete with the run-down connotation that this concept implies. To this day the economic and social profile of Five Points remains overwhelmingly bleak.[11]

Five Points, however, does not represent the economic and social profile of the majority of Denver blacks, for a large portion of them are overwhelmingly middle class and resemble the white population of Denver with respect to fundamental social and economic indicators. The uniquely middle-class character of Denver's black population and their patterns of residential mobility may have helped give rise to the school desegregation lawsuit.

Unlike blacks in northern cities such as Chicago, Detroit, New York, and Buffalo, the blacks who migrated to Denver in recent decades were not poor, southern, rural blacks seeking employment in heavy industry. Rather, they were the sons and daughters of these poor, rural, southern blacks. They came to

8. In 1970, 51 census tracts of Denver contained 400 or more persons of Spanish language or Spanish surname. By way of contrast, only 16 census tracts contained 400 or more blacks. Most census tracts containing Hispanos are located north and west of the city's center.

9. C. Cortese, The Impact of Black Mobility: Selective Migration and Community Change (final report to the National Science Foundation, Department of Sociology, University of Denver, 1974), at 12.

10. *Id.* at 12–15. During the 1960–1970 decade, 43 percent of this increase was natural increase; 57 percent was due to net in-migration. The population increase of whites and other combined races in the period 1940–1970 was less than one-tenth the black rate (314,576 to 467,491, an increase of 48.6 percent), and during 1960–1970 all this increase was natural increase, since there was a net out-migration of whites.

11. The preceding paragraph is based on the U.S. Bureau of the Census, *supra* note 5. In 1970, the median number of school years completed by residents of the three census tracts that comprise Five Points (tracts 16, 24.01, 24.02) was 9.1 years. Only 24 percent of the adults residing in Five Points were high school graduates, and only 22.2 percent were employed in white-collar occupations. The median income of families located in the three Five Points census tracts was $4,014.

Denver via the urban centers of the North and West. According to one analyst, "black population growth (. . . [was] brought about by the in-migration of up-wardly mobile offspring of earlier migrants from the South and they were drawn to Denver by the relatively greater occupational opportunity offered by its economic base."[12]

The middle-class character of Denver blacks is enhanced by the presence of the large number of federal government installations in the city. Denver is second only to Washington, D.C. in the number of federal agencies which have offices in the city. The proportion of the total Denver labor force employed in federal agencies is twice the national average. Through the Civil Service System, black employment has reached into professional, supervisory, administrative, and clerical areas. Federal agency employment for blacks alone is nearly four times the national average, and in 1960 the government employed about 15 percent of employed Denver blacks.[13]

With the post-World War II influx of blacks to Denver, Five Points became more heavily segregated: the Five Points census tracts that had been 26.7 percent black in 1940 were 52.9 percent black in 1960.[14] Concurrently, however, there was a movement of blacks eastward and northward. To some degree the movement of blacks eastward was made possible by the Colorado Fair Housing Law of 1959, which made discrimination in housing illegal. By 1950 the black population had extended eastward to a major north-south thoroughfare called York Street, and a decade later it had crossed another principal thoroughfare called Colorado Boulevard. Thereafter, black population movement entered a predominantly white neighborhood known as Park Hill.

Park Hill has been characterized as consisting of "fine, large brick homes accommodated by wide, well-planted parkways and tree-shaded streets."[15] Between 1960 and 1967, the black population in Park Hill increased about 67 percent per year.[16] By 1970, 52 percent of the population in the six census tracts that comprise Park Hill were black.[17] This black population was not uni-

12. Cortese, *supra* note 9, at 54. Denver's economic base consists primarily of professional services, trade, and public administration, rather than manufacturing and raw-resource extraction. Once in Denver, the black population took advantage of this base. Black employment in Denver is particularly high in SIC classifications for Railroad Transportation, Banking, Finance, Insurance and Real Estate, Business and Repair Services, Medical and Health Services, Postal Services, Federal and Public Administration, and State and Local Administration. These classifications represent professional, technical, business, and administrative occupations associated with the white collar and the middle class.

13. The preceding two paragraphs are based on Cortese & Leftwich, *A Technique for Measuring the Effect of Economic Base on Opportunity for Blacks,* 12 Demography (May 1975).

14. George E. Bardwell, Park Hill Areas of Denver: 1950–1966 (Denver Commission on Community Relations, 1966), at 5.

15. *Id.* at 6.

16. *Id.*

17. Doyal D. O'Dell, The Park Hill Area of Denver: An Integrated Community? (Denver Urban Observatory, 1973), at 12.

formly distributed throughout the six census tracts.[18] The black residential increase occurred mostly in the northern sections of Park Hill.

Although the influx of blacks east of Colorado Boulevard occasioned rapid panic selling by white residents and rapid residential turnover, the neighborhood did not experience the normal deterioration associated with such phenomena. Nor did Park Hill become an all-black ghetto. Although vacancy rates during the 1960s tended to be highest in areas with the highest black occupancy, at no point was the Park Hill vacancy rate seriously out of line with other Denver residential areas.[19] In addition, sales prices for improved residential properties in all areas of Park Hill throughout the era of heavy black in-migration increased fairly steadily at rates between 1 and 2 percent per year.[20] Whites, however, are continuing to move to Park Hill, and in recent years Park Hill has become one of the tightest and most desirable housing markets in the city.

The character of the black population that migrated to Park Hill is relevant to why Park Hill did not become an all-black slum. Since the impetus for school desegregation originated in Park Hill, it is also relevant to understanding the course of the desegregation controversy in Denver.

Socioeconomic Characteristics of Park Hill Blacks. A look at such socioeconomic indicators as income, education, and occupation shows that Park Hill blacks resemble the white population of Denver more than they do the non-Park Hill black population and the black population in other U.S. metropolitan cities of comparable size.[21]

In 1970, Park Hill blacks had completed 12.5 median school years. This compared favorably with the 12.8 years of school completed by Park Hill whites and was identical to the median number of school years completed by whites in the more affluent Denver Standard Metropolitan Statistical Area (SMSA). The educational accomplishments of Park Hill blacks were somewhat greater than the 12.1 recorded for Denver city whites as a whole; and well above the 10.9 median number of years of school completed by blacks in cities of comparable size to Denver.[22]

The income profile of Park Hill blacks shows much the same pattern. Although in 1970 Park Hill blacks earned less than Park Hill whites, less than whites in the city of Denver, and less then whites in the metropolitan area as a whole, the gaps are relatively narrow. Far broader income gaps appear between the 1970 income of Park Hill blacks and the 1970 income of the overall black population in Denver, blacks in the Denver SMSA, and blacks in U.S. metropolitan cities of comparable size to Denver.[23]

The statistics on Park Hill blacks employed in white-collar occupations pro-

18. *Id.*
19. Bardwell, *supra* note 14, at 11.
20. *Id.* at 19–23.
21. The following three paragraphs are based on Cortese, *supra* note 9, at 8–11.
22. *Supra* note 5.
23. *Id.*

duce substantially similar results: 44.7 percent of Park Hill blacks were white-collar workers in 1970. Although this fell short of the 57.2 percent for Park Hill whites in 1970, short of the 58.3 percent for Denver city whites and short of the 52.8 percent for whites in other metropolitan cities with similar sized populations, it far exceeded the 38.7 percent for blacks in the city of Denver as a whole and the 30.6 percent for blacks in similar sized U.S. metropolitan areas comparable to Denver.[24]

Demographic and Economic Prospects for Denver

In recent years, Denver's pattern of population change has begun to resemble that of older urban core cities, especially in the East and West.[25] Relative to the four-county suburban ring, Denver is increasingly populated by the poor; the less educated, the minorities; the less easily employed; the elderly; and the working young adult households. When Denver is compared to the suburban ring, it lags with respect to the educational level, professional classification and income of its labor force. It is projected that Denver's population growth will begin to decline by about 1980, and until that time Denver's share of total regional population growth will steadily taper. Families in childbearing ages will continue to migrate into the suburbs, while young adults and the elderly migrate into Denver. It is projected that Denver's economy will continue to grow at about the national rate, although its share of economic activity will lag behind that of the suburban counties. This is the demographic and economic setting in which the school desegregation controversy occurred.

HISTORY OF THE DENVER SCHOOL DISTRICT

The Creation of School District No. 1

School District No. 1 and the city and county of Denver are geographically coterminous.[26] Fiscally and politically, the district and the city are independent. The city has a mayor-council form of government, and, until 1967, had exclusive control over annexation of surrounding lands. The district is govered by a seven-member board of education elected for staggered six-year terms; since 1967 the district has had the power to veto contemplated annexations by the city.[27]

To date the school district has also operated independently of surrounding school districts. There are indications that this situation might change in the near future either by state legislative action or by Colorado State Board of Education activity.[28] In the meantime, the Denver school district will continue to function totally apart from surrounding school districts.

24. *Id.*
25. The following two paragraphs are based on Rahe, *supra* note 1, at 17–30.
26. Both were created by an amendment to the Colorado Constitution in 1902, Art. 20, §7.
27. CRS 31-8-105.
28. Fred Holmes, State Department of Education, Personal Interview, April 17, 1974.

School districts are largely free from state controls.[29] The Colorado Department of Education is a permissive, as opposed to a regulatory, board. The state education department lacks statutory authority to mandate directly education policies and practices in the local districts. State funding formulas stipulate that state aid be based solely on pupil enrollments in the various school districts—not on the adoption or abandonment of specific educational programs or policies.[30]

The local district school board is authorized to enter into contracts with a chief executive officer, commonly called a superintendent, for day-to-day administration of the schools.[31]

The School Board and the Superintendent

In practice, however, the actual power wielded by the school superintendent in Denver has been greater than the statutory language would predict. From 1947 to 1967 the Denver public schools were under the control of a very strong and popular superintendent, Kenneth Oberholtzer. Observers say that during this period decision-making resided exclusively in the hands of the superintendent and his staff.[32]

In the same 1947–1967 period, the election of school board members came under the school superintendent's supervision. For most of this period school board elections were conducted separately from all other municipal contests. Education decision-making was viewed as the domain of the local board of education, the superintendent, and his close associates.[33]

In 1959 the Colorado Legislature voted to hold school board elections in conjunction with other municipal elections. One result of this was that voter turnout for school board elections was higher when school board and municipal elections coincided every four years than during off-year school board elections.

Electoral turnout for school board elections *per se,* however, mushroomed only in 1969 as school desegregation emerged as an issue. That year there was a record turnout for the school board election even though it did not coincide

29. By law, all Colorado school districts, including School District No. 1, are bodies corporate, §22-32-101, CRS 1973. Governance of each district by a board of education is prescribed in §22-32-103, CRS 1973; board members, once elected, select their own officers. §22-32-104, CRS 1973.

30. The only statutory authorization for direct intervention by the state in local district affairs is §22-2-107, CRS 1973, giving the state board the power to "provide consultative services to the public schools and boards of education of school districts." Otherwise, the state board's powers are limited to such matters as requiring census takings, reporting, and various other "health and welfare" activities.

31. CRS §22-32-110(g).

32. Rocky Mountain News, June 20, 1949.

33. *See id.,* June 16, 1951. In this article entitled "School Board Elections Flaunt Democracy," the *Rocky Mountain News* accused the school administration of calling its own elections, setting up the precincts, appointing judges and clerks, and counting the ballots and certifying the results. The article urged that school elections be placed in "impeccably disinterested hands."

with a municipal race. The election coincided with intense community and school board conflict over school desegregation issues.[34]

In addition to increasing voter turnouts, the controversy over desegregation increased the number and varieties of persons that became candidates in school board races.[35] Until recently, persons who chose to run for the school board tended to be upper-class professionals, executives, and independent business-people.[36] Since 1965 (the first year for which detailed information is available), a trend may be noted of greater numbers of people of varied backgrounds seeking office.[37]

The ensuring desegregation controversy greatly altered the race, class, and

34. Harriet Tammings, A Decade of Controversy in School Policy-Making: The Desegregation Issue, a paper presented at the Rocky Mountain Social Science Association meetings, El Paso, Texas, April 25–27, 1974.

35. By law, candidates for the school board must submit a petition signed by 50 electors of a school district. Traditionally, successful candidates for positions on the school board were persons who were acceptable to the school administration. As late as 1965, a newspaper article reported that school board candidates critical of the superintendent generally lost the election, while those who had praised him were successful. *See* Rocky Mountain News, May 20, 1965.

36. Paul Hamilton, director, Black Educators United, Personal Interview with Harriet Tammings, 1972.

37. Denver Post, April-May, 1965. In 1965, approximately three-quarters of the 28 candidates for school board positions were professionals, managers, executives, independent businesspeople, and government bureaucrats. The single largest occupational group represented among the candidates was attorneys (25 percent). An additional 25 percent were managers, executives, and independent businesspeople, and another 25 percent were upper-level bureaucrats in government service. The remainder were women at home, school teachers, or persons engaged in voluntary service.

Thus, among the 1971 candidates, there was a worker for a health center in an Hispano neighborhood, two equal-employment-opportunity counselors in community centers, a member of the Denver County Judicial Commission, a former public health nurse who was engaged in a variety of voluntary activities, and an Hispano activist. The candidate pool also included three school teachers or retired school teachers, a student, a photographer, a manager of a meat store, a medical secretary, and a truck driver. Denver Post, April-May 1971.

The background of successful school board candidates has also tended to become more varied. During 1973–1975, the school board included an Hispanic city government administrator; a former head of the Denver League of Women Voters; a black equal-employment-opportunity counselor at a federal government installation in Denver; a sales manager; an executive of a real estate firm who was formerly a Republican state senator and an unsuccessful candidate for the U.S. Congress in November 1974; an attorney who was also a former Republican state senator; and a truck driver. Denver Post, April-May 1971. In the 1975 school board elections, two male members of the board, both former Republican state senators, were replaced by the two female, activist candidates.

The racial composition of the school board has also undergone striking changes. In 1965 Rachel Noel, a black consultant for the Mayor's Commission on Community Relations, was elected to the board. She was the first successful black candidate. In 1973 a second black, Omar Blair, was elected to the board. Blair is an equal-employment-opportunity counselor for the Air Force Finance and Accounting Center. Two Hispanos have served on the board; however, neither of them has been endorsed by the exclusively Hispano political organization, La Raza Unida Party. Both Hispanos are Republican.

occupational composition of the school board candidates. In 1971, of 21 school board candidates, only two were attorneys, two were independent businessmen, and two were college instructors. The largest occupational classification represented among the candidates were voluntary service employees and activists.

Financing School District No. 1

The Denver public schools receive their income from federal, state, and local sources.[38] School construction is financed through the approval of bond-issue pledges by the voters.

Traditionally, the local property tax has been the mainstay of the Denver school district. In 1966, local revenues accounted for approximately 77 percent of the total revenues available to the school district. Despite this the Denver school levy has been among the lowest in the state, and in 1970 its levy of 49.94 actually was the lowest among the state's major school districts. Since the passage of the Public School Finance Act of 1973, local contributions to school finance have decreased somewhat. In 1974 the Denver mill levy dropped nearly 14 percent to 45.77. In 1975, local revenues accounted for approximately 58 percent of total school revenues, and the school mill levy was 50.93. In 1976 the mill levy was 50.925 and local revenues comprised 66.98 percent of total school funds.[39]

State funding of local education has traditionally been weak in Colorado.[40]

38. The following paragraphs are based on Denver Public Schools, Adopted Budgets for the years 1967–1975, and the Colorado Department of Education, Consolidated Report on Elementary and Secondary Education in Colorado, 1972–1975.
  39.

Mill Levies and Rates of Change of Mill Levies: School District No. 1, 1966–1976

	Mills	*Percent Change*
1966	40.83	
1967	43.77	+ 7.2%
1968	46.94	+ 7.2
1969	49.27	+ 5.0
1970	49.94	+ 1.4
1971	53.80	+ 7.7
1972	56.29	+ 4.6
1973	53.05	− 5.8
1974	45.77	−13.7
1975	50.93	+11.3
1976	50.925	0.0

Source: Compiled from *Denver Public Schools, Adopted Budgets,* 1966–1976.

40. In 1967, receipts from state sources accounted for approximately 12 percent of the total revenues needed by the district. This figure was well below the average of 39 percent received from state funds by all school systems in the United States. In 1968 the state contribution amounted to approximately 11 percent of total revenue available to School District No. 1. This was well below the average of 40 percent received from state funds by all school systems.

In recent years the contributions of the state have increased considerably, and under the Public School Finance Act of 1973, the 1976 state contribution was approximately 30 percent, more than twice the proportion it contributed in 1966.

Federal revenue received has more than doubled in the ten years since 1966, from $5.2 million to $13.9 million in 1976. The proportion of total revenues contributed by federal sources, however, has remained relatively constant at approximately 8 percent. These federal funds must be used to supplement local funds in providing special instructional services and facilities to schools—Headstart and vocational training programs, for example. Federal funds are also available for programs to desegregate minority schools in appropriate cases.

Both state and federal funds were available to District 1, beginning in 1971, for implementation of desegregation plans and for purchase of transportation. The district steadfastly refused to seek and obtain these funds, maintaining that to apply while the lawsuit was in the appeals process would be premature. Millions of dollars of special assistance were lost to the district through these refusals, even though under federal law the federal money involved would not have been required to be refunded in the event the courts reversed the requirement to desegregate the Denver public schools.[41]

During calender year 1974, School District No. 1 applied for and received more than $200,000 of federal funds for school desegregation. During 1975 the district received $1.9 million for this purpose from federal sources. The 1976 federal funds for desegregation amounted to $2.3 million.[42]

The Pupils of School District No. 1

As of September 1975, School District No. 1 operated 122 schools.[43] Of these, 93 were elementary schools, 18 junior high schools, 9 high schools, and 2 special schools, the last category consisting of an opportunity school and a metropolitan youth education center. Although the number of schools has steadily increased from 1964-1974 (from 113 to 122), the enrolled population

---

41. The preceding paragraph is based on news articles that appeared in the *Denver Post*, 1971–1973, and personal interviews with Fred Thomas, former chief of elementary and secondary education, Office of Education, Department of Health, Education and Welfare, Region VIII, on April 17, 1975, and George Bardwell, professor of mathematics, University of Denver, and key researcher for the plaintiffs on April 7, 1975.

42. Denver Public School, *ADOPTED BUDGET*, 1976. In 1966 School District No. 1 received 7.4 percent of its funding from federal sources, 12.9 percent from state sources, and 76.9 percent from local sources. By 1975 the federal funding had increased marginally to 7.9 percent, while state funding increased to 25.4 percent and local funding dropped to 57.9 percent. Estimates for 1976 suggest that federal funding will increase to 9.2 percent, state funding to 29.6 percent, and local funding to 61.2 percent. A complete table of all survey summaries mentioned in this study are on file at the Institute of Judicial Administration.

43. The following three paragraphs are based on Denver Public Schools, Report of Estimated Ethnic Distribution of Pupils, 1964–1974.

has been steadily diminishing. In 1964 there were 96,428 students enrolled in regular district schools. In September of 1975 the number of students enrolled in the regular schools decreased to 76,503, an absolute loss of 19.925 students and a percentage decline of approximately 20.7 percent. The biggest drop in student enrollment occurred in 1974, immediately after the desegregation plan went into effect. That year the district lost 7,157 pupils, a 10.8 percent loss. In 1975, enrollment figures indicate that the district losses were at the lowest level since 1971. There were 1,778 fewer pupils in October 1975 than in October 1974—a decline of only 2.3 percent.

In ethnic and racial terms the attrition may be attributed almost entirely to Anglo student out-migration. For the first time, in 1972 the Hispano school population also declined. In 1973 a similar decline was noted for the black student population. The Hispano and black declines, however, have been fairly modest and, proportionately, the Hispano and black population continues to increase in the schools. Blacks made up 11.6 percent and Hispanos comprised 17 percent of the school population in 1964; they now comprise 19.1 percent and 27.2 percent, respectively. At the same time, Anglos, who made up more than 70 percent of the school population in 1964, now comprise only 50.7 percent of the enrolled population.[44]

In recent years the rate of white student attrition in the schools has accelerated considerably. Prior to 1969, the year the desegregation case was filed, the decline in white enrollment occurred at an average annual rate of 1.66 percent. In the years since 1969, white attrition in the schools has taken place at an average annual rate of 6.73 percent. In 1974 the school district lost its most sizable number of Anglos to date: 7,622. This translated into an annual rate of decline of 15.27 percent. The 1975 Anglo attrition rate was sizable, but considerably lower. Public School District No. 1 lost 3,539 Anglo pupils, an annual rate of decline of 8.4 percent.[45]

The Teachers of School District No. 1

In 1974, Public School District No. 1 employed 4,031 classroom teachers. The overwhelming majority of these teachers were Anglo, although in recent years the number of Hispano and black teachers has steadily risen. In 1962, less than 1 percent of the district's classroom teachers were Hispano; in 1974, 4.5 percent were Hispano. In 1962, black teachers comprised 5.6 percent of the district's classroom teachers; in 1974, they made up 9.7 percent. Between 1962 and 1974 the Anglo teaching population declined from 93.5 percent of the total to 84.8 percent of the total.[46]

44. *Id.*
45. *Id.*
46. The preceding paragraph is based on Denver Public Schools, Estimated Ethnic Distribution of Classroom Teachers, 1962–1973, and Denver Public Schools, Reports Required by the Final Judgment and Decree, Civil Action No. 1499, Court Order November 18, Section (2), October 15, 1974.

Since 1963 the Denver Classroom Teacher's Association (DCTA) has been recognized as the sole negotiating agent for the teachers of School District No. 1.[47] The Denver Classroom Teacher's Association is affiliated with the Colorado Education Association at the state level and the National Education Association at the national level. In 1974, approximately 70 percent of the district's 4,200 teachers, counselors, and nurses belonged to DCTA.

During the long period of controversy over school desegregation in Denver and the long court battle, DCTA refrained from taking any position or making any public comment. In 1970, however, it voted to include on its board of directors educators representing two teachers' associations that had been more vociferous on the issue: the Black Educators United and the Congress of Hispanic Educators. In 1974, following the issuance of the final order and decree concerning desegregation, DCTA voted to assist the superintendent of schools in implementing the court-ordered integration program.[48]

Under the 1969 agreement negotiated between DCTA and the school district, teacher assignments and reassignments are required to be made by the district without regard to "race, creed, color, national origin, sex, marital status, or membership in any teacher organization."[49] The only valid considerations in assignment of teachers are competence and the scope of teaching certificates, experience levels, and—other qualifications being equal—seniority in the school district.[50]

As noted below however, the federal courts have concluded as petitioners claimed that the district had maintained a deliberate racial policy in the assignment of teachers to schools. In court, Superintendent Oberhotzer confirmed that black classroom teachers have been almost always initially assigned to those schools where black pupils are concentrated, on the grounds that such teachers would have "immediate empathy" for such students and that the teachers would be "role models."[51]

The Administrators of School District No. 1

Persons who have held administrative or supervisory positions in the Denver public schools has been overwhelmingly Anglo.[52] Although there has been a

47. Rocky Mountain News, February 14, 1963.
48. Preceding information based on a personal interview with Robert A. Anderson, president, Denver Classroom Teachers Association, April 18, 1975.
49. Denver Classroom Teachers Association and School District No. 1, Agreement, 1969, article 9-4.
50. The agreement also specifically notes that both the "Board and the Association recognize that students with slow achievement rates need the expertise of experienced teachers as much as do students with rapid achievement rates." *Id.,* article 9-6.
51. On writ of *certiorari* to the United States Court of Appeals for the Tenth Circuit, Brief for Petitioners, at 12.
52. The paragraphs in this section are based on Denver Public Schools, Estimated Ethnic Distribution of Administrators, Social Workers, Nurses and Psychologists, 1962–1964; and Estimated Ethnic Distribution of Other Certified and Classified Personnel 1965–1973.

fairly regular increase in the number of minorities in such positions, the changes have been relatively modest. In 1962, 95 percent of 307 school administrators were Anglo. There were only two black principals in the district, and three Hispano administrators—a supervisor, an assistant principal, and a coordinator. In addition, there was one school coordinator of Asian derivation.

In 1973, the last year for which such information was available, 87 percent of the district's administrators were Anglo. Approximately 8 percent of the district's administrative staff were black (33), and approximately 4 percent (16) were Hispano. There were 4 school administrators of Asian derivation.[53]

Among the district's classified service personnel[54] the proportions of black and Hispano employees begin to resemble their distribution in the city labor force.[55]

The Quality of School District No. 1

Although it is difficult to gauge the quality of a school district, various impressionistic evaluations as well as statistical indicators suggest an erosion of educational quality. During the past several years, for example, the teacher turnover rate in the Denver school district has consistently declined. This is largely attributed to the improved salary schedule negotiated in 1969 which rewarded career teachers and reduced teacher mobility. At the same time the pupil-teacher ratio has steadily dropped from 24 pupils per teacher in 1969 to 19.3 pupils in 1975. These indicators suggest improved quality.[56]

On the negative side, however, the student drop-out rate has risen from 5.5 percent in 1971/72 to 6.6 percent in 1972/73 to 7.8 percent in 1973/74 to 8.5 percent in 1974/75.[57] Pupil achievement test scores have dropped in these years, and students in more and more of the district's schools fail to meet or exceed national achievement norms.[58] Furthermore, public satisfaction with the school district has also eroded.[59] More recent achievement test comparisons

53. *Id.*
54. "Service personnel" include those in operations, maintenance, transportation, warehouse, and lunchroom.
55. In 1973, 14.6 percent of the district's low-level classified service personnel were black, 17.6 percent were Hispano, and 67.2 percent were Anglo.
56. Colorado Department of Education, Consolidated Report on Elementary and Secondary Education, 1972–1976.
57. *Id.*
58. From 1968 to 1972 the number of Denver junior high schools with achievement scores below the national norm rose from 6 to 13. During the same period the number of high schools with achievement scores below the national norm doubled from 2 to 4. Denver Post, April 22, 1973.
59. In 1968, 14 percent of the Denver population reported that the school district was doing an excellent job, 44 percent felt that the district was doing a good job, and only 19 percent rated the school district performance as fair. In 1972, a comparable survey revealed greatly altered proportions: only 5 percent rated the district excellent, 39 percent good, and 36 percent fair. *Id.*

covering the 1972-1975 period, however, fail to suggest continued patterns of decline.[60]

THE DEVELOPMENT OF THE
DESEGREGATION CONTROVERSY

Although the battle for school integration was not fully launched in Denver until 1968, momentum had been building for a much longer period of time. For years there had been controversy about the techniques the school board and school administration used to regulate distribution of students. One technique was the construction of schools in locations which predictably became racially segregated on the basis of long apparent trends in black population movement. A second technique was the establishment of school attendance zones which assigned black pupils to predominantly minority schools. A third technique was the use of mobile classroom units to increase pupil capacity at predominantly minority schools rather than assigning them to nearby, underutilized Anglo schools.

Newspaper accounts[61] indicate that a series of boundary changes resulting from the construction of a new high school in 1953 provoked protest from the black community, as did a 1957 school boundary change. Protest mounted once again in 1959, after the board of education approved preliminary plans for the construction of a new elementary school in the section of northeast Denver, known as Park Hill. Critics of the plan said that the construction site would lead to the creation of an all-black school. According to the superintendent, the proposed building was designed to relieve overcrowding in adjacent schools and provide a school within walking distance in the area. Notwithstanding the opposition, the Barrett Elementary School was built and shortly after it opened became overwhelmingly black in composition.

In 1962 a new school construction plan again became an issue of controversy among proponents of school integration.[62] The new plan was for a junior high school in northeast Denver. In view of trends in the migration of blacks, it was widely acknowledged that the new school would be all-black. CORE and the NAACP led the attack against the construction of the junior high in the proposed location.[63] Churches in the black community helped to solidify opposition to the plan within the black community. As a result of the ensuing controversy, plans for the construction of the school were suspended, and a special study committee was created to examine the problems of equal educational opportunity

60. Denver Public Schools, A Comparative Study of National Percentile Achievement by Interquartile Distributions, June 12, 1975.
61. Denver Post, April 9, 1959.
62. *Id.*, February 14, 1962.
63. *Id.*, April 5, 1962.

in the Denver public schools and to make recommendations. It was known as the Special Study Committee on Equality of Educational Opportunity in the Denver Public Schools.[64]

As a result of these and other school boundary changes and new school construction, the segregation of the Denver public schools became a concern of several Denver organizations, including traditional civil rights agencies like the Urban League, CORE, the NAACP, and the Colorado Anti-Discrimination Commission. In addition, several church and neighborhood associations from Park Hill were central actors in the segregation controversy. One of the most important neighborhood associations in this struggle was the Park Hill Action Committee (PHAC). A biracial organization formed in 1960 to prevent the deterioration of Park Hill as a neighborhood and to combat the mass flight of whites in the wake of black in-migration to Park Hill, PHAC received support from the black and white Park Hill area churches.[65]

In 1964 a school board-appointed special committee released its long-awaited report.[66] The report criticized the board's school boundary policies as designed to perpetuate racial isolation as well as to concentrate minority faculty in minority schools. The report also concluded that segregated schools resulted in inequality of educational opportunity and recommended a policy of considering racial and ethnic factors in setting boundaries to minimize segregation. At the same time the report upheld the neighborhood school concept and rejected as impractical the transportation of pupils for the sole purpose of integrating school populations. Substantively, the report contained approximately 155 recommendations for improving educational opportunity in minority schools.

The board of education adopted Policy 5100 in May 1964, which upheld the principle of educational equality and cited the desirability of reducing concentrations of racial and ethnic minority groups in the schools. It also established an open-enrollment program designed to reduce racial imbalance. The plan permitted parents to file transfer requests to fill approximately 1,809 places, some 2 percent of the public school enrollment.[67] Students were required to provide their own transportation. Aside from this limited open-enrollment program, nothing else was undertaken to implement a policy of racially heterogeneous schools.

64. A committee of 32 persons, representing various segments of the community, was selected from over 500 names of interested citizens. James Vorhees, an attorney and unsuccessful candidate for the school board in 1950, was appointed as committee chairman. Also on the committee was Rachel Noel, a black consultant for the Mayor's Commission on Community Relations.

65. Cohen & Robnett, *Organizational Evolution,* in C. Cortese, The Impact of Black Mobility: Selective Migration and Community Change (Final report to the National Science Foundation, University of Denver, Department of Sociology, 1964), at 60.

66. This paragraph is based on the special study committee, Advisory Council on Equality of Educational Opportunity in the Denver Public Schools, Report and Recommendations to the Board of Education (1964).

67. Denver Post, May 21, 1964.

In the school board election of 1965, James Vorhees and Rachel Noel, both of whom had served on the special study committee, were elected as board members, along with James Amesse, a doctor. Edgar Benton, who had previously been the lone "civil rights liberal" on the board, was now joined by Ms. Noel, the first black ever to be elected to the Denver School Board, and two other members sympathetic to minority pupil problems.

The steady increase of blacks in northeast Denver meant even greater concentrations of minorities in the Park Hill schools. School overcrowding, the use of mobile classroom units, and unabated racial segregation led to more pressure by civil rights groups and black community leaders for action. In response, the school board created a second study committee in February 1966, the Advisory Council on Equality of Educational Opportunity, which was directed "to examine the 'neighborhood school' policy in its application to building new schools or additions to relieve northeast Denver and to suggest changes or new policies if needed necessary to eliminate 'de facto' segregation."[68] William Berge, an attorney, was appointed committee chairman. The advisory council's report was published in February 1967. Frequently a mere reiteration of the 1964 report, the 1967 report recommended that no new schools be built in northeast Denver until plans had been developed to reduce concentrations of minority pupils. The report also advocated that heterogeneity in schools be increased to improve the quality of education for all students. It suggested the establishment of special programs in schools which would attract students of a variety of racial backgrounds; the creation of an educational center, or a multipurpose building to which students would be drawn for special purposes; and the creation of superior programs in several all-black junior high schools.

A member of the advisory council, Stephen Knight, Jr., wrote a minority report which contested plans for an educational center and what he termed "busing." That spring (1967), he and William Berge ran as candidates for the school board with the support of the Republican Party. Their leading opponents were backed by an interracial group of civil rights liberals and supported by the Democratic Party Executive Committee. Knight and Berge were elected to the school board in May 1967.

Shortly before the election, the voluntary open-enrollment program was reviewed and declared unsatisfactory as a method of achieving racial balance. Most transfers, it was noted, involved the movement of Anglo students to new Anglo schools and black students to different all-black schools.[69]

Around the election period several attempts were made in the state legislature to pressure school districts into eliminating racial segregation[70] and to commit additional attention to instruction in Hispanic culture.[71] All three bills were postponed indefinitely.

68. Advisory Council on Equality of Educational Opportunity in the Denver Public Schools, Final Report and Recommendations to the Board of Education (1967), at 8.
69. Denver Post, March 19, 1967.
70. HB 1351, SB 417.
71. SB 280.

Under mounting pressure to act positively to desegregate schools, the school board voted in June 1967 to halt additional school construction in northeast Denver where the likelihood of racial isolation was very high.[72] Several months later, the school board issued a plan for school construction in northeast Denver based on the concept of an intermediate school drawing from larger attendance areas. Estimated to require the busing of 4,700 students per year, the intermediate school plan was designed to foster racial mixture in northeast Denver by possessing a school boundary sufficiently large to contain a racially heterogeneous population. The plan was seen as a politically feasible response to the complaints of the black community as well as the proponents of neighborhood schools.[73]

The intermediate school plan was submitted for public approval in a capital bond election in November 1967. For the first time in the history of the school district, a bond issue did not pass. The $32.5 million school bond issue was defeated approximately seven to three. According to former school board member Jim Vorhees, the bond issue was transformed into an integration fight. The business community, which normally distributed support in bond elections, refused to approve the "forced busing" component of the intermediate school plan and withheld financial support.[74] As a result of the bond defeat, the intermediate school concept was never implemented.

In 1968, protest about racial imbalance in the schools reached a new pitch. Several events were critical in setting this tide of protest into motion. For the first time the school administration released comparative achievement test score data.[75] These scores disclosed not only a great disparity between achievement levels at predominately Anglo and predominately minority schools, but they also reflected very low achievement levels at the minority schools, which became even lower as the minority children advanced through the grades. There was also evidence that the predominately minority schools had a disproportionate number of minority teachers, fewer experienced and more inexperienced teachers, and much higher rates of teacher turnover than the predominately Anglo schools.

Outrage over this new information and the events of the last decade came to a head on April 5, 1968, the day Martin Luther King was assassinated.[76] The following week, a minister, a social worker, and a juvenile court judge formed Citizens for One Community, which adopted a petition calling for national unity and racial balance in the schools.

72. Denver Post, June 1967.
73. *Id.,* October 17, 1967.
74. Personal interview with Jim Vorhees, April 22, 1975. (Subsequent surveys showed that busing and other integration factors were responsible for the defeat of the bond among the electorate.) Denver Post, January 19, 1968.
75. The following paragraph is based on the writ of *certiorari* to the United States Court of Appeals for the Tenth Circuit, Brief for Petitioners, at 47–50.
76. The following three paragraphs are based on a personal interview with Jules Mondschein, April 4, 1975. Mondschein was co-director of Citizens for One Community.

The organization rapidly recruited supporters, and on the night of April 25, 1968, thousands of middle-class whites and Park Hill blacks attended a public school board meeting where Rachel Noel, the only black member of the school board, introduced a resolution instructing then Superintendent Gilberts to submit an integration plan by September 30, 1968, with consideration for the use of transportation. The meeting and the turnout in support of the resolution received full coverage in the press. The board voted to table the resolution for one month.

During the following month, relentless organizational activity continued. The homes of school board members who were uncommitted to the resolution were picketed, as was the school administration building. Speak Out for Integration groups attempted to educate the public on the deleterious consequences of segregated education.[77] Community, religious, political, and social leaders were approached to lend support to the resolution. Indeed, the Denver Chamber of Commerce and the Denver City Council, among other organizations, voted to support the Noel Resolution. Two nights before the May school board meeting, an association of black school teachers, Black Educators United, announced its intention to boycott in support of the resolution. Then, James Voorhees, the last school board member needed to pass the resolution, was persuaded to vote affirmatively. The boycott was officially cancelled, but thousands of public school children were absent. In black schools, more than half the students boycotted classes. However, in predominantly Anglo schools absenteeism was only 68 percent.[78]

On May 16, 1968, the school board voted 5-2 (another "doubtful" vote had gone in favor of the resolution) to pass Resolution 1490, the Noel Resolution, and philosphically committed itself to the desegregation of the schools.

Pursuant to Resolution 1490, Superintendent Gilberts presented a report for the board's consideration on October 10, 1968. At a school board meeting on November 21, 1968, the superintendent was directed to come up with more specific planning options, particularly for the possible desegregation of a junior high school in Park Hill and the amelioration of crowding in that school by means of limited busing. The superintendent reported back to the board. The result, termed the Gilberts Plan,[79] involved the creation of elementary, junior, and senior high model-school complexes. On all levels, schools forming a complex would be selected so as to include a wide representation of racial and ethnic groups. A further component of the plan was the sharing of educational resources, equipment, and opportunities in a central-city school to encourage integration while retaining the individual character of other schools. Busing would be employed for the voluntary transfer of students to achieve racial balance; the

77. Personal interview with George Bardwell, April 7, 1975.
78. Denver Post, May 16, 1968.
79. The Superintendent Reports: Planning Quality Education—A Proposal for Integrating the Denver Public Schools (Denver, Colorado: School District No. 1, October 10, 1968).

nonvoluntary transfer of pupils to predominantly Anglo schools with available space; and the transportation of students of all races for special educational programs. Later in November 1968, the board adopted a new voluntary transfer program, called "voluntary" rather than "limited" open enrollment (VOE), whereby the district provided transportation for children voluntarily choosing to fill limited spaces in cross-town pupil exchanges.

Extensive public hearings and board-administration deliberations occurred through the early months of 1969 on the proposals formulated by the superintendent. These proposals ultimately became known as Resolutions 1520, 1524 and 1531, adopted by the school board on Janaury 30, March 20, and April 17, 1969, respectively. Collectively the resolutions provided for concrete measures by which to alleviate school segregation in Park Hill.[80] Combined, they would have meant integrated education for 33,151 students.[81]

Such was not to happen. May 1969 was occasion for another school board election, in which two new members were to be elected. Closely following the formal adoption of Resolutions 1520, 1524 and 1530, the May election was dramatic and emotional. The dominant theme of the election was busing versus neighborhood schools.

Election day was a disaster for the pro-busing forces. Busing opponents were elected by a margin of two and one-half to one. Voting patterns were strictly along racial lines, and the pro-busing pair lost soundly in predominantly Anglo sectors of the city.[82]

The first action of the new school board on June 9, 1969, was to rescind Resolutions 1520, 1524 and 1531.[83] But the desegregation embers were far from cool. For even on the eve of the disastrous school board election of 1969, plans were underway for new actions to remedy the segregation problems in School District No. 1.

COMMENCEMENT OF THE LAWSUIT: BACKGROUND

Many people, of course, were involved in the years and months prior to the bringing of the plaintiffs' lawsuit in June of 1969 in laying the groundwork for legal action.

Plaintiffs' attorneys were Robert Connery, Craig Barnes, and Gordon Greiner.[84]

---

80. Resolution 1520 dealt with high-school level racial stabilization; 1524 was concerned with the junior-high-school level; and 1531 with the elementary-school level.
81. Denver Post, May 11, 1969.
82. Jackson, *Discrimination and Busing: The Denver School Board Election of May, 1969,8* Rocky Mountain Social Science J. (October 1971).
83. Denver Post, June 9, 1969. The rescission was by a 5–2 vote, and the vote was conducted over the opposition of the school superintendent.
84. All were originally with the Denver law firm of Holland and Hart; by the time serious consideration of a lawsuit was underway, Barnes had left Holland and Hart to form his own practice.

The two professionals were Paul Klite, a medical doctor and researcher, and George Bardwell, a mathematician and statistician. Prior to the school board election of May 1969, there had been some contact through Connery with representatives of the NAACP Legal Defense Fund (LDF) in New York. But, in reflecting on the events leading up to the filing of the lawsuit, Barnes recalled that little serious thought had been given to the actual commencement of legal action prior to the night of the school board election in May of 1969.

During the late fall of 1968 and the winter of 1969 when the school board, the school administration, and the general public were involved in hearings and other deliberations about Resolutions 1520, 1524, and 1531, Craig Barnes was devoting his primary efforts toward the recruitment of pro-desegregation candidates for the May election. Gordon Greiner was not even peripherally involved with the legal or political ferment over desegregation in Denver. Robert Connery was also working to make the desegregation effort succeed through electoral strategies. George Bardwell and Paul Klite were generally making themselves experts on the subject of school desegregation and, in the course of organizing testimony on the Gilberts proposals, were involved in accumulating extensive information about the history and statistical complexion of the Denver schools.[85]

On election eve in May 1969 at the Benton-Pascoe headquarters, Barnes recalls approaching Robert Connery and saying "If you ever decide to bring a lawsuit, let me know." It was commonly understood, Barnes says, that the election of the anti-busing candidates would immediately lead to the rescission of Resolutions 1520, 1524, and 1531.

Connery called Barnes the next day. Did Barnes, Connery asked, have time the next weekend to come over and help draw up a complaint? Barnes said he was busy. Connery persisted. Barnes gave in. They thought, working together and with the help of others, to have a complaint done by Sunday night. They were wrong.

The following weeks were frantic for Barnes, Connery, Bardwell, Klite, and others they worked with, and, after Memorial Day 1969, for the newcomer to the group, Gorden Greiner. Conrad Harper of the Legal Defense Fund was called in. The LDF played a continuing advisory role. Prior to the May election, no legal research had been coherently drawn together, although various people, including those associated with LDF, had collected cases and theories. The attorneys worked frantically to pull together a complaint; Bardwell and Klite worked closely with them and supplied factual underpinnings. The most hopeful factor in favor of the plaintiffs-to-be, from a purely legal standpoint, was the virtual certainty that the new school board would rescind the three resolutions. A tangible thread of state action wove its way into the legal theorizing.

Neither Barnes nor Connery had much trial experience. Connery felt strongly that they needed help from someone who did. Connery approached Greiner on

85. Bardwell, claims Barnes, became the local authority, bar none, on the educational effects of segregation and the findings of the 1966 Coleman report, *Equality of Educational Opportunity* (1966).

Memorial Day. Greiner at the time had never been involved in civil rights causes or litigation; he was an anti-trust litigator for Denver's largest and perhaps most prestigious law firm. Greiner for the first time read all the cases in the desegregation litigation area. He was convinced there was a good case and joined the others in the job of putting together a complaint and legal strategy.

Fred Thomas and Martha Radetsky spearheaded an effort on behalf of the plaintiffs to put together a group of representative plaintiffs to name in the complaint. The objective was to find students in each school who had in the past been or would in the future be affected by acts of segregation or desegregation under authority of the school board or the courts.[86]

After commencement of the lawsuit, the Legal Defense Fund continued to play an active role. Conrad Harper assisted in the drafting of a complaint.[87] At various stages, apparently, there was some disagreement between the local Denver attorneys and the attorneys for LDF about the strategic merits of the plaintiffs' claims regarding unequal educational opportunity. However, to the extent that these disagreements were important, they never significantly disturbed the cordial and beneficial relationship of the local group to LDF. Finally, LDF was instrumental in putting together for plaintiffs a group of expert witnesses for the hearing on the preliminary injunction and the trial on the merits itself.

One of the biggest strategic decisions facing the attorneys was whether or not to go after an immediate preliminary injunction and what effects such an effort would have on a subsequent trial on the merits. The data developed by Bardwell and Klite was sufficient to convince the attorneys that the whole district, not just its so-called Park Hill enclave, was ripe for legal attack on both de jure and de facto grounds. Yet, Resolutions 1520, 1524, and 1531, the rescission of which occurred on June 9, 1969, addressed desegregation in the Park Hill area alone. From the standpoint of attorneys drafting a complaint in May of 1969, an immediate injunction against an official rescission was necessary to get the resolutions back in effect by fall. Yet the hearing on such a temporary injunction would limit the presentation of evidence to the alleged segregation in the Park Hill area. Not until a trial on the merits would the plaintiffs be able to in-

86. Along with Bardwell and Klite, other citizens in the community, on behalf of the plaintiffs, had been gathering general information about school board history, test and achievement data, and other information relevant to the "quality" of individual Denver schools.

87. Velma Singer of LDF met with the plaintiffs' Denver attorneys prior to the hearing on the motion for preliminary injunction and, according to Gordon Greiner, significantly influenced the order of presentation of evidence therein. Singer was present for the part of the hearing on the preliminary injunction itself. Later, during the course of the trial on the merits, Harper returned to Denver to assist with the litigation. According to Greiner, LDF continually supplied suggestions for litigation strategy and research materials about new cases in the desegregation area. Attorneys for LDF wrote the entirety of the plaintiffs' petition for *certiorari* to the Supreme Court, and James Nabrit of LDF divided the authorship of the plaintiffs' brief and argument before the Supreme Court with Greiner.

troduce their evidence on the alleged segregation in other parts of the system. The prospect of two separate evidentiary hearings raised the unpleasant prospect of two different results. On the other hand, it was paramount to obtain some immediate relief in Park Hill. Therefore, the motion for a preliminary injunction accompanied the complaint when the latter was filed on June 19, 1969.

Another strategic problem confronted the attorneys: whether to sever a distinct claim for relief based on the educational consequences of desegregation, a claim of unequal educational opportunity largely traceable in an empirical sense to the Coleman report and in a legal sense to the *Brown* decisions. It was the feeling of the attorneys that the complaint already incorporated almost all shadings of previously tried legal theories in desegregation lawsuits. The unequal educational opportunity claim they envisioned would be novel. LDF expressed certain reservations about such a claim. Eventually, it was in fact added. In retrospect, Greiner, for one, feels its inclusion was important and beneficial, especially at the Supreme Court level where arguably its prominence in the posture of the plaintiffs' case provided a strong incentive for the Court to go as far as it did in order not to reach the question of unequal educational opportunity itself.

THE BRINGING OF THE LAWSUIT: THE COMPLAINT

The complaint and motion for preliminary injunction were filed simultaneously in U.S. District Court for the District of Colorado on June 19, 1969. The complaint listed as plaintiffs eight individual citizens and residents of the city of Denver, Colorado, and their wards or children who were students in the Denver public schools. Included were blacks, Anglos, and Hispanos. Listed as defendants were the school district itself, the then-superintendent of the Denver public schools, and all the individual members of the school board in their individual and official capacities. In the complaint, the plaintiffs sought permanent injunctive relief and a declaratory judgment under 28 *U.S.C.* §2201. Jurisdiction of the district court was invoked under 28 *U.S.C.* §1343(3) and (4), based on the allegation of the existence of a civil action under 42 *U.S.C.* §1983 and the Fourteenth Amendment to the Constitution of the United States.

The plaintiffs' action was brought as a class action pursuant to Rules 23(b) (1)(B), 23(b)(2) and 23(b)(3), *Federal Rules of Civil Procedure*. The complaint itself stated two claims for relief. As to both claims, the plaintiffs purported to represent that class of school children who, as a result of actions of the Denver School Board, would be (and had been) attending segregated schools and who would be (and had been) receiving an unequal educational opportunity.

The relief prayed for in the first claim was dual in nature: First, the plaintiffs prayed that the rescission of Resolutions 1520, 1524, and 1530 be temporarily and permanently enjoined; second, the plaintiffs prayed for a declaratory judgment that the rescission by the board constituted a violation of the equal protection clause.

The second claim for relief addressed itself to alleged segregation in those portions of the Denver school system which became known during litigation as the "core-city" schools, not merely the Park Hill schools; this claim involved the following four separate counts:

First. An allegation of certain deliberate and purposeful actions by the school board, allegedly undertaken with the intent to "create, foster and maintain racial and ethnic segregation within the School District," the effect of which was to produce such segregation in core-city schools.[88]

Second. An allegation that the core-city schools were segregated and that the school board had taken certain actions, the consequences of which were to create unequal educational opportunities in the core-city schools.[89]

Third. An allegation that the school board had adopted and maintained a "neighborhood school" policy (albeit without discriminatory intent) which in fact produced racial and ethnic segregation of students, such segregation being further alleged to deny equal educational opportunity to students assigned to predominantly black and/or Hispano schools and to deny equal protection of the laws to such students.

Fourth. An allegation that effects from a so-called "track system" similar to those which were alleged to have accrued from the "neighborhood school" policy, was subsequently abandoned by the plaintiffs and did not figure in the litigation.

The second claim for relief prayed for general injunctive relief and for declaratory judgments as to the unconstitutional and void nature of the complained of acts of the school board, and further demanded affirmative equitable relief in the nature of requiring the school board to submit various plans and programs no later than September 1, 1970 to deal in a comprehensive and effective fashion with all the alleged factual characteristics and consequences of segregation within the school district.

The bulk of the allegations contained in the first claim for relief were tried fully at the hearing on the preliminary injunction; the bulk of the allegations in the second at the trial on the merits.

---

88. Specifically, the court alleged maintenance of a "neighborhood school" policy, creation and alteration of school attendance boundaries, allowance of optional transfers by Anglo children outside of certain school attendance areas, assignment of black and Hispanic faculty and staff to segregated schools, and the creation of optional attendance areas which retained and confined black and/or Hispanic pupils to predominantly segregated schools.

89. The court alleged the provision of physical plants, equipment materials, supplies, and curricula inferior to that provided to schools with predominantly Anglo student pupil populations; and the assignment of a disproportionately large number of less experienced faculty.

The Litigation: Chronological Summary

For ease of reference in reading later sections of this essay, the reader is given the following chronological summary of the course of the litigation.

June 19, 1969. Plaintiffs filed their complaint in the United States District Court for the District of Colorado whereby commencing Civil Action No. C-1499. The complaint, discussed in more detail above, sought both a declaratory judgment and injunctive relief. Simultaneously, plaintiffs filed a motion for a preliminary injunction which sought to enjoin certain actions of the defendant school board during the pendency of the principal action.

July 16-22, 1969. Hearings on the motion for the preliminary injunction were held before District Judge William E. Doyle.

July 31, 1969. By order and opinion Judge Doyle granted the motion for the preliminary injunction (303 F.Supp. 279). (On appeal by the defendants, the circuit court of appeals vacated the preliminary injunction and remanded the case to the district court for further proceedings, holding the injunctive order lacked "specificity" as required by Rule 65(c), F.R.Civ.P.)

August 7, 1969. The district court proceeded with hearings pursuant to the remand.

August 14, 1969. The district court issued its supplemental findings, conclusions and temporary injunction (303 F.Supp. 289). Defendants immediately applied to the court of appeals for a stay.

August 27, 1969. The court of appeals stayed the preliminary injunction pending further review and order. Plaintiffs immediately moved the Supreme Court of the United States for an order vacating the stay of the court of appeals.

August 29, 1969. Justice Brennan granted plaintiffs' motion for a stay (396 U.S. 1215). Justice Brennan's order vacating the stay of the court of appeals further directed the reinstatement of the preliminary injunction of the district court.

February 2-20, 1970. Trial on the merits of plaintiffs' complaint before Judge Doyle.

March 21, 1970. Pursuant to said trial, the district court entered its opinion and findings on the issues and made permanent the preliminary injunction. The court reserved ruling on remedies until consideration of proposed remedial plans to be submitted by both plaintiffs and defendants.

May 11-19, 1970. The court held additional hearings on proposed remedial plans.

May 21, 1970. The court issued an opinion regarding remedies (313 F.Supp. 90).

June 11, 1970. Pursuant to the order and opinion of March 21, 1970 and pursuant to the opinion regarding plans and remedies of May 21, 1970, the district court issued its final decree and judgment. Both the defendants and the plaintiffs appealed the final decree and judgment to the court of appeals.

March 2, 1971. The court of appeals granted said motion for stay as to all judgment.

March 26, 1971. The court of appeals granted said motion for stay as to all proceedings pertaining to the plan envisioned by the district court's final decree and judgment not yet implemented as of the date of the stay. *Per curiam,* the United States Supreme Court vacated the stay ordered by the court of appeals (402 U.S. 182).

June 11, 1971. The court of appeals issued its opinion and judgment regarding the appeal and cross-appeal from the final decree and judgment of the district court. The court of appeals affirmed the decision of the district court in part and reversed and remanded in part to the district court (445 F.2d 990).

Plaintiffs appealed to the Supreme Court of the United States, and their petition for *certiorari* was granted (404 U.S. 1036).

October 12, 1972. Plaintiffs' appeal was argued before the Supreme Court.

June 21, 1973. The Supreme Court, in an opinion delivered by Justice Brennan, modified the judgment of the court of appeals so as to vacate instead of reverse the relevant portions of the final decree of the district court (413 U.S. 189). The case was remanded to the district court for further proceedings.

December 11, 1973. Pursuant to the remand, and hearings held thereon, the district court issued its opinion and order. The court's opinion included orders to both plaintiffs and defendants to submit to the court their remedial plans in order to effectuate the district court's order itself.

April 24, 1974. After substantial hearings on proposed plans, the district court entered its final judgment and decree, selecting a desegregation plan developed by one John A. Finger, Jr., and rejecting the plans proposed by both plaintiffs and defendants.

Both plaintiffs and defendants appealed this final judgment and decree to the United States Court of Appeals for the Tenth Circuit.

February 10, 1975. The appeals of the plaintiffs and defendants reached the court of appeals.

August 11, 1975. The appeals were decided by the court of appeals (521 F.2d 465). The court of appeals affirmed the district court as to the bulk of the latter's final judgment and decree and reversed as to portions thereof dealing with bilingual-bicultural education and "pairing."

The defendants petitioned the United States Supreme Court to review the decision of the Tenth Circuit Court of Appeals, as did intervenors in the case representing the Congress of Hispanic Educators (CHE), the party to the suit primarily concerned with bilingual-bicultural matters.

November 11, 1975. The petitions for review by the defendants and CHE intervenors were docketed with the Supreme Court (44 USLW 3351).

January 12, 1976. The Supreme Court denied the petitions for review. (As of the date of this writing, the district court is left with minor portions of the case not finally determined—the bilingual-bicultural issue as to which the Tenth Circuit Court of Appeals reversed, pairing, and the East-Manual Complex.)

The Litigation: The Preliminary Injunction

When the plaintiffs filed their complaint on June 19, 1969, they also filed a motion for a preliminary injunction. The preliminary injunction was aimed at stopping implementation of the rescission of Resolutions 1520, 1524 and 1531 during the litigation. Since the resolutions dealt exclusively with the schools in Park Hill, as noted above, the preliminary injunction motion and its later hearing were limited to the plaintiffs' case as it related to segregation in Park Hill, not in Denver as a whole. The motion was heard and argued and testimony was taken during July 16 through 22, 1969. Judge Doyle for the district court found that the preliminary injunction was justified in his opinion of July 31, 1969 (303 F.Supp. 279). The judge considered the rescission of the three resolutions by the school board in light of voluminous evidence of actual segregation in Park Hill. He described "the purpose and effect" of the rescission as "designed to segregate" and ordered the school board to cease from putting the rescission into effect.

The decision of the district court on the preliminary injunction was appealed, and the appeals court sent the matter back for further hearing. At the hearing, the preliminary injunction was reinstated by the district court. And this time, the United States Supreme Court upheld the district court, even though the court of appeals was prepared to prevent the preliminary injunction again. The preliminary injunction disposed of, the district court had to proceed with a trial on the merits of the plaintiffs' complaint.

The Litigation: Trial on the Merits

The trial on the merits proceeded during February 2 through 20, 1970, again before Judge Doyle. This phase of the proceedings raised many of the same issues for determination that had been before the court in the hearing on the preliminary injunction. One issue at the trial on the merits regarded Park Hill: the making permanent of the preliminary injunction. But the chief questions not previously before the court involved: (1) whether there was in fact segregation in other than the Park Hill schools, especially in what came to be called the core-city schools; (2) whether, if such segregation existed, it had been intentionally created and maintained by the defendants, under guise of a "neighborhood school" policy or otherwise; and (3) whether, if such segregation existed either by intentional or nonintentional acts, it was accompanied by measurable and intangible consequences which inevitably resulted in a deprivation of equal educational opportunity.

After considerable testimony by both sides, on March 21, 1970, Judge Doyle issued his opinion (313 F.Supp. 61). He ordered that the plaintiffs should have the full benefit of Resolutions 1520, 1524 and 1531, thus in effect finalizing his preliminary injunction order as to the Park Hill schools. Second, he concluded that the segregation shown by the evidence to exist in the core-city (non-Park Hill) schools was not intentionally created; it was de facto, not de jure. He held that "the evidence establishes . . . that an equal educational opportunity is not being provided" at the core-city schools, and set a hearing on remedies to consider the "serious and difficult problem" of alleviating that unequal educational opportunity.

The Litigation: 1970 Hearing on Relief

The hearings on relief pursuant to Judge Doyle's opinion of March 21, 1970, occurred May 11 through 14, 1970. The issue, what Judge Doyle had called "a serious and difficult problem," was the development of an appropriate plan to overcome inferior educational opportunity in the core-city schools. Judge Doyle had indicated in his opinion a reluctance to consider compulsory busing in any final plan, although he had not ruled it out. He had left the door open to both plaintiffs and defendants to come up with proposals.

At the hearings, both plaintiffs and defendants submitted lengthy plans for improving educational opportunity in the core-city schools. In his opinion of May 21, 1970, Judge Doyle considered the evidence offered about these plans and made a final order with regard to relief.

Findings. On the basis of the evidence and testimony presented at the hearing on relief, Judge Doyle made the following findings:

1. A program of desegregation and integration was necessary to improve the quality of education in the so-called core-city schools.
2. The segregated setting in the core-city schools did in fact stifle and frustrate the learning process.
3. To attempt to carry out a compensatory education program within minority schools without simultaneously desegregating and integrating those schools would prove unsuccessful.
4. A system of so-called voluntary open enrollment, or free transfer to designated Anglo schools of minority group students, would constitute a minimal but insufficient fulfillment of the constitutional rights of the persons involved.
5. Prior to a program of integration, the core-city schools had to be drastically improved in order not to impose inequity on white students required to attend those schools through the integration process.

The Court's Plan. Judge Doyle rejected the plans proposed by both the plaintiffs and the defendants and instead set forth the plan described below. It should be noted that the court's plan applied to only fifteen so-called core-city schools. These schools were selected for subjection to the remedies in the plan on the basis of their possession of a 70–75 percent concentration of *either* Negro or Hispano students, not both. In the opinion of May 21, 1970, the court agreed to add two more schools to the core-city designation, making a total of seventeen schools, on the basis of their success in meeting the above-limited 70–75 percent criterion. The court refused plaintiffs' request that a school which possessed a *combined* percentage of Hispano and Negro students in the 70–75 percent range also be included in the plan. Within this context, the provisions of the court's plan were as follows:

1. *Elementary Schools.* At least 50 percent of the court-designated elementary schools must be desegregated by September 1, 1971; the balance of the court-designated elementary schools to be desegregated by September 1, 1972. Desegregation for the purposes of this aspect of the plan was deemed by the court to consist of an Anglo component in each school in excess of 50 percent of the total racial composition of the student body. Details of this aspect of the plan were left to the plaintiffs and the school board subject to ultimate court review.

2. *The Junior High Schools.* There were two junior high schools affected. With regard to one, the court called for "substantial" desegreation "along the lines set forth" for the elementary schools by the beginning of the school year in the fall of 1972. With regard to the other junior high school, the court set forth two options: first, to desegregate in the manner proposed for the first junior high school; second, to make the other junior high school an open school for special education and other special programs then in effect or which the board might wish to put into effect in the future.

3. *The High Schools.* There was only one high school affected by the court's findings with regard to unequal educational opportunity, and with regard to this high school, the court ordered implementation of the plans set forth by both defendants and plaintiffs for making this high school an open school for vocational and pre-professional training programs already instituted there.

4. *Preparation.* Beginning immediately, the court ordered an "intensive program" of education to be carried out within the community and the school system. This program was to include orientation for teachers in the field of minority cultures and problems and how to deal effectively with minority children in an integrated environment. The court also urged education of the community as to the educational benefits and values to be derived from desegregation and integration.

5. *Free transfer.* As an interim measure only, the court approved the board's program for voluntary open enrollment with respect to all the designated core-city schools.

6. *Compensatory Education.* For the 1970/71 school year, the court ordered implementation of the compensatory education programs already in effect.[90]

90. These programs included the following:

Integration of teachers and administrative staff.
Encouragement and incentive to place skilled and experienced teachers and administrators in the core-city schools.
Use of teacher aides and paraprofessionals.
Human relations training for all school district employees.
In-service training on both district-wide and individual school bases.
Extended school years.

Finally, the court noted that only grades one through six of the elementary schools covered by the plan were to be included therein. Kindergarten students were to be excluded.

The defendants appealed the final decree and order of the district court on June 16, 1970, to the Court of Appeals for the Tenth Circuit. On June 24, 1970 the plaintiffs cross-appealed on the following specific issues: (1) the court's failure to grant relief to the core-city schools whose combined black and Hispano enrollment was in excess of 70 percent; (2) the court's failure to find intent in the school district's setting of school attendance boundaries with regard to the core-city schools; (3) the court's failure to find that a neighborhood school system is unconstitutional where it produces segregated schools in fact, regardless of intent; (4) the court's failure to require that all desegregation and integration be accomplished by September of 1971. The Court of Appeals for the Tenth Circuit issued its opinion for both the appeal and the cross-appeal on June 11, 1971 (445 F.2d 990 [1970]).

The court first dealt with the defendants-appellants' attack on the district court's decision that found intentional segregation in the Park Hill schools. The court of appeals came down in support of the conclusion of the district court:

> In sum, there is ample evidence in the record to sustain the trial court's findings that race was made the basis for school districting with the purpose and effect of producing substantially segregated schools in the Park Hill area. This conduct clearly violates the Fourteenth Amendment and the rules we have heretofore laid down in the Downs and Dowell cases. [445 F.2d at 1002.]

As to whether, as contended by the plaintiffs, the rescission of the three resolutions itself was an act of de jure segregation, the court of appeals dodged the issue, saying:

> It is sufficient to say that the Board's adoption of those resolutions was responsive to its constitutional duty to desegregate the named schools and the trial court was within its powers in designating those resolutions as the best solution to a difficult situation. [455 F.2d at 1002.]

As to the issue of unequal educational opportunity in the so-called core-city schools, which the district court had found to require the relief designated above, the court of appeals noted that "the trial court's findings stand or fall on the power of federal courts to resolve educational difficulties arising from circumstances outside the ambit of state action" (445 F.2d at 1004). The court of

---

Early childhood programs.
Classes in black and Hispanic culture and history.
Spanish language training.
Continuation of special programs for children with deficient reading skills.

appeals then noted that the district court correctly stated the law of the district "that a neighborhood school policy is constitutionally acceptable, even though it results in racially concentrated schools, provided the plan is not used as a veil to further perpetuate racial discrimination" (*id.*). Notwithstanding its correct observation and statement of the law in the Tenth Circuit, said the court of appeals, the district court then fell into an error:

In the course of explicating this rule and holding that the core area school policy was constitutionally maintained, the trial court rejected the notion that a neighborhood school system is unconstitutional if it produces segregation in fact. However, then, in the final analysis, the findings that an unequal educational opportunity exists in the designated core schools must rest squarely on the premise that Denver's neighborhood school policy is violative of the Fourteenth Amendment because it permits segregation in fact. This undermines our holdings in the Tulsa, Downs and Dowell cases and cannot be accepted under the existing law of this Circuit. [445 F.2d at 1004.]

While refusing to dispute the evidence offered by the plaintiffs and while further refusing to dispute the opinion of other cases in other circuits to the effect that segregation in fact may create an inferior educational atmosphere, the Court of Appeals for the Tenth Circuit attempted to distinguish and refused to follow the statements in those other federal cases, suggesting that federal courts should play a corrective role in the system.

Our reluctance to embark on such a course stems not from a desire to ignore a very serious educational and social ill, but from the firm conviction that we are without the power to do so. . . . Unable to locate a firm foundation upon which to build a constitutional deprivation, we are compelled to abstain from enforcing the trial judge's plan to desegregate and integrate court designated core area schools. [445 F.2d at 1005.]

The court of appeals took solace from the fact that since the commencement of the litigation the new school board had passed Resolution 1562, stating that regardless of the final outcome of the litigation the school board would attempt to improve the quality of education offered in the school system. "The salutary potential of such a program cannot be minimized, and the Board is to be commended for its initiative" (445 F.2d at 1005).

The court of appeals gave short shrift to the cross-appeal of the plaintiffs. As to the assertions of the plaintiffs that they were required to labor under too high a burden of proof in proving state action in the segregation of the core-city schools, the court of appeals held as follows:

Where, as here, the system is not a dual one, and where no type of state imposed segregation has previously been established, the burden is on plaintiffs to prove by a preponderance of the evidence that racial imbalance exists and that it was caused by intentional state action. Once a prima facie case is made, the defendants have the burden of going forward with the evidence [citations omitted]. They may attack the allegations of segregatory intent, causation and/or defend on the grounds of justification in terms of legitimate state interest. But the initial burden of proving unconstitutional segregation remains on plaintiffs. Once plaintiffs prove state imposed segregation, justification for such discrimination must be in terms of positive social interests which are protected or advanced. The trial court held that cross-appellants failed in their burden of proving (1) a racially discriminatory purpose and (2) a causal relationship between the acts complained of and the racial imbalance admittedly existing in those schools. [455 F.2d at 1006.]

The court of appeals found that although there was some evidence to sustain the position of the plaintiffs, there was also evidence to support the findings of the district court, and that under Rule 52, F.R.Civ.P., the district court's decision must be affirmed.

Accordingly, the case was remanded to the district court as to that part of the district court's opinion pertaining to the core-city schools and reversed as to the legal determination that such schools were maintained in violation of the Fourteenth Amendment because of the unequal educational opportunity afforded by them.

The Litigation: The Supreme Court Enters

In the fall of 1971, the plaintiffs petitioned the Supreme Court of the United States for a writ of *certiorari* to review the final judgment and opinion of the Court of Appeals for the Tenth Circuit. According to Gordon Greiner, the entire 26-page petition was authored by the Legal Defense Fund. Beginning at page 14 of the petition, the plaintiffs noted the distinctiveness of their case:

The issue in this case is not *de facto* versus *de jure* segregation. Whatever the term "de facto" may mean, this case involves a school district in which segregation has been brought about by regular, systematic and deliberate choice of the school authorities.

This is the first case of this sort before this Court from an area where officially required segregation was not previously authorized by statute.

. . . .

The cases in which the lower courts have determined that a school district has maintained a policy of segregation should be governed by the same rules, regardless of geography or the source of the official segregation, as cases where the initial source was State law. But there is a division among the lower courts; and this is reflected in the opinions of the courts below in this case, applying different rules to different geographical parts of the same school system. Whereas this Court and the lower courts require desegregation throughout a southern school district where segregation was imposed by law (even though it persists only in certain portions of that district), the lower courts here (and in some other places) have confined desegregation to discrete areas where particular segregating deeds have been uncovered and identified.

Consideration of the Park Hill area school separately from the rest of the Denver school system resulted from the lower courts' insistence that petitioners demonstrate a segregating act at every school in order to justify relief. This narrow focus facilitated compartmentalized consideration of the different areas of the district. But the court's concern should have been school authorities' actions anywhere in the district creating or maintaining racial and ethnic segregation.

In addition to seeking review from the Supreme Court on the issue of state action in the segregation of the core-city schools in Denver, the plaintiffs requested review of the ruling of the court of appeals as to the effect of unequal educational opportunity. The essence of the plaintiffs' contention on this score is set forth at page 22 of the petition for *certiorari*:

> We think the Court of Appeals misconstrued the basis of the District Court's ruling, but, moreover, its own opinion drains the concept of equal educational opportunity (recognized by this Court in *Brown*) of its meaning by declaring segregation-related inequalities irremediable in the federal courts unless that segregation is proved to have been caused entirely by school authorities. [Emphasis in original.]

On January 17, 1972 the Supreme Court of the United States granted the plaintiffs' petition for *certiorari*. The case was argued on October, 12, 1972, and decided on June 21, 1973 (413 U.S. 189, 37 L.Ed.2d 548 [1973]). James M. Nabrit III, of the NAACP Legal Defense Fund, and Gordon C. Greiner argued the case for the plaintiffs; William K. Ris, of the Denver firm of Wood, Ris and Hames, argued the case for the defendant. Justice Brennan delivered the opinion of the Court.

The opinion is divided into four principal parts. The essence of the first portion of the opinion was that Judge Doyle erred in failing to combine the number of black and Hispano students in any school in determining the concentration of minorities in a school (70–75 percent) likely to produce an inferior educational opportunity. The Court cited findings of various reports of the United States Commission on Civil Rights and stated that "Negroes and Hispanos in Denver suffer identical discrimination in treatment when compared with the treatment afforded Anglo students" (37 L.Ed.2d at 557).

In Part II of the opinion, Justice Brennan considered the contention of the plaintiffs that the district court imposed an unreasonable burden on the plaintiffs with regard to proof of unconstitutional state action in the segregation found to exist in the so-called core-city schools. Justice Brennan found that the proof produced by the plaintiffs about segregation and state action in the Park Hill area sufficed to meet plaintiffs' burden in a case not involving de jure segregation by statute:

> Nevertheless, where Plaintiffs proved that the school authorities have carried out a systematic program of segregation affecting a substantial portion of the students, schools, teachers and facilities within the school system, it is only common sense to conclude that there exists a predicate for a finding of the existence of a dual school system. [37 L.Ed.2d at 559.]

Therefore, Justice Brennan directed the district court, on remand, to "decide in the first instance whether respondent School Board's deliberate racial segregation policy with respect to the Park Hill schools constitutes the entire Denver school system a dual school system" (37 L.Ed.2d at 560).

In Part III of the opinion, Justice Brennan elaborated. He first pointed out that Judge Doyle, for the district court, had mistakenly failed to take into account the already-proven intentional school segregation in the Park Hill schools when evaluating the admitted factual segregation in the so-called core-city schools.

> Plainly, a finding of intentional segregation as to a portion of a school system is not devoid of probative value in assessing the school authorities' intent with respect to other parts of the same school system. On the contrary, where, as here, the case involves one school board, a finding of intentional segregation on its part in one portion of a school system is highly relevant to the issue of the board's intent with respect to other segregated schools in the system. This is merely an application of the well-settled evidentiary principle that "the prior doing of other similar acts, whether clearly a part of a scheme or not, is useful as reducing the possibility that the act in question was done with innocent intent." II Wigmore, Evidence 200 (3d ed. 1940). [37 L.Ed.2d at 562–63.]

Justice Brennan went on to hold that a finding of intentional segregative school board action in a "meaningful" portion of a school system creates a "presumption" that other segregated schooling within the system is not accidental. "In that circumstances, it is both fair and reasonable to require that the school authorities bear the burden of showing that their actions as to other segregated schools within the system were not also motivated by segregative intent" (37 L.Ed.2d at 563). The opinion went on to identify the exact burden to be shifted to the defendants as one not satisfied by the aducement of "some allegedly logical, racially neutral explanation" for school board actions. Rather, Justice Brennan said, the burden required submission of proof sufficient "to support a finding that segregative intent was not among the factors that motivated" school board action (37 L.Ed.2d at 564). Justice Brennan also rejected those portions of Judge Doyle's opinion below that attributed significance to the alleged remoteness in time of certain of the new admitted segregative acts of the school board. The Supreme Court thus summarily rejected the primary defense of the school board that its "neighborhood school policy" combined with residential segregation were the primary justification for all previous acts of the board that resulted in fact in segregated schools in the core-city area.

In Part IV of the opinion, Justice Brennan set forth in capsule form the duties of the district court on remand. As a first item, Justice Brennan directed the district court to "afford respondent School Board the opportunity to prove its contention that the Park Hill area is a separate, identifiable and unrelated section of the school district that should be treated as isolated from the rest of the district" (37 L.Ed.2d at 566). Second, assuming that the school board failed to prove that contention, Justice Brennan directed the district court to "determine whether respondent School Board's conduct over almost a decade after 1960 in carrying out a policy of deliberate racial segregation in the Park Hill schools constitutes the entire school system a dual school system" (*id.*). Citing *Green v. County School Board,* 391 U.S. 430, 20 L.Ed.2d 716 (1968), Justice Brennan stated that if the district court were to determine that the Denver school system was a dual school system, "respondent School Board has the affirmative duty to desegregate the entire system 'root and branch'" (*id.*). Finally, Justice Brennan directed the district court, in the event that the Denver school system was shown not to be a dual school system, to afford the school board the opportunity to rebut the plaintiffs' prima facie case of intentional segregation in the core-city schools. There, the school board's burden would be to show that its "neighborhood school" concept was not utilized in order to effect a policy creating or maintaining segregation in the core-city schools or was not a factor in causing the existing conditions of segregation in those schools. "If respondent Board fails to rebut petitioners' prima facie case, the District Court must, as in the case of Park Hill, decree all-out desegregation of the core-city schools" (*id.*).

The Litigation: The Proceedings in December 1973

After the decision of the Supreme Court on June 21, 1973, the case was remanded for further hearings before the district court in accordance with the Supreme Court's decision. Initially, in December of 1973, hearings were held on the limited actual issue set forth in Part II of the Supreme Court decision: whether the uncontested segregation in the Park Hill schools constituted the Denver School District a "dual" system, or whether the Park Hill situation was "a case in which the geographical structure of, or the natural boundaries within, a school district [had] the effect of dividing the school district into separate, identifiable and unrelated units" (413 U.S. at 203).

Judge Doyle's memorandum opinion and order arising out of the December 1973 hearings before the district court was issued on December 11, 1973 (368

F.Supp. 207 [1973]). The opinion consists primarily of a restatement of the findings and guidelines set forth by the Supreme Court in its earlier 1973 decision on the case (413 U.S. 189 [1973]). Judge Doyle carefully interwove findings from the evidence in the December 1973 hearing with verbatim quotations of the Supreme Court decision. He first considered the issue of whether the Park Hill portion of the Denver school system was a "separate, identifiable and unrelated" system in either a geographic or a nongeographic sense.

Judge Doyle noted that the substantial impact of the racial segregation in Park Hill on schools outside of Park Hill "was settled in earlier decisions in this case, and is additionally supported by the presumption enunciated in Mr. Justice Brennan's Opinion of the Supreme Court" (368 F.Supp. at 210). Nevertheless, he said, the defendants had "contended that these issues are proper for retrial here" (*id.*). Elaborating, Judge Doyle stated:

> We have fully considered all of this evidence presented by defendants, both that offered in this hearing and all evidence of record from previous proceedings in this case. Insofar as that evidence was offered to support defendants' contention that the Denver school district is not a dual system, we conclude that it is merely conclusory and is lacking in substance. The intended thrust of that evidence has been that segregated conditions in individual schools outside the Park Hill area are wholly the product of external factors such as demographic trends and housing patterns, and are in no way the product of any act or omissions by the defendants. We are not persuaded by the evidence presented, nor have defendants succeeded in dispelling the presumption that segregative intent of the School Board was clearly evidenced by its actions in Park Hill permeating the entire district. The affirmative evidence is to the contrary, that defendants' actions in Park Hill are reflective of its attitude toward the school system generally [368 F.Supp. at 210.]

Judge Doyle proceeded to find the conclusion "inescapable" that the Denver school system was a dual school system within the Supreme Court's definitions.

Pursuant to order, hearings were conducted February 19 through March 27, 1974, before the district court, regarding proposed desegregation plans. In these hearings the plaintiffs submitted two plans; the defendants submitted one; and a plan was submitted by court-appointed consultant, John A. Finger; and plans complementary to the plaintiffs' plans were submitted by the Congress of Hispanic Educators (CHE) about bilingual and bicultural education.

THE FINAL JUDGMENT AND DECREE

Judge Doyle entered his final judgment and decree on April 17, 1974 (380 F.Supp. 673). A central part of the decree is its incorporation by reference of Finger's plan of April 5, 1974, with minor modifications. Implementation of the

Finger plan was mandated for the 1974–75 school year. As to the discretionary aspects of the Finger plan, the court formally instructed the defendant board to exercise its discretion in good faith, to forthwith consider and to report to the court about contemplated alternative courses of action on enumerated administrative and educational details. Balancing the need for court administration with the desirability of unhampered school board implementation, the judge noted, at page 5 of his decree:

> If defendants are uncertain concerning the meaning or intent of the plan, they should apply to the Court for interpretation and clarification. It is not intended that the school authorities be placed in a single "strait jacket" in the administration of the plan, but it is essential that the Court be informed of any proposed departure from the sanctioned program. The Court is committed to the principles of the plan, but it is not inflexible concerning the details. . . .

In addition to permanently enjoining the defendants from "discriminating on the basis of race or color in the operation of the school system," the court reminded the defendants that the "duty imposed by the law and by this Order is the desegregation of schools and the maintenance of that condition. The defendants are encouraged to use their full 'know-how' and resources to attain the described results, and thus to achieve the constitutional end by any legal means at their disposal . . ." (page 5 of the decree).

The other key provisions of the decree included:

1. *Voluntary Open Enrollment.* The board was instructed to hold in abeyance its voluntary open-enrollment program pending resolution of various details of the Finger plan, but, in any event, subject to elimination of current restraints on participation in the program by minority students (refusal of voluntary transfers to minority students to Anglo schools having combined black-Hispano enrollments exceeding the district-wide average).
2. *Collateral Services.* The board was instructed to maintain "to the extent feasible" on-going programs of "collateral" services such as hot breakfast programs, free lunches, tutorial programs, health services, remedial and compensatory education programs.
3. *Busing.* The board was instructed to file plans with the court and to make immediate purchases of equipment for implementation of the busing required in the Finger plan.
4. *In-Service Teacher Training.* The board was instructed to implement its own proposals for orientation and training of parents, pupils, school personnel, and staff as proposed to the court in the February hearings.
5. *Monitoring Commission.* This key aspect of the decree required both parties to submit to the court nominees for appointment to a commission, initially

to serve until June 1, 1975, at the expense of the district, to act as a liaison between the court and the "community" as to such matters as: coordination of community efforts to implement the plan; community education; receipt and consideration of criticism and suggestions from the community regarding the plan; assisting the community in working out programs with the school administration; reporting to the court as to the nature and resolution of such problems; and generally reporting on a periodic basis to the court about implementation of the plan.

6. *Bilingual-Bicultural Education.* The school district was ordered to implement the model plan presented by CHE or a plan "substantially and materially similar," retaining a qualified consultant to develop the program and implement the plan on a pilot basis at three elementary schools and one junior high and one senior high school.

7. *New School Construction.* The defendants were enjoined from locating new schools or additions thereto in a manner conforming to patterns of residential segregation and were required to submit all plans for new schools or additions thereto to the court, with notice to counsel for the plaintiffs and provision for hearings to air objections within thirty days of reporting to the court.

8. *Reporting.* The court set forth formal and detailed reporting requirements on a monthly schedule beginning May 1, 1974, through September of 1974 as to plans and administrative details regarding implementation of the Finger program.

9. *Additional Reporting.* The defendants were instructed to report within thirty days of the commencement of the fall semester in 1974 and the second semester in 1975 on an extensive array of statistical phenomena including ethnic distribution of pupils and teachers, distribution of tenured and probationary teachers, student dropouts and suspensions, the number and nature of special administrative and hardship transfers, and actions taken to implement the bilingual-bicultural program.

10. *Desegregation of Faculty and Staff.* The school district was instructed in detail as to the permissible standards for assignment of faculty and staff among all schools in the district and required to implement immediately an affirmative action program for hiring minority teachers, staff, and administrators with the objective of attaining a ratio of Hispano and black personnel within the district corresponding to the overall black and Hispano student population of the district.

11. *Foot Dragging.* The Board was instructed to "take steps to prevent the frustration, hinderance or avoidance of this Decree, particularly with regard to spurious transfer and falsification of residence to avoid reassignment."

12. *Harassment.* "Any attempt to hinder, harass, intimidate, or interfere with the School Board, its members, agents, servants, or employees in execution

of this Order shall be reported to the Department of Justice through the United States Attorney for the District of Colorado."

13. *Fees of Dr. Finger.* These fees were taxed to the school district, "since the services of Dr. Finger were necessary to the development of an adequate and acceptable plan."

14. *Plaintiffs' Attorney's Fees and Costs.* The school district was ordered to pay an award of attorney's fees and costs to plaintiffs' attorneys accruing since the inception of the lawsuit in June of 1969.

COMMUNITY REACTION TO THE DESEGREGATION PLAN

Community Opposition to the Desegregation Plan

Even before the court issued its final order and decree, community reaction to desegregation began to crystallize. The most vociferous organized opposition to school desegregation was a group known as Citizens Association for Neighborhood Schools (CANS). An outgrowth of a variety of neighborhood associations opposed to busing, CANS was incorporated in January 1974.[91] According to the first president of CANS, Nolan Winsett, Jr., CANS enjoyed a membership of approximately 15,000 individuals, and by November 1974 it had raised approximately $12,000.

Since its inception, CANS expressed its opposition to busing in a variety of ways.[92] Initially it held numerous meetings at local schools throughout Denver to protest busing. Most meetings featured members of the school board who opposed busing; citizens were encouraged to write school, local, state, and federal officials to express their objections to busing and to demand federal and state constitutional amendments to halt it. CANS also sponsored a rally featuring Congressman Norman Lent (R-NY), proponent of a constitutional amendment against busing, and Lawrence Hogan (R-MD). Both speakers voiced their oppositon to court-ordered busing to approximately 3,200 Denverites.

In the political arena, CANS succeeded in organizing a successful drive to put an anti-busing amendment on the November 1974 election ballot in Colorado.[93] In July 1974 CANS also prepared a pamphlet describing the history of the court

91. Personal interview with Nolan Winsett, Jr., April 3, 1975.

92. The following four paragraphs are based on Citizens Association for Neighborhood Schools, Education by Judicial Fiat, July 1974, Denver, Colorado; a personal interview with Nolan Winsett, Jr., former president of CANS (April 3, 1975); and various newspaper accounts, which will be noted *infra.*

93. More than 94,167 signatures were collected, fully double the requisite number needed to place the amendment on the ballot. It appeared as Amendment No. 8 on the ballot and read as follows: "To prohibit the assignment or transportation of students to public educational institutions in order to achieve a racial balance of pupils at such institutions." Persons who voted in favor of the amendment totaled 102, 654; 60, 681 opposed it. Denver Post, November 5, 1974.

order, entitled "Education by Judicial Fiat," and became intervenors in the desegregation litigation.

CANS also encouraged a number of boycotts to demonstrate citizen opposition to busing. The first and most successful one was a one-day demonstration in February 1974. More than half of Denver's pupil school population participated in the boycott, and approximately 36,000 students were absent from school.[94]

Soon after the opening of the 1974/75 school term, CANS announced plans to conduct a series of boycotts on Fridays during the month of October. The action was designed to communicate citizen opposition to the court order, as well as reduce the level of federal and state support conveyed to the schools on the grounds such monies were devoted to "the indoctrination of parents and students and teachers in the workings of the plan rather than pure education."[95] The first boycott was planned in cooperation with a Boston citizens organization known as ROAR (Return Our Alienated Rights), also confronted with a court-ordered desegregation plan.

In contrast to the February 1974 action, the October boycotts were never executed. Prior to the first Friday boycott scheduled in October, the plaintiffs obtained a temporary restraining order prohibiting CANS leaders from encouraging the boycott. As a result, it was leaderless, and attendance in the schools was reduced only about 8 to 10 percent.[96] The restraining order also prohibited CANS from encouraging additional boycotts, and they were cancelled. In addition, at least 375 members of CANS resigned from the organization to protest plans to coordinate boycott actions with Boston's ROAR.[97]

Although CANS was the only group to display mass resistance to desegregation planning, other events were indicative of community opposition.[98] For example, in 1970, Craig S. Barnes, a trial attorney for the plaintiffs, was severely defeated in a race for a seat in the U.S. House of Representatives in a campaign that aroused much pro- and anti-busing sentiment. In the 1971 Denver mayoral race, the successful candidate conducted an advertising campaign that linked his opponent with Craig S. Barnes and a pro-busing stance. And in the 1973 Colorado Democratic primary for the U.S. Senate, Floyd Haskell won the nomination after placing advertisements in suburban newspapers linking his opponent with busing and amnesty.

Community opposition has continued since the promulgation of the order, too. In April 1974, members of the Colorado state legislature passed House Joint Resolution No. 1012 calling for an amendment to the Constitution of the

94. *Id.*, February 22, 1974.
95. *Id.*, September 24, 1974.
96. *Id.*, October 3, 1974.
97. The resignations were spearheaded by the Hampden Heights Association. According to its spokesman, Wally Becker, it was felt that it was a mistake for CANS to associate with the ROAR organization and its "KKK and Neo-Nazi" elements. *Id.*, September 21, 1974.
98. Material in the following paragraph is based on Meadow's *Busing: It Has Been Five Long Hard Years,* Cervi's Rocky Mountain J., May 8, 1974, at 23–26.

United States prohibiting the assignment of students to schools on the basis of race, creed, or color and granting to Congress the power to enforce this prohibition by appropriate legislation.

On the federal level, in 1974 Colorado's members of congress split on bills that would have limited busing for integration to the next closest school. Both of Colorado's U.S. Senators voted for a similar bill and for another bill that would have prohibited cross-districting busing.[99]

In 1975, Congressmen Schroeder (D) and Wirth (D), both with constituencies in Denver, voted against an amendment to the Energy Conservation and Oil Policy Act that would have prohibited the use of gasoline- or diesel-powered vehicles to transport school children to public schools other than the grade school closest to the student's home in his or her school district.[100]

An amendment to the HEW Labor Appropriations Bill (H.R. 8069) also contained an anti-busing provision. The two Colorado senators took different positions on this amendment. Floyd Haskell (D) voted for it, while Gary Hart (D) voted against it.[101]

Locally, the voters have also expressed their positions on busing for integration purposes. As noted above, Colorado approved a citizen-initiated anti-busing constitutional amendment in November 1974. In addition, Denver voters rejected a Denver school mill levy increase (by 61,181 to 38,605), which was widely described as money to pay for court-ordered busing.[102]

In 1975, two new candidates were elected to the Denver School Board. The election involved two candidates closely identified with the CANS organization and a third who expressed strong opposition to court-ordered desegregation. While one of the CANS candidates did get elected and the other came in fourth, it should be noted that the CANS victory was extremely narrow. A mere 1,064 votes separated Bradford from runner-up Larry McLain, and the latter was firmly committed to implementing the court-ordered plan.[103]

Violent modes of expressing opposition to the court-ordered plan had earlier arisen in the city.[104] In February 1970, shortly after Judge Doyle's first busing order, 46 buses were destroyed or damaged by dynamite blasts. Race-related

99. [Denver] Citizens Association for Neighborhood Schools, Education by Judicial Fiat, July 1974.

100. Telephone conversations with staff people at Representatives Patricia Schroeder's and Tim Wirth's offices, February 6, 1976.

101. Telephone conversations with staff persons at Senators Gary Hart's and Floyd Haskell's offices, February 6, 1976.

102. Denver Post, November 5, 1974.

103. *Id.,* May 21, 1975. Community opposition to busing has also been expressed in new legal action. In May of 1975, 10 Denver area residents brought suit on behalf of what they claimed to be "dozens" to force the attorney general of Colorado and the Colorado Board of Education to enforce the citizen initiated and approved anti-busing amendment. *Id.,* May 7, 1975. (Shortly after it was filed, however, the case was dismissed.) Telephone interview with Mary Malarky, February 6, 1976.

104. Material in the following paragraph is based on Meadow, *supra* note 98, at 23–26; and [Denver] Citizens Association for Neighborhood Schools, Education by Judicial Fiat, 1974.

tensions flared in various schools at various times during the course of the controversy. The latter part of 1973 saw the bombing of the school administration building, bombings at other school facilities, and bombs mailed to some school board members. In addition, several key participants in the plaintiffs' case were harassed by bomb threats and menacing phone calls; plaintiff Wilfred Keyes was the victim of a bomb attack on his home. On June 9, 1974, shortly after system-wide busing orders, four flares taped together to imitate a bomb were found under the hood of a bus at the school bus lot which had been the site of the dynamite blast in 1970.

Recently published opinion survey information from a variety of sources indicates that while three out of four Denver residents are in favor of integrating schools, most Denverites, with the exception of blacks, categorically reject the theory of busing children to achieve racial balance.[105]

Opposition to busing appears to have intensified in recent years;[106] and when asked for solutions to the problems of unequal educational opportunity, broad support from all racial groups is indicated for spending more money in disadvantaged schools and only weak support is found for the transportation of pupils.[107]

A survey of 200 Denver and 200 suburban-ring homeowners residing in homes sold during 1973 and 1974, and of 90 Denver and 90 suburban-ring renters residing in multifamily units, suggests the significance of busing in the decision to move out of Denver. Although the most important reasons for moving were the "home" and its financing and its amenities, Denverites who moved were also influenced by busing considerations. Busing was opposed by 77 percent of the Denver Metropolitan Area respondents, and of those who had moved to the suburban ring from Denver, 23 percent indicated busing was a problem at their previous address.[108]

105. Denver Urban Observatory, Citizen Attitude Survey (1970), and Majority-Minority Citizen Voter Attitudes in Denver (1972). Opposition to busing appears to be about the same for parents with bused children and for the general public; and in 1974, 73 percent and 72 percent voiced opposition, respectively. The most frequently cited reason (in a sample of 350 respondents) among those opposing busing was "family inconvenience or hardship." This involved such factors as "getting children ready earlier in the morning, accessibility to the school, distance from the school and difficulty in getting involved with the school for extra-curricular activities." Rocky Mountain News, June 8, 1975. Report on study conducted by Rocky Mountain Research Institute during fall 1974.
106. *Id.*
107. A 1972 survey reveals that while 66 percent of those questioned opposed busing as a means of providing quality education to a maximum number of school children, 83 percent favored spending more money to improve the quality of schools in the disadvantaged areas. Denver Urban Observatory, Majority-Minority Voter Attitudes in Denver (1972).
108. G. Von Stroh, Denver Metropolitan Area Residential Migration: Why Citizens are Moving In and Out of Denver and the Suburban Ring (Denver Urban Observatory 1975). A *Denver Post* survey of headmasters and admissions officers in five metro private schools indicates that applications in 1974 were unusually high and overrepresented by Denver-area residents. In the case of one K-12 school, Colorado Academy, inquiries for enrollment more than doubled between 1973 and 1974 (from 70 to 147). The Kent-Denver

Community Support for the Desegregation Plan

Despite the evidence of fairly substantial opposition to school desegregation, community reaction in Denver must be characterized as relatively peaceful and mild. Fortunately, the violent hysteria that has gripped other cities confronted with similar problems has not appeared. Indeed, numerous organizations and actions indicate that support for implementing the plan in a peaceful and orderly manner is the goal of a generous segment of the population. In addition to the traditional civil rights groups and Park Hill neighborhood associations, several groups have formed specifically for the purpose of facilitating implementation of the desegregation plan. One such group is the organization called PLUS (People Let's Unite for Schools).[109] PLUS boasts a membership list that includes such prestigious organizations as the Denver Bar Association, the League of Women Voters, the Metro YMCA, the Anti-Defamation League of B'nai B'rith, various neighborhood associations, and organizations representing teachers and other school personnel. It takes no position on the litigation in the desegregation controversy and is purely committed to making the plan and order promulgated by the court effective.

A second such organization is CHUN-DECCA (Capitol Hill United Neighborhoods and Denver East Central Civic Association). Like PLUS, CHUN-DECCA is committed to the implementation of the decree.

In the political arena, events suggest less intense opposition to the court order. U.S. Congresswoman Patricia Schroeder was successfully reelected in November 1974 in a campaign against state legislator and school board member Frank Southworth.[110] An opponent of busing, Southworth campaigned on a one-plank anti-busing platform. Despite Congresswoman Schroeder's record in support of court-ordered desegregation plans, she won by a healthy margin.

In 1974 the Colorado voters elected Gary Hart (D) to the Senate over incumbent Peter Dominick (R). Hart has consistently voted against anti-busing amendments. Dominick's voting record showed clear support for the prohibition of busing to achieve racial integration in schools.

In the 1975 school board elections, Virginia Rockwell, an outspoken supporter of implementing the court-ordered desegregation plan in Denver, won a decisive victory. The 46,812 votes cast in her favor exceeded those received by the second-place candidate, CANS candidate Naomi Bradford, by more than 10,000 votes.[111]

Activity in the Colorado legislature suggested widespread, bipartisan accep-

---

Country Day School estimates that it received 50 to 60 Denver-area students in 1974 who probably would not have come had the desegregation decree not gone into effect. The survey also reports that applications to private schools in 1975 were on the whole back to normal levels, an indication of waning "panic" among Denver parents over desegregation. *Denver Post*, June 8, 1975.

109. *Id.*, May 22, 1974.
110. *Id.*, November 5, 1974.
111. *Id.*, May 21, 1975.

tance, if not support, for the court-ordered desegregation plan. Two pieces of legislation are relevant. One is S.B.2, signed into law July 14, 1975, concerning state reimbursements to local districts for expenditures in the acquisition of school buses. S.B.2 (now Secs. 22-51-101, *et seq., Colorado Revises Statutes, 1973*) somewhat modifies the operation of a special state fund historically used to assist the local school districts with bus purchase expenses. First, the new law gives state assistance not only to district purchases of buses used in transporting pupils from home to school and back; but also to purchases of buses used in school-to-school busing, such as in the court's final plan. Second, the new law adds the hitherto unseen condition to state assistance that applicant school districts make known not only funds they have received for bus purchases from other sources, but also funds they were *entitled* to receive from other sources. Both provisions are clearly directed at the Denver school district. S.B.2 received extensive bipartisan support; the extent of the funding of its pupil transportation fund by the legislature is yet to be determined.

H.B. 1295, a major bilingual-bicultural bill, was signed into law June 30, 1975. The bill creates the mechanics by which the state board of education, the state department of education, and a special appointive statewide steering committee can administer a new bilingual-bicultural policy. The policy requires local districts to canvass their pupil population for "linguistically different" (bilingual) pupils and to offer the parents of these pupils the opportunity of participating in a bilingual-bicultural program. Each district develops its own program for pupils electing to take advantage of it: courses, community participation, administration, and so on. The act is effective for the 1975/76 school year, but more stringent planning requirements are first imposed on local districts after 1975/76. An approved district plan qualifies for substantial state financial support. For the 1975/76 fiscal year, the legislature appropriated $2.35 million for implementation of the act. It is noteworthy that the court of appeals did not take formal notice of this new law in justifying its reversal of the district court's final provision for bilingual-bicultural programs in Denver. The court of appeals' decision, however, does appear to notice the act implicitly.

IMPLEMENTING THE COURT ORDER

Creation of a Monitoring Network

The most significant factor in the implementation of the court-ordered plan has been a body created by the order itself. Subsequently known as the Community Education Council (CEC), the monitoring commission created by Judge Doyle in his final order and decree of April 1974 was composed of court-appointed members of the community who were nominated by the parties to the case. The order provided that CEC be furnished with secretarial services by the school district and instructed the district to cooperate with the commission in full.

As defined by the order, the duties of CEC were to coordinate efforts of community agencies and persons interested in the implementation of the desegregation plan; to educate the community on the constitutional requirement of desegregation and the court's findings and conclusions; to educate the public on the services and facilities needed to implement the plan; to receive suggestions and comments of the community regarding the implementation of the plan; to assist in working out problems with the school administration concerning the plan; to report periodically to the court and the parties on the progress of the plan and its implementation; and to provide continual monitoring of such implementation.

University of Denver Chancellor Maurice B. Mitchell was selected by the judge to be chairman of the monitoring commission. Chancellor Mitchell, among other things, is a past commissioner to the U.S. Civil Rights Commission.

As originally constituted, the Community Education Council consisted of 41 persons. Currently there are 61 members. Council members include the president of the Denver Classroom Teachers Association, members of the League of Women Voters, state legislators, ministers and other religious leaders, members of the business community, academics, the president of the Denver Chamber of Commerce, representatives of the local media, labor leaders, members of the Colorado Department of Education, housewives, and high school students.[112]

CEC met for the first time on May 10, 1974, and received instructions from Judge Doyle. Subsequently it has met approximately twice a month as a group and more often in smaller groups and subcommittees. Meanwhile, CEC organized itself, elected officers, and appointed standing committees and subcommittees. Currently CEC members are organized into six committees. These are an executive committee, a monitoring committee, a transportation committee, a bilingual-bicultural committee, an affirmative action committee, and a community education and information committee.[113]

In order to discharge its monitoring responsibilities, CEC decided to appoint volunteer monitors from the community to be assigned to each school.[114] Under the system, two monitors are assigned to each school or school pair at the elementary, junior and senior high school level. Ideally, monitors are expected to visit their schools on a weekly basis and to report to a specific member of the monitoring committee of CEC at least once a month. As of January 28, 1976, there were 210 volunteer monitors chosen by the CEC members in the Denver public schools.[115]

The responsibilities of monitors[116] include fact-finding, information-gathering, observation, information evaluation, and reporting. Fundamental is the respon-

112. Community Education Council, Membership Roster, August 1, 1975.
113. *Id.*
114. Letter of Maurice Mitchell to Judge Doyle, September 20, 1974, at 2.
115. Community Education Council, office files, January 28, 1976.
116. Community Education Council, A Guide for Denver Public School Monitors (August 1, 1974).

sibility to discern commitment on the part of the school administration, teachers, staff, students, and parents to honest and effective implementation of the court plan. In so doing, monitors are encouraged to develop harmonious relations with the school and CEC. Monitors are further instructed not to betray personal opinions on matters affecting the school, not to assume an advocacy role, and not to become involved in school matters that have no bearing on the desegregation plan.[117]

By August 15, 1974, the monitoring network in the Denver public schools was intact and functioning. Within the next two weeks, monitors arranged to meet with school principals to obtain basic information about the school and programs related to the court order, as well as to identify difficulties that might impede implementation of the order. Not insignificantly, the monitor-principal meeting was also designed to acquaint the principal with the scope of monitoring activities.

Monitor activity was particularly intense during the opening of school in 1974, and monitors aware of serious tensions or problems relayed this to the school principal and the member of CEC most directly responsible for his or her school. In subsequent visits, monitors observed classrooms, in-service training programs, parent gatherings, staff meetings, and transportation arrangements. After each visit they completed a report sheet about the school situation they encountered; these were submitted to CEC. Regular reports on monitoring activities were conveyed to the court.

Several actions by the court were indispensable to strengthening CEC and making its monitoring network effective. For example, when the school administration initially insisted that all monitoring services be conducted by the court-appointed members of CEC and not by council-supervised volunteers recruited from the community, the matter was referred to the judge who ruled in favor of the council. When the administration refused to allow monitors to enter schools without identification, which would have impaired their ability to monitor unobtrusively, the matter was referred to the court, and the administration was required to distribute identification badges making for easy and rapid identification. Finally, when the administration wanted to circumscribe school matters and places subject to monitor overview, the issue was referred to the court. Once

---

117. All school monitors were trained during the summer preceding the 1974 fall commencement of school, and supplied with packets of information to facilitate the discharge of their responsibilities. This included information on the constitutional basis of the court order and the provisions of the final order and decree. Monitors were also supplied with detailed information on the school boundaries, community characteristics, and programs for the implementation of the court order of schools to which they were assigned. In addition, each monitor was supplied with an evaluation report form and the name of a council member directly responsible for his or her school. (This information is based on an interview with the chairman of the Community Education Council, Maurice B. Mitchell, May 7, 1975, and a series of letters sent from Chancellor Mitchell to Judge Doyle about the council's findings, on July 12, 1974, September 20, 1974, October 15, 1974, and February 10, 1975.)

again the court decided in favor of the council, thereby permitting the operation of an autonomous monitoring system with sufficient independence and freedom to achieve effective supervision.

CEC's effectiveness also results from a number of internal organizational and procedural decisions which facilitated its operation. According to the council's chairman, Chancellor Mitchell, two decisions at the start were critical to its successful operation. Noting the variety of members that composed the Community Education Council, including groups with diametrically opposing constituency bases and political persuasions, Mitchell established that the chairperson was the only one who could speak for the council in any public of official occasion. This eliminated the problem of individual council members making conflicting and provocative statements to the press and public. The heterogeneity of the council members also led Mitchell to dispense with strict parliamentary procedures; the chairperson has the right to determine consensus among the commission members.[118]

According to several persons interviewed in this study, CEC has been the single most important factor in the implementation process.[119] At the close of the first school year (1974/75) under the desegregation plan, Judge Doyle himself lauded CEC members, the 200 voluntary monitors and CEC Chairman Mitchell, for their efforts. Noting the time-consuming nature of the voluntary monitoring responsibilities, he termed it "the greatest bargain the community could have." And he attributed the success of the program "in large measure to the magnificent leadership furnished by Chancellor Mitchell."[120] Asked by Mitchell several months later about the future of CEC, Doyle replied that CEC must continue to function and report to him until the school district shows "more responsibility in the field of desegregation, of which there is no convincing evidence yet." He reported that he expected CEC to run at least another year and that he hoped it would continue indefinitely as a community-sponsored group.[121]

Of course, not everyone is enthusiastic about the Community Education Council. According to Superintendent Kishkunas, monitoring is totally unnecessary since the schools are staffed with professionals who have demonstrated both an ability to implement the court decree and have a commitment to the law.

118. Personal interview with Maurice B. Mitchell, May 7, 1975.

119. Gordon Greiner, the plaintiffs' chief trial lawyer, feels the CEC has made the relative success of the Denver plan possible. (Personal interview with Gordon Greiner, April 9, 1975). George Bardwell, key researcher for the plaintiffs, feels that at least part of the reason Denver has avoided the violence and hostility that desegregation decrees have met in other cities may be attributed to the widespread involvement of the community in the implementation of the plan through CEC. (Personal interview with George Bardwell, April 7, 1975.)

120. Denver Post, May 17, 1975.

121. Maurice B. Mitchell, notes on telephone conversation with Judge Doyle, January 23, 1976.

Moreover, according to Kishkunas, monitors are often highly critical and enthusiastic to discover problems, and their reports are selective and prejudiced.[122] Southworth, an ex-school board member elected in 1969 on an anti-busing plank and an unsuccessful 1974 candidate for the U.S. Congress who emphasized busing in his campaign, feels that CEC is less than neutral.[123] According to Southworth, Judge Doyle appointed the dean of the Denver Law School and managers of the major newspapers to allow the organization to pose as an impartial and widely representative group of citizens and community organizations. But in fact, he says, CEC members are tightly knit by their residence in the same communities, membership in similar associations, and shared political and social beliefs.[124] And in July, 1975, CANS (Citizens Association for Neighborhood Schools) demanded that Mitchell and five other CEC members resign from the council on grounds that they were not Denver residents—a demand brushed off by Judge Doyle and the six CEC members.[125]

Despite the differences in view expressed by advocates and opponents of the court order, the Community Education Council must be recognized as unique. Neither a plaintiff nor a defendant, it enjoys the position of being independent and of never having been embroiled in the bitter legal controversy over the formulation of the final plan. But independence has not been sufficient for the council to avoid a variety of serious dilemmas in the course of discharging its responsibilities. These problems have decreased as implementation has moved into its second year, but the problems are still real.

Problems in the Implementation of the Court Order

CEC's chief obstacle in implementing the order is the opposition of the school board and members of the school administration to the desegregation order and decree.[126] The court's and CEC's involvement is said to be viewed as a fundamental political threat to the autonomous powers of the district. By some, CEC is feared, resented, and loathed. The board's strategy has been one of delay. Because the final order and decree is currently under appeal, the administration feels that it does not have to fully comply with the order. The appeal is regarded as an excuse for lax or at best reluctant enforcement of the law. Thus, in a letter to Judge Doyle on September 20, 1974, CEC reports the school board president at that time, James Perrill, freely admitted that the school board would pursue every possible avenue leading to the delay or reversal of the court order.[127]

The school board's attitude has been evidenced in several other substantive

122. Personal interview with Superintendent Louis Kishkunas, April 8, 1975.
123. Southworth sees the members of the CEC as individuals in collusion with one another to effect social reform through the schools.
124. Personal interview with Frank Southworth, April 17, 1975.
125. Denver Post, July 30, 1975, and July 31, 1975.
126. Personal interview with Maurice B. Mitchell, May 7, 1975.
127. Letter of Maurice Mitchell to Judge Doyle, September 20, 1974, at 6.

matters. In May of 1975, three weeks before the school board elections, a four-man majority approved three-year contract extensions for Superintendent Kishkunas and three top aides, despite the fact that none of the contracts was due to expire before the election.[128] In November 1975 the school board voted a $100,000 cut in the school budget and indicated that this decrease was in the funds "designed for desegregation costs."[129] During the first school year the plan was implemented (1974/75), the Denver School Board ignored invitations to meet with the Community Education Council.[130] During the 1975/76 school year, a meeting of three school board members, Superintendent Kishkunas, and the CEC members has taken place. In January 1976, however, a resolution[131] was introduced before the board prohibiting the superintendent and members of his administrative staff from attending any private meetings with CEC members, committees, or chairpersons, unless the meetings are announced and open to the public, taped, and transcriptions and verbatim written minutes furnished to the board of education. The resolution was defeated, but formal action by the board to open up communication with CEC is yet to come.

The ramifications of fundamental opposition to the decree and order by the school administration and the school board have been critical. One major consequence has been the reluctance on the part of teachers and school administrators to fully support the plan. Knowing the administration invests so little interest in its successful implementation, there is little incentive for the individual principal or teacher to wrestle with the problems arising from the plan.[132]

A second problem has been the dilatory response of the school administration to two programs in the decree: the creation of bilingual-bicultural programs[133] and the so-called East High–Manual High Complex.[134] Both are outlined in rough in the plan; timetables for implementation are not specified. As a result, negligible progress has been made toward successful implementation. Indeed, the school administration moved to undermine the bicultural-bilingual program by transferring qualified and experienced teachers of Hispanic background to schools not involved in the bilingual-bicultural program, despite assurances by the administration that such transfers were to be based on the needs of the program. Although the court order calls for specific kinds of activities and planning programs preparatory to the commencement of the school year, monitor reports indicated that the district was both behind schedule and inaccurate in statements about these programs. For example, the job of supervisor for the

128. Denver Post, May 1, 1975.

129. Maurice B. Mitchell, Letter to Judge Doyle, November 24, 1975.

130. Community Education Council, Report to Judge Doyle—Denver Public School Year 1974–1975, May, 1975, at 10.

131. Resolution, Board of Education of School District No. 1, January 1976.

132. Personal interview with Maurice B. Mitchell, May 7, 1975.

133. Letters of Maurice Mitchell to Judge Doyle, September 20, 1974, at 7–10; February 10, 1975, at 2–4.

134. Doyle Report, East-Manual Complex (January 1975); letter of Maurice Mitchell to Judge Doyle, February 10, 1975, at 4–5.

bilingual-bicultural program was posted only a few days before the first of September, making it impossible to put a planning program in effect in time to comply with the court's wishes. The plan's affirmative action program was violated when the administration interviewed applicants for the post of supervisor in advance of posting the job. With respect to the East-Manual Complex, the council reported to the judge as late as January 1975 that the administration was only "going through the motions" regarding the Complex, and that "in truth they do not support or promote the general idea of the Complex."[135] During the first semester, only about 10 percent of the pupils in each school were involved in joint courses, and these were mostly consolidations of low enrollment units in each school.

Difficulty was encountered in the nature of the in-service training program supplied by the school administration for teachers and school staff members. Chancellor Mitchell notes that the in-service training procedure as it currently exists alienates teachers. Training sessions are offered during after-school hours. Although teachers are reimbursed for their time, all training that occurs during nonschool hours is widely resented by the teaching staff and meets with stiff opposition.[136]

Other problems noted by the council have included the "failure of the School Board to act to request funding under certain Federal Programs"[137] that entitle school districts to assistance in achieving racial balance. One anticipated result of this failure was the impaired ability of the district to comply with the final decree. Still other problems have emanated from the frequent shifting of school boundaries under the plan and consequent shuffling of students. Finally, the school board has consistently refused to compensate CEC for expenses incurred in the course of discharging its court-ordered responsibilities.[138]

In some areas, however, such as the development of procedures to deal with parents who refuse to allow their children to participate in paired situations, the administration has been helpful.[139] Most monitors report that school principals are exceedingly cooperative. In general, the CEC reports characterize their relationship with the administration as a "workable" one,[140] and, it appears,

135. Doyle Report, East-Manual Complex (January 1975), at 1.
136. Personal interview with Maurice B. Mitchell, May 7, 1975.
137. Letter of Maurice Mitchell to Judge Doyle, July 12, 1974, at 2.
138. Although the school board pays the salary for a secretary to coordinate the activities of the council, all members of the council serve on a volunteer, unpaid basis, as do school monitors. In addition, the Community Education Council is housed in the Office of the Chancellor at the University of Denver, where it pays no rent or overhead expenses. According to Mitchell, the school board is only billed for expenses such as mailings that are directly linked to its court-ordered activities. Without fail, he has been forced to obtain a court order to assure reimbursement for such expenses. Indeed, Mitchell recently possessed a check from Judge Doyle to cover duplication expenses for CEC activities incurred at Mitchell's own expense. Personal interview with Maurice B. Mitchell, May 7, 1975; Denver Post, November 13, 1974.
139. Community Education Council, Report to Judge Doyle (October 30, 1975, at 11.
140. Community Education Council, Report to Judge Doyle—Denver Public School Year 1974–1975 (May 1975), at 9.

certainly better in year two of implementation than in year one. Moreover, it should be noted that numerous problems arising from the implementation of the plan do not arise alone from the reluctance of the school board and the school administration to participate in its successful effectuation. Many are inherent in the nature of the plan, and their solution may not be accomplished short of a court revision of the plan under question.

Examples of fundamental problems associated with the plan that may not necessarily be blamed on the reluctance of the school district to cooperate are the problem of Title I federal programs, the paired school situation and the limited geographical scope of the desegregation order and decree. Title I programs provide allocations of special services to students in low-income neighborhoods. The handicaps of the students are not in themselves a qualifying condition. When students from such low-income areas are bused to a higher-income area, the new area does not qualify for programs funded by Title I, and students are deprived of such services as a result of being bused. While the problem associated with children in a paired situation was resolved by allowing the student to receive such additional help in his or her home school, the problem for the "satellite" student full time at another school remains unresolved.[141]

The problems in the operation of the paired school programs are considerable.[142] Although reports for the 1975/76 school year show that pairing is working more smoothly, much confusion is associated with the assignment of support personnel such as nurses, social workers, and librarians to both members of the typical pair of schools. Pairing has been blamed for the underutilization of school facilities. Curriculum is often not coordinated between schools, and students receive duplicated instruction in both school settings. Hispano students at times do not benefit from bilingual-bicultural programs because of pairing. The time lost in busing under part-time pairing has been a source of complaint. Students, it is argued, do not get the supplementary help they got previously and must relate to double the number of persons they formerly had to relate to. As a result there is at least some sentiment for all-day pairing (as proposed by the plaintiffs).

Finally, the loss of pupils the district has experienced in the past two years has created concern, particularly in 1974 when 7,157 fewer pupils were enrolled in the schools. This is a decline of 3,857 more than would be expected on the basis of past trends in shrinking enrollment. Such pupil loss has led many to question the ultimate feasibility of a desegregation plan limited to the city and county of Denver. Declines in Anglo enrollment have meant that many of the enrollment boundaries developed by consultant Finger are no longer operative. New boundaries are needed to attempt to restore ethnic balance.[143] More fundamentally, the losses of Anglo students have made it impossible for the

141. Letter of Maurice Mitchell to Judge Doyle, February 10, 1975, at 6.
142. Letter of Maurice Mitchell to Judge Doyle, October 15, 1974.
143. Community Education Council, Report to Judge Doyle—Denver Public School Year 1974–1975 (May 1975), at 2.

schools to meet the ethnic balances called for in the original court order, no matter what boundary changes are made.[144] Future ethnic trends, and the ability to move to the suburbs to avoid participation in school desegregation, have ominous implications. In the words of the Community Education Council, "a white noose has been forming around the city for years."[145] In the long run, the enforcement of the decree might depend on challenges of the political boundaries that make this possible.

SUMMARY AND CONCLUSIONS

The desegregation of the Denver public schools involved nearly two decades of community controversy and six years of court battles. The formulation of the actual desegregation plan occupied another six months, and its implementation to date has consumed another two years. The story began with the migration of blacks eastward from the central city, away from traditional black neighborhoods, into traditional white neighborhoods of Denver. The school board's response was to maintain racial segregation in the schools in the wake of neighborhood change. Although this scenario is common to a number of communities that have experienced desegregation controversies, certain factors unique to Denver may help to explain the course of community mobilization and legal confrontation that transpired.

Analysis of Community Mobilization
Although panic selling and white flight accompanied the arrival of blacks in northeast Denver neighborhoods (Park Hill), circumstances were quite different from those to be found in other northern cities. Principally, blacks who migrated to Denver tended to be educated and skilled members of the labor force. As a result, high proportions of blacks were homeowners and high levels of black political participation were common. This meant that the black population was more equipped to exert pressure to improve the quality of education in its schools. The middle-class status of the black population also meant that there was less social distance between whites and blacks in Park Hill, which was to become the seat of the desegregation controversy. As a result, in addition to the traditional civil rights groups such as CORE, the NAACP, and black politicians, a variety of biracial community organizations dedicated their efforts to the preservation of stable, integrated neighborhoods in northeast Denver.

The response of the school board to broadly based community pressure about segregation and educational inequality was initially one of acquiescence, rather than of resistance. In 1962, faced with widespread protest over the proposed construction of a school in Park Hill, the school board halted its construction

144. Community Education Council, Report to Judge Doyle (October 30, 1975), at 12.
145. Community Education Council, Report to Judge Doyle—Denver Public School Year 1974–1975 (May 1975), at 3.

plans and created a committee to study school segregation and educational quality. The board subsequently initiated a voluntary open-enrollment program, a second study committee, and some compensatory educational programs in minority schools. The board also developed a plan to foster racial mixture in the schools by creating intermediate schools that drew students from larger attendance areas than had been previously delineated. Finally, under extreme community pressure, the school board approved a resolution directing the school superintendent to develop an integration plan with consideration for the use of transportation to achieve racial balance. And subsequently the school board adopted three resolutions to alleviate school segregation in Park Hill on the high school, junior high school, and elementary school level.

Changes in the personal socioeconomic and ideological composition of school board members and the politicization of civil rights issues both explain why resistance to school desegregation hardened so dramatically. As numerous studies show, socioeconomic status is related to race liberalism.[146] High-status persons are more likely to be liberal and sympathetic to civil rights demands, while low-status persons tend to be conservative and resistant to civil rights demands. In the late 1960s and early 1970s, the upper-class profile of the school board began to change, and persons of lower socioeconomic status were elected to the school board. This coincided with stiff board resistance to civil rights demands.

Concurrently, school matters became highly politicized. School board races and school bond elections became focal points for highly charged and dramatic confrontations between community members opposed to and supportive of school desegregation. The earliest instance of this was in 1967 when two persons clearly identified as opposed to busing students were elected to the school board with the support of the Republican Party. Their leading opponents were backed by an interracial group of civil rights liberals and supported by the Democratic Party Executive Committee. Several months later, a school bond issue for the construction of intermediate schools designed to foster racial balance was defeated. The defeat was attributed to busing and other integration factors. In 1969 another school board race featured the busing controversy. The pro-desegregation candidates were endorsed by the Democratic Party; the victorious anti-busing opposition received the support of the Republican Party. Throughout the period busing was an issue in a variety of campaigns for state and national office, and with few exceptions, pro-busing candidates were defeated.

With the politicization of the desegregation issue, individuals who could be identified as political professionals rather than civic-minded elitists sought positions on the school board. As other studies have shown,[147] political professionals, in contrast to school board members recruited from the civic elite, tend to be more conservative on civil rights issues. This contributed to the board's reversed position on desegregation matters.

146. *See, e.g.,* L. Rubin, Busing and Backlash: White Against White in a California School District (1972); and M. Tumin, Desegregation, Resistance and Readiness (1958).
147. *See, e.g.,* R. Crain, The Politics of School Desegregation (1968).

Another consequence was the development of constituency-based school policy-making. In place of circumspect, nonpartisan, education administration, decision-making became highly public and visible. And school board members saw themselves as elected to uphold a pro- or anti-busing position.

With the politicization of the desegregation issue and the attraction of professional politicians and lower-class individuals—less tolerant to civil rights demands—to positions on the school board, the barriers to community acceptance of desegregation became insurmountable. In fact of this the proponents of desegregation turned to the courts.

Analysis of the Litigation

The plaintiffs in the Denver case came to the courtroom in 1969 equipped with an arsenal of legal and academic expertise. They came with reams of computerized statistical information, maps, charts, graphs, and documentary evidence. They were directly assisted by the foremost organized and activist legal counsel in the desegregation area in the country (the Legal Defense Fund). They and their sympathizers, perhaps, epitomized the strongest impulse of the liberal civil rights movement which had developed during the 1960s.

Nevertheless, what may distinguish the Denver plaintiffs more than anything else is the adventitious timing with which they sought legal relief. They chose to sue because of the resounding electoral defeat of a cause in which they believed. Yet it so happened at the time they made this choice that their primary adversary, the school board for the district, had just taken the first open and official action to reverse a policy designed to desegregate, which had been evolving for nearly a decade. This action was the rescission of Resolutions 1520, 1524, and 1531. Resolutions 1520, 1524, and 1531 were themselves the culmination of the decade's growing recognition of the need to desegregate schools. The resolutions were official acts. Their rescission on June 9, 1969, was another official act.

But the rescission of Resolutions 1520, 1524, and 1531 clearly, indeed almost brazenly, fell within the category of actions against which the equal protection clause of the Fourteenth Amendment was intended to be a shield.

As a result, at least as to the portion of the school district that would have been affected had the three resolutions been allowed to stand, the plaintiffs' burden of proof at trial as civil rights complainants was greatly reduced. If they could demonstrate the existence of segregation in schools, the opportunity befell them to prove causative state action directly rather than circumstantially. Few manifestations of official state policy implementation could be more overt than the rescission of the three resolutions.

Challenging this manifestation of state action head on, however, required the seeking of injunctive relief: the effects of the rescission had to be halted immediately. It also required bifurcating what was, in embryo, a comprehensive and all-out attack on the entire school system. First came an injunctive relief hearing on the relatively small Park Hill component of the system. Trial on the rest of the system did not come until later. Due to the fortuities of the state of law, the bifurcation arguably added four years to the lawsuit. Judges argued expansively about the significance of the relationship between the two parts of the case. On the other hand, it is just as arguable, and probably more likely that the bifurcation—or, rather, the rescission of the resolutions which precipitated it—more than anything else led the plaintiffs to a convincing legal victory. For it was precisely the plaintiff's clear and convincing case on official state action in the hearing on injunctive relief that became the touchstone of a Supreme Court decision which mandated the desegregation of the Denver schools and probably will affect the desegregation of schools in northern cities for years to come.

Analysis of the Plan and its Implementation

The recalcitrance of the school board and the school administration defendents in the Denver lawsuit forced the federal Judge to make an end-run around these defendants in both the formulation and the implementation of the desegregation plan. In the formulation, the judge retained his own expert. Since the school board and administration had given him no help, his only other alternative was to turn to the plaintiffs. This alternative the judge eschewed. No one will ever know exactly why. It is logical speculation, however, that, knowing whatever plan he adopted would be unpopular with large numbers of citizens, he hoped at least to avoid the appearance of partiality in his final decision. Thus, through the court-appointed expert, a compromise plan was adopted which, in the eyes of many, fell short in sophistication and workability to the plaintiffs', which involved full-time busing and virtually equal sharing of the burdens of busing as between minorities and Anglos. But the court of appeals has said (and the Supreme Court has refused to review the statement) that equal sharing of such burdens is not constitutionally required. The part-time pairing aspect of the plan, however, will be required to be replaced by full-time busing under the court of appeals latest reversal.

In the implementation of the plan, the judge has similarly by-passed the school board and the school administration. He had no choice. Neither the board nor the administration was any more willing to put an unwanted plan into practice than they were to go through the motions of dreaming up an unwanted plan in the first instance.

The judge created his own monitoring council, the Community Education Council. In effect, he empowered CEC to act—under the imprimatur of the court—as the superego of the board and administration. While obviously the administration continues to carry out day-to-day operations of the district, in one important regard it is no longer as autonomous as it would otherwise be by custom and law. The prolific network of school monitors created by CEC is constantly peering over the administration's shoulder. The network draws from a cross-section of the community. It reaches into every school. It is, like every superego, greatly resented, but it cannot be escaped.

Through the network, CEC possesses an effective, ingenious capacity to fulfill its monitoring responsibility. Through CEC the court possesses a practical and relatively convenient instrument for maintaining meaningful jurisdiction over its plan. The court relies on the council. The council gives it information. Orders to the administration or board based on information from the council, since such information is ultimately that produced by the network and the network is the community, are more likely to have community support. Having community support they are more likely to be implemented and peaceably abided.

This is the success of the plan in Denver and its implementation. Now that the appeals process has been exhausted, the school administration and board may hopefully put their resources and authority behind the spirit as well as the letter of the plan.

Sealing Off the City: School Desegregation in Detroit

Elwood Hain

The Detroit litigation occasioned a significant decision of the Supreme Court in Milliken v. Bradley. *This essay examines the way in which the metropolitan-wide remedy, rejected by the Supreme Court in that decision, arose in the litigation and the effort to create a remedy in a predominantly black school district in the aftermath of that rejection. It is, among other things, a study of judicial frustration as the limits placed on remedy approach the point of compromising the goal of desegregated education.*

Elwood Hain was a professor of law at Wayne State University Law School. He was a co-chairman of the Metropolitan Coalition for Peaceful Integration in Detroit. He is now Visiting Professor of Law at the University of San Diego. —Eds.

Detroit is a city much maligned by public opinion, local and national. It is known as a dirty factory town, the scene of bitter strikes and race riots, and there are facts to support that image. Automobile workers still exhibit some of the militance of the 1930s, although the UAW leadership has mellowed somewhat. While blacks hold an unusually high number of positions in public office, in government employment, and in labor, race relations are tense, a fact which for years has sustained a wide array of membership organizations and service agencies dealing with racial problems. While today little thought is given to the 1943 race riot that left 34 dead,[1] the effects of the even deadlier 1967 riot are still evident in the burned-out buildings that line some streets and in the armed guards conspicuously posted in grocery stores and pharmacies.

1. National Advisory Commission on Civil Disorders, Report 244 (Bantam Books ed. 1968).

There is, however, another Detroit, less well known but equally significant for an appraisal of events in the city. Wages are high, even for the unskilled, although the recession largely eliminated overtime and sharply increased unemployment. Detroit is not a crowded city; it has a low population density for a major American city.[2] It is predominantly a city of homeowners, not of tenants. It has the highest rate of owner-occupancy of housing found among the ten largest American cities.[3] Its city government has a strong, relatively corruption-free civil service. Its citizenry, black and white, is politically sophisticated and assertive. It is laced together with organizations devoted to the public good, ranging from citywide and metropolitan groups to thousands of block clubs in all parts of the city.

Both faces of Detroit have been seen during the six-year battle over school desegregation. The struggle erupted amid racial hysteria in 1970. When the city's schools were desegregated in January 1976, all was calm. As the issue of metropolitan desegregation remains unresolved, Detroit's struggle with itself continues.

THE DEMOGRAPHY OF DETROIT

Detroit has been a major center of heavy industry since the end of the Civil War. When the automotive industry began to grow, Detroit boomed. The city's population increased 63 percent between 1900 and 1910, and another 113 percent between 1910 and 1920. In 1920 it contained just under a million persons and continued to grow until the Crash in 1929. Despite the severity of the Depression in Detroit, the 1930 census showed 1.57 million residents, 58 percent more than a decade earlier. With partial recovery in the late 1930s and the intense production effort generated by World War II, the city's population peaked at almost 2 million. About 1945, a decine began that has not yet stopped.

The expansion of the Detroit suburbs began a decade later than that of the city, but has never stopped. Each decade since World War I the suburbs have grown at a faster rate than the city. The 1960 census showed that suburbia was for the first time more populous than Detroit. The 1970 census revealed a standard metropolitan statistical area (SMSA) of approximately 4.2 million persons, of whom 1.51 million lived in the city. With the automobile industry again suffering hard times and with gloomy long-range forecasts for all heavy manufacturing, the population of the Detroit SMSA is expected to be stable or to decline in the next few years.[4]

Detroit has had a black community since before the Civil War. Until World War I it was small, growing at about the same rate as the general population. Although World War I cut off the flow of European immigrants to Detroit, at the same time it demanded stepped-up production from heavy industry. Southern black workers were recruited to fill the need. Even so, only 4 percent of the

2. U.S. Bureau of the Census, County and City Data Book 1972 at 814 (1973).
3. *Id.*

City's population was black in 1920. The black population grew rapidly during the twenties, was almost stable in the thirties, and climbed steadily thereafter. By the 1970 census, 44 percent of the city's population was black. It is generally accepted that today slightly more than half the city's population is black.[5]

The changing complexion of the Detroit population has resulted from both in-migration by blacks and out-migration by whites. The whites left the city at a fairly constant rate throughout the 1950s and 1960s. The black in-migration has been smaller than the white departure, and was much higher in the 1950s than in the 1960s. During the 1960s the city had a net loss of 400,000 whites and a net gain of 100,000 blacks. Migration of both whites and blacks has been heaviest among persons of child-bearing age, a fact of significance for school enrollments.[6]

Detroit, of course, does not rest in isolation on the flat plains of southeastern Michigan. The "real city," as George Romney used to refer to urbanized areas, has expanded to fill all but the outer reaches of Wayne, Oakland, and Macomb counties. The area is tied together by an elaborate network of freeways, all converging on downtown Detroit. Indeed, the spreading out of the city has been possible largely because of the freeways.[7]

Nearly all of the black population in the metropolitan area has been channeled into the city of Detroit. Within the city, blacks have been concentrated in an expanding core area. The black core area and surrounding transitional areas today include about two-thirds of the city. The white population of the city is concentrated in the western and northeastern sectors, although some whites remain in transitional areas. Indexes of dissimilarity show the extent of residential segregation to be quite high. In 1970 the indexes were 78 for the city of Detroit, 94 for suburban Detroit, and 89 for the combined urbanized area (the SMSA less the few remaining rural areas). The lower index for Detroit reflects the presence of transitional neighborhoods.[8]

The black population of suburban Detroit rose slowly but steadily during the fifty years between the 1920 and the 1970 censuses. In 1920 the 4,000 blacks in suburban Detroit were 1 percent of the suburban population. By 1970 the number of suburban blacks had increased to 97,000, but they were still only 4 percent of the persons living in suburbia.[9] The presence of almost 100,000 blacks in the Detroit suburbs should not be interpreted as a breakthrough for open housing. Nearly all of them are in eight well-defined black areas: two small cities totally surrounded by Detroit (Highland Park and Hamtramck); two small indus-

4. Farley, *Population Trends and School Segregation in the Detroit Metropolitan Area,* 21 Wayne L. Rev. 867, 870–71, 892 (1975) [hereinafter cited as Farley].

5. *Id.* at 867, 892.

6. *Id.* at 869–70.

7. J. Humphrey, Segregation and Integration: A Geography of People in Metropolitan Detroit 12 (1972).

8. *Id.* at 872. The index was calculated on the basis of census tract data rather than block data. Block data normally shows a higher degreee of segregation than census tract data does.

9. *Id.* at 892.

trial cities tucked in between southwest Detroit and the Detroit River (River Rouge and Ecorse); Pontiac and Mount Clemens, two old industrial towns recently reached by the expanding Detroit suburban area; Inkster, a Wayne County suburb divided by railroad tracks into a black half and a white half; and Royal Oak Township, an unincorporated area abutting Detroit in Oakland County where, at the beginning of World War II, the federal government sponsored the building of substandard segregated housing for black workers in war industries.[10]

THE SCHOOLS

The public schools of metropolitan Detroit are as racially identifiable as the residential patterns. Professor Reynolds Farley's recent careful study of residential and school segregation statistics concludes:

> First, all the indexes suggest high levels of racial segregation in the schools. Most whites attend exclusively or principally white schools while blacks go to largely black schools.
>
> Second, there are city-suburban differences in segregation. Suburban school districts, considered together, have higher levels of segregation than city schools. At the same time, less of an effort would be required to desegregate the suburban schools.
>
> Third, since city and suburban schools are both racially segregated, the indexes based on all schools in the area are also high.
>
> Fourth, levels of racial segregation in secondary schools are similar to those in elementary schools. Even though they draw their students from broader geographical areas, there is no evidence that high schools are more integrated than grammar school.
>
> Fifth, no large increases or decreases in segregation were recorded between 1967 and 1972.[11]

Within the Detroit School District, which is coterminous with the city of Detroit, the racial composition of enrollment has shown a steady shift from white to black.[12] In 1970 it was 63.6 percent black. By September 1975 the black percentage had increased to 75.2 percent.[13] Most of the city's schools have long been racially identifiable, although Michigan law since 1869 has clearly

10. *Id.* at 873.

11. *Id.* at 879.

12. Of the nonblack pupil population, 2 percent is Spanish-surnamed, Oriental, or American Indian. The rest are white, non-Spanish-surnamed. Michigan State Department of Education, Department of Research and Evaluation, Office of Research, Planning, and Evaluation, Racial-Ethnic Distribution of Students and Employees in the Detroit Public Schools, September 26, 1975 at 1 (Jan. 1976) [hereinafter cited as 1975 Fourth Friday Count]. With possible minor exceptions discussed *infra* (text accompanying notes 351–354) "other minorities" have been treated as white in the desegregation case.

13. 1975 Fourth Friday Count at 1. *Cf.* Bradley v. Milliken, 338 F. Supp. 582, 586 (E.D. Mich., 1975), giving the 1970 black percentage as 63.8 percent. The minor difference appears to be the result of a typographical error by the court.

prohibited racial segregation in schools.[14] Most of the citizenry, including school officials, have operated on the assumption that the racial separation of pupils was a fortuitous result of residential segregation and have assumed that racially identifiable schools presented no constitutional problem.[15]

During the 1960s the Detroit Board of Education was sued often on allegations of racially discriminatory practices in particular schools. George E. Bushnell, Jr., the board's attorney during those years, recalls that suits alleging discrimination by building administrators ran as high as 10 or 12 a year, at a time when the board employed over 3,000 persons and enrolled almost 300,000 pupils. The board carefully investigated each complaint. If the board's investigation showed board personnel to be guilty of discrimination, strong measures were taken to correct the matter, including the demotion or reassignment of administrators. When the board was convinced that the charges were groundless, it went to trial. According to Bushnell, the board's approach in court was not to argue about the legal standards, but to press for a full airing of the facts. The combination of self-policing and candor in court led, Bushnell reports, to the board's never losing such a lawsuit.[16]

In the early sixties several suits were filed in state courts challenging specific textbooks adopted by the school board on the ground that they either ignored or unfairly stereotyped minorities. After losing several of these suits and after a change in school board membership, the Detroit district became more forceful in pressing publishers for better-balanced texts. A particularly promising step was the adoption of a procedure for reviewing proposed texts for their human-relations sensitivity. Until 1968 the board largely relied on exhortation; the result was a series of compromises.[17] Where adequate texts were unavailable, the district prepared its own. In 1968, Assistant Superintendent Arthur Johnson, a former executive secretary of the Detroit Branch of the NAACP, instituted a get-tough policy that led to substantial changes by publishers wanting to do business with Detroit and the other urban school districts which were by then following Detroit's lead.[18]

14. Mich. Pub. Act 34 § 28 (1867); People *ex rel.* Workman v. Board of Education, 18 Mich. 400 (1869). After *Workman,* Detroit eliminated one of its two all-black schools but continued the other with a totally black enrollment. At least one black school had existed in the city from the original establishment of public schools in 1838. *See* People *ex rel.* Workman v. Board of Education, 18 Mich. 400, 418 (1869) (Campbell, J., dissenting); Grant, *The Detroit School Case: An Historical Overview,* 21 Wayne L. Rev. 851, 854 (1975), *citing* C. Burton, The City of Detroit 743 (1922).

15. *Cf.* Deal v. Cincinnati Bd. of Educ., 369 F.2d 55 (6th Cir. 1966), *cert. denied,* 389 U.S. 847 (1967), 419 F.2d 1387 (6th Cir. 1969). At the trial in *Bradley v. Milliken,* counsel for the Detroit Board of Education conceded the racial identifiability of many schools, but denied that the board had caused it.

16. Interview with George E. Bushnell, Jr., in Detroit, Michigan, Aug. 26, 1975 [hereinafter cited as Bushnell interview]. Mr. Bushnell is a partner in the Detroit law firm Miller, Canfield, Paddock and Stone.

17. Interview with Freeman Flynn, divisional director, School-Community Relations, Detroit Public Schools, in Detroit, Michigan, May 22, 1975 [hereinafter cited as First Flynn interview].

18. Bushnell interview; First Flynn interview.

The most important school suit in the sixties was one brought in federal court by parents at Sherrill Elementary School in 1962.[19] The suit sought to enjoin a proposed redrawing of feeder patterns which would have removed Sherrill graduates from a predominately white high school area and reassigned them to a predominately black school. Once in court both sets of attorneys and their clients sought to use the case as a lever to end the inertia of the school bureaucracy in a whole range of racially significant areas. District Judge Fred Kaess, to whom the case was assigned, reportedly cooperated in that effort. While the case was never actually tried, the court at one point made "interim findings," which included a series of recommendations aimed at resolving the grievances of blacks against the school system.[20] The case was eventually dismissed by consent of the parties after some changes were made by the school system and after a liberal majority was elected to the board of education.[21]

In the decade between 1957 and 1966 the board created a series of study commissions, and they advised it that the schools were racially identifiable, that black schools had poorer programs, that the black community felt excluded from the operations of the schools, and that the practices of the school bureaucracy promoted those results. As a result of recommendations of the first committee, chaired by George Romney in the late 1950s, the board stopped routinely assigning black teachers only to schools with large black pupil populations and white teachers to predominantely white schools.[22] As there was no affirmative integration program and teachers' requests for reassignment were not evaluated for racial effect, the change did not produce dramatic results. The board forced the nominal integration of craft union apprenticeship programs conducted in the schools. Several years before other districts or even the federal government put nondiscrimination clauses into contracts with suppliers, the Detroit School Board insisted that its contractors engage in affirmative action in employment.[23]

When a more liberal board took office in 1965 it implemented more changes recommended by the study groups. It changed some pupil assignment patterns to promote integration, but as these were minor adjustments between neighboring schools, their impact was small and short-lived. The board's open-enrollment policy was revised to permit pupil transfers only if they improved the racial balance of the receiving school.[24] Any busing to relieve overcrowding was required to be desegregative as well. These policies of the board were not always

19. Sherrill School Parents' Committee v. Board of Educ. of the School District of the City of Detroit, Civ. No. 22092 (E.D. Mich., filed Jan. 22, 1962).

20. Interim Findings, Sherrill School Parents' Committee v. Board of Educ. of the School District of the City of Detroit, Civ. No. 22092 (E.D. Mich. Sept. 18, 1964).

21. Order of Dismissal, May 3, 1968. First Flynn interview; Bushnell interview.

22. First Flynn interview.

23. Bushnell interview. *See* Bradley v. Milliken, 338 F. Supp. 582, 591 (E.D. Mich. 1971).

24. The impact on the sending school was not considered. Hence racially isolated students could and did transfer to other schools where their race, while outnumbered, was better represented.

implemented as written. Notable exceptions later haunted the board's attorney in defending against charges of segregation.[25]

Starting in 1965, the board also took steps toward more balanced faculties. It negotiated with the Detroit Federation of Teachers to move toward racial balance through racially conscious initial assignments and a racial impact review of transfer requests. In addition, acting largely in response to swelling enrollments and a shortage of teachers, but also out of a desire to secure a more balanced staff, the board actively recruited teachers from southern black colleges.[26]

After several years of informally ignoring written promotion criteria when it wanted to promote blacks to administrative posts,[27] the board raised the issue in the mid-1960s with the newly certified bargaining agent for the principals and other supervisors. The board sought the union's agreement to the creation of a class of black "special" principals who lacked the regular qualifications. The union leadership, aware of the tension resulting from such an arrangement in New York City, declined, but suggested that revised qualifications be established for all principals. The board accepted the idea with alacrity. Since then the Detroit board has pursued a promotion policy aggresively preferential to blacks.[28] For nearly a decade the Detroit Board of Education has maintained one of the highest rates of minority administrators in the country. For most of that time it boasted that it had more black regular principals then Chicago and New York combined.

WINDS OF CHANGE

Most of the innovations in the system were the result of the election of a team of three liberals to the seven-person school board in 1964. The slate was supported by a liberal-labor-black coalition. When the three took office in January 1965 they joined with Remus Robinson, the first black person ever to serve on the board, to form a solid majority dedicated to racial equality. The new majority soon concluded that Superintendent Samuel Brownell lacked sufficient commitment to the new goal. When his contract expired in 1966 the board replaced him with Norman Drachler, the assistant superintendent for community

25. See Bradley v. Milliken, 338 F. Supp. 582, 588 (E.D. Mich. 1971) (pupil assignment and transportation); *but see id.* at 589–91 (teacher assignment).

26. Bushnell interview; First Flynn interview. Bradley v. Milliken, 338 F. Supp. 582, 589–91 (E.D. Mich. 1971). In February 1961 the Detroit board employed 2,275 black teachers who were 21.6 percent of the total teaching staff. By October 1970 black teachers numbered 5,106 and constituted 41.6 percent of the total faculty. Bradley v. Milliken, 338 F. Supp. 582, 590 (E.D. Mich, 1971).

27. Bushnell interview.

28. First Flynn interview. *See,* Bradley v. MIlliken, 338 F. Supp. 582, 590 (E.D. Mich. 1971). Educational levels were not reduced, but time in the system and time spent as a supervisor were. An oral examination was added to the written one. All persons on the existing eligibility list were guaranteed a position, although perhaps not as soon as once expected.

relations. Drachler proved to be the aggressive integrationist the board wanted.[29] Even so, the school bureaucracy did not uniformly bend itself to the new tasks. Such progress as was made frequently resulted from community pressures and from decisions by persons other than professional educators. The textbook disputes demonstrate how that worked. After several years of community pressure the district established a committee of educators to review books for their racial context. That committee was relatively ineffectual until a civil rights leader, newly hired as a school administrator, took decisive action.[30]

By 1968 the big-city school systems of the country were seriously considering decentralization as a means of making the schools more accessible to the public, especially the black public. In Detroit the school board majority favored greater openness but frankly feared a repetition of the chaos it associated with the Oceanhill-Brownsville experience in New York City. After successfully opposing a proposal by a flamboyant black Detroit legislator to carve up the Detroit school system into 16 completely separate school districts, it began a serious study of how to structure some form of community input. The November 1968 election of Andrew Perdue gave added impetus to the study. Perdue was a black attorney pledged to work for decentralization and community control.[31]

By the spring of 1969 some black groups in Detroit were pressing hard for decentralization, although most of the public was apathetic about the issue. More because the board was committed to public accessibility then because of overwhelming public pressure, the board conducted a series of hearings on the subject in all parts of the city. The hearings were poorly attended, but most of those who spoke favored some type of decentralization.[32] Their reasons were often contradictory. The NAACP, struggling to reconcile its integrative goals with the new value of community control, proposed giving significant decision-making powers to local school building councils of parents, teachers, students, and administrators. It opposed the creation of internal political boundaries and regional school boards, as it saw decentralization as an educational device, not a political one.[33] An assortment of black parent groups and political groups, often based in federal poverty programs, had a different view of decentralization. They called for black control of black schools, rejecting any concept of integration.

29. *See* Grant, *Community Control v. School Integration—The Case of Detroit,* 24 Public Interest 62, 64–65 (Summer 1971) [hereinafter cited as Grant].

30. *See* text at note 18, *supra.*

31. Grant at 67–68. In the same session of the legislature a more responsible decentralization bill was introduced by a white liberal Democratic representative from Detroit. It got little public notice and died in committee. *Id.*

32. Interview with Norman Drachler in Palo Alto, California [hereinafter cited as Drachler interview].

33. Interview with Jesse Goodwin, chairman, Education Committee, Detroit Branch, NAACP, in Detroit, Michigan, May 27, 1975 [hereinafter cited as Goodwin interview]; G. LeNoue & B. Smith, The Politics of School Decentralization 121–22 (1976) [hereinafter cited as LaNoue & Smith].

Some white homeowner groups and parent organizations also supported decentralization.

Responding to the growing popularity of the concept, State Senator Coleman Young[34] introduced a bill in the legislature authorizing the Detroit Board of Education to decentralize its functions and to draw boundary lines for subordinate "regions." Key provisions of the bill were worked out with persons close to the Detroit board, although board members themselves were apparently not consulted. The board decided not to oppose the bill which, after all, left it with the power to determine most of the features of decentralization. The teachers' union withdrew its objections to the bill when job security provisions were written in to avoid confrontations such as those in New York. Thereafter the bill, Act 244, was approved by lopsided margins in both houses with almost no debate. It was signed by the governor in August 1969.[35]

After the passage of Act 244, the board of education conducted further hearings on where to draw boundary lines for the new regional school districts and how to divide authority between central and regional boards.[36] The NAACP, the Urban League, and the board's own attorney were about the only commentators to suggest that integration, or at least avoiding further racial isolation, should be a major criterion.[37] Most other groups—black and white—assumed racially identifiable schools would continue to exist and pressed for racially identifiable regions to govern them. The assumption was not groundless, as the sincerley integrationist board had been unable during the last four years to take any major step toward pupil integration. Given racially identifiable schools and a predominately white electorate, even an integrationist might at that point have settled for "black control of black schools," the rallying cry of the more assertive community-control proponents.

The liberal bloc on the school board saw the matter differently. Its leader, A.L. Zwerdling, claimed homogeneous decentralization would lock the city into the existing racially separate schools. He believed that whites and blacks would learn to work together in heterogeneous districts and would then move to eliminate segregation in their own regions. Zwerdling therefore proposed a set of regions that would each include both black and white high schools and their feeder schools.

By the time they had to decide the matter, the liberal bloc had lost its automatic majority. Robinson, the key fourth vote, was hospitalized wtih cancer. While Swerdling delayed a vote on his decentralization plan, it finally became

34. Young was Minority Leader of the Michigan Senate as well as the recognized leader of black legislators in both houses. He was also Michigan's Democratic National Committeeman. He is presently mayor of Detroit.

35. *See* Grant at 66–69; LaNoue & Smith at 123–24. *See also* Mich. Pub. Act 244 (1969).

36. For detailed discussions of the process, *see* Grant at 69–71; Lanoue & Smith at 124–28.

37. Goodwin interview; Bushnell interview.

clear in early 1970 that Robinson would never be able to attend another board meeting. Swerdling then had to win a vote from one of the other three board members. Two were white attorneys, Patrick McDonald and James Hathaway, who for somewhat different reasons opposed Zwerdling's decentralization plan and seemed unshakable. The other board member, Andrew Perdue, was a staunch supporter of decentralization who felt the Swerdling plan combined continued segregation with continued white domination. If the board was not seriously going to pursue integrated schools, he felt it should create separate black and white regions. His position was one of "put up or shut up" about integration.[38]

Zwerdling put up. In late March 1970 he asked Superintendent Drachler to redraft the decentralization plan to include some immediate desegregation. Drachler delegated the job to a small group of community-relations specialists on a Saturday afternoon. By the end of the day the staff group had mapped out a high school desegregation plan. On the following Monday afternoon the staff gave the superintendent a report containing a detailed recitation of the new boundaries, a map of the new boundaries, and a ten-page introduction adapted from a position paper on integration the staff had been drafting when Drachler reassigned them.[39]

The plan redrew attendance boundaries for 12 of the 22 geographically based high schools, changing the racial composition of 11 of them. None of the reassignments crossed the regional boundaries proposed by Zwerdling. The plan proposed two-way integration for the first time, placing black pupils in the three remaining white high schools and reassigning white pupils to heavily black schools. Only tenth graders without older siblings were to be reassigned the first year of the plan; eleventh and twelfth grade students would finish school where they had started. It would, therefore, take three years for the plan to be completely implemented. When fully implemented the plan would have reassigned only 12,000 of the 190,000 pupils in the system, though it would have changed the racial character of over half the high schools. The plan did not include a transportation component. Rather it assumed that all pupils would make their own transportation arrangements, as historically had been the practice in Detroit.[40] The new attendance zones were designed to make it easier to get to school by public bus. Most of the new zones were rectangles running from east

---

38. *See* Grant at 69–71.

39. First Flynn interview; Drachler interview.

40. Although the state of Michigan furnished 75 percent of the funds for transporting school children in most school districts, it provided no transportation aid to city school districts. Most, but not all, metropolitan Detroit suburban districts qualified for state transportation funds. *See* Mich. Comp. L. Ann . § 388.621; Bradley v. Milliken, 338 F. Supp. 582, 589 (E.D. Mich. 1971); *aff'd,* 484 F.2d 215, 238, 240–41 (*en banc*) (6th Cir. 1973); *rev'd on other grounds,* 418 U.S. 717 (1974). At that time about 25,000 school children in Detroit rode public transportation to school. LaNoue & Smith at 127.

to west, the direction of most bus routes in the city. The old zones had been more compact but were less adapted to public bus routes.[41]

Drachler presented the plan at a private dinner meeting of the board the following evening, March 31, 1970. Four members of the board endorsed it, the three members elected in 1964 as integrationists, plus Perdue, elected as a community control advocate. Robinson sent word that he, too, supported it. Board members Hathaway and McDonald opposed the plan. On Friday, April 3, copies of the plan were distributed to each board member at the request of Patrick McDonald. McDonald promptly gave his copy to the *Detroit News*. The *Free Press* also secured a copy and both Sunday papers reported the plan in bold headlines.[42] Crowds of angry whites demonstrated at the Schools Center Building on Monday and Tuesday. Two hours before its regular Tuesday meeting on April 7, the board met privately with Superintendent Drachler and Attorney Bushnell to discuss the plan. Two members were absent. Remus Robinson was hospitalized and Patrick McDonald was in the foyer of the building addressing the hundreds of protestors who had assembled. At the private meeting Bushnell was for the first time asked his opinion of the proposal. He assured the board that it was completely within its power to redraw attendance zones, and that there was nothing in the decentralization law that precluded combining decentralization with revision of attendance boundaires. But he volunteered the political advice that it would be wiser to separate the two issues, postponing changes in pupil assignments until later.[43] Member Hathaway argued against the proposal, citing the public uproar and the probability of a white flight so severe as to cripple the district financially while destroying any chance for integration. He also criticized the plan as giving too little power to the newly created regional boards.[44] The other four members of the board pledged their votes for the plan. In the five-hour public meeting that followed, most of the thirty citizens who spoke opposed the plan, but spokes-persons for the NAACP, the Urban League, the American Civil Liberties Union, and the Michigan Civil Rights Commission supported the plan and the board.[45] Superintendent Drachler explained the proposal and its educational, moral, and legal rationale. Board president Zwerdling explained that the superintendent did not need board approval to make attendance zone changes, but had elected to seek it in this case because of the importance of the matter. Each member of the board then explained his intended

41. First Flynn interview. *See* Bradley v. Milliken, 338 F. Supp. 582, 588 (E.D. Mich. 1971).

42. Detroit News, April 5, 1970, at 1; Detroit Free Press, April 5, 1970, at 1A; Grant at 71.

43. Bushnell interview; Grant at 72.

44. Bushnell interview; Detroit Free Press, April 8, 1970.

45. The NAACP endorsed the plan as a promising first step toward really meaningful desegregation. Goodwin interview. The spokeswoman for the Michigan Civil Rights Commission asserted there was a legal duty to consider integration in drawing any new boundaries. The ACLU praised the board's courage. Detroit News, April 8, 1970, at 1.

vote. The board majority made it clear that even if the legislature were to repeal the decentralization statute, the attendance boundary changes would remain in effect. As was predicted before the meeting, the measure carried 4–2. The plan was thereafter known as the April 7 Plan.[46]

OPPOSITION TO VOLUNTARY DESEGREGATION

Addressing the white opponents of the April 7 Plan who gathered outside the board's meeting room minutes before the crucial vote, board member McDonald suggested that a recall election was a feasible means of controlling wrong-headed public officials. On May 4 a recall drive was formally launched against the four board members supporting the April 7 Plan. Six weeks later recall petititons containing 130,000 signatures were filed with the city clerk. The total far exceeded the 114,000 required (25 percent of the city's vote for governor in the last election). Never before had a recall campaign in the district succeeded in securing the required number of signatures.[47]

Both houses of the legislature moved quickly, too, although in different ways. On April 9 the Michigan House passed a bill requiring a city referendum on decentralization and mandating the assignment of pupils to the schools nearest their homes. The bill carried by more than a 2–1 margin, with heavy support from suburban, rural, and white Detroit representatives. No black legislator voted for it. The Michigan Senate simply voted to repeal the act authorizing decentralization. That vote was equally decisive.

The black legislators and their handful of liberal white allies were faced with losing both decentralization and partial desegregation. They knew the votes were then largely because of the integration issue. If they could separate the issues they might salvage decentralization. Negotiating simultaneously with conservative whites and unhappy blacks while delaying action by the conference committee, the Democratic leadership of the legislature secured a compromise on a measure that effectively prohibited desegregation and withdrew from the Detroit Board of Education the power to draw boundaries for decentralization. The dis-

---

46. Detroit News, April 8, 1970, at 1; Detroit Free Press, April 8, 1970. In the days that followed, the plan was endorsed by several "national and local agencies and organizations, including the United States Office of Education, the defendant Michigan State Board of Education. . . the Michigan Civil Rights Commission" and the Michigan Association for Supervision and Curriculum Development. Bradley v. Milliken, 433 F.2d 897, 900 (6th Cir. 1970).

Senator Young, the author of the decentralization bill, was reportedly furious that the board had been foolish enough to jeopardize decentralization by attaching a "chicken-shit integration plan" to it in an election year. Grant at 73. Senator Young's remark reveals a fundamental difference in perspectives about desegregation. The black community generally saw the reassignment of less than 3 percent of the system's students as more symbolic than substantive integration. The white community saw the board's initiative as a sweeping change in the nature of the school system, not just because of the number of children affected and the cost allegedly involved, but because, for the first time, integration was to be sought by sending some white children into predominately black schools.

47. Grant at 72, 74–75.

trict was to be divided into eight decentralized regions by the legislature or, if it could not agree within a week after the bill became law, by a panel appointed by the governor.[48]

To eliminate any need for a recall, the bill shortened the terms of three of the supporters of the April 7 Plan so they would leave office in December 1970 rather than a year later.[49] The compromise, Act 48, passed with but a single dissent in the lower chamber and none in the other, and was signed by Governor Milliken on July 7.

The legislature did not even try to agree on internal boundaries for the district, so the governor appointed a three-man commission. The commission's decision, issued two weeks later, was structured to create four white-dominated regions and four black-dominated regions, a result approved by both black and white politicians.[50]

In the meantime the recall campaign was in high gear. Traditional political leaders, fearing that a hard-fought recall would trigger another summer of riots, had secured the promise of the recall leadership to abandon the recall if Act 48 were passed. After the statute passed, the recall leaders reneged on their promise. Lulled into complacency until the last minute, the opposition to the recall focused on the courts, not the electorate, and failed in both arenas.[51] In light voting on August 4, 60 percent of the voters favored the recall. The vote was divided along straight racial lines: about 90 percent of the whites voted yes, and 90 percent of the blacks voted no, but the black turnout was lower. It was the first successful recall campaign in the 128-year history of the school district.[52]

48. Mich. Pub. Act 48 (1970). *See* Grant at 72–74. The critical provision of the statute abolished the April 7 Plan in one sentence and in the next directed the Detroit board to assign pupils on the basis of neighborhood schools or freedom of choice:

> Sec. 12. The implementation of any attendance provisions for the 1970/71 school year determined by any first class school district board shall be delayed pending the date of commencement of functions by the first class school district boards established under the provisions of this amendatory act but such provision shall not impair the right of any such board to determine and implement prior to such date such changes in attendance provisions as are mandated by practical necessity. In reviewing, confirming, establishing or modifying attendance provisions the first class school district boards established under the provisions of this amendatory act shall have a policy of open enrollment and shall enable students to attend a school of preference but providing priority acceptance, insofar as practicable, in cases of insufficient school capacity, to those students residing nearest the school and to those students desiring to attend the school for participation in vocationally oriented courses or other specialized curriculum.

The entire text of Act 48 is reprinted in Bradley v. Milliken, 443 F.2d 897, 905–909 (6th Cir. 1970).

49. Mich. Pub. Act 48, §3-A (1970).

50. Grant at 75. In fact blacks gained control of only two of the eight regions in the first school board election held under the new statute. That result was generally regarded as due to the widespread disorganization of traditional political groups at the time. *Id.* at 76–77. For a somewhat different view see LaNoue and Smith at 141–44.

51. Grant at 75; Bushnell interview.

52. Detroit Free Press, Aug. 6, 1970 at 1A; Michigan Chronicle, Aug. 15, 1970; Grant at 75.

Prelude to the Suit

In early July 1970 the Detroit branch of the NAACP had secured passage by its national convention of a resolution condemning legislative efforts to repeal Detroit's voluntary desegregation plan.[53] After the passage of Public Act 48, well-founded rumors abounded that the NAACP was going to file suit to require the integration of the Detroit schools. Superintendent Crachler sought the NAACP's help in challenging Act 48, which he saw as a "classic" example of rescinding an integration plan for the purpose of perpetuating school segregation. With encouragement from Rev. Darneau Stewart, who was then serving as school board president, he contacted the national NAACP leaders who had cooperated with the Detroit Board of Education during the years of liberal ascendancy. On short notice he directed two of his key administrators, Arthur Johnson and Aubrey McCutcheon, and the school board's attorney, George Bushnell, Jr., to fly to New York to meet with representatives of the NAACP. He informed only Stewart and former school board president Zwerdling of the meeting.[54]

The school board's representatives were not segregationists. Johnson had been executive secretary of the Detroit branch of the NAACP before Drachler hired him as an assistant superintendent for community relations. McCutcheon was a labor lawyer hired, on Zwerdling's recommendation, to conduct the board's labor relations under a new Michigan public employee collective bargaining statute.[55] Neither was a professional educator; both were strong-willed men who valued competence and results. Both are black. Bushnell had been the school board's attorney for eight years. He was at the time a life member of the NAACP and one of only three whites serving on the board of the Detroit branch of the NAACP. He had been heavily involved in a series of difficult efforts to make the school system more responsive to the needs of blacks. As he himself has said, he had become so heavily involved in the administrative decisions of the board that he no longer had the detached view expected of legal counsel but instead was emotionally involved in any judgment passed on it.[56]

The NAACP was represented primarily by June Shagaloff, the director of educational matters for the organization, and Louis Lucas, a white attorney from Memphis, Tennessee, who had represented the NAACP in several major school desegregation suits since leaving the Justice Department's Civil Rights Division in 1967.[57]

At the meeting the Detroiters reviewed the school district's progressive record

53. Goodwin interview.
54. Drachler interview.
55. McCutcheon became the executive deputy superintendent of the Detroit school system in July 1973 and held that post until he resigned in June 1976. Until mid-1975 he was widely viewed as the leading candidate to replace the superintendent. In 1975 Arthur Jefferson was elected superintendent by a coalition of seven central board members united primarily by a desire to stop McCutcheon. Johnson is now a vice-president of Wayne State University.
57. Bushnell interview.

and its recent effort to integrate, followed by the state's intervention. They sought to determine the likelihood that the NAACP would challenge the statute in court. Lucas wondered if perhaps the organization should go further and sue the Detroit board, too. The school administrators advised against that step. They asserted that for the NAACP to sue the Detroit board would jeopardize a prominent liberal superintendent, destroy the advances that had been made, and lose the case on the merits as well. In the meantime, white flight would be overwhelming. Decentralization would not be given a chance to work.[58]

Lucas, at least, was skeptical and pressed Bushnell. In his opinion there was a clear case against both the state and the Detroit board. Besides, he asked, if the board were so dedicated to desegregation, why wouldn't it want the plaintiffs to seek a sweeping desegregation order rather than have a fight every time the school board wants to desegregate another 3,000 of its 290,000 pupils? Why not solve the whole problem at once.[59]

Bushnell reacted strongly, "I told Mr. Lucas I would whip his ass."[60] Attacking what many would call the country's most progressive school district would not only fail, he argued, it would deter other districts from attempting to solve racial problems. After the recall was defeated in court or at the polls, a result he predicted, the board would be ready and able to resume its quest for integrated quality education. But it should be allowed to do so at its own pace. Lacking any knowledge of the Detroit political situation, Lucas did not press the point further.[61]

The negotiators left the meeting uncertain about what had been achieved. Bushnell assumed the NAACP would sue the state to set aside Act 48. He was fearful that it would also sue the Detroit school board but he never doubted the board would be vindicated.[62] Lucas, on the other hand, thought the parties had agreed to cooperate in a suit against the state, challenging Act 48. The board would furnish Lucas statistical data, information about the April 7 Plan and the legislative history of Act 48, as well as assist in finding witnesses. The local NAACP would be a plaintiff and would identify other potential plaintiffs.[63] The agreement to cooperate was sufficiently tenuous that Lucas promised to notify Bushnell if the NAACP decided to sue the Detroit board after all.[64]

Shortly after the New York meeting, the Detroit NAACP branch conducted a meeting of potential plaintiffs, including some identified by the school district's staff. The named plaintiffs, black and white school children and their

58. Bushnell interview; Lucas interview. Lucas was a stand-in for Nathaniel Jones, National Counsel for the NAACP, who was unable to make the meeting because of other business outside the city.
58. *Id.*.
59. Lucas interview.
60. Bushnell interview.
61. Bushnell interview; Lucas interview.
62. Bushnell interview.
63. Lucas interview.
64. Bushnell interview.

parents, were selected at that time. The Detroit NAACP was also to be a plaintiff. The school staff supplied Lucas with some basic school racial data and the promised information about the April 7 Plan and Act 48. But while Lucas was drafting the petition, the majority of the school board was recalled. The school board consisted of only three persons, too few to muster a quorum necessary to select replacements to the board or to conduct other business for the district. After consulting with his clients and the national office of the NAACP, Lucas altered the draft petition to include the Detroit Board of Education, its three remaining members, and Superintendent Drachler as defendants.[65] Before he filed the complaint, Lucas called Bushnell to advise him that Bushnell's clients would be defendants. Bushnell was shown the complaint that night when the two attorneys, with some of their associates, met over dinner. Lucas filed the complaint in the U.S. District Court for the Eastern District of Michigan the next morning, August 18, 1970.[66]

The Complaint and Preliminary Motions

In addition to the Detroit defendants, the complaint named as parties defendant Governor William G. Milliken, Attorney General Frank Kelley, the Michigan Board of Education, and State Superintendent of Public Instruction John Porter. It asserted that by their actions and policies the defendants and their predecessors in office had subjected plaintiffs and the class they represented to racially segregated schools. It alleged that segregation was perpetuated by familiar devices, including pupil assignment, faculty and staff assignment, building construction and abandonment, grade structures, and transportation policies. The only significant variation from any of a dozen northern school desegregation complaints was the allegation of intentional segregation by statute, Act 48, and the request that, as interim relief, the April 7 Plan be ordered into effect that fall.[67] There was no mention of a multidistrict remedy, the issue on which the Supreme Court decided the case in 1974.[68]

The case was assigned by a blind-draw system to Judge Stephen J. Roth,[69]

65. Lucas interview. Mr. Bushnell, though a member of the Detroit NAACP Board of Directors, was not advised by his fellow board members that the matter was under discussion, a fact he still resents. The suit led directly to his resignation from the organization. Bushnell interview.

66. Bushnell interview; Lucas interview.

67. The petition asserted that both Section 2a and Section 12 were unconstitutional. Section 2a was the section that authorized the division of the city into regions. That division, plaintiffs asserted, was done with the purpose and effect of segregating the district into black and white regions. Section 12 was attacked on the ground that it both prevented the school board's effort to desegregate and mandated continued segregation. *See* Complaint at 8–10, Bradley v. Milliken, 338 F. Supp. 582 (E.D. Mich. 1971).

68. *See* Milliken v. Bradley, 418 U.S. 717 (1974).

69. Judge Roth was a product of the ethnic, blue-collar wing of the Michigan Democratic Party. Born in Hungary, he had moved at the age of 5 to a melting-pot neighborhood in Flint, Michigan where his father worked in the Buick plant. Several years after finishing high school he returned to college at Notre Dame and then to law school at the University

who sat in Flint and Bay City, Michigan, as well as in Detroit. Judge Roth, after hearing argument in his courtroom in Flint, denied plaintiffs' request for a temporary restraining order and set the hearing on the preliminary injunction for August 27. At that time he heard three days of testimony dealing primarily with the background of the April 7 Plan and of Act 48. Much of that information was introduced through the testimony of Superintendent Drachler. There was also brief testimony demonstrating the racial identifiability of most Detroit schools and statistical evidence tending to show that achievement test scores were lower in the predominately black schools. On September 3, Judge Roth denied the motion for a preliminary injunction and granted a motion to dismiss the governor and the attorney general. Before the day was over, plaintiffs' attorneys had filed a notice of appeal and a motion for an injunction pending appeal. On September 8, the day the Detroit schools opened, Chief Judge Phillips of the Court of Appeals for the Sixth Circuit heard oral arguments in Nashville on the motion for an injunction pending appeal. He denied the injunction and advanced to October 2 the hearing before a regular panel of the court.[70] Acting with dispatch, the panel issued its decision eleven days later.[71]

The court of appeals' decision covered three basic issues. It held unconstitutional Section 12 of Act 48, which prohibited Detroit from implementing the April 7 Plan for a year and required pupils to be assigned only to neighborhood schools or to other schools chosen by the pupils.[72] It held that the district court had not abused its discretion in denying a preliminary injunction on the basis of the three days' testimony it had heard. In this respect the court of appeals noted that the case raised issues and sought relief going beyond the April 7 Plan.[73] Finally, it held that the governor and the attorney general were proper parties "at least at the present stage of the proceedings."[74]

---

of Michigan. Immediately upon graduation in 1935, he plunged into politics. He was elected attorney general in the Democratic sweep of 1948, but lost the post in the Republican resurgence of 1950. Governor G. Mennan Williams appointed him to a state judgeship in 1952. In 1962 President Kennedy named him to the federal bench. *See* Detroit Free Press, October 11, 1971 at 7; Grant, *The Detroit School Case: An Historical Overview,* 21 Wayne L. Rev. 851. 856 (1975).

70. *See* Bradley v. Milliken, 433 F.2d 897, 901–902 (6th Cir. 1970). *See* Fed. R. App. P. 8. The appeal was based on 28 U.S.C. §1292(a). 433 F.2d at 898.

71. Bradley v. Milliken, 433 F.2d 897 (6th Cir. 1970). The panel consisted of Chief Judge Harry Phillips of Nashville, Tennessee; Judge John W. Peck of Cincinnati, Ohio; and Judge George C. Edwards, Jr., of Detroit. As a district court judge, Judge Peck had heard Deal v. Cincinnati Bd. of Educ., 244 F. Supp. 572 (S.D. Ohio 1965), *aff'd* 369 F.2d 55 (6th Cir. 1966), *cert. denied,* 389 U.S. 847 (1967); 419 F.2d 1387 (6th Cir. 1969), *cert. denied,* 402 U.S. 962 (1971), a case heavily emphasized by defendants throughout the litigation in Detroit. Chief Judge Phillips had served on the appellate panel in the *Deal* case.

72. 433 F.2d at 902–904. In actual terms the act was effective only until Jan. 1, 1971, but the board's attorney, in an opinion dated July 28, 1970 had acknowledged that the practical effect was to preclude the implementation of the April 7 Plan for a full school year. The opinion is quoted at 433 F.2d 897, 900–901.

73. *Id.* at 904–905.

74. *Id.* at 905.

After the remand by the court of appeals, plaintiffs filed a motion for implementation of the April 7 Plan at the start of the winter semester. The district court scheduled the hearing on that motion for November 4, the date it had originally set for trial on the merits and postponed for a month the trial on the issue of segregation.[75] At the hearing the plaintiffs argued that as the court of appeals had held the rollback of the April 7 Plan unconstitutional, plaintiffs should promptly be restored to the position they would have been in but for Act 48. Appearing to accept the logic of that argument, the court, on November 6, ordered the Detroit Board of Education to submit a plan for new high school attendance areas "consisting of the April 7 plan 'or an updated version thereof which achieves no less pupil integration.'"[76]

The Detroit Board of Education was ill-equipped to cope with the political pressures the court's order created. Only three of its members had been elected. Two, McDonald and Hathaway, had opposed the original April 7 Plan. A third member, Cornelius Golightly, had been appointed by the liberal-dominated board to fill the vacancy created by the death of Robinson.[77] He had just been elected in his own right to an at-large seat in the November 3, 1970, election. The other four members had been appointed by the governor to fill the vacancies created by the recall.[78] By November 6 all four were lame ducks; none was on the new board that had been elected three days earlier. The newly expanded board, which would take office in January, included eight members elected from the decentralized regions, three members elected at large, and Hathaway and McDonald, the two holdovers who had not been required by Act 48 to run for

75. *See* Bradley v. Milliken, 438 F.2d 945, 947 (6th Cir. 1971).

76. *Id., quoting* the district court's unpublished November 6, 1970 order.

77. Golightly, Associate Dean of the Wayne State University College of Liberal Arts, was elected to a three-year term as a central board member in the November 1970 election. He was reelected in 1973. He was serving his third term as president of the Detroit board when he died unexpectedly in early 1976. A philosopher with a keen sense of the ridiculous, he generally failed in his repeated efforts to get his colleagues on the board to understand the philosophical implications of what they were about.

78. Act 48 had anticipated the possible recall of the board members but had provided an unworkable solution. It provided that any vacancy on the central board which occurred after the effective date of the act was to be "filled by majority vote of all persons serving as regional board and first class district board members. . . ." Mich. Pub. Act 48, §3a (1970). The act had been given immediate effect to prevent desegregation in September 1970. As the forty members of regional school boards (five members in each of eight regions) would not be elected until November or take office until January, it was impossible for the board to comply with the literal requirements of the statute. As the recall had removed four of the seven members of the existing central board, there was no quorum for that board to act even if it had attempted to operate under the general school law applicable to it before the passage of Act 48. That absence of a quorum, in fact, rendered the board incapable of acting for any purpose. Using the exigency of the situation to support a colorable interpretation of other statutes, the attorney general rendered an opinion that the governor had the power to fill the vacancies. Letter from Att'y. Gen. Frank J. Kelley to Sen. Coleman A. Young, Aug. 6, 1970, on file in the office of the Michigan attorney general. While the district court was hearing evidence on the motion for a preliminary injunction in late Aug. 1970, Governor Milliken appointed two blacks and two whites to the vacant seats.

reelection. Only three of the thirteen members of the in-coming central board were black, as compared with three of seven members of the out-going board.[79]

Perhaps because of its handicaps, the lame-duck board responded flexibly to the pressures on it. It invited the newly elected board members to sit in at all its meetings, public or private, dealing the segregation case.[80] After a majority of the new board opposed submitting any desegregation plan, they were not invited to participate further.[81] After first indicating that there would be no public hearings on the issue, as no useful purpose would be served, the board yielded to fears in the white community that the board was "planning another April 7" and conducted a public hearing. That meeting confirmed the board's original notion that a hearing would not be helpful. The almost all-white crowd of 600 persons fervently opposed any desegregation plan and verbally attacked Judge Roth— ignoring the fact that he had consistently upheld the school board's position in the case.[82]

After finding no support either from the new board or from the vocal public, the board nevertheless adhered to its announced determination to obey the court order to recommend an interim plan. As no one on the board was truly happy with the April 7 Plan, several board members proposed alternatives. In a six-hour closed meeting, the board settled on three plans to be submitted to the court. The first priority plan was sponsored by member McDonald. Labeled the "magnet plan" it consisted of two parts, a high school plan and a middle school plan. Under the high school portion, the city was divided into quadrants. Each high school in each quadrant would develop a specialized curriculum designed to attract students interested in that speciality. Each school would continue to offer all the programs it had formerly offered. The process would, McDonald claimed, lead 20,000 of Detroit's 55,600 high school students to switch schools voluntarily in the next 18 months.[83] The other part of the plan called for the creation of an experimental middle school for grades 5 through 8, in each of the eight decentralized regions of the district. Admission to the middle schools would be by application only and would be controlled to assure that half the students in each would be white and half would be black.[84]

The second priority plan was proposed by gubernatorial appointee Carol Campbell. It included the middle school proposal of the magnet plan but replaced the high school portion with a plan that would assign each high school student to two high schools. Each student would have a "base" high school in his or her regular attendance area where required subjects would be taken. Additional

79. Detroit Free Press, Nov. 7, 1970 at 12A.
80. Detroit News, Nov. 9, 1970, at 11A; *id.,* Nov. 10, 1970, at 20A.
81. *Id.,* Nov. 11, 1970 at 9A.
82. *Id.,* Nov. 12, 1970, at 20A; *id.,* Nov. 15, 1970, at 14A; Detroit Free Press, Nov. 15, 1970, at 8A.
83. Detroit Free Press, Dec. 4, 1970, at 1A.
84. *Id.,* Dec. 5, 1970, at 1B, 3B.

courses would be taken at one of several other schools offering a specialized curriculum. The proposal was hazy on the mechanisms for deciding which schools would offer what curricula and which students would take each specialized curriculum. It contemplated that students would be bused from one school to another. The board had not yet attempted to resolve the admittedly difficult class scheduling problems that plan would create.[85]

The third priority plan submitted to the court was the April 7 Plan, which redrew high school attendance boundaries to achieve some desegregation.

At the time the three plans were submitted to the court, the Detroit *Free Press* reported that the listing of the magnet plan as first priority was the result of hard bargaining between McDonald and moderates on the board who wanted to submit the April 7 Plan as well, and, to avoid a political backlash, wanted to be sure the entire board recommended it. To get McDonald's vote for submission of the April 7 Plan, the moderates agreed to list the magnet plan as first priority even though most of the board preferred Campbell's plan. Most board members frankly believed there was no likelihood the court would approve the magnet plan as it closely resembled freedom-of-choice plans that had been rejected as unworkable in southern districts.[86]

At the hearings in late November, the board's attorneys pressed for the magnet plan as a noncoercive plan with promise for lasting desegregation. They suggested it be implemented in September 1971 in order to minimize disruption of classes. The NAACP insisted the plan could not possibly induce whites to change schools. As a result the plan was, according to the plaintiffs, a freedom-of-choice plan that did not "promise realistically to work."[87] As proof of its lack of promise, they cited an unsuccessful effort in the mid-sixties to retain whites in three racially changing high schools. Although the district had spent a million dollars upgrading the curricula at the three schools, it had failed to stem the tide. The only proper interim remedy, the plaintiffs argued, was the adoption of the April 7 Plan, effective February 1971.

The court ruled on December 3 that the board should implement the magnet plan the following September. Judge Roth held a news conference to explain his decision and to rebut the NAACP's ciriticism of the magnet plan.[88] Board of Education Vice President Golightly was quoted as commenting acidly, "If the court wanted an integration plan with a lot of form and no substance, then this was the plan. It will cost nothing and it will do nothing."[89] Judge Roth's order postponed indefinitely a hearing on the merits of the case. The NAACP promptly appealed.[90]

85. Detroit News, Nov. 17, 1970, at 3B.

86. Detroit Free Press, Nov. 17, 1970, at 1A. *Cf.* Green v. County School Board of New Kent County, 391 U.S. 430 (1968).

87. Green v. County School Board of New Kent County, 391 U.S. 430, 439 (1968).

88. Detroit Free Press, Dec. 4, 1970, at 1A, 8A.

89. Detroit Free Press, Dec. 4, 1970, at 1A.

90. *See* Bradley v. Milliken, 438 F.2d 945 (6th Cir. 1970). The indefinite postponement may not have been as irresponsible as the Sixth Circuit's opinion made it sound. Bushnell

While the appeal was pending, the new school board took office in January 1971. Some of the blacks and at least one white board member favored desegregation, but the majority of the newly elected members had campaigned against busing and the liberal Drachler administration. The new board elected Patrick McDonald president. Curiously, however, McDonald thwarted last-minute plans to appeal to the Supreme Court the Sixth Circuit's October ruling that the legislative repeal of the April 7 Plan was unconstitutional. At a special meeting called the day before the deadline for an appeal, seven votes were required to authorize the appeal. One newly elected member was absent. Outgoing board president Hathaway abstained. The three black members and the one white integrationist opposed an appeal. To the amazement of the six remaining white members, McDonald refused to vote for an appeal, suggesting instead a meaningless vote to appeal if the court of appeals upset the magnet plan ordered implemented by Judge Roth. The conservatives had no choice but to accept McDonald's proposal. McDonald's position was widely seen as an attempt to protect his magnet plan, then being challenged in the court of appeals.[91]

At the new board's first regular meeting, Superintendent Drachler announced that he was resigning his post, effective in June, to establish the Institute for Educational Leadership at George Washington University, funded by the Ford Foundation.[92]

The court of appeals on February 22, 1971, issued its *per curiam* decision on the appeal from the order implementing the magnet plan. The opinion expressed annoyance with counsel and the district court for not having gone promptly to trial on the central issue of segregation after the first appellate decision.[93] The appeals court refused to grant summary relief to the appellants, noting, "The trouble with this procedure is that there has never been an evidentiary hearing on the charges set forth in the complaint nor any findings of fact with respect to these charges."[94] The court explicitly refrained from expressing an opinion about the merits of the magnet plan or the other two interim plans that had been considered, but it pointedly footnoted three Supreme Court decisions holding various freedom-of-choice desegregation plans to be unacceptable remedies for proven school segregation.[95] Finally the court remanded the case to the district court with instructions that it be tried on the merits forthwith.[96]

---

attributes the postponement to his plea for a few weeks delay to learn whether he would continue to represent the board after the new members took office Jan. 1, 1971. There was a good chance that he would be replaced as he was strongly identified with the liberal policies a majority of the new board was pledged to oppose. Bushnell interview.

91. Detroit Free Press, Jan. 9, 1971, at 4B, col. 1; *id.,* Jan. 13, 1971, at 2A; Northeast Detroiter, Jan. 14, 1971, at 1; Redford Record, Jan. 20, 1971. The state defendants had consistently said they would not appeal the October decision. Detroit Free Press, Oct. 16, 1970; Detroit News, Oct. 16, 1970.

92. Detroit Free Press, Jan. 27, 1971, at 9C.

93. Bradley v. Milliken, 438 F.2d 945, 947 (6th Cir. 1971).

94. *Id.* at 946–47.

95. *Id.* at 947, n.1.

96. *Id.* at 947.

Trial on the Issue of Segregation

The case had been moving along even before the remand. The district court had conducted a hearing on the standing of the named black and white plaintiffs to represent the class asserted. At the conclusion of the hearing the court defined the class represented by plaintiffs as "all school children of the City of Detroit and all Detroit resident parents who have children of school age."[97] The district court permitted the local NAACP branch to remain a party as its standing had not been contested.[98]

The district court had also received two petitions for intervention. In early November it had permitted the Detroit Federation of Teachers to intervene as a party defendant.[99] Shortly after the second remand from the court of appeals, it permitted the intervention of a group of white parents active in Concerned Citizens for Better Education, the group that had organized the recall election.[100] Both intervenors played an active part in the trial, which started April 6, 1971, one day short of the first anniversary of the April 7 Plan.

By the time the trial started, both sides were fully prepared. They had on two or three dates in the past year appeared in court ready to go to trial on the merits and each time they had been delayed. Each time they had renewed their preparations. The NAACP in particular put almost unprecedented effort into preparation for the case. On the first day of the trial it had over 2,000 exhibits ready to offer. Such an effort was necessitated by its internal politics, by the way in which the case arose, and especially by the size of the Detroit school system. The Detroit branch of the NAACP was one of the largest and most prosperous. For years it had contributed generously to oppose school segregation in other parts of the country. Neither the Detroit branch nor the national organization could sit idly by while resegregation was openly imposed in Detroit. Indeed, the course of events in Detroit was becoming painfully familiar in district after district, and the NAACP felt forced to challenge school boards that, under public pressure, retreated from voluntary desegregation programs.[101] The critical factor governing the extent of prepartion, however, was the size of the school system. For example, Detroit had over 300 school buildings in 1970.[102] Plaintiffs' experts and attorneys had to analyze every attendance boundary

97. Order, Feb. 16, 1971, *quoted in* Bradley v. Milliken, 338 F. Supp. 582, 584 (E.D. Mich. 1971).

98. Bradley v. Milliken, 338 F. Supp. 582, 584 n.1 (E.D. Mich. 1971). Appellate courts noted that fact without passing judgment on it. *See* Milliken v. Bradley, 418 U.S. 717, 722 n.2 (1974); 484 F.2d 215, 219 (6th Cir. 1973).

99. Order Granting Motion of Detroit Federation of Teachers Local 231, AFT, AFL-CIO, to Intervene as Party Defendant (Nov. 2, 1970).

100. Order Granting Motion for Intervention (March 22, 1975).

101. Other recent cases involving "rollbacks" of board-adopted desegregation plans included Oliver v. School Dist. of the City of Kalamazoo, 346 F. Supp. 766 (W.D. Mich.), *aff'd* 448 F.2d 635 (6thCir. 1971); Keyes v. School District No. 1, Denver, Colorado, 313 *F. Supp.* 61 (D. Colo. 1970), *modified,* 445 F.2d 990 (10th Cir. 1971), *modified,* 413 U.S. 189 (1973). *See also* Aaron v. McKinley, 173 F. Supp. 944 (E.D. Ark. 1959), *aff'd per curiam, sub nom.* Faubus v. Aaron, 361 U.S. 197 (1959); Bush v. Orleans Parish School Board, 188 F. Supp. 916 (E.D. La. 1960), *aff'd per curiam,* 365 U.S. 569 (1961).

change for three decades. It was a major task to master the names and locations well enough to read intelligently the minutes and reports of the school board. The preparation of the case was aided, however, by the reports of a series of study commissions appointed by the school board and by the files of the local branch. Plaintiffs also took depositions from many of the officers and employees of the school district.[103]

Counsel for the board of education Bushnell had concentrated on revealing the board's actions in a favorable light. He engaged in no discovery of defendants. However, he too, directly and through employees of the board, spent a great deal of time digging out information buried in the board's files. Bushnell had a free hand in preparing the case. While the board was intensely concerned about the outcome of the case, it lacked the time and background to get into the details. All but two of the thirteen members had come onto the board after the adoption of the April 7 Plan. Bushnell, by contrast, had represented the board for a decade and had been intimately involved in decision-making. Besides, the board was distracted by a $51 million dificit, by organizing a national search for a new superintendent, and by coping with decentralization, which meant different things to different groups.[104]

At the trial the plaintiffs first set out to demonstrate that housing in Detroit was racially segregated and that the acts of public bodies and officials had played a substantial part in creating housing segregation. Judge Roth, seeing the general thrust of the housing case, encouraged counsel for the school board to stipulate that the residential patterns of the city were racially segregated, but the suggestion was declined.[105] The plaintiffs therefore developed the roles of the Federal Housing Administration, the Detroit Housing Commission, judicially enforced restrictive covenants, and semiprivate agencies such as real estate brokers and financing institutions. They called Professor Karl Taeuber to demonstrate statistically the differences between the level of residential separation of nationality groups and that of blacks. Taeuber also testified as to the possible causes of black residential separation and negated the possibility that choice or economics was primarily responsible.[106] The plaintiffs then demonstrated that many of the segregatory practices continued at the time of trial and that the effect of the rest was still felt.

At the conclusion of their "housing" proof, the NAACP lawyers were con-

---

102. Milliken v. Bradley, 418 U.S. 717, 729 n.10 (1974).

103. Lucas interview.

104. Bushnell interview.

105. Defense counsel's refusal to stipulate was accompanied by a demand that the NAACP prove its case in detail. The plaintiffs did so. The overwhelming evidence of how housing and other aspects of life were deliberately segregated in Detroit went far to change Judge Roth's view of the problem. Thereafter defense testimony about neutral reasons for school decisions—which all seemed to separate blacks and whites—was heard more skeptically. See Grant, *The Detroit School Case: An Historical Overview,* 21 Wayne L. Rev. 851, 862–64 (1975).

106. For a convenient statement of his views *see* Taeuber, *Demographic Perspectives on Housing and School Segregation,* 21 Wayne L. Rev. 833 (1975).

vinced they had presented the most thoroughly documented housing case ever made in a school desegregation case.[107] Plaintiffs then explored the racial practices of the school board and the bureaucracy that worked for it. Brushing aside the liberal policies of recent years, they demonstrated that in years past the board had consistently acted to segregate teachers, administrators, and students. Indeed, the defense hardly contested charges of segregation before 1960. The plaintiffs went further, however, to adduce evidence that even after 1960, when "crunch points"[108] occurred, the board or the bureaucracy had yielded to community pressures for racial separation. They also argued that the effects of the earlier blatant segregation had not been eliminated by the later, more liberal, policies.

In a process Lucas calls a "forensic autopsy" of a school district,[109] plaintiffs systematically explored every device by which they believed the schools had been segregated. They offered evidence of pupil segregation by means of gerrymandered attendance boundaries, feeder zone changes, optional attendance areas in changing neighborhoods, the construction and location of new schools to "contain" black expansion, intact busing of children from overcrowded black schools to undercapacity white schools, and busing of black children from overcrowded schools to other black schools when white schools with space available were closer. They showed that for a period in the 1950s high school students from the all-black Carver District, a K–8 district abutting Detroit in suburban Oakland County, were bused to a black high school in Detroit, although white schools in Detroit and adjoining suburbs were closer. They explored the tracking system allegedly used in Detroit, although the district claimed all tracking was contrary to its policies. There was testimony that achievement levels in predominately black schools were substantially below those in white schools. The plaintiffs demonstrated that for many years black teachers were assigned only to schools with black pupils. A black superintendent of a region was called to testify that as the system began to liberalize, it assigned some black teachers to white schools, subject to removal if the community objected. While the district was by 1971 no longer following overtly discriminatory practices, the plaintiffs introduced evidence that the assignment of teachers still correlated strongly with the racial makeup of the student body, despite the adoptionof a "balanced staff" approach to reassignments and new assignments. Finally, plaintiffs explored the racial consequence of the state of Michigan's failure to finance school transportation in the city of Detroit while it paid 75 percent of the cost of transportation in most other districts.[110]

107. Lucas interview. For an adversary's interpretation of the NAACP housing strategy, see Beer, *The Nature of the Violation and the Scope of the Remedy: An Analysis of Milliken v. Bradley in Terms of the Evolution of the Theory of the Violation*, 21 Wayne L. Rev. 903 (1975).

108. A term used by plaintiffs' chief counsel, Lucas. Lucas interview.

109. Lucas interview.

110. For a compact summary of the points plaintiffs believed they had proved, *see* [Plaintiffs' Proposed] Findings of Fact and Conclusions of Law.

At the conclusion of the plaintiffs' proof, the state defendants filed motions asking that they be dismissed. The court, after hearing argument, denied the motions.[111] It did, however, grant plaintiffs' motion for an injunction *pendente lite* forbidding school construction, site acquisition, and other steps toward the building or expansion of school facilites. Neither the motion nor the order applied to construction already begun. In its order the court pointedly noted that counsel for the board of education had misrepresented the district's construction program in August when plaintiffs had first asked for a construction injunction. According to the court, counsel for the school district had denied that there was any construction under way or planned, but the evidence brought out at the trial showed that the district was "proceeding apace" with such projects.[112]

Trial resumed with the Detroit board presenting its defense. Counsel for the board were confident that if they laid the entire record before the court their client would be completely vindicated by a decade of good works. The defense had three major goals. It sough to show that there were valid, racially neutral, reasons for recent acts branded by palintiffs as segregatory.[113] It emphasized the increasing tempo of affirmatively integrationist actions during the 1960s.[114] And in a hazily reasoned way, it sought judicial help in changing the state's school finance system to recognize the needs of districts with high concentrations of poverty-level pupils.[115] In developing its case against the state, the Detroit board

111. Motion to Dismiss on Behalf of Defendants William G. Milliken, Governor of the State of Michigan and Frank J. Kelley, Attorney General of the State of Michigan (filed May 21, 1971); Motion to Dismiss on Behalf of Defendants Michigan State Board of Education and John W. Porter, Superintendent of Public Instruction (filed May 21, 1971); Proposed Findings of Fact and Conclusions of Law Submitted on Behalf of State Defendants (filed May 28, 1971); Order, June 25, 1971.

112. Ruling and Order on Motion for Construction Injunction *Pendente Lite,* Bradley v. Milliken, Civ. No. 35257 (E.D. Mich., June 8, 1971). Lucas, chief counsel for plaintiffs, has stated that he, like the court, had accepted as true the representations of opposing counsel, only to discover during preparation for trial that those representations had been "an error of many, many millions of dollars." Lucas interview. The injunction permitted certain projects to continue as plaintiffs and the Detroit board agreed that they would have no segregative effect.

113. The defense did not seriously attempt to refute or explain away pre-1960 acts of segregation. Rather it denied their present relevance. In Bushnell's words, they sought to show that "we are not guilty *now.*" Bushnell interview.

114. *See* text accompanying notes 22–28, *supra.*

115. Bushnell interview. Mr. Bushnell, the board's chief counsel, has since stated:

> . . . I really didn't know what kind of relief we awere after specifically. But we were after generally a revisitation of *Rodriguez* and the funding question, a debate within the judicial framework of state responsibility for education as opposed to local responsibility. A recognition judicially . . . of the responsibility of educational systems to care for the whole child, not just attempt to teach the basic skills. . . . We really wanted to raise all of those kinds of things since we were in that [judicial] environment, secure in the knowledge that we could *never* be found guilty of wanting a segregated school district.

Id. The interest in litigating the school finance issue was not a new one for the Detroit board or for Bushnell as they had filed, but not pursued, the first of the school finance cases that culminated in San Antonio Ind. School Dist. v. Rodriguez, 411 U.S. 1 (1973). *See,* Detroit Board of Education v. Michigan, General Civ. No. 103342 (Cir. Ct., Wayne

expanded on the notion of state financial discrimination against Detroit and the racial effect thereof. As the attorney general's lawyers seldom appeared in court after the denial of their motion for dismissal at the end of plaintiffs' case, much of the testimony against the state defendants came in without cross-examination by—and possibly without the knowledge of—the state's lawyers.

The state defendants made little factual contribution to the case, choosing to rely primarily on their assertion that the plaintiffs had failed to make out a case against them and on their denial that the state exercised control or responsibility over the Detroit Board of Education. They also maintained that the Eleventh Amendment precluded an action against state officials, repeatedly renewing the claim after the court had ruled adversely on it.[116] The logic of their position led their attorneys to risk absenting themselves from the courtroom during much of the Detroit Board's defense.

The two intervenors made more of a contribution to the case. The Detroit Federation of Teachers (DFT) hammered away at the efforts made by both the union and the school board to eliminate racial bias in hiring, assignments, and promotions. While not denying the discrimination of the past, nearly all of which occurred before the DFT became the recognized bargaining agent for the teachers, it insisted that an adequate remedy for employment discrimination had already been achieved through collective bargaining.

The intervenors from the Concerned Citizens for Better Education (CCBE) made a very different sort of contribution. Their attorney, Alexander Ritchie, had a dramatic change of perspective during the trial. He had entered the case as the spokesperson for a group of white homeowners, convinced that there had been no segregation in Detroit and suspecting that the school board might not defend itself vigorously enough. Before the NAACP had finished its housing evidence he began to see that it might succeed in making a case for segregation. At that point, believing the plaintiffs would be entitled to a remedy, he began exploring the possibility of a metropolitan remedy as he cross-examined the witnesses called by the plaintiffs and later those called by the defense. With the decision in the *Swann* case on April 20, 1971, be became even more concerned with the remedy.[117]

He persisted in that vein despite the great reluctance of Judge Roth to broaden the scope of the trial. Even the NAACP was loathe to embrace the wider remedy, fearing that to do so would deny plaintiffs the speedy remedy

County, Mich., *filed* Feb. 2, 1963), *dism'd for lack of progress,* May 11, 1970; *reinstated,* May 8, 1972. There has been no action in the case since it was reinstated. *Cf.* Milliken v. Green, 389 Mich. 1, 203 N.W.2d 457 (1972), *vacated,* 390 Mich. 389, 212 N.W.2d 711 (1973).

116. Judge Roth, a former Michigan attorney general, was privately upset at the refusal of the present attorney general's office to accept his Eleventh Amendment ruling as the law of the case, pending appeal.

117. *See* Swann v. Charlotte-Mecklenburg Bd. of Educ., 402 U.S. 1 (1971).

they sought.[118] Shortly before the close of testimony, Ritchie moved to join as parties defendant all the other eighty-six school districts in the Detroit Standard Metropolitan Statistical Area of Macomb, Oakland, and Wayne counties.[119] The court conducted a hearing on the motion and took it under advisement. The CCBE had planted a seed that was to change the nature of the case and make constitutional history. Whether it will ever bear the intended fruit is still uncertain.

After 41 days of trail, stretching from April 6 to July 26, 1971, the hearing on the issue of segregation was closed and the parties were asked to submit proposed findings of fact and conclusions of law, as well as briefs. Judge Roth then began preparing his decision,[120] while trying simultaneously to catch up on the backlog of cases in Bay City and Flint caused by the lengthy trial in Detroit. Two months later he released his decision with a calculated absence of fanfare.[121] At a September 27 conference with attorneys in the case to deal with some routine matters, he almost casually announced that the decision was available in the clerk's office. Rather than holding a press conference as he had the previous December, he avoided public comment.

THE FINDINGS OF SEGREGATION

After tracing the history of the litigation, the opinion outlined how the populations of Detroit and its suburbs had changed since 1940, concluding: "Detroit today is principally a conglomerate of poor black and white, plus the aged. Of the aged, 80% are white."[122] It found that the city schools were changing from white to black at a rapid rate.[123] It then traced the devices by which all levels of government and the private real estate industry had segregated the city and the metropolitan area into black and white residential areas.[124] Judge Roth then turned to the methods by which he found the school district had separated black and white youngsters.

The judge ruled that the Detroit Board of Education had utilized attendance boundary changes, optional attendance zones, transportation from overcrowded schools, grade structures, feeder patterns, building site selection, and construction practices to segregate the children.[125] The court noted pointedly that a

118. The fear has proved well-founded. It took four and a half more years before any schools were desegregated in Detroit. Most of the delay was due to proceedings revolving around the proposed multidistrict remedy.

119. Motion to Join Additional Parties Defendant (filed July 16, 1971). *See generally* Grant, *The Detroit School Case: An Historical Overview,* 21 Wayne L. Rev. 851, 863–64 (1975).

120. Bradley v. Milliken, 338 F. Supp. 582 (E.D. Mich. 1972).

121. *Id.*

122. Bradley v. Milliken, 338 F. Supp. 582, 585 (E.D. Mich. 1971).

123. *Id.* at 585–86.

124. *Id.* at 586–87.

125. *Id.* at 587–89, 592–93.

higher percentage of black students were in 90 percent black schools in 1970/71 than a decade earlier.[126] The court also mentioned briefly that the state had also made a contribution to school segregation, most obviously by Act 48, Section 12, requiring Detroit to forego partial integration, but also by refusing transportation assistance to Detroit, by imposing lower bonding limits on Detroit than other school districts, and by the operation of the school-aid formula.[127] In short, the court was persuaded by the NAACP evidence on housing segregation, pupil segregation, and state support of school segregation. But it also accepted the defendants' case with respect to the school board's aggressive pursuit of better race relations, as in textbook selection, and its affirmative action program for faculty integration.[128]

The court concluded that its findings made out a case of purposeful segregation of pupils by the state and Detroit defendants.[129] Holding in abeyance the CCBE intervenors' request to join the suburban distircts, the court scheduled a conference with counsel for the following week to discuss problems of formulating a remedy.[130]

Public Reaction to the Findings of Segregation

The finding of segregation was fully reported by both of the daily newspapers and by the neighborhood newspapers that blanket large areas of Detroit and the suburbs.[131] Editorial reaction was split. Most neighborhood papers agreed with the conservative Detroit *News* that the ruling was "unreasonable." The *News* was particularly concerned with Judge Roth's failure to disavow the possibility of including suburban districts.[132] The relatively liberal *Free Press* took a more moderate tack, finding it "impossible to challenge [the court's] findings," and calling for a remedy that also resolved the "inequity" of the

126. "Whereas 65.8% of Detroit's black students attended 90% or more black schools in 1960, 74.9% of the black students attended 90% or more black schools during the 1970–71 school year." *Id.* at 588.

127. *Id.* at 589.

128. *Id.* at 589–92. Judge Roth's views on faculty segregation contrasted sharply with those of the United States Department of Health, Education and Welfare. A month after Judge Roth's ruling, HEW denied Detroit a grant to assist in implementing the interim desegregation order because the faculty assignments were badly imbalanced. Detroit Free Press, Oct. 30, 1971. The two rulings were not necessarily inconsistent. Judge Roth based his on 1969/70 data and earlier statistics. HEW ruled on the basis of 1971/72 data. When the decentralization plan was inaugurated in January 1971, control of faculty assignments passed to regional boards. While all regions drew from a central pool of teachers and administrators, two did so in a notoriously discriminatory fashion. Region 4 took whites almost exclusively and Region 1 took almost no one but blacks. Both regions reflected the race and the bias of their boards in their faculty policies. As a result of decentralization, Detroit's balanced faculty policy had begun to deteriorate even before Judge Roth began hearings on the violation issue.

129. Bradley v. Milliken, 338 F. Supp. 582, 592–94 (E.D. Mich. 1972).

130. *Id.* at 594–95.

131. *See* Detroit Free Press, Sept. 28, 1971, at 1A, 2a; Detroit News, Sept. 28, 1971, at 1; Eastside Shopper, Sept. 29, 1971.

132. Detroit News, Sept. 29, 1971.

state's school finance system.[133] Remarkably, one chain of neighborhood papers centered in conservative white areas of Detroit and Macomb County also supported the court's factual findings and tried to defuse the furor about suburban desegregation by pointing out that the court had not ruled on the question and that white Detroiters, not Judge Roth, were proposing metropolitan busing.[134]

The initial reaction of the Michigan Democratic Party was almost unparalleled in states with major desegregation cases. At a meeting the weekend after the segregation ruling, the Democratic State Central Committee adopted a ringing resolution in support of busing as a solution to segregation.[135] Even more remarkably the resolution was signed by most of the party's top officeholders and obvious contenders, including Attorney General Frank J. Kelley, a defendant in *Bradley v. Milliken* and a potential candidate for U.S. senator.[136] By contrast, most Democratic legislators and congressmen representing white constituencies had already committed themselves to oppose busing. Unlike Kelley, who spent much time in his unsuccessful senatorial campaign trying to explain away the statement, Republican leaders generally restated their opposition to "forced busing" and their support of legislation to eliminate it. As the controversy over busing grew in the following months, the Republicans were much more likely than the Democrats to cite the Democratic policy statement on the issue. Those Democrats who did not recant generally avoided public comment on school segregation.

Suburban school superintendents and board members immediately discovered that busing was a dangerously volatile issue. Anti-busing groups existed in almost all white suburbs. Within days of Judge Roth's finding that Detroit was segregated, 20,000 children were kept out of school in Macomb County.[137] A 500-person anti-busing rally in western Wayne County was given prominent treatment in the Detroit *News.*[138] Less then 48 hours after the court's ruling was an-

133. Detroit Free Press, Sept. 29, 1971, at 6A. On the morning of the segregation ruling, the *Free Press* had editorially wrung its hands over the near-bankrupt condition of the Detroit schools. Detroit Free Press, Sept. 27, 1971.

134. *See* Eastside Shopper, Sept. 29, 1971. Despite severe pressures from advertisers and readers, the Eastside Shopper and other community news publications consistently took a constructive matter-of-fact posture on the case, in marked contrast to the hysteria of some of their competitors. *Compare* text at note 434, *infra.* Economic pressure finally killed the Eastside Shopper. The Nathanson family, which owned it, sold it to the highly conservative Panax chain. The newspaper is now ardently anti-integrationist.

135. The [Detroit] Sunday News, Oct. 3, 1971, at 1. The resolution read in part:

. . . .

The education of a child cannot wait until every school in every neighborhood provides a quality education.

The court's answer in some cases has been bussing. It is an imperfect answer. But it is an answer for today.

We accept the decisions of the courts and Congress. We accept bussing as an instrument for immediate implementation of the courts' rulings. We accept bussing as an imperfect and temporary mechanism to help erase the imbalances in our educational system. . . .

136. *Id.*
137. Detroit Free Press, Oct. 2, 1971, at 1A.
138. Detroit News, Sept. 30, 1971, at C1.

nounced, 65 suburban superintendents met for a legal briefing and strategy discussion. The president of the state board of education issued a strongly worded statement condemning boycott organizers, pointing out that no desegregation order had been issued yet.[139]

While public leaders struggled to regain their balance, Judge Roth conducted a pretrial on October 4 to discuss how to develop a remedy. At its conclusion, he directed the Detroit Board of Education to prepare within 60 days a plan for desegregating the city's schools. Within 30 days the Detroit board was also to report on the success of the "magnet school" interim desegregation plan. The state board of education and the state superintendent of public instruction were directed to prepare, within 120 days, a plan for desegregating Detroit plus some or all of the surrounding suburban school districts.[140] Again the suburban school superintendents met hurriedly.[141] Scores of rallies voiced opposition to desegregation. Legislators were flooded with mail. Within a week anti-busing petitions had collected tens of thousands of signatures.[142] Again the press divided editorially. The *News* denounced the decision to consider multidistrict desegregation plans as "casual justice."[143] The *Free Press* cautiously warned that however troubling busing might be, "the barriers between the races have to be broken down" to avoid "another 100 years of racial separation and hostility."[144] U.S. Senator Robert P. Griffin introduced in the Senate a proposed constitutional amendment banning court-ordered busing.[145]

In the meantime another storm had arisen. The day after the court found Detroit guilty of school segregation, *Free Press* reporter William Grant revealed for the first time that representatives of the school board had negotiated with the NAACP in New York before the suit started.[146] A conservative school board member called for the dismissal of all concerned. The issue was quietly dropped after a hurried investigation proved all had acted under orders from then Superintendent Drachler and had tried to prevent a suit against Detroit.[147]

The investigation did not resolve the tension between George Bushnell and the board's conservatives. Indeed, some of them had campaigned on a promise to replace him.[148] A month later, while Bushnell was in Washington meeting with

139. Detroit Free Press, Oct. 2, 1971, at 1A.
140. Order, Nov. 5, 1971.
141. Detroit News, Oct. 5, 1971.
142. Detroit Free Press, Oct. 10, 1971, at 1A.
143. Detroit News, Oct. 6, 1971, at 24A.
144. Detroit Free Press, Oct. 6, 1971.
145. S. Res. 164, 92d Cong. 1st Sess. (1971); Detroit News, Oct. 7, 1971, at 1.
146. Detroit Free Press, Sept. 29, 1971, at 1. Grant, who has followed the desegregation case closely from its inception to date, is unusually well informed on education developments and very sophisticated on legal matters. His restraint in witholding an explosive but legally irrelevant story for weeks after he learned of it demonstrates his sensitivity to the dynamics of the case and of Detroit politics.
147. Detroit Free Press, Sept. 30, 1971, at 1; Detroit News, Sept. 30, 1971; *id.*, Oct. 2, 1971.
148. Bushnell intetview.

HEW officials, Patrick McDonald led the seven conservatives on the board in voting to appoint McDonald's administrative intern as co-counsel in the desegregation case. It was obvious to all concerned that his appointment was a vote of no confidence in Bushnell rather than a serious selection of counsel for the case.[149] Bushnell, called by Detroit *News* reporter Harry Salsinger after the vote, promptly announced his resignation and withdrew his firm from the desegregation case and approximately one hundred other matters it was handling for the board.[150]

The board was then in the midst of preparing a desegregation plan to be considered by the court on December 3, 1971, less than four weeks away. Bushnell's resignation put great pressure on the board to find new counsel at once. The board's solution was to divide its legal work among five Detroit firms and a Cincinnati firm with a reputation in school desegregation matters. Two of the Detroit firms were black, three were white.[151] The firm that would up with the lion's share of the work was a white firm, Riley and Roumell, which was assigned to be local counsel on the desegregation case. George Roumell, a partner in the firm, was a leading arbitrator and mediator in school district labor disputes. When the key attorney from the Cincinnati firm suffered a severe heart attack in mid-December, Roumell became responsible for the entire school desegregation case.[152]

The Desegregation Plans

In the midst of the political maneuvering, the school bureaucracy filed its report with the court on the effectiveness of the interim magnet plan of "voluntary" integration. The report showed the magnet plan was a total failure at the high school level; results in the middle schools, while unsatisfactory, reflected some desegregation. In the high schools, most student transfers under the magnet curriculum program either had no racial effect or increased racial separation. The eight middle schools, which offered innovative programs and lower student-

---

149. The man's legal experience was the subject of a battle of semantics between the Detroit *News* and the *Free Press*. The conservative *News* reported that he had been "with a Detroit law firm for ten years" before coming to the board as a federally financed education intern. Detroit News, Nov. 19, 1971; *id.,* Nov. 11, 1971, at 24A. The moderate *Free Press,* while not discussing the man's role at the law firm, reported that he had graduated from law school six years earlier and had been admitted to the bar the next year. Detroit Free Press, Nov. 11, 1971.

150. Bushnell interview; Detroit Free Press, Nov. 11, 1971; Detroit News, Nov. 10, 1971; *id.,* Nov. 11, 1971, at 24A. Bushnell's resignation was not a surprise to the board. A week before the appointment of co-counsel, Acting General Superintendent Charles Wolfe, Superintendent Drachler's successor, had told Bushnell that board member McDonald wanted his intern assigned to monitor Bushnell's handling of the case. At that time Bushnell had refused to accept the arrangement and had threatened to quit if co-counsel were appointed. Wolfe did not press the issue. Bushnell interview.

151. One of the white firms was chosen as bond counsel only.

152. Detroit Free Press, Nov. 24, 1971; *id.,* Dec. 14, 1971; Detroit News, Nov. 24, 1971; *id.,* Dec. 14, 1971.

teacher ratios, used racially controlled admissions to achieve a reasonable level of integration. Half the whites and 88 percent of the blacks in magnet middle schools were in a more racially mixed environment than if they had remained in their neighborhood schools. On the other hand, the magnet middle schools contributed to greater imbalance in mixed but predominantely black "regular" schools. Thirty-eight percent of the whites in middle schools were getting out of even more heavily black schools. Furthermore, the price of integrating eight middle schools was high for the debt-ridden school district. The cost per pupil in the magnet middle schools was 38 percent higher than the average for the other pupils in the school district.[153]

Despite the poor performance in the initial test of the magnet concept, the Detroit Board of Education reported to the court in December 1971 that the board's preferred method of desegregating the city schools was an enlarged magnet plan. The alternative suggested by the board offered only part-time pupil mixing. It provided for 38,000 upper elementary pupils to have racially mixed classes two half-days a week.[154] The board, made slightly less conservative by changes in personnel, also advised the court that it preferred a metropolitan integration order to one affecting only the city. It did not offer an actual metropolitan plan until February, after the state department of education had submitted its multidistrict plans. Measured by the standards of *Swann*,[155] the Detroit board had clearly defaulted on its obligation to produce an effective plan for desegregation within its own boundaries.[156]

The plaintiffs reacted strongly to the Detroit board's proposals. They asked the court to order the board to pay the costs of hiring experts to prepare a plan for the plaintiffs to submit.[157] After hearing arguments on the motion, the court took it under advisement but never ruled on it.[158] Rather, taking an intermediate course, it instructed the board to give plaintiffs copies of all plans it had considered but rejected.[159] In February the NAACP introduced its plan for desegregating the city schools.

153. Detroit Free Press, Nov. 3, 1971, at 3A; *id.,* Nov. 5, 1971, at 1A; Detroit News, Oct. 4, 1971; *id.,* Nov. 3, 1971, at 3A. The plaintiffs criticized the magnet middle schools as creating a dual school system, part of which was integrated and reasonably well financed but most of which was blacker and further impoverished as a result. Lucas interview. *See* note 286, *infra.*

154. *See* Findings of Fact and Conclusions of Law on Detroit-Only Plans of Desegregation (E.D. Mich. Mar. 28, 1971, at 2, *quoted in* Bradley v. Milliken, 484 E2d 215, 243 (6th Cir. 1973). *See also* [Detroit] Sunday News, Dec. 5, 1971; Detroit News, Dec. 4, 1971, at 1.

155. Swann v. Charlotte-Mecklenburg Bd. of Educ. 402 U.S. 1 (1971).

156. *Id.*

157. Plaintiffs' Response to the Board's Plans and Motion for Order Allowing Plaintiffs to Present a Desegregation Plan at the Board's Expense (filed Dec. 13, 1971). *See* Detroit Free Press, Dec. 11, 1971; *see also* editorial, Detroit Free Press, Nov. 27, 1971 (accusing the Detroit Central Board of trying to force the district court to make the unpopular decisions about the nature of desegregation in Detroit).

158. *See* Ruling and Order on Motions and Other Matters Heard June 14, 1972, at 3 (June 29, 1972) (holding the motion in abeyance pending further proceedings).

159. Record at 34, Dec. 20, 1971.

The NAACP plan sought a 65–35 black-white ratio in each school in the district. At the high school level it was patterned after the school board's abortive April 7 Plan, which redrew attendance boundaries. The NAACP went further and redrew boundaries for junior high and elementary schools. In the elementary schools it proposed to pair schools so that each school would have only first and second grades or only third through sixth grades. As a result of the pairings, each elementary student would attend a neighborhood school for two or four years and be bused to another school for the rest of his or her elementary years. The plan estimated that a total of 100,000 pupils would be reassigned. Bus transportation was planned for those who needed it.[160]

In early February the state board of education, responding to the court order to offer a metropolitan plan, presented six plans prepared with the help of consultants. Despite the protests of two of its members, the state board refused to express a preference for any of the plans.[161] Five of the plans were patently unresponsive to the court's order. Some of the plans did not even purport to desegregate schools anywhere.[162] They served a political purpose, however, in

160. [Plaintiffs'] Desegregation Plan of Detroit Public Schools, (filed Feb. 22, 1971). *See* Detroit Free Press, Feb. 23, 1972.

161. Michigan State Board of Education, A Summary of Six Plans to Achieve Racial Desegregation in Public Schools of the Detroit Metropolitan Area (filed Feb. 3, 1972). The board's motion specified that the transmittal was without recommendation. Excerpt of Minutes of Regular Meeting of State Board of Education, held in Lansing on Feb. 1, 1972. One dissenter, Annetta Miller, would have submitted all six plans but with "some evaluation." *Id.* The other, Marilyn Jean Kelly, felt the board should submit a single plan that should actually be fit for use. Hence she preferred Plan No. 3, the Metropolitan School District Reorganization Plan, although it was admittedly imperfect. The other plans, in her view, were not metropolitan desegregation plans. *Id.* at Exhibit B. A third member of the board, James F. O'Neill, seemed to oppose the submission of any plan at all. *Id.* at Exhibit A.

The titles of the six plans, with the state board's brief description of them, were as follows:

1. Detroit Metropolitan Racial Proportion Criteria Plan: "Would call for establishment of criteria for metropolitan racial desegregation which could be applied in each building in the appropriate designated metropolitan area."
2. Metropolitan One-way Movement Plan: "Would call for movement of minority students from Detroit schools to other metropolitan area schools."
3. Metropolitan School District Reorganization Plan: "Would establish six new Regional School Districts directly involving 36 of the 86 school districts in the tri-county (Wayne, Oakland, Macomb) Detroit metropolitan area, and put all 86 districts under a three-member Authority."
4. Metropolitan Magnet Plan: "Would extend the 'magnet school' concept now applied in Detroit to other schools in the metropolitan area."
5. Neighborhood School Based Metropolitan Plan: "Would involve moving every student in a desegregated metropolitan area at least twice a week to a school having a racial majority different from the 'home' school."
6. Metropolitan Equal Educational Opportunity and Quality Integration Plan: "Discusses the judicial perception of integration and suggests ways in which equalized educational opportunity might be accomplished to bring about quality integrated education."

Id. at 2–3.

See Detroit Free Press, Oct. 6, 1971; *id.,* Oct. 8, 1971; *id.,* Feb. 2, 1972; *id.,* Feb. 3, 1972, at 3A; Detroit News, Feb. 2, 1972.

162. *See* Plans 1, 2, 4, 5, and 6, *supra* note 161.

that they provided a camouflage for Plan 3, the one plan that could be called responsive to the court's directive. That plan, entitled the School District Reorganization Plan, proposed to replace Detroit and thirty-five nearby suburban districts with six new districts, each including part of Detroit and contiguous suburbs. While each of the new districts would have its own elected school boards, the plan proposed the creation of a three-person metropolitan area education authority to oversee the implementation of the desegregation order. The authority would have had the power to add any of the fifty remaining districts in the three county areas to add any of the fifty remaining districts in the three county areas to the integration plan if that became necessary to preserve integrated schools. About 35 percent of the pupils in the original 36 districts were black. School taxes would be reallocated throughout the tri-county area to assure equal funding for all pupils.[163]

A rival metropolitan plan was submitted by the intervening white Detroiters who initially proposed to include the suburbs in the case. That plan would have included 66 school districts in a pupil assignment area. Ninety percent of the public school students in the metropolitan area would have been included, but no pupils would be reassigned before the fifth grade. Seven geographic "boroughs," with elected boards, would have been created to assign pupils for desegregation purposes, but school governance would otherwise have been undisturbed.[164] All existing school districts, including Detroit's eight regional districts, would have remained in existence. The existing tax system would have continued unchanged.[165]

Remedy Hearings

In reaction to the multidistrict plans submitted to the court, many of the suburban school districts moved to intervene as defendants. Forty districts were represented by a single firm. Three other firms represented the remainder of the intervening districts. In addition, the city of Warren (a major suburb),[166] two

163. Michigan State Board of Education, Metropolitan School District Reorganization Plan, Bradley v. Milliken, (E.D. Mich., dated Feb 1, 1972).

164. Two of the boroughs did not include any part of Detroit. Rather, it was planned that they would draw black students from the suburban industrial cities of Mount Clemens and Pontiac.

165. [Intervenors'] Motion to Join Additional Parties Defendant (filed July 16, 1971); Memorandum Brief in Support of Intervening Defendants' Motion to Join Suburban School Districts (filed July 16, 1971). *See* Detroit Free Press, Jan 28, 1972; Detroit News, Jan. 28, 1972. For an insight into the process by which a homeowner's group secured the expertise necessary to develop the plan, *see* Detroit News, Jan. 30, 1972; East Side Shopper, Feb. 2, 1972. The consultants who drafted the plan explicitly dissociated themselves from the political and educational views of the Concerned Citizens for Better Education. *Id.* Their starting point was one of several internal discussion drafts prepared by the School-Community Relations staff of the Detroit board, which was given to Alexander Ritchie, attorney for the CCBE, by the chairperson of one of Detroit's regional school boards. First Flynn interview.

166. School districts in Michigan are seldom coterminous with municipal boundaries. The city of Warren, for instance, is served by a total of six school districts, three of which

organizations of suburban residents, and an independent teachers' union sought to intervene. Not all school districts petitioned to intervene. The cost was a consideration for some. Others stayed aloof on advice of counsel.[167] At least one district, Inkster, apparently sympathized with the plaintiffs but, being in desperate financial condition, could not afford the cost of litigation.[168]

Judge Roth invited the parties and the applicants for intervention to recommend the conditions, if any, upon which intervention should be permitted. The plaintiffs and the Detroit board opposed intervention, arguing that suburban districts were agencies of the state whose interests were adequately represented already. But if intervention were to be allowed, they wanted the newcomers to join the case as they found it, not to relitigate the issue of segregation. The white Detroiters who had raised the question of metropolitan desegregation pressed for all suburban districts to be joined, not just those that sought to intervene. They agreed, however, that relitigation should not be permitted. The suburban districts and the state defendants, on the other hand, sought almost unfettered intervention.[169]

In March 1972, on the day after hearings began on the feasibility of a remedy limited to Detroit alone, the court ruled on the petitions to intervene. All the suburban districts that wanted to intervene were allowed to, but the court re-

extend outside the city limits. The Grosse Pointe school system, by contrast, serves all five of the separate municipalities named Grosse Pointe, *viz.,* Grosse Pointe Park, Grosse Pointe Woods, Grosse Pointe Shores, Grosse Pointe Farms, and the City of Grosse Pointe, plus part of the adjoining suburb of Harper Woods. School districts are equally indifferent to county boundaries. At least 17 districts in metropolitan Detroit lie in two counties and two lie in three counties. *See* Milliken v. Bradley, 418 U.S. 717, 795 (1974) (Marshall J., dissenting).

167. As general suburban interests would be represented by those who did intervene, the inclination to stand apart offered a rare opportunity to have the best of two worlds—representation by surrogate and a strong claim never to have been subjected to the jurisdiction of the court.

168. The inference is based on the strongly pro-integration position taken by the Inkster school superintendent in meetings of suburban representatives. *See* Detroit News, Oct. 5, 1971. Inkster is an 85 percent black district surrounded by white districts in western Wayne County. Its tax base is almost exclusively residential. Although a very high percentage of Inkster residents work at the Ford Motor Company's giant Rouge Works, that plant pays no taxes in Inkster as it is located in overwhelmingly white Dearborn. Inkster's financial squeeze was twofold. It lacked ready funds for litigation and it badly needed special state assistance with its other bills. Prudent local leaders might well have feared their chances of state help would be jeopardized by opposing the state political leadership in a desegregation case.

169. Notice to Counsel (filed Mar. 6, 1972); Intervention Conditions Submitted by Applicants Green, *et al.* (filed Mar. 13, 1972); Letter from Counsel for the Southfield Public Schools to the Court (filed Mar. 14, 1972); letter from Counsel for the Grosse Pointe Public Schools to the Court (filed Mar. 14, 1972); Letter from Counsel for Bird *et al.* to the Court (filed Mar. 14, 1972); Conditions of Intervention Submitted by Professional Personnel of Van Dyke (filed Mar. 14, 1972); Statement of State Defendants' Position Re Pending Intervention Motion (filed Mar. 14, 1972; Intervening Defendant Magdowski's Recommendations for "Conditions of Intervention" (filed Mar. 14, 1972); Plaintiffs' Recommendations for Conditions to be Placed on Interventions (filed Mar. 14, 1972); Recommendations of Defendant Board of Education for the City of Detroit and Other Defendants for "Conditions of Intervention" (filed Mar. 14, 1972).

frained from ruling on the CCBE motion to join all the suburban districts. One group of individual suburban residents and the organization they belonged to were permitted to intervene, but another such group was refused.[170] The city of Warren and the independent teachers' union were denied intervention. In drafting the terms upon which intervention would be permitted, the court was obviously concerned to avoid additional delay.[171] It prohibited the intervenors from raising factual or legal issues already adjudicated. It subordinated their participation to that of the earlier parties and required them to agree on a single attorney to examine each witness. It emphasized that their function was to help the court decide whether to consider a metropolitan plan and to help shape such a plan if the court decided one was appropriate.[172] The intervenors objected strongly to the conditions.[173]

During the hearing on what was known as a "Detroit-only" remedy, the plaintiffs pressed for immediate adoption of a plan limited to the city. They reasoned, rightly it turned out, that a metropolitan remedy would involve long, complex litigation about novel issues. The plaintiffs wanted immediate relief while that litigation wound through the courts.[174] The Detroit board argued fervently for

170. Ruling and Order on Petitions for Intervention, Bradley v. Milliken (E.D. Mich., March 15, 1972).

The court reasoned that since the NAACP, as well as individuals, had appeared as plaintiffs, the Tri-County Citizens for Intervention should be allowed to be a defendant. Besides, admitting the group's members as individual defendants was tantamount to admitting the group anyway. The other citizens' group was denied intervention on the ground its interests would be adequately protected by the other group. Petitioners who were denied intervention were permitted to appear as amicus curiae. *Id.* at 2. The order does not reflect that the group denied leave to intervene was affiliated with the National Action Group (NAG), which had figured prominently in the explosive Pontiac desegregation case.

171. Its concern was hardly surprising. A year earlier the court of appeals had rebuked it for being too slow. Bradley v. Milliken, 438 F.2d 945, 947 (6th Cir. 1971). Judge Roth, a few days later, publicly acknowledged the time limits he felt imposed on him. At the end of the hearing on plans limited to Detroit, the court referred to the pressure from the court of appeals as a reason for considering the legal propriety of a multidistrict remedy before the court had made a decision on the feasibility of a Detroit-only remedy. Ruling on Propriety of Considering a Metropolitan Remedy to Accomplish Desegregation of the Public Schools of the City of Detroit, at 2 (E.D. Mich. Mar. 24, 1972).

172. Ruling and Order on Petitions for Intervention, at 2–4. (Mar. 15, 1972). The court's conditions of intervention closely parallel those recommended by the plaintiffs. *See* Plaintiffs Recommendations for Conditions to be Placed on Interventions (filed Mar. 14, 1972).

173. In reviewing the district court's decision, the Court of Appeals for the Sixth Circuit directed that the intervening school districts and any other school districts which might later be joined would have an opportunity to offer additional evidence and to cross-examine witnesses who had previously testified on any issue relevant to the question of the multidistrict remedy. The court of appeals, however, expressly ruled that there was no need to allow those districts to submit additional evidence about the issue of segregation or the feasibility of a Detroit-only remedy. Bradley v. Milliken, 484 F.2d 215, 251–52 (6th Cir. 1972). The Supreme Court found it unnecessary to reach the issue. Milliken v. Bradley, 418 U.S. 717, 752 (1974).

174. Lucas Interview. Lucas, who was also counsel in the Richmond, Va. case, was very familiar with the metropolitan concept, which had not yet been considered by the Supreme Court. *See* School Bd. of the City of Richmond v. State Bd. of Educ., 412 U.S. 92 (1973),

the adoption of "metro," claiming that a Detroit-only plan would simply create a totally black city district surrounded by white suburbs, making all desegregation more difficult because the political boundaries would coincide with racial ones.[175]

The court did not wrestle long with the Detroit-only proposals. It rejected both of the board's plans. One was criticized for being modeled on the unsuccessful magnet plan and, in some respects, for increasing segregation. The other was dismissed as a "token or part-time desegregation effort."[176] While it thus accepted plaintiffs' criticisms of the board's plans, the court also agreed with the board's attack on the thoroughgoing desegregation plan of the NAACP. Judge Roth rejected that plan because "the racial composition of the student body is such that the plan's implementation would clearly make the entire Detroit public school system racially identifiable as black".[177] The court then concluded that true relief from segregation was impossible within the city limits of Detroit.[178]

The court began hearings on possible metropolitan plans the same day it issued its ruling that no Detroit-only plan would work. In reporting the hearings, the press focused on the geographic scope of the various metropolitan plans.[179] The court and the parties emphasized the rationales and methods as well.[180]

The hearings began with three multidistrict proposals before the court, submitted by the Detroit board, the CCBE intervenors, and the state board.[181] During the hearings, the NAACP suggested a modification of the other plans, drawing a more compact perimeter than the Detroit board or the CCBE proposals, and specifying high school clusters.[182] The suburban intervenors made no effort to

---

aff'd by an equally divided Court sub nom. Bradley v. School Bd. of the City of Richmond, 462 F.2d 1058 (4th Cir. 1972). He was not looking for a second test case for that remedy. If he had been, he would not likely have chosen one from a northern school district or from a major metropolitan area.

175. *See* Objections of Bd. of Educ. for the City of Detroit and Other Defendants to the Alleged Plan of Desegregation Filed by Plaintiffs, Bradley v. Milliken (E.D. Mich. dated Mar. 12, 1972).

176. Findings of Fact and Conclusions of Law on Detroit-only Plans of Desegregation, at 2 (Mar. 28, 1972), *quoted in* 484 F.2d 215, 243 (6th Cir. 1973).

177. Findings of Fact, *supra* note 176, at 3, 5; 484 F.2d at 243–44.

178. Findings of Fact, *supra* note 176, at 5; 484 F.2d at 244.

179. *See* Detroit Free Press, March 30, 1972 (with maps); April 9, 1972, at 9D; April 12, 1972; Detroit News, March 29, 1972 (with maps); March 30, 1972; March 31, 1972; April 12, 1972.

180. *See* Bradley v. Milliken, 345 F. Supp. 914, 916, 922 (E.D. Mich. 1972).

181. Five of the state's six plans cannot be called metropolitan desegregation plans. See text at note 161, *supra*. The Detroit board's plan had been submitted along with its objection to the state defendants' plans. *See* Basic Guidelines for a Metropolitan Detroit Area Integration Plan *attached to* Objections of Board of Education for the City of Detroit and Other Defendants to the Metropolitan Plan Submitted by the State of Michigan and by Way of an Alternative, A Submission Herein by Said Board of a Metropolitan Detroit Area Integration Plan (dated Mar. 4, 1972).

182. *See* Bradley v. Milliken, 345 F. Supp. 914, 922 (E.D. Mich. 1972). Plaintiffs felt the state defendants had defaulted on their obligation to prepare a meaningful metropolitan

suggest either areal limits or techniques for successful multidistrict desegregation. Instead they stuck to their position that no metropolitan plan was permissable.[183]

Ruling on the Desegregation Area

On June 14, 1972, the court issued its key decision on a metropolitan plan.[184] The court tentatively described the area to be included in the remedy,[185] appointed a panel of experts to work out the details of pupil and faculty reassignment subject to guidelines set by the court,[186] and ordered the state defendants to prepare plans for "governance, finance and administrative arrangements" necessary to implement a desegregation plan, both in the short run and indefinitely.[187] First the court analyzed the desegregation areas proposed by the various plans. It rejected out of hand five of the state board's plans,[188] and dismissed the sixth as based primarily on an arbitrary racial ratio rather than "relevant factors, like eliminating racially identifiable schools; accomplishing maximum actual desegregation of the Detroit public schools or on any practical limitation of reasonable times and distances for transportation of pupils."[189] Turning to the other three proposals, the court noted that they had in common

plan. They responded as they had to the Detroit-only plans of the Detroit board by filing a Motion for Order Requiring State Defendants to Cooperate Fully and Openly and for State Defendants to Pay Costs of a Metropolitan Plan to be Prepared by Plaintiffs (filed April 4, 1972). The court avoided ruling on the motion until the end of the hearings when it dismissed as moot both motions to require a defendant to finance plaintiffs' counterplans. Rulings and Order on Motions and Other Matters Heard June 14, 1972, at 3 (June 29, 1972).

183. *See* Bradley v. Milliken, 345 F. Supp. 914, 924 (E.D. Mich. 1972). The district court suggested:

> The failure of the group of 40 districts to even comment that the court should exclude certain districts under any number of available rationales may in part be explained by the awkward position chosen by them and their counsel of having single representation for districts on different sides of the various suggested perimeters.

Id.

184. Bradley v. Milliken, 345 F. Supp. 914 (E.D. Mich. 1972).

185. *Id.* at 918–20.

186. *Id.* at 916–17.

187. *Id.* at 920; *see also id.* at 933–35, 937.

188. *Id.* at 922–23.

189. *Id.* at 923. Judge Roth was openly unhappy with the role of the state defendants in the hearing:

> At the hearings, moreover, the State defendants did not purport to present evidence in support, or even in opposition, to the State Proposal. The State, despite prodding by the Court presented only one witness, who merely explained what appeared on the face of the various State "Plans" submitted. The State's cross-examination of witnesses was of no assistance to the court in ascertaining any preference, legal or educational. Put bluntly, State defendants in this hearing deliberately chose not to assist the court in choosing an appropriate area for effective desegregation of the Detroit Public Schools. Their resistance and abdication of responsibility throughout has been consistent with the other failures to meet their obligations noted in the court's earlier rulings. Indeed, some of the submissions spoke as clearly in opposition to desegregation as did the legislature in Sec. 12 of Act. 48 of 1970, . . . ruled unconstitutional by the Sixth Circuit.

Id. at 923–24. The majority of the Supreme Court later criticized Judge Roth for being

two premises: that the three-county area was the "relevant school community" for testing the adequacy of plans and that parts of the metropolitan area could be excluded either if they imposed unreasonable transportation burdens or if they were unnecessary to eliminate racially identifiable schools.[190] Accepting those premises, the court adopted the plaintiffs' proposed perimeter, the most conservative proposal that would effectively eliminate racially identifiable schools. That area included 153 school districts with 780,000 students, 25.3 percent of whom were black.[191] The court refused to expand the perimeter, as urged by the Detroit board in order to raise the average socioeconomic status of some clusters of schools.[192] The court's one concession to the Detroit board on the matter of geographic scope was to concede that it would permit the court-appointed panel to suggest modifications.[193]

The court named a panel of nine experts "broadly representative of the parties and their interest" to refine the plan of desegregation outlined by the court.[194]

---

himself overly concerned with racial ratios rather than with simply dismantling a dual school system. 418 U.S. 717, 738–41 (1974). *But see* Justice Marshall's dissent, *id.* at 784–89, concluding: "There is simply no foundation in the record . . . for the majority's accusation that the only basis for the District Court's order was some desire to achieve a racial balance in the Detroit Metropolitan Area." *Id.* at 788. Justice Marshall was clearly correct.

190. Bradley v. Milliken, 345 F. Supp. 914, 925 (E.D. Mich. 1972).

191. *Id.* at 925, 928 The court's order named 54 districts, but during the pendancy of the suit two suburban districts had merged. The voters in the Fairlane District had voted to merge with the Dearborn District. The Dearborn board, without putting the issue to the electorate, had voted to accept Fairlane into Dearborn. The inconsistency of the suburban merger with the rhetoric of the anti-busing forces was ignored by press and courts.

192. *Id.* at 927. Despite the Detroit board's evidence that the average socioeconomic status of a student body is an important factor for the success of desegregation, the NAACP opposed basing a plan on socioeconomic data. It did not want to complicate the case further or to add to the list of novel issues for appeal.

193. *Id.* at 918, 927.

194. *Id.* at 937. *See also id.* at 916–17. The panel was shortly expanded to eleven by adding representatives of the Detroit Federation of Teachers and the Michigan Education Association. Order Modifying Order for Development of Plan of Desegregation, to Add Additional Panel Members (dated June 29, 1972). The original nine members included an educational expert to be designated by the state superintendent of public instruction; the state department of education's transportation director; the Detroit Board of Education's deputy superintendent; its school housing chief and its director of school-community relations; an expert for the plaintiffs; a representative of the white Detroit intervenors who was both a professor of education and a member of a regional school board; the superintendent of the Oakland County Intermediate School District as the designee of the intervening suburbs and suburban parents; and an education expert from the Michigan Civil Rights Commission.

Chief Justice Burger, while not saying the district court had erred in the selection of panel members, later commented rather critically that the suburbs, with three-fourths of the children, were under-represented on the panel. Milliken v. Bradley, 418 U.S. 714, 733 n.14 (1974). In reaching that conclusion, he ignored the close alignment of state and suburban interests. In fact three persons represented state interests, one spoke for the suburbs, three represented the Detroit board, and a fourth was closely allied with the Detroit board. The two representatives of organized teachers were also identified with the defendants. If anyone had objective grounds for complaint it was the plaintiffs, who were allocated only one seat. In point of fact the panel did not disagree along city-suburban lines. The one public dissent from its report was filed by the two labor representatives—one from the suburbs, one from the city. For a discussion of the workings of the panel see text *infra* at notes 214–227.

The court felt that "the time constraints, . . . the State defendants' default in assisting this court to determine the appropriate desegregation area, and the State defendants' asserted and evident lack of available planning capacity suited to the task" required it to rely on some planning agency other than the state department of education.[195] It charged this panel with developing a plan of pupil assignment, a transportation plan, and a faculty reassignment system, all within 45 days. The panel was to provide for the greatest feasible integration in September 1972 and completion of the job by September 1973. Its last task was to consider how best to avoid white flight from the desegregation area by controlling school construction throughout the entire metropolitan area.[196]

Despite its obvious lack of confidence in the state defendants, the court directed them to produce both an interim and a long-term plan for overhauling the political and financial structure of local education to cope with multidistrict desegregation. The state superintendent of public instruction was to file a progress report in 15 days and a final set of recommendations within 45 days.[197] Recalling the state board's failure to recommend or defend any of its six metropolitan plans, the court directed the superintendent to "choose one appropriate interim arrangement to oversee the immediate implementation of a plan of desegregation."[198]

Looking ahead, the court announced that it would conduct hearings on the interim plan 15 days after it received the reports it was ordering. Reacting to its experience with some of the defendants in the most recent hearings, it put the parties on notice that it would not "consider objections to desegregation or proposals offered 'instead' of desegregation."[199]

PARALLEL POLITICAL DEVELOPMENTS

While the court was conducting its hearings, the politics of desegregation had reached a boil. In March, President Nixon called for a moratorium on busing.[200] A week later the Justice Department filed a motion to intervene in the Detroit case. It was at first ignored, assertedly for failure to comply with local court rules. Later the court denied the motion but let the government participate as *amicus curiae.*[201]

195. Bradley v. Milliken, 345 F. Supp. 914, 937 (E.D. Mich. 1972).
196. *Id.* at 916–19, 929–33, 936–37.
197. *Id.* at 920, 937.
198. *Id.* at 920.
199. *Id.*
200. Detroit Free Press, March 18, 1972 at 1.
201. Motion of United States of America for Leave to Intervene (filed March 23, 1972); Ruling (May 9, 1972). *See* Detroit Free Press, Mar. 31, 1972, at 9A; *id.,* May 10, 1972; Detroit News, April 13, 1972, at 22A. In mid-summer 1972 the court of appeals allowed the Justice Department to intervene as a party to defend the constitutionality of the newly enacted Broomfield Amendment, Pub. L. No. 92–318, §803, 86 Stat. 235, which the Justice Department asserted had been challenged as unconstitutional. *See* Bradley v. Milliken, 484 F.2d 215, 221 (6th Cir. 1973); Brief for the United States, *id.* at 1.

In May and June Congress debated and passed the Broomfield Amendment, which purported to postpone the effectiveness of any federal busing order until all appeals had been exhausted.[202] The amendment, introduced by Republican Congressman William Broomfield of Michigan, had strong bipartisan support from the once strongly liberal Michigan delegation.[203] President Nixon approved the amendment despite his assertion that it would be ineffectual.[204] The amendment had not gone into effect at the time Judge Roth ordered the panel to prepare a plan, and the sixth circuit court never ruled on it in the Detroit case.[205]

One additional sign of strong white opposition to desegregation, whether within or across city boundaries, was the defeat by Detroit voters of a critical millage proposal in May. While white areas in Detroit are traditionally more reluctant than black areas to support millages,[206] the white "no" vote was unusually strong that year.[207]

Anticipating the millage defeat, the Detroit Board of Education had given tentative dismissal notices to 1,548 teachers. After the millage vote and the June 14 ruling on the desegregation area, the board voted also to reduce the number of school days in 1972/73 from the 180 days required by state law to 117. The Detroit Federation of Teachers promptly secured a preliminary injunction from Judge Roth prohibiting both reductions as they would have made impossible a metropolitan desegregation plan premised on "'schools of substantially like quality, facilities, extra-curricular activities and staffs.'"[208]

Less excited voices were also raised during the hearings. In March a consortium of Detroit civic and church groups sponsored a one-day conference on desegregation and school finance problems.[209] The Detroit Coordinating Council on Human Relations conducted another conference on busing two months later.[210] A widely based group of 33 religious, labor and civic groups announced in April

202. Education Amendments of 1972, §803, Pub. L. No. 92–318, 86 Stat. 235 (effective July 1, 1972; expired Jan. 1, 1974).

203. Senator Philip Hart and Detroit's two black Congressmen, Charles Diggs and John Conyers, were notable exceptions.

204. Public Papers of Richard Nixon, 1972, at 701 (June 23, 1972). His analysis seems valid from the face of the Amendment. The statute applied to district court orders requiring student transfers for racial balance. As a result it was not applicable to transfers for the purpose of desegregation. *See* Drummond v. Acree, 409 U.S. 1228 (1972) (Powell, Cir. J.); NAACP v. Lansing Bd. of Educ., 485 F.2d 569 (6th Cir. 1973); United States v. Board of Educ., Indep. School Dist. No. 1, Tulsa County, 476 F.2d 621 (1973).

205. *See* Bradley v. Milliken, 484 F.2d 215, 258 (6th Cir. 1973). *But see* NAACP v. Lansing Bd. of Educ., 485 F.2d 569 (6th Cir. 1973). The amendment had expired by its own terms by the time the Supreme Court decided the Detroit case in July 1974.

206. Drachler interview.

207. Detroit Free Press, May 17, 1972; Detroit News, May 17, 1972.

208. Preliminary Injunction, at 2 (July 7, 1972), *quoting* Bradley v. Milliken, 345 F. Supp. 914, 919 (E.D. Mich. 1972). *See* Mich. Comp. L. Ann. §388.641. *Cf.* Swann v. Charlotte-Mecklenburg Bd. of Educ., 402 U.S. a, 18–19 (1971).

209. The Joint Action Committee on Education held its conference at the University of Detroit on March 25, 1972. It focused on desegregation, community, control and school finance.

210. Michigan Chronicle, May 20, 1972.

they had formed the Metropolitan Coalition for Peaceful Integration, dedicated to the successful implementation of whatever plan the court might order.[211]

DEVELOPMENT OF A PLAN

While political leaders denounced Judge Roth and lawyers sought stays and filed appeals from the June 14 order,[212] the panel of experts and the state department of education went to work on their assigned tasks.

The panelists contacted each other unofficially shortly after learning of their appointment. A week later John Porter, the state superintendent of public instruction, chaired their first meeting in the Lansing offices of the state board of education. After pledging the panel his full cooperation, he left it to organize itself. Over the dissent of the suburban representative, the group voted to conduct its business in private. As the press would not leave, the panel arranged to move to another room. A state trooper was stationed outside to assure privacy.[213]

When they reassembled, the group agreed that a different member would chair the meeting each day. The chair would make any announcements to the press on that day. After preliminary maneuvering, the group took a businesslike attitude toward their charge.[214]

The panel gave first priority to developing pupil assignment plans and to establishing transportation routes. On July 5 it reported to the court that for an interim plan to be implemented in September 1972, more buses would have to be secured. The panel's investigation showed that no more than 295 buses were available for September delivery if bought immediately. Consequently the panel asked the court to order the purchase of 295 buses with state funds.[215] At a hearing on the recommendation, the court learned that only the state treasurer had the legal power to sign warrants to pay the state's obligations. Being other-

211. Detroit Free Press, April 12, 1972; Detroit News, April 12, 1972. The first steps toward the formation of the coalition had been taken in January 1972. The coalition, by design, included several groups based primarily in the suburbs, as its leaders felt there was no existing organization both willing and able to bring city and suburban residents together so long as public officials refused to plan for the contingency that a multidistrict desegregation order would actually be implemented. *See also* text at notes 430–37, *infra.*

212. See text accompanying notes 236–41, *infra.*

213. Interview with Rita Scott, supervisor of the education program, Michigan Department of Civil Rights, in Detroit, Michigan, May 19, 1975 [hereinafter cited as Scott interview]. Scott was a member of the panel.

214. *Id.* Fellow panelists are quick to give Oakland County intermdiate School District Superintendent William Emerson credit for helping to set that tone. After restating his opposition to the whole notion of metropolitan desegregation, Emerson reportedly added that if there was to be multi-district desegregation, he wanted the court to use the best possible plan. In the development of that plan, he and Detroit Deputy Superintendent Aubrey McCutcheon established themselves as dominant personalities on the panel.

215. Recommendation of Desegregation Panel Regarding Additional Transportation Equipment Needed for the Implementation of an Interim Desegregation Plan (July 5, 1972). The court had instructed the panel to give it an early report on the need to acquire additional transportation equipment. Bradley v. Milliken, 345 F. Supp. 914, 917 (E.D. Mich. 1972).

wise persuaded that the purchase was wise, the court joined the treasurer as a party defendant and ordered the buses purchased.[216] The state defendants promptly moved for a stay of the purchase order, which was denied by the district court[217] but granted by the court of appeals.[218] This was the beginning of the appellate process. Nothing significant was before the district court for the next two and a half years.

In the meantime the panel continued its work. Before submitting its final report to the court, it recommended changes in the clusters of schools and school districts initially approved by the court. Its purpose was to improve the racial composition of some clusters, to minimize travel time, and to make the clusters as small as possible.[219]

In a final report in late July, the panel made detailed recommendations for reorganizing grade structures and feeder patterns. In general, pupils who started together in elementary school, though living in different districts, would have remained together through high school. The report admittedly suffered from insufficient data about building capacities and new construction, but frankly relied upon the litigation process to identify and correct such shortcomings. It recommended that only elementary schools be included in the first year of desegregation but that as many clusters be desegregated as possible.[220] It suggested criteria for deciding which clusters to integrate first, and following those criteria, suggested timetables for each cluster.[221] The panel also made detailed recommendations about special education, state and federal compensatory education programs, and pupil transfers. It recommended that transportation be provided by the three intermediate school districts under the supervision of the state superintendent of public instruction.[222] It suggested standards for the integration of faculty, who would at first be exchanged under memoranda of agreement but would later become employees of the districts to which they were reassigned.[223] The report contained an elaborate affirmative action plan[224] and a

216. Order Adding Defendant Allison Green (July 11, 1972); Order for Acquisition of Transportation (July 11, 1972).

217. Order Denying Motion for Stay of Order for Acquisition of Transportation (July 11, 1972).

218. Order, Bradley v. Milliken, No. 72-8002 (6th Cir. July 13, 1972), *extended by* Order, Bradley v. Milliken, No. 72-8002 (6th Cir. July 17, 1972). *See* Bradley v. Milliken, 484 F.2d 215, 218 (6th Cir. 1973).

219. Recommendations of Desegregation Panel Regarding Cluster Reorganization, (dated July 12, 1972, filed July 27, 1972). No hearings were held about the proposed changes.

220. The Panel's Response to the Court's Ruling on Desegregation Area and Order for Development of Plan of Desegregation, at 3–5 (July 29, 1972) [hereinafter cited as Panel's Response].

221. As a stay had been entered by the court of appeals, the report listed alternate timetables based upon different starting dates. *Id.* at 6–12.

222. Each county in metropolitan Detroit constituted an intermediate school district. The panel suggested rather detailed regulations for the transportation system, many of which paralleled state law. *Id.* at 20–25.

223. *Id.* at 26–30.

224. *Id.* at 31–37.

very general proposal for equitably reallocating revenues among the school districts included in the order.[225] Finally the panel suggested that the state board of education be required to issue a uniform code of student conduct.[226] The two representatives of the teachers' unions gave notice that they would file a minority report on the reassignment of teachers and other terms of employment.[227]

Superintendent of Public Instruction John Porter also filed his reports by the deadline. In a letter of submission he cautioned that the court should allow more than a year's experience with the interim plan before implementing the proposed final arrangements for finance, governance, administration, and personnel.[228] Porter's proposed interim arrangements relied very heavily on memoranda of agreement between school districts exchanging pupils and staff,[229] and foreswore proposals that would have required legislative action. He carefully avoided volunteering to supervise, coordinate, or evaluate the desegregation process.[230] He did, however, suggest that evaluations and recommendations be submitted by the three county intermediate school districts and by advisory councils chosen by the school boards in each cluster.[231]

Superintendent Porter's proposed final arrangements called, very tentatively, for the creation of an elected "area-wide authority" to supervise and coordinate the desegregation effort. The report insisted that there was no intention to alter the status of existing local school districts, Detroit's decentralized regions, or the three intermediate school districts. Yet the proposal allocated so much power to the area-wide authority that all the other entities would have been subordinated to it. The area-wide authority, for instance, would determine the

225. *Id.* at 38.
226. *Id.* at 51–52.
227. Dissent from the Final Report of the Desegregation Panel (July 29, 1972). In due course they filed their minority report. Minority Report and Dissent from the Final Report of the Desegregation Panel (Aug 31, 1972).
228. Letter from John W. Porter to Judge Stephen A. Roth, July 29, 1972. While clearly no decision had been made on the matter, the court did seem to contemplate that the final plan for *pupil assignments* would be put into effect after only a year. Such delay in those assignments as the court anticipated was apparently due to logistics rather than to a desire to experiment with governmental forms. *See* Bradley v. Milliken, 345 F. Supp. 914, 936–37 (E.D. Mich. 1972).
229. Matters he suggested be handled by the memoranda included the terms of the pupil exchange, pupil conduct codes, the terms of faculty exchanges (in consultation with the appropriate unions), affirmative action programs, in-service training, curriculum, student activities, and the appointment of bi-racial committees. [Superintendent of Public Instruction John W. Porter's] Recommendations Regarding the Financial, Administrative and Governmental and Contractual Arrangements for Operating the Public Schools in the Desegregation Area During the Period of *Interim* Desegregation (dated July 28, 1972, filed July 29, 1972) [emphasis in original].
230. By contrast, the court-appointed panel forewaw a more active role for the state superintendent and state board. *See* Panel's Response at 8, 15–16, 20, 22–25, 30, 31–32, 35, 39, 41–43, 46, 51–52.
231. [Superintendent of Public Instruction John W. Porter's] Recommendations Regarding the Financial, Administrative and Governmental and Contractual Arrangements for Operating the Public Schools in the Desegregation Area During the Period of *Interim* Desegregation, *supra* note 229, at 12–13.

area-wide tax rate, receive state aid, oversee the budgetary process, realign territory and clusters, employ faculty, conduct labor negotiations, adopt affirmative action plans, and oversee curriculum and extracurricular activities.[232]

The parties submitted their responses to the reports of the superintendent and the panel, receiving extra time from the court because of the delayed minority report from the panel.[233] By mid-September, when the responses were filed, the appellate process was well under way. Despite the urgent pleas of the plaintiffs to refine the plan during the delay caused by the appeals, [234] no hearings were conducted. Judge Roth was working hard at reducing his backlog of other cases when a severe heart attack in early November removed him from the bench for many months. Although he later returned to work, he died of a heart attack two weeks before the Supreme Court issued its decision in *Bradley*.[235]

THE APPELLATE PROCESS

Immediately after the June 14, 1972, decision on the desegregation area, all defendants appealed. They also applied to the district court and the court of appeals for stays of the order to prepare desegregation plans. No stays were granted until Judge Roth ordered the purchase of buses necessary to start desegregating in the fall. The court of appeals stayed the purchase order until Judge Roth had passed on the application for a stay.[236] When he refused to stay the purchase order,[237] the court of appeals renewed its stay to "remain in effect . . . until entry by the District Judge of a final desegregation order or until certification by the District Judge of an appealable question as provided by 28 U.S.C. § 1292(b)."[238] At the behest of both plaintiffs and defendants, the district court certified its five key rulings as final orders under Rule 54(b), *Federal Rules of Civil Procedure,* and as presenting controlling questions of law under 28 U.S.C. § 1292(b).[239] Later the same day, the court of appeals granted the interlocutory

232. [State Superintendent of Public Instruction, John W. Porter's] Recommendations Regarding the Financial, Administrative and Governmental and Contractual Arrangements for Operating the Public Schools in the Desegregation Area During the Period of *Final* Desegregation, at 19–20, 32–34, 45 (filed July 29, 1972) [emphasis in original].

233. Order, Bradley v. Milliken, Civ. No.35257 (E.D. MIch., September 7, 1972). The court had earlier denied the state defendants' request for a time extension in which to file objections, Order, Bradley v. Milliken, Civ. No. 35257 (E.D. Mich., Aug. 15, 1972), but in a separate order had granted such a request by intervening school districts. Order, Bradley v. Milliken, Civ. No. 35257 (E.D. Mich., Aug. 15, 1975).

234. Plaintiffs' Supplemental Responses, Objections and Proposed Modifications to Reports Submitted, at 3–4, 21 (Sept. 15, 1972).

235. *See* Grant, *The Detroit School Case: An Historical Overview,* 21 Wayne L. Rev. 851, 866 (1975).

236. Order, Bradley v. Milliken, No. 72-8002 (6th Cir., July 13, 1972).

237. Order, Bradley v. MIlliken, Civ. No. 35257 (E.D. Mich., July 13, 1972).

238. Order, Bradley v. Milliken, No. 72-8002 (6th Cir. July 17, 1972).

239. Order, Bradley v. Milliken, Civ. No. 35257 (E.D. Mich., July 20, 1972). The rulings certified were: Ruling on Issue on Segregation, Bradley v. Milliken, 338 F. Supp. 582 (E.D. Mich., 1971); Ruling on Propriety of Considering a Metropolitan Remedy to Accomplish

appeal.[240] The court of appeals' order also continued the stay of the bus purchase order and enlarged it to cover all orders dealing with interdistrict reassignment of pupils and faculty. It expressly authorized "planning proceedings" in the district court and the continuation of the planning work of the court-appointed panel.[241]

The Sixth Circuit Decision

In December 1972 a unanimous panel of the court of appeals decided the case. In January the court granted the defendants' request for an *en banc* hearing, a rarity in the sixth circuit court.[242] The full court reissued the original opinion, with minor changes, on June 12, 1973. Three judges dissented from all or part of the decision.[243]

The court of appeals upheld the district court's ruling that the Detroit schools were segregated by acts of the state and acts of the Detroit Board of Education which were attributable to the state.[244] Keeping its ruling as narrow as possible, it expressly refrained from basing its conclusion on the evidence of housing segregation.[245] Turning to the remedy problem, it found ample support for the district court's conclusion that a "Detroit-only" plan of desegregation would not work.[246] It set out in detail its understanding of the status of school districts

Desegregation of the Public Schools of the City of Detroit (March 24, 1972); Findings of Fact and Conclusions of Law on Detroit-only Plans of Desegregation (March 28, 1972), *quoted in* Bradley v. Milliken, 484 F.2d 215, 242–45 (6th Cir. 1973); Ruling on Desegregation Area and Development of Plan, and Findings of Fact and Conclusions of Law in Support Thereof, Bradley v. Milliken, 345 F. Supp. 914 (E.D. Mich., 1972); Order for Acquisition of Transportation (July 11, 1972).

240. Order, Bradley v. Millken, No. 72-8002 (6th Cir. July 20, 1972).

241. *Id.* at 2–3, *quoted in part in* Bradley v Milliken, 484 F.2d, 215, 218–19 (6th Cir. 1973). As noted above (see text at notes 234–35 *supra*), the district court did not conduct "planning proceedings" after the submission of the panel's and the state superintendent's reports. Because of this, the panel was never reconvened after submitting its July 29, 1972 report.

242. Bradley v. Milliken, No. 72-1809 (6th Cir., Dec. 8, 1972) *rehearing en banc granted* Bradley v. Milliken, No. 72-1809 (6th Cir. Jan 16, 1973). Under the rules of the Sixth Circuit, the effect of granting a *rehearing en banc* is "to vacate the previous opinion and judgment of the court, to stay the mandate and to restore the case on the docket as a pending appeal." 6th Cir. R. 3(d). *See* Bradley v. Milliken, 484 F.2d 215, 218 (6th Cir. 1973). The original panel consisted of Chief Judge Phillips and Judges Edwards and Peck who had been the appellate panel in the case from its inception. It was widely assumed that the court felt the need to reconcile the approval of a broad remedy in Detroit with another panel's October 11, 1972 disapproval of a more limited remedy in Chattanooga, Tenn., as it granted *en banc* hearings in both cases. The *en banc* court, two judges dissenting, reversed the panel and upheld the district court order in Chattanooga. Mapp v. Board of Educ. of City of Chattanooga, 447 F.2d 851 (6th Cir. 1973) (*per curiam*).

There had been a good deal of idle speculation in Detroit whether the court of appeals panel would act before the November 1972 presidential election, which President Nixon won on an anti-busing platform.

243. Bradley v. Milliken, 484 F.2d 215, 250 (6th Cir. 1973) (*en banc*).

244. *Id.* at 221–50.

245. *Id.* at 242.

246. *Id.* at 242–50.

under Michigan law, finding that local school districts are merely instrumentalities of the state created for the state's administrative convenience.[247] From the facts of the violation, the inadequacy of a Detroit-only remedy, and the state's pervasive control over education, the court of appeals concluded that a metropolitan remedy was called for.[248] There was, it found, no other way to protect plaintiffs' constitutional rights. However, it reversed the district court's orders dealing with metropolitan relief because all school districts to be affected by the remedy were necessary parties to the hearings on relief.[249] Some of the districts had neither intervened nor been joined.[250] The court of appeals specified that the district court on remand would not be required to take further evidence about the existence of segregation or the futility of a Detroit-only remedy. This implied what the panel had specified: that the inclusion of the suburbs need not be premised on a finding that each suburb was independently guilty of acts of segregation.[251]

SUPREME COURT REVIEW

The state and suburban defendants promptly applied for writs of *certiorari,* which were opposed by the Detroit board as well as by the plaintiffs. When *certiorari* was granted, due process claims and other issues were before the Supreme Court, but it was clear the key issue was the remedy. That issue pitted

247. *Id.* at 245–49. Most of the court's rationale was based on statutes and cases, but included with it was an extensive discussion of the major role of state agencies in the recent history of school district mergers in Michigan. *Id.* at 247–48. While based largely on public records, the source of the court's information was not the trial record—which was silent—but the Detroit board's brief. Brief of Appellant Board of Education of the School District of the City of Detroit, at 46–51; Bradley v. Milliken, 484 F.2d 215 (6th Cir. 1973). Mr. Justice White, in noting this history, was careful to attribute it to the court of appeals. Milliken v. Bradley, 418 U.S. 717, 768 n.4 (1974) (White, J, dissenting).

248. Bradley v. Milliken, 484 F.2d 215, 250–51 (6th Cir. 1973). The Supreme Court did not accept the rulings of the court of appeals and the district court that the state of Michigan has and exercises plenary control over its school districts, although two of the lower court judges overruled by the Supreme Court were uniquely knowledgeable on the subject. They were District Judge Roth, a former Michigan attorney general, and Circuit Judge George Edwards, Jr., a former justice of the Michigan Supreme Court. *See* Milliken v. Bradley, 414 U.S. 717, 742–43 (1974). The Supreme Court's disregard of local judges on a critical point of state law and practice stands in marked contrast with the Court's position in Bishop v. Wood, 44 U.S.L.W. 4820, 4821–22 (June 8, 1976), which gives great deference to a merely "tenable" district court reading of a local ordinance. While the two cases are irreconcilable in approach, they are consistent in result: a narrow reading of the protection of the Fourteenth Amendment.

249. *Id.* at 251–52. The orders vacated were: Ruling on Propriety of a Metropolitan Remedy to Accomplish Desegregation of the Public Schools of the City of Detroit (Mar. 24, 1972); Ruling on Desegregation Area and Development of Plan, Bradley v. Milliken, 345 F. Supp. 914 (E.D. Mich. 1972); Order for Acquisition for Transportation (July 11, 1972).

250. See note 167 and accompanying text, *supra;* Bradley v. Milliken, 484 F.2d 215, 251 (6th Cir. 1973).

251. Bradley v. Milliken, 484 F.2d 215, 252 (6th Cir. 1973). *Compare* the opinion of the original panel, Bradley v. Milliken, slip opin. at 68, No. 72-188009 (6th Cir. Dec. 8, 1972).

the NAACP and the Detroit board against the state and suburban defendants.[252] The Justice Department, as *amicus curiae,* allied itself with the suburban viewpoint.[253]

The Supreme Court's decision has been widely commented upon,[254] a task that need not be repeated here. In brief, the Court sustained the findings of segregation,[255] but not the remedy or the rationale upon which the remedy was based. The majority opinion by Chief Justice Burger held that while it was permissible in a proper case to order schools desegregated across district boundaries, there must be a showing of "a constitutional violation within one district that produces a significant segregative effect in another district."[256] Somewhat incon-

252. Although they were allied at this point of the case, the Detroit board and the NAACP were still adversaries. For this and possibly other reasons, the NAACP, which controlled the allocation of time for respondents' oral argument, refused to allot time for the attorney for the Detroit School Board to make an oral argument.

In the court of appeals the Detroit board had argued both that it was not guilty of segregation and that, if it were, a metropolitan remedy was appropriate. *See* Brief of Appellant Board of Education of the School District of the City of Detroit, Bradley v. Milliken, 484 F.2d 215 (6th Cir.1973). Counsel for the board found those two positions very difficult to defend simultaneously. Consequently, in its brief to the Supreme Court, the Detroit board pressed its claim that the state of Michigan had contributed significantly to segregation within Detroit and that a metropolitan remedy was the only feasible one. It somewhat awkwardly abandoned its claim of innocence:

> Although the Detroit Board of Education maintains that, as a local state agency, it had taken no actions which resulted in the current condition of segregation forming the basis of the original complaint, but instead had taken positive steps to promote integration in its schools, it has not appealed the lower court findings for the following reasons: (1) the consistent findings of violations in the Courts below; (2) this Honorable Court's recent decision in *Keyes*; and (3) a recognition by the Detroit Board that it is a mere instrumentality of the State under Michigan law and therefore, regardless of whether violations were found to have been committed either by State officers at the State level alone, or by State officers at the local level, the result would be the same. It is incumbent upon the State of Michigan ultimately to remedy the violations.

Brief for the Respondent Board of Education for the School District of the City of Detroit, at 8–9, Milliken v. Bradley, 418 U.S. 717 (1974). Abandoning George Bushnell's original strategy as impractical, George Roumell, the new counsel for the Detroit board, made no attempt to relitigate the issues decided in San Antonio Ind. School Dist. v. Rodriguez, 411 U.S. 1 (1973). *Cf.* note 115 and accompanying text, *supra.*

253. *See* Brief of the United States of America as *Amicus Curiae,* Milliken v. Bradley, 414 U.S. 717 (1974). While the federal government had been allowed to intervene as a party in the court of appeals (*see supra* at note 201), the basis of its intervention had been the constitutional defense of a federal statute. As that issue was not before the Supreme Court the government did not have the standing of a party there.

254. *See, e.g., Symposium: Milliken v. Bradley and the Future of Urban School Desegregation,* 21 Wayne L. Rev. 751 (1975); *Symposium: The Courts, Social Science, and School Desegregation,* 39 Law and Contemp. Prob. 1, 217 (1975); Amaker, *Milliken v. Bradley: The Meaning of the Constitution in School Desegregation Cases,* 2 Hastings Const. L.Q. 349 (1975).

255. The Court relegated this aspect of its decision to a curiously mimimal affirmance in a footnote, holding "this court's Rules 23(1)(c) and 40(1)(d)(2), at a minimum, limit our review of the Detroit violation findings to 'plain error' and under our decision last term in Keyes v. School District No. 1, Denver, Colorado, 413 U.S. 139 (1973), the findings appeared to be correct." Milliken v. Bradley 418 U.S. 717, 738 n.18 (1973).

256. *Id.* at 744–45.

sistently he added, "without an interdistrict violation and interdistrict effect, there is no constitutional wrong calling for an interdistrict remedy."[257] The Court found that in this case the violations and their effects were limited to the boundaries of the Detroit district, despite the participation of the state in those violations.[258] In the last sentence of the opinion, the Court—almost mockingly— remanded the case "for further proceedings consistent with this opinion leading to prompt formulation of a decree directed to eliminating the segregation found to exist in the Detroit public schools, a remedy which has been delayed since 1970."[259]

Four members of the Court angrily dissented, largely agreeing with the court of appeals.[260] Justice Marshall branded the Court's decision "a giant step backward."[261] But the most intriguing position was taken by Justice Stewart, who joined the majority decision but filed a separate concurring opinion.[262] Unlike Chief Justice Burger, he thought the case involved only the "appropriate exercise of federal equity jurisdiction," not substantive constitutional law.[263] As there was no constitutional violation shown to affect more districts than Detroit, he felt the remedy should be limited to Detroit. But, again unlike the Chief Justice, he was willing to consider constitutional violations by officials not directly charged with operating the schools. He suggested, for example, that schools might be desegregated across district lines if state officials had used state housing or zoning laws in a "purposeful, racially discriminatory" fashion.[264] As the swing vote on a strongly divided court, his suggestion received even more attention than the usual concurrence.

PREPARATION FOR AN ORDER

The Supreme Court's decision was issued July 25, 1974, a full month after the usual end of the term. During the long wait for a decision the conviction had grown in Detroit that the Court would disapprove a metropolitan plan. Sharing

257. *Id.* at 745.

258. *Id.* at 748–52. The Court dsismissed as an "isolated instance" the most clearly interdistrict act of segregation, the busing of black suburban high school students to a black Detroit high school. *Id.* at 749–50. See text at notes 109–110, *supra.*

259. 418 U.S. at 753.

260. The dissents were by Justice Douglas, *id.* at 757; Justice White, joined by Justices Douglas, Brennan, and Marshall, *id.* at 762; and Justice Marshall, joined by Justices Douglas, Brennan, and White, *id.* at 781.

261. *Id.* at 782.

262. *Id.* at 753.

263. *Id.* By contrast the opinion of the Court argued that a multidistrict remedy premised on a single district violation could "be supported only by drastic expansion of the constitutional right itself. . . ." *Id.* at 747.

264. *Id.* at 755. *Cf.* the majority opinion, *id.* at 728 n.7, refusing to consider the proof of housing segregation as a basis for school desegregation on the grounds that although the district court had relied on the housing testimony, the court of appeals had expressly refused to. This narrow, technical ruling has been criticised in Taylor, *The Supreme Court and Urban Reality: A Tactical Analysis of Milliken v. Bradley,* 21 Wayne L. Rev. 751, 764 n.48 (1975).

that feeling, Executive Deputy Superintendent Aubrey McCutcheon began early in July planning to implement a Detroit-only desegregation decree. He drafted a plan for the creation of the Office of Effective Desegregation, for which he proposed a $135,000 budget and a staff of four. The office would report directly to the Office of the General Superintendent.[265] He scheduled two public meetings, one in August and one in September. After the decision was issued, McCutcheon carefully chose speakers to explain it and to outline the alternative ways to respond to it. Both meetings were well attended. Both were dominated by persons who opposed desegregation, but by the end of the second meeting the discussion was much less explosive and more conducive to planning. Shortly thereafter the central board of education voted to create the Detroit Office of Desegregation with a $175,000 budget.[266]

The board moved slowly in staffing the new office. It at last chose Margaret Ashworth, a professor of education at Wayne State University. Ashworth, a veteran of the black community's struggle for power in the school system, was a former teacher and administrator in the Detroit public schools.[267] Her first assignment was to conduct a final citywide desegregation meeting. In addition she inherited McCutcheon's plan for a series of seminars in January 1975 aimed at key groups: business, labor, clergy, and the media.[268] The attendance at those meetings was disappointing in the extreme. Each attracted only a handful of persons, most of whom were already unusually knowledgeable.[269] Ashworth's office there-

265. Under Detroit's decentralized system, there is a general superintendent for the entire district, while each of the eight regions has a regional superintendent. At the time the Supreme Court's decision was pending, the general superintendent worked very closely with the executive deputy superintendent. It is more accurate to say they shared authority than to say that one was the other's supervisor. This unusual arrangement was primarily a result of the personalities of the two men who held the offices at that time. General Superintendent Charles Wolfe was a quiet, soothing man who had risen through the ranks to his position. Executive Deputy Superintendent Aubrey McCutcheon was an aggressive, ambitious lawyer who had entered the school system near the top when he was hired to handle its labor relations.

272. Remarks of Aubrey V. McCutcheon, Jr., to the Consultation on Problems and Issues in School Integration/Bussing and the Role of the Churches, in New York City, Nov. 22, 1974, in Division of Education and Ministry, National Council of Churches of Christ in the U.S.A., A Tale of Seven Cities: Report of Consultation, at 9 (mimeo, 1975) [hereinafter cited as McCutcheon remarks, Tale of Seven Cities]. The name of the office was changed from Office of Effective Desegregation to Office of Desegregation because one board member disliked the term "effective desegregation." *Id.* at 10.

267. Interview with Margaret Ashworth, in Detroit, Michigan, July 29, 1975 [hereinafter cited as Ashworth interview].

268. McCutcheon originally formulated the idea of these seminars while attending a National Council of Churches consultation among persons actively involved in desegregating northern urban schools. McCutcheon remarks, Tale of Seven Cities, at 11.

269. At the first of these seminars the author upset Ashworth by bluntly warning that she should not wait for community input before drafting a plan, because the district court was likely to want a complete integration plan presented to it by mid-March or early April 1975. While the warning proved accurate, much of the board's plan was hastily written in the last two weeks before the court's April 1, 1974 deadline. The court was displeased with the quality of the work. *See* Memorandum Opinion and Remedial Decree, at 46–47, Bradley v. Milliken (E.D. Mich., Aug. 15, 1975).

after planned and conducted seminars in most of Detroit's eight regions while collecting necessary data for a comprehensive desegregation plan. For the next few months, seven-day workweeks were the norm for her and her staff.[270]

ACTION ON THE REMAND

The remand to the district court was delayed by a dispute over the payment of costs in the Supreme Court. The Supreme Court resolved the dispute by taxing the costs to the NAACP.[271] On remand then to the district court, the case was reassigned by a blind draw system on January 7, 1975, to Judge Robert DeMascio.

Judge DeMascio had been appointed to the federal bench by President Nixon upon the recommendation of Senator Robert Griffin. He had earned a "law-and-order" reputation as a judge of Detroit's Recorders Court, the local criminal court. John Conyers, one of Detroit's two black congressmen, had taken the unusual step of opposing his nomination.[272] At the time he was assigned the case, Judge DeMascio was almost totally uninformed on the law of school desegregation. As he candidly told the author, in all his years as a lawyer, state judge, and federal judge, he had never read the desegregation decisions. Assuming he would never have any litigation in that area, he had concentrated on other cases that might have some relevance to him. His one brush with school desegregation matters had been in November 1972, when he was part of a three-judge panel assigned to hear an emergency motion in the Detroit case while Judge Roth was hospitalized.[273]

A week after he was assigned to the case, Judge DeMascio ordered the attorneys to meet with each other to prepare a status report on the case.[274] After getting the status report, he directed both the Detroit board and the NAACP to present desegregation plans to the court on April 1, 1975.[275]

The Court's Experts: At the first pretrial after receiving the plans, Judge DeMascio announced that he wanted the assistance of expert advisors. After receiving suggestions from the parties, he appointed three nationally recognized

270. Ashworth interview.
271. Milliken v. Bradley, 419 U.S. 815 (1974). The Justices who had dissented in the case on the merits also dissented as to the costs.
272. Detroit Free Press, July 23, 1971, at 1B.
273. Interview with Judge Robert E. DeMascio, in Detroit, Michigan, June, 1975, [hereinafter cited as First DeMascio interview]; *see* Hearing on Emergency Motion of Board of Education to Order State of Michigan Officials To Provide Funds for 180 days of Instruction in the Detroit Public Schools, Bradley v. Milliken (E.D. Mich., Dec. 11, 1972), *motion denied*, Dec. 18, 1972.
Judge DeMascio declined to discuss the substance of the case pending before him. He was, however, most helpful in discussing matters peripheral to the suit and in furnishing the author with a copy of his Aug. 15, 1975 decision on the remedy.
274. Order, Jan. 13, 1975.
275. Order, Feb. 18, 1975.

educators to secure additional information—off the record—from the defendants and to weigh the merits of the various education components.[276] Only one of the experts, John Finger, attended hearings with any frequency. The experts did not file separate reports and were not subject to examination in the courtroom. Neither were they masters. Rather, they discussed the case with the judge in private and sometimes debated with each other the merits of various proposals. Those discussions did not always produce agreement among the experts and the judge on the relative importance of various educational components of preparatory steps, such as teacher training. The experts' written report to the court, which arrived too late for incorporation in the opinion, reflected the judge's resolution of their different views rather than the opinion of each man. The report was not distributed to the parties. Judge DeMascio believes the experts supplied him with valuable insights and saved him enormous amounts of time in digesting the board's educational proposals. However, he says he sought no advice from them on the central issue of the remedy hearings, the racial objectives to be sought in the desegregated schools. The judge relied on his own judgment there.[277]

The court also formally designated the Community Relations Service of the Justice Department to assist it. The service was to focus on the potential for violence: coordinating the efforts of the school board and police agencies and quietly encouraging opponents of desegregation to express their opposition in ways that were unlikely to lead to violence. It was also assigned to secure data for the court on student violence and vandalism in Detroit schools. The court was later to refer to the resultant data in pressing hard for a stern student conduct code.[278]

The Plans: The NAACP and the board of education submitted drastically different plans. Both parties seemed to take extreme positions on the assumption the court would strike a compromise between them.

The board's plan proposed to desegregate the eighty remaining majority-white schools, along with as many black schools as were necessary to do the job. Over a hundred black schools, 40 percent of the city's schools, were left untouched. The board utilized attendance-zone changes, new feeder patterns, noncontiguous

276. The experts were Wilbur Cohen, dean of the College of Education, University of Michigan and formerly secretary of Health, Education and Welfare; John Finger, professor of education at Rhode Island College and author of pupil assignment plans used in Charlotte, N.C. and Denver, Colo.; and Francis Keppel of the Aspen Institute in New York and former U.S. Commissioner of Education. *See* Detroit Free Press, April 16, 1975. The court wanted especially to clarify the board's proposal and to get hard cost data on it, as it believed the cost estimates in the formal plan to be inflated. *See* Memorandum Opinion and Remedial Decree, at 8-9 (Aug. 15, 1975) [hereinafter cited as Mem. Op., Aug. 15, 1975]. Had it not been for the large number of "education components" in the board's proposal, the court would have been satisfied to retain only Dr. Finger. Interview with Judge Robert E. DeMascio, in Detroit, Michigan, Sept. 3, 1975 [hereafter cited as Second DeMascio interview].

277. Second DeMascio interview.

278. *Id.*

zoning, pairing and clustering, and revised grade structures to desegregate the 60% of the district covered by its plan. The plan affected schools at every grade level. About 51,000 of the district's 257,000 pupils would have been transferred. Few of the students would be required to cross Detroit regional school boundaries. In addition to the pupil reassignments, the plan included thirteen "components" designed to improve education or to smooth the transition to a desegregated system.[279] A budget submitted with the Detroit board's plan estimated it would cost $54.9 million.[280] The board asked that the state be required to pay the cost of its plan.[281] It set the cost of buying 425 buses and operating them for a year at $11.1 million.[282]

The senior NAACP attorney scornfully referred to the "components" as "an opium dream of what they would like to have in the way of education improvements." He claimed the high figure was designed "to obscure the relatively minor costs associated with desegregation."[283] The plaintiffs' plan did not propose any of the education components suggested by the board. It reassigned about 20,000 more students than the board's plan and reached almost every school in the system. The rationale underlying it was that the entire system should be desegregated. For planning purposes, the plaintiffs' expert, Gordon Foster, defined a desegregated school as a school having the same racial composition as the district, plus or minus 15 percent. As the district was then 71.5 percent black, he tried to assure that each school was between 57.5 percent and 87.5 percent black.[284] He admittedly was unable to adhere strictly to his rationale. Under his plan, schools ranged from 41.4 percent to 89.8 percent black.[285] The plan completely ignored regional boundaries.[286]

279. Those components were entitled: In-Service Training; Guidance and Counseling; Vocational Education; Career Education; Student Rights and Responsibilities; School Community Relations; Parental Involvement; Testing; Accountability; Curriculum Design; Bilingual; Multi-Ethnic Curriculum; Co-Curricular Activities. Detroit Board of Education, Office of Desegregation, Desegregation Plan 1975/76 (April 1, 1975) [hereafter cited Detroit Board, April 1, 1975 Plan].

280. Detroit Board, April 1, 1975 Plan, at 15; *see* Detroit News, April 1, 1975 at 1A. Within a week that estimate was reduced by almost $5 million to $49,993,461. *See* Detroit Board, April 1, 1975 Plan, at 15, *as revised* April 5, 1975.

281. Detroit Board, April 1, 1975 Plan, at 13. *See* Detroit Free Press, April 2, 1975, at 1A.

282. Detroit Board, April 1, 1975 Plan, at 41–43. *See* Detroit Free Press, April 2, 1975 at 1A. Within a month a more optimistic calculation of the average number of pupils per bus reduced the estimated number of buses to 335 and the cost to $9 million. *See* Detroit Board, April 1, 1975 Plan, at 41–43, *as revised* April 25, 1975.

283. Detroit Free Press, April 2, 1975, at 10, quoting Louis Lucas.

284. *See* Mem. Op., Aug. 15, 1975, at 29–30. The plan was in fact slightly more complex, as the guideline ratios were adjusted to reflect the marginal differences in the racial composition of Detroit's elementary, junior high, and high school populations. *Id. See* Detroit Free Press, April 2, 1975, at 1A; Detroit News, May 29, 1975, at 16.

285. Revised and Supplemental Plaintiffs' Desegregation Plan for the Assignment of Pupils 1975–1976 Detroit Public Schools, at 3A, 4A, April 30, 1975 [hereinafter cited as Plaintiffs' Revised April 1975 Plan]; Mem. Op. Aug. 15, 1975, at 30. *See* Detroit Free Press, April 2, 1975 at 1A.

286. Plaintiffs' Revised April 1975 Plan; Mem. Op., Aug. 15, 1975, at 30. The plaintiffs have consistently refused to concede any legitimacy to the regional boundaries, insisting that

Judge DeMascio directed the parties to meet to identify points of agreement and to try to agree on a single plan. The effort was completely unsuccessful.[287]

In the hearings that followed, the board's attorney, George Roumell, emphasized that Detroit was "unique" in being a very large, decentralized, urban school district with a majority black school population and a majority black school board that was acting completely in good faith to comply with the law. He argued strongly that the plaintiffs' plan would not successfully desegregate the schools because it would lead to massive resegregation.[288] He also attacked the plaintiffs' plan as moving many children for marginal changes in racial composition.[289]

The plaintiffs derided the claim that Detroit was unique.[290] To them the fact that a majority of Detroit's students were black was irrelevant. If 70 percent white districts are totally desegregated, so should 70 percent black districts be. The plaintiffs maintained that there was no legal basis for leaving 40 percent of the school system solidly black. In their view the board's plan created a dual system of schools, one integrated and one strictly segregated. The plaintiff's plan, on the other hand, applied equally to all.[291]

Under either plan the court faced the issue of buying buses in time for use in September. Plaintiffs wanted them ordered at once. The Detroit board was quite

---

they were created in 1970 as part of the legislative effort to prevent the desegregation of Detroit's schools. *See* Complaint, at 8–9; Plaintiffs' Response to Submission by Detroit Board, at 12–13, Bradley v. Milliken (E.D. Mich., Apr. 21, 1975); Brief for Appellants, at 23, Bradley v. Milliken, No. 75-2018, (6th Cir., dated Dec. 22, 1975).

287. Detroit Free Press, April 14, 1975, at 1A; *id.,* April 22, 1975 at 5A.

288. Detroit News, May 2, 1975 at 5A; Detroit Board, April 1, 1975 Plan, at 2.

289. Detroit News, June 5, 1975 at 16A. For a summary of his position, *see* Defendant Detroit Board of Educ., Proposed Findings of Fact and Conclusions of Law Following Remand Hearing on Detroit-only Remedy, at 56–63 (dated June 26, 1975).

290. Plaintiffs' attorney and demographer, both of whom have worked on many cases, were monumentally unimpressed with the asserted uniqueness of Detroit. "You have no idea how many 'unique' school systerms there are in the country." Lucas interview. Lamson added:

> When we come into a city and we have local people tell us that this is different and yet in fact we can see on the face of their presentation the same sort of approach, the same sort of dynamics, and the same sort of anticipated effect that we have seen time after time, city by city, coast to coast, we cannot take them seriously. . . . They are all variations on the same theme. . . . We have been there before, starting with 5% systems, 10% systems, 25% systems, 50% systems, the whole spectrum of minority systems. We have heard the same story, the same reasons and the same excuses for non-action or mis-action on the part of local authorities.

Interview with William Lamson, demographer, in Detroit, Michigan, May 22, 1975.

291. Lucas interview; Plaintiffs' Proposed Ruling on Detroit-Only Desegregation Plans, at 3–10, 59, 68–69 (dated June 1975). Plaintiffs contended:

> [The Detroit Board's] plan is based on the premise that black children should be housed in schools which are blacker, older and more overcrowded than those schools which most white children would attend. Indeed . . . the articulated premise of the Detroit Board's Plan is that there are too many blacks for whites to stand.

Plaintiffs' Response to Detroit Board's Motion to Strike, at 2 (dated May 6, 1975).

willing, provided the state paid for them.[292] The state, predictably, was unwilling to do so. When the district court did order the state to buy 150 buses, the attorney general secured a stay from the court of appeals. After argument, the court of appeals imposed a compromise solution. It directed the state to pay 75 percent of the cost of the buses on the same formula and payment schedule applied to districts routinely receiving state transportation assistance.[293]

The Court's Order: Judge DeMascio's major decision in the case was issued on Saturday, August 16, 1975. It is difficult to say which was more remarkable, the decision or the process of releasing it. On Friday August 15 Judge DeMascio met privately with Detroit board president, C. L. Golightly, its general superintendent, Arthur Jefferson, and counsel, George Roumell. The stated purpose of the meeting was to discuss the status of labor negotiations with the teachers' union. While no one has ever publicly admitted that the meeting also covered the forthcoming remedy order, Roumell was able that evening to give a closed meeting of the board a detailed briefing on what to expect in the order. The forecast was quite accurate. A board member leaked the details to the Detroit *News,* which published them the morning of the day the court released its decision.[294] An hour before the decision was officially released, Dean Wilbur Cohen, one of the court-appointed experts, briefed the media on the guidelines the board of education would have to follow in desegregating its schools. The media were forbidden to release any information before six o'clock that evening, effectively assuring coverage on the evening news broadcasts and in the Sunday morning newspapers.[295]

292. *See* Detroit Free Press, May 14, 1975 at 9A.

293. Bradley v. Milliken, 519 F.2d 679 (6th Cir. 1975), *modifying and aff'g* Order, Bradley v. Michigan, Civ. No. 35257 (E.D. Mich., May 21, 1975). Michigan has since modified its school transportation funding statute to conform to the court order and to treat city districts the same as other districts. Mich. Pub. Acts 1975, No. 261, Sec. 71, *amending* Mich. Comp. L. Ann. 388.1171.

294. Detroit News, Aug. 16, 1975 at 1. The *News* is an evening paper except on Saturday and Sunday, when it publishes in the morning.

This meeting and others Judge DeMascio conducted with business and civic leaders before issuing his decision eventually led the NAACP to ask Judge DeMascio to excuse himself from further participation in the case. The NAACP made the motion in November 1976, after the Sixth Circuit had decided appeals from DeMascio's August 15, 1975 order. The essence of the NAACP's charge was that Judge DeMascio had shown himself to be partial to the defendants and had violated the judicial canons of ethics by meeting privately with some of the parties in the case without the knowledge or presence of the plaintiffs. Detroit Free Press, Nov. 24, 1976. Two months later Judge DeMascio issued an opinion refusing to recuse himself from *all* future participation in the case but agreeing that it might be preferable for another judge to hear future arguments dealing with teacher reassignments. The opinion conceded that he had met privately with school board and teachers union officials and had given school board attorney George Roumell a copy of the August 15, 1975 opinion a day before it was available to other parties. The opinion also admitted the meetings with business and civic leaders, but Judge DeMascio felt those meetings involved no impropriety. The NAACP promptly announced that it would appeal. Detroit Free Press, Jan. 22, 1976, at 3, col. 3.

295. Detroit News, Aug. 17, 1975, at 10C.

To the surprise of almost everyone, the court did not order any plan into effect that September or at any stated time in the future. Rather it rejected the plaintiffs' entire plan and major portions of the school board's plan. It directed the board to revise its plan in accordance with guidelines in the opinion and to file with the court a timetable for the submission of reports and detailed proposals.[296] The NAACP immediately announced that it would appeal.[297]

In Judge DeMascio's view, the contested part of the case was over, except for appeals. Hence he abandoned the usual litigation process. Between August 16 and January 26, 1976 (the date subsequently set for reassigning pupils) the court issued a steady stream of supplemental orders in response to the submissions by the board.[298] Those orders variously approved, revised, or rejected detailed plans for implementing components of the general desegregation plan. The process resembled negotiation rather than litigation. But the negotiations were between the judge and the school board; the plaintiffs were consciously excluded.[299] On some issues, particularly pupil reassignment, initial negotiations were conducted between John Finger, representing the court, and staff members of the school board. Unresolved issues were presented to the court by counsel. The board fought hard against some projects dear to the court's heart, announcing from time to time that if the court did not yield on key issues the board, like the NAACP, would appeal. As the court presumably wanted at least one party to defend its decree on appeal, the board's position was a strong one. At any rate, the negotiations led to major, albeit often unacknowledged, concessions by both the court and the board.[300]

296. Partial Judgment and Order (Aug. 15, 1975). The order was accompanied by a much more detailed Memorandum Opinion and Remedial Decree. Although physically released on Aug. 16, both documents bear the date Aug. 15, 1975.

Possibly through oversight, the court did not direct the board to prepare a revised pupil reassignment plan. It merely ordered the board to include in its proposed timetable a "date for submission of a revised student reassignment plan." Partial Judgment, at 12 (Aug. 15, 1975). If the omission was an oversight, the court corrected it shortly by directing that a revised pupil assignment plan be submitted on Sept. 19, 1975. Order (Aug. 27, 1975).

297. Plaintiff's Notice of Appeal (filed Aug. 28, 1975). *See* The [Detroit] Sunday News Aug. 17, 1975, at 10C.

298. *See* Memorandum and Order, at 1–2 (Oct. 31, 1975). The district court, in a supplemental order issued while the case was awaiting argument before the court of appeals, amplified its reason for excluding the plaintiffs:

> While the revised plans were under consideration, the plaintiffs requested a hearing to document their objections. However, it was our view, that a hearing would not be appropriate. The adversarial phase of this litigation ended with the August 15, 1975 partial judgment; the issue of the conformance of the revised plan with our guidelines was an issue solely between the defendant Detroit Board and the court. Thus, our failure to include plaintiffs in the process of shaping the details of the transportation plan was not motivated by indifference to their views, but rather reflected the fact that the adversarial phase of this litigation had ended. Plaintiffs' review of the validity of the guidelines was on appeal.

Memorandum, Order and Judgment (May 11, 1976).

299. *Id.*

300. Two of the judge's primary goals were the immediate funding of a major vocational education program and a stricter student discipline code. See text accompanying notes 388–404, *infra.*

The plan hammered out by the court is openly solicitous of the fears of Detroit's remaining white population and tries to minimize occasions for white concern.[301] It requires much less actual desegregation than even the defendants thought was legally required.[302] It puts the burden of that desegregation mainly on the black children. It creates a uniform, strict student conduct code and a uniform grade structure throughout the district. It holds out a judicial promise of quality education. As Detroit is broke, the value of that promise is no greater than the court's willingness or power to order the state to pay for the "quality" features in the order.

The Rationale: In framing the decision, Judge DeMascio faced a basic problem. Like Judge Roth before him[303] he was convinced that "the Detroit Public Schools could not be adequately desegregated within the corporate limits of the city."[304] Furthermore, he believed the Supreme Court's decision in the case had not disturbed Roth's finding on that point.[305] Yet he no longer had available the choice Roth had made, to seek desegregation on a wider scale.[306] He chose then to reduce the numbers of pupils desegregated in hope of making desegregation work for some rather than fail for all. The tone of his opinion, however, suggests great sensitivity to many socially acceptable white objections to urban desegregation.[307]

The court's legal rationale was based on the premise that the Supreme Court had "left this court to determine what constitutes desegregation in this particular school district."[308] Believing there were no other guidelines for desegregating

301. *See* note 364, *infra.*
302. *Compare* McCutcheon interview.
303. *See* Findings of Fact and Conclusions of Law on Detroit-Only Plans of Desegregation, Bradley v. Milliken (E.D. Mich., Mar. 28, 1972). Judge Roth had ruled: "The conclusion . . . is inescapable that relief of desegregation in the public schools of the City of Detroit cannot be accomplished within the corporate geographical limits of the City." *Id.* at 5.
304. Mem. Op., Aug. 15, 1975, at 8.
305. *Id. But cf.* Milliken v. Bradley, 418 U.S. 717, 738–741, 747 n.22 (1974).
306. The issue of a metropolitan remedy based on evidence conforming to the requirements in the Supreme Court's opinion in this case still waits to be tried. *See* Memorandum and Order (Dec. 19, 1975).
307.

[R]igid and inflexible desegregation plans too often neglect to treat school children as individuals, instead treating them as pigmented pawns to be shuffled about and counted solely to achieve an abstraction called 'racial mix.' . . . We are aware of the adverse educational and psychological impact upon black children compelled to attend segregated schools . . . but . . . the remedy devised should not inflict sacrifices or penalties upon other innocent children as punishment for the constitutional violations exposed.

Mem. Op., Aug. 15, 1975, at 2.
Referring to the usual techniques of desegregation, the opinion objected that: "All of these techniques require children to spend more time going to school and divert educational dollars and energy from *legitimate* educational concerns." *Id.* at 3 [emphasis added].
The decision repeatedly used segregationist catch phrases such as "massive busing" (*id.* at 3, 58) and "forced reassignments" (*id.* at 4) to refer to transportation for the purpose of desegregation. It worried that the cost of buses "would financially cripple the Detroit School System" and that the system "does not presently possess the expertise to manage,

majority black urban districts, he announced his own guidelines, in part to force appellate courts to address the problem more specifically.[309] He rejected the plaintiffs' concept of desegregation based on the elimination of all racially identifiable schools, regardless of whether the system is majority black or majority white.[310] Instead he believed desegregation only required that blacks be represented in significant numbers in every school in the district, as evidence they were no longer excluded.[311] It was not necessary, he believed, for whites to be as widely distributed. The presence of a relatively small number of whites in the same school would be of no educational benefit to the blacks. Indeed the court felt white children would not even be necessary to the perception of black children that they were part of a desegregated school system. "Equal facilities, integrated faculties and meaningful guarantees that every student is welcome in any school" were, in Judge DeMascio's view, sufficient indicia of a desegregated system.[312] He cited no authority.

In deciding what constituted desegregation in Detroit, Judge DeMascio felt he should pay particular attention to the "practicalities of the situation."[313]

route, maintain and store such a large fleet of buses." *Id.* at 64. It feared that the "establishment of such a vast transportation network would bring chaos and financial destruction to the school system. . . ." *Id.* at 65.

Ignoring the strong proof of deliberate housing segregation in the city, it suggested that "the shifting demography [*sic*] occurring *naturally* in the school district" was a factor limiting the amount of school desegregation the court should order. *Id.* at 4 [emphasis added].

For other indications that Judge DeMascio had an affinity for the views of white opponents of desegregation, see text at notes 311–19, 324, 364, 367.

308. Mem. Op., Aug. 15, 1975, at 2.

309. Second Demascio interview.

310. Partial Judgment and Order, at 1 (Aug. 15, 1975); Mem. Op., Aug. 15, 1975, at 29–39, 60–65. In rejecting the plaintiffs' plan, the court commented: "The basic fallacy underlying Plaintiffs' contentions . . . lies in their definition of a desegregated school." Mem. Op., Aug. 15, 1975, at 61.

311.
. . . [B]ecause Plaintiffs' represent a class of blacks and not a class of whites, desegregation requires only that Plaintiffs themselves be represented in significant proportions through the school district through the elimination of identifiably white schools. . . .
". . . However, when blacks are represented in all schools throughout the system, i.e., when white identifiable schools are eliminated, . . . [the psychological impact of segregation on black children] no longer exists. There is no longer a denial of their right to equal protection when there are no schools from which they are excluded.
Mem. Op., Aug. 15, 1975, at 83.
Cf. Briggs v. Elliott, 132 F. Supp. 776 (E.D.S.C. 1955). *But cf.* Green v. New Kent County School Bd., 391 U.S. 430 (1968); Swann v. Charlotte-Mecklenburg Bd. of Educ., 402 U.S. 1 (1971); Davis v. Board of School Comm'rs of Mobile County, 302 U.S. 23 (1971).
Judge DeMascio was wrong in saying the plaintiffs represented only blacks. Not only was one of the *named* plaintiffs white, Judge Roth had certified the plaintiff class as "all school children of the City of Detroit and all Detroit resident parents who have children of school age." See text *supra* at note 97.

312. Mem. Op., Aug. 15, 1975, at 79.

313. *Id.,* at 4, 84, *citing* Davis v. School Comm'rs of Mobile County, 402 U.S. 33, 37 (1971).

Among those practicalities he included a concern to avoid harming the educational system by causing it either financial hardship or administrative disorder.[314] He also took into account his perception that the black-dominated board and its biracial staff were unlikely to repeat the discriminatory practices of the past.[315] While conceding that it is impermissible to take threatened "white flight" into account in designing a remedy,[316] he believed he had to avoid resegregation "at all costs."[317] He thought a "self defeating exodus of the middle class white and black" would result if the school system became, "as a result of desegregation orders, . . . chaotic and hostile to intellectual achievement" and "incapable of delivering basic educational services."[318] Other "practicalities" mentioned in the opinion were "the undesirability of forced reassignment" when it would achieve "only negligible desegregative results"; "the persistent increase in black student enrollment"; the fact that a majority of the population in the district is now black; the declining tax base of the city and school district; "the volatile atmosphere" created by high unemployment; and the "overriding community concern for the quality of educational services."[319]

Criticism of Plans Submitted: In rejecting the plaintiffs' plan, the court criticized the techniques it used,[320] but elsewhere conceded it used the same methods as the board's plan.[321] It was clearly the rationale and scope of the plaintiffs' plan that caused the court to reject it. In a nutshell, the court was of the opinion that the type of thorough desegregation plan appropriate for a majority white district was inappropriate for a majority black district.[322] It absolutely rejected the plaintiff's target of 56.5-86.5 percent black in every school.[323] The court was especially critical of busing black children into schools

314. Mem. Op., Aug. 15, 1975, at 65.
315. *Id.* at 65–66.
316. *Id.* at 76.
317. *Id.* at 4, 65.
318. *Id.* at 78.
319. *Id.* at 4–5.
320. *Id.* at 29–39.
321. *Id.* at 58.
322.

If the white population were predominant, Plaintiffs' plan could achieve desegregation. Under the practicalities at hand, however, Plaintiffs' plan is unsatisfactory because it does not distinguish between busing black students to majority black schools and majority white schools.

Id. at 63–64.
323.

Plaintiffs contend that there is only one constitution equally applicable to all school districts. Thus, they argue that since we would not hesitate to apply their parameters to a 72.5% [*sic*] white school district, we should equally apply them to a 72.5% [*sic*] black school district. We think such an argument in the context of this school district is superficial. The argument ignores the fact that the "practicalities of the situation," which the Constitution requires that we take into account, would be different if the school district were 72.5% [*sic*] white.

Id. at 81.

that, while whiter than the district as a whole, were already more than 50 percent black.[324] The plaintiffs' plan, the court felt, would almost guarantee resegregation.[325]

The court was more favorably impressed by the board's objectives, but rejected major parts of its detailed plan.[326] The court heartily endorsed the board's proposal to improve the educational process, although it suspected the board's cost estimates were unreliable.[327] The court was much less satisfied with the desegregation aspect of the board's proposal. It insisted upon a major *reduction* in the number of pupils and school buildings desegregated. It initially ruled it had no legal justification for integrating faculties as requested by the board. Two weeks later, acting on its own motion, it reversed itself and ordered faculties reorganized to assure that no more than 70 percent of the teachers in a building were of the same race.[328]

Pupil Reassignment: The board's stated goal was "maximum effective desegregation," a concept designed to reduce the chances of resegregation by ordering no more integration than the white population would endure.[329] The court, however, thought the board's pupil assignment plan was too demanding and imposed too great a burden on the children and the school system. The court also felt the board's plan adhered too rigidly to the goal of 40-60 percent black pupils in each school affected by reassignments. As a result, the court held the plan in that respect "not only undesirable but constitutionally infirm."[330] A school should be considered already desegregated, the court held, if between 30 and 50 percent of the students drawn from the neighborhood were black. In such cases no changes in assignments were necessary.[331]

In desegregating other schools, the court had no objection to the board's using a 50-50 racial mix as a starting point.[332] But here, too, the court believed the board had been too vigorous, too intent on racial results. The board should

324. *Id.* at 63–65, 81.
325. *Id.* at 65.
326. Partial Judgment and Order, at 1 (Aug. 15, 1975); Mem. Op., Aug. 15, 1975, at 47–48, 67–69, 83.
327. Mem. Op., Aug. 15, 1975, at 46–48, 67, 73.
328. *See* text at notes 367–78, *infra.*
329. For succinct descriptions of the pupil reassignment portion, *see* Detroit Board's April 1, 1975 Plan, at 3–6, and Appendix A; Mich. State Board of Education, A Critique of the Desegregation Plan Filed by the Detroit Board of Education, at 5–11, Bradley v. Milliken (E.D. Mich., April 21, 1975); Mem. Op., Aug. 15, 1975, at 39–45.
330. Mem. Op., Aug. 15, 1975, at 68. *But cf.* McDaniel v. Barressi, 402 U.S. 39 (1971); Swann v. Charlotte-Mecklenburg Bd. of Educ., 402 U.S. 1, 16 (1971).
331. Mem. Op., Aug. 15, 1975, at 91. The board's plan had treated as a racially identifiable white school any school in which the white enrollment exceeded 50 percent. The Detroit board had not defined the term in its plan, but upon inquiry gave that definition to the state board. *See* Mich. St. Bd. of Educ., A Critique of the Desegregation Plan Filed by the Detroit Bd. of Educ., at 7 n.2, Bradley v. Milliken (E.D. Mich., April 12, 1975).
332. Mem. Op., Aug. 15, 1975, at 85. *Cf. id.* at 68, noting that the board's 40 to 60 percent range was "in reality 50%–50% plus or minus 10%."

have been less ready to bus children. Instead it should have given more careful attention to other techniques. Devices the court instructed the board to investigate more thoroughly included re-zoning (across regional lines if necessary),[333] satellite zones,[334] and one-way busing.[335]

Transportation for the purpose of racial desegregation was obviously distasteful to Judge DeMascio. More than once he referred to it as an "extraordinary remedy."[336] Nevertheless, after exhausting all other possibilities, the board was permitted to transport children.[337] The distance of travel was in all cases to be minimized.[338] The court directed the board to avoid busing any child more than five of his first eight years in school. Any unavoidable exceptions were to be reported to the court.[339] With that end in view, he ordered that children in paired schools be "rotated" every year or half year.[340] The board was permitted to rotate the teachers or not, as it wished.[341]

The board submitted a revised plan to the court on September 19. The court returned it for modifications, mainly further reductions in the number of

333. *Id.* at 69, 88, 91. The court openly suspected the Detroit Central Board of succumbing to regional politics in minimizing reassignments across regional boundaries. *Id.* at 69, 72. That suspicion set off a lengthy discourse on the shortcomings of decentralization. It ended in a suggestion that the legislature reexamine the actual results of decentralization. *Id.* at 69–72. The plan ordered implemented by the court is not noticably less respectful of regional boundaries than the plan it criticized. *See* Detroit Board of Education, The Detroit Public Schools Report to the Hon. Robert E. DeMascio, U.S. District Court, Eastern District of Michigan, Southern District in Response to Court Order Dated November 4, 1975, Bradley v. Milliken (E.D. Mich., Dec. 19, 1975), Appendix as revised Jan. 24, 1976 [hereafter cited as Detroit Board, January 1976 Plan]. Nevertheless the court renewed its criticism of decentralization in another lengthy opinion the following spring. Memorandum, Order and Judgment, at 9–14 (May 11, 1976).

334. Mem. Op., Aug. 15, 1975, at 91. The court expressed concern that satellite zones be designed so as not to disturb "housing stability." *Id.* at 91, 92, 94. In establishing satellite zones the court directed that "there should not be great variation in the transportation burden on adjacent areas because such variations will influence residential patterns." *Id.* at 92. After the board submitted revised plans, the court took no testimony about their probable impact on housing patterns.

335. *Id.* at 69. It is difficult to reconcile the court's suggestion of heavier use of one-way busing with its professed concern for the cost of the plan. Two-way busing between paired schools is generally more efficient and more economical than one-way busing from satellite areas to schools. The fact that the plan ultimately implemented by the court used one-way busing primarily to take black pupils to formerly white schools suggests that the court's emphasis on one-way busing was designed to minimize hardships of white pupils rather than to minimize costs. *See* text at notes 359–60, *infra.*

336. *Id.* at 65, 75, 85.

337. *Id.* at 69, 88, 92.

338. *Id.* at 88–90, 97.

339. *Id.* at 94. This permitted busing a child one way throughout elementary school. As finally developed, all one-way busing of elementary pupils is from black schools to white ones. *See* below at notes 359–60.

340. *Id.* at 92, 97. The board of education has not yet devised a rotation plan for paired schools. The court order does not contemplate a rotation system for children bused one way even where only part of the sending school is involved in the busing program. Such rotation would obviously be destructive of any social benefits to be derived from desegregation as lasting friendships between children would not be possible.

341. *Id.* at 93. The board has given no sign that it might attempt to do so.

schools affected. The court at that time directed the board to have its staff work with Finger, the court's expert, to revise the plan.[342] When the board submitted its third plan, the court refused to conduct a hearing on plaintiffs' objections[343] and approved it, but only after making substantial alterations. The court ordered the plan, thus amended, into effect.[344]

The court's desegregation plan reassigned 27,524 students for desegregative purposes; 21,853 of them required transportation to their new school. Those reassigned constituted 11 percent of the total pupil population of 249,596; those bused, less than 9 percent. In a major revision of the grade structure that accompanied desegregation, 25,389 additional students changed schools without significant impact on racial distributions.[345] The court's plan thus moved slightly more students than the Detroit board's April 19, 1975 plan, but achieved about half as much desegregation.

Eighty percent of Detroit's black students are omitted from the plan.[346] At the outset the court excluded virtually all of the three blackest administrative regions, containing 42 percent of the district's black students.[347] One hundred forty-nine of the city's 280 geographically zoned schools were 90 percent or

342. Memorandum and Order (Oct. 8, 1975). This directive was a restatement of a suggestion the court had made earlier. *See* Partial Judgment and Order, at 1 (Aug. 15, 1975).

343. Memorandum and Order (Oct. 31, 1975).

344. Memorandum and Order (Nov. 4, 1975).

345. Detroit Free Press, Jan. 24, 1976, at 3A, col. 2. As of September 1975 the pupil population of the district was 75.2 percent black, 22.8 percent white, and 2.0 percent other minorities. 1975 Fourth Friday Count, *supra* note 12, at 1. The data used by the parties and the court in the summer of 1975 were based on 1974 statistics, which indicated that the district was 71.5 percent black, 26.4 percent white, and 2.1 percent other minorities. *See id.*

346. Detroit Free Press, February 1, 1976 at 1A, col. 1, 2.

347. Mem. Op., Aug. 15, 1975, at 73-75.

348. *See* Detroit Free Press, Feb. 1, 1976, at 1A, col. 1, and at 9A, col. 4; Detroit Board, January 1976 Plan.

The conversion of the black St. Clair Elementary School into an all-black middle school was one of the most unfortunate aspects of the court's order. The court divided the St. Clair School's 675 first through fifth graders among three previously white elementary schools. The building thus emptied was then converted into a middle school for students transferred from all-black Joy Junior High School. As Joy was to become a desegregated—but majority white—middle school, some of its black pupils had to be moved out to make room for the incoming whites. Joy is one of the newest, best-equipped junior high schools in the city. It has fully equipped industrial arts shops, home economics kitchens, sewing and typing rooms, and a swimming pool. The St. Clair School had none of those advantages. Joy also had an excellent full-sized gym with showers and locker rooms for both boys and girls. The St. Clair gymnasium is a tile-floored lunchroom with no showers or lockers. The library at Joy as 12,000 books suited for middle school youngsters; the St. Clair library as 2,200 elementary school books. *See* Detroit Free Press, Feb. 1, 1976, at 1A, col. 1, and at 9A, col. 4. Despite the fact that almost all the burdens of the change were imposed on the blacks, some of whom remained totally segregated, while the whites were moved to an outstanding building, the Joy Middle School has lost more white students than any other middle school in the district. *See* Detroit Free Press, Mar. 12, 1976, at 6A, col. 1. *Compare* note 364, *infra.*

347. *See* Plaintiff's [*sic*] Response to Submission by Detroit Board, at 10, Bradley v. Milliken (E.D. Mich., April 21, 1975), referring to the smaller number of black schools left under the board's plan.

more black in 1974. Only 12 of those 149 schools are desegregated by the plan. Five others are affected but not desegregated. One of the five was closed and its pupils bused to the only two Latino-majority schools in Detroit. Three sent some of their pupils to schools in white neighborhoods, but receive no white pupils in return. They therefore remain all-black schools with reduced enrollments. The fifth school buses all its elementary pupils to formerly white schools and has been converted into an all-black middle school.[348] The NAACP has referred to the excluded heavily black schools as "warehouses" from which black children are shipped when needed in white schools.[349]

Sixty-two white majority schools increased their black enrollment. Fifty of the sixty-two maintained white majorities; twenty did not attain the board's stated goal of at least 40 percent black pupils. In Regions Four and Seven, where white opposition was strongest, no formerly white school has a black majority. Neither of the predominantly white high schools in those two regions attained a 40 percent black population. By contrast only two of the newly integrated black schools failed to meet the goal of at least 40 percent white. A third of them became majority white.[350]

In revising the board's elementary school proposals the court ordered that two white schools be excluded even though their black population was below 30 percent. A black school was necessarily eliminated from the plan at the same time. The court's rationale was that the presence in the two white schools of a large number of Chaldeans, Middle Eastern immigrants, raised the "minority" population of the schools over 30 percent.[351] The validity of that rationale

---

350. *See* Detroit Board, January 1976 Plan.

The method of counting schools used herein is based in large part on the calculations of Detroit *Free Press* reporter William Grant, a copy of which is in the files of the author. No single system of counting schools is agreed upon within the school system. An assortment of annexes, small satellite schools with assistant principals, and consolidated elementary/ junior high, or junior high/senior high schools causes the definition of a school to change with the purpose of the enumerator.

The Detroit board represented to the district court in the summer of 1975 that, as of the preceding September, "there were 326 schools . . . of which 22 were high schools, 55 junior high schools, 226 elementary schools and the remaining 24 specialized and primary schools." Defendant Detroit Board of Education, Proposed Findings of Fact and Conclusions of Law Following Remand Hearing of Detroit-Only Remedy, at 15, Bradley v. Milliken (E.D. Mich., June 26, 1975), *citing* documents introduced in evidence. By subtracting from the Board's total of 326 the 24 specialized and primary schools, the 8 magnet middle schools (counted as elementary schools by the board), and the 1 citywide high school, there is still a difference of 13 schools between reporter Grant's count and the one submitted to the court.

351. The court ruled:

The Detroit Board is directed to re-evaluate the assignments at Grayling and Greenfield Union. These reassignments appear to be inconsistent with the court's directive that integrated neighborhoods not be disturbed. . . . Grayling and Greenfield Union are 28% and 25% black respectively and contain a significant number of other minorities as well. The presence of other minorities in significant numbers is a permissible practicality to be taken into account when deciding whether a school board should be included in a reassignment plan.

Memorandum and Order, at 4–5 (Oct. 8, 1975).

is suspect in light of the contrasting treatment of schools with large Latino populations.

The Latino minority, unlike the Chaldeans, have been treated by the courts as an educationally distinctive minority group.[352] Late in the remedy hearings before Judge DeMascio, a group of Latinos had sought to intervene to protect their interest in bilingual-bicultural education. They had no objection to desegregation but wanted their children to be concentrated in a few integrated schools with bilingual programs. Judge DeMascio had angrily refused to permit the intervention, both because it was late and because a language minority had no interest to defend in a desegregation case.[353] In contrast with the Chaldeans, the Latinos received no special consideration in the pupil assignment portion of the final plan. The two majority Latino elementary schools, the only two schools with bilingual programs, received a large number of black children. One became a majority black school with less than two dozen non-Spanish-surnamed white children in attendance. Eleven other elementary schools had been more than 10 percent Latino before the court order; in six of them, the combined Latino and black populations had equaled or exceeded 30 percent. All eleven were desegregated by the court's order. In at least seven of these schools, 50 percent or more of the student population appears to be Latino or black.[354]

While the school board had been trying to scale down its desegregation plan to meet the court's guidelines, anti-busing parents from the two schools had disrupted a school board meeting and had maintained a noisy picket line around the board's headquarters.[355] The lesson appeared to be that to have the federal court consider a group's concerns, one avoids litigation in favor of disruption; Latino leaders in Detroit are painfully conscious of that lesson.

The great puzzle of the court's plan is the requirement that all schools be reorganized as K-5, 6-8, or 9-12 schools, except where a deviation is specially justified. Unlike the desegregation plan, the grade reorganization affects almost

---

The NAACP's appeal briefly mistakenly assumed that the "other minorities," were Latinos. *See* Plaintiffs' Brief, at 11, Bradley v. Milliken, No. 75-2018 (6th Cir., filed Dec. 22, 1975). That error was corrected, but not acknowledged, in a later submission to the court of appeals. *See* Plaintiffs' Motion to Supplement the Record on Appeal, at 5 n.4, Bradley v. Milliken, No. 75-2018 (6th Cir., filed June 1976.)

352. *See* Keyes v. School Dist. No. 1, Denver, Colo., 413 U.S. 189, 197–98 (1973); U.S. Texas Educ. Agency, 467 F.2d 848 (5th Cir. 1972) (*en banc*); Cisneros v. Corpus Christi Indep. School Dist., 467 F.2d 142 (5th Cir. 1972) (*en banc*); *cf.* Serna v. Portales Municipal Schools, 351 F. Supp. 1279 (D.N.M. 1972).

353. The decision was announced orally but no written order was issued and counsel for the Latinos did not press the issue further. As to the interest of Latinos in school desegregation, *contrast* Keyes v. School Dist. No. 1 Denver, 413 U.S. 189 (1973); Cisneros v. Corpus Christi Ind. School Dist., 467 F.2d 145 (5th Cir. 1972); United States v. Texas, 467 F.2d 848 (5th Cir. 1972).

354. Derived from 1975 Fourth Friday Count, *supra* note 12, at 26–80; Detroit Board, January 1976 Plan. As the January 1976 Plan reports all minorities except blacks as if they were white, it is impossible to know exactly how many Latinos are in each desegregated school.

355. *See* Detroit News, Aug. 27, 1975.

every school in the system. Although the court referred to the new system as "traditional," the Detroit system had in fact been based on a K–6, 7–9, 10–12 structure, somewhat obscured by numerous exceptions.[356] No party had proposed such a reorganization. Under questioning by the court, no education expert would recommend it. The change eliminated a major desegregation device as it precluded the pairing and clustering technique used by both plaintiffs and the board in their desegregation plans, plans the court found too drastic.[357] In fact the court's stated rationale was not a desegregative one but, despite the contrary testimony of experts, an educational one: "Irregular grade structures hamper school curriculum offerings."[358]

Unconvinced by the public rationale, those close to the case have sought others. Some suggest privately that the bewildering variety of schools offended the judge's sense of order. The plaintiffs in their emergency appeal suggest a less happy theory: that the reorganization is a device to minimize the busing of white elementary pupils. By removing all sixth graders from elementary schools, many formerly white majority elementary schools can attain the 40 percent black minimum by one-way busing of black pupils.[359] That allegation, made before the details of the court's plan were worked out, is now bolstered by the statistics. Of 13,939 elementary pupils bused, 5,441 are bused "one way," that is, not in exchange for pupils from the other school. Even though black schools have many more vacant seats than white schools, *all* the one-way busing is from black schools to white schools.[360] Unless they lost their sixth graders or bused some white pupils out to formerly black elementary schools ("two-way busing"), the

356. Mem. Op., Aug. 15, 1975, at 67, 97. *See* Defendant Detroit Board of Education, Proposed Findings of Fact and Conclusions of Law Following Remand Hearings on Detroit-Only Remedy, at 15, Bradley v. Milliken, (E.D. Mich., June 26, 1975), *citing* documents introduced in evidence. Judge Roth had found that in Detroit one of the techniques of segregation was manipulation of grade structures. Bradley v. Milliken, 338 F. Supp. 582, 588 (E.D. Mich. 1971). The Detroit board was in fact employing some 29 different grade structures at the time Judge DeMascio conducted the remedy hearings. Interview with Freeman Flynn, Divisional Director, School Community Relations, Detroit Public Schools, in Detroit, Michigan on January 9, 1976. The most common grade combinations in buildings were K–6, 7–9, 10–12. The court seemed to acknowledge that it was ordering a substantial change in existing grade structures when it noted that a K–5 system would create excess capacity in the elementary schools. Mem. Op., Aug. 15, 1975, at 92, 97.

357. *Cf.* Dimond, *School Segregation in the North: There Is But One Constitution*, 7 Harv. Civ. R. Civ. Lib. L. Rev. 1, 26–27 (1972); Foster, *Desegregating Urban Schools: A Review of Techniques*, 43 Harv. Educ. Rev. 5, 18–19 (1973).

358. Mem. Op., Aug. 15, 1975, at 67. Witnesses for both the Detroit board and the plaintiffs had testified, without contradiction that varying grade structures have no adverse educational effect on the children. See Record, vol. 9 at 15 (Margaret Ashworth, Director, Office of Desegregation, Detroit Public Schools); vol. 17 at 38 (Gordon Foster, plaintiffs' expert), Bradley v. Milliken, Remand Hearing on Detroit-Only Remedy, Civ. No. 35257 (E.D. Mich.).

359. Brief for Appellant, at 11 n.7, Bradley v. Milliken, No. 75-2018 (6th Cir., filed Dec. 22, 1975).

360. Statistics derived from Detroit Board, January 1976 Plan. Not quite all of the students bused one way are black; 199 are whites bused along with their more numerous black neighbors.

elementary schools receiving those black pupils would not have the physical capacity to accept the transferees, to say nothing of the black sixth graders they would also need.

Except for minor changes in feeder patterns, the order ignores high schools, the level at which the desegregation battle had started almost six years earlier. At one point, however, the court actually planned to reduce the number of black high school students in biracial schools. In amending the board's third draft plan in November 1975, the court proposed to reassign some of the black pupils at two biracial high schools to totally black high schools. The court's purpose was to reduce the black population in the two integrated schools from 89 percent and 61 percent to less than 55 percent without reassigning additional whites to them. The school board threatened to appeal and submitted its final plan to the court on the assumption that the court would back down. Two weeks before the pupil reassignments were to take effect, the court yielded to the board's judgment, noting that while it still believed its approach would promote racial stability, it recognized it conflicted with the court's August 15, 1975, guideline prohibiting the transfer of blacks to predominantly black schools.[361]

The magnet middle schools, first established in 1972 as an alternative to more extensive desegregation, remain in existence. The plaintiffs have consistently attacked the magnet middle schools as "islands of privilege" that allow whites to escape from blacker, less well-funded schools.[362] The court's only concession to that criticism was to change the racial objectives for these schools from half black and half white to between 55 and 70 percent black.[363]

361. *See* Memorandum and Order, at 36–37, 42–44, 48–49 (November 4, 1975); Order (Jan. 14, 1976); Detroit Board, January 1976 Plan, at 1. *See also* Detroit Free Press, January 15, 1976, at 1A, col. 2. One of the high school changes that the court proposed but later abandoned would have reassigned students from Pershing High School in Region 6 to Northern High School in Region 1. To reach their proposed new assignments the students would have to go through either the Highland Park or the Hamtramck School District. Both of those school districts are independent enclaves totally surrounded by Detroit. The court's other proposed high school change would have sent black students from Finney High School in Region 7 to Southwestern High School in Region 8. The school board successfully proposed a more integrative alternative which would take black students from Finney and assign them to Denby High School which, like Finney, is in Region 7. The school board's approach changed the black percentage at Denby from 19.6 percent to 33. Both the school board's method and the judge's reduced the black population at Finney to 55 percent.

362. *See, e.g.,* Plaintiff's Proposed Ruling on Detroit-Only Desegregation Plans at 16, Bradley v. Milliken (E.D. Mich. 1975), attributing the expression to Detroit Board of Education President C.L. Golightly; Plaintiffs' Response to Submission by Detroit Board, at 74, Bradley v. Milliken (E.D. Mich., Apr. 21, 1975).

363. Mem. Op., Aug. 15, 1975, at 93–94. Compliance with the previously established judicial guidelines for the racial composition of middle schools had been uneven. In September 1975 the Region 6 middle school was 23 percent black, although two-thirds of the pupils in the region are black. By contrast, the middle schools in Regions 5 and 3 are 90 percent and 93 percent black, respectively. Region 1, recognizing its shortage of whites, let the black enrollment in its magnet school rise to 66.7 percent rather than have spaces go unused. The other four regions' middle schools ranged from 51 to 58 percent black. Data derived from 1975 Fourth Friday Count, *supra* note 12.

Judge DeMascio has assured the white population that the plan takes their concerns into account.[364] Anti-busing activists did not believe these assurances,[365] but the more sophisticated white leadership clearly did.[366] How well he protected whites is only suggested by the retention of majority white schools, by the small number of pupils bused, and by the number of blacks left in overwhelmingly black schools. The workings of the plan cause blacks to bear a vastly disproportionate share of the inconvenience associated with it. Furthermore, the court rewrote the school board's third and final draft plan to appease the noisiest white protesters.

Faculty Reassignment: The court's position toward faculty desegregation was inconsistent. In the end the plaintiffs, the Detroit board, and the Detroit Federation of Teachers all appealed the faculty reassignment aspect of the case.[367]

The Detroit board had proposed to reassign teachers throughout the district, seeking approximately a 50–50 black-white balance in each school. The board's faculty reassignment proposal, unlike its pupil plan, applied to all the schools. Its purpose was explicitly to help the board qualify for federal assistance by elimi-

364. In its order modifying and accepting the school board's third draft of a pupil assignment plan, the court emphasized its concern:

> We are fully aware of the community concern for the hardships involved in forced reassignments, particularly through the use of school bussing. This awareness influenced the court to scrutinize every school involved in the plan carefully to ascertain that the desegregative results achieved warranted the burdens imposed. . . .
>
> While some members of the community may be displeased over some of the reassignments the court has deemed essential, it is our hope that their burden will be made easier to bear by the knowledge that the court has given full consideration to every reassignment and has permitted the reassignment of students only where it has concluded that the desegregative results achieved justify the burdens imposed. Moreover, Detroit citizens can be further assured that the court has taken steps to improve the quality of education and has not permitted transfers where the receiving school is not comparable in all respects to the sending school.

Memorandum and Order, at 6–8 (Nov. 4, 1975).

365. See Detroit Free Press, Jan. 25, 1976; ("Busing Opponents Stage Mock Funeral"); *id.,* Jan. 26, 1976, at 1.

366. *See, e.g.,* editorial, Detroit Free Press, Aug. 18, 1976, at 8A, col. 1; editorial, Detroit News, Aug. 19, 1975, at 6B ("the first real opportunity for a reasonable settlement"; "a victory for good sense in a wasteland of nonsense about school desegregation"). Richard Gerstenberg, chairman of the Board of New Detroit, Inc., and immediate past chairman of the General Motors board, called the decision "a practical framework for bringing about school desegregation reasonably and peacefully." Michigan Chronicle, Aug. 23, 1975.

School Board President C.L. Golightly was a good deal blunter in speaking to newspeople who came to Detroit for the first day of desegregation. He was quoted as saying: "[T]he whole plan is minimal tokenism," and that Judge DeMascio "has done all he can to protect the white community." Detroit Free Press, January 27, 1976, at 6A, col. 3.

367. *See* Brief for Appellants, at 27, Bradley v. Milliken, No. 75-2018 (6th Cir., dated Dec. 22, 1975); Brief for Appellee Detroit Board of Education, at 7, 87–90, Bradley v. Milliken, No. 75-2018 (6th Cir., dated Jan. 29, 1976); Brief for Appellee Detroit Federation of Teachers, Bradley v. Milliken, No. 75-2018 (6th Cir., dated Jan. 27, 1976).

nating faculty imbalance, although the board also asserted it would be helpful in desegregating pupils.[368] In the remedy hearings the teachers' union opposed involuntary reassignments and successfully objected to the introduction of any evidence pertaining to faculty desegregation. It based its opposition primarily on Judge Roth's affirmative finding that there was no faculty segregation.[369]

When the court issued its August 15 decision, it appeared the union had won a clear victory. The court, referring to the board's proposal to balance all faculties racially, said:

> This approach is overly simplistic. It fails to take account of the qualifications of a teacher to teach the subject and grade level, the necessity of balancing schools with respect to teacher experience, and the necessity of considering the sex of the teacher, all of which are necessary ingredients for quality desegregated education. To seek a racial mix, without more, is undesirable and arbitrary.[370]

368. Detroit Board, April 1, 1975 Plan, at 192–94. The latest statistics available during the remedy hearing indicated that 49.5 percent of the teachers in Detroit were black. Mem. Op., Aug. 15, 1975, at 116. In the fall of 1975, the black percentage rose to 50.9 percent. 1975 Fourth Friday Count, *supra* note 12, at 2.

The plaintiff's desegregation plan had ignored teachers to concentrate solely on pupil reassignment. Revised and Supplemental plaintiff's [*sic*] Desegregation Plan for the Assignment of Pupils 1975–76 Detroit Public Schools, Bradley v. Milliken (E.D. Mich., Apr. 30, 1975). *See* Mem. Op., Aug. 15, 1975, at 56. In their April 1975 response to the Detroit board's faculty reassignment proposal the plaintiffs took a cautious position. They asserted that the board had a continuing obligation to maintain balanced faculties in all schools in order to avoid creating a pattern of racial identifiability of faculties. They also argued that Judge Roth's earlier approval of the board's faculty assignment was premised upon the progress then being made. Such progress was no longer occurring, according to plaintiffs. They concluded their response by suggesting that it would be necessary to reach the issue only if the faculty assignments necessitated by the pupil reassignment plan failed to adequately integrate faculties. It will be recalled that both plaintiffs and the Detroit board had suggested fairly drastic reorganizations of grade structures, which would have reassigned approximately half the elementary school teachers in the district. Plaintiffs' final thought on the subject in April 1975 was:

> Plaintiffs want no part in the resolution of collective bargaining disputes unless and until they interfere with Constitutional rights of pupils. This court should be equally loath to intervene, unless necessary.

Plaintiff's [*sic*] Response to Submission by Detroit Board, at 20–21, Bradley v. Milliken, (E.D. Mich., Apr. 21, 1975).

369. Bradley v. Milliken, 338 F. Supp. 582, 589–91 (E.D. Mich. 1971). The DFT argued that the Supreme Court's remand limited the district court to "eliminating the segregation *found to exist.*" Brief for Appellee Detroit Federation of Teachers, at 5, Bradley v. Milliken, No. 75-2018 (6th Cir., dated Jan. 29, 1976), quoting Milliken v. Bradley, 418 U.S. 717, 753 (1974) [emphasis added by counsel]. The union claimed that no faculty segregation had been found, so the court had no power to reassign teachers. It also claimed that it was improper for a defendant school board to seek a remedy for a wrong it had successfully denied. *Id.* at 6. In addition, the DFT asserted the contractual seniority rights of teachers, while conceding that in a proper case they would have to yield to a desegregation order. *Id.* at 19–20.

370. Mem. Op., Aug. 15, 1975, at 54–55.

It is dismissed as unfounded the board's concern for federal funding, suggesting that earlier applications for federal assistance had been rejected for poor documentation rather than for faculty imbalance.[371] Noting that there had been no evidence in the remedial hearing dealing with faculty segregation, it ruled that "it would be inappropriate for this court to order any reassignment of faculty at this time."[372] Nevertheless the board had not lost entirely. Because of the grade restructuring, many teachers would have to be reassigned. The court suggested that those reassignments should promote a better racial mix and directed the board and the union to "immediately begin negotiations concerning reassignments necessitated by [the grade structure changes]."[373]

Three days later, reacting to "reports in the media that contract negotiations between the Detroit Board of Education and the Detroit Federation of Teachers [had] stalemated and [might] not be resolved in time for the opening of schools," the court on its own motion ordered the two parties to conduct daily negotiations and to present a status report to the court on August 27, 1975.[374] The day after receiving the report the court changed its mind and ordered that teachers be reassigned so that no more than 70 percent of the teachers at any school would be of the same race.[375]

The court's order was a compromise between positions which neither labor nor management wished publicly to abandon. The order had all the earmarks of a mediated settlement, privately negotiated under pressure from the court and publicly maligned by the leadership of the two bodies. The compromise helped the union and the board reach final agreement on a contract within a week. Then both of them appealed from it, as did the NAACP. The union was offended because its members were to be reassigned on the basis of race and in derogation of their seniority rights. The board was worried because the 70 percent standard set by the court was more lax than HEW requirements.[376] The NAACP, which had not been consulted before the order was issued, was unhappy that the court had once again ordered less thorough desegregation than it wanted or the board was willing to accept.[377] The state defendants, with no obvious stake in the issue, agreed with the union.[378]

During the short break between fall and winter semesters in late January 1976, 1,200 teachers reported to new buildings as required under the court's 70 percent formula. They were chosen on the basis of race, specialty, and seniority.

371. *Id.* at 55–56.
372. *Id.* at 116.
373. *Id.*
374. Supplemental Memorandum and Order, Aug. 18, 1975.
375. Order, Aug. 28, 1975.
376. The Detroit board understands the Department of Health, Education and Welfare to require that in a system with a 49.5 percent black staff, each school's faculty should be between 37.1 and 61.9 percent black. Brief for Appellee Detroit Board of Education, at 89, *Bradley v. Milliken*, No. 75-2018 (6th Cir., dated Jan. 29, 1975).
377. *See* Brief for Appellants, at 27, *id.* (dated Dec. 22, 1975).
378. Brief of Appellees Milliken *et al.*, at 22–24, *id.* (dated Jan. 26, 1976).

Others, to avoid reassignment, exercised their seniority rights to "bump" newer teachers of their race in the same building but in other grades.[379] And the board began negotiating with the Department of Health, Education and Welfare for federal assistance with the new court-ordered reading program.[380]

Education Components: The court was as enthusiastic about revitalizing the educational process as it was reluctant to desegregate it. In the first blush of that enthusiasm it embraced most of the board's proposed "education components," drastically recast one and added one of its own.

Reading: The court was especially impressed with the need to put new stress on the teaching of reading. The board was directed to make the development of a new reading program its "top priority."[381] The program was to "be characterized by excellence and . . . instituted in every school in the system."[382] Openly snubbing the regional boards of education, which the judge felt had developed into eight dysfunctional bureaucracies,[383] the court made the development of the reading program "the direct responsibility of the General Superintendent and a committee to be selected by him."[384]

The court stressed that part of the reading program must be remedial, especially for minority youngsters. Its rationale assumed a close association among race, reading, and discipline:

> Statistical data establish that minority youngsters lag significantly behind their white counterparts in reading skills, which in turn affects the ability of minority students to . . compete. . . . Moreover, when such conditions persist, there is a direct effect upon the school environment. Students become disciplinary problems when in reality their problem is directly associated with an inability to conceptualize due to a lack of proper reading and communication skills. As a consequence, teachers and staff assume that such minority students are uneducable, thus further deteriorating the school environment for these students. To eradicate the effects of past discrimination, a remedial reading program should be instituted immediately to correct the deficiencies of those mid-way in their education experience.[385]

The court derived its emphasis on reading as a component of the desegregation plan from a standpoint of the NAACP.[386] The Detroit board did not even suggest it. The court-appointed experts were less enthusiastic than the judge.[387]

379. Detroit Free Press, Jan. 14, 1976.
380. Interview with Freeman Flynn, in Detroit, Michigan, Jan. 9, 1976.
381. Mem. Op., Aug. 15, 1975, at 100.
382. Partial Judgment and Order, at 5 (Aug. 15, 1975).
383. Mem. Op., Aug. 15, 1975, at 70–72.
384. *Id.* at 100.
385. *Id.* at 99–100.
386. Second DeMascio interview. *See* Plaintiffs' Proposed Ruling on Detroit-Only Desegregation Plans, at 27, 29–30, which suggests the rationale adopted by the court.
387. Second DeMascio interview.

Vocational Education: The court, its experts, and the Detroit board all agreed, however, that an expanded vocational education offering was important.[388] On the basis of that concensus the court ordered the board to establish three vocational centers and two technical high schools. The technical high schools are to concentrate on business education. Each of the vocational centers is to emphasize trades in one of three general categories: construction, transportation, and health services. In two years they are supposed to serve 10,000 eleventh and twelfth graders, over 67 percent of the juniors and seniors in the district. All are to be open to students from throughout the city. Each is to seek a racial ratio of approximately 60 percent black and 40 percent white.[389] Ironically, the court did not direct the board to change the racial makeup of the two biggest vocational programs already functioning in the district, the Construction Trade School, presently 11.1 percent black, and the Aero Mechanics Schools, 31.7 percent black.[390]

The court, in support of its plan, reasoned that vocation training would "compensate for past discrimination, at the same time it serves as an effective tool for desegregation."[391] It would also prepare black students for entry into occupations often closed to blacks, thus dovetailing with federal employment discrimination laws.[392]

The court had hoped to see quick action on vocational education, and initially it had wanted two existing high schools closed in September 1975 so they could be converted to trade schools. The court therefore ordered the state board and the Detroit board jointly to develop a plan of vocational education.[393] That hope was quickly dashed. The existing high schools did not have enough room for all the ninth graders the court had ordered transferred to them. Closing two high schools would have left 7,000 pupils nowhere to go.[394] The two boards' first submission was rejected, but their second was heartily endorsed by the court and ordered implemented.[395] The court was dismayed to learn that the

388. Second DeMascio interview; Mem. Op., Aug. 15, 1975, at 103–107; Partial Judgment and Order, at 5–8 (Aug. 15, 1975); Detroit Board, April 1, 1975 Plan, at 187–91, 210–11. The Michigan Board of Education and the NAACP, while supporting other "education components," refrained from either endorsing or opposing vocation education. Michigan State Board of Education, A Critique of the Desegregation Plan filed by the Detroit Board of Education, at 38–39, Bradley v. Milliken (E.D. Mich., April 21, 1975); Plaintiff's Response to Submission by Detroit Board, at 1–2, *id.*

389. Mem. Op., Aug. 15, 1975, at 103–107; Mem. and Order, at 2 (Nov. 10, 1975). The opinion does not explain why the court expects whites, who are presently about 25 percent of the total student population, to constitute 40 percent of those seeking vocational education. Neither does it explore the probable impact of the vocational programs on the racial makeup of other high school curricula or buildings.

390. *See* 1975 Fourth Friday Count, *supra* note 12, at 77. The omission was no oversight. The board had recommended that the court order it to limit new admissions to existing vocational programs to "the city-wide racial ratio." Detroit Board, April 1, 1975 Plan, at 3; *see id.* at 211.

391. Mem. Op., Aug. 15, 1975, at 103.

392. *Id.* at 103–104; Second DeMascio interview.

393. Mem. Op., Aug. 15, 1975, at 105–106.

394. Detroit Free Press, Aug. 30, 1975, at 7B, col. 2.

395. Memorandum and Order, Nov. 10, 1975; Judgment, Nov. 20, 1975.

two boards were still unwilling to implement the plan because each wanted the other to pay for it. Early in the second semester the court held a hearing on the subject but broke it off shortly to lecture counsel for the boards in chambers. Under pressure from the court the boards agreed to divide the cost of vocational education equally between them.[396]

Student Discipline: The court, with strong support from the teachers' union, began pressing early in the remedy hearing for a strict student conduct code. The Detroit board's desegregation plan had included a vague description of measures necessary to prevent the discriminatory use of discipline that often accompanies school desegregation.[397] With that goal in mind the board had proposed to spend $283,000 of the state's money to inform students, parents, and staff of the student's rights and responsibilities.[398] Judge DeMascio was clearly shocked at the board's emphasis on rights and its vagueness about standards of behavior and penalties for infractions. He was also concerned about reports of vandalism and violence in Detroit schools.[399] He asked the board to revise its code of student conduct to deal with those concerns.

In mid-summer 1975 the court rejected the board's first revision of its code of conduct and ordered it stiffened. The court had not reviewed the second effort by the time it issued its major opinion, but it emphasized in the opinion that the board must tolerate no violence in the schools. It stressed its intention to order a uniform code of conduct to "be administered uniformally [*sic*] without regard to regional lines."[400] It promised, however, to "ensure . . . that all Detroit students are afforded minimal right [*sic*] of due process. . . ."[401]

Alarmed by the emphasis the judge placed on prohibitions, penalties, and uniformity, spokespersons for the board let it be known that the board would appeal if the court pressed the issue. After reviewing critiques of the board's second draft prepared by the other parties and after argument by counsel, the court chose to compromise. It rewrote the board's second draft code, detailing offenses, procedures, and a uniform system of reports. It ordered the code printed and distributed to all parents and students before it was put into effect at the beginning of the second semester in January 1976.[402] Reacting warily, three bar associations and the Michigan Civil Liberties Union announced that they were prepared to provide legal assistance for any student threatened with discipline under the new code.[403]

396. *See* Memorandum, Order and Judgment, at 3–6, May 11, 1976.
397. Detroit Board, April 1, 1975 Plan, at 216–18.
398. *Id.* at 27.
399. *See* Second DeMascio interview; Mem. Op., Aug. 15, 1975, at 109–10; Order, July 3, 1975.
400. Mem. Op., Aug. 15, 1975, at 109.
401. *Id.* at 110.
402. Memorandum and Order, Oct. 29, 1975; Judgment, Nov. 20, 1975.
403. Detroit News, Jan. 27, 1976. The bar associations were the Detroit Bar Association, the Wolverine Bar Association, and the Detroit Chapter of the National Lawyers Guild. The Michigan Civil Liberties Union has for several years been a leading defender of students' rights.

The school board remained unenthusiastic. Early in the second semester Judge DeMascio learned that the implementation of the Uniform Code of Student Conduct had been less uniform than he had wished. In a subsequent order he castigated all concerned and suggested that he would conduct hearings to establish personal responsibility if his instructions were not followed precisely in September 1976.[404]

Bilingual Education: With one exception, the other education components were noncontroversial. That exception was bilingual-bicultural education. By refusing to let Latino parents and groups intervene, the court spared itself a detailed hearing on the controversy. As Latinos had persuaded the Office of Desegregation to propose a bilingual program and had gotten the NAACP lawyers to acquiese, the court order did direct the board to institute a bilingual program. Due almost certainly to the inability of the Latinos to present their case directly, the court misunderstood the problem. State law, passed in response to *Lau* v. *Nichols,*[405] requires each district with 20 or more students to provide bilingual instruction for children of limited English-speaking ability, unless their parents sign a written request that they remain in a totally English program.[406] (Detroit has 4,268 Spanish surnamed students, a high percentage of whom have limited English-speaking ability. Fifteen schools were at least 10 percent Latino in September of 1975.)[407] The Latino parents wanted that statute implemented in all Detroit schools with sizable Latino populations, not just in the two schools which had special state and federal grants. They also wanted to change the emphases of the two programs that were in existence.

The courts' response to those unheard desires was to order the board to comply with state law. Elaborating, it then reduced the board's obligations to less than the state statute requires. It directed the general superintendent to "provide bilingual instruction for all kindergarten students requesting such instruction" and to assure that such students are assigned to classes of at least 20 students.[408] Under the statute, of course, it is not the *class* that must have 20 students but the *district.* Furthermore the statute puts the burden on the district, not on the parents, to identify such children and to place them in bilingual classes. Under the statute a parental request is necessary to prevent such an assignment, not to instigate it. The court also directed the board to re-apply for federal funds to continue its bilingual programs, thus casting some doubt on its duty to provide bilingual education if outside funding should become unavailable.[409] Certainly

404. Memorandum, Order and Judgment, at 6–9, Bradley v. Milliken (E.D. Mich., May 11, 1976); *see* Judgment, at 4, Bradley v. Milliken (E.D. Mich., May 11, 1976).
405. 414 U.S. 563 (1974).
406. Mich. Comp. L. Ann. § § 340.360; 340.390-95 (1975/76 Supp.). The Michigan statute closely resembles the Massachusetts statute discussed in Lewis, *The Massachusetts Transitional Bilingual Education Act,* 19 Inequality in Education 31 (Feb. 1975).
407. *See* 1975 Fourth Friday Count, *supra* note 12, at 4, 26–80.
408. Partial Judgment and Order, at 9, Aug. 15, 1975.
409. Mem. Op., Aug. 15, 1975, at 115.

the board feels under no compulsion to expand its bilingual program, for it has taken no steps to do so.

The court has, at best, left the Latino population to seek bilingual education through political channels. Those channels hold little promise. While most members of the Detroit board and its staff are indifferent, some, both blacks and whites, are as opposed to bilingual education as many whites once were to black history, and for similar emotional reasons. A fair indication of the level of support for bilingual education may be found in the fact that, despite a state law mandating bilingual education, the only two bilingual programs in the district owe their existence to outside funding.[410] When federal funding was reduced for one of them in 1975/76, the program was cut back accordingly.

Monitoring Commission: In structuring a monitoring commission, the court adroitly avoided the Detroit board's effort to control the court's access to information. The board had proposed the creation of a monitoring commission whose members would be appointed by the board subject to the approval of the court.[411] The court approved the monitoring concept but not the board's effort to control it. Citing its own obligation to audit the implementation of its orders and the state's Fourteenth Amendment obligations, it ordered State Superintendent of Public Instruction John Porter to submit a design for a court-appointed monitoring system utilizing the talents of a broad cross-section of the citizenry. The court also directed Porter to seek "supervisory and expert support staff from state universities . . . to analyze and report" information developed by the monitoring process.[412]

Inexplicably, the superintendent submitted a plan that would have had the court name the monitoring committee but would have made it dependent on the board's internal channels for information. To provide that information it recommended that the "Detroit Board of Education establish various committees, set up on the school, district and regional levels to communicate input for study and analysis by a 7-10-member commission."[413] The court rejected that proposal

410. The existing bilingual programs are in Preston and Webster elementary schools, the only two schools that had Latino majorities in the fall of 1975. The desegregation order converted Preston from 61.4 percent Latino and 25.4 percent black to 54 percent black. Webster, which had been 56 percent Latino and 14.1 percent black, was 37 percent black after desegregation. *See* 1975 Fourth Friday Count, *supra* note 12, at 28, 33–38; Detroit Board, January 1976 Plan. The board has not published the number or percentage of Latinos in individual schools as reconstituted by the desegregation order.

411. Detroit Board April 1, 1975 Plan, at 243–46. The only substantial change made by the elected board members in the desegregation plan prepared by its Office of Desegregation before the plan was submitted to the court concerned the process of selecting members of this commission. The Office of Desegregation had planned for the court to make the appointments. The board changed the process to that described in the text. Ashworth interview.

412. Mem. Op., Aug. 15, 1975, at 118–19; Partial Judgment and Order, at 9 (Aug. 15, 1975).

413. Memorandum Order, at 1–2, Oct. 24, 1975. *See* Superintendent of Public Instruction, A Proposed Plan for Monitoring the Court's Desegregation Effort, Milliken v. Bradley (E.D. Mich., Aug. 29, 1975).

but in general accepted the next one, which followed the court's guidelines more faithfully.

The plan approved by the court created a 55-member monitoring commission to be appointed by the court. It does not anticipate that all 55 members are ever to operate as a unit. Rather, 14 persons are named to an executive committee and the rest are to serve on 12 subcommittees which are to report to the executive committee. Members of the executive committee do not routinely serve on subcommittees. Each subcommittee is to focus on the implementation of a particular component of the court's desegregation order.[414] In its order establishing the commission, the court named the executive committee and chairpersons for nine of the subcommittees. The executive committee consisted of seven blacks and seven whites, eleven men and three women. Only two of the whites live in the school district; all of the blacks do. The interim chairman designated by the court is William Wattenberg, a 65-year-old white education professor who lives in suburban Bloomfield Hills.[415]

The NAACP publicly attacked the court for ignoring the plaintiffs in appointing the commission. According to Jesse Goodwin, education chairman of the Detroit branch, the court asked all parties to suggest persons for service on the commission but accepted only one of the plaintiffs' 50 nominees; the one exception was on several other lists as well.[416]

The monitoring commission, loosely patterned after one in Denver, was charged with observing not only the desegregative aspects of the court's order but also the "education components" such as vocational education. The state board of education was ordered to provide a staff and offices for the commission. In fact it has loaned only one professional and two clerical employees to the commission, while refusing to commit itself further. The commission has used offices in the Detroit Federal Building furnished by the district court.[417]

414. Memorandum Order, at 3–5, Oct. 24, 1975. Subcommittees were named to oversee reading, in-service training, vocational education, testing, school-community relations, counseling and career guidance, co-curricular activities, bilingual and multi-ethnic studies, and the uniform code of conduct. It will be noted that all those subcommittees concern matters peripheral to the actual desegregation effort. Sometime later a chairperson was chosen for a subcommittee to monitor the reassignment of pupils and to train monitors for individual schools. *Compare,* Mich. Superintendent of Public Instruction, A Proposed Plan for Monitoring the Courts Desegregation Effort, Milliken v. Bradley (E.D. Mich., Aug. 29, 1975, *revised and resubmitted* Sept. 12, 1975).

415. *See* Detroit Free Press, Jan. 26, 1976, at 12C.

416. *Id.*

417. *Id.* Staff and budget proposals for the monitoring commission, while never adopted by the court or the board, have reinforced the professional educator's image as an inveterate empire-builder. The chairman of the commission wanted a staff of six professionals and four secretaries at a cost of $375,000 in the first full year of operation. *Id. Cf.* Detroit Board April 1, 1975 Plan, at 28, proposing a budget of $183,712 for a differently constituted monitoring commission and $82,243 for the board's in-house desegregation evaluation program. Detroit, of course, wanted the state to pay the bill. By contrast, Denver's successful monitoring commission had a budget of $9,360, which covered only the cost of a secretary and duplicating. The school district paid those costs. Address by Sally Geiss to the Coalition for Peaceful Integration in Detroit, Michigan, April 26, 1975.

When the pupil reassignment plan was implemented in late January 1976, most of the subcommittees had vacancies and were still trying to get organized. Only one professional staff person had been assigned, Ken Harris, an employee of the state department of education. Initially it was understood that Wattenberg and Harris, with the assistance of the school board staff, would identify potential monitors to serve in schools, and that a subcommittee on pupil reassignment and transportation would train them. That subcommittee one of the last formed, consisted of Reginald Wilson, president of Wayne County Community College, and Marcia Pitcole, executive director of the Coalition of Peaceful Integration. Wattenberg and Harris never found time to do any recruiting. Less than a month before the pupils were to change schools, Wilson and Pitcole realized that they had to recruit monitors as well as train them. Utilizing the personnel and contacts of their two organizations, plus the school board's Office of School Community Relations, they provided about 200 trained monitors in the last weeks before January 26.[418]

The court has not relied on the monitors to provide it with data on how the board is complying with the pupil reassignment aspects of the court order. Rather it has indicated it will use the commission to evaluate educational components the court wants more aggressively implemented.[419]

Community Relations: A community-relations effort was included in the Detroit board's initial desegregation plan and the court ordered the board to take action in that area,[420] but it gave no precise direction to the board until May 1976. On May 11, 1976, Judge DeMascio ordered the creation of a three-tiered, school community-relations organization, with councils sitting at the school, regional, and district level.[421] Ignoring a board proposal to enhance the role of existing school-community councils, which are often strongly dominated by parents, he directed that each school have a twenty-person community-relations committee composed of school personnel, students, and community representatives. The community is to have only ten of the twenty seats; apparently the other ten are reserved for school employees and, perhaps, students. The result will often be a committee, half of which is under the control of the principal. Each committee must reflect the racial makeup of the school's student body. At least two community representatives must be persons not associated with the local PTA or parents club and in newly desegregated schools, at least two must be parents of reassigned children. It is unclear how the ten parents are to be chosen. It is possible the court expects the principal to pick them.

It is also uncertain who is to create the regional committees: they are to be

418. Interview with Marcia Pitcole in Detroit, Michigan, Feb. 23, 1976.
419. *See* Memorandum, Order and Judgment, at 3, 9, 15, 17–18, 22–24, Bradley v. Milliken (E.D. Mich., May 11, 1976).
420. Detroit Board, April 1, 1975 Plan, at 219–21; Mem. Op., Aug. 15, 1975, at 111–12; Order, Aug. 26, 1975.
421. Memorandum, Order and Judgment, at 19–24, May 11, 1976.

composed of members selected "from" (not "by") local committees. The chairpersons, however, are to be appointed by the regional boards of education. The citywide council is to consist of ten persons named by the general superintendent, and ten selected by the court's Monitoring Commission, plus, at the initiative of the first twenty members, representatives from "such organizations as New Detroit, NAACP, the Chamber of Commerce, the League of Women Voters, the Coalition for Peaceful Integration, etc."[422] No representation of local or regional boards is mandated.

The school-level committees are to "strengthen communication between school personnel and parents, . . . increase understanding among parents from different communities [and] . . . aid in resolving conflicts arising from the desegregation process."[423] Unresolved problems, "whether created by desegregation or not," are to be taken to the regional committee or the city-wide council.[424]

The role of the regional committees is "to discuss problems arising in the desegregated schools, such as discipline and academic achievement,"[425] and to make recommendations for resolving the problems. Presumably committees in regions having no desegregated schools are nevertheless to discuss discipline and academic achievement.

The central council is to be a mediator of conflicts from local or regional committees. Surprisingly, it is also to set the agendas for local and regional committees, evaluate their programs, and report on their progress to the school boards and the Monitoring Commission. The court directed the central council to organize six named subcommittees and determined how often the council and its subcommittees were to meet. A representative of the Community Relations Service of the Justice Department was directed to attend open and executive meetings of the council.[426]

The effect of the court's intervention is not yet certain. In regions with anemic community relations programs, it should provide a major stimulus to action. In regions with very active programs, it seems likely to increase the power of board employees at the expense of parents. The court-ordered program may also compete with other programs in the district for the ever-scarce supply of dedicated citizen volunteers. It is a mystery why the court revamped the board's proposal to strengthen existing programs. No other party suggested it. Neither did the Community Relations Service or the Monitoring Commission. Even the court's unhappiness with the bureaucratic confusion of decentralization[427] does not

422. *Id.* at 22. Early indications are that representatives of the general superintendent and the monitoring commission will jointly agree on the members of a well-balanced committee. The superintendent and the commission will each then appoint half of the agreed members.

423. *Id.* at 21.

424. *Id.*

425. *Id.* at 22.

426. *Id.* at 19-24.

427. In the same order the court had renewed its criticism of decentralization and its call for the legislature to reexamine the issue. *Id.* at 9-14.

logically explain the order. The creation of a new channel for appeals from the field and directives from the top only increases opportunities for the irresponsibility deplored by the court. The board of education, surprised by the nature of the order, plans to seek clarification and perhaps modification by the fall of 1976.

PREPARING THE PUBLIC

In September 1971, when Judge Roth found the Detroit schools to be segregated, a few people realized the need to prepare the public for the inevitable remedial order. They badly underestimated the complexity of the task and the time it would take, but they plunged into it. Wayne State University held a symposium on desegration and school finance a month after the ruling. About 150 persons, mostly senior school administrators and attorneys, attended the program, which was designed to inform them of the state of the law on the two topics then blazoned across the newspapers.[428] During the remedy hearings the following spring two other conferences were organized by ad hoc groups of human rights organizations. These meetings frankly advocated integrated schools and equal funding. No action program came out of any of those programs.[429]

Some of the planners of the conferences, which tended to involve the same persons, thought a different kind of advocacy was needed. Noting the absence of a local government with responsibility for education or law enforcement throughout the metropolitan area, and the abdication of leadership by state officials, these persons feared that preparation would lose out to politics. A few of them met early in January 1972 to organize a coalition of existing groups to fill the gap between the plaintiffs and the political opponents of desegregation. The goal of the group was simply the peaceful implementation of whatever orders the court issued. The initial meetings were devoted to identifying groups with a stake in the outcome and quietly persuading them to affiliate. The new group was named the Metropolitan Coalition for Peaceful Integration (MCPI).[430] The recruiting was aimed at key groups of differing outlooks and constituencies, including labor, business, churches, and social agencies. Churches and social agencies joined wholeheartedly, unions, more quietly. One exception, the Michigan Federation of Teachers, was prominent even while its most important affiliate was a defendant in the case.[431] The Chamber of Commerce was cordial, but

428. *See* Busing, Taxes, and Desegregation (R. DeMont, L. Hillman, & G. Mansergh eds. 1973) for the text of the three principal presentations by John E. Coons, Gordon Foster, and Elwood Hain.

429. See text at notes 209–10, *supra*.

430. The name detracted from the coalition's effort to avoid identification with either side in the litigation. Opponents of desegregation especially saw it as a pro-integration group and used the name as proof.

431. Coalition meetings may have been unique in providing occasions for cooperation among representatives of the NAACP, the Federation of Teachers, and the Detroit Board of Education during the long years of litigation.

kept its distance. Surprisingly, New Detroit, Inc., the urban alliance created in 1967 to prevent future riots, showed little interest in desegregation and less in publicly working for peaceful change involving the metropolitan area. The usual "power brokers" in town were not drawn in, despite efforts of MCPI leadership.[432]

MCPI set a strenuous agenda for itself. Working with small local grants and part-time staff loaned by member groups, but relying heavily on volunteers, it sought to provide accurate information throughout the tri-county area, using pamphlets, newsletters, the media, and a speakers' bureau.[433] The information dealt primarily with the current status of the Detroit case, the alternatives available to the court, and possible solutions to the nonracial objections to "busing." Satisfactory experience in other places was prominently mentioned. The group also made an unsuccessful effort to encourage the Detroit *News* to be more even-handed and less inflammatory in its reporting and editorializing. An inter-denominational delegation of clergy who visited the paper was blandly assured that the newspaper simply reported the news and that the particular examples cited by the visitors were the result of the exercise of journalistic freedom by the staff.[434]

Great care was taken to contact suburban school leaders and to provide reliable information while tactfully avoiding political embarrassment to them. Local coalitions, largely based in church groups and the League of Women Voters,

432. New Detroit ignored an MCPI request that it publicly endorse obedience to court orders and good-faith preparation by public officials. It declined to work openly with the MCPI or to help fund it until the courts had reached a final decision. Until that time, it said, its emphasis would be on improving the quality of education within the existing public school system. It kept its word; in 1975, once a desegregation order was inevitable, it did give the Coalition for Peaceful Integration an $8,000 grant to finance its work until federal money became available.

New Detroit never took an official position on metropolitan desegregation, Board Chairperson Lynn Townsend later admitted, because the issue threatened to tear the organization apart. Detroit News, Mar. 20, 1973. Reflecting the tenacious view that truly equal schools, though separate, would prevent desegregation suits, Townsend said, "I personally think the cross-busing issue would not have been an issue if we had moved to equalize the financing of our schools . . . and that is what the probusing people are really saying. . . . [T]hey're trying to point out the inequality of educational opportunities for their children in the present situation." *Id.*

433. For several critical months it had a paid executive director, Maxine Rose, who had worked almost full time as a volunteer in bringing the coalition into existence.

434. The coalition was not alone in its concern over reporting by the *News. See* Eastside Shopper, April 12, 1972, reporting that many persons knowledgeable about the evidence in the case were angry over "what Detroit's largest daily newspaper, *The Detroit News,* had implied with an astonishing series of front page headlines and stories: '50% Detroit tax boost for bussing?,' 'Some pupils would be bussed 3 hours under cluster plan,' 'School buses: How safe are they?,' 'Wider metro busing plan is urged.' . . .

The *Eastside Shopper* went on:

To be sure, nothing *The News* said was patently untrue. It simply had focused on the extremes of hardship that some people would experience if some of the most disputed and speculative aspects of the desegregation plans now under discussion should ever be approved by the judge and upheld by the superior courts.

Nevertheless, the headlines and stories were strangely misleading. . . .

were organized in several middle-class suburbs to press local school officers to begin contingency planning. The assumption was that local suburban voters could be more aggressive than the central organization.

Tenuous contacts were also established with the Governor's Office and the Detroit Police Department. Efforts to spur the state board of education into action were unsuccessful. A formal presentation asking that body to exercise its power of educational leadership resulted only in a vague thank-you letter.

Realizing the leadership void was even greater than it had thought, MCPI turned to working with those who could not evade the impact of a court order, the parents of the students. In mid-summer 1972 the court-appointed planning panel designated 16 clusters of schools for purposes of metropolitan desegregation. The panel gave first priority to a cluster consisting of Martin Luther King High School in Detroit, with its feeder schools, and the Grosse Pointe Public Schools. The MCPI and the Grosse Pointe Interfaith Action Center brought parents from both areas together, first at a black church in Detroit and later at King High School, to discuss their concerns and to create a framework for cooperation.[435] After it became clear no remedy would be implemented in the fall of 1972, the parents' group disbanded. Sometime later the MCPI suspended most active operations, awaiting the outcome of the appeals.

After the Supreme Court decision limiting the remedy to Detroit, the MCPI reorganized, dropping suburban groups and adding other city-based ones. It omitted "Metropolitan" from its name. Still lacking clout with major power brokers in the city, it concentrated on building local coalitions in each region of the district. It emphasized parent and student participation while providing public support for preparations by school officials. It secured an $85,000 HEW grant to help with grassroots organizing in three designated regions.[436] The proposal, which emphasized the process of stimulating citizen involvement rather than specific tasks for citizen volunteers, has since been successfully copied by groups

435. Black parents were surprised at the depth of the Grosse Pointers' fear of physical violence by black children and youth in general. The whites were even more surprised to learn that black parents dreaded the "psychic violence" they expected their children would have to endure if they were assigned to schools in the (literally) exclusive suburb.

436. HEW regulations require independent groups seeking grants for desegregation work to state whether the local school board has approved their proposals. Proposals without board approval are almost never funded. The white members of the Detroit board, as part of their general opposition to desegregation, tried to prevent the Coalition for Peaceful Integration from getting a grant. They were initially joined by a couple of black board members, one of whom made clear that his concern was to get control of the patronage he imagined would become available. Seeing that a vote of support would not carry, board member Herbert McFadden successfully moved to have the matter tabled for two days. (McFadden, the most astute politician on the board, was also co-chairman of the coalition.) The next morning NAACP attorneys brought the issue to Judge DeMascio's attention, challenging the board's contention that it was eager to cooperate in every way with the court. DeMascio left no doubt in the mind of the board's counsel that he saw the vote on the coalition's application as a test of that claim. At the board's next meeting, the motion to endorse the coalition's application was approved without debate.

in other cities.[437] More significantly, the coalition has been consulted by citizens groups and government officials from a score of cities across the country for help in establishing effective programs in the community.

In late March 1975 another group announced with great fanfare the formation of a coalition with two goals: to help shape the order and to assure that it was peacefully implemented.[438] Prominent among the leadership of the group were persons who had been leading a drive to get the NAACP to drop the case.[439] Some 300 organizations were invited to join the new coalition. Among those invited were the NAACP and the Coalition for Peaceful Integration. The NAACP furiously denounced the new group as an "unholy alliance" trying to gain by indirection what it had failed to get by frontal assault.[440]

The CPI executive board had a stormy meeting over the issue. Some members were outraged that leaders of the new group would "steal" CPI's program after years of ignoring the need. To add insult to injury, the leaders of the new effort had not even acknowledged their debt to CPI. The CPI officers, initially outnumbered on the issue, finally persuaded the board that results were more important than public credit or control of a cause. The new group obviously had the political and media contacts that CPI had never acquired. They should be welcomed, not shunned. CPI should join, the officers urged, and influence the behavior of the newcomers. As the first item of business they proposed that the new group

437. The bulk of the proposal was prepared by Marcia Pitcole, president of the Detroit League of Women Voters. She got vital technical assistance from the National Center for Quality Integrated Education and from a former Detroit board employee. As a direct result of her hard work, Pitcole was hired as the coalition's executive director once federal money was available.

438. See Detroit Free Press, Mar. 26, 1975, at 3A, col. 7.

439. For several months before Judge DeMascio began hearings on the remedy issue in April 1975, a group of prominent citizens had waged a public and private campaign to persuade the NAACP to abandon the suit. Although only a few of them had publicly espoused metropolitan desegregation, all were concerned that a city-only remedy would be pointless because it would drive whites out of the city and undercut the tax base. The group included Mayor Young, several union leaders, both black and white, and the leadership of New Detroit, Inc. The press supported them wholeheartedly. The leadership of the school system was, at a minimum, kept well informed. The explicit assumption of the campaign was that the local NAACP branch would readily agree that a city remedy was futile and would help persuade the national NAACP. That premise was fallacious. The local NAACP board was dominated by black professional men who felt the labor men, though devoted to civil rights, were too imbued with the union notion that everything is negotiable. One strong-willed physician on the board has been credited with single-handedly preventing the local and national NAACP from even talking with the mayor about a compromise. Detroit Free Press, Mar. 9, 1975; *id.,* Mar. 10, 1975. National NAACP leaders were not surprised that even black politicians, faced with threats of white flight, might try to preserve the political conditions that had elevated them. But the national organization, like its local affiliate, was determined not to back off. It saw the talk of white flight as an attempt to "hold the constitution hostage" to white fears. To have yielded in Detroit would have weakened its position in cases all over the country. Lucas interview; Detroit Free Press, Mar. 9, 1975; *id.,* Mar. 10, 1975.

440. Detroit Free Press, Mar. 26, 1975, at 3A, col. 7.

trim the agenda to peaceful implementation, abandoning all claim to influence the content of the court order.

At the first meeting of the steering committee of the new coalition, dubbed Pro-Detroit[441] by its public relations firm, the CPI representative successfully pressed for dropping the notion of influencing the court. The majority of the other representatives agreed that that would be both futile and divisive. Thereafter CPI and Pro-Detroit leaders met and agreed on a division of functions. Pro-Detroit was to handle media relations, and coordinate public statements by prominent persons. CPI was to work with parents, pupils, and teachers in local schools and regions. While there was some overlap in fact, the division of labor coincided so nicely with their respective competences that both groups were more successful for it.

After the remedial order was issued, Pro-Detroit produced television and radio spot announcements supporting obedience to the law, and orchestrated more news stories favorable to the order. The stories emphasized the limited nature of the busing order and the potential of the education components. In the last weeks before the order was implemented, Pro-Detroit managed the almost daily release of appeals by political, educational, and religious leaders for public calm and cooperation. The media treated each appeal as a straight news item. Stories of police preparedness were prominently featured, as was the announcement by John Cardinal Dearden that Roman Catholic schools in the archdiocese would not be a haven for those fleeing public school desegregation.

CPI, able at last to function in a city where nearly everyone expected the schools to desegregate soon, organized affiliated groups of parents, teachers, and students in most of the eight regions. In areas affected by pupil reassignments, the regional groups organized neighborhood meetings, made presentations to regional school boards, contacted each principal and parents' club president, and developed an excellent resource packet for use in every school in the region. They organized open houses between paired schools. They demonstrated "barrier-breaking" techniques for school staffs to use. They also recruited volunteers to monitor individual schools, to assist at bus pick-up points, and to staff telephone information centers.

The central CPI office, in addition to coordinating and advising the regional groups, conducted four citywide meetings. The first focused on Denver's pioneering experience with monitoring. The second featured the success of Impact, a creation of the Memphis Chamber of Commerce and the Memphis Board of Education, in organizing community forces in Memphis. The third and fourth discussed the details of the desegregation order and the preparations of various public agencies to implement it.

The Coalition for Peaceful Integration and Pro-Detroit were no longer alone in the quest for peace. Church leaders in all parts of the city worked for months to prepare their parishioners for change. Their efforts ranged from condemning the

441. An acronym for People and Responsible Organizations for Detroit.

sin of segregation to counseling nonviolence. (Generally, pastors reported their congregations were more swayed by prudence than by guilt.) Religious groups conducted several conferences on "Pastoral Ministry and School Desegregation," which emphasized ministering to church members with a dozen different perspectives on desegregation. Each month the first weekend was designated as "Days of Prayer to Ask God's Guidance Through the Process of School Desegregation." Prayer led to discussions which sometimes led to volunteer action groups. Public statements in support of peaceful implementation were issued by clergy associations, denominational groups, local churches, and individual religious leaders. The media cooperated in publicizing these pro-compliance activities. But the religious leaders were able to get even more media time. To counteract the coverage invariably given groups protesting desegregation, they supplied local television stations with ideas for more positive coverage, such as meetings to organize welcoming parties for students transferred to new schools.[442]

Public officials at least were openly working to make desegregation function. While the limited nature of the desegregation plan disheartened integrationists, others were cheered by the education components. The nine black members of the school board, though badly divided by personalities and political outlook, were forced by the noisy objections of the four white members into a fairly cohesive majority for vigorous compliance with the court order. The newly appointed general superintendent, Arthur Jefferson, took a no-nonsense attitude toward preparations for compliance even as he worked with the school board's counsel to oppose the court's wishes on key issues. Each regional school superintendent and each principal had fully developed plans for a range of contingencies. They arranged enthusiastic welcomes for new students, reassigned teachers, perfected bus routes, calmed parents, and met with police.

Mayor Coleman Young, once the proponent of the decentralization bill that had precipitated the April 7 Plan, the recall, and the desegregation suit, gave his unequivocal public support to full enforcement of the law. The police department created and trained a special detachment to deal with school desegregation. The media gave prominent treatment to the fact of police preparation while remaining discretely obscure as to details.[443]

White opposition did not vanish in the face of the forces of compliance, but it was far less volatile than four years earlier. Anti-busing leaders settled for rallies, parades, and rhetoric, but carefully eschewed inflammatory calls to action. Representatives of the Community Relations Service of the Justice Department discreetly discussed possible protest activities with anti-busing leaders. Perhaps as a result of CRS encouragement, those leaders decided not to risk confrontations by picketing at school buildings on January 26. They confined their last-ditch opposition to a call for a boycott of schools, a tactic that promoted peace

442. J. Radelet, Religious Leadership and Detroit School Desegregation (Mar. 27, 1976) (mimeo).
443. *See* Detroit News, Jan. 20, 1976, at 3, col. 1.

by temporarily removing from school children from the most inflamed households.

January 26 arrived, a miserable day for demonstrations if any had been planned. After six weeks of frequent snow and unusually bitter cold, it had rained and refrozen the day before. Driving was hazardous; the air was raw. But the buses ran and 68 percent of the district's elementary pupils went to school.[444] The next day, high school and middle school students returned to school after the semester break. There was not an untoward incident in the entire city. The hundreds of out-of-town reporters packed their bags and left. No violence meant no story.

By the end of the week, boycotting students were drifting back to class. A month later the district reported that it had lost 800 students because of deseg-regation.[445] Some had moved to the suburbs; others had registered in private schools;[446] and some simply quit attending. In a district that has lost over 6,000 white students a year since 1960, the change is minor.[447]

SUMMARY

The die is cast for Detroit. The decades-long abandonment of the city by whites is almost completed. Nearly all suburbs remain closed to blacks. Barring a major change in social policy, such as that accepted by Judge Roth, no one expects whites to return to the city or blacks to be able to leave it in numbers. The Supreme Court has reinforced existing racial barriers with a legal wall between the city and the encircling suburbs, offering only a faint hope of penetration. The district court, while forced to order some school desegregation within the city, has minimized the inconvenience for those whites who have not yet left.

But while the judiciary has written the city off, the citizenry has not. Rough, maligned Detroit has shown a grace more genteel cities might envy. That spirit, however, offers no hope of truly desegregated education for the black school children of Detroit. Only inclusion of the suburbs in a desegregation plan has that potential.

EDITORS' POSTSCRIPT

On August 4, 1976, the United States Court of Appeals for the Sixth Circuit filed its opinion in Bradley v. Milliken *reviewing Judge DeMascio's remedial order dis-*

444. Detroit Free Press, at 10c, col. 1, Jan. 27, 1976. Absenteeism ranged from 15–60 percent in schools directly affected by the desegregation. The normal absentee rate is about 15 percent. *Id.*

445. Most of the loss of attendance was in Region 7, the area most carefully protected by the court's revision of the Detroit board's desegregation proposal.

446. Detroit Free Press, Jan. 22, 1976, at 12c. Reacting to the reports of the secular press, the education director of the Archdiocese of Detroit announced that no Detroit public school pupils had enrolled in Catholic schools at the beginning of the second semester. The Tidings [a local parish newspaper], Feb. 1, 1976, at 1, col. 2.

447. *See* 1975 Fourth Friday Count, *supra* note 12, at 1.

cussed by Professor Hain in the foregoing essay.[1] *Its judgment may be character-ized as a reluctant and qualified affirmance. The court of appeals made manifest its belief, in common with the late Judge Roth and Judge DeMascio, that no effective desegregation of Detroit's schools is possible without involvement of the entire metropolitan area.*[2] *It is clear that the Court of Appeals for the Sixth Circuit expects further proceedings on the subject of metropolitan remedy.*[3]

In the meantime, however, that court has remanded to Judge DeMascio the student assignment portion of the remedial order for Regions 1 (90.3 percent black), 5 (96.7 black) and 8 (95.2 percent black).[4] *These regions had been ex-cluded from the order without, in the judgment of the appellate court, "adequate justification."*[5] *Judge DeMascio's attempted justification had been what he re-garded as the futility of such an order. The court of appeals also, however, rejected the plaintiffs' plan which would, as the court perceived it, require sub-stantial transportation but would still "leave a majority of Detroit's students in schools 75 to 90 percent black."*[6] *Furthermore: "Our considered judgment is that plaintiffs' plan would accelerate the trend toward rendering all or nearly all of Detroit's schools so identifiably black as to represent universal school segrega-tion within the city limits."*[7]

And yet the appeals court, having rejected alike the district court's plan (now supported on appeal by the Detroit Board of Education) and the plaintiffs' plan had no advice to guide the district court in proceeding under the remand. The absence of guidelines, Chief Judge Phillips wrote for the court, "is based upon the conviction which this court had at the time of its en banc *opinion in this case—and for the reasons carefully spelled out therein—that genuine constitu-tional desegregation cannot be accomplished within the school district bound-aries of the Detroit School District."*[8]

The court of appeals sustained those parts of the remedial order styled "edu-cational components," finding them "essential to the effort to combat the ef-fects of segregation."[9] *These were supported on appeal by the Detroit board but opposed by the state defendants who argued that no constitutional violation had been found justifying these remedies. A similar attack on compulsory teacher reassignments was also made on appeal by the Detroit Federation of Teachers (intervenors), and the state defendants; it too was rejected by the court of appeals:*

The reassignment of faculty is similar to the reading and counseling "Edu-cational Components" which we have upheld in Part III of this opinion. It helps to mitigate the fact that the majority of Detroit's children are left in schools that are overwhelmingly one race. Reassignment of faculty serves

1. 540 F.2d 229 (6th Cir. 1976).
2. *Id.* at 236.
3. *Id.* at 240.
4. *Id.* at 237–40.
5. *Id.* at 238.
6. *Id.* at 239.
7. *Id.*
8. *Id.* at 240.
9. *Id.* at 241.

to provide these children with the maximum desegregative experience possible under the circumstances.[10]

The sixth circuit opinion explicitly left open the matter of whether changes should be made by the district court in the faculty reassignment formula to permit the Detroit School Board to comply with applicable federal regulations under the Emergency School Aid Act, 20 U.S.C. Section 1602.[11]

Finally, the court of appeals rejected the contention of the state defendants that Judge DeMascio's order compelling the state to pay one-half of the cost of the education components and three-quarters of the cost of school bus acquisition violated the Eleventh Amendment. Rejection of this assertion rested apparently on two grounds: first, that a prospective court decree that has an impact on a state's treasury does not violate the Eleventh Amendment since it is not an award of money damages against the state;[12] *second, that state officials, including the legislature, had helped to create the de jure segregation which this order was designed to correct.*[13] *The court of appeals made it clear that if the Detroit board could not finance its share of the costs of the decree, then the district court ought to increase the state's share as required.*[14]

On June 27, 1977 the Supreme Court affirmed the appellate court decision in the two respects on which review had been sought. The Court held that the remedial order could include matters broader than pupil assignment and that the State could be compelled to contribute to the costs of the order.[15]

10. *Id.* at 247.
11. *Id.*
12. *Compare* Edelman v. Jordan, 415 U.S. 651 (1974) *with* Scheuer v. Rhodes, 416 U.S. 232 (1974).
13. Compare Ex parte Young, 209 U.S. 123 (1908).
14. 540 F.2d 229, 242–46.
15. 45 U.S.L. Week 4873.

United States v. Board of School Commissioners

William E. Marsh

United States v. Board of School Commissioners of City of Indianapolis *was the first case, after the Supreme Court decision in* Milliken v. Bradley (Detroit), *to consider and order a metropolitan remedy. It is also one of the few desegregation cases that involved not only proof of the impact of housing segregation on school segregation but also a judicial effort at a partial housing remedy. This study examines the legislative and administrative history of the Indianapolis school system in the light of the adjudication that arose from it.*

William E. Marsh is an associate professor of law at the Indiana University School of Law at Indianapolis.—Eds.

BACKGROUND

Demography

The Indianapolis Public School Corporation (IPS) is located in the central part of Marion County, Indiana. Until 1969 its boundaries were coterminous with those of the city of Indianapolis. The "Univ-Gov" Act of 1969[1] consolidated the civil governments of Indianapolis and Marion County to create a metropolitan city government.[2] It expressly excepted the schools from the

---

1. 1969 Ind. Acts, ch. 173, §101 at 357; Ind. Code §§18-4-1-1 to 18-4-5-4 (1971); Ind. Code Ann. §§48-9101 to 48-9507 (Burns Supp. 1974).

2. Three enclaves, situated on the boundaries of the old city, were only partially subsumed in the new city; Beech Grove, an industrial community of 13,432 in 1970, had a black population of 19; Speedway, an industrial community of 14,951 with a black population of 68; and Lawrence, with 216 blacks in a population of 18,997. United States v. Board of School Commissioners of the City of Indianapolis, Indiana, 332 F. Supp. 655, 663 (S.D. Ind. 1971), *aff'd*, 474 F. 2d 81 (7th Cir.), *cert. denied*, 413 U.S. 920 (1973). [Hereinafter cited as Indianapolis I]

territorial expansion, however, so that the area served by the IPS remained limited to that of the former city of Indianapolis.[3] Moreover, by its acts of 1961 and 1969, the Indiana General Assembly made it virtually impossible for IPS to extend its boundaries.[4]

Center Township lies at the heart of IPS and comprises over half its area. In 1970 the population of Center Township was 273,598, of which 166,622 (61.2 percent) were white and 106,112 (38.8 percent) were black. The population of the newly legislated city of Indianapolis was 518,400, of which 28,500 (5.5 percent) were black. Thus, about 79 percent of the blacks and only 10 percent of the whites of the civil city lived within the confines of IPS.[5] Furthermore, the number of blacks in IPS appeared to be increasing significantly.[6]

This imbalance reflects a tradition of geographical racial segregation that has roots in the mores of the slaveowning Virginians, Kentuckians, and Carolinians who settled, during the course of the eighteenth century, the land that was to become Indiana. At least through 1869, blacks were effectively prevented from purchasing property in white neighborhoods by realtors, lending institutions, and threatening landowners. Deed covenants restricting ownership of lots to whites were upheld by law until 1948. In 1963, newspapers were still advertising real estate with the designation, "for colored only"; after 1963, "for anyone" became a popular term meaning that black purchasers would be considered. In addition, low-rent housing projects were uniformly situated on the boundaries of established black residential areas, attracting almost total black occupancy. The result of these housing practices was the Indianapolis's black ghetto was located and virtually confined within the boundaries of Center Township.

Segregation of School Facilities

Segregation of school facilities in Indianapolis has equally deep historical roots. Prior to 1869, Indiana state laws prohibiting blacks from attending public

---

3. District Judge S. Hugh Dillin described the school city in the following terms:

The shape of the School City resembles that of a trussed fowl, with its head to the north, its bound feet to the south, and its flapping wings extending east and west. The east-west wing spread, at its greatest, is about 16 miles. The north-south dimension of the School City is about 13 miles.

Id. at 656.

4. 1961 Ind. Acts, ch. 186, § §1, 10 at 431; Ind. Code § §20-3-14-1, 20-3-14-10 (1971); Ind. Code Ann. § §28-3610, 28-3619 (Burns 1970); 1961 Ind. Acts, ch. 186, §9 at 431, Ind. Code Ann. §28-2346 (Burns Supp. 1968), *repealed* 1969, ch. 52, §2; 1969 Ind. Acts, ch. 52 §3 at 47, Ind. Code §20-3-14-9 (1971), Ind. Code Ann. §28-3618 (Burns 1970).

5. Accurate census figures for the school city are not available, because it includes parts of eight other townships annexed before the 1961 act. However, the Marion County Index of Dissimilarity, a comparision of percentages of blacks and whites in each census tract to percentages of blacks and whites in the entire county, is 81 percent, one of the highest in the United States, indicating the radical degree of segregation in Indianapolis. The index for the geographic area with the school city of Indianapolis is 87 percent.

6. Indianapolis I, 332 F. Supp., at 663.

school were strictly enforced.[7] The adoption of the Fourteenth Amendment caused the state to pass a statute in 1869 providing for the education of blacks,[8] but it was interpreted by the Indiana Supreme Court in 1874 to mean that blacks were not entitled to attend public schools unless a black school was available in the district where they lived. In other words, blacks and whites could not attend the same schools, even if it meant that the black child was deprived of education.[9] A dual school system was adopted throughout the state, and Indianapolis implemented it by building a new school for white pupils and assigning black pupils to the old one.[10] Segregation was upheld by law in the elementary schools of Indianapolis for the next hundred years.

From 1877 to 1927, however, high school students of either race were permitted to attend the school of their choice on an integrated basis. Then, in 1927, a "colored high school," built at the instigation of the Indianapolis Chamber of Commerce and named Crispus Attucks after a black patriot who was killed by the British during the Boston Massacre, was completed. All black high school students were compelled to attend it regardless of their place of residence.[11] The burden of finding transportation, where necessary, was placed on the pupils. Not until 1935 was legislation enacted which mandated paid transportation for black students who lived a specific distance from the school.[12]

Some members of the black community supported the construction of Crispus Attucks on the basis that it would provide jobs for black teachers who previously had not been permitted to teach at the high school level.[13] A suit was brought against the Indianapolis Board of School Commissioners in 1926 in an attempt to halt construction of Crispus Attucks on the basis that a single all-black school could not possibly provide an educational program equal to that provided white students in the existing three specialized high schools, "technical, manual and classical and academic." The Indiana Supreme Court, however, refused to halt the project saying that the lawsuit was premature. It stated:

> When some colored child who is sufficiently advanced demands and is denied educational advantages accorded white children of equal advancement, then it will be time enough to take such proceedings as are necessary to secure the constitutional rights of such child.[14]

7. The Supreme Court of Indiana held that a person was eligible for admission to public school only if he or she was between the ages of 5 and 21, unmarried and was "neither a negro, a mulatto nor the son of a mulatto." Draper v. Cambridge, 20 Ind. 268, 269 (1863).
8. 1869 Ind. Acts (Spec. Sess.) ch. 16, §3, at 41, *repealed* 1949 Ind. Acts, ch. 186, §10 at 603.
9. Cory v. Carter, 48 Ind. 327 (1874).
10. Leary, Indianapolis: The Story of a City 118 (1970).
11. Indianapolis I, 332 F. Supp., at 664.
12. *Id.*
13. Thornbrough, *Segregation in Indiana During the Klan Era of the 1920s,* 47 Miss. Valley Hist. Rev. 594, 601 (1961).
14. Greathouse v. Board of School Commissioners of the City of Indianapolis, 198 Ind. 95, 151 N.E. 411 (1926).

Governance of Indiana Schools

The Indiana Constitution states that the ultimate responsibility for the public schools and the duty to provide a "general and uniform system of Common Schools, wherein tuition shall be without charge, and equally open to all," is vested in the state.[15] School corporations organized to run the schools are therefore but agents of the state. Thus, the Indianapolis public schools are managed by the local Indianapolis Board of School Commissioners, but ultimately controlled by the Indiana Board of Education. School funds, nevertheless, are mainly derived from local property taxes.

Until 1929, members of the IPS Board of School Commissioners were selected in a partisan political election. But, in response to alleged Ku Klux Klan domination of the board during the 1920s, leaders of the Indianapolis community obtained enactment of legislation which made the election nonpartisan. At the same time they formed the Citizen's School Committee, a candidate-slating committee, which until the 1976 election maintained virtually absolute control over the selection of members of the Indianapolis Board of School Commissioners.[16] One of the founders, John L. Niblack, a Marion County judge from 1941 to 1975 and an overt segregationist, was a leader of the committee for over forty years. The committee has tended to restrict its efforts to campaigning for the election of "leading members of the community" to the board, after which it has generally given the board independence in operating the schools.

The Desegregation Act of 1949

Prior to 1949 the official policy of the state of Indiana and of its agent, the Board of School Commissioners of the City of Indianapolis, was one of de jure segregation. Faculty and staff as well as pupils were separated. New construction, renovation, attendance zones, and grade structures were planned to promote isolation of the white from the black race.

Then, in 1949, the Indiana General Assembly passed an act which required Indiana public schools to begin desegregating on a phased basis. It permitted students enrolling for the first time in kindergarten, first grade, and the first junior and high school grades (6 and 9) to attend the school nearest their homes, regardless of race.[17]

The IPS Board of School Commissioners was not moved to change its ways; it responded to the 1949 legislation by instituting construction and pupil-transfer policies that would minimize desegregation. Crispus Attucks remained an all-black high school, and in 1953 the board established attendance-zone boundary lines for all elementary schools, which tended to solidify past segregation pat-

15. Ind. Const. art VIII, §1.

16. J. Niblack, The Life and Times of a Hoosier Judge 191, 331-332 (1973). [hereinafter cited as Niblack]

17. 1949 Ind. Acts, ch 186, § §1-6, 8, at 603 *as amended by* 1965 Ind. Acts, ch. 101, §1, at 149; Ind. Code § §20-4-1-7 to 20-4-1-13 (1971); Ind. Code Ann. § §28-6106 to 28-6112 (Burns 1970), *repealed* 1973 Ind. Acts, Pub. L. 218 §4.

terns. Some of the boundary lines were clearly gerrymandered; all were based on a census of school children, taken by the IPS, in which race was recorded.[18] Further, under an optional attendance-zone plan, pupils in the few existing integrated neighborhoods were given a choice of two or more schools; most enrolled in a school identified with their own race.[19]

In 1953, Arthur Boone, a black father, filed a lawsuit to obtain a transfer of his children from the all-black school to which they were assigned to a school which was 75 percent white. The grounds were that the white school was closer to his home, that the only two white children on his block were permitted to attend it, and that his children's lives were endangered by having to cross a railroad track to get to the black school; a child had been killed crossing those tracks.[20] Unfortunately, the records of the trial have been misplaced so that the decision of the court is not known. It is clear, however, that segregation persisted after the 1949 legislation.

Post-Brown v. Board of Education Policies—
1954–1967

In 1954 the *Brown* decision of the United States Supreme Court rendered racially segregated school facilities unconstitutional, but it did not drastically change the Indianapolis Board of School Commissioners' policies or practices. The school system underwent an extraordinary period of growth in the ensuing decade, and the techniques employed by the board to deal with overcrowding were clearly chosen to foster rather than to reduce segregation. New schools were constructed. Additions were made to old ones. Busing privileges were extended. Attendance zones were changed. Grade structures were altered, and special education classes were relocated. The net result was that segregation increased. Between 1954 and 1968 the number of institutions with 90 percent or more black students had doubled. Faculty and staff in these schools were virtually all black; in white schools they were virtually all white.

In 1967 the Indiana Civil Rights Commission adopted a resolution urrging IPS to take steps to obtain a more favorable racial balance in the schools. The resolution specifically sought action toward several overcrowded schools with large black enrollment which were in close proximity to all-white schools in

18. There have been a large number of minor changes since 1953, but the basic plan was still used in 1976. In 1971, Judge Dillin found that "[a]ccording to the evidence there have been approximately 350 boundary changes in the system since 1954. More than 90 percent of these promoted segregation." Indianapolis I, 332 F. Supp., at 655, 670.

19. The ingenuity expended on putting these policies into practice is evident in the case of Elementary School 19, which was converted from an all-black non-neighborhood school to an all-white non-neighborhood school in September 1953. The school was made to serve two noncontiguous white areas, although it was located in neither of them. The blacks who had attended the school were sent to Elementary School 64, the attendance zone of which had been redrawn to include almost all the black students in the area. *Id.* at 655, 666.

20. Testimony of Arthur Boone, Record of Proceedings at Trial (Indianapolis I), vol. IV, at 793 (July 15, 1971). [Hereinafter cited as Trial Record I.]

which space was available.[21] There is no indication that IPS responded to this request. The Indianapolis Mayor's Commission on Human Rights also expressed concern about the effect of the board's racial practices and conducted an investigation of them.[22] However, like the Civil Rights Commission, it took no action having the force of law.

A Complaint is Filed

Meanwhile, in March 1967, a black parent whose children attended the Indianapolis public schools filed a complaint with the United States Department of Justice stating that the children were being denied equal protection of the law because of the dual school system. The parent did so at the instigation of the Indianapolis Metropolitan Council for the National Association for the Advancement of Colored People (NAACP), acting principally through its president, Andrew W. Ramsey.[23] Ramsey had been a teacher at the Crispus Attucks High School and, at the time of the complaint, was teaching at the Shortridge High School, a high school that was predominantly black, but which was located in what was formerly an elite white neighborhood.

On the basis of the complaint the Justice Department investigated the IPS system and found it guilty of unlawful segregation. On April 18, 1967, it advised the school board that a suit would be filed against it unless corrective action was taken before May 6, 1968.[24]

The School Board's Denials. On April 26, 1968, the president of the board of school commissioners denied that Indianapolis's schools were segregated, and insisted that Indianapolis had, in fact, been in the forefront in achieving equal treatment for all races in its schools.[25] He cited the IPS board's resolution of March 12, 1968, setting forth its commitment to neighborhood schools and to integration, and attributing the racial imbalance in the schools to "housing restrictions, certain inequalities of job opportunity, legacies of history, unfounded prejudice and considerable self-segregation by groups in our city."[26]

A week afterward, the school board issued a resolution ordering the superintendent to submit a plan for voluntary integration, and on May 23, 1968, he reported a plan to the board which called for each school principal to request

21. Indianapolis Star, Nov. 17, 1967, at 23, col. 2.

22. *Id.,* Aug. 23, 1968, at 32, col. 8.

23. Indianapolis News, June 17, 1968, at 4, col. 1.

24. Board of School Commissioners of the City of Indianapolis, Indiana, Minutes, Book iii at 2053. [hereinafter cited as Minutes] *See also,* Indianapolis Star, April 27, 1968, at 25, col. 4.

25. Minutes, *supra* note 24, Book iii, at 2058. The letter stated, in addition, that the deadline established for corrective action exhibited unfortunate timing since it came the day before the scheduled school board election. As it turned out, the 1968 school board election was held without racial integration having become a major issue in the campaign.

26. *Id.* at 1453.

teachers to transfer voluntarily to schools where the race opposite to their own was dominant.[27] The plan stated that such a transfer would be considered an affirmative action in promotion evaluations because it would indicate that the teacher wanted a broader experience. No stronger encouragement was provided, and the plan was largely unsuccessful.

Complaint by the Department of Justice.   Finding this plan insufficient, the United States Department of Justice filed a complaint on May 31, 1968, in the United States District Court for the Southern District of Indiana, against the Board of School Commissioners of the City of Indianapolis, Indiana; George F. Ostheimer, superintendent of schools; Mark W. Gray, president of the board of school commissioners; and the six other members of the board of school commissioners.[28]

The complaint alleged that the Indianapolis public schools were segregated in violation of the Fourteenth Amendment to the Constitution of the United States and the Civil Rights Act of 1964, and that the defendants had instituted racial discrimination by:

> assigning students, designing attendance zones for elementary schools, establishing feeder patterns to secondary schools, and constructing new schools on the basis of policies and practices which in some instances have the purpose and effect of segregating students on the basis of race. . . .[29]

and by:

> assigning faculty and staff members among the various schools and the Indianapolis School System on a racially segregated basis so that as a general practice white faculty and staff members have been assigned on the basis of their race to schools attended only or almost entirely by white students and Negro faculty and staff members have been assigned on the basis of race to schools attended only or almost entirely by Negro students.[30]

The complaint further stated that of the one hundred seven elementary schools, five junior high schools, and eleven senior high schools in IPS, the Crispus Attucks High School and sixteen elementary and junior high schools were attended solely or predominantly by black students and staffed solely or predominantly by black teachers; and sixty-eight elementary schools and senior high schools were attended solely or predominantly by white students and were staffed solely or predominantly by white teachers.

27. *Id.* at 2052.
28. Complaint of Plaintiff, United States v. Board of School Commissioners of the City of Indianapolis, Indiana, No. IP 68-C-225 (S.D. Ind. May 31, 1968).
29. *Id.* at 2.
30. *Id.* at 3.

The Justice Department concluded by asking the court to:

enter an order enjoining the defendants, their agents, officers, employees, successors, and all persons in active concert or participation with them, from discriminating on the basis of race or color in the operation of the Indiana Public School System and from failing to adopt or implement a plan for the elimination of the aforementioned discriminatory practices in the Indianapolis Public School System in compliance with the Fourteenth Amendment to the United States Constitution.[31]

Pursuant to the selection procedure which assigns cases on a random basis to one of the four federal district judges of the Southern District of Indiana, the action was assigned to the court of Judge S. Hugh Dillin. A former member of the Indiana House of Representatives and the Indiana Senate of which he had been floor leader and president pro tem, Judge Dillin had also been a candidate for governor in 1956, and had been appointed to the federal bench in 1961.

The School Board's Legal Response. The defendants filed a response to the Justice Department's complaint on June 19, 1968. Its attorneys were Baker & Daniels, one of the oldest and among the three largest law firms in Indiana; it had been counsel for the Indianapolis public schools during most of this century.

Although the response conceded that the Indianapolis public schools had at one time been racially segregated, it denied that any racial discrimination had occurred since 1949. It asserted that in 1968 "students are assigned, attendance zones designated, feeder patterns established, new schools constructed and faculty and staff members assigned solely on the basis of sound nonracial education principles and neighborhood consideration."[32] It affirmed that Crispus Attucks High School was built in 1927 as an all-black school, but maintained that the school had not been de jure racially segregated for many years. The racial balance between teachers and students in each school, it alleged, reflected the composition of neighborhoods surrounding the school and resulted primarily either from residential housing patterns or the private choice of the individual faculty members and students.

The response further insisted that the defendants had operated a unitary nonracial school system for more than twenty years and, moreover, that the unitary system had been established prior to the 1949 Indiana legislation requiring desegregation of public schools, thus prior to the *Brown* decision. It pointed out that the school district had been providing compensatory education for inner-city children, a program which principally benefited black children. In addition, it had voluntarily engaged the services of an impartial outside agency

31. *Id.* at 4.
32. Answers of Defendant at 1, United States v. Board of School Commissioners of the City of Indianapolis, Indiana, No. IP 68-C-225 (S.D. Ind. June 19, 1968).

in order to "verify and maintain" the school system's objectivity in drawing attendance zones to implement the neighborhood school concept. In conclusion, the response stated that the voluntary teacher transfer plan had resulted in more than 100 applications for transfer for the upcoming 1968/69 school year. In short, the defendants all said that they had sought to afford every pupil in the public school system a superior educational opportunity completely without regard to race, color, or national origin.

The School Board's Early Strategy. The defendants knew, of course, that although their general denial of racial segregation was an appropriate plea, they would be obliged to respond to the suit. The school board and their lawyers felt that their legal posture and the practicalities of eliminating the segregation dictated a division of the case into three distinct categories: teachers, high school students, and elementary school students. They aimed first to eliminate the assignment of faculty and staff in a racially identifiable manner, because they believed there was no legal defense for this practice and it was easier to change than were student assignment practices. After this was accomplished, the board planned to deal with segregation in the high schools. Members of the school board were not as opposed to the busing of high school students. Finally, they would approach the issue of desegregation of the elementary schools, the area which they felt they had the most chance of defending successfully.

Desegregating Faculty and Staff. At the time the complaint was filed, the Indianapolis public schools were racially identifiable by faculty distribution. A formal stipulation[33] shows that there were eighteen schools in the IPS system with black principals. Of these, seventeen had at least 97 percent black students; fourteen had 99 percent or more black students, and none had less than 91 percent black students. Eleven of the eighteen schools had all black teachers and only one had less than 92 percent black teachers.

The voluntary transfer plan instituted in May 1968 had not resulted in enough requests for transfers to eliminate the racial identification of schools; nor did it satisfy the Justice Department which, on July 14, 1968, filed a motion for preliminary injunction requiring the IPS to make this a priority so that substantial reassignments leading to integration would take place before school opened in September.

Counsel for the school board and for the Justice Department entered into a series of pretrial conferences about the teacher portion of the law suit, with Judge Dillin acting as mediator. A settlement was reached and the IPS board approved it on July 30, 1968.[34] The settlement was the basis for a stipulated

33. Stipulation IX at 2, United States v. Board of School Commissioners of the City of Indianapolis, Indiana, No. IP 68-C-225 (S.D. Ind. Aug. 5, 1968).
34. The IPS Board approval was contained in the resolution number 5851-1968. *See* Minutes, *supra* note 24, Book iii, at 257.

judgment entered by the court on August 5, 1968, technically granting the Justice Department's motion for a preliminary injunction requiring reassignment of teachers. The plan required assignment of at least 83 white teachers to the 16 all-black schools, and required all schools to have at least one black regular classroom teacher for the 1968/69 school year. This settlement left three to four times as many black teachers as white teachers in all-black schools.

Teacher Reaction. As was not surprising, the transfer plan was unfavorably received by the teachers, who in their dissatisfaction turned for help from the Indianapolis Education Association (IEA), the leading (but not exclusive) local organization representing teachers. The IEA, which did not retain counsel on an on-going basis, engaged Irving Fink, an Indianapolis lawyer with labor-relations experience, to represent it in its response to the teacher transfer program. Fink's first step was to advise the IEA that in order to be effective it must first view itself as a union rather than simply as a professional organization, and be prepared to take strong measures including litigation, if it was to have an impact on the plan. Fink's second step was to confer informally with Judge Dillin. At the end of the conference he concluded that the teachers could not successfully intervene in the pending school desegregation case, and so he filed a separate action against the board of school commissioners in the superior court of Marion County alleging that the teacher transfer program was a violation of the teacher's right to due process of law. This suit did not succeed in blocking the teacher transfer program, but it did enable the IEA to participate in the formulation of the transfer plan.

The out-of-court settlement of the dispute between the IEA and IPS did not mean that all the teachers were satisfied or that they were agreeable to the reassignment program. A sizable number of teachers left the IPS system, some for suburban schools, rather than be transferred within IPS, and the school system experienced a teacher shortage when schools opened in the fall of 1968. It was reported there were approximately 170 substitute teachers in classrooms as compared to approximately 70 in preceding years.[35]

Teacher resignations had an undesired and unexpected impact on black schools. The plan had intended that transferred teachers would be replaced by teachers of equal experience and level of competence. At Crispus Attucks High School what actually happened was that experienced black teachers were replaced by inexperienced white teachers because the experienced white teachers refused to be transferred to an all-black school. The president of the student body appeared before the board to protest this fact.[36] Furthermore, there was very little actual interaction between the white teachers and the black teachers within the school, at least during the first year of the transfer program.

35. Indianapolis Star, Sept. 4, 1968, at 23, col. 4; *see also,* Indianapolis News, Sept. 5, 1968, at 27, col. 4.
36. Also, Niblack reports that "[t]he president of the student body of Crispus Attucks,

At the Northwest High School, a predominantly white school, the PTA supported teachers who were scheduled to be transferred. Its action led to the formation of Citizens of Indianapolis for Quality Schools, Inc. (CIQS), an organization of conservative whites. Eventually CIQS was able to intervene in the lawsuit as a party defendant, buttressing the efforts of the Indianapolis public schools which, it believed, was not resisting the Justice Department's attacks forcefully enough.[37]

High Schools. As soon as the settlement with the teachers had been agreed upon, the school board turned its attention to the high school component of the suit. The neighborhood concept gave it little legal support in this area, but as members of the board were not strongly opposed to busing high school students —in fact it was traditional practice in Indianapolis—they hoped that some solution to the problem could be found. Pressure was on the board from the court which, in December 1969, had filed a pretrial order expediting the trial.

After a great deal of deliberation, the school board formulated a proposal for desegregating the system's eleven high schools. On January 27, 1970, it passed a resolution to close two predominantly black high schools—Crispus Attucks and Shortridge—and desegregate the nine white high schools by transporting the black students to them. The court agreed that this was a good-faith proposal and vacated its pretrial order.

The proposal to close Crispus Attucks High School was strongly challenged by blacks throughout the city. They formed Concerned Citizens for Crispus Attucks High School, a coalition bringing together all segments of the black community, from its most conservative members to the Black Panthers. The response of the school board was to continue its plan to close the Attucks facility, but preserve the Attucks heritage by giving it a new building. It argued persuasively that since the existing structure was over forty years old and was located in a neighborhood gutted of students by an interstate highway which passed by its front door, relocation of the physical plant would be beneficial.

The black community agreed. Two possible sites were selected for the new high school. The first was abruptly rejected as excessively expensive by the

---

our all-colored High School which had brought fame to the city, a lad named Crenshaw, appeared before the board [of school commissioners] to protest transfer of 38 negro teachers of long standing out of Crispus Attucks, to be replaced by 38 white strangers." *See* Niblack, *supra* note 16, at 332.

37. CIQS moved to intervene on February 6, 1970. Judge Dillin denied the motion to intervene on April 29, 1971, more than 14 months after the motion was filed. CIQS appealed to the U.S. Court of Appeals for the Seventh Circuit.

The Seventh Circuit held that the district judge had not abused his discretion in denying intervention, but that in light of subsequent developments the court should reconsider the motion. United States v. Board of School Commissioners of the City of Indianapolis, Indiana, 466 F.2d 573 (7th Cir. 1972), *cert. denied,* 410 U.S. 909 (1973).

On remand, Judge Dillin reconsidered the motion, and on September 13, 1972 he granted CIQS leave to intervene as a party defendant.

board at its meeting in July 1970. (There had been school board elections in May and its membership had changed on July 1, 1970.)[38] The board then proposed a site in the northwest section of the city which was being used as a tree-growing station by the city of Indianapolis. However, in order to build a new high school at this location it was necessary to obtain a zoning change from the Marion County Metropolitan Development Commission. The CIQS group opposed the building of the new Crispus Attucks at this site. CIQS supporters appeared *en masse* at a hearing of the Metropolitan Development Commission and pressured the commission to deny the zoning change. The effect of the denial was to interfere with the desegregation of the schools.[39]

Shortridge High School, the oldest high school in Indianapolis, is located in the north-central part of IPS, an area which is now predominantly black, but which was once the home of the city's wealthiest white citizens. It enjoyed a reputation as an excellent academic high school and, in an effort to maintain a racial balance among its students, plans had been formulated to make it a magnet school with a strong college preparation curriculum. This plan was never fully funded or implemented and was abandoned in 1968.[40] Nevertheless, Shortridge retained its reputation for academic excellence, and its closing was opposed by the community, including the mayor, a graduate of the school, who, as a member of the school board, had been an originator of the magnet plan.[41]

The cumulative effect of black opposition to the closing of Crispus Attucks, establishment opposition to the closing of Shortridge, and the CIQS opposition to a new Crispus Attucks was that the school board gave up its efforts to desegregate the high schools and accepted the inevitability of a trial. The consensus was that no plan to desegregate even the high schools could be effected by the politically sensitive board without an order from the federal court.[42]

38. The school board election was held in May 1968. Because of staggered terms, four persons elected in 1968 took office July 1, 1968, and the three remaining members elected in 1968 began their four-year terms on July 1, 1970. Sammy Dotlich was appointed to fill the unexpired term of Richard G. Lugar effective July 11, 1967. Dotlich was elected in May 1968, and his four-year term began July 1, 1968.

39. Indianapolis I, 332 F. Supp., at 679. The Metropolitian Development Commission was subsequently made a party to the case. The issue which brought the commission into the case was whether past zoning practices would provide the basis for an interdistrict remedy.

40. Under the plan, Shortridge was not completely a magnet school. It was rather a combination of students from the neighborhood and students attracted from other neighborhoods. The reluctance of IPS to "go all the way" may have been fatal to the plan.

41. Some of the same people are disgruntled by the fact that Shortridge is the apparent model of Shortley High School in Dan Wakefield's novel, *Going All The Way*. Wakefield is a Shortridge graduate.

42. The IPS Board was politically sensitive in that community groups had been successful in blocking contemplated board actions. In retrospect, it seems surprising that the board was not more independent. Unlike some cities, such as Boston, the school board in Indianapolis is not commonly used as a springboard to higher political office. Of the thirteen different persons who served on the board between July 1967 and 1971, only one, Robert DeFrantz, has subsequently been a candidate for public office. DeFrantz was an unsuccessful candidate for reelection to the IPS Board in 1972 and was reelected to the board in

The school board apparently believed that any attempt to desegregate the schools without a court order could only fail because it had no method, other than a court order, of assuring that a subsequent board would not reverse its efforts.

Elementary Schools. The school board's inability to desegregate the high schools discouraged it from attempting to desegregate the elementary schools. No concrete proposals were forwarded and the attitude of the board about what should be done about the segregated elementary schools is not clear. If they had been successful in desegregating the high schools, the board could have defended the legality of their segregated elementary schools on the basis of the neighborhood concept and the community's opposition to busing.

THE TRIAL

The teacher assignment issue having been settled, the issues of the racial segregation of elementary and high school students raised by the Justice Department's complaint went to trial before the United States District Court for the Southern District of Indiana on July 12, 1971, more than three years after the complaint was filed. Judge S. Hugh Dillin presided.

The Government's Case

The approach of the lawyers for the Justice Department was to prove that the Indianapolis public schools had always been segregated that the school board had never acted to eliminate segregation and had indeed taken numerous specific actions over a period of years which cumulatively had served to promote and perpetuate segregation.[43] From 1954 to 1968 when—despite official change in policy—the school board allegedly continued to operate the dual school system, became the critical period under scrutiny.[44]

Government evidence of de jure segregation concentrated on several categories of school board activity: (1) construction, both new schools and additions to existing schools; (2) boundary changes for elementary school districts; (3) high school feeder school patterns; (4) optional attendance zones; (5) alteration in grade structures; (6) transportation policies and practices; and (7) special education classes.[45]

1976. Richard G. Lugar, who left the IPS Board in 1967 to run for major of Indianapolis, is the only notable exception to the rule. Lugar was elected mayor in 1967 and reelected in 1971. He was unsuccessful as the Republican nominee for U.S. Senate in 1974, but was elected to the Senate in 1976. The election contest was against incumbent Vance Hartke.

43. Closing Argument of John D. Leshy, Trial Record I, vol. VIII, at 1349-50, July 21, 1971.

44. Indianapolis I, 332 F. Supp., at 659.

45. At the conclusion of the trial Judge Dillin found IPS actions in each of these categories had in fact promoted segregation within IPS. Indianapolis I, 332 F. Supp., at 655, 677-78.

Although the government called IPS administrators to testify, it did not make a serious attempt to show purposeful racial discrimination on the part of the defendants. Rather, the government emphasized that, in the absence of rational or minimal explanations for actions which in fact promoted segregation, the inference could be established that the motivation for the action was racial segregation. The government maintained that: (1) the effect of specific actions and the cumulative effect of the school board actions generally was to promote segregation; (2) in some instances, particularly for boundary changes, there was no rational motivation other than racial separation for taking certain action; and (3) the overall pattern of school board activities was such that when the school board was faced with a choice, a decision most likely to promote segregation was customarily chosen.[46]

School Construction
It had been stipulated that of the sixteen new schools constructed in the IPS system between 1961 and 1968, only one was significantly integrated on the day it opened.[47] Fourteen of the sixteen new schools opened with at least 99 percent white population, one school opened with 820 black students and 20 white students, and another with 997 white and 318 black students.

Some of the new schools were constructed adjacent to schools attended primarily by students of the opposite race, thereby preventing integration of neighboring school districts. Two new high schools were located at the extreme northeastern and northwestern boundaries of the city so as to serve virtually all white areas.[48] Furthermore, even while the trial was taking place the school board was planning a new middle school (Forest Manor—grades 6, 7, and 8), the anticipated enrollment of which was 90 percent black.[49]

The construction of additions to existing schools had also allegedly been used to promote segregation.[50] Additions had been made to large black elementary schools when integration could have been increased by adding classrooms to smaller, nearby white schools. IPS records of construction projects and enrollment figures were provided as evidence of these acts of de jure segregation.[51]

Optional Attendance Zones
The government submitted that optional attendance zones, for both elementary and high school assignments, were used to promote segregation in

---

46. Closing Argument of John D. Leshy, Trial Record I, vol. VIII, at 1349-50, July 21, 1971.
47. Stipulation XI, Record on Appeal, United States v. Board of School Commissioners of the City of Indianapolis, Indiana, No. 72-1031 (Aug. 5, 1968).
48. Indianapolis I, 332 F. Supp., at 669.
49. The school would be located at 4501 E. 32d Street.
50. Indianapolis I, 332 F. Supp., at 667.
51. *See* government exhibits number 48 and 171.

several neighborhoods where the residential housing patterns were integrated. The optional attendance zone permitted students in the zone (a part of a school district) to attend one of two or more schools. Generally, one was white and one black. IPS records and testimony of teachers and principals were used to prove that such students customarily attended the school in which most of the students were of their race, even where this involved crossing physical barriers such as railroad tracks, arterial highways, or rivers.[52]

IPS administrators testified that there had been approximately 350 changes in the boundaries of elementary school districts since the districts were established in 1953.[53] They maintained, however, that the changes were necessitated by the rapidly expanding school population and were aimed at alleviating overcrowding at some schools. No direct evidence that any of the boundary changes was motivated by a desire to perpetuate segregation was presented, but government counsel argued that an inference of racial motivation could be established because there was no other rational basis for some of the changes. They cited specific examples of unusually shaped districts, of districts which ignored natural barriers, and of districts which drew lines between the black and white communities. In addition, lines had been moved when the racial composition of the communities changed. The emphasis of the evidence about boundary changes, however, was on their effect, which was to perpetuate segregation.

High School Feeder Patterns

In the Indianapolis Public School System, all students graduating from a specified group of elementary schools are assigned to the same high school. Thus, by adjusting the boundary lines of the elementary school groups, the school board can exercise a significant measure of control over the racial composition of the high schools. The government maintained that in several instances the board had altered the boundary lines of the feeder school in response to changes in neighborhood racial composition, and in doing so had perpetuated segregation. IPS records showing changes in feeder school assignments were offered as evidence of this.[54]

Busing

In order to allevaite overcrowding, the school board had also resorted to busing. The government produced evidence, again drawn from IPS records, showing that generally students were bused to a school where most of the students were of their race, in some cases even when there was space available in schools closer to the students' homes.[55]

52. Trial Record I, vol. II, at 208-14, 244-46 (July 13, 1971); vol. IV, at 821-25 (July 15, 1971).
53. *See* government exhibit number 27.
54. *See* government exhibit number 88.
55. Trial Record I, vol. IV, at 839 (July 15, 1971).

The IPS Defense

The Indianapolis Board of School Commissioners based its defense on two principles. First, it asserted that its elementary school districts were determined by the neighborhood school concept and that, therefore, the schools were de facto segregated because of housing patterns in the community and not because of acts promoting segregation on the part of the school board or the administration. They cited the policy on integration issued by the board on March 12, 1968 as making this clear.[56]

Second, the board conceded that the school system had at one time been racially segregated, but maintained that this practice had been abandoned.[57] It proposed that the legal issue was, or should be, whether the board was presently (in 1971) acting to promote segregation in the schools. It stated that IPS had attempted to eliminate a dual school system, and at the time of the trial was no longer acting in a manner which would promote a dual system. The board also maintained that actions such as the construction of new schools, which the government suggested were evidence of de jure segregation, were necessitated by a rapid growth in school population. Furthermore, the defense sought to demonstrate that failure or refusal to build the Forest Manor Middle School, although it was in a totally black neighborhood, would constitute an act of discrimination against the residents of the neighborhood because the school was badly needed. It argued that the proposed location was chosen on a racially neutral basis, and that it was legally irrelevant that the school would be nearly all back when it opened.[58]

General Conclusions

The trial was concluded on July 21, 1971, and on August 18 Judge Dillin announced his decision in favor of the plaintiffs.[59] He found that IPS was operating an unlawfully segregated school system on May 17, 1954 (the date of *Brown*), that IPS was continuing to operate an unlawfully segregated school system on May 31, 1968 (the date the complaint was filed against IPS), and that this unlawful segregation had not been eliminated as of the trial of the case.[60]

The court rejected the IPS theory that it should be judged on the basis of current rather than past practices and also rejected its factual justifications for existing de facto segregation. It found that the board had committed acts of de jure segregation when it had:

> built additions at Negro schools and then zoned Negro students into them from predominantly white schools; it has built additions at white schools

56. *See, e.g., id.,* vol. II, at 371 (July 13, 1971).
57. *See id.,* vol. VIII, at 1380-81 (July 21, 1971).
58. *Id.* at 1393.
59. Indianapolis I, 332 F. Supp., at 655.
60. *Id.* at 658.

for white children attending Negro schools; it has generally failed to reduce overcrowding at schools of one race by assigning students to use newly built capacity at the schools of the opposite race. The Board has also constructed simultaneous additions at contiguous predominantly white and Negro schools, and has installed portable classrooms at schools of one race with no adjustment of boundaries between it and the neighboring schools of the opposite race.[61]

As evidence that the school board's policies regarding new construction activity promoted segregation, Judge Dillin pointed to the proposed Forest Manor Middle School; planning to build a school in a location which guaranteed its student body would be virtually all black, he found, constituted an act of incontrovertible de jure segregation.[62] Boundary changes and the use of optional attendance zones reinforced by busing were found to be part of the same pattern perpetuating segregation.

Having decided that the IPS system was unlawfully segregated, Judge Dillin concluded that the school board was "clearly charged with the affirmative duty to take whatever steps might be necessary to convert to a unitary system in which racial discrimination [will] be eliminated root and branch."[63] Any revision of local laws and regulations and revision of school districts required to achieve this end should be undertaken.[64] Furthermore, the court had continuing jurisdiction and a broad scope of powers to make and enforce decrees in equity which would remedy the existing unconstitutional segregation.[65]

Judge Dillin went on to state that although the easy way out would be "to order a massive 'fruit basket' scrambling of students within IPS during the coming school year and then go on to other things," such a "simplistic solution" would not work in the long haul.[66] He cited the mandate of *Green* to formulate a plan that "promises realistically to work now," emphasizing the verb *work* rather than, as other courts had done, its modifier *now*.[67]

Dillin had been impressed by the testimony of Theron A. Johnson of the Office of Education, Department of Health, Education and Welfare, that when a school's black population reached approximately 40 percent, an accelerated and irreversible white flight from the neighborhood in which the school was located took place.[68] Since the IPS system already contained 37.8 percent black students, it became central to Judge Dillin's concept of a workable remedy

61. *Id.* at 667.
62. *Id.* at 671.
63. *Id.* at 678.
64. *Id.,* citing Brown v. Board of Education [Brown II], 349 U.S. 294 (1955).
65. *Id.,* citing Swann v. Charlotte-Mecklenburg Board of Education, 402 U.S. 1 (1971).
66. *Id.*
67. *Id.* at 678-79.
68. Trial Record 1, vol. V, at 995-96 (July 16, 1971). *See also* government exhibit number 178, at 14.

that the 40 percent tipping point be avoided.[69] This would be easily possible, he believed, if areas adjoining the board's jurisdiction were added to it. He raised the basic question of the constitutionality of the Uni-Gov Act, which had united the governments of Indianapolis and Marion County with the express exclusion of the IPS, and further suggested that it might be necessary to provide either legislatively or by judicial decree "for the creation of a metropolitan school district embracing all of Marion County, together with all or some substantial part of the other counties going to comprise the Indianapolis Metropolitan Statistical Area, in order to purge the state of its role in contributing to de jure segregation in the Indianapolis School System."[70] Judge Dillin, therefore, ordered the plaintiff to secure the joinder as parties defendant of the necessary municipal corporations which would be involved.[71]

Judge Dillin also raised the question of whether the Metropolitan Development Commission of Marion County had power to deny the school board its choice of sites for Crispus Attucks or other new schools, and the question of whether his court had power to override the rulings of the commission or any other agency about the location of schools and low-rent housing projects; if it found that its rules interfered with desegregation, the plaintiff was ordered to join such agencies as third-party defendants. In addition, Dillin stated that the Indiana attorney general should be served by the plaintiff, because of the interest of the state of Indiana in the constitutionality of its laws. He concluded this section of his opinion by suggesting that other questions might well occur to the parties which would involve additional parties, and that they should feel free to seek whatever relief seemed appropriate; he openly solicited new petitions of intervention.[72]

Court Orders

Pending the decision of the questions the case had posed, Judge Dillin ordered the defendants to take several actions, at a minimum, "to fulfill their affirmative duty to achieve a nondiscriminatory school system."[73] First, he ordered the defendants to redress the situation which had arisen because faculty and staff reassignments had "tended to result in more experienced Negro faculty and staff being transferred and/or assigned to schools attended predominantly by white students and more inexperienced white faculty and staff being transferred and/or

69. During the trial, Judge Dillin repeatedly demanded, but never got, HEW statistics showing the resegregation effect of desegregation remedies in other cities. The judge expressed disbelief that such statistics were not available. *See, e.g.,* Trial Record I, vol. V, at 1019-23 (July 16, 1971); vol. VII, at 1337 (July 20, 1971). Judge Dillin was apparently influenced by Calhoun v. Cook, 332 F. Supp. 804 (N.D. Ga. 1971), which indicated that as a consequence of desegregating Atlanta's public schools, the system had gone from 70 percent white students in 1961 to 70 percent black students in 1971.

70. Indianapolis I, 332 F. Supp., at 679.

71. *Id.* at 680.

72. *Id.*

73. *Id.*

assigned to schools attended predominantly by Negro students." Second, he ordered the defendants to continue with their plans to desegregate and relocate Crispus Attucks High School; third, to amend immediately its "majority-to-minority" transfer policy so as to conform with the *Swann* decision, eliminating the requirement that such transfers be dependent on the availability of space. The transfer option was to be publicized to eligible students and their parents, and transportation was to be provided upon request. In addition, the court ordered the defendants to attempt to negotiate with school corporations outside the IPS for possible transfer of minority race students. This order was the first indication of the court's inclination toward a remedy that would desegregate the inner-city black schools by transportation of black students to white suburban schools with no reciprocal transportation of white students to black schools in the city.

In order to prevent schools that had a reasonable white-black ratio from reaching a tipping point, Dillin ordered the IPS to re-survey the probable racial make-up of all schools for the 1971/72 school year and to provide transportation in and out of schools as required. This was the first court-ordered busing in Indianapolis. In a footnote, Dillin wrote: "This Court regards the outcry made in some quarters against 'bussing' as ridiculous in this age of the automobile. Most students in the outside school corporations have been bussed for years with never a complaint about bussing *per se.*"[74]

Finally, the court ordered the IPS to halt construction of the Forest Manor Middle School until it could hear further evidence on the subject.

In conclusion, Judge Dillin recognized that the orders would not result in significant desegregation unless the voluntary transfers were unusually effective. He also noted that more black than white students would be affected by the transfers. But he stated that "there is a limit to what can be accomplished at one time and final plans cannot be made until answers [to the legal questions were found].[75]

Political Repercussions

Virtually all the political leaders in Indianapolis responded promptly and adversely to Judge Dillin's decision. The opinion was issued approximately ten weeks prior to the mayoralty election for the city-county of Indianapolis and, since it raised doubts about the legality of Uni-Gov, the case immediately became a campaign issue.

Mayor Richard B. Lugar, the Republican candidate, announced several times that the school desegregation cause was a bogus issue in the mayoralty campaign because the mayor had no legal power or influence over the schools, but he continued to oppose court-mandated integration of schools, speaking vigorously

74. *Id.* at 681, n.100.
75. *Id.* at 681.

against "forced busing" to obtain racial balance. His Democratic opponent, John F. Neff, a lawyer, tried to give the impression that Lugar, both as mayor and previously as a member of the IPS board, was responsible for the school segregation. Five days after the decision was handed down, Neff filed a petition to intervene as a party to the IPS desegregation case. Neff's stated reasons for seeking intervention were to "challenge the constitutionality of Uni-Gov" and to "have the court order a referendum on Uni-Gov" for the November ballot. This revival of the Republican-Democratic controversy over Uni-Gov was a blatant political ploy as both the United States District Court for the Southern District of Indiana[76] and the Indiana Supreme Court[77] had held it to be constitutional. Judge Dillin denied Neff's petition on September 1, 1971, commenting that the petition raised "sham issues put forward in the interest of political opportunism."[78]

The Indianapolis *Star* and the Indianapolis *News,* the city's two major newspapers, had been consistently sharp critics of Judge Dillin's actions in the school desegregation case. The friction was not one-sided for, in open court, Judge Dillin had once called an editorial in the *News* "asinine."[79] The press had also criticized the school board's lawyers for not pressing its case strongly enough.

Some public support for the decision did come from the Indianapolis chapter of the NAACP and from the Indianapolis Urban League, whose president was the Right Reverend John P. Craine, Bishop of the Episcopal Diocese of Indianapolis. Bishop Craine hailed the decision as a "landmark for all cities, since it talks of the inclusiveness of the metropolitan area in all our planning and working."[80]

But the most vocal supporter of Judge Dillin's decision was Stanley Campbell, the IPS superintendent of schools, who expressed confidence in Dillin's thinking[81] and stated that although he doubted that a metropolitan school system would solve segregation problems in Indianapolis or elsewhere, school officials could live with the decision. At an Indianapolis Rotary Club meeting held on August 31, Campbell said:

I have some criticisms, but I was tremendously impressed with the way

76. Bryant v. Whitcomb, No. IP 69-C-115, slip. op. (S.D. Ind. Feb. 3, 1970).

77. Dortch v. Lugar, 255 Ind. 545, 266 N.E.2d 25 (1971).

78. Indianapolis Star, Sept. 1, 1971, at 1, col. 3. Judge Dillin's sharp rebuff of candidate Neff may have been prompted by charges that the judge's decision was politically motivated. The day after the decision was announced, the *Indianapolis Star* quoted L. Keith Bulen, Marion County Republican chairman, as saying that "the former democratic state senate leader, now federal judge, has a fine political as well as legal mind. We will study immediately and carefully his dictum and findings in order to evaluate more fully his talents in both arenas, as we coincidentally approach the last two months before our city elections." Indianapolis Star, Aug. 20, 1971, at 1, col. 5.

79. *See* Record on Appeal, United States v. Board of School Commissioners of the City of Indianapolis, Indiana, No. 73-1968 to 73-1984, at 237 (Aug. 20, 1973).

80. Indianapolis Star, Aug. 20, 1971, at 1, col. 5.

81. *Id.,* Aug. 19, 1971, at 11, col. 5.

he got to the heart of the problem and particularly its long range implications. I personally have thought this is a great challenge for the community. The community, Dillin's ruling indicates, has a guilty conscience and the school system has been the focus of segregated practices. As superintendent, I feel the decision was reasonable and has pointed us toward improved educational practices.[82]

IPS Reaction

At an IPS board meeting on August 31, 1971, the board voted 4–3 to appeal Judge Dillin's decision to the United States Court of Appeals for the Seventh Circuit. Because of the long list of essentially uncontroverted acts of unlawful segregation found by the court, and the fact that, in the absence of a remedy order, there was no final judgment, the vote to appeal came as a surprise to many persons. Three black board members voted against an appeal.[83] Two board members, however, were quoted as saying that the appeal was "more to keep options open in the event of further rulings by the court than to attempt to block what the Judge had already decreed."[84] Moreover, there was some sentiment on the board that the community was entitled to an appellate review of the decision, without regard to the board's feelings about the merits of the case, because the decision was of such crucial importance.

Immediately after voting to appeal the court's decision, the board defeated a motion to request a stay of the court's orders. This action followed advice from the attorneys for the board that a motion for a stay would be a waste of time because they are so rarely granted.

When school opened on September 7, 1971, few of the court's orders had been carried out. After a bitter dispute between IPS and teachers, 132 teachers had been reassigned in such a way as to promote desegregation. The required changes were made in the IPS student transfer policy, but they had little effect on the racial composition of the schools. Nine hundred white ninth- and tenth-grade students were assigned to Crispus Attucks High School but, discouraged by the widespread opposition to its efforts to find a new site for the school in 1970, the board made no serious attempt to relocate it in 1971. On the basis of projected declining enrollments, the IPS resolved on January 11, 1972 to abandon any plans to construct a new building for Attucks, and Judge Dillin approved the action. In September, Judge Dillin had set aside his order to cease and desist from building the Forest Manor School, and construction went ahead at the original planned site. However, although it was in an all-black neighborhood, when it opened as a junior high school, students were assigned to it from a much broader area, giving it a black student body of about 35 percent.

IPS promptly initiated contact with the Marion County public school corpora-

82. *Id.*, Sept. 1, 1971, at 10, col. 3.
83. Indianapolis News, Sept. 1, 1971, at 1, col. 7. The three board members voting no were Landrum E. Shields, Jessie Jacobs, and Robert DeFrantz.
84. Indianapolis News, Sept. 1, 1971, at 1, col. 7.

tions outside IPS jurisdiction and the Carmel Clay and Greenwood school corporations, adjoining Marion County, as specified in the opinion. It proposed that each school corporation accept black students from IPS equal in number to 2 percent to 5 percent of each corporation's total school enrollment. Suburban parents of the non-IPS school students were strongly opposed to the busing of black IPS students to the suburbs, and eventually all the school corporations rejected the IPS proposal.

In response to the court's order to prevent schools with a reasonable black-white ratio from reaching the tipping point, IPS identified several elementary schools as likely to go beyond the 40 percent tipping point if not adjusted. Less than 1,000 elementary pupils were reassigned for the 1971/72 school year, some of whom were bused to their new school. This was about 1 percent of the total IPS enrollment, but it constituted a beginning of school desegregation in Indianapolis.

Added Parties Defendant

Meanwhile, on September 7, 1971, the United States Department of Justice filed a motion to add parties defendant to the case; the motion was approved by Judge Dillin on the same day. These twelve defendants fell into three categories: (1) the Marion County school corporations not included in the IPS jurisdiction (Franklin Township Community School Corporation and the seven separate Metropolitan School Districts of Lawrence, Perry, Pike, Warren, Washington, and Wayne Townships); (2) the two Municipal School Districts which lie within Marion County (Beech Grove City and the town of Speedway); and (3) two county school corporations whose boundaries were outside of, but contiguous to, Marion County (the Carmel-Clay schools from Hamilton County and the Greenwood Community School Corporation from Johnson County).

Because the government did not charge these added defendants with acts of de jure segregation or seek relief against them,[85] the parents of Donny Burrell Buckley and Alycia Marquese Buckley petitioned, on September 14, 1971, to intervene on their own behalf and on behalf of all black school-age children residing in the area served by the IPS. The court granted the petition on the same day and subsequently the Buckleys added the governor, attorney general, the superintendent of public education of the state of Indiana, the Indiana State Board of Education, and nineteen school corporations within and without Marion County, including the ten in-county corporations joined by the government.

The added defendants responded to the joinder through counsel, for the most part independently.[86] This led to duplication of thought and legal research

85. The Justice Department merely had each defendant served with a summons accompanied by a copy of the judge's order that the defendant be made a party to the case.

86. One prominent Indianapolis law firm, Bose, McKinney and Evans, represented Wayne, Warren, and Lawrence Townships. Professor Marshall J. Seidman of the Indiana University School of Law–Indianapolis represented five out of the ten Marion County

by the individual defendants, but did not result in substantially different arguments.

Each of the added school defendants made a prompt and vigorous effort to dispose of the case. They raised two principal issues. First, they contended that it was a violation of due process to bring new defendants into a lawsuit after three years of litigation in which they had not taken part; and, second, they charged that the court had no judicial power over them until a finding was made that they had been guilty of unlawful segregation.[87]

Within six weeks of the order of September 7, 1971 there were at least six efforts to obtain dismissal from the United States Court of Appeals for the Seventh Circuit. The added defendants also attempted to dilute Judge Dillin's power by demanding a three-judge court, pursuant to 42 U.S.C., Sec.2281. This effort was unsuccessful since a three-judge court was appropriate only if there was at issue a state statute or regulation that had statewide application. Judge Dillin held that there were no statewide issues in the case and denied all petitions for a three-judge court. He was upheld by the court of appeals.[88]

Pretrial Conference

On December 20, 1971, Judge Dillin held a pretrial conference with all the attorneys, reportedly to persuade the parties to negotiate a voluntary desegregation plan. Over the public objection of the Indiana attorney general, the session was closed to the public and the press.

On December 31, 1971, Judge Dillin entered an order denying all motions to dismiss, to docket the action separately, to obtain more definite statement (because the action was not properly prosecuted as a class action), to strike, to extend time. This sweeping end-of-the-year order forced the defendants to accept the fact that they would have to litigate. Within two weeks several of the defendants voluntarily withdrew appeals pending before the seventh circuit court and began to file answers to the complaint made by the intervening plaintiffs, Buckley.

The IPS 111 and 114 Controversy

IPS Elementary Schools 111 and 114 are situated within three blocks of each other in the extreme southeastern section of the IPS district. Until two low-income housing projects, inhabited almost totally by blacks, were opened in

---

school corporations. These school corporations, generally represented by local attorneys, joined together in hiring Seidman in an effort to procure a litigation specialist at the lowest possible cost. The remainder of the defendants had individual representation, in many cases more than one lawyer.

87. Some of the defendants alleged that this procedure denied them every aspect of their pretrial and trial rights. Additionally, some contended that their joinder violated Federal Rules of Civil Procedure 4(d), 8(a), 10, 11, 20, 24, 60(d) and 79(a), Federal District Court Rule 7 for the Southern District of Indiana, Title IV, Civil Rights Act of 1964, as amended, 42 U.S.C. § 2000 c-6 (1972), and the Ind. Const., art. VIII, § 1.

88. Indianapolis I, 474 F.2d 81 (7th Cir. 1973).

1971, elementary School 111 had an all-white enrollment. School 114 had been built to relieve overcrowding in School 111, occasioned by increased population in the housing projects; it was planned as a model, experimental elementary school with open classroom design. It opened in September 1972.

On June 20, 1972, the school board approved a resolution establishing School 114 as a K-6 school, with all seventh- and eighth-grade students from the district attending School 111. The board predicted that School 111 would be 38.4 percent black and that School 114 would be 39.5 percent black.

On July 1, 1972, however, four new school board members, elected in May on an anti-busing, anti-forced-integration platform, took office. One of the first acts of the newly constituted board was to fire Superintendent Stanley Campbell, who had spoken favorably about Judge Dillin's 1971 decision and had devised the plan for School 114. He was replaced by Karl Kalp, a career IPS teacher and administrator of more conservative bent. On August 21, 1972, the new board appealed the June resolution and adopted a new resolution which would make School 111 and School 114 K-8 schools, and would give kindergarten pupils a choice as to which school they would attend. On the testimony of Superintendent Kalp that there was no evidence that open classrooms provided superior educational advantage, it called for immediate construction to convert IPS 114's open classrooms to closed classrooms, a four-month project. The planned experimental programs were cancelled. Facilities were to be added to accommodate the seventh and eighth grades, and since there were not enough students for two full junior high programs, some junior high teachers were assigned to teach at both School 111 and School 114. Classes opened as specified under this resolution on September 5, 1972 with an enrollment of 37 percent black students at School 111 and an enrollment of 52 percent black enrollment at School 114.

Some of the black residents from the housing projects felt that these changes were racially motivated and that the elimination of the innovative programs would adversely affect the quality of their children's education. They contacted the Indianapolis Legal Service Organization (LSO), and on September 7, 1972, its lawyers filed on behalf of three black mothers from one of the projects and their children a motion to intervene in the IPS desegregation case. The intervenors sought to enjoin the changes and to have the board members held in contempt of court for acting contrary to the court's orders of August 18, 1971.[89]

89. Plaintiffs alleged that the optional kindergarten zone was inconsistent with the new IPS transfer policy, adopted pursuant to the court order of August 18, 1971. This policy provided that transfers were available to students when they were in the racial majority in their school. They could transfer only to a school in which they would be in the racial minority. The plaintiffs also alleged that the opening of School 114 with 47.7 percent black students violated the court's order prohibiting any school, not already over the 40 percent tipping point on August 18, 1971, to go over that point pending formulation of the final remedy for the case. Finally, plaintiffs asserted that the elimination of the innovative features of School 114 denied them an equal educational opportunity which was tantamount to a denial of equal protection of the law.

The intervenor's application for a temporary restraining order was denied, but Judge Dillin set the motion for a preliminary injunction to be heard by the court on the following Wednesday, September 12, 1972. At the hearing, IPS board members and administrators testified that discipline was so deteriorating at School 111, especially among the black seventh- and eighth-grade students from the housing projects, that it was necessary to transfer some of them to School 114; that the open classrooms at School 114 would hinder efforts to control students; and that it was their understanding that the court's tipping point order did not apply to new schools. They cited for support the fact that in September 1971, immediately after the order, the opening of new School 48 with over 90 percent black enrollment was unchallenged. Optional enrollment for kindergarten students was defended on grounds that some of these young pupils could avoid crossing a busy street by exercising the option.

At the conclusion of the hearing on Saturday morning, September 16, 1972, Judge Dillin gave his ruling as part of a wide-ranging two-hour oration from the bench, in the presence of all seven members of the school board; it was issued in written form on September 28, 1972.

Judge Dillin found that the school board had succumbed to pressure from white parents in the district to make School 111 a white school and School 114 a black school, and that in responding to these demands the board had violated the court's order of August 18, 1971, and had committed a new separate act of unlawful segregation. He annulled the changes and reinstated the original plans. This meant that all the junior high students would be assigned to School 111, the kindergarten pupils would attend the school in their district, and School 114 would utilize open classrooms. Construction plans were reversed.

The court did not hold the board members in contempt of court, but severely reprimanded them for taking the action without approval from the court.[90] Judge Dillin characterized his two-hour lecture as a civics lesson for board members; he told the board members that he understood the facts of political life and that they could campaign on any platform they wanted, but if their proposals were unlawful, as they were in this case, the campaign promises could not be carried out.

In promulgating a remedy, Judge Dillin went further than the requests of the Legal Services Organization lawyers. He believed that the substantial rise in black enrollment over the figures projected in June demonstrated substantial white flight from the area during the summer of 1971. The tipping point, at least for this neighborhood, he said, was obviously lower than 40 percent.

The judge ordered IPS to submit a plan for reducing the enrollment at both schools to not more than 35 percent black students immediately, adding the proviso that this level was not to be reached by one-way busing of black students out of Schools 111 and 114.

90. Trial Record I, vol. III, at 397-441 (Sept. 15, 1972).

The School Board's Response

The school board's response was to exchange black students at the two schools with white students from Schools 21 and 82, which were located nearby. On Thursday, September 21, 1972, it met to discuss a plan to be submitted to the court. At the same time, IPS administrators met with parents of each of the four schools. A large number of white parents, mostly from School 21, left the meeting at their school and descended on the school board meeting. They were angry and disruptive and their reported purpose was to advise the board that they would boycott the school if the court's order was implemented. The Indianapolis police were called and responded with a sizable force.[91]

Nevertheless, the board voted to approve the staff proposal for complying with the court order. The seven-member board voted 4-0 in favor of the plan with three of the four newly elected board members abstaining. One of the abstaining members was quoted by the Indianapolis *Star* as saying she could not vote for the plan because it contemplated busing, but she would not vote against it for fear of a contempt-of-court citation.[92] The board also voted to appeal the court's order.

On the following day, IPS attorneys traveled to Terre Haute, Indiana, where Judge Dillin was conducting a trial, to plead for a stay, alleging a volatile and potentially uncontrollable situation existed at the schools. Judge Dillin granted a stay of the portion of the order which involved the two additional schools, and that portion of the plan was never implemented. The remainder of the order affecting schools 111 and 114 remained intact.

LSO and Urban League Chastised

The participation of LSO in the case was very unpopular politically, and when the question of its refunding by the Department of Housing and Urban Development Model Cities program, which was controlled by the Indianapolis City-County Council, came up, the opposition was formidable. It was approved only after stringent restrictions were placed on the activities of LSO lawyers. A year later the debate was renewed and the funding was withdrawn. These monies constituted one-third of the LSO budget, the rest was provided directly by the Office of Economic Opportunity.

The Indianapolis Urban League, which operated a social service program at one of the housing projects in the 111–114 school district, was also harassed because it had petitioned to participate as *amicus curiae*. The Urban League receives nearly all of its funds from the Indianapolis United Way, which, pressured by Indianapolis industrial workers who threatened to withhold their pledges to the 1973 fund-raising campaign, made plans to impose restrictive guidelines on the advocacy activities of affiliates. At one point a lawsuit was

---

91. Indianapolis Star, Sept. 22, 1972, at 1, col. 2.
92. *Id.* The three board members who refused to vote were Paul E. Lewis, Lester Neal, and Constence R. Valdez.

filed in Marion Circuit Court to enjoin the United Way from funding the Urban League.

The Failure of Indianapolis

By the end of the 1972 it was clear that the cooperative effort of officials, administrators, teachers, and parents required to carry out Judge Dillin's orders of August 1971 would not be forthcoming and that the federal court would be forced to accept the burden of devising and implementing a meaningful desegregation plan for the Indianapolis school system. The geographical scope of the case had been greatly expanded by the addition of the suburban school districts; political and emotional pressures had greatly expanded as well. A second major trial had become inevitable.

INDIANAPOLIS II—"THE REMEDY TRIAL"

Indianapolis II began on June 12, 1973 and lasted for fourteen days. Although this portion of the case is commonly called the remedy trial, the added school defendants consistently objected to this designation. They maintained that a remedy involving them could not be ordered before a finding had been made that they were guilty of a constitutional violation.

The length of the trial was attributable more to the number of attorneys participating (at least twenty-five) and the absence of clearly defined legal principles than to the amount of significant evidence introduced. The large number of lawyers complicated the proceeding, particularly in such matters as authenticating evidence. The lack of clear controlling principles of law resulted in the introduction of a great deal of essentially immaterial evidence.

Ranged against the intervening plaintiffs Buckley were twenty school districts, the governor, the attorney general, the superintendent of schools of the state of Indiana, and the Citizens for Quality Schools, Inc. Coalition for Integrated Education participated as *amicus curiae*. The United States Department of Justice, although theoretically still the plaintiff, was, as a practical matter, aligned with the defendants.[93]

93. One of its two lawyers, Brian Lanberg, said in his opening statement:

. . . [T]he United States has stated no claim against the added defendants here, such as the claim stated by the plaintiff intervenors. As we stated in our pre-trial submission in December 1971, if it is shown that the added defendants have engaged in inter-district violation, that is to say a constitutional violation that in some manner involved two or more school systems, then some relief against them may be warranted. On the other hand, if no inter-system violation is shown, we do not believe that either the facts to be adduced at this hearing or the laws of the United States would authorize the imposition of an inter-district remedy. The record will show that an intra-system desegregation plan can feasibly be fashioned and implemented in Indianapolis.

United States v. Board of School Commissioners of the City of Indianapolis, Indiana, Record of Proceedings at Trial, vol. I, at 8-9 (June 12, 1973) [Hereinafter cited as Trial Record II]

Issues

The issues of *Indianapolis II* were: (1) whether a plan involving only IPS schools would result in the racial integration of the IPS system that would satisfy *Brown II* and *Green;* and (2) whether there was a legal basis for an interdistrict remedy. In his 1971 opinion, Judge Dillin had concluded that because of the rising percentage of black pupils in IPS, "a massive 'fruit-basket' scrambling" within IPS exclusively would not work.

The legal and practical consideration of a metropolitan plan, therefore, became the central focus of *Indianapolis II*. This was a particularly difficult issue to formulate because at the time of the trial, the law relating to interdistrict remedies, still in the early stages of development, was unclear. As Judge Dillin aptly stated from the bench, "really, we are out in the wilderness without much precedent one way or the other."

In 1972 the United States Court of Appeals for the Fourth Circuit had reversed an order of the district court for a metropolitan desegregation plan for the city of Richmond, Virginia, on the basis that the operation of public schools within the different counties of Virginia was a matter of local option and that, in any case, "the root causes of the concentration of blacks in the inner cities of America are simply not known . . .";[94] but in Indiana it was clear that the operation of the public schools was vested in the state government.

More pertinent was *Bradley v. Milliken,*[95] in which the United States Court of Appeals for the Sixth Circuit had upheld the district court's opinion that a metropolitan remedy would be an appropriate means of desegregating the public schools of Detroit. As in Indiana, the public schools of Michigan are ultimately under the jurisdiction of the state, and the acts of segregation committed by it were similar to those charged against the defendants in *Indianapolis I.* The sixth circuit court decision in *Bradley v. Milliken* was not handed down, however, until the opening day of *Indianapolis II,* so there was little time for the opposing lawyers to incorporate its findings into the strategies they had devised for the trial.

During the course of the trial the United States Supreme Court decided the case of *Keyes v. School District No. 1, Denver, Colorado.*[96] Applied to the Indianapolis case, it laid to rest the dispute over which specific schools in the IPS system had been found de jure segregated; the *Keyes* decision meant that, at a minimum, all the schools in the IPS system must be involved in the desegregation plan. During the trial the Supreme Court denied IPS petition for *certiorari* on Dillin's 1971 decision finding IPS unlawfully segregated.[97]

94. Bradley v. School Board of the City of Richmond, Virginia, 462 F.2d 1058 (4th Cir. 1972), *aff'd by an equally divided court,* 412 U.S. 92 (1973).

95. 484 F.2d 215 (6th Cir. 1973), *reversed,* 418 U.S. 717 (1974).

96. 413 U.S. 189 (1973).

97. Board of School Commissioners of the City of Indianapolis, Indiana v. United States, 413 U.S. 920 (1973).

Strategies

The Intervening Plaintiffs' Arguments. The intervening plaintiffs' amended complaint served, at least partially, to frame the issues. First, it asked the court to declare Uni-Gov unconstitutional insofar as it affected racially separate public schools and school systems in Marion County. Second, it asked that the defendants be ordered to take "all steps reasonably necessary to secure to plaintiff-intervenors their right to attend racially non-segregated and non-discriminatory schools and school systems, including, if necessary: (a) the consolidation or merger of the defendant school systems in all respects of school operation and administration . . . requiring that each defendant by withholding funds or accreditation, and by the exercise of any and all powers available to each, insure the full cooperation of the other defendants in the prompt accomplishment of said consolidation or merger. . . ."

Their attorneys, John O. Moss and John Ward, submitted that both the state of Indiana and the suburban schools[98] had an affirmative responsibility to eliminate unlawful segregation in the Indianapolis metropolitan area, and that their failure to fulfill this affirmative responsibility was a basis for including suburban schools in the desegregation plan ordered by the court. This theory of affirmative obligation did not necessitate any showing of unlawful acts of segregation by either the state defendants or the school defendants.[99]

98. The term suburban school is used to cover the non-IPS Marion County schools and the outside-Marion County schools which were named as defendants.

99. However, Moss and Ward called twenty suburban school superintendents to the witness stand. Their testimony provided a vivid picture of an essentially all-white school system—students, teachers, administrators, and employees—in all but two of the suburban schools, but the testimony did not have any direct bearing on the two basic issues being tried and was probably attributable to an effort by the intervening plaintiffs to develop a legal basis for an interdistrict remedy.

The testimony elicited attempted to show that the suburban schools were guilty of discriminatory practices in the hiring of teachers and noncertified staff personnel. It was suggested that the suburban schools had located their school buildings in such a way as to perpetuate all-white schools, but the point was not pursued. (At the time of the trial, only two suburban districts had large enough black populations to make segregation a factor in decisions about location of schools. One of these, Washington Township, had an excellent record of race relations, causing Judge Dillin to comment during the course of the trial that, if the other school systems had displayed the same sense of community responsibility, none of them would be in court.)

The attorneys for the intervening plaintiffs also established that there were no significant black studies programs in the suburban schools, that the suburban schools had land available for expansion, and that 78.5 percent of all the students in the defendant school districts were bused to school. All of the Marion County township schools bused more than 75 percent of their students in 1971/72, six of the eight township schools bused more than 80 percent, and two bused more than 90 percent. Speedway had no busing and Beech Grove bused 62 percent of its students in 1971/72. These statistics cast serious doubts on the credibility of citizens groups which oppose "busing" but do not provide a basis for an interdistrict remedy. In addition, they asked each school superintendent about their receipt of federal funds, but they did not argue this point as legal grounds for an interdistrict remedy.

Counsel for intervening plaintiffs referred to acts of segregation by the Housing Author-

It is difficult to evaluate the presentation of the plaintiffs' lawyers, but the fact that they were lacking the resources available to their opponents or indeed to most attorneys in major lawsuits cannot be ignored. John Moss was a member of a two- or three-lawyer firm in Indianapolis and John Ward was a sole practitioner, and it is not surprising that the case for a metropolitan plan was not as expertly presented as it could have been. Moss and Ward were frequently prodded by the court and needled by the opposing lawyers. In the words of the Indianapolis *News*, Judge Dillin frequently interrupted questioning by the plaintiffs' counsel and took over the examination of a witness himself.[100] This practice drew the ire of defense counsel who charged in open court that the judge was acting as an advocate rather than as a judge.[101] During the course of the trial, Moss and Ward were frequently criticized by witnesses, the press, courtroom observers, and even by the court, for not preparing witnesses prior to calling them to the witness stand.[102]

The Defendants' Arguments. The twenty defendant subsurban school districts were served by over twenty-five lawyers, and there was serious discussion among them about choosing a chief counsel for the group and delegating principal trial responsibility to him. Because of what was perceived to be "diverse interests," this was not done.[103]

---

ity of the City of Indianapolis arising from its siting of public housing projects, but this issue was not fully litigated. Although they continued to press a Uni-Gov theory, no clear specification was given.

100. Indianapolis News, June 13, 1973, at 1, col. 5.

101. *Id.*

102. Some witnesses commented that they did not know why they had been called to testify. The deputy director of the Indiana Civil Rights Commission, for instance, testified that he was in court because "Mr. Moss showed up in my office this morning looking for the Director of the Civil Right Commission. She was unavailable so he was directed to me, and he asked me to come and testify." Trial Record II, vol. I, at 7 (June 12, 1973). Seidman implored the judge to speed up the direct examination of witnesses by Moss and Ward, reminding the court that since there were twenty school corporations represented at the trial and they were paying their lawyers at least $50 an hour, the trial was costing the taxpayers of central Indiana at least $1,000 an hour. Judge Dillin at one point candidly pleaded with Moss and Ward to prepare their witnesses before putting them on the stand, saying, "Gentlemen, I've done it all my life." Trial Record II, vol. II, at 382 (June 13, 1973).

103. Each of the defendant school corporation's lawyers formally preserved complete freedom to call witnesses, present evidence, cross-examine witnesses, raise objections, and otherwise participate fully in the trial. Nevertheless, they developed a manner of loose cooperation by assigning areas such as factual presentation and cross-examination of witnesses. According to one of the unofficial leaders, all the attorneys acted with great restraint. The school districts lying outside of Marion County did not participate in this cooperative effort. It was the strategy of these schools, led by Marshall J. Seidman, to emphasize the difference between Marion County and outside-Marion County defendants. In fact, Seidman even demanded, and got, a separate counsel table for non-Marion County school defendants. Their position was based on the pragmatic reasoning that even if the court decided to order a metropolitan plan, it could be persuaded to stop at the county line.

On the first day of trial, Judge Dillin established a ground rule whereby when an objection was made by a defendant, that objection would be deemed to have been raised by each defendant, unless a defendant opted to be excluded from the objection. It was prompted by the potential delay envisioned when, the second time an objection was made, nineteen lawyers automatically stood and said, "Your honor, we join in that objection."

The strategy of the state defendants is difficult to evaluate. It appears that their approach was to resist as forcefully as possible whatever the court tried to do, and to defend, for the record and as a matter of principle, the honor and integrity of the officials of the state of Indiana and the right of state officials to act without federal review.

John Moss and John Ward were clearly outnumbered, and one of the favorite items of gossip among lawyers in downtown Indianapolis during June of 1973 was the "massacre in federal court." The absence of national NAACP counsel during the trial was a major drawback for the plaintiffs.

Expert Witnesses. The intervening plaintiffs called two expert witnesses, Charles Albert Glatt, professor, demographer, and director of the Midwest Institute, a desegregation center at the Ohio State University,[104] and John T. Liell, a professor of sociology and demographer at Indiana University–Purdue University, Indianapolis.

Glatt's opinion was that whenever a school or a school system exceeds 25 percent to 33 percent black, white flight will accelerate and the school or the system will resegregate to all, or nearly all, black. For this reason, Glatt testified that IPS could not be effectively desegregated within its own boundaries.

Liell testified that an IPS-only plan would result in the resegregation of IPS. His opinion was based on 1970 census data and an analysis of demographic trends in metropolitan Indianapolis.

The defendants called two expert witnesses, Clifford P. Hooker, a professor of educational administration at the University of Minnesota, and Ernest van den Haag, a professor of sociology and psychology at New York University.

Hooker testified on behalf of the suburban schools that an IPS-only plan was preferable to a metropolitan plan. He favored an IPS-only plan because he believed that larger school systems encounter more complex problems and are less effective educationally, and because he also believed that "white flight is grossly overstated." IPS would not resegregate, Hooker testified, because black migration is essentially over and because the birth rate is declining. Both John Moss, counsel for the intervening plaintiffs, and Judge Dillin cross-examined Hooker in order to show that he had expressed views opposite to these in articles he had published in 1968.[105]

Van den Haag was called by suburban schools to testify that integration does not reduce prejudice or promote racial harmony. Objections to his testimony were sustained and he was not permitted to testify. The defendants also offered to present David J. Armor, who would testify similarly. The United States Court of Appeals for the Seventh Circuit upheld the exclusion of the evidence as an attempt to challenge the underpinnings of *Brown v. Board of Education.*[106]

104. In 1975, Professor Glatt was tragically murdered in Dayton, Ohio, while preparing a desegregation plan for that city.

105. United States v. Board of School Commissioners of the City of Indianapolis, Indiana, 368 F. Supp. 1191, 1198 (S.D. Ind. 1973), *aff'd* 503 F.2d 68 (7th Cir. 1974), *cert. denied,* 421 U.S. 929 (1975). [Hereinafter cited as Indianapolis II.]

106. Indianapolis II, 503 F.2d 68, 83-84 (7th Cir. 1974).

The Department of Justice, which occupied an ambivalent position in the adversary proceedings, also called two expert witnesses, Dan W. Dodson, professor of sociology at Southwestern University, Georgetown, Texas, who had testified in many desegregation cases, and Jane R. Mercer, professor of sociology at the University of California at Riverside.

The essence of Dodson's testimony was that straight-line projections of racial composition in metropolitan areas were not valid in 1973 because the trend of blacks moving into the inner city and whites fleeing it was over. He testified that the birth rate for both blacks and whites was declining and that due to those changes "we are in a completely different era, a different ball game than three years ago."[107]

Mercer stated that she did not believe that the existence of a desegregation plan prompted white flight. She had done extensive work on the desegregation of schools in Riverside, California. But as Judge Dillin was quick to point out, the Riverside experience differed widely from the situation in Indianapolis because in Riverside minority students comprised less than 25 percent of the school population, the desegregation plan was voluntary, and implementation of the plan was accompanied by unusual community cooperation.[108]

Both Mercer and Dodson testified that no studies had been made exploring the effects of a desegregation plan on demographic patterns.

The Decision

Judge Dillin announced his decision on July 20, 1973.[109] He found, as he had suspected in 1971, that no plan confined only to schools within the IPS jurisdiction would succeed in vindicating the Fourteenth Amendment rights of black school children living in the IPS area. He stated that since the IPS black census had reached over 41.1 percent, only two IPS-only plans were possible, and ultimately neither was workable.[110] One would fix the racial balance at each of the schools at approximately 60 percent white and 40 percent black, a plan he had referred to in 1971 as a "massive fruit basket scrambling." This was not viable because all of the schools would be beyond the tipping point; the exodus of white students would be inevitable and resegregation irreversible. The alternative would desegregate less than all of the IPS schools so that the desegregated schools were below the tipping point, leaving other schools all or predominantly black. Judge Dillin held that neither of these solutions was a constitutionally permissible remedy.

Moreover, because of evidence adduced at the trial, Judge Dillin had become convinced that in the area served by IPS, a tipping point of 25 percent to 30 percent was more realistic than the 40 percent he had believed feasible in 1971.

107. Trial Record II, at 2582 (June 29, 1973).
108. Indianapolis II, 368 F. Supp., at 1198-99.
109. *Id.* at 1191.
110. *Id.* at 1198.

Desegregation in IPS schools could only be achieved, he stated, by means of a plan which included school districts outside of the IPS area.

Judge Dillin held that the legal basis for an interdistrict remedy was to be found in the fact that Indiana school corporations are the agents of the state government, and that, therefore, the unlawful acts of segregation committed in IPS were the responsibility of the state.[111] He found that although the state exercises broad powers over the educational process and had an affirmative duty to act to eliminate segregation, it had "done almost literally nothing and certainly next to nothing, to furnish leadership, guidance, and direction in this critical area."[112] As an example Dillin cited the location of three new high schools in the outer reaches of the district, as far removed as possible from the black ghetto in its center.[113]

The court did not find the suburban schools guilty of any acts of unlawful segregation. As he put it, "In fact, the evidence shows that, with a few exceptions, none of the added defendants have had the opportunity to commit such overt acts because the Negro population residing within the borders of such defendants ranges from slight to none."[114]

The court did find, however, that the outside-IPS Marion County schools were culpable because they had unanimously opposed the reorganization of schools in Marion County pursuant to the Indiana School Reorganization Act of 1959, which resulted in freezing all existing school corporations in Marion County according to their then existing boundaries.[115] The court asserted that "confining IPS to its existing territory had the effect, which continues, of making it first difficult and now impossible to comply with the law requiring meaningful desegregation."[116]

In response to the plaintiffs' prayer for a declaration that state Uni-Gov and the school boundary statutes be found unconstitutional, the court said only that although the court itself had posed these questions in the *Indianapolis I* decision:

> In the opinion of the Court such statutes, along with the application or the misapplication of the School Reorganization Act of 1959, certainly placed IPS in a strait jacket. However, in view of the Court's other findings and conclusions, it is unnecessary to consider the question of unconstitutionality.[117]

111. Ind. Const., art. VIII § 1.
112. Indianapolis II, 368 F. Supp., at 1203.
113. In 1971, Judge Dillin had found the location of these two new high schools to be an act of unlawful segregation by IPS, and in 1973 he found approval of the site selections by the Indiana Department of Public Instruction to be acts of de jure segregation by the state of Indiana. This provided the legal basis in Judge Dillin's opinion for an interdistrict remedy. Indianapolis II, 368 F. Supp., at 1205.
114. *Id.* at 1203.
115. *Id.*
116. *Id.* at 1204.
117. *Id.* at 1208.

The Remedy. Instead of immediately imposing a judicial remedy as a result of the 1973 trial, the court provided the Indiana General Assembly "a reasonable time" in which to devise and implement its own remedy. No rational, politically aware person in Indiana believed that the General Assembly would relieve Judge Dillin of this burden, but it is possible that the court acquired at least a small amount of support by giving the General Assembly one last chance to solve the problem legislatively.

The court, however, left no doubt about the alternative to legislative action. The opinion states unequivocally that "if the Indiana General Assembly fails to act in the manner described within a reasonable time, this Court has the power and the duty to devise its own plan, and to order the defendant(s) . . . to implement the same."[118]

Interim Measures

Pending action by the Indiana General Assembly, the court ordered interim measures to be implemented prior to the beginning of the 1973/74 school year. The court ordered that black students be transferred from IPS to each of the defendant suburban schools in Marion County and outside Marion County, in such number as equal 5 percent of the enrollment of each suburban school corporation.[119]

Desegregation efforts in IPS were to be increased so that, when school opened in the fall of 1973, each IPS elementary school would have a minimum black enrollment of 15 percent. The court ordered that this should be done by first pairing and clustering schools which were in close proximity. If, after utilizing these procedures, the required 15 percent level was not reached, pairing and clustering of schools in "non-contiguous zones" should be undertaken. In addition, the court ordered that high school feeder patterns be altered.

If busing were required, the court ordered that the "transportation of students of the two races shall be generally proportionate."[120] The court recognized, however, that the burden of busing would not be "proportionate," and qualified this requirement by stating that because nothing in the order would prevent IPS from closing obsolete, heavily black schools "in some cases, a disproportionate number of black students will require transportation."[121]

Finally, the court ordered all defendants to institute "appropriate inservice training courses for their respective faculties and staff, and otherwise to orient their thinking and those of their pupils toward alleviating the problems of segregation."[122]

118. *Id.* at 1205.
119. The court order excepted kindergarten students and high school seniors. Washington Township, which in 1973 had an 11 percent black enrollment, would receive only 1 percent black student transfers; and Pike Township, which had a black enrollment of 8 percent, would receive only 2 percent black student transfers. Indianapolis II, 368 F. Supp., at 1209.
120. *Id.*
121. *Id.*
122. *Id.* at 1210.

The Public's Response

The public's response to Judge Dillin's opinion was immediately and uniformly in opposition to the court's orders. Those in Indianapolis who supported Judge Dillin kept silent, as had been typical throughout the case.

The leaders of the black community were initially united in their disapproval of Judge Dillin's opinion, because of the decision to bus black students to the suburban schools without a reciprocal return of white students to IPS schools.[123]

White residents of the suburbs were, of course, negative, and some circulated a petition asking for the impeachment of Judge Dillin. The petition drive was headed by Marion Circuit Judge John L. Niblack.[124]

Interim Plans

On August 8, 1973, Judge Dillin stayed those portions of the decision which required transportation of students outside IPS for the 1973/74 school year

123. Rev. Boniface Hardin, director of the Martin Center, a black cultural organization, said: "I think it is naive to think that black parents will send their children out there. I am very much afraid these children will be harmed, given the behavior pattern manifested at this time." David Mitcham, president of the Indianapolis chapter of the NAACP, was quoted by the *Indianapolis News* as saying the decision "shows we haven't come a darn bit since the 1954 separate but equal decision." Indianapolis News, July 20, 1973. On July 31, 1973, however, Mitcham announced that the local board of directors of the NAACP had voted to support Judge Dillin's decision and stated that he, too, would support it.

124. Niblack, who had been a Marion County judge for over thirty years, said, in reference to the appointment of commissioners to prepare a school desegregation plan, that Dillin had "seized the reins of civil authority and deposed a duly elected qualified school board of this state as effectively as Castro took power of Cuba or Russia in Czechoslovakia without any more legal warrant" and that, furthermore, Dillin was "acting as chief advocate, judge, jury, and executioner in the case, ordering new parties added to the case on his own motion and putting them to large expense with taxpayers' money to defend themselves."

Moreover, Niblack charged that Dillin had "deliberately violated the 1964 Civil Rights Act passed by Congress which forbids discrimination against citizens and school children by race or color or drawing of school districts to correct racial imbalance.

The *Indianapolis News* reported on August 25, 1973, that Niblack was asked at the news conference why he didn't also call for the impeachment of the U.S. Court of Appeals for the Seventh Circuit, which had, to that time, upheld all of Judge Dillin's decisions in the case. The *News* reported that Niblack responded, "because I didn't choose to. I will say this about the Seventh Circuit Court. I think it is a rotten Court. They let the Chicago Seven and Kunstler go. Maybe they should be impeached." Niblack added that he was concerned with the "oligarchy of federal judges who have seized power in the United States without regard to the law."

When Niblack was asked at the news conference whether he was violating any canons of professional ethics by speaking out against another judge, Burton responded that "the answer would be up to the electorate to determine whether Niblack was right in speaking out in that Niblack's present six-year term would expire on January 1, 1975."

Niblack was not reelected to the circuit court bench in 1974, but it is not believed that the movement to impeach Judge Dillin had any impact on the election. At the 1974 election, all of the incumbent state court judges in Marion County—all Republicans—were defeated, and the entire slate of democratic hopefuls was elected.

Two days after the press conference, Representative Bales was quoted as saying that Judge Dillin was, through his school desegregation orders, seeking to "establish legal credentials for a possible appointment to the United States Supreme Court." It was a no-holds-barred campaign.

and ordered IPS to submit, in one week, an interim plan for the upcoming school year in which no elementary school would have less than 15 percent black enrollment, which would reduce Shortridge High School to 60 percent black, and which would make Howe High School about 25 percent black, instead of the predicted 6 percent black. On August 14, 1973, the IPS board submitted its plan to the court. The plan did not satisfy any of these criteria. It left nearly fifteen all-white elementary schools with less than 15 percent black enrollment, and did not fulfill the ratios established for the two high schools.

Judge Dillin held a hearing on August 20, 1973, to hear evidence on the IPS plan. After listening to testimony for several hours, Judge Dillin rejected the plan because none of the requirements had been satisfied, because

> most importantly, the plan is in complete disregard of the Court's order of July 20, 1973 as to method of desegregating the elementary schools. That order, agreeable to the policy of the Supreme Court of the United States as announced in *Swann v. Charlotte-Mecklenburg Board of Education,* 402 U.S. 1 (1971), required the Board to give first consideration to the changing of the attendance zones and to such devices as pairing and clustering before giving consideration to the transportation of pupils. The Board's plan does not provide for the use of any of these Supreme Court approved devices.[125]

Having found that IPS was in default of the July 20, 1973 order, the court, upon the motion of the intervening plaintiffs Buckley, appointed two court commissioners to formulate an interim plan for the 1973/74 school year and a final plan.[126] They were Joseph T. Taylor, dean of the School of Liberal Arts, Indiana University–Purdue University at Indianapolis (a black man), and Charles A. Glatt, professor of education and director of a desegregation center at Ohio State University. Glatt served as a consultant for IPS and was the expert witness who had most impressed Judge Dillin at the 1973 trial.

IPS was directed to cooperate fully with the commissioners, to provide them space at the Education Center in the IPS Administration Building, to pay all their fees and expenses, and to provide office support. The court ordered that the commissioners have full access to the maps, drawings, reports, statistics, computer studies, and all information about the school system necessary to their preparation of a plan. The court specifically ordered that "until such time as the Commissioners may have completed their assignment to the satisfaction of the Court, the defendants are ordered and directed to assign their professional

---

125. United States v. Board of School Commissioners of the City of Indianapolis, Indiana, Order of Judge Dillin, at 2 (Aug. 27, 1973). *See also* Indianapolis II, 503 F.2d, at 74 n.9.

126. *See* Record on Appeal, *supra* note 79, at 256-57 (Aug. 20, 1973).

planning staff wholly to the services of the Commissioners, except as Commissioners or the Court may otherwise permit or direct."[127]

Finally, Judge Dillin ordered that IPS formally apply to the United States Department of Health, Education and Welfare for funding under the Civil Rights Act of 1964, Title VII, for a comprehensive human relations program. As he put it, "[L]ittle bitty systems that I never heard of . . . are collecting, in some instances, over a million dollars a year for this type of thing, but you have not applied at all."[128] No order of the court in the entire case created more animosity with the IPS board than the order to apply for federal funds; it was viewed as an unprincipled invasion of the administrative prerogative by the judiciary. At a special board meeting on August 21, 1973, the IPS board voted to apply for the federal funds as ordered by the court, but four of the members of the board read a public statement which said that they were voting to apply for the funds only because the court had so ordered and that they still disapproved of accepting federal funds.[129] The initial application for the funds was denied because it was, as some observers commented, so defective as to be bordering on contempt of court. Judge Dillin ordered IPS to reapply for the federal funds and the funds were ultimately received.

Meantime, the board filed a petition in the court of appeals for review of the order, which affirmed it,[130] then unsuccessfully sought a writ of *certiorari* from the United States Supreme Court.[131]

The commissioners found themselves faced with the formulation of a desegregation plan which would be implemented when school started in fifteen days, in the words of the court of appeals, a "Herculean task within a minuscule period of time."[132] There were 44 elementary schools in IPS which were at least 90 percent white, and 22 which were at least 90 percent black. Although they were not formally bound to do so, the commissioners used the guidelines from the July 20 decision because they were resolved that the interim plan should be one that could be developed into a final plan without further reassigning those children affected by the interim plan. The interim plan paired and clustered the peripheral black schools with white schools in outlying areas of IPS on the assumption that the black children attending the schools in the innermost core of the city would, in the final plan, be transported to suburban schools. There remained, under the interim plan, 19 all-black schools in the center core of the city which were left to be desegregated by the final plan.

---

127. *See* Order of Judge Dillin, *supra* note 125, at 4-5. *See also* Record on Appeal, *supra* note 79, at 123-24.

128. *See* Record on Appeal, *supra* note 79.

129. Indianapolis Star, Aug. 22, 1973, at 52, col. 3. The board members were the four new members elected in the 1972 election: Lester Neal, Carl J. Meyer, Constence Valdez, and Paul E. Lewis.

130. Indianapolis II, 503, F.2d, at 78.

131. Indianapolis II, 421 U.S. 929.

132. Indianapolis II, 503 F.2d, at 77.

Despite the fact that the board had vigorously resisted the court's desegregation efforts, and had, in Judge Dillin's judgment, not done anything until they were forced to do so, the IPS staff had indeed accomplished a considerable amount of work without which the commissioner would never have been able to prepare a plan in the short amount of time available. After some initial difficulties, such as the commissioners not being provided a telephone because the court had not explicitly ordered that they be given a telephone, the commissioners established a viable working relationship with IPS staff. In fact, the commissioners found that the staff personnel had more faith in the law prevailing than did the board. The board was consistently hostile to the commissioners, apparently holding the commissioners personally responsible for intruding on their former hegemony. While the plan was being prepared, the IPS board reportedly met every day to query staff members about what the commissioners were doing. On the other hand, the commissioners believed that the board was leaking the information to the press. The only meeting of the commissioners and the board occurred when the commissioners presented the interim plan to the board the night before presenting it to the court. At that meeting, the members of the board reportedly demonstrated very strong and emotional resentment of the commissioners.

When the commissioners' plan was presented to the court on August 30, 1973, the IPS board requested the kindergarten and high school pupils be excluded from the plan. Kindergarten students were to be excluded so as not to require busing of the youngest children, and high schools because the board believed the potential for violence and disorder increases as the age of the students increases. The commissioners accepted these alterations and they were approved by the court. The plan, as approved by the court, called for the reassignment of 9,300 students, 80 percent of whom would be bused. However, IPS, apparently believing that their continuing efforts to obtain a stay from the court of appeals or the Supreme Court would be successful, had not made any provisions to obtain buses, and they pleaded with Judge Dillin that they could not possibly institute the plan when school opened on September 4 because they did not have the necessary transportation facilities. Judge Dillin agreed to permit school to open on the scheduled date, but ordered that all reassignments of the interim plan be completed within about six weeks; the first of these took place on September 17, 1973.[133]

The student reassignments were divided into eight phases for the initial transfer. IPS made a last-minute effort to prepare the school personnel, at both the sending and receiving school, and also the students, parents, community or-

133. The delay of the reassignments until after school opened had both disadvantages and advantages. The greatest disadvantage was that students started school in one building and then, within six weeks, were assigned to another building. This created uncertainty and anxiety for the parents. On the other hand, IPS administrators believe that the added time gave them a chance to implement the interim plan more efficiently.

ganizations, and churches.[134] Although there were some public demonstrations and rumors of school boycotts, neither type of action had significant effect. Within a few days after all transfer had been completed, attendance was reported to be normal[135] and the public outcry had dissolved.

Nevertheless, IPS, even while implementing the interim plan, continued its efforts to obtain a stay. Supreme Court Justice William H. Rehnquist denied two separate petitions.

The Indiana General Assembly Does Not Act

The Indiana General Assembly met in November 1973 to organize itself for a session that would convene in January 1974. Public statements by the governor and the legislative leaders indicated that the Indiana General Assembly would not accept Judge Dillin's invitation to devise a desegregation plan for metropolitan Indianapolis. The most commonly stated reason was that the problem was a "local one," not one of state concern,[136] but it was evident that the issue was a difficult one politically; the Republican-controlled General Assembly would be well served to leave the burden of action with Judge Dillin.

In an effort to move the Indiana General Assembly, Judge Dillin issued, on December 6, 1973, a "Supplemental Memorandum of Decision,"[137] expounding on his belief that the General Assembly had a duty to provide a metropolitan plan, resolving the issue of what was a responsible time for the state to act, and advising the General Assembly of what standards would be acceptable to the court. He also vacated the orders contained in the July 20, 1973 opinion which required transfer of students to the suburbs on an interim basis. This order had previously been stayed, but the judge did not want any question about it to hinder legislative action.[138]

---

134. A specific administrator from central administration was assigned to each school to assist in the transfers. Switchboard operators at the education center were advised of these assignments and incoming calls were referred accordingly. Each newly assigned student was assigned a "buddy" at the receiving school, and IPS attempted to send a "personalized letter" to each parent involved. In at least one white school, School 84 (but probably not many more than that), the principal and the parents worked diligently to make the incoming black students welcome.

135. Indianapolis News, Sept. 18, 1973, at 2, col. 1.

136. *See e.g.,* Indianapolis News, Dec. 8, 1973, at 21, col. 5.

137. United States v. Board of School Commissioners of the City of Indianapolis, Indiana, 368 F. Supp. 1223 (S.D. Ind. 1973) (Supplemental Memorandum of Decision) [hereinafter cited as Indianapolis III].

138. Judge Dillin's proposition that the Indiana General Assembly had a duty to devise a plan to dismantle the dual school system in IPS was based on the principles of Brown v. Board of Education, 347 U.S. 483 (1954), the supremacy clause and the oath, prescribed by Article Six, clause three, of the Constitution of the United States, taken by members of the General Assembly. The court quoted extensively from *Brown;* Swann v. Charlotte-Mecklenburg Board of Education, 402 U.S. 1 (1971); Green v. County School Board, 391 U.S. 430 (1968); and other Supreme Court school desegregation cases to the effect that school systems segregated by law were unconstitutional and must be dismantled.

Judge Dillin suggested that possible solutions to the desegregation problem were: to combine all the school districts in the metropolitan Indianapolis area into a single metropolitan school district; to replace the present "24 school districts" with 6 or 8 new school districts; or to provide for an exchange of pupils within the existing school corporations.[139] He advised the General Assembly that one-way busing of black students to the suburban schools would not be acceptable unless there were "compelling reasons" to support it—for instance, the closing of some of the old, unsatisfactory school buidlings in the Indianapolis inner city. A reasonable time within which the General Assembly should act, Judge Dillin stated, was the end of its January 1974 session or February 15, 1974, whichever date was sooner.[140]

The Indiana General Assembly did not accept the court's challenge. Not only was no metropolitan plan forthcoming, none was introduced and there was very little public discussion of the issue.[141]

On the same day as Dillin issued his "Supplemental Memorandum of Decision," the court relieved the commissioners from preparing a final plan for desegregation, released the IPS planning staff to the complete control of the board, and ordered the IPS board to prepare a metropolitan plan of desegregation to be available as a contingency plan in the event the General Assembly failed to act.[142]

The IPS Staff Plan

In January of 1974, the IPS staff prepared a proposed metropolitan plan as ordered by the court. On February 12, 1974, the IPS board voted 5–2 not to approve the plan, but to permit the plan to be submitted to the court in accordance with the court's order. The plan proposed to close most of the remaining all-black schools and some integrated schools in stable neighborhoods. Some of these schools were new and others had been extensively remodeled.

Judge Dillin entered several other orders compelling IPS to begin preparations for a final desegregation plan in the fall of 1974, among them the purchase of sufficient buses to implement the final plan.

Since by March 21, 1974, it was still not known whether the appellate courts would approve a metropolitan plan, Judge Dillin ordered IPS to submit three contingency IPS-only plans. IPS responses with a basic plan which, with two minor variations, were presented as three plans. IPS subsequently sub-

139. Indianapolis III, 368 F. Supp., at 1227–28.
140. *Id.* at 1224.
141. The only legislation enacted by the Indiana General Assembly at this session, which was applicable to the case, was Senate Enrolled Act No. 119, a statute providing for "the adjustment of tuition among transferor and transferee schools and for the reimbursement of transportation cost by the state and rigidly limited in its application." *See* Indianapolis II, 503 F.2d, at 74.
142. Judge Dillin subsequently ordered IPS to pay Glatt $29,925 and Taylor $13,950 for their services as commissioners. In addition, IPS was required to pay $5,000 to John O. Moss and John Preston Ward for legal services the two attorneys performed for the commissioners in defending an action against the commissioners in state court.

mitted a fourth plan it stated was based on plans proposed in Memphis and Knoxville. This plan would have left a number of IPS elementary schools predominantly black and provided far less integration than Judge Dillin had consistently indicated would be required.

Appeals

The defendants appealed Dillin's decision of June 11, 1973 to the United States Court of Appeals for the Seventh Circuit, which heard oral arguments on February 20, 1974. An immediate decision was not expected since, at the same time, the United States Supreme Court was deliberating *Bradley v. Milliken.* The Sixth Circuit's ruling that an interdistrict desegregation remedy was necessary and permissible in the Detroit area was being reviewed, and the anticipated decision would have strong bearing on what remedy would be possible for Indianapolis. It was believed, however, that both decisions would be handed down early enough in the year so that final desegregation plans could be formulated and put into effect by the opening of school in September 1974.

In anticipation of the appellate decision, two new groups petitioned to intervene as plaintiffs so that they might have a voice in the design of the final plan. They were the Indiana State Teacher's Association (ISTA) and Community Coalition for Schools (CCS).

ISTA Intervenes

ISTA intervened as an affiliate of the National Education Association whose local affiliate, the Indianapolis Education Association, consists of more than 1,800 teachers employed by IPS. It raised several objections to the metropolitan plan submitted by IPS on March 8, 1974. It complained that the plan was "obviously incomplete" in that it was "limited to demographic factors and contains nothing pertaining to the impact of desegregation, such as curriculum development, guidance and other school personnel in dealing with issues incident to desegregation." It alleged also that the plan was "further deficient in that it contains no data whatever concerning teacher displacement, and no indication whether or not displaced teachers, if any, could or would be absorbed elsewhere in the desegregation area, either in Indianapolis or the suburban schools." ISTA was particularly concerned because the IPS had announced, on April 10, that the contracts of all probationary teachers would not be renewed, although those who wished to do so could apply for reemployment after May 1, 1974. IPS's reasoning was that if a plan calling for one-way transfers of students out of IPS were implemented, IPS would need as many as 1,000 fewer teachers. ISTA alleged that this approach—"wholesale dismissal to be followed by selective rehiring pursuant to new applications"—was not in accord with the procedure for staff reduction required in other desegregation cases.[143] It was also contrary

143. ISTA specifically cited Singleton v. Johnson Municipal Separate School District, 419 F.2d 1211 (5th Cir. 1969).

to Judge Dillin's opinion of July 20, 1973, which provided that "if any teachers presently employed by IPS are rendered surplus as a result of this order, and additional teachers are needed by any added defendant as a result thereof, first consideration shall be given by such added defendant to employ a qualified IPS teacher."[144]

ISTA asked to participate in the formulation of a comprehensive plan covering all aspects of desegregation impact. Specifically it asked that the court "enjoin defendant Board of School Commissioners of the City of Indianapolis to reinstate all teachers who have been notified of non-renewals contract for the 1974–75 school year . . . pending the approval of this court of a comprehensive Desegregation Impact Plan," and that it "enjoin all school corporation defendants to offer contracts for the 1974–75 school year to all teachers on the same terms and conditions as such contracts would have been offered if no desegregation orders had been pending, subject, however, to the right of the school corporation to terminate or change such contracts pursuant to a comprehensive Desegregation Impact Plan approved by this Court." Judge Dillin did not rule on the ISTA petition to intervene during this critical period of time. Rather, he waited nearly two years until the first day of the second remedy trial, March 17, 1975, when he denied the petition from the bench.[145] ISTA was, however, subsequently granted leave to intervene by Judge William E. Steckler on August 8, 1975.

The Community Coalition for Schools (CCS), a group of northside Indianapolis neighborhood associations, petitioned to intervene in the name of the neighborhood associations and individual members thereof,[146] which had coalesced around the fact that the metropolitan plan filed by IPS contemplated closing all the schools on the north side of Indianapolis. This included 19 predominantly black schools and several integrated schools in the north-central part of Indianapolis. CCS sought to protect the residents' educational, environmental, social, recreational, and financial interests that would be directly affected by the final desegregation plan. Primarily it asked that any plan should retain all schools which had adequate physical facilities for an on-going educational program; only schools with deficient physical facilities should be closed.

The coalition also opposed one-way busing, an issue directly related to the closing of schools, since if a substantial number of IPS students were transported to other school corporations, and none returned to IPS, it was inevitable that some IPS schools would not have sufficient enrollment to remain open. The petition sought a plan that would assure that both the benefits and burdens of desegregation would be shared by all children and parents in all neighborhoods.

144. Indianapolis II, 368 F. Supp., at 1209.
145. United States v. Board of School Commissioners of the City of Indianapolis, Indiana, Trial Record, vol. I, at 2 (March 17, 1975). [Hereinafter cited as Second Remedy Trial Record]
146. The petition to intervene was filed by this writer as counsel for the group on June 10, 1974.

In addition, it maintained that the final desegregation plan should be concerned with the total educational program of the affected students. Students "reassigned to new schools outside their neighborhood [should] be provided an educational environment and programs in their new schools which are equal or superior to the educational environment and programs in schools which they previously attended." Human relations programs and other teacher and staff training should be designed to "assure a receptive and friendly environment for transfer of pupils in their new schools."

The coalition submitted that the final desegregation plan should, to the greatest extent possible, continue student reassignments established by the 1973/74 interim desegregation plan. The proposed metropolitan plan, it asserted, completely ignored the interim plan and would have resulted in a second reassignment for most of the students included in the interim plan.[147]

As an alternative, the coalition proposed that, when schools were paired or clustered, the grades should be split among the schools so that all students would be bused out of their neighborhood part of the time, but no children would be bused out all the time.[148]

In conclusion, CCS asked the court to appoint an advisory committee "representing all racial, economic, and geographic interests of the City of Indianapolis to study all proposed plans and advise the court before the adoption of the final plan." It also asked the court to name, at the time the final plan was ordered, a "bi-racial committee" to assist the court in monitoring the operation of the plan.

None of the parties to the desegregation case opposed the petition of the CCS to intervene on its merits; but at the December 2, 1974 pretrial conference, IPS orally opposed the petition on the grounds that it was premature because the court was not ready to consider a final plan. Like the ISTA petition to intervene, the CCS petition was not ruled upon for nearly nine months. On March 17, 1975, the first day of the second remedy trial, Judge Dillin denied the intervention from the bench.[149]

---

147. Among the individuals joining the petition to intervene was a white mother, on behalf of her children, who had very vocally opposed having her daughter bused to a previously all-black school under the interim plan. This same mother was now just as violently opposed to having her daughter reassigned again. In less than one year the family had developed a strong identification with the new school, and were just as upset about having their daughter transferred out of this school as they were about having her transferred out of her neighborhood school in the fall of 1973.

148. For example, if School 1, a black school, and School 2, were paired, all students in grades 1–4 might go to School 1 and all those in grades 5–8 might go to School 2. This approach differed from the IPS approach, which would send all of these students from a portion of the School 1 district and all of the students from a portion of the School 2 district to School 1; or all of grades 1–8 with the remaining portion of the two districts going to School 2 for all of grades 1–8. IPS favored this approach because it resulted in all children from the same family attending the same school.

149. Second Remedy Trial Record, vol. I, at 2 (March 17, 1975).

Milliken v. Bradley

Weeks passed and still no decision was reached on the appeals from the Indianapolis and Detroit cases. And so at the beginning of July, Judge Dillin entered an order staying the metropolitan transfers for the 1974/75 school year and continuing the interim plan for another year with only minor adjustments.

The United States Supreme Court finally announced its decision in *Milliken v. Bradley*[150] on July 25, 1974. It held against a metropolitan-area remedy for the Detroit school district, but the vote was 5 to 4, and Justice Stewart, in his decisive concurring opinion, stated: "Were it to be shown . . . that state officials had contributed to the separation of the races by drawing or redrawing school district lines . . .; or by purposeful, racially discriminatory use of state housing or zoning laws, then a decree calling for transfer of pupils across district lines or for restructuring of district lines might well be appropriate."[151]

A month later, the Court of Appeals for the Seventh Circuit reversed Judge Dillin's findings relating to a metropolitan remedy beyond the Marion County boundary, and vacated and remanded those findings relating to a metropolitan remedy within Marion County.[152] In vacating the inter-county remedy, the seventh circuit court stated that "the district court should determine whether the establishment of the Uni-Gov boundaries without a like re-establishment of IPS boundaries warrants an inter-district remedy within Uni-Gov in accordance with *Milliken.*"[153]

Seventh Circuit Upholds Dillin

The court of appeals affirmed Judge Dillin with respect to his orders holding the IPS board in default for not submitting an acceptable plan, appointing commissioners to prepare the interim plan, assigning IPS staff to the commissioners, and ordering IPS to apply for federal funds. It rejected the notion that the Eleventh Amendment barred prosecution of the action "without the state's consent or waiver of consent,"[154] and affirmed his ruling of July 11, 1973, that the city of Indianapolis's operation of a de jure segregated school system was *res judicata.*[155]

In addition, the circuit court affirmed the exclusion of "sociological evidence" which the suburban schools offered through the testimony of David J. Armor and Ernest van den Haag—to wit, that "contact between the races does not reduce prejudice; and integration (as distinguished from desegregation) may heighten racial identity and reduce the opportunity for actual contact between the races"—as being an attempt to challenge the underpinnings of *Brown v. Board of Education.*[156]

150. 418 U.S. 717 (1974).
151. *Id.* at 755.
152. Indianapolis II, 503 F.2d, at 68.
153. *Id.* at 86 n.23.
154. *Id.* at 82.
155. *Id.* at 83.
156. *Id.* at 84.

Finally, the circuit court refused to order that Judge Dillin be recused, as state officials had petitioned, on the grounds that he had evidenced a prejudgment of liability on the part of the defendants in a newspaper interview. The court of appeals found that his statements were based on the record of *Indianapolis I* and thus derived from proceedings before the court.[157]

As soon as this opinion was handed down, the defendant state officials, IPS, and some of the Marion County suburban schools petitioned the United States Supreme Court for a writ of *certiorari* to review what for them was a partial victory.

The Supreme Court of the United States denied *certiorari* on all of these petitions. These same parties also filed a motion with Judge Steckler, the chief of the Southern District of Indiana, asking that a new judge be appointed to hear the remainder of the case pursuant to Rule 23, Local Rules of the United States Court of Appeals for the Seventh Circuit.[158] Judge Steckler referred the motion to the court of appeals for instruction, and on November 14, 1974, the court of appeals denied the motion to have a new judge appointed to the case.

Pretrial Conference

At a pretrial conference held on December 2, 1974,[159] Judge Dillin ruled that there would be a trial permitting all parties to present additional evidence on the issues of whether Uni-Gov, zoning laws, or location of public housing projects might constitute grounds for imposing a multidistrict remedy within Marion County. At the same time he continued his efforts to persuade the parties to settle the case voluntarily, saying, "I have consistently pointed out that if suburban schools would accept 15 percent new minority students from IPS this would solve the problem, preserve their local autonomy and end this case." The judge accused the suburban schools of wanting "to hang out on an all-or-nothing basis. If you want to shoot dice with this Court, the Seventh Circuit and the Supreme Court," he stated, "this is your prerogative, but if you wake up some morning and find you are out of existence, it is your problem and not mine." He was alluding to the possibility of the court creating a single school district for the entire county, or dissolving the IPS corporation and distributing its territory to the township school corporations. These proposals had been made as early as 1971, and had been consistently rejected. Since the Supreme Court in *Milliken* had severely restricted the availability of an interdistrict remedy, and the circuit court had set aside one such remedy in the *Indianapolis*

---

157. *Id.* at 80.

158. This rule provides that "whenever a case tried in a District Court is hereafter remanded by this court for a new trial, it shall be reassigned by the district for trial before a judge other than the judge who heard the prior trial unless the remand order directs or all parties request that the same judge retry the case." 7th Cir. R. 23, 28 U.S.C.A. (West Supp. 1976).

159. This writer attended the pretrial conference as counsel for the community coalition of schools. The quotations are taken from the writer's personal notes of that conference.

case, the suburban schools evidenced a surge of confidence and Judge Dillin could not have been optimistic that a settlement would be reached.

He assured the lawyers, however, that a voluntary metropolitan plan would be stayed if there were an appeal by the intervening plaintiffs to challenge the constitutionality of the one-way busing. Then Judge Dillin ordered the intervening plaintiffs to file with the court a statement of the issues which they intended to raise at the upcoming trial. He also ordered the Justice Department to "decide which side it is on and file a statement accordingly." Within three weeks, all schools were to list the number of spaces available in each classroom and the number of students in each class.

In the court's pretrial entry of December 13, 1974, he ruled that "in addition to the Univ-Gov issue, the issue of the effect, if any, of the housing and zoning laws, rules, regulations, and customs in Marion County, Indiana, and its various political subdivisions upon the *de jure* segregation of IPS, would be considered."

The Housing Authority of the City of Indianapolis

The second remedy trial concluded on March 24, 1975; the greater part of the evidence introduced centered on the issue of public housing location, thus enlarging the scope of the case. It was anticipated that a decision would soon be forthcoming since at the pretrial conference Judge Dillin had said that he "did not want to get into another summer trial pushed up to a deadline by school starting." The decision was not handed down, however, until August 1, 1975, approximately one month before school was to reopen. The "Memorandum of Decision" reiterated the need for an interdistrict remedy stating that "when the General Assembly expressly eliminated the schools from consideration under Uni-Gov, it signalled its lack of concern with the whole problem and thus inhibited desegregation with IPS."[160] Judge Dillin held that the issues of housing and zoning laws were not controlled by *Milliken,* and attacked the policies of the Housing Authority of the City of Indianapolis (HACI) asserting that "the evidence is undisputed that each and every public housing project constructed and operated by the added defendant HACI is located within IPS territory, in some instances just across the street from territory served by one of the added defendant school corporations. . . ."[161]

Because the residents of the public housing projects were approximately 98 percent black (except in projects for the elderly), HACI actively promoted a segregated school system. The opinion stated that both the Metropolitan De-

---

160. United States v. Board of School Commissioners of the City of Indianapolis, Indiana, 419 F. Supp. 180, Memorandum of Decision, at 5 (Aug. 1, 1975), *aff'd,* 541 F.2d 1211 (7th Cir. 1976), *vacated and remanded,* 45 U.S.L.W. 3508 (Jan. 25, 1977). [Hereinafter cited as Indianapolis IV.]

161. *Id.* at 2–3.

velopment Commission of Marion County and the HACI had been guilty of acts "confining poor blacks to the inner city [and] has directly and proximately contributed to cause the suburban school districts within Marion County, other than Washington Township and Pike Township, to be and remain segregated white schools, with segregated white faculties and administrative staffs."[162]

Based on its findings, the court ordered black students from IPS grades 1–9 transferred to each of the suburban school districts in such numbers as would cause the total enrollment of pupils in each suburban school, after the transfers, to be approximately 15 percent black. Washington Township, which already had a black enrollment of approximately 15 percent, and Pike Township, which had a black enrollment of approximately 12 percent, were excluded from the plan. All other Marion County suburban school defendants were ordered to accept the transfers for the 1975/76 school year and each year thereafter. Furthermore, the court ordered that students would continue to attend the school to which they were transferred until graduation from high school, as long as they remained students within the IPS territory.

The opinion said this would amount to the transfer of 6,533 black students in grades 1–9 to suburban schools for the fall of 1974, increasing in each of the next four years with the addition of high school students until approximately 9,525 black students would be transferred each year to schools in the suburban districts.

In addition, Judge Dillin ordered IPS to submit, on or before October 15, 1975, a final plan for desegregation of the remaining IPS schools to be put into effect within IPS at the beginning of the second semester of the 1975/76 school year. "Fortunately," the opinion stated, "the reports on classroom space filed by the added defendants reflects that, without exception, there is ample space available in which to house transferees. Also, IPS has ample transportation facilities available."[163]

The memorandum also enjoined HACI from locating any additional public housing units within the boundaries of IPS and from reopening a vacant project to tenants other than the elderly.

Since Judge Dillin had stayed the transfer of IPS students to suburban schools in August 1973, it was widely and erroneously assumed he would do so again. Immediately after entering his order, Judge Dillin left Indianapolis to attend an ABA convention in Montreal. The motion for a stay was therefore filed with Judge William E. Steckler, the chief judge of the Southern District of Indiana, and on August 8, 1975, Judge Steckler, reportedly after consultation with Judge Dillin, denied the motion. But before school started, the United States Court of Appeals for the Seventh Circuit stayed the interdistrict portion of the August 1, 1975 order.

162. *Id.* at 4.
163. *Id.* at 10.

CONCLUSION

Although the desegregation of the Indianapolis school system has been under litigation for eight years, the termination of the case is not in sight. There is presently no plan for meaningful desegregation. Moreover, no structure by which community groups can cooperate in the preparation and implementation of desegregation plans has been developed. Public resistance to integration is still vocal, although perhaps slightly more restrained than in 1971.

The only significant step toward a unitary school system has been the reduction of racially identifiable faculties. Many schools which were near the 40 percent tipping point, which Judge Dillin's orders consistently tried to avoid, are now predominantly black. It is doubtful that the school system will become integrated in the immediate future.

A potentially significant event for the future occurred when a new IPS school board was elected in May 1976. For the first time since 1930 the Citizens' School Committee was defeated *in toto* by a more progressive slate of candidates. Four of the newly elected board members took office on July 1, 1976. One of the new members, Mary Busch, was promptly elected president. At the first board meeting the board voted 4–3 (the new members for, the carryover members against) to recognize the birthday of Martin Luther King as a school holiday.

POSTSCRIPT

On July 16, 1976, a divided United States Court of Appeals for the Seventh Circuit affirmed the interdistrict remedy ordered by Judge Dillin on August 1, 1975.[164] The court held that on the principles of *Milliken v. Bradley*,[165] the interdistrict remedy ordered by Judge Dillin was legally permissible.

The court concluded that the exclusion of the public schools from the territorial expansion of Uni-Gov constituted an interdistrict violation which justified an interdistrict remedy. Uni-Gov, and its companion legislation,[166] which repealed the law automatically extending school district boundaries upon ex-

---

164. Indianapolis IV, 541 F.2d, at 1211. The appeals court action came just fifteen days less than one year after the district court's decision. In a footnote to his opinion, Judge Tone, the dissenter, attributes the delay to the fact Tone initially voted to affirm and was assigned to write the opinion. During the preparation of the opinion Judge Tone "came to the view reflected in this dissent." The opinion was reassigned to Judge Swygert who, with Chief Judge Fairchild, voted to affirm Judge Dillin's opinion.

165. 418 U.S. 717 (1974). The Seventh Circuit relied mainly on Mr. Justice Stewart's concurring opinion. Reliance was also placed on Evans v. Buchanan, 393 F. Supp. 428 (D. Del.) (three-judge court), *aff'd*, 423 U.S. 963, *reh. denied*, 423 U.S. 1080 (1975).

166. 1969 Ind. Acts, ch. 52 §§1, 3, 4, at 57; Ind. Code §§20-3-14-4, 20-3-14-9, 20-3-14-10 (1971); Ind. Code Ann. §§28-3613, 3618, 3619 (Burns 1970).

pansion of the civil city, "had an obvious racial segregative impact."[167] The court stated:

> Because, in 1969, 95 percent of the blacks in Marion County lived in the inner city and segregation in its schools was under attack in federal court, it is clear to us that Uni-Gov and its companion 1969 legislation were [a] substantial cause of interdistrict segregation [Milliken v. Bradley, 418 U.S. 717, 745 (1974)]; and [c]ontributed to the separation of the races by . . . redrawing school district lines. . . ." [*Id.* at 755 (Steward, J., concurring).][168]

The court of appeals seems to hold that since the Uni-Gov package had an "obvious racial segregative impact,"[169] the exclusion of IPS schools from Uni-Gov would be an interdistrict violation unless there were a "compelling state interest that would have justified the failure to include IPS in the Uni-Gov legislation."[170] Given the segregative effect, the court holds, the absence of racial motivation does not preclude a finding of an interdistrict violation.

The court suggests throughout the opinion that the actions of the Housing Authority of the City of Indianapolis in locating all public housing (the occupancy of which is 98 percent black) within the boundaries of IPS constituted an interdistrict violation. Judge Dillin found this action to be an interdistrict violation within the principles of *Milliken.* Despite all the discussion of the housing issue the court of appeals seems to affirm the interdistrict remedy solely on the Uni-Gov issue and not on the basis of the location of public housing. The court's discussion of the public housing issue is in support of the court's affirmance of Judge Dillin's injunction against the building of any additional public housing projects within IPS.[171]

The court concludes its opinion by "suggesting" that "the court [Judge Dillin] monitor the transference of black pupils from IPS to other school districts periodically, perhaps on a yearly basis, in order that modifications, if necessary, may be made."[172] As is discussed earlier in this paper, annual modifications of a plan have been a frequently expressed fear of suburban school officials and their lawyers. Judge Dillin partially allayed those fears when he told the lawyers at the pre-trial conference on December 1, 1974, that he did not intend to "exercise continuing jurisdiction to alter the plan every year."[173] Judge Swygert's opinion will likely rekindle these fears.

167. Indianapolis IV, 541 F.2d, at 1221.
168. *Id.* at 1220.
169. *Id.* at 1221.
170. *Id.* at 1220.
171. *Id.* at 1223.
172. *Id.* at 1224.
173. At the pretrial conference Judge Dillin characterized these fears as a "paranoid attitude."

On August 20, 1976, Justice Stevens granted the suburban schools a stay of the interdistrict portion of Judge Dillin's August 1, 1975 order, pending possible review by the United States Supreme Court.[174]

On January 25, 1977, the United States Supreme Court granted the petitions for writs of *certiorari* of several defendants, summarily vacated the judgment and remanded[175] to the United States Court of Appeals for the Seventh Circuit for reconsideration in light of *Village of Arlington Heights v. Metropolitan Development Corp.,*[176] and *Washington v. Davis.*[177] *Washington v. Davis* was decided by the Supreme Court prior to the decision of the court of appeals in the *Indianapolis* case. Judge Tone, dissenting from the decision of the court of appeals, relied on *Washington v. Davis.*

174. Metropolitan School District of Perry Township v. Buckley, No. 76-212, 45 U.S. L.W. 3183 (Sept. 14, 1976); Metropolitan School Districts of Lawrence, Warren and Wayne Townships v. Buckley, No. 76-468, 45 U.S.L.W. 3319 (Oct. 26, 1976).
175. 45 U.S.L.W. 3508 (Jan. 25, 1977).
176. 429 U.S. __, 45 U.S.L.W. 4073 (Jan. 11, 1977).
177. 426 U.S. 229 (1976).

With All Deliberate Delay: School Desegregation in Mount Vernon

James J. Fishman, Laura Ross, and Steven R. Trost

Mount Vernon, a city of 73,000, is located a few miles north of New York City. Efforts to desegregate Mount Vernon's schools began in 1963, and court actions are still pending. This case study is the only one in which the litigation occurred in a state—as opposed to a federal—forum, and illustrates the interplay of the judicial, legislative, and administrative process. Mount Vernon demonstrates how procedural strategy can delay desegregation efforts.

James J. Fishman is associate director of the Courts' Roles in Desegregation of Education Litigation Project. Laura Ross is a member of the New York Bar. Steven R. Trost is a 1977 graduate of the New York University School of Law.—Eds.

Since 1963, Mount Vernon has been involved in a controversy over integration of its elementary schools. The controversy is still unresolved. Delay has been due to poor legal strategy by the pro-integrationists, an intransigent school board with access to political power, tactical errors, the failure of two commissioners of education and their staffs to provide leadership, and long-run demographic changes in the city.

THE SETTING

An understanding of the demographics of Mount Vernon gives one an insight into why a twelve-year battle for integrated elementary schools has not been decided. The demographics show a city divided not only along racial and class lines (as most urban cities are), but more significantly severed geographically by a clearly demarcated zone—railroad tracks which cut the city in half. Railroad tracks have figured significantly in American history and language as symbols of both deprivation or affluence. In Mount Vernon, the tracks form a barrier, symbolizing the separation of races, and an atmosphere in which a school board and northside community refuse to order one white child to cross to go to school with black children on the south side of the tracks.

Demographic History of Mount Vernon

Mount Vernon has changed from a white suburban community in the 1940s to an economically and perhaps socially unviable city of the 1970s, divided racially and residentially. Mount Vernon is located in Westchester County, contiguous to the Bronx, a borough of New York City. To the north is Bronxville; to the east is Pelham; and to the west is Yonkers. The city is rectangularly shaped, encompassing an area of approximately four and one-quarter square miles. The tracks of the New Haven division of the Penn Central Railroad bisect the city from west to east at about the geographical midpoint. The railroad tracks—the symbolic focal point of the desegregation dispute—separate Mount Vernon into a white community on the north side and a black community on the south side of the tracks.

From 1910 until the end of World War II, Mount Vernon developed and established itself as an attractive suburb in fashionable Westchester County. However, by 1960 when the city reached its maximum population growth, the community had become "urbanized."[1] The characteristics of the city's population were more a microcosm of New York City than suburban Westchester. By that time, Mount Vernon was a commercial and industrial center with business areas located in the southern and central areas of the city. But Mount Vernon never attained the affluence of the neighboring white residential suburbs. Overall it is the poorest city in Westchester County, one of the nation's wealthiest counties.[2]

The 1960s was a decade in Mount Vernon—of change in the racial, ethnic, class, and age mix of the city, dramatically evidenced by the composition of the elementary schools. From 1950 to 1960, the minority population of Mount Vernon remained constant at about 20 percent of the total population. By 1965 it had risen to 27 percent of the total population. By 1970 this figure had increased to 35.6 percent. In real numbers, the past decade has seen a growth in the minority population of Mount Vernon from 15,000 to over 26,000. During the same period the white population decreased from 61,000 to 46,000.[3]

---

1. From 1950 to 1960, Mount Vernon grew from a city of 71,899 to 76,010. By 1970 the city's population had shrunk to 72,778. A statistical appendix of tables and charts utilized for this study is available upon request from the Institute of Judicial Administration, One Washington Square Village, New York, New York 10012.

2. Westchester is the thirteenth-wealthiest county in the United States. Bureau of the Census, County and City Data Book 333 (Statistical Abstract Supp. 1972).

3. In this paper "minority" refers to blacks, Hispanics, and Orientals. Almost all of Mount Vernon's nonwhite population is black. In the 1970 census only 531 residents of a

The transition from an all-white community to a racially mixed one was logical in light of expected migration patterns. Mount Vernon is just across the border from New York City and there is ready access to the central business districts of New York City through public transportation. Thus, it was easy for inner-city blacks to move to Mount Vernon, yet still be able to commute inexpensively to their jobs in New York City. In addition, Mount Vernon has been itself a commercial and industrial center which attracted blacks to jobs in the southern areas of the city. The initial settlement of Mount Vernon occurred on the south side. Large numbers of small, low-priced one- and two-family houses within the price range of middle-class black people were available when whites moved out of this section. The city had long been regarded as a temporary stopover for young white families. After a few years in Mount Vernon, they would move to the more attractive communities, such as Scarsdale, farther north in Westchester County.

The migration of blacks to the area south of the tracks contributed to an existing exodus of Mount Vernon's southside whites. Most of the white community remaining in the south side are the elderly, whose children have either left Mount Vernon or moved north of the tracks. The housing units of those whites who had left were replaced by young black families with school-age children. Between 1960 and 1970, there was a gain of 3,984 units by black occupants, and a 3,656 loss by white occupants.[4] This residential pattern divided the city into two racially unbalanced parts, so that 90 percent of Mount Vernon's black population lives on the south side of the city.[5]

As blacks moved into the city, the phenomenon of white flight appeared. In 1954, 25,000 Jews comprised 33 percent of Mount Vernon's population. By 1969 they had diminished to only 12,000, a mere 15 percent of the city's population. Of the other large groups in Mount Vernon, the Italian community comprised about 45 percent of the city's population while the black community accounted for 30 percent.[6]

Whites who fled were mainly those in the prime earning age group of 25–64, who took their school-age children with them. The loss of white urban youths had a profound effect upon the composition of Mount Vernon's elementary schools. The population of black children up to the age of 14 increased from 4,500 to almost 8,000 (in percentages from 24 to over 46 percent) during the past decade. The comparable young white population dropped from 14,000 to 9,200.[7] And since the black community of Mount Vernon is made up of a much

total of 72,778 were not classified as black or white. Englehardt and Englehardt, Inc., Education Consultants, in association with Fuller and Wenning, Architects, Master Plan for the the City School District of Mount Vernon, New York 162 (December 1972). [Hereinafter cited as Englehardt Report.] The Master Plan was commissioned by the Mount Vernon Board of Education.

4. *Id.* at 11.
5. *Id.* at 5.
6. New York Times, October 24, 1969, at 49, Col. 1.
7. *See* Englehardt Report, *supra* note 3, at 4.

younger component than its white counterpart, this will further affect the present and future make-up of the public school population. The Engelhardt Report, a master plan for Mount Vernon's schools issued in 1972, points out that "the major shift in the ethnic characteristics of the City has occurred within the past decade. If continued at the present rate, the black population will be in the majority within a decade."[8]

The median income of black families who live on the south side is far lower than the white northside families.[9] But the black community of Mount Vernon cannot be considered a monolith. There is a substantial number of solidly middle-class families as well as a growing number of welfare families.[10] There are many more white-collar, college-educated residents on the north side,[11] which points out the division between upper-middle-class whites and lower-middle-class blacks in Mount Vernon. These differences in class, when combined with the age and race differences, that exist on each side of the railroad tracks, reflect the change in composition of and social distance between Mount Vernon's elementary school population over the last decade. These demographic differences reveal in part why the twelve-year unsuccessful struggle for desegregating the city's public schools on both sides of the tracks has been so bitter and divisive.

Racial Composition of Mount Vernon's Elementary Schools

The focus of the struggle for integrated education has been on the eleven elementary schools in Mount Vernon; six on the north side of the railroad tracks, and five on the south side. Mount Vernon's schools are administered by the city's board of education. The board, composed of nine trustees, no more

8. *Id.* at 4.

9. It should be noted that three of the southside districts had median income levels above the median income of white families in the United States, which was, according to the United States Census, $10,236 in 1970. All ten of the southside census tracts of Mount Vernon had median income levels which were higher than the median income of a black family in the United States, which was $6,516 in 1970.

10. *See* Englehardt Report, *supra* note 3, at 129, 132.

11. In the northside census tracts, the number of professional, technical, and kindred workers of all races is 3,094 out of a total of 16,637 residents who are employed and over age 16. This figure of almost 18 percent compares with the southside total of 1,405 out of a total of 12,926 residents, approximately 11 percent. A more valuable indicator is that in Mount Vernon's northernmost and most affluent census tract (44), 36.2 percent of the 1,566 residents employed in the labor force are employed in white-collar occupations.

In the census tract 33, which contains the greatest number of southside residents employed in white-collar occupations, only 16.2 percent of the 1,737 residents are employed in white-collar jobs. Of those residents who have had four years or more of college, a comparison of northern tract 44 and southern tract 33 shows that on the north side of the tracks, 31.3 percent of the 2,514 residents 25 years of age and older are college educated, while on the south side only 10.0 percent of 2,143 residents over 25 have college degrees.

than two of whom are elected each year for a five-year term,[12] has full control over budgetary matters, subject only to the state limitation on school taxes.

The policy of dividing the city into attendance zones, so that children residing in an area were assigned to a school near their homes, was devised and implemented as early as 1922, when the present city charter was adopted. The neighborhood school concept is firmly established in Mount Vernon.[13]

In the past decade the racial composition of Mount Vernon's elementary schools has changed from 58.8 percent white in 1963 to 63.9 percent nonwhite in 1973.[14] As of 1973 the five public schools on the south side had an average enrollment of 94.5 percent nonwhite students, while the six north side schools had an average enrollment of 71 percent white students. Every public school on the south side has an enrollment of nonwhite pupils which exceeds 90 percent.[15]

During these past twelve years, not one white child living on the north side has been direct by the Mount Vernon Board of Education to go to school south of the tracks. One of the results of this intransigence against enforcing the orders of the commissioner of education or voluntarily re-zoning the attendance lines has been to assist in the creation of a completely segregated school system on the south side while preserving a majority school population of white students on the north side.

When the integration controversy began, Mount Vernon's school system started on an irreversible path of becoming populated with an overwhelming majority of black pupils even though whites of school age constituted a majority within the city.[16] This trend will probably continue whether or not the attendance zones are changed in the future. After the mid-sixties, the flight of white families out of the city or into private schools had taken its course, but Mount Vernon could no longer return to the demographics of the early part of the decade. The school board, after fighting desegregation for over a decade, will

12. The school trustees are elected on a citywide basis rather than a ward or school attendance-zone basis. Due to the nature of this electoral system, the board has been dominated by northside whites throughout the period of the desegregation dispute.

13. *See* Englehardt Report, *supra* note 3, at 169.

14. *Id.* at 164, 167.

15. *Id.* at 166, 167, 169, 170, 207.

16. It is important to note that even with the vast exodus of whites from the city, white school-age children still constituted a "technical majority." That is, if all the white children in Mount Vernon attended the elementary public schools of the city, the majority of those in class would be white. However, as well as the white out-migration that occurred during the sixties, there was a corresponding removal of many white children from the public schools to the parochial schools. In 1972, 1,440 white children were enrolled in parochial school, grades kindergarten through eight, while only 197 black children were so enrolled. This removal increased the proportion of minority children in Mount Vernon elementary schools so that by 1970 the public school enrollment in grades kindergarten to six was 63.9 percent minority and only 36.1 percent white.

eventually be faced with a school system where 75 percent or more of the public school enrollment will be black.

One cannot necessarily assume that if an integration plan had been adopted in the early sixties, Mount Vernon's elementary schools would be more racially balanced than they are today. A total integration plan instituted in the sixties might have hastened white flight from the north side at a higher rate, causing even further segregation in the schools than exists today. But the failure to adopt any plan, the length of time the integration struggle took, and the ensuing racial tensions, brought an uncertainty to Mount Vernon that probably encouraged a white exodus.

However, if white children had to attend a school where racial proportions were similar to those of any other school in the city (whether it be north or south of the tracks), there would be less of a premium upon northside residency. In 1964 this might have exerted a stabilizing influence upon the demographic and residential patterns of Mount Vernon.[17] Instead, the neighborhood school concept has preserved a segregated system.

While black families now live on the north side, there are few living outside the easternmost and westernmost northside attendance zones. Thus, the imbalance in much of the north side exists just as strongly as it did in the previous decade.[18]

When one examines the allocation of resources, inputs, and utilization for the elementary schools, the differences are not as great as one might expect.[19] But the community is of the belief that the northside schools are "better." This may be reflected in the open-enrollment program which accounts for about 40 percent of the total black student population on the north side. All the integration plans that have been promoted have included an expansion of the open-enrollment program. As long as a higher quality in northside schools is perceived by the community and reflected in reading scores,[20] some southsiders will press for integration, and northsiders, led by the board, will do everything they can to delay re-zoning.

Many whites have chosen to remove their children entirely from the turmoil of the public school system and have enrolled them in the city's seven parochial schools. Over *one-third* of Mount Vernon's whites, who attend grades kindergarten through eight, attend parochial schools within the city's limits.[21]

17. The possibility of this phenomenon is discussed in text accompanying footnotes 30-33, *infra*.

18. By deducting the open-enrollment schools from the nonwhite totals in the schools, Lincoln had 102 students who went to the school as their neighborhood school; Traphagen had 51; Columbus had 27; and Pennington had only 11. A total of 191 nonwhite out of a nonwhite enrollment of 3,992 attended neighborhood schools in the north side in 1972. (This excludes Hamilton and Holmes, which are located in the far eastern and western districts north of the tracks.)

19. *See* Englehardt Report, *supra* note 3, at 42, 45, 172.

20. *Id.* at 127, 133.

21. *Id.* at 22, 164.

In addition to the parochial school population, between 1,000 and 2,000 white children between the ages of five and fourteen attend schools outside the city's limits. While these alternative school sources do not foster racial balance in the city's schools, the easy access to white parochial schools in the northside neighborhoods and private schools outside the city give white residents an incentive to remain as residents of Mount Vernon. The Engelhardt Report points up the dual effect of the nonpublic schools:

> . . . even if the parochial or non-public schools in Mount Vernon were to close, the white youngsters might not return or go to the public schools. Experience indicates that they would either enter other parochial schools or move out of the community. A desire expressed in Mount Vernon is to keep the City a biracial one. If the City is to remain biracial, the parochial school system appears to be desirable. It provides the holding power. As long as there is a parochial school predominantly white, certain whites will remain. Closing of a parochial school or schools in Mount Vernon would probably hasten the exodus of the whites from the community. Public school officials and City and state officials should be vitally concerned in maintaining a dual private and public system in Mount Vernon if they want the City to remain biracial.[22]

Integrated education will have a minimal effect upon Mount Vernon's school system, for there are not enough white children left in the public school to hold out the promise of integrated education put forward more than a decade ago. The statistics detail the changes of the last twelve years. They strongly suggest that Mount Vernon's public school system has a bleak future in store.

THE ERA OF GOOD FEELINGS: THE DODSON PLAN, 1963–1964

Unlike other efforts to eliminate racially imbalanced school systems, the initial impetus in Mount Vernon came not from the courts or federal action, but from the New York State Legislature and state law. The New York State Board of Regents is entrusted by statute[23] with the making of educational policy for the state of New York. In 1960 the regents declared that segregated education had a damaging effect on minority-group children:

> Schools enrolling students largely of homogeneous ethnic origins may damage the personality of minority group children. Such schools decrease their motivation and thus impair the ability to learn.[24]

---

22. *Id.* at 23.
23. N.Y. Education Law §305(2) (McKinney 1969).
24. New York Times, January 28, 1960 at 10, col. 5.

Pursuant to his authority to execute the board of regents' promulgation, in 1963 New York State Commissioner of Education James E. Allen, Jr., wrote to all boards of education in New York state ordering every local board to examine the extent of racial imbalance in its public schools and to determine ways in which to eliminate it.[25]

In response to this request, on July 5, 1963, the Mount Vernon Board of Education declared that elimination of racial imbalance was "one of the keys to greater educational opportunity and greater achievement for all [its] school children, and, therefore to greater personal fulfillment in life and meaningful participation in a democratic society." It resolved "as a firm expression of policy" to take such measures as were required to carry out the objective of Allen's letter.[26]

In support of this pledge, the board of education first appointed the twelve-member Citizen's Advisory Committee on racial imbalance, made up of the most prominent citizens of the city.[27] This committee was to work with the board in fulfilling the goal of equal educational opportunity. However, by September 10 Mount Vernon was but one of three school districts in the state that had failed to file plans with the commissioner. They were subsequently granted a delay. Commissioner Allen was told by the board that it would do everything possible to end imbalance, but "would not rush into stopgap remedies" and that ultimate remedies would be so costly (in part due to the construction of the first lunch-rooms in the eleven elementary schools, then attended only by neighborhood children) that "big state aid would be required."[28]

A standing-room-only public hearing held the week of September 22 displayed a community split into two unorganized factions. Before any plans had been presented, black speakers protested that the board was moving too slowly to

25. New York Times, June 19, 1963 at 1, col. 6.

26. Black Community Planning Board of Mount Vernon, The Bi-racial Parental Participation, Equality of Educational Opportunity Superior Curriculum, Total Integration Plan, at 1 (February (1968). [Hereinafter cited as BEST Plan.]

27. Included in the advisory committee: Sandford Solender, a former president of the school board, presently executive vice president of the New York Federation of Jewish Philantrophies, and Catherine Rhodes, retired assistant superintendent of the Mount Vernon Schools.

28. New York Times, September 22, 1963, at 73, col. 3. Specifically, Commissioner Allen requested the Mount Vernon Board of Education to report on:

1. The situation in the district with regard to any problem of racial imbalance regardless of the number of negro children enrolled, or to the actual existence of or trend toward racial imbalance. At this time and for the purpose of this report, a racially imbalanced school is defined as one having 50 percent or more Negro pupils enrolled.

2. A statement of policy by the Board of Education with respect to the maintenance of racial balance.

3. In districts where racial imbalance exists, or is a problem, a report of progress made toward eliminating it.

4. In such districts, the plan for further action, including estimates of additional costs, if any, and the time required for carrying out a plan.

end racial imbalance and that segregation was so harmful to black and white pupils that almost any price should be paid to end it. White speakers argued that integration would not be worth the price of transferring children from neighborhood schools to distant ones and that taxpayers should not have to finance "something special for Negroes."[29]

It was within this already antagonistic atmosphere that the board also in 1963 employed the services of the Center for Human Relations and Community Studies of New York University to work with both the board and the Citizen's Advisory Committee and to report to the board on how to deal with the problem of racial imbalance. The center was under the direction of Dan W. Dodson, and on February 6, 1964, he presented his forty-page report.

The most severe racial imbalance perceived by the Dodson report[30] was found in the city's eleven elementary schools. Those on the south side were predominantly black, while those on the north side were overwhelmingly white. After outlining a series of alternatives—open-enrollment, special-ability schools, one school for all sixth graders—the Dodson report concluded that the most efficacious method of eliminating racial imbalance would be to integrate the elementary schools by assigning all first-, second-, and third-grade children to the northside schools, and all fourth, fifth, and sixth grades to the southside schools.

While Dodson noted that busing of small children and development of school lunch facilities would be required to implement the plan, he felt great educational benefit would accrue from such a program. The report also warned that the plan could cause an exodus of whites from the city or could have the effect of stabilizing the city as a whole. For, if whites in the north side did not want their children going to school in the south side, they would leave the city entirely or enroll their children in private schools. Implementing the plan would also mean that the sizable number of whites still residing on the south side could not move to the north of the city to have their children attend the "segregated" northside elementary schools. Dodson believed that one of the biggest stumbling blocks to adopting the plan was the cost of busing, estimated annually at $250,000.

Although the Citizen's Advisory Committee approved of the plan 11-1, the proposal divided Mount Vernon's residents. At the time the plan was promulgated, many thought there was a good chance of its adoption by the board. In 1964 there was substantial white support for integration. Community opposition was not as cohesive as it would become in the near future. The board could have voted to move slowly into the busing plan over a three-year period as recommended by the advisory committee. Instead, on March 12, 1964, they rejected the pairing plan by a 7-2 vote and formulated their own program called "open enrollment" or "free choice."

The board's announced reason for rejecting the Dodson plan was that it would

29. *Id.*
30. New York University Center for Human Relations and community studies, Racial Factors in Public Elementary Education: Mount Vernon, New York (February 1964).

cost too much—more than $1 million the first year, and the city had already expended its school spending power to the statutory limit. This excuse would provide the basis for the board's defense against all future integration orders.

Dodson's report altered the framework of discourse. The pairing plan went further than the NAACP position at the time. Politically, the proposal permanently separated the black and white communities. It moved too far too soon. The plan's rejection marked the "official" beginning of the dispute in Mount Vernon. Since then, those who originally favored the Dodson plan have used almost every legal means to compel the board to adopt some variation of the pairing proposal.

Under the board's free-choice plan, children on either side of the city could attend elementary schools on the opposite side of the city on a voluntary basis provided there was available space in the receiving school. The free-choice program was adopted only after a number of parent-teacher associations had voted to retain the neighborhood school policy which would have been vitiated by acceptance of the Dodson report.[31]

The most serious obstacle to the success of the free-choice plan was the lack of free transportation. As the city's schools were based on the neighborhood concept, Mount Vernon had not provided school buses except for handicapped children. Since the estimated cost to a parent of voluntarily transporting his or her own child was $100 annually, the free-choice plan was never successfully implemented, and was only an illusory step toward the elimination of racial imbalance.[32]

The era of good feelings was over in Mount Vernon. On April 10, 1964, fourteen black and white parents whose children attended northside and southside schools, filed an Article 310 proceeding with the New York State Commissioner of Education challenging the Mount Vernon Board of Education's rejection of the Dodson plan.[33]

USE OF THE ADMINISTRATIVE REMEDY

The Power of the State Commissioner of Education

Although the local school boards were given the first opportunity to cure racial imbalance, ultimate authority remains with the state. Section 310 of the New York Education Law provides for an administrative remedy by way of a direct appeal to the commissioner for persons dissatisfied with the action of the

---

31. The Free Choice plan also included an extension of an after-school elementary reading program for black children in the most severely imbalanced schools; the establishment of a special elementary remedial reading school; employment of ten special reading teachers in the most severely imbalanced schools; and the addition of nurse-teachers services at four elementary schools.

32. Note, *Black and White: Desegregation Dispute in Mount Vernon,* 5 Col. J. Law & Soc. Problems 112, 119 (1969) [hereinafter cited as Black and White].

33. Matter of King, 5 N.Y. Ed. Dept. Rep. 85, Decision No. 7579 (1965).

local school boards.[34] Once an appeal to the commissioner has been instituted, the commissioner's power is quite broad. He may, in his discretion, substitute his judgment for that of the local board,[35] and his decision, unless purely arbitrary, is not subject to judicial review.[36] Local board members who refuse to obey his order may be removed from office,[37] or the local board's school districts may have its state funds cut off.[38] Although the power is rarely used to its fullest extent, the commissioner can exercise almost complete control over the affairs of a school district.[39] The commissioner has quasi-judicial power to promulgate and enforce desegregation orders. This power has been sustained in both the state and federal courts.[40]

It has been suggested in one article that the choice of proceeding via Article 310, as opposed to court action, was necessitated by the then uncertainty of the law over the need for affirmative state action.[41] Mount Vernon's actions could not be classified as an overt intention to establish and maintain a dual school

34. N.Y. Education Law §310 (McKinney 1969) states:

Any person conceiving himself aggrieved may appeal or petition to the commissioner of education who is hereby authorized and required to examine and decide the same; and the commissioner of education may also institute such proceedings as are authorized under this article and his decision in such appeals, petitions or proceedings shall be final and conclusive and not subject to question or review in any place or court whatever. . . .

35. Vetere v. Allen, 15 N.Y.2d 259, 267, 206 N.E.2d 174, 176, 258 N.Y.S.2d 77, 80, *cert. denied,* 382 U.S. 825 (1965).

36. Vetere v. Allen, *supra* note 35, first formulated the principle of "pure arbitrariness":

Where the commissioner of education found racially unbalanced schools to be inadequate from the viewpoint of educational soundness, his determination in directing the school board to reorganize attendance areas in the school district was not arbitrary or illegal, but conclusive. Where the Board of Regents under authority of Section 207 declared racially unbalanced schools to be educationally inadequate, decisions of the commissioner implementing such policy by directing local boards to take steps to eliminate racial imbalance was final, absent a showing of pure arbitrariness.

37. N.Y. Education Law §306 (McKinney 1969) states:

(1) Whenever it shall be proved to his satisfaction that any . . . member of a board of education . . . has been guilty of . . . willfully disobeying any decision, order, rule or regulation of the regents or of the commissioner of education, said commissioner, after a hearing at which the school officer shall have the right of representation by counsel, may by an order . . . remove such school officer from his office.

38. *Id.,* §306(2) (McKinney 1969) states:

Said commissioner of education may also withhold from any district or city its share of the public money of the state for willfully disobeying any provision of law . . . decision, order or regulation. . . .

39. Black and White, *supra* note 32 at 117. In most cases, the state education department merely tries to aid local districts administratively, by offering advice and, occasionally funds to bring about better racial balance.

40. The power of the commissioner was up held by the highest New York court in Vetere v. Allen, *supra* note 35. *See also* Olson v. Board of Education, 250 F. Supp. 1000

41. Black and White, *supra* note 32 at 115.

system. The issue in the courts at that time was the quantum of governmental activity necessary to constitute a discriminatory course of conduct.[42] Notwithstanding the fact that a federal court in the Eastern District of New York had held two years earlier that the mere fact that an education system is compulsory and publicly financed is sufficient state action to render the system subject to the Fourteenth Amendment's protection,[43] Lloyd King, one of the petitioning parents and chairman of the Mount Vernon chapter of the NAACP, decided to proceed with an Article 310 remedy. He was influenced by the commissioner's strong policy in favor of desegregating New York's school systems, a policy vigorously supported by the New York State Board of Regents, as well as the broad statutory powers of the commissioner.[44] In April of 1964, Section 310 seemed a better tool for the NAACP than a suit in federal court.

The Community Splits

While waiting for the commissioner's decision,[45] the NAACP and other community groups began an active campaign for free transportation. They were joined by CORE and an ad-hoc group called Free Choice Parents for Better Education. The president of Free Choice Parents sent a letter to the board in February 1965 arguing that economic status should not be a barrier to voluntary school transfers, and demanded free school bus transportation. In June of that same year, the NAACP and Free Choice Parents sponsored a demonstration for free transportation.

Countering these activities was a group called Parents and Taxpayers (PAT), a white organization dedicated to the preservation of neighborhood schools, whose position was that the board of education should not give discriminatory preference to a small group of parents. This stance was shared by the Italian Civic Association (ICA). In May 1965, shortly after the election of two board members who sympathized with the views of PAT and ICA, the board declined to provide free school transportation. In September they passed a resolution providing for free bus transportation for students who lived more than a mile and a half from their schools. The board rescinded that resolution in October by a 5-4 vote, touching off protests among black parents. The rescinded resolution and subsequent protests deepened the hostility between the two groups. At a raucous board meeting, Clifford Brown, Education Chairman of CORE, admonished the board members: "I would like nothing better than to walk up on

42. Since 1968 the government cannot countenance a racially unbalanced school system, but must take affirmative steps to desegregate it, root and branch. *See e.g.,* Green v. County School Board, 391 U.S. 430 (1968); Raney v. Board of Education, 391 U.S. 443 (1968); Monroe v. Board of Commissioners, 391 U.S. 450 (1968).

43. Branche v. Board of Education, 204 F. Supp. 150 (E.D.N.Y. 1962).

44. By 1965 these powers included the power to impose a desegregation plan on a local school system. *See* Vetere v. Allen, *supra* note 35.

45. The delay between oral argument in June 1964 and the decision in 1965 was occasioned by the commissioner, who was awaiting the outcome of Vetere v. Allen, *supra* note 35.

that podium and spit in your faces."[46] Brown was later forced to resign as a member of CORE after making an outrageous anti-Semitic remark at a school board meeting. Mr. Brown said: "Hitler made one mistake when he didn't kill enough of you."[47]

Commissioner Allen issued his decision in response to the *King* petition on December 21, 1965. While declining acceptance of the Dodson plan, the commissioner found that the board's free-choice policy was inadequate compliance with his directive on June 14, 1963. He therefore ordered the board to submit to him by March 15, 1966 a plan to eliminate racial imbalance "to the fullest extent possible within educational principles."[48]

THE ACADEMY PLAN

"The Board spent six weeks formulating the new plan required by the commissioner. Neither interested individuals nor community groups were consulted during the Board deliberations, nor were community suggestions solicited. Meetings were held in closed session with Superintendent of Schools, Dr. John Henry Martin, the author of the final draft of the new plan."[49]

There might have been good reason for lack of consultation by the board for, as the *New York Times* described, the city was "polarized into positions of hate and fear."[50] March 15, the day the plan was due, was seen by some "as a day of doom."[51] *New York Times* reporter William Borders summed up what the board faced on March 15:

> If the integration plan that the board proposes is too broad for them, more whites are likely to move out and then, in an expression popular with the white conservatives, "the Negroes won't have anyone left to integrate with."

46. New York Times, November 5, 1965, at 23, col. 1.
47. *Id.,* February 8, 1966, at 22, col. 7.
48. Matter of King, *supra* note 33.
49. Black and White, *supra* note 32 at 122.
50. New York Times, February 14, 1966, at 22, col. 5.
51. *Id.*

Today it is a city divided—divided not only by the New Haven Railroad tracks but also by two opposite worlds. . . . Except for chance encounters at places like the railroad station in the middle, the two sides seldom meet, certainly not in the public schools. . . .

At a recent school board meeting, one Negro speaker urged the board to act on integrating the schools "before Mount Vernon becomes a city of blood." [After a] Negro pleaded with the board . . . "For God's sake heed us, for this may well be the last time you will have the calm and thoughtful opportunity" . . . [a] white man in the [standing room] audience . . . called out: "Why don't you wave a gun at them?" And a woman of Italian descent yelled, "Majority rule! Majority rule!"

. . . [s]cores of young families have left the white area of the city. Sometimes they have sold their houses to Negroes, thereby multiplying the fears of those who stay behind.

If it is not broad enough, there is certain to be more Negro discontent. And that is why, as a minister who has observed the turmoil from both sides of the racial barrier put it, "Mount Vernon is a city holding its breath."

"After March 15," he continued sadly, "you may see a couple of hundred northside houses suddenly on the market. And that would be the end for Mount Vernon."[52]

On February 24, 1966, the board announced its new plan, "The Board of Education's Plan for the Renaissance of Education in Mount Vernon," later known as the Children's Academy plan. It had four essential features: (1) the ninth grade would be added to the single high school population; (2) grades seven and eight were to be consolidated in an existing junior high school complex; (3) the free-choice program would continue for the elementary schools, and the board of education would now offer free transportation; (4) pupils of all eleven elementary schools would spend 40 percent of their daily elementary schooling together on one site—a newly constructed integrated facility called the Children's Academy.[53] This last feature was the major innovation in the new plan.

The academy would be constructed upon a 33-acre site to be acquired from a local Lutheran-sponsored orphanage, the Wartburg Farm. The academy would emphasize individual learning and offer a variety of special programs: an advanced scholarship center for science, mathematics, history, and art; a center for the performing and creative arts for the children; an educational and medical clinic center for diagnosis of individual needs; a children's library center; a 5-acre farm; and a teacher-training center. The estimated $5.98 million cost was expected to be contributed by the state, the federal government, and private foundations. The academy plan concluded that the Dodson program was unworkable because of the large percentage of black children in the Mount Vernon School District.

Only two of the nine board members voted against the plan. One of the negative votes was cast by the only black member of the board, Mary Ellen Cooper. Her objection was the plan's failure to make a direct attack on racial imbalance. The other board member who opposed the plan, E. Gene Orsenigo, felt the plan was too expensive and not worth the cost to the community.[54]

Politics of the Plan

In retrospect, the failure to involve the community in the academy plan's formulation was a fatal mistake. Superintendent Martin misjudged the political atmosphere and overestimated his own prestige vis-à-vis the black community. He believed he could not get the board's approval if he discussed the plan prior

52. *Id.*
53. Daily Argus, February 25, 1966.
54. *Id.*

to its publication with the local black leadership; the board would vote against it because it was supported by the black community. The board was split and Martin thought he could carry a comfortable majority if the board believed it was their plan.

The writer, Charles Silberman, had just moved to Mount Vernon. Martin had indicated to a number of black leaders that Silberman would support the black community in their aims. Silberman did become a leading proponent of the academy plan, but his influence on the black community was not what Martin expected. Blacks thought that Martin was too manipulative and they became suspicious of Silberman. The academy plan, despite its merits, appeared as another case of whites defining what should be good for blacks.

When the plan was announced to the public and the board responded positively, Lloyd King publicly attacked the plan. Roy Wilkins, executive director of the NAACP, privately indicated his opposition. Psychologist Kenneth Clark suggested a meeting with Martin to discuss the plan.

At that time, the national office of the NAACP was supporting a "4-4-4 plan" in New York City which did not attack racial imbalance until the fifth grade. The academy plan was in conflict with the national NAACP position. At a meeting hosted by Wilkins, Silberman says he convinced Wilkins and Clark that the plan was a good one.[55] Wilkins then reversed himself and supported the plan, indicating his belief that the local chapter was making a mistake.

At this time, some of the NAACP's local chapters and the national organization were in dispute. The problem was whether the local chapter could back down and then support the plan without seeming to bow to the national organization. The Mount Vernon chapter refused to change its position. After the plan was opposed by the local NAACP chapter, the white liberal community became silent.

Pursuant to his continuing jurisdiction created in the *King*[56] case, Commissioner Allen held a hearing on the academy plan on March 6, 1966. By that time, public opinion had crystallized. Although the Urban League approved of the plan as a first step, the NAACP, CORE, and Free Choice Parents opposed it.[57] At the hearing the NAACP, through its attorney, Robert L. Carter, objected to the plan because there were no substantial steps to eliminate racial imbalance in 1966. Full implementation was not possible before three years; there was no concrete attack upon racial imbalance; and the plan was too expensive.[58] Instead, the NAACP urged the commissioner: (1) to adopt the Dodson plan or in the alternative send a team of experts to Mount Vernon to work out

55. Interview with Charles Silberman, August 26, 1975.
56. Matter of King, *supra* note 33.
57. Daily Argus, March 1, 1966; March 4, 1966.
58. Daily Argus, March 17, 1966. The NAACP more specifically objected that the plan dealt only with "extras" and seemed to say to the blacks, "Stay on your side of town except for some cultural window-dressing."

for all concerned a viable integration plan that would be consonant in all respects with the order of December 21, 1965; and (2) to retain jurisdiction of this matter until a viable plan was finally approved by the board, adequately financed and reasonably assured of implementation.[59] PAT appeared at the hearing as *amicus curiae*. They too opposed the plan, but on the grounds that it would necessitate "increased taxes and excessive busing," and suggested that it be used only in the summer with voluntary attendance.[60]

The third source of opposition was from Wartburg Farm, the Mount Vernon Council of Churches, and the YMCA, who argued against the plan because the officers of Wartburg wanted to keep their land.[61] Due to the turbulence at the open board meetings, and heightened tensions among all factions, the president of the school board instituted a series of rules that warned against any disruption of the meeting or breach of the peace, and implied that policemen present at the meeting were empowered to remove and arrest violators.[62]

Despite the opposition, on April 29, 1966, Commissioner Allen, calling the proposal "an imaginative practical approach to the solutions of difficult and complex problems of eliminating the educational disadvantages of racial imbalance in Mount Vernon," approved the academy plan.[63] The commissioner retained jurisdiction and ordered the board to submit periodic progress reports.

Shortly thereafter, on May 3, 1966, the board held its annual election. Two outspoken critics of the plan (one the former president of PAT), both endorsed by PAT and ICA, were elected. Now, four of the nine members opposed the academy plan. On May 7, a fifth board member, citing the immense community pressure put upon him, changed his mind and said he would oppose the academy program.[64]

Even if the board had supported the plan, it was now confronted with the

---

59. Petitioner's Brief in Opposition to Respondent's Integration Plan Before Commissioner Allen, Matter of King, 5 N.Y. Ed. Dept. Rep. 185, Decision No. 7636, (1966).
60. Daily Argus, March 21, 1966.
61. *Id.,* April 2, 1966.
62. *Id.,* April 8, 1966.
63. Matter of King, 5 N.Y. Ed. Dept. Rep. 185, Decision No. 7636, (1966).
64. New York Times, May 7, 1966, at 33, col. 6:

Mr. Pierce said he did not oppose the academy program, but the confiscation of church property. He declared:
"Never in all my seventeen years on the School Board has any action I've taken been so criticized, nor have I personally encountered such abuse, condemnation, and castigation as I have over my support of taking the Wartburg property.
Mount Vernon residents are 99 percent against it. I have been accused by church members of being Godless, a hypocrite and unworthy of being considered a professing Christian. I have been accused by members of the Masonic fraternity of being untrue to my obligations.
Even at a convention of school board members in Minneapolis last month, where delegates saw by my badge that I came from Mount Vernon, they expressed their utter disapproval of the action of the Mount Vernon Board of Education.
Should the board stand firm in its plan to acquire the Wartburg property by condemnation, I feel I must respectfully resign from the board."

purchase of the Wartburg Farm in the face of their reluctance to sell. On May 12, 1966, the Mount Vernon City Planning Commission unanimously disapproved the Wartburg site. On June 8, 1966, the school board, by a 6-3 vote, decided that the entire 33 acre Waterburg property was not required for the academy and determined to seek only 17 acres. On July 17, 1966, the Mount Vernon Planning Commission rejected the modified site for the academy. In October 1966 the board officially abandoned the Wartburg site in favor of a smaller piece of land adjacent ot the high school. The planning commission immediately approved the alternative site.

Meanwhile, in the midst of the attempt to purchase the Wartburg Farm, superintendent of schools and author of the academy plan, John Henry Martin, announced his resignation effective November 30, 1966. Although the board heard numerous appeals from citizens not to accept his resignation, they accepted Martin's resignation by a vote of 6-3. Martin's resignation exacerbated the tensions in the community. His supporters viewed his resignation as disgust at the board's procrastination. Martin later explained that he resigned "in order to give the integration plan the only chance it had."[65]

The Move to Other Legal Forums to Speed Integration

Suit in Federal Court. It had been a little over six months since the board had announced the academy plan, and those seeking to desegregate the school system were growing impatient with the board's efforts to acquire land. In September 1966 a group of forty southside black parents, called Citizens United for Education, who were not affiliated with the NAACP, brought suit in federal court alleging that the school board had deliberately fostered a segregated school system by gerrymandering attendance zones. The group sought an injunction against the neighborhood school plan and an order for the adoption of the Dodson plan.[66]

The board retained the New York law firm of Paul, Weiss, Rifkind, Wharton & Garrison to defend the suit. On November 1, 1966, Citizens United for Education lost on their request for a preliminary injunction. On September 27, 1967, Judge Frederick van Pelt Bryan held that the Mount Vernon board was not guilty of purposeful de jure segregation. The judge pointed out that the complaint only charged the board with fostering intentional race discrimination; there was no allegation by the plaintiffs that charged the board with failing to alleviate the conditions of de facto segregation, so as to constitute a violation of the Fourteenth Amendment. Judge Bryan indicated that while there was racial imbalance, a solution to the problem was being adequately supervised by

---

65. *Id.,* September 14, 1966, at 36, col. 6.
66. Bryant v. Board of Education, 274 F. Supp. 270 (S.D.N.Y. 1967).

the New York State Commission of Education. Therefore, intervention by a federal court was not warranted.[67] The judge then granted summary judgment to the school board.[68]

Petition to the Commissioner for Receivership. On October 5, 1966, seven proponents of the Dodson plan instituted an administrative proceeding before Commissioner Allen to remove the Mount Vernon School Board and to place the school system in receivership under the authority of the New York State Board of Regents. The plaintiffs also requested that the commissioner appoint an overseer for future school board elections and that all campaign literature approved by him before distribution.[69] Oral argument was heard on December 13, 1966, and on April 7, 1967, the commissioner dismissed the petition and terminated the action indicating that the issues raised in this proceeding were already dealt with adequately by the 1964 petition of *King.*[70]

The End of the Academy Plan

The school board in early 1967 instituted a pilot phase of the academy plan. They temporarily utilized a vocational school which 73 fourth-grade students attended two days per week. The free-choice aspect of the program, supplemented now with free transportation, had been immediately instituted. Although the number that transferred was twice as many as those participating in the program prior to transportation, the total number of transfers was but 325, less than 15 percent of the eligible black students. And not one white elected to transfer from the north side to the south side.[71]

The academy plan was in danger. In June of 1967, Deputy State Commissioner of Education Ewald B. Nyquist wrote to the school board criticizing them for their delay in implementing the plan and for their adoption of an abbreviated program. Under the pilot phase, only 20 percent of a child's school day was spent at the academy whereas the program had been approved on the basis of 40 percent of the school day.

Because the pilot phase of the program did not provide for sufficient integration of a large enough number of children, federal funds had been denied. In August, therefore, the board prepared a new application for federal funds and a new proposal that would have satisfied the 40 percent attendance rate by 1970. The board also requested $55,000 from the state to finance the pilot phase of

67. "Intervention by this court is not justified nor would such intervention further the solution." *Id.* at 280.

68. A student commentator took the view that "Judge Bryan implied that if the State, through the Commissioner, had not been actively involved in finding a solution, he might have looked further to find a basis for court intervention." Black and White, *supra* note 32, at 128.

69. Daily Argus, April 7, 1967.

70. Matter of Davis, 6 N.Y. Ed. Dept. Rep. 106, Decision No. 7735, (1967).

71. Daily Argus, September 6, 1966.

the academy. When the board first instituted its pilot phase of the academy program, they hired IBM as planning consultants. Their study proved conclusively, in the board's opinion, that full implementation of the academy plan would be beyond the financial resources of the city. Moreover, the academy plan would not sufficiently reduce racial imbalance. As a result of IBM's findings and the lack of a positive response to its requests for financial assistance, the board requested Commissioner Allen to suspend the plan.[72]

On January 29, 1968, the commissioner consented to termination of the academy plan on the grounds that fiscal limitations would prevent the academy plan from being a viable solution to racial imbalance in the schools,[73] and directed the board to develop an alternative plan, this time involving members of the community. The plan was ordered to be submitted by April 12, 1968. It was now five years since Commissioner Allen's letter had directed local boards of education to end de facto segregation. The feelings of fear of white families who still remained in the city were reflected in the statement of a white resident who was also a school official:

> We figure if it gets 30 percent Negro, that's the tipping point, that's the time to move out. I say, one or two families on the block, all right.[74]

The white members of the board held to that same view as they were pressed to formulate an integration plan to present to Commissioner Allen.

NEW APPROACHES

In meeting the directive of the commissioner, the board held two round-table discussions with local leaders. The Italian Civic Association proposed that several Westchester communities institute cross-busing to achieve integrated schools in a greater area. The local PTA recommended that children in kindergarten through third grade be kept in neighborhood schools, but that grades four through six should be fully integrated in a new building or by combining existing schools.

72.

Dr. E. Swanson's report charged organized crime backed the 1966 Mount Vernon Academy plan in order to keep federal attention from being focused on the city. He said the underworld was infuriated when Negroes rejected the plan. Then [the Mafia] withdrew their support to insure defeat of the plan. . . . "You make more money from a Harlem than a Scarsdale"—unidentified crime figure.
New York Times, June 21, 1967, at 1, col. 2.

73. By November 7, when Deputy Commissioner Nyquist warned the school board not enough children were attending the Academy, it was assumed that the decision to end state aid had already been made and new integration plans would be mandated in the near future.
New York Times, November 7, 1967, at 26, col. 3.

74. New York Times, May 5, 1968, at 51, col. 4.

The new superintendent of schools, Paul Smith, suggested closing some south-side schools and enlarging schools on the north side.

In February 1968 an ad-hoc council of black parents, the Black Community Planning Board of Mount Vernon, with the assistance of the Sarah Lawrence College Institute for Community Studies, issued a plan entitled the Bi-Racial Parental Participation, Equality of Educational Opportunity, Superior Curriculum, Total Integration Plan (known as the BEST plan). This group was headed by Garnett Young and included Lloyd King, petitioner in the Article 310 action. A consensus in the black community was reached after a series of open community meetings. The plan contained the following essential features:

1. All students in grades one through three would attend elementary schools on the north side of town; all children in grades four through six would attend elementary schools on the south side of town. Busing and school lunches would be provided.
2. A new community school would be developed to absorb part of the kindergarten population while making facilities available for adult education and cultural and community endeavors.
3. Elementary children would be grouped according to ability for some courses, and mixed heterogeneously for other subjects.
4. New staff members would be added, including social workers, nursing staff, and librarians. Teacher aides would be placed in all elementary classrooms with an effort to place a black teacher aide with a white teacher and vice-versa.
5. Parental participation would be increased by creation of an elected parent community council.[75]

The school board's third plan was made public at an open meeting on April 10, 1968—two days before Commissioner Allen's deadline. The timing of the presentation of the plan, plus the eclipse of the steering committee formulated to oversee the plan, suggest that the board was unwilling to have it discussed at a public debate.[76]

75. BEST Plan, *supra* note 26 at 6.
76. The board's alleged fear of public debates was not without cause as indicated by this eyewitness account of a board meeting:

Four hundred people had filed into the auditorium of the Holmes School in Mount Vernon, New York. After everyone was seated, a tall man, well-groomed and in his thirties, insisted that the pledge of allegiance be recited as an affirmation of Americanism. When the chairman refused, giving as a reason the absence of the procedure in the by-laws, the tall man rose and began to recite the pledge himself. He was immediately joined by about half of the audience and several of the men on the podium. After brief shouts of protest, those still seated began singing "We Shall Overcome." The brief peace that followed this noisy exchange was ended twenty minutes later by a squabble over seats between two blacks and two whites, which ultimately brought police intervention. The meeting was prematurely ended.

Black and White, *supra* note 32, at 112.

The board rejected the BEST plan[77] and adopted the "Mount Vernon Plan for Quality Integrated Education 1968-1971," which contained the following provisions: (1) a single high school serving all children in grades nine through twelve; (2) two middle-school complexes: one—utilizing already existing school structures—would house all children in grades five and six; the other—to be built in 1971—would house all children in grades seven and eight; (3) grades kindergarten through four would continue unchanged as neighborhood schools. The critical difference between the two plans was that the BEST plan offered total integration, while the board's plan maintained the separate school system in the elementary grades kindergarten through four.[78]

Although there were then two black board members, the vote was 8-1. The black who voted for the plan had been appointed by the board to fill a vacancy and felt that the board's goal of maintaining community peace was supportable.[79] Superintendent Smith resigned his post citing "frustration" in formulating an integration plan.[80] The board clearly indicated that they considered their endorsement of the plan a real, as well as their last, concession.[81] On April 16,

---

77. The board stated in its written report that it rejected the BEST plan because:

The pairing of schools, either direct or by region, would destroy the neighborhood school concept, and as a corollary [sic] would result in the busing of small children. This plan was rejected by the Board in 1964, and the community is more opposed to it now than in 1964.

78. City School District, Mount Vernon, New York, Mount Vernon Plan for Quality Integrated Education, 1968-1971 (1968).
The board considered the following plans:

1. Central Educational Park of one building in the center of the city over the railroad tracks for grade K to 6.
   Rejected.—Prohibitive cost.
2. Pairing of Individual Schools.
   Rejected.—(Destroys neighborhood school concept; extensive busing of small children).
3. Pairing of Schools by Region (Princeton Plan).
   Rejected.—(Same reasons as above.)
4. Open Enrollment.
   Rejected.—(Insufficient integration.)
5. Academy Plan
   Rejected.—(Prohibitive cost.)
6. All Schools Northside K-5, 6-8, 9-12 (except Grimes and Longfellow).
   Rejected.—(Considered by some as a threat to the residential nature of the south side.)
7. K-4, 2, 2, 2
   Accepted.—(Neighborhood schools for grades K to 4; grades 5 to 6 and 1 school for all pupils; grades 7 to 8 at 1 school for all pupils; senior high for all pupils.)

79. Daily Argus, April 16, 1968.
80. New York Times, April 11, 1968, at 33, col. 1.
81. E. Gene Orsenigo warned that "this is no invitation for new pressures and negotiations, that is it. I will move no more." He continued:

If in the future there are created more tensions which result in the tipping point being reached, the ruin and dishonor of this city will be on the heads of those mili-

1968, a hearing was held in Albany on the two plans. In addition, a task force of fourteen educators was appointed by Commissioner Allen to review the two plans. Although they were unable to agree on a single plan, the task force did conclude that full implementation of the BEST plan was financially unfeasible. The task force submitted two alternative approaches—one, a modified board plan, the other a modified BEST plan.[82]

THE ALLEN ORDER

On June 13, 1968, Commissioner Allen issued his third opinion in the *Matter of King*.[83] The commissioner found that the board's latest plan contained no provision for the reduction of racial imbalance in grades one through four, and that it therefore failed to meet the urgent needs of the children in those grades for quality education in an integrated environment. Instead of giving the board another opportunity to devise a plan, the commissioner directed:

> As early as possible in the school year commencing in September 1968, but not in any event later than November 4, 1968, the Board of Education provide for full integration in grades one through six by assigning all pupils in grades one through three to existing elementary schools in either the north or south half of the district.[84]

This was the integration plan promulgated by the Dodson report and repeated in the BEST plan. Lastly, the commissioner again retained jurisdiction and ordered that the board submit quarterly reports to him beginning August 1, 1968.[85] The order's effect on the community was immediate and divisive, as whites also split into organized camps.[86] On June 23, Mount Vernon State Assemblyman

---

tants who prefer total victory at any price rather than an honest compromise with honor.

Daily Argus, April 16, 1968.

82. Modifications of the board's plan included the addition of teacher aides, additional efforts to integrate faculty assignments, greater parental involvement, and pairing of two middle school grades pending completion of a new middle school complex. Modifications in the BEST plan entailed retention of the 1-3, 4-6 pairing proposals, but a decrease in other provisions to the extent of financial aid available.

83. Matter of King, 7 N.Y. Ed. Dept. 145, Decision No. 7877, (1968).

84. *Id.*

85. Allen also noted that the steps he called for would require funds not presently budgeted by the school district. He pointed out, however, that recently enacted programs were dispensing funds for special aid for urban school districts having a heavy concentration of pupils with special educational needs associated with poverty, and particularly for programs designed to correct racial imbalance.

86. Opposed to Commissioner Allen's directive were: PAT, the 800-member Italian Civic Association; Italian Women Civic Association; and the Guardia-Lombardi Association, as well as the major and eight of the nine board members. Mothers Against Busing and the Citizens' Union were formed in response to the order. In favor of the order were: The American Jewish Congress; Concerned Clergy; United Negro Clergy; Southside Civic Associ-

George Van Cott called the plan absolute suicide: "White people aren't going to permit it," he said, as 500 white demonstrators protested the busing plan.[87] On June 28, over one thousand whites staged a rally protesting the Allen order, as Mayor August P. Petrillo forecast "an exodus from the city should the busing plan go through."[88] Fifteen hundred persons turned out at a stormy school board meeting on July 2 where many whites threatened to sell their homes if the Allen order went into effect. The president of PAT called for legal action in order to block the commissioner's order. The anti-integrationists had always been conscious of the effective use of poltiical influence and exerted pressure on state politicians.[89] Though there was confusion on what the Allen order entailed,[90] this did not diminish the nature of the vehement opposition to it and the demand for a court fight on the order. Despite this opposition, many whites supported the order and organized the Committee for Responsible Compliance to help allay fears that northsiders might have over southside schools. This group contained a substantial number of Jews, which intensified the tensions among white residents of the city.[91]

The board of education did not move to implement Commissioner Allen's order. Six days after the commissioner's decision, the board requested attorney

---

ation, the Ad Hoc Council which had drawn up the BEST plan; and a new group calling itself the Committee for Responsible Compliance. Daily Argus, February 5, 1969.

87. New York Times, June 23, 1968, at 62, col. 3.

88. *Id.,* June 28, 1968, at 26, col. 7.

89. Harvey Felton, an attorney and the board's vice president (and later its president), was an ex-legislative assistant to Mount Vernon's state senator. In another showing of political pressure, the Mount Vernon Citizens Union urged fifty state delegation leaders at the Republican National Convention not to vote for Governor Rockefeller on the grounds that "he is guilty of confiscation of neighborhood school systems by refusing to intervene in the Allen order." New York Times, August 7, 1968, at 21, col. 4.

90. The chairman of the Mount Vernon Citizens Union told the *New York Times* that the plan would cost taxpayers from $6 million to $8 million a year to get buses to transport pupils, to hire the extra school personnel needed, and other requirements. New York Times, July 3, 1968, at 19, col. 2. "On August 18, 1968, the Mount Vernon Board of Education's counsel was quoted as saying the BEST plan would cost $3.1 million in additional teachers' salaries. However, Allen did not order the Board to hire those additional teachers—yet the Board has persisted in using that cost figure to string everyone along." Letter from Leonard Rosenfeld, Legal Redress Chairman of the Mount Vernon NAACP Branch, to Sylvia Drew, Attorney for Petitioners, August 1, 1969.

91. An article in the *New York Times* illustrated the split among white residents:

Some parents have been upset by the appearance at recent school board meetings of a group of about ten white men dressed in T-shirts and slacks who silently stand near the back of the auditorium.

At a recent meeting a reporter asked one of the men, who refused to give his name, why he was in the auditorium.

"I'm protecting the school board," he said.

What was he protecting it from?

"The Jews and the Negroes," he said, alluding to the support of the Allen order by many of the city's Jews.

New York Times, October 24, 1969, at 49, col. 1.

Richard Ross (who later became Mount Vernon's state assemblyman), to look into legal means of thwarting his order.[92] The board spoke in open defiance against the commissioner, claiming they would ignore the order when schools were due to reopen. Taking an extreme view of the situation, E. Gene Orsenigo, the newly elected president of the board, wrote to his board colleagues on July 27:

> Dr. Allen proposes these steps toward a Police State Education Department like those of the Fascist, Nazi, and Communist countries which have no local control of public education . . .[93]

In August 1968 the board refused to submit its first quarterly progress report. An application to reopen the commissioner's decision was made by the board, and denied on November 1, 1968.[94] In September the board decided to appeal the commissioner's decision in state court claiming the order would cost $3.5 million to implement, and that waiting at bus stops and bus travel would jeopardize the children's safety, academic achievement, and happiness. The board hired the New York City law firm of Demov, Morris, Levin & Shein, mainly known for their real estate expertise. Eight members voted an appropriation of $50,000 from the city's school budget to present its suit seeking reversal of the Allen order. The board's previous counsel, Paul, Weiss, Rifkind, Wharton, & Garrison, declined to take the case, as did some other Wall Street firms.

There was also a shift in counsel representing those in favor of integrating the schools and enforcement of the Allen order. During the summer of 1968 (after the issuance of the Allen order), the NAACP legal staff—headed by Robert L. Carter,[95] counsel for the petitioners—resigned en masse. This was the result of a dispute with the NAACP National Board of Directors over a controversial article written by Lewis Steele, one of the staff lawyers.[96] Steele remained as counsel as the case proceeded to state court, but after the original lower state court decision in January of 1969, the NAACP Legal Defense and Education Fund, Inc.[97] took over as sole counsel, representing the "integrationists."[98]

92. *Id.,* July 7, 1968, at 36, col. 5.

93. Letter from E. Gene Orsenigo to members of Mount Vernon Board of Education, July 27, 1968.

94. Matter of King, 8 N.Y. Ed. Dept. Rep. 151, Decision No. 7962 (1968).

95. Robert L. Carter later became a U.S. district judge.

96. Steele's article, *Nine Judges in Black Who Think White,* appeared in the New York (Sunday) Times, October 13, 1968, Section 6 (Magazine), at 56.

97. The Legal Defense Fund is an independent organization which split from the NAACP many years ago.

98. The NAACP's attorneys again entered the case in February 1975 when they took over as head counsel for the petitioners, although the Legal Defense Fund has continued as associate counsel.

DELAY IN THE COURTS

On October 9, 1968 an Article 78 proceeding[99] was brought by the Mount Vernon School Board in the Supreme Court of Albany County to annul the determination made by Commissioner Allen. The Board's motion for a preliminary stay of Commissioner Allen's order was granted on November 1—three days before the commissioner's order was to go into effect, foreclosing the possibility of implementing the order for the 1968/69 school year.[100]

99. The N.Y. CPLR Article 78 (McKinney 1974), proceeding is set forth below in its relevant parts: §7803—what questions may be raised; §7804—the procedure involved. Section (g) deals with the hearing, and Section (h) with the trial (which never occured during the time Mount Vernon's case was in the courts); §7806—the judgment.

§7803. Questions raised.
The only questions that may be raised in a proceeding under this article are:
. . . .
(3) whether a determination was made in violation of lawful procedure, was affected by an error of law or was arbitrary and capricious or an abuse of discretion including abuse of discretion or mode of penalty or discipline imposed;
§7804. Procedure.
(a) Special proceeding.
A proceeding under this article is a special proceeding.
. . . .
(f) Objections in point of law.
The respondent may raise an objection in point of law by setting it forth in his answer or by a motion to dismiss the petition, made upon notice within the time allowed for answer. . . .
(g) Hearing and determination; transfer to appellate division.
Where an issue specified in question four of Section 7803 is not raised, the court in which the proceeding is commenced shall itself dispose of the issues in the proceeding. Where such an issue is raised, the court shall make an order directing that the proceeding be transferred for disposition to a term of the appellate division held within the judicial department embracing the county in which the proceeding was commenced; the court may, however, itself pass on objections in point of law. When the proceeding comes before it, whether by appeal or transfer, the appellate division shall dispose of all issues in the proceeding, or, if the papers are insufficient, it may remit the proceeding.
(h) Trial.
If a triable issue of fact is raised in a proceeding under this article, it shall be tried forthwith. Where the proceeding was transferred to the appellate division, the issue of fact shall be tried by a referee or at a trial term of the supreme court and the verdict, report or decision rendered after the trial shall be returned to, and the order thereon made by, the appellate division.
. . . .
§7086. Judgment.
The judgment may grant the petitioner the relief to which he is entitled, or may dismiss the proceeding either on the merits or with leave to renew. If the proceeding was brought to review a determination, the judgment may annul or confirm the determination in whole or in part, or modify it, and may direct or prohibit specified action by the respondent.

100. The black community illustrated their displeasure with the Board by handing to each person who attended the December board meeting the following "ticket" in a Christmas envelope:

"Pure Arbitrariness" and Financial Impossibility

On October 30, 1968, before a hearing was held, the New York State Education Department moved to dismiss the board's petition for failure to state a cause of action. The hearing was held on December 13, 1968 before Judge T. Paul Kane in Albany. The board argued that the commissioner's order of June 13, 1968 was purely arbitrary, in excess of his jurisdiction, and unconstitutional for the following reasons: (1) his plan contravened the informed judgment of the duly elected and constituted local board of education; (2) his plan was financially impossible to implement; and (3) his plan was not ordered for educational purposes but solely to achieve racial balance.[101] The same group of black and white parents who initiated the original Article 310 action with the commissioner moved to intervene as respondents and, with the respondent commissioner of education, moved to dismiss the board's petition.

Represented by the NAACP Legal Defense Fund, the intervenors argued that (1) the policies and practices of a locally elected school board in conflict with the public policy of the state may not be maintained simply because they are preferred by a locality or by its school board; (2) the commissioner's plan was not financially impossible because not only were there available to the city additional funds in the budget for transportation and school lunches as verified by the board's own accountants, but there are a number of state and federal programs to provide funding for these purposes as delineated by the commissioner in his order.[102] Finally, the intervenors maintained that the commissioner's decision was not blind to educational purposes since numerous authorities, including the New York State Board of Regents, have found that "the elimination of racial imbalance is not sought as an end in itself but stands as a deterrent and handicap to the improvement of education for all."[103]

The state did not argue the merits of the ordered pairing plan, but instead insisted on its right to issue orders with court review only in extreme cases. Buttressing its argument, the state cited *Vetere v. Allen*[104] and the broad statutory

ADMIT ONE

PRESENTING
THE MOUNT VERNON PRODUCTION
"RACISM IN ACTION"
SEE YOUR NEIGHBORHOOD PERFORM IN
AMERICA'S LONGEST RUNNING DRAMA
SPECIAL HOLIDAY PERFORMANCE
IN THE USUAL SPIRIT
OF BROTHERHOOD & GOOD WILL

101. Brief of Petitioners, at 6, Board of Ed. of City Sch. Dist of Mount Vernon v. Allen, 58 Misc.2d 762, 296 N.Y.S.2d 890 (Sup. Ct. 1969).

102. Brief of Intervenors, at 4, Board of Ed. of City Sch. Dist. of Mount Vernon v. Allen, *supra* note 101.

103. *Integration and the Schools,* State of New York Board of Regents Policy Statement, January 1968.

104. Vetere v. Allen, *supra* note 35.

power the commissioner has to impose policy judgments involving the educational system, absent a showing of pure arbitrariness, even where the action of the local board was not arbitrary.[105]

In countering the arguments offered by the intervenors and the state, the board of education contended that Commissioner Allen here acted in a judicial capacity. According to the board, the purpose of Section 310 was to give a remedy to an individual aggrieved by a local board's action such as a teacher being discharged by a principal. Then and only then could the commissioner substitute personal judgment for that of the principal. On the other hand, the board argued, when the commissioner acts in an administrative capacity, that is reviewable *de novo* by a court to determine whether or not the commissioner's action was arbitrary.[106]

The board also contended that the intervenors' arguments about the financial capacity of Mount Vernon to institute the desegregation plan were irrelevant in a hearing on a motion to dismiss, for all allegations are deemed to be true in response to such a motion. But even if the arguments were not premature, the board argued, the intervenors were wrong in thinking that the school district had the means to implement the plan. The board felt that the cost of "responsibly implementing" the commissioner's June 13, 1968 order would exceed $3 million.[107]

On January 31, 1969, Judge Kane handed down his decision. The court considered the crucial issue to be "whether the efforts of the Commissioner to correct racial imbalance possess the required educational purpose that will vest him with the necessary jurisdiction to act in the manner indicated in the order of June 13, 1968."[108] Judge Kane answered the question emphatically in the affirmative: "The conclusion is inescapable that it does."[109] The court held that because the commissioner's plan has an educational purpose, the order was not arbitrary and hence the petition of the school board was dismissed.[110]

On November 1, 1968, Mary Ellen Cooper, the black school board member, talked of consulting with the Department of Justice about the possibility of a federal court order to get compliance with the Allen order.[111] By February of

---

105. *Id.* at 267.

106. Petitioner's Answering Memorandum to Respondent—Intervenors Brief, at 6, Board of Ed. of City Sch. Dist. of Mount Vernon v. Allen, 58 Misc.2d 762, 296 N.Y.S.2d 890, (Sup. Ct. 1969).

107. *Id.* at 9.

108. Board of Ed. of City Sch. Dist. of Mount Vernon v. Allen, 58 Misc.2d 762, 764, 296 N.Y.S.2d 890, 892 (Sup. Ct. 1969).

109. *Id.*

110. *Id.* at 765, where Judge Kane noted:

Reasonable men may have an honest difference of opinion as to the efficacy of the Commissioner's determination and the extent of the financial burden it will impose upon the district, but these conflicts as developed in this proceeding do not warrant judicial interference.

111. New York Times, November 2, 1969, at 37, col. 1.

1969 it seemed that the state court had vindicated the intervenors' position and all that was left was implementation of the integration order. To that end, Catherine Rhodes, a retired assistant superintendent of Mount Vernon public schools, formulated a plan in preparation of effecting the order. The plan included an examination of staff, curriculum, preschool training, books and equipment, school organizations, parental committees, and participation of lunchroom facilities necessary to execute the order. Included in the study was an analysis of busing needs and costs, estimated at $180,000 per year.[112]

However, the board would not order a northside child to go to a school south of the tracks. In response to a question about contingency plans in the event the

112. C. Rhodes, Mount Vernon School Busing Data, at 1 (February 1969):

Study of bus requirements for busing Mount Vernon elementary school children of grade 1-to-3 from the south side of the city to schools on the north side and vice-versa for grades 4-to-6. The assignment shown of children to schools does not, in most cases, necessarily represent other than arbitrary assumptions for the purpose of estimation only.

It was assumed, for this purpose, that, in the morning, buses would operate along various routes through the north side picking up children near their homes to take them to southside schools. There children from the south side would be assembled at the schools to be taken to northside schools. The need for southside children to be picked up at the schools rather than nearer to their homes is to minimize the difference in school starting times between bus arrivals at south and north schools. This imbalance is corrected, however, in the afternoon when the northside children, who started earlier, are taken home first; they must be delivered to northside schools where southside children are picked up who can then be delivered closer to their homes.

Assuming that each bus in the morning makes only this one trip to the south and north, the bus requirements, governed by the south-to-north traffic which is slightly larger, are (for 60-passenger school buses):

From	To	Children	Buses
Grimes	Columbus	76	1½
Hale	Traphagen	283	5
Fulton	Lincoln	195	3½
Fulton	Traphagen	71	1½
Fulton	Columbus	30	½
Fulton	Pennington	70	1½
Graham	Columbus	125	2
Graham	Holmes	172	3
Longfellow	Pennington	165	3
Total	1,187	1,187	22

At the prevailing cost for school bus operation of $8,000 per bus per year, the total cost would be about $180,000. This sum could be cut about in half if each bus were to make two such trips in the morning and afternoon. This would require a difference in starting times for various schools ranging from 30 to 45 minutes.

commissioner's directive was upheld, member-trustee Louis Lacerra answered, "The Board will not comply under any circumstances and the status quo will be maintained in the school system."[113] The board had only one option. On the evening of February 6, 1969, in a closed session after the public meeting was suspended due to "scuffling" between whites and blacks, by an 8-1 vote the board decided to appeal Judge Kane's decision.[114]

The board flexed its political muscle and sought help from the state legislature. Leading the fight was Mount Vernon State Assemblyman George Van Cott. Subsequently, on May 2, 1969, while the appeal was pending and prior to oral argument, the New York State Legislature passed a new amendment to the Education Law requiring school plans for integration to have the approval of the locally elected board of education.[115] The law was to go into effect September 1, 1969, and purported to divest the commissioner of any authority to require compliance by the Mount Vernon Board of Education with the outstanding order of June 13, 1968.[116] Despite this legislation favoring the board, the appeal was argued only on the facts of the Mount Vernon situation.[117]

The appellants argued that the plan of the commissioner lacked not only an educational purpose, but funding provisions as well. As a result, according to the board, the pairing of elementary schools would wreak havoc on the financial and social structure of the city. In responding to the board's contention that financial disaster was imminent in Mount Vernon if pairing were implemented, the NAACP intervenors argued that the board had inflated the cost of the commissioner's plan. Although both groups were citing accountants' reports, the NAACP argued that the $3 million figure was the estimate given to implement the entire BEST plan, not pairing alone; the board maintained that this figure reflected the cost of "responsibly implementing" the Allen plan.[118] And the commissioner of education argued that the financial issue was bogus because he had not ordered any busing, so there were no transportation costs whatsoever.[119]

113. Black and White, *supra* note 32, at 134.
114. Daily Argus, February 7, 1969. For a vivid account of the board's public meetings, *see* note 76 *supra*.
115. Ch. 341, §1 (1969) Laws of New York 504.
116. Indicating the still-present white support for integrated education, American Jewish Congress Executive Director Abraham Maslow sent a letter to the New York State Senate Majority Leader which opposed the proposed ban on busing. Maslow, whose group supported the Allen order, said that the basic educational policy rulings of the state commissioner are supreme. Letter from Abraham Maslow to Perry Duryea, February 18, 1969.
117. The law had no significant effect on Mount Vernon, since the appellate decision was handed down on July 1, 1969 before the law was in effect, and the amendment was declared unconstitutional on October 1, 1970. *See* Lee v. Nyquist, 318 F. Supp. 710 (W.D. N.Y. 1970). Even without legislation, the school board argued, the commissioner was not *required* to force their compliance with his order.
118. *See* note 90 *supra*.
119. It seems that if anyone was using a bogus issue it was the commissioner's own attorneys. They used the same argument before Judge Kane in the lower state court, and he strongly noted:

It appeared, however, that the commissioner's lawyers had made a critical legal error. Since the commissioner moved to dismiss on the grounds that there was no triable issue of fact, it was treated as a demurrer. As a result, the facts alleged in the board petition were taken in their most favorable light and were deemed true, as a matter of law. The board said it was financially impossible for the city of Mount Vernon to implement the commissioner's order. Therefore, since the figures alleged by the Mount Vernon board were considered incontrovertible, "to require implementation of a plan which is financially impossible to obey is clearly [an order of] 'pure arbitrariness.'"[120] The appellate division reversed the order to dismiss and remanded it to the lower state court since there was an issue to be resolved, the financial feasibility of the plan.

Following submission of answers by respondents to the petition, the matter was renoticed for a hearing on September 12, 1969, before Judge Harold Koreman in New York State Supreme Court in Albany. The positions of the three parties remained the same: the board thought the pairing of schools was too costly; the NAACP intervenors believed that busing would not unduly burden the financial resources of Mount Vernon; and the commissioner argued that he had mandated pairing, not busing. Fundamentally, the three parties were unable to agree on the scope of the commissioner's order. The intervenors suggested that the board's petition be dismissed since the board had not sought to determine the amount of financial resources available from the state prior to filing in court as the commissioner had suggested they do in his June 1968 order. The board, however, felt there should be a hearing so that they could show that the cost of the plan was economically prohibitive.

On September 30, 1969, Judge Koreman issued his opinion.[121] He agreed with the board that there should be a hearing on the question of the financial feasibility of the plan. However, since the board had not sought to determine what financial aid would be available from the state, a hearing would be premature, since without this information it would be impossible to determine the actual cost to the board. Judge Koreman therefore dismissed the petition, but held it could be renewed after the board determined the extent of financial assistance available to it.

The court is not persuaded otherwise, nor is it impressed with the argument by counsel for the Commissioner that the order of June 13, 1968 does not require cross-busing but leaves it at the discretion of the petitioner. Such a position is an unrealistic attempt to ignore the serious financial burden that is being imposed upon the taxpayers of the Mount Vernon School District by the Commissioner, one which he fully recognized and for which he offered several areas of solution which were contained within the very order now under attack.

Board of Ed. of City Sch. Dist. of Mt. Vernon v. Allen, supra note 108, at 766.

120. Board of Ed. of City Sch. Dist. of Mt. Vernon v. Allen, 32 A.D.2d 985, 301 N.Y.S. 2d 764 (1969).

121. Board of Ed. of City Sch. Dist of Mt. Vernon v. Allen, 60 Misc.2d 926, 304 N.Y.S. 2d 410 (Sup. Ct. 1969).

Subsequently, the lawyers for the three parties began to negotiate upon an order, but no agreement was reached. An in-chambers conference was held with Judge Koreman in February 1970, where he informed attorneys for the commissioner and the intervenors that a statute of limitations had been brought to his attention by the school board attorneys which would bar renewal of their petition after four months. In order to avert this, Judge Koreman withdrew his September 30 opinion, and substituted a further opinion.[122] Judge Koreman again held that a hearing was necessary to determine whether it was financially impossible for the board to carry out the plan of the commissioner. However, the judge felt that prior to a hearing it was essential that the board request from the commissioner the amount of funding available. Accordingly, the court ordered the board to submit a plan for implementing the commissioner's order to the commissioner within thirty days after service of a copy of the order upon the board. Thereafter, the court ruled, the commissioner must advise the board of the available funding within thirty days after the board submits its plan. Afterward, either party could then renotice the proceeding for a hearing on the petition.

On April 7, 1970, the board submitted to the commissioner a plan for the implementation of his 1968 order and a request for information about funding available. The board's plan was divided into three parts: Parts Two and Three dealt respectively with school transportation and a lunch program. Busing costs were estimated to be $345,000 annually; the lunch program $448,580 annually. Part One of the plan dealt with a series of "improvements and innovations" in the Mount Vernon educational program. Included in these improvements were reorganization of the homeroom and classroom structure for all elementary schools; employment of art, music, and physical education teachers; changing the library to a multimedia center with both additional equipment and personnel; hiring assistant principals, reading consultants, and nurses; and the construction of new facilities. The estimated cost of this part of the program was in excess of $3 million. The board was still strongly backed by the white community.[123]

On May 8, 1970, the commissioner of education responded to the application of the Mount Vernon board with a statement of aid available for the implementation of the plan. In that response, the commissioner stated that there would be funds available for transportation and the lunch programs to meet the needs of Mount Vernon. A more limited amount of the monies requested for construction and alteration of facilities would be allocated. The commissioner reiterated his position that none of the funds requested were required by his June 1968

122. Board of Ed. of City Sch. Dist. of Mt. Vernon v. Allen, 64 Misc.2d 200, 314 N.Y.S. 2d 550 (Sup. Ct. 1970).
123. John Debellis was reelected in May, running on the board's record: "The Board has helped stop white people from moving out of Mount Vernon." He pledged to appeal "all the way up to the United States Supreme Court," if the state court ordered Mount Vernon to bus school children. New York Times, May 3, 1970, at 62. col. 4.

order. Allen continued to insist on a position unaccepted by Judge Kane in the initial decision in state court.[124]

On July 7, 1970, following a request of the commissioner and the NAACP-intervenors for the setting of a trial date, Judge Koreman invited all parties to meet with him for a pretrial conference. The attorneys for the Mount Vernon School Board argued that although there was no longer any substantial controversy about the financial feasibility of the busing and school lunch plan, there did need to be a trial on the necessity of including Part One of their program. The program of construction and supplemental school personnel were essential, the board contended, to prevent the deterioration of the educational level as a result of integration. The board's lawyers wanted to present experts to testify that the present educational levels would not be maintained without new money and programs due to integration. The commissioner and the NAACP-intervenors contended that no trial was necessary because the additional programs were not mandated by the order. On July 10, 1970, Judge Koreman called the parties to notify them that the trial date on financing the plan had been set for September 1, 1970.[125]

On August 18, 1970, thirteen days prior to the opening of the trial term, the NAACP-intervenors, fearing further opportunities for delay by the board at a trial, brought a motion for summary judgment to dismiss the board's Article 78 petition. Although the commissioner's attorneys submitted papers in support of the motion, they were less than enthusiastic about such a motion. The intervenors contended that in view of the financial assistance available to the board, there could no longer be any question as to its financial ability to carry out the commissioner's order; therefore, no further triable issues of fact existed. After exchange of memoranda and oral argument, Judge Koreman, on October 17, 1970, issued his opinion.[126] He held that the order of the commissioner direct-

---

124. *See* note 119 *supra.*
125.

Following submission of a plan by a petitioner and the responses by the Commissioner as to the amount of financial aid available to the Board, the parties agreed that a trial was to be held on the issue of the Board's financial ability to comply with the Commissioner's order.

Board of Ed. of City Sch. Dist. of Mt. Vernon v. Allen, 64 Misc.2d 379, 314 N.Y.S.2d 773 (Sup. Ct. 1970).

126. *Id.*

The question to be determined here is whether evidence sought to be adduced by petitioner relating to the services it claims it would be required to furnish to achieve soundness of education in its school system in correcting racial imbalance would be relevant and material to the issue of petitioner's alleged financial inability to comply with the Commissioner's order. Correlatively, may petitioner make an independent determination of the considerations and assumptions necessary to correct racial imbalance and to achieve educational soundness? The answer must be in the negative. To hold otherwise would result in a delegation by the courts to every local school board the responsibility and authority vested by statute in the Board of Regents and the Commissioner of Education.

ing the local board of education to eliminate racial imbalance by the pairing of schools was not purely arbitrary and this was final and conclusive. The order granting the motion for summary judgment by NAACP-intervenors was entered November 9, 1970.

In short, it had been established by judicial decree that the commissioner—not the board—had the power to determine the scope of his order and that the commissioner had the money to finance implementation of the order. It seemed that the "integrationists" had finally triumphed and all that was left was the plan's actual enforcement.[127]

Legal Tactics and the Utilities Tax

The granting of summary judgment eliminated the two questions which even now still remain unanswered: (1) What must the board of education reasonably do to implement the commissioner's order? and (2) What will it cost? Instead of proceeding to trial, the lawyers for the intervenors asked for summary judgment in the hopes of speeding up compliance with the order, rather than engage in a long trial which would let the board present numerous experts and studies.[128] Though it could not be foreseen at the time, the decision to avoid further delay by a motion for summary judgment ironically allowed the board to cover up its potential for raising money to finance integration. The summary judgment avoided a trial at which the board's capacity for raising money would have been brought out. The contention that the board did not have the money to institute the Allen plan had always been at the core of their defense. It was not until December 1972, two and one-half years later, that the board's ability to finance the school system was revealed to the intervenors, not in any court trial, but on the next-to-last page of a consulting firm's master plan for Mount Vernon public schools, known as the "Engelhardt Report."[129]

---

127. Leonard Rosenfeld, Legal Redress Chairman of the Mount Vernon NAACP branch, an attorney involved in the case, wrote, "The judicial phase had concluded—successfully for us, we believed. . . ." Letter from Leonard Rosenfeld to Petitioners, April 17, 1974.

128. The attorneys for the intervenors discussed the option of moving under N.Y. CPLR 3036 (5) to clarify and define the issue of the board's capability to raise money:

At a pre-trial conference or at any time on motion of any party or on its own motion, or notice to the parties, and upon such terms and conditions as in its decision may seem proper, the court may:

. . . .

(b) Direct pre-trial disclosure of evidence and discovery and inspection of books, records, and documents.

. . . .

(d) limit or restrict the number of experts to be heard as witnesses.
(e) clarify and define the issues to be tried.

. . . .

(g) grant summary judgment.

N.Y. CPLR §3036 (5) (McKinney, 1974).

129. Engelhardt Report, *supra* note 3, at 237.

The board's claim of financial difficulties would seem to have had some validity, in that without significant state aid it appeared impossible for the city to raise sufficient funds to implement the Allen order. Mount Vernon had exhausted its ordinary school budget, the maximum it could have raised by taxing local residents given the New York State constitutional tax limitation of 2 percent assessed valuation. However, since 1965 the board had had the power to levy a 3 percent tax on utilities bills in Mount Vernon. This utilities tax, though regressive, since it would be most burdensome to the poor of the city, would have financed any of the plans promulgated since 1964 even in the absence of state aid for busing.

More importantly, though the attorneys for the intervenors did not know of the tax's existence, the commissioner and his attorneys and the board's attorneys were conscious of the tax, and the commissioner had the *statutory power to direct the Mount Vernon Board of Education to levy it.*[130] The commissioner never revealed the existence of the tax to his co-party intervenors during the years of litigation. Had the intervenors not moved for summary judgment, this ability to levy the tax would have been revealed in a trial to determine the financial capability of the board. This would have made the next two years of litigation (1970–1972) and two years of inactivity (1972–1974) on the part of the integrationists unnecessary. In a brief filed in March 1974 petitioning the commissioner for further action, Legal Defense Fund's Attorney Sylvia Drew noted:

130. New York Tax Law §1212 (McKinney, 1974) states:

(a) Any school district which is coterminous with, partly within or wholly within a city having a population of less than one hundred twenty-five thousand, is hereby authorized and empowered, by majority vote of the whole number of its school authorities, to impose for school district purposes, with the territorial limits of such school district and without discrimination between residents and nonresidents thereof, the tax described in subdivision (b) of section eleven hundred five, including the transitional provisions in subdivision (b) of section eleven hundred six, so far as such provisions can be made applicable to the tax imposed by such school district and with such limitations and special provisions as are set forth in this article, such tax to be imposed at the rate of one-half, one, one and one-half, two, two and one-half or three percent which rate shall be uniform for all portions and all types of receipts subject to such tax. In respect to such tax, all provisions of the resolution imposing it, except as to rate and except as otherwise provided herein, shall be identical with the corresponding provisions in such article twenty-eight, including the applicable definition and exemption provisions of such article, so far as the provisions of such article twenty-eight can be made applicable to the tax imposed by such school district and with such limitations and special provisions as are set forth in this article. The tax described in such subdivision (b), including the transitional provision in subdivision (b) of such section eleven hundred six, may not be imposed by such school district unless the resolution imposes the tax described in such subdivision so as to include all portions and all types of receipts subject to tax under such subdivision.

In addition, 21 Opinions of the State Comptroller 39 (1965), states: "A city school district may impose a full three percent tax on the consumption or use of utility services, notwithstanding the fact that the city also taxes utilities."

Mount Vernon has had the financial capacity to correct racial imbalance. . . . The Board has argued before the Commissioner, the courts, and the public that it could not in any way meet the operational expenses required by busing to eliminate racial imbalance. There has not been mere silence, there has been unconscionable misrepresentation. Nor did the Commissioner's staff which must be presumed to know of the existence of such a statutory power point it out. The Board hid the tax while unconscionably arguing at the same time its financial inability.[131]

However, since there was no trial in 1970 and the commissioner failed to reveal the tax, litigation and delaying tactics by the board continued unabated.

One can only speculate why Commissioner Allen did not disclose the tax or order its imposition. Integrationists felt that the commissioner applied a double standard, one for school districts run by white boards and another for boards controlled by blacks. These critics point out that Commissioner Allen was quick to take strong action against the predominantly black Ocean Hill-Brownsville board by superseding it in 1969. Yet both Commissioner Allen and his successor, Ewald Nyquist, have consistently refused to take such drastic action against the Mount Vernon board even though their removal was requested as far back as 1966.

Another view is that the New York State Board of Regents has always held to the notion that local control over education is paramount and state intervention should only be used as a remedy of last resort. Both commissioners of education have followed that policy since their vast potential powers over local boards have been utilized only gradually and cautiously. The policy letter in 1963 did not suggest specific action and left the formulation of a plan in local hands. Commis-

---

131. N.Y. Education Law §3114 (4) (McKinney, 1970) states:

The Commissioner in reference to such appeals, petitions or proceedings, shall have power:

. . . .

(4) To make all orders by directing the levying of taxes or otherwise which may, in his judgment, be proper or necessary to give effect to his decision.

The legal precedent for a Commissioner ordering the school board to institute a tax comes from People *ex rel.* Board of Education v. Graves, 243 N.Y. 204, 153 N.E. 49 (1926), in which the court said the commissioner of education has the power to direct a board of education of a union free school district to provide, by levy of a tax, funds for the transportation of children of school age living so remote from the school building in such district that they cannot otherwise attend school. "The power to regulate all appeals and to make all orders by directing the levying of taxes or otherwise which may be necessary to give effect to his decisions is expressly conferred upon the commissioner under subdivision 4 of this section and is essential for the proper administration of the school system." The Suffolk County school district involved in the *Graves* case refused to provide transportation to a village three miles from the school. The parents of the students petitioned to the commissioner on September 28, 1923. On March 21, 1924, he directed the board of education to provide transportation for the children and to pay for it; in the event no moneys were available, he directed the board to raise the money by a tax upon the taxable property of the district.

sioner Allen later assumed jurisdiction pursuant to the *King* suit,[132] but for three years he required only periodic reports, leaving the board with primary responsibility. Finally, five years after the initiation of the dispute, he imposed a plan similar to the one rejected by the board in 1964. It is clear that Commissioner Allen thought that a community solution was preferable to one imposed from Albany.[133] Commissioner Nyquist continued to follow Allen's philosophy even though both were confronted with an intransigent school board.

A third view is that the state board of education has been politically sensitive to the pressures brought upon it by the New York State Legislature and the governor's office. Mount Vernon's officials have been consistently able to go to the legislature for help.[134] It is clear that the statutory power given to the commissioner's office could be divested and was subject to increasing attacks by the legislature. For a commissioner, an unelected official, to have ordered imposition of an unpopular and costly tax against the wishes of the regents or the governor, would have been suicide. In addition, Mount Vernon's legislators were leaders in the right wing of the state Republican Party, and it was this faction which then Governor Rockefeller had to placate for a variety of political reasons.[135] In many instances the commissioner's hands were tied by the governor's office as he took only minimal actions in view of the gross violations and misrepresentations of the Mount Vernon board. Neither the commissioner nor his staff ever introduced the tax as refutation of the board's contention that it lacked the financial capability to impose a pairing plan.

The Litigation Continues

While the possibility of a utilities tax remained hidden for the next two years, the litigation continued as the board used the courts to delay integration and buy time in the legislature. On November 12, 1970, the board filed a notice of appeal from Judge Koreman's order. The NAACP filed a motion to dismiss the board's appeal for failure to timely prosecute. The board moved for an extension of time on the grounds that the United States Supreme Court was issuing an opinion in the *Charlotte-Mecklenburg School* cases,[136] which might have a direct

---

132. Brief of Petitioners in Support of Motion for Further Proceedings, at 36, Matter of King, 13 N.Y. Ed. Rep. 224, Decision No. 8801 (1964).

133. Black and White, *supra* note 32, at 135.

134. To a large extent the utility tax was invulnerable to being eliminated by the legislature since a number of cities in New York State were using the tax; therefore, the tax could not be repealed without providing for many millions of dollars in state education aid to those cities. If the tax's existence had been revealed at a trial in 1968, 1969, or 1970, the tax—though unpopular—might have been instituted. However, by the time the intervenors knew of the tax, utility rates had risen to such a level that even the Mount Vernon Teachers Union opposed implementing the tax to save the jobs of its members. So by delay and coverup, the board had been able to eliminate a potentially effective weapon.

135. One of the major political reasons was to build an image as a "mainstream Republican"; someone who the National Republican Party could support.

136. Swann v. Charlotte-Mecklenburg Board of Education, 402 U.S. 1 (1971).

bearing on the Mount Vernon case. The NAACP filed an affidavit in opposition to the board's motion for an extension of time saying, *inter alia*:

> If the pendency of the *Swann* decisions in federal cases is not permitted to delay implementation of desegregation orders in federal suits presenting identical questions, certainly, it cannot be used to postpone resolution of school suits which do *not* raise federal questions.
>
> . . . The decision in the *Swann* case in no way involves the permissible latitude of a state administrative officer to carry out the educational policy of the state.[137]

On April 12, 1971, the court denied the NAACP's motion to dismiss the board's appeal and, in addition, granted the board an extension of time. The state court refused to speed up the legal process even though the case had been in the courts since 1968.

The board took full advantage of the additional time by lobbying in Albany for the elimination of funds from the state budget that assisted in desegregation efforts. Their efforts were successful. The New York State Legislature deleted $3 million from the budget that had been previously allocated for aid in the elimination of racial imbalance from the Mount Vernon schools.

Instead of pressing their appeal, the board quickly moved for reargument to have the summary judgment order recalled and a hearing ordered as to whether it was financially impossible for the board to implement the order, since the funds that were to provide the assistance to the board were eliminated from state budget for the current year.

In an unreported opinion on June 23, 1971, Judge Koreman was receptive to this argument and granted summary judgment to the board, and vacated his order. He remanded the matter to the commissioner for further consideration in light of the changed circumstances and for his determination of the financial assistance available to implement the Allen order.[138] The order was dated July 8, 1971, and the board withdrew its appeal on that date.

---

137. Brief of Intervenors, at 3, Board of Ed. of City Sch. Dist. of Mt. Vernon v. Allen, Unreported Opinion (Sup. Ct. June 23, 1971).

138.

> Insofar as this court has determined that the maintenance of a proper level and standard of education is within the sole responsibility and authority of the Commissioner of Education and that petitioner [board] may not make an independent determination of the considerations and assumptions necessary to correct racial imbalance and to achieve educational soundness, that principle is reiterated and adhered to. Nor may the court substitute its judgment for that of the Commissioner in a matter of educational policy and soundness. As to the issue of whether it would be financially impossible for petitioner to implement the Commissioner's order so as to render his order purely *arbitrary*, the matter is remanded to respondent Commissioner's for his determination of the consideration required and the financial assistance available to implement his order of June 13, 1968.

Board of Ed. of City Sch. Dist. of Mt. Vernon v. Allen (Sup. Ct. June 23, 1971) (Unreported Opinion of Judge Koreman).

On October 6, 1971, Commissioner Nyquist (successor to Commissioner Allen) issued an interim order requesting the board to submit plans for implementing the 1968 Allen order, a statement of the additional services needed, and the funds the board had available for such purposes. On October 7, Mount Vernon testified against federal aid for busing at Senate committee hearings.[139]

On November 24, 1971, the board wrote the commissioner refusing to comply with his order. In its letter, the board argued that Judge Koreman's decision on June 23, 1971 made a final disposition of the Article 78 proceeding by remanding the matter to the commissioner. Therefore, the board said, there was no longer any need to comply with the June 13, 1968 order of Commissioner Allen. This argument was to be continually reiterated throughout the remaining efforts to force the board to comply with the Allen order.

Thereafter, Commissioner Nyquist moved by an order to show cause why the board should not comply with his order of October 6, 1971. The motion was returnable on January 14, 1972, and Judge Koreman scheduled a hearing on that date. In response to the commissioner's motion, the board filed a new Article 78 proceeding to annul and set aside the commissioner's order of October 6, 1971 as arbitrary and barred by *res judicata* and filed a cross-motion requiring the commissioner to show cause why the terms of his order should not be stayed pending the determination of the new Article 78 action.

In an unreported opinion on April 13, 1972, Judge Koreman denied the commissioner's motion since the proceeding on which it was based was terminated. He also dismissed the board's motion without prejudice, but the motion could be renewed by the board and a new proceeding scheduled following a reevaluation by the commissioner of the necessary funds available.[140]

---

139. New York Times, October 7, 1971, at 24, col. 1.
140.

The stated purpose of the [June 23, 1971] order was for his [Commissioner's] determination of the considerations required and the financial assistance available to implement the Commissioner's order of June 13, 1968: [Judge Koreman then reaffirms the independence of the Commissioner, repeating the language of his first unreported opinion, *supra* note 138.] Remanding this matter to the respondent Commissioner terminated the original Article 78 proceeding and requires a determination by the Commissioner *de novo* as to the considerations required and the financial assistance available to achieve educational soundness and to correct racial imbalance.

   The Commissioner's motion is denied and the petition seeking to review and annul the Commissioner's orders of October 6, 1971 is dismissed without prejudice to a renewal by petitioner if so advised of a new proceeding pursuant to Article 78 following a new and final determination by respondent Commissioner. (Matter of Bethlehem Auto Laundry v. Murphy, 55 Misc.2d 401, 285, N.Y.S.2d 218, (1967).)

Board of Ed. of City Sch. Dist. of Mt. Vernon v. Allen (Sup. Ct. April 13, 1972) (Unreported Opinion of Judge Koreman).

   There seems to be no question as to what Judge Koreman meant—even the board and the intervenors agreed that Commissioner Nyquist had to make a *de novo* consideration and the case was now out of the courts. This view is further borne out by Judge Koreman's citing of the *Bethlehem Laundry* case, where the court said:

THE ROLE OF HEW

While the New York State Education Department was prodding the Mount Vernon School Board into action, the board was also receiving inquiries from federal agencies. During the end of October and beginning of November 1970, the Civil Rights Office of the United States Department of Health, Education and Welfare visited the school district to determine their compliance with Title VI of the Civil Rights Act of 1964. Under that law, the federal government may terminate the granting of federal funds to the school districts if it finds that a school district is maintaining discriminatory practices.[141]

On March 24, 1971, the director of the Office of Civil Rights wrote Alfred Franko, superintendent of the Mount Vernon Public Schools, that Mount Vernon was in noncompliance wth legal requirements, most notably in the area of employment, assignment, and promotion of minority professional staff. The letter also noted that there was an undue concentration of black and Hispanic students in some of the schools and that these schools showed educationally inferior results as compared to the white schools.

But, because of the legal proceedings, HEW did not at that time request any action regarding this last observation. However, in a letter at the end of the following month, HEW officials stated that since the school board was able to obtain a continuance in their legal battle because of the United States Supreme Court decision in *Swann*,[142] HEW staff felt they would be derelict if they neglected to correct certain present disparities in the Mount Vernon schools. They therefore officially informed the superintendent of Mount Vernon schools that the school district was in noncompliance with Title VI, and sought voluntary compliance.

A little over a year later, on May 31, 1972, HEW threatened to initiate enforcement proceedings unless the school board responded in ten days with a proposal to remedy the situation.

Within the framework of statutory authority [CPLR §7806: . . . if the proceeding was brought to review a determination, the judgment may annul or confirm the determination in whole or in part, or modify it and may direct or prohibit specified action by the respondent], there is no question that this Court can remit the matter to the Commission to make a specific determination.

The instant determination is annulled and remitted to the Commissioner [of Taxation and Revenue] and is made without prejudice to a renewal by the petitioner if so advised of a new Article 78 proceeding within the required statutory period following a new determination.

Matter of Bethlehem Auto Laundry v. Murphy, *supra.*

Judge Koreman also precluded any question of administrative law by holding that the original Article 78 proceeding was terminated leaving the Allen order intact but requiring a new determination by the Commissioner.

141. Civil Rights Act of 1964, 42 U.S.C. §2000d *et seq.* (1964), and the regulations promulgated there-under; 45 C.F.R. §80 *et. seq.*

142. 402 U.S. 1 (1971).

Finally, in June 1973, HEW wrote to the new Mount Vernon superintendent of schools, William C. Prattella, and informed him that since efforts to secure compliance by voluntary means had failed, administrative enforcement proceedings would be initiated. The letter stated that there were two areas of noncompliance with Title VI: (1) in employment, assignment, and promotion of minority professional staff; and (2) in the poorer physical conditions and facilities in the predominantly minority schools. In addition, the May 1973 letter informed the superintendent that any request for federal funds for new programs and activities would henceforth be deferred until ninety days after an administrative hearing.[143]

One month later, the General Counsel's Office at HEW sent a notice of allegation to the Mount Vernon School Board and informed them that they had a right to request a hearing. Contained in the list of charges were the following:

> For many years, the respondent school district has applied a discriminatory pattern of assigning teachers to its various schools based on the race or ethnic origin of the teachers and of the pupils in particular schools. During 1971, the average percentage of black teachers assigned to northside, predominantly white, schools was approximately six percent. The percentage of black teachers assigned by the school district to the southside, predominantly black, schools during the same period was approximately 27 percent.
>
> During the 1972–1973 school year, 86.8 percent of the racial or ethnic minority teachers and principals employed in the elementary schools were assigned to the five southside elementary schools each of which has a minority pupil component exceeding 90 percent of total attendance.[144]

Though HEW charged the board with the failure to alter racial inequality in the schools, the enforcement proceedings did not confront this issue. Since the problem of integrating the schools was already before the courts and the commissioner, an administrative remedy would have been inappropriate. Additionally, by taking this stance HEW was not directly involving itself with desegregating the schools and a busing order.

A ruling against the board would have meant the suspension of nearly $2 million in federal funds. The president of the Mount Vernon board responded to the charge of discriminatory teacher assignments by saying, "We did assign most of the black teachers to black schools, but we felt we were doing the right thing. We thought they could relate to each other that way. In fact, most of the new black teachers we hired requested assignments in black schools."[145]

143. Matter of the City School District of City of Mount Vernon, New York and State Department of Education, New York, Docket No. CR-1002, Notice of Opportunity For Hearing, at 4-5 (1973).
144. *Id.*
145. New York Times, January 13, 1974, at 22, col. 1.

On December 21, 1973, the hearing before Administrative Law Judge Green-ridge resulted in a decision by the Office of Civil Rights for HEW that the Mount Vernon school system was operated in noncompliance with Title VI of the Civil Rights Act of 1964. This was the first suspension of funds involving faculty discrimination in a school district in the North. On February 11, 1974, the school board appealed the decision, thereby preserving federal funding.

THE ENGELHARDT REPORT

In response to the legal proceedings with the New York State Department of Education and to the administrative action with HEW, and prior to the April 13, 1972 decision of Justice Koreman, the board hired an education consulting firm, Engelhardt and Engelhardt, Inc., to prepare a master plan for the Mount Vernon schools. The state department of education accepted the board's actions.

While the report was being prepared, representatives of the state education department met with the board of education, school personnel, and the con-sultants "to render assistance and advice and to encourage improvement of the schools of the district and reduction of racial imbalance."[146] September 1, 1972 had been established as the target date for the Mount Vernon board to submit the plan to the commissioner. The educational consultants did not, however, file their plan with the board until January 1973. The state education department— at the board's request—reviewed these proposals and made further comments and suggestions.

One wonders why the commissioner did not send one of his monitors to Mount Vernon immediately after the Koreman decision of April 13, 1972 to work directly with the staff there in developing a program and to determine what financial resources were available. After this informal investigation, the commissioner could then have issued a formal order satisfying the court's order of a *de novo* consideration. But Nyquist preferred to work as informally as he could with the board on the Engelhardt Report rather than issue another formal order. Nyquist explained the reason why he decided to collaborate with the board in this fashion:

> An important corollary to the principle of equal educational opportunity—and responsibility to achieve it—rests with the respective school districts of the State. My commitment to that belief has led me to explore every avenue which might lead to voluntary action on the part of school districts. . . .[147]

146. Matter of King, 13 N.Y. Ed. Dept. Rep. 224, Decision No. 8801 (1974).
147. *Integration: Is the Bus Out of Gas?* Empire State Report 36, 39 (December 1974) [hereinafter cited as *Integration*] explained Commissioner Nyquist's approach:

> While Nyquist has not mounted an all-out attack on racial imbalance in the state, he has followed a deliberate approach to the problem. Appointed Commissioner in 1969, shortly after the passage of the state law prohibiting busing, Nyquist has

The Engelhardt Report contained eleven alternatives, and even though three public meetings had been held on the options, the board was still not ready at the end of August 1973 to adopt any of the suggested alternatives. In a statement to the state board of regents about desegregation-integration activities in New York state, Commissioner Nyquist said that the Mount Vernon board would hold final discussions on their plan on October 9, 1973 and present their plan to him on the following day.

On November 15, 1973, the board adopted Alternative II of the master plan, the plan recommended by the consultants.[148]

At a cost of $20 million, Alternative II proposed to change the current grade structure from K–6, 7–8, 9–12 to pre-K–5, 6–8, 9–12, by adding the sixth grades to the middle school. In addition, the school district would be divided administratively east-west, so that both middle schools (but not the elementary schools), would have almost equal porportions of black pupils. Attendance zones would be altered and northside school capacities expanded, so more black children from the south side could go to elementary schools north of the tracks, but there would be no zoning of northside students to southside schools.[149]

The Mount Vernon branch of the NAACP immediately opposed the plan because it did not aid in integrating the elementary schools. The NAACP objected to the plan because it was totally inconsistent with the 1968 order of Commissioner Allen—the schools on one side of the district to be devoted to grades 1–3 and on the other side, 4–6, creating a north-side administrative division.[150]

---

operated in a milieu of explicit and explosive hostility. He frequently explains that he chose a strategy of persuasion, emphasizing voluntary local participation and action. "I was right," he said recently of his coax-and-cajole method, "but it didn't get the job done."

148. The board spelled out the criteria upon which the alternatives were considered:

1. The plan should promise hope for Mount Vernon's being a biracial community and school system.
2. The plan should provide opportunities for biracial experiences and opportunities for all children to be educated with and to associate with one another.
3. The plan should include improved educational opportunities for all youngsters.
4. The plan should be acceptable to a majority of the Mount Vernon citizens.
5. The plan should be such that the school situation will remain operational after its implementation; that is, sufficiently free from conflict so that the educational program operates normally.
6. The plan should promise the support of the courts and by the State Education Department authorities.
7. The plan should promise a long-term solution.
8. The plan should be financially feasible for Mount Vernon.

City School District, Mount Vernon, New York, Summary of Master Plan, at 2 (1973).

149. Engelhardt Report, *supra* note 3, at 183–87.

150. *Id.* at 176, estimated that a busing program from north to south would "hasten the exodus of white families from Mount Vernon." This increase could be slowed down, on the other hand, the consultants said, through "educational leadership, confidence in the educational program and resolution of uncertainties in the school system."

THE CHANGING ATMOSPHERE FOR
SCHOOL DESEGREGATION

New Petition to the Commissioner

The NAACP petitioners, tired with the commissioner's refusal to make the *de novo* determinations of financial assistance available called for by Judge Koreman, and now armed with the knowledge of the utilities tax, which had been cited in the Engelhardt Report,[151] resorted to a renewal petition in the *King*[152] action under Section 310 of the New York Education Law[153] on February 22, 1974, two months shy of the tenth anniversary of the original petition. The petitioners sought: (1) to enjoin the board from implementing any master plan other than one encompassing Commissioner Allen's 1968 order; (2) to determine that implementation of the Allen order was financially within the board's capabilities; and (3) to order implementation of the Allen directive within a time certain.[154]

Commissioner Nyquist responded to the renewal petition on March 29, 1974. He agreed with the contention that Commissioner Allen's order had been sustained by the courts and that the only issue remaining was the cost of implementing the order. To that end, the commissioner directed the school board to show what, if any, additional personnel, facilities, or services would be needed to implement the 1968 Allen order.[155] This hearing was scheduled for April, 23, 1974.

---

151. *Id.*

152. Matter of King, *supra* note 146.

153. *See* note 34 *supra.*

154. Brief of Petitioners in Support of Motion for Further Proceedings, at 34, Matter of King, *supra* note 146, bluntly pointed out to the Commissioner:

> Judge Koreman's order imposed a legal duty upon the Commissioner to make a *de novo* determination of considerations required and financial assistance available to correct racial imbalance and achieve educational soundness. The Commissioner's interim order of October 6, 1971 failed to comply with the express directive and the Commissioner's petition to the Board was denied. In short, the Commissioner indicated his intent to implement the order without taking account of the financial burden of busing and lunch program costs so imposed. This was not in the spirit of the 1968 order—and the point cannot be too often stressed, was not along the lines spelled out by Judge Koreman!

The petitioners continued, *id.* at 35:

> Should the Commissioner find that funds are necessary which are not now available to implement the Allen order, he should direct the Board to levy the maximum tax on utilities receipts to raise such funds permitted by Section 1105(b) of the Tax Law under authority conferred by Section 1211(a) and 1211(b) of the Tax Law.

155. Matter of King, *supra* note 146. Nyquist took the view that:

> The 1968 order has been sustained by the courts in all respects, except the matter of possible additional cost to the district. That is the only issue remaining.

The Board of Regents Steps Back

One response to Commissioner Nyquist's order came from two Republican state legislators, Senator Joseph Pisani (R-New Rochelle and Mount Vernon), and Assemblyman Richard Ross (R-Mount Vernon), who wired the state board of regents urging it to overturn or modify Nyquist's order.[156]

The board of regents controls the state education department. The commissioner of education is appointed by the regents, serves at their pleasure, and is answerable only to them. As chief executive officer of the education department, he implements their policies. The regents issue regulations which carry the force of law.

The legislators felt that the city would become all black if the Allen order were implemented and argued that the ethnic composition of the area and elementary school student body had changed since the 1968 order. They were asking the regents to modify their policy of eliminating racial imbalance in the schools, at least in districts where black children form a high proportion of the student body and where implementation of the policy promises to drive white children out of the system, if not out of the community. Nyquist in his March 29 order stated that the long-standing state policy on integration was the "establishment of school-attendance areas that make possible wherever feasible a student body that represents a cross-section of the population of the entire school district."[157]

In response to this, the president of the Mount Vernon chapter of the NAACP wrote to Roy Wilkins, executive director of the NAACP, urging the national office to meet with them for fear the board of regents would weaken their prior pro-integration policy unless there was a strong response. In the past year, the members of the board of regents had changed, and there were rumors that the new majority might modify its previous policy.[158]

156.

The legislature moved in another area to curtail busing by taking action on a bill to repeal Section 310 of the State Education Law, which provides that the Commissioner's decisions in educational disputes are not subject to review in the courts. It is under the authority of this section that Nyquist and his predecessor, James E. Allen, Jr., have issued integration orders to thirteen school districts since 1963, including Mount Vernon.

The bill, sponsored by Assemblyman George J. Farrell of Floral Park (R-N.Y.), would have made court challenges possible. It passed both houses handily, but was recalled to the Assembly for amendments, a procedure that killed it. According to education officials, this was done at the request of Governor Wilson, who had been convinced by Chancellor McGovern, an old friend, that the bill should not become law.

The Governor used the recall method to bury the bill, these officials said, to lessen the ire of Conservative Party politicians who had made it an item of top priority and who would have been highly offended by an outright veto.

Integration, supra note 147.

157. Matter of King, *supra* note 146.

158. Letter from Percy Somerville to Roy Wilkins, April 5, 1974.

Not content with lobbying efforts, the school board directed its attorneys on April 16, 1974, to initiate a new Article 78 proceeding to annul and set aside Commissioner Nyquist's order of March 29, 1974 on the grounds that it was arbitrary; that the 1968 order had been supplanted by Justice Koreman's remand in 1971 to the commissioner; and that the commissioner still had not made a *de novo* determination as required by the remand. A month later, the NAACP Legal Defense Fund intervened in the action and then moved to dismiss the proceeding for failure to state a claim.

On August 2, 1974, the matter was resolved. Commissioner Nyquist suspended implementation of the integration order for Mount Vernon. There was speculation that the decision may have been in response to pressure by some members of the board of regents.[159]

On June 27, 1974, the board of regents had made the decision to reevaluate the fourteen-year-old policy favoring busing as a tool for integration. Six of the fifteen regents were publicly opposed to busing. Because the Mount Vernon desegregation orders were initiated by the state education commissioner, implementing regents' policy, another opportunity for delay and resistance was found. Since the Allen order was not a court order, it would be completely within the commissioner's power to withdraw it. Three regents pressured the commissioner to suspend all current busing orders in New York State. One of the regents who approached the commissioner said, "If these orders had come from the courts, we would not attempt to interfere in any way."[160]

The failure to obtain a federal court order to desegregate impaired the implementation of any integration plan by placing the issue into state court and administrative forums. This lesson was realized ten years too late, as the chairman of the local NAACP chapter of Mount Vernon, Percy Somerville, issued a frustrated warning that no matter what the regents did, the chapter would ultimately take the issue to federal court.[161]

With the suspension of the order and review being conducted by the board of regents, the school board decided to withdraw its Article 78 proceeding. On October 25, the regents issued a statement on school integration policy that busing was still an appropriate measure for education officials to employ provided that there be established a procedure for parents of students challenging integration orders if they believed the bus ride (necessary to implement the order) would endanger their children's health and safety or lower the quality of their education.[162] These are the same grievances that the Mount Vernon board has made since 1964 in their rejection of any plan which contained busing in it. The provision opens the possibility for additional delays before any final assignment changes can take place. Commissioner Nyquist considered the regents' statement

159. Daily Argus, August 3, 1974.
160. New York Times, June 30, 1974, at 14, col. 3.
161. *Id.* As of this writing, the ultimate has not occurred.
162. *Id.,* October 26, 1974, at 1, col. 4.

a sufficient affirmation of busing to permit him to issue another integration order for Mount Vernon.[163]

On January 16, 1975, the commissioner issued a new order to the board of education to show cause why the Allen desegregation order should not be implemented by September 1975. It also directed the board to show·what additional personnel, facilities, or services were needed to implement the plan. A hearing was scheduled for February 7. This new order was issued on the strength of the October 25 regents policy statement. To this end, commissioner Nyquist in his January statement ordered the board to advise parents of students to be reassigned that if they felt opposed to the change for the designated reasons that they should write the school authorities and the board would issue an opinion, meet with the parents if requested, and submit the decision to the commissioner for final approval. Once again, Commissioner Nyquist did not directly order the use of busing of any student to the school to which he or she would be assigned. But a uniform declaration in the plan added: "However, the transportation of some students not presently transported may well be desirable."[164]

Suddenly,[165] on January 22, 1975, the board of regents, by a vote of 9–4, adopted a new policy rejecting the use of racial enrollment quotas or ratios in judging a school district's degree of compliance with integration orders. The "clarification" of earlier integration policies said: "In short, racial integration does not imply quantitative racial balance in the schools within a district."[166] The January 22 board of regents' statement created confusion[167] with Com-

163. *Id.*

164. *Id.*, January 17, 1975, at 31, col. 6.

165. Apparently, Commissioner Nyquist had angered some of the regents because of the abruptness of his January 16 integration orders and his failing to give them more notice that the orders were coming. *Id.*, January 23, 1975, at 6, col. 1.

166. *Id.* The statement read:

Integration does not, by definition, require that racial quotas be used in determing the proper or desirable composition of population within a school.

If a school district is making, and has made, a serious effort to bring about equal opportunity for children of various ethnic groups to intermingle and to share a common learning environment, then the Regents maintain that the population of a school within a school district need not be required to be comprised by, or be measured by ratios of quotas of white to black (or Hispanic) students.

In short, racial integration does not, in the Regents' statement of policy, imply quantitative racial balance in all schools within a district.

167. The board battled with the state department of education on still another front. In July, the board sought approval for construction of a new elementary school to replace the Lincoln School. On August 30, 1974, the department refused to approve the construction because it was not consistent with the Allen order. Moreover, approval would not be forthcoming, the department said, unless the board complied with the Allen order and the subsequent Nyquist orders. In December, therefore, the board commenced a new Article 78 proceeding to direct the state education department to approve construction of the school. The commissioner answered on January 9, 1975, stating that the proposed reconstruction of the Lincoln School, a racially identifiable facility, would foster existing segregation.

After the January 22 board of regents statement rejecting the use of racial quotas, the board of education wrote to Justice A Franklin Machoney, before whom their Article 78

missioner Nyquist's previous order of January 16, 1975 to the Mount Vernon Board of Education, since most of the evidence of segregation in the schools was based upon the numerical imbalance of blacks and whites in their schools on the opposite sides of the tracks. On January 30, 1975, Commissioner Nyquist postponed the hearing date in the Mount Vernon proceeding pending clarification of the regents' statement.

Since the January 22 declaration had been presented only as a "statement" by the regents, its force in guiding the commissioner in following the regents' policy was not clear. Nyquist pointed out to the regents the inconsistencies of the statement and its questionable legality since it came close to embracing the "separate-but-equal" concept.

> How, he asked in effect, can anyone discover whether a school is segregated without comparing the ratio of blacks to whites with the racial compositon of the district as a whole? And how can goals for imbalances be set without establishing a new ratio?[168]

The board of regents was forced to back down on February 21, 1975, and returned to the concept of requiring schools to reflect approximately the racial composition of the district as a whole. The new policy statement dropped the January language about quotas and ratios and instead defined an "integrated school" as "one in which the racial composition of the student body reflects the pupil population of the school district without necessarily attempting to be proportionate to it."[169] What constitutes that "reflection" appeared to be left to the commissioner to decide. The statement also included the "judicious use of" busing for small children and changing attendance zones in the list of measures that may be taken to effect integration. The new policy permits the schools of a given district to vary in racial or ethnic composition from that of the district as a whole, within a range to be decided by the commissioner on a case-by-case basis. Nevertheless, the reverse-and-back policy shifts indicate a changing attitude toward affirmative state education department action against school districts.

MORE PROBLEMS WITH HEW

During the time the commissioner postponed his integration order of January, the Board had not been totally relieved of pressure to desegregate the schools.

---

petition was pending, that in view of the regents' new policy, the reason for the department's refusal to approve of the construction of the Lincoln School was no longer applicable. The board argued that compliance with the Allen order, which was solely concerned with racial quotas, was not followed by the regents any longer. As part of the plan ordered December 4, 1975, the Lincoln School is to be replaced with a new building with capacity for 50 more students, intended as space for open-enrollment pupils.

168. New York Times, February 22, 1975, at 52, col. 4.
169. *Id.,* February 21, 1975, at 1, col. 8.

On January 27, 1975, the final decision of the reviewing authority by the Office of Civil Rights for HEW was handed down. The authority found that the disparities in the facilities of the southside and northside schools did not constitute a *prima facie* case of race discrimination. This reversed the finding of the lower administrative judge's ruling. Other findings as to the practice of assigning black faculty to predominantly black schools were affirmed.[170] The board complied with HEW's regulations on teacher assignments, and federal funding continued.

In February HEW threatened to suspend approximately $100,000 in federal aid because of the failure of the board to integrate the Grimes School when it was reopened. In the past the Grimes School had been closed, since the parents of pupils in Grimes wanted their children to go to the Washington School. The school board agreed, but then to alleviate the overcrowding of the Washington School, which had occurred over a period of years, the board reopened Grimes.

HEW complained that the reopening of Grimes, a racially identifiable black school, was an act of de jure segregation in that it reestablished an old attendence zone which had 90 percent minority-group children. The board filed a complaint in federal court in response to HEW's action to contest the threatened suspension of funds. The board urged the court to declare that the reopening of Grimes was not an act of de jure segregation. The action in federal court was prompted by HEW's failure to bring proceedings while still threatening the deferral of funds.

On November 13, 1975 the Office for Civil Rights notified Pratella that the board's plan to comply with Title VI was unacceptable and that HEW was instituting enforcement proceedings. On that same day, HEW issued a Notice of Opportunity for Hearing which was duly answered by the board, who requested a hearing. The board's action in federal court was discontinued by consent as moot.

HEW attorneys have admitted that their department has gone slower and wanted much less in terms of re-zoning and integrating the schools than the state education department. The administrative hearing, extended by stipulation, took place in July 1976.

THE COMMISSIONER GIVES IN

In February Commissioner Nyquist reopened the January 16 integration order and sent representatives to Mount Vernon to assess the racial balance in the city's schools. The commissioner felt he could order integration under the regents' guidelines. However, in formulating these new plans, Nyquist and his representatives "took care" not to go further than what the regents would consider appropriate. Nyquist commented that he was nearly alone among top education officials still calling for integration:

170. Matter of the City School District of City of Mount Vernon, H.E.W. Civil Rights Docket No. CR-1002 (January 27, 1975).

It's a lonely position to have these days. Hell, you don't even get any open advocacy on the part of the country's other chief school officers.[171]

During the spring of 1975, Nyquist was subject to increasing pressure from the board of regents. On February 28, 1975, a regent announced he would introduce a resolution at the next meeting to require the commissioner of education to consider the possible harmful effects of busing in any future integration orders he may issue.[172]

Individual regents continued to speak out against busing as misguided and ineffectual as an integration tool. The regents were also somewhat upset with the attitude taken by the commissioner that the regents "clarification" of February 21 would let him proceed relatively unfettered in the enforcement of his integration orders. They felt Nyquist was ignoring the prefatory warnings in the February 21 statement, which expressed skepticism about the educational benefits of busing and frowned on the use of "quantitiative measures" to assess segregation in a school district.

In April 1975 the commissioner's representatives were in the final stages of implementing the integration plan during which "cooperative reviews" of the plans were conducted in light of recent changes softening the pro-busing policies of the board of regents.[173] "In place of the generally supportive atmosphere for integration a decade ago, the State Education Department"[174] found itself trying to enforce another integration plan faced with a hostile local school board, "an unsympathetic legislature, an aloof national Administration, local opposition that has been strengthened by economic recession," fear of further white flight, "cries of community control by blacks and a lack of fresh thinking about strategies for racial integration."[175]

In addition, the feeling was that the board of regents would toughen their views on school busing and probably try to block enforcement of the school busing orders pending in Mount Vernon, as well as other cities in New York state. On June 7, James S. Coleman's remarks about busing[176] buttressed the arguments of those who claimed implementation of the 1968 Allen order could not work without driving the remaining whites out of Mount Vernon. The black community was resigned to the impossibility of "meaningful integration" of the city's public schools, for almost 70 percent of the school district was populated by minority students. Willing to settle for something rather than no order, the president of the local NAACP chapter, Percy Somerville, said: "We know we can't get a 50–50 ratio or even a 60–40, but if we get going on this thing at least we will end up with a better cross-section for our kids to grow up

171. New York Times, January 22, 1975, at 35, col. 1.
172. *Id.,* February 28, 1975, at 37, col. 4.
173. *Id.,* April 3, 1975, at 39, col. 7.
174. *Id., supra* note 171.
175. *Id.*
176. *Id.,* June 7, 1975, at 1, col. 4.

with.''[177] The twelve-year delay had caused the system to run out of "white chips."

Faced with changing demographics and a new political and social atmosphere, Commissioner Nyquist issued a modified integration plan on July 29, 1975 which would go into effect in September 1976. Essentially the commissioner accepted Alternative II of the master plan (plus a "dash" of the academy plan), the plan the board reluctantly had adopted in 1973. This plan provides that: (1) The district would be divided on a north-south axis into two separate attendance zones, one east and one west, for the city's elementary schools. The two areas would include roughly the same number of students and in the same racial proportions as for the city as a whole. (2) Open enrollment would be utilized by giving students of each area the option to attend any school in their area that has room for them. (3) Each of the Mount Vernon attendance areas would also seek to combine nonclassroom functions—such as dramatic productions, sports, clubs, and outings—"to foster greater mingling of students of different races." (4) A new school building would be constructed and a special "magnet school" offering enriched programs would be established.[178]

After hearings were held in August, on December 4, 1975 the board was ordered to implement the modified plan over the vehement objections of the NAACP.[179] The finalized plans include the above provisions. Additionally, the reopened Grimes School on the south side[180] will be developed into a magnet elementary school planned for four hundred students, 50 percent white and 50 percent minority. Although, as of this writing, there has been no administrative decision in the HEW proceedings, this plan will apparently satisfy the HEW complaint about Grimes and federal funding will be maintained.[181] The Lincoln

---

177. *Id., supra* note 173.

178. *Id.,* July 29, 1975, at 33, col. 7.

179. *Id.,* December 4, 1975, at 1, col. 1:

The NAACP argued that the plan would promote further deterioration of predominantly black schools by siphoning off the best black students to the magnet and open-enrollment schools and would do little more than create two new segregated districts in place of one.

180. Grimes is located on the horizontal border between census tracts 29 and 30, just a few blocks south of the railroad tracks.

181. At the July 1976 hearing, HEW's position was that the reopening of the Grimes Elementary School, using the old elementary school attendance zones as boundary lines, created a racially identifiable facility and thus was an act of de jure segregation that violated Title VI of the Civil Rights Act of 1964.

The board responded that it neither engaged in any discriminatory practice prohibited by Title VI nor had the intent thereto, and that all activities were administered without regard to race, color, or national origin. The board further contended that it was under order of the commissioner of education to implement a plan to promote a greater interrelation among the students of all segments of the school district (see discussion *infra*) and that the federal government should not contravene the authority of the commissioner. Finally the board raised the point that since the school district will have a district-wide attendance zone for Grimes as a "magnet" school HEW's position has been rendered moot.

School will be replaced with a new facility that has an increased capacity for fifty more students, intended as space for open-enrollment pupils.[182]

WHAT WENT WRONG

Why did the twelve-year effort to integrate fail? One must conclude that the NAACP petitioners made a critical mistake on April 10, 1964 by bringing the Article 310 proceeding before the state commissioner. Once he took it under his continuing jurisdiction, the NAACP lawyers were trapped into choosing the state courts as its forum. Once the suit moved into the state administrative process, a myriad of political pressures could be exerted upon the commissioner, upon the state courts, and upon any remedial actions.

The Mount Vernon School Board was able to get help from the legislative and executive branches in Albany. They were able to get support from the New York State Board of Regents. Their attorneys were superior in their use of legal tactics to delay through the fullest use of the legal process. Due to local and state pressures, state court judges do not appear to be as "forceful" in their order as federal court judges, who are potentially more independent. But, with jurisdiction still being retained by state court judges, it does not seem that a federal judge would be too amenable to interfere today. With the commissioner's ruling, it appears the administrative route is also blocked. If there is still any impetus to achieve integration (and there is little reason to believe there will be), a new legal strategy could be initiated involving a multidistrict, Westchester County-wide approach. But that is not contemplated at present, and it is doubtful that such an approach could succeed in light of expected opposition.

The future for Mount Vernon's public schools is bleak. So is the future for the city, which is irrevocably scarred by twelve years of racial tension.

182. New York Times, *supra* note 179.

Multitudes in the Valley of Indecision: The Desegregation of San Francisco's Schools

David L. Kirp

San Francisco is often regarded as one of the success stories of school desegregation. This thoughtful and thorough essay presents an analysis not only of the litigation itself but of the social and political structure of San Francisco. It provides an opportunity to consider both the apparent and real roles of the participants in school desegregation litigation. It also provides an opportunity for the author and reader to consider the possibilities and limitations of such litigation.

David L. Kirp is an Associate Professor at the Graduate School of Public Policy at the University of California at Berkeley and a Lecturer at its School of Law. He was formerly the director of the Law and Education Center at Harvard University.—Eds.

The Dynamics of Desegregation

Any litigation requires that complicated histories be rendered into a form which makes them judicially comprehensible. The process is necessarily one of simplification; behind such conclusory legal terms as "reasonable" and "intentional" lurks the resolution of a welter of incidents, or conflicting accounts of

The title is loosely borrowed from Joel 3:14: "Multitudes, multitudes in the valley of decision."

Doris Cohen, Ph.D. candidate in sociology and education, functioned as substantially more than an ordinary research assistant. She drew on her knowledge of the San Francisco public school system to ferret out unpublished material and conduct unusually candid interviews with school personnel. Her draft of a portion of this piece was itself of publishable quality.

The Teachers Professional Library in San Francisco made available much of the primary source material. Quentin Kopp, lawyer for the Chinese intervenors, allowed the author to use his copy of the record in the *Johnson* case, and Assistant City Attorney George Krueger shared his copy of the transcripts. Without that help the research task would have been substantially harder.

411

incidents. In desegregation cases, as in all other cases, the chief task for a court is to simplify without undue distortion, to describe a sequence of events, identify a legal framework within which those events can properly be fit, and—if appropriate—devise a remedy. At each stage the court must remain faithful both to the legal mandate that makes its judgment authoritative and to the realities of the situation the court has been called upon to address. Success at this enormously difficult task affords legitimacy to what the court is doing; it makes resolution of the dispute, and implementation of the remedial order, more likely to succeed.

During the year that the San Francisco school desegregation case[1] was before it awaiting judgment, the district court sought to fulfill the demands of this role. The court gathered in the strands of community conflict, identifying and making constitutional sense of diverse and competing perspectives; it tried through its order to reflect both the constitutional command for equal treatment and the idiosyncracies of the school district. It avowedly attempted to co-opt the larger community in its venture, recognizing that without such support its decree might prove a futile gesture.

If, in the end, the court's success was only mixed, this result may be partially attributable to a stress on the political—at the expense of the traditionally judicial—dimensions of the task. But the inherent limitations of *any* court's authority afford a more significant guide to the outcome. No court can be simply a political entity, endorsing the expedient; but expediency has a way of shaping whatever a court says. No court can substitute itself for those who manage complex governmental system such as schools; but the responses of those who do bear management obligations often prove of critical importance. No constitutional decree can merely reflect ideological vagaries; but, particularly with respect to desegregation, diminished enthusiasm both on the part of minority groups and activist white liberals for the kind of order issued in San Francisco has to influence the way in which a court order is followed.

THE SAN FRANCISCO DESEGREGATION CASE

The July 1971 federal district court order in *Johnson v. San Francisco Unified School District*,[2] which desegregated San Francisco's elementary schools, marked the culmination of one decade-long political struggle and the beginning of another which has yet to be concluded. The first, pre-decision phase of the struggle centered on the meaning of racial equality in the school context; the

---

More than 50 people willingly submitted to interviews, some of which lasted several hours; several provided valuable unpublished material from their libraries. Although some will not like—and others will not recognize—their portraits, their help was invaluable.

The author as founding Director of the Law and Education Center between 1969 and 1971, had considerable involvement in desegregation litigation, including the Detroit suit. If parts of this piece read as a *mea culpa,* that is not unintentional.

1. Johnson v. San Francisco Unified School District, 339 F. Supp. 1315 (N.D. Calif. 1971), *vacated and remanded,* 500 F.2d. 349 (9th Cir. 1974).

2. *Id.*

court decision imposed a legally authoritative definition upon a community unable, in the end, to resolve the question itself. Although San Francisco appealed that decree, it came to accept the court's formal view of equality as its own. While the specifics of the remedy adopted in *Johnson* have evoked continuing unhappiness, there is no real possibility that San Francisco will in the foreseeable future restructure its schools along wholly neighborhood lines. In that sense the court's role was decisive, and decisively successful.[3] Yet the second phase, the attempt to give content and meaning to the order, lay ahead. That task has been undertaken largely outside the control or even the purview of the court, and it has been decidedly less successful. San Francisco's schools are numerically more desegregated than prior to the decision, but little attempt has been made to move beyond numerology in order to create a genuinely integrated school system.[4] If the public schools are the "sick man" of San Francisco municipal government, as is often asserted, problems traceable to the implementation of desegregation constitute a major cause of that sickness.

The focus of this article is judicial management of San Francisco's desegregation dispute: how desegregation came to be perceived as a legal rather than a wholly political, matter; how the court went about the task of resolving the legal issues and framing a decree. This inquiry is intelligible only if placed in the context of both the earlier aspects of the controversy and what has taken place in the years since the *Johnson* decision. The critical question can be simply put: why did a city whose political elite had, prior to the court decree, accepted the rightness of desegregation fail to fulfill the aspirations of *Johnson?* This simplicity is, however, deceptive. A thorough response requires at least some understanding of the dynamics of "official" politics (as embodied both in the school board and the mayor's office), minority community politics, and bureaucratic politics. The account which follows attempts that task.

The Idiosyncracies of San Francisco

San Francisco prides itself, and not without some justification, as different from—better than—most other American cities.[5] It is not just the elegance of the place—that rare coupling of physical and man-made beauty, the machine *and* the garden—which distinguishes San Francisco, although the city trades shamelessly on its mystique. San Francisco thinks of itself as that *rara avis,* a politically progressive and tolerant community. State Democratic politicians count on its votes to offset those of the more conservative South; gay men and women have long regarded it as a haven and a refuge; a host of ethnic groups, the arrived and politically dominant Western Europeans and the rapidly expanding, arriving groups of Asians and Latinos,[6] decidedly unassimilated, enjoy both a community and

3. See text at notes 373–80, *infra.*
4. See text at notes 394–96 and 425–35, *infra.*
5. *See generally* Culture and civility in San Francisco (H. Becker ed. 1971), especially Davis, *The San Francisco Mystique* at 151.
6. "Arrived" and "arriving" are the terms used in F. Wirt, Power in the City: Decision-Making in San Francisco (1974) [hereinafter cited as Wirt].

political life of their own. If all of these communities are ghettos, it is only an outsider's perspective that makes them so.

This image conceals important demographic and political realities. Although the effects have not been so serious or so visible, San Francisco has not been immune to the dilemmas—notably those of racial and ethnic conflict—which have beset other urban communities. San Francisco's population has declined in recent years—from 740,316 in 1960 to 679,200 in 1974—as former residents have moved to the surrounding suburbs, continuing to use the city as a work-place. The racial and ethnic composition of the city has changed notably: there are almost a quarter of a million fewer whites and about 125,000 more non-whites in San Francisco today than in 1950; the city, 90 percent white in 1950, was about 60 percent white in 1974.[7] The change is even more marked in the schools. Between 1965—the first year for which racial data are available—and 1975, the proportion of whites declined from 46.4 percent to 24.5 percent.[8] In the wake of this dramatic demographic change have come new—and newly perceived—problems.

Blacks constitute the largest single minority group, almost 15 percent of the population. San Francisco long enjoyed a reputation of tolerance toward black people, in good part because there were not many of them; as late as 1940 only 4,806 residents (less than 1 percent of the population) were black.[9] But blacks in substantial numbers were drawn to San Francisco by the promise of wartime employment in the U.S. Navy's Hunter's Point shipyards, and found temporary housing in that isolated corner of the city; they have remained clustered there, as their temporary housing has become permanent, and have also settled in other pockets of the city.

It was Asians, rather than blacks, who until recently were the have-not group. As political scientist Fred Wirt has stated, "It is not overdrawn to suggest that sinophobia has been San Francisco's substitute for the anti-Semitism of eastern cities."[10] The traditional kinship ties of the Chinese and Japanese, coupled with the outright prejudice of San Franciscans, encouraged both groups to withdraw into their own enclaves. San Francisco's Chinatown remains intact, one of the most densely populated districts in the country. The Japanese community, dispersed by the ruthless expedient of World War II "evacuation," has remained relatively stable in size during the past two decades; but, particularly since the liberalization of immigration laws in 1965, the Chinese (and Filipino and Samoan) populations have increased rapidly. In 1974, about 9 percent of the population (62,400) was of Chinese origin, many of them first-generation peasant refugees from Taiwan, and about 4 percent of the population (28,100)

7. L. Austin, Around the World in San Francisco: A Guide to the Racial and Ethnic Minorities of the San Francisco-Oakland Area (1955) [hereinafter cited as Austin].
8. Status Report of the Office of Integration, San Francisco Unified School District 6 (1975) [hereinafter cited as Status Report].
9. *Austin, supra* note 7, at 4.
10. Wirt, *supra* note 6, at 241.

was Filipino.[11] In addition, one out of every nine persons in the city was of Hispanic—primarily Mexican and Central American—descent, concentrated in the Mission District.[12]

For the most part the arriving ethnic groups were poor, unskilled, and unable to speak English. Unlike their predecessors, who had either withdrawn or—in the case of Western Europeans—worked within the traditional political system, these groups began to make their voices heard outside formal channels; they organized into literally countless groups. The demands they began, during the mid-1950s, to make on city government generally, and the public school particuarly, were novel and potentially threatening. They sought better jobs, better schools, and— perhaps most important—deference, the political recognition of their worth in the urban scheme of values. The school desegregation issue was one important focus of this new politics. It was initially pressed by civil rights groups, coalitions of old-line white liberals and blacks, but came subsequently, and in very different ways, to involve the Chinese and Latinos as well.

THE SYMBOLIC POLITICS OF DESEGREGATION: 1960-1970

In 1960, Superintendent of Schools Harold Spears could honestly report to the United States Civil Rights Commisson that racial discrimination was not a problem, that San Francisco's "liberal attitude . . . in respect to neighbors" had produced a wide and presumably salutory "scattering of the various racial elements throughout the city's schools."[13] Seven years later, when Spears stepped down after a dozen years in the superintendency, such a reading of the situation would have been untenable. School officials and the school board had been brought to the realization that racial isolation in the schools existed, and indeed was a problem. But the change which had occurred was largely symbolic; a great deal of study and report-writing had been done, but it was not accompanied by any demonstrable shift in policy, or any action which affected the lives of schoolchildren.

The Stirrings of the San Francisco Civil Rights Movement: 1960-1967

The Professional as Educational Leader. For 50 years, from 1922-1972, the San Francisco Board of Education consisted of seven citizens, appointed by the mayor and subsequently ratified by the electorate for five-year terms. The school board is formally independent of the city and county governments; it sets

11. San Francisco Department of Public Health.
12. Wirt, *supra* note 6, at 41.
13. Hearings of the U.S. Commission on Civil Rights 816-17 (1960) [hereinafter cited as 1960 Hearings].

its own tax rate and adopts its own budget, without the necessity of approval of any other city agency. The board has not, however, been politically isolated: its school construction bonds must be approved by the San Francisco Board of Supervisors; unofficially, the mayor's office has often sought to influence school policies.[14] The board of itself has been, at different times, more or less concerned with the intimate details of school operations: while everyone could agree with the maxim that a board of education sets policy which school administrators are responsible for carrying out, the line between policy and operations, the distinction between careful purview and officious intermeddling, has never been clear.

San Francisco's superintendents have sought, with varying success, to avoid both outside pressure and board of education intervention. Their common strategy, most artfully pursued by Superintendent Spears, has been to insist that school governance was a matter of professional—not political—judgment. If successful, that tactic insulates school officials from everyone, leaving them free to pursue what they perceive as the schools' mission. Harold Spears, superintendent from 1955 to 1967, epitomized this point of view.[15] He saw the task of school administration as best left to the experts. Schools served a vital but narrowly conceived social purpose: they prepared the young to become useful, productive citizens. The task of the school board was to obtain public support for the professional administration's policy, not to be armchair quarterbacks.

The superintendent prided himself on his administration's responsiveness to changes that were taking place in San Francisco. In a statement delivered to the U.S. Commission on Civil Rights, which held hearings in San Francisco early in 1960, Spears pointed out:

> The public schools, especially the elementary schools, actually represent barometers of changes in this city. Personally, I think that for a city to see what actually goes on . . . it can find no better barometers than the elementary schools of that city, because they are very conscious of the economic aspects of the neighborhood and the racial makeup of that neighborhood. . . . We do feel that we are very close to the changes in the city here.[16]

Spears's perception of the changing racial composition of San Francisco's public schools did not entail any distinct administrative reaction. His attitude reflected the classic liberal position: race or other group attributes should be irrele-

14. *See, e.g.,* F. Dohrmann, Three Years on a Board (1924); L. Dolson, Administration of the San Francisco Public Schools (unpublished Ph.D. dissertation, University of California, Berkeley, 1964).

15. For an astute discussion of the Spears era, *see* L. Cuban, School Chiefs Under Fire: A Study of Three Big City Superintendents Under Outside Pressure 109–151 (unpublished Ph.D. dissertation, Stanford University, 1974, to be published by University of Chicago Press) [hereinafter cited as Cuban].

16. 1960 Hearings, *supra* note 13, at 816–17.

vant, individual characteristics controlling, with respect to any institutional decision. Thus, while the district's hiring policy "emphasizes the selection of the best qualified teachers available, as is evidenced by our use of civil-service examinations,[17] and its educational policy stressed quality education geared to the capabilities of the individual student,[18] the racial implications of such policies constituted an inappropriate line of inquiry. Spears offered the Civil Rights Commission the off-the-record impression that more than three-quarters of all public schools had black pupils, an estimate based on the visible migration of black families into heretofore white sections of the city.[19] There existed no official statistics to document the impact of such trends; policies of objective school management, which were premised on equal treatment, precluded official notice of racial differences.

To Spears the neighborhood school policy that had been in existence for many years epitomized this racial neutrality. During the 1957 Little Rock confrontation, he took the opportunity to contrast that shameful situation with the nondiscriminatory practices of the local schools. "Integration No Problem Here" was the newspaper headline for Spears's comments: "Everyone living in a certain area, regardless of race, goes to the school in that area. . . . We have all races in our schools."[20] Nor was San Francisco like New Rochelle, New York, whose boundary-line gerry-mandering had led a federal court in 1961 to question the neutrality of the neighborhood concept.[21] In response to a reporter's query, Spears stated flatly: "We have not manipulated boundaries to segregate racial groups nor to integrate them. . . . We are conscious of our problems and are trying to treat everyone fairly."[22]

"The Proper Recognition of a Pupil's Racial Background." Superintendent Spears's desire to treat questions about race, if at all, as professional questions failed to reckon with the talismanic concept of equal opportunity, a concept whose bounds are unfixed but which was then (and remains today) capable of evoking strong political response. To those whose objective was the elimination of racial injustice, Spears's avowals of nondiscrimination were inadequate if only because they implied that no problem existed. On January 23, 1962, leaders of CORE and the Council for Civic Unity urged the board of education to recog-

17. *Id.* at 817.
18. Spears commented to the Civil Rights Commission:

We have a variety of practices where we encourage some of the brighter children to take more work, or to move ahead faster, but it is not the track system that Washington, D.C., has.

Id. at 822.
19. *Id.* at 820.
20. Quoted in Cuban, *supra* note 15, at 130.
21. Taylor v. Board of Education, 294 F.2d 36 (2d Cir. 1961), *cert. denied,* 368 U.S. 940 (1961).
22. San Francisco Examiner, March 16, 1961, at 6.

nize that de facto racial segregation existed in San Francisco; to declare that segregated schools (by which the civil rights advocates meant predominantly black
schools were educationally undesirable; and to prepare a program for their
elimination.[23]

The civil rights leaders offered no clear alternative programs of their own.
Despite their professed concern for the "elimination" of school segregation, it
appears—at least at this stage—that no one had in mind the abandonment of the
neighborhood school concept; certainly no one thought to propose sending substantial numbers of students out of, much less into, Hunter's Point. What was
really being sought was a token of official concern, admission that there was a
problem and that *something*—however symbolic that something might be—was
being done about it.

The civil rights groups had been encouraged to make their request by their
earlier success in preserving one city high school as an academic, rather than a
comprehensive, high school (academic excellence was, at least in 1961, perceived as a civil rights issue). The board had acceded to the civil rights group
pressure—an "unexpected surprise" for the advocates, who had not realized that
they could be quite so effective—and reversed the superintendent's recommendation to convert the school into a comprehensive school.[24] With respect to desegregation, however, the board was more politically prudent. It deferred to the
professional judgment of the superintendent, and asked him to report back on
the matter.

Spears's report, issued on June 19, 1962,[25] was not similarly prudent. He met
the de facto segregation accusation head-on, and flatly rejected it; his remarkably
candid report became a focus for disaffection.

As the superintendent described his task, it was a "rational and deliberate
treatment" of the problem of "the proper recognition of a pupil's racial background by the school."[26] Spears did his homework: his twenty-five-page report
included a substantial bibliography on the subject; accompanied by School
Board Commissioner Claire Lilienthal, he visited eight large city school districts
and, under the auspices of the U.S. Office of Education, conferred with representatives of others; he attended over a dozen civic functions to gain a sense of
community sentiment; he also obtained from each of the district's 135 schools a
good working estimate of its racial composition.

The report recognized that a problem existed: "Providing the nonwhite child
a proper education . . . is a highly complicated educational matter. . . ."[27] But
the problem was not of the schools' making; it stemmed rather from "dispro-

23. San Francisco Board of Education, Transcript, January 23, 1962, at 46.

24. *Id.,* December 5, 1961, at 23–24; interview with Ruth Kadish, president of SCOPE
and founder of the Coordinating Council for Integrated Education.

25. H. Spears, The Proper Recognition of a Pupil's Educational Background, Superintendent's Report to the Board of Education (June 19, 1962) (Mimeo). June 19, 1962.

26. *Id.* at 1.

27. *Id.* at 19.

portionate housing, indifferent parents, limited job opportunities for youth, and unresponsive pupils."[28] Blunt words, indeed; and the rejection of a racial census —sought by civil rights groups in order to prove with numbers what was apparent to the unadied eye, that blacks and whites attended separate schools—was even more blunt.

> We are now faced with the movement to emphasize differences in the color and races of pupils. . . . In some school systems, such records are now prepared annually. One asks for what purpose do we so label a child, and in turn, post a sign on his school indicating the racial makeup of the student body at the moment? If we are preparing to ship these children to various schools, in predetermined racial allotments, then such brands would serve the purpose they have been put to in handling livestock. But until somebody comes up with an educationally sound plan for such integration, then this racial accounting serves nothing but the dangers of putting it to ill use.[29]

Spears recognized the symbolic importance of the question that had been put to him, but he resisted using children as "the tools" in a process of social change. Racial labeling was, in his judgment, a perversion of the schools' purpose, namely instruction in the pedagogical basics of "reading, writing, spelling, arithmetic, English, geography, history, civics, and so on."[30] His conclusion simply dismissed the issue: "I have no educational sound program to suggest to the Board to eliminate the schools in which the children are predominantly of one race. . . ."[31]

The superintendent's declaration personalized the issue: a debate over the meaning of equal opportunity had given way to a battle between the school board and superintendent on one side, and the civil rights movement on the other.

The Persistence of Pressure. In what has been described as the most stormy meeting in the history of San Francisco's public schools, 1,400 persons jammed the auditorium of Galileo High School variously to denounce and defend Spears's position.[32] Angry threats alternated with supportive statements, as a total of 52 speakers addressed the board.

The position of the civil rights groups was epitomized by NAACP attorney

---

28. *Id.*
29. *Id.* at 23–24.
30. *Id.*
31. *Id.* at 25.
32. San Francisco Examiner, September 19, 1962, at 1. CORE's statement declared: "The American Negro is demanding action now. . . . It's later than you think." San Francisco Board of Education, Transcript, September 18, 1962, at 94; Citizens for Neighborhood Schools stated: "San Francisco has a tradition of neighborhoods. . . . The average parent wholeheartedly favors neighborhood schools." *Id.* at 12, 14.

(and subsequently a member of the city's board of supervisors) Terry Francois, who pleaded that:

> racial composition of the schools become a matter of concern to this Board and its administrators. We do advocate that, where students are transported to relieve overcrowding, the effect upon the racial composition of the receiving school should be considered. We do advocate that the achieving of maximum desegregation be given a prominent place in all of the decisions of this Board having to do with zoning, site selection, pupil and teacher assignment, selection of feeder schools, optional transfers and in all administrative concerns.[33]

Francois and the other civil rights spokespersons were not urging wholesale changes in student assignment. To them, as to the superintendent, it was important to retain "to the maximum extent possible . . . the basic character of the neighborhood schools. . . . We have never advocated a particular percentage. . . ."[34] That point was reiterated by CORE and the Council for Civil Unity; in statements delivered to the board, both groups urged the board to take race into account as *a* legitimate basis for decision-making, to do so voluntarily and not in response to a court order:

> Time is running out. The Board of Education has an opportunity to take the role of leadership at a crucial time, now. . . . *We most earnestly hope that here in San Francisco, "The City That Knows How," our Board of Education will not wait for the force of a judicial decision.*[35]

The configuration of opinions expressed at that September 1962 board meeting reflected the range of views and interests that were to be expressed repeatedly during the decade. There were, first of all, the white liberals for whom San Francisco was so famous, veterans of housing and employment discrimination battles, seeing education as but one more civil rights issue. Also heard were the white conservatives, advocating preservation of neighborhood schools—indeed, of their neighborhoods. Individuals, as well as several neighborhood-improvement clubs and merchants' associations, were fearful that changing the racial composition of the school population, through the adoption of race-conscious policies, would threaten the character of the communities they had struggled to enter. Those criticizing the civil rights groups' position were themselves the arrived minorities —Italian, Dutch, Irish, German, and French[36] —unwilling to extend to this new

---

33. *Id.* at 20.

34. *Id.* at 26.

35. CORE, *Relationship Between Racial Balance and Sound Education in the San Francisco Unified School District* 17, 10 (September 1, 1962) (on file at the Alexander Meikeljohn Library, Berkeley, California) [emphasis added].

36. The speakers praising Spears's report included Cognetta, Farrieggio, Van Skike, Bogard, Duffey, Bushnell, and Vipiana. San Francisco Board of Education, Transcript, September 18, 1962, at i-ii.

minority benefits which they themselves had not been offered in their efforts to become middle-class, assimilated citizens. With the exception of one speaker —Herman Gallegos, a member of the recently organized Community Service Organization, who spoke on behalf of the "ignored" Spanish-surnamed population[37]—none of the other nonblack groups was represented at the meeting. Racial discrimination was perceived as an exclusively black-white issue.

A hint of the division within the black community also emerged from the September meeting. While the pro-desegregation position was most frequently advanced, two members of the Afro-American Association argued not for desegregation but rather for black teachers and a curriculum that would instill "racial pride and motivation in the black child."[38] A member of Phi Delta Sigma, a black educators' fraternity, urged that black teachers in increasing numbers be assigned to predominantly black schools to serve as role models for the students.[39] The faintest concern for community control of education could also be detected. A representative of the Hunter's Point–Bayview Citizens Committee declared: "Parents want to be involved."[40]

The voices heard at this September board meeting—middle-class whites, both liberal and conservative; blacks, pressing a variety of positions—were to remain dominant throughout the decade. Neither the other minorities, who saw racial discrimination as someone else's issue, nor the social and business elite, were to enter in significant numbers a fray whose denouement was the 1971 *Johnson* decision.

The School Board Responds. The civil rights groups sought, during the fall of 1962, to repudiate the Spears report on the "proper recognition of a pupil's racial background by the schools." They insisted upon the device of a citizens' advisory committee as the most likely vehicle for formulating and legitimizing a policy which committed the school district to overcoming racial isolation.[41] The demand reflected distrust both of the board of education and the superintendent, a fact which the board itself recognized. Some response to this rapidly escalating issue more satisfactory than the superintendent's statement was called for; but the board chose to appoint an ad hoc committee composed of its own members, rather than creating a citizens' group, in order to keep the issue under its control.[42]

That action did not satisfy the civil rights organizations. CORE staged a sit-in following the meeting, and its president declared to the press that more picketing

37. *Id.* at 41.
38. *Id.* at 96–105.
39. *Id.* at 147.
40. *Id.* at 77.
41. *See generally id. See also* Council for Civic Unity, *Race and the Schools,* September 5, 1962 at 21 (submitted but not orally presented to the board).
42. San Francisco Board of Education, Transcript, September 18, 1962, at 172, 176-79. The motion was made by Commissioner James Stratten, the board's one black member.

and demonstrations would follow.[43] The NAACP, acting on a suggestion advanced several months earlier by national legal counsel Robert Carter, filed suit against the school district, charging that San Francisco had discriminated against black students through its pupil assignment and transfer policies; "indifference" to segregation, the complaint charged, was no different from complicity in segregation.[44]

The *Brock* suit was essentially another move in the political chess game. The NAACP gave little serious support to its active pursuit. Nonetheless, the board was anxious to defend itself; it hired local attorney and former School Commissioner Joseph Alioto as counsel, paying him a $10,000 retainer.[45] Alioto sought to defuse the issue. In a private meeting with Alioto and Council of Civic Unity Chairman Frank Quinn, NAACP attorney Terry Francois conceded that there had been no overt action taken by the school district to create or maintain racial imbalance. What the NAACP really wanted, Francois stated, was a policy statement committing the district to work toward desegregation, coupled with the appointment of an administrator to whom the NAACP could take individual grievances.[46]

The board's ad hoc committee was the instrument for just such a resolution. Its report, issued in April 1963, constituted a gentle rebuke to the superintendent. It admitted that, although the school district did not intend or practice segregation, segregation persisted nonetheless; it recommended that the district take unspecified measures to respond to the educational problems that it caused: that —in the patrician language of the report—the schools should act to brighten the "graceless" lives of minority children.

> . . . There exist a considerable number of schools having a preponderance of one or another race. It is recommended that wherever practicable and reasonable and consistent with the neighborhood school plan, the factor of race be included in the criteria used in establishing new attendance zones and in redrawing existing boundaries.[47]

In the context of 1963, the committee's suggestion (which was embraced by the board) was indeed radical. The hedged language of the report could not obscure the civil rights organizations' success. The district also intimated that it was willing to act on its altered convictions: black students had recently been reassigned from overcrowded black schools to neighboring schools in the wealthy and white Marina and Pacific Heights areas, and it was announced that 300 black

43. San Francisco Examiner, September 20, 1962, at 1.

44. Brock v. Board of Education, Civ. No. 71034 (N.D. Calif., October 2, 1962).

45. A taxpayers' suit protesting the payment of public moneys for Alioto's services was dismissed by Superior Court Judge Bryon Arnold. San Francisco Examiner, December 11, 1962, at 11.

46. *Id.,* January 1, 1963, at 1.

47. Final Report of the Ad Hoc Committee, April 2, 1963, at 7–8.

students from the Fillmore and Hunter's Point areas would be sent to nearby predominantly white schools.[48]

The board's policy statement, and the reassignment of several hundred students, could not "cure" the problems of racial segregation; nor were the actions intended to. But they nonetheless satisfied—at least for the moment. The reassignments were praised by the president of the Council for Civic Unity: "It is commendable that the schools are taking racial balance into account."[49] And the endorsement of racial criteria by the board was hailed by spokespersons for the NAACP and CORE as a "real step forward."[50] The *Brock* litigation was permitted to lapse, in good part because the NAACP no longer felt that it had a case to press. Superintendent Spears hoped that the year-long debate had come to an end. He urged that differences be reconciled, that everyone unite in support of a school system which "reflects the public interest and likewise reflects the educational welfare of every child in the school system. There is nothing to fear and everything to hope for. . . . The spirit of the Report provides a common point of departure."[51]

The ad hoc committee had successfully closed the rift between the board and the liberal community in San Francisco. Even some conservative spokespersons had softened their position. The head of the Committee for Neighborhood Schools was soon to suggest that limited desegregation "experiments" be tried.[52] A process of mutual accommodation seemed to be working, as new tactics—demonstrations and lawsuits—were incorporated into the traditional pattern of negotiation and compromise.

The Perception of Administrative Recalcitrance. Issues as volatile as segregation are never resolved in any permanent fashion. Organizations whose primary concern is the furtherance of minority civil rights do not admit to final successes; they recognize only the stage-by-stage resolution of continuing controversies, disputes in which the meaning of the operant terms—here, equal educational opportunity—are constantly changing, the demands constantly expanding, the inequality about which objection is voiced constantly becoming less readily detectable. The school desegregation issue in San Francisco was no exception to this iron law of social movements.

During much of the 1963/64 school year, civil rights organizations did not continue to press the school system with specific demands. The focus of the movement shifted, albeit briefly, to the employment front;[53] the outright refusal

48. San Francisco Chronicle, January 30, 1963, at 1; February 5, 1963, at 3.
49. *Id.,* January 31, 1963, at 2.
50. *Id.,* April 4, 1963, at 1.
51. *Id.*
52. 1 Transcript of the Joint Conferences 51–54, 95–97 (August 23 and 26, 1965) [hereinafter cited as Joint Conferences].
53. R. Crain, The Politics of School Desegregation 92 (1969 ed.) [hereinafter cited as Crain].

of dealers on "automobile row" to hire blacks became the subject of primary attention. The NAACP felt it appropriate to give William Cobb, who had been appointed human relations officer of the district in response to their demands, time to maneuver.[54] Within six months of Cobb's appointment, the liberals began to realize they had won an empty victory. Spears and his staff had taken no further steps to desegregate the schools, and Cobb, who had effectively been frozen out of the administration's decision-making process, appeared more concerned with educational standards than civil rights ideals. On April 7, 1964, the school administration building was again picketed. Spears complained to the press: "They don't give us credit for the many fine things we are doing for minority groups."[55] A racial census was again sought, but a divided board chose not to vote on the question.[56]

Spears took one action he thought would appease civil rights groups. He proposed that there be a bond issue to permit the construction of a new high school in a location that would guarantee its integration. But Spears, who had not raised the matter with the NAACP, failed to reckon with the divergence within the black community. The NAACP, responding to pressure from its Hunter's Point constituency, reversed its earlier stand and insisted that new schools be built in the ghetto; the powerful Central Labor Council announced that it would recommend rejection of the bonds unless the NAACP supported the plan. With understandable bewilderment, Spears found himself neogitating a plan which included construction on sites he "would never have dreamed of asking for."[57] The accommodation was ultimately a costly one. Six years later the plaintiffs in *Johnson* would point to the construction of ghetto schools as evidence of the school district's "deliberate" segregation of black students.

A year later, civil rights leaders were still complaining: "All we get from San Francisco after repeated correspondence, visits and converences are policy statements, not facts."[58] The racial census remained a key issue: without data, it was felt, the extent of segregation could not be made plain. By the summer of 1965, the board was under new pressure to make public the racial composition of its schools. Newly elected Supervisor Francois proposed that the school board become an elected—and, it was presumed, more liberal—body. This position received warm endorsement from black Assemblyman Willie Brown, who saw it as a way of affording citizens "fundamental participation in the affairs of the school."[59] The civil rights organizations, determined to present a united front, regrouped into the Coordinating Council for Integrated Schools; from the roster of member groups, it appeared that everyone except the Chamber of Commerce

54. San Francisco Chronicle, April 30, 1963, at 6.
55. *Id.,* April 26, 1963, at 2.
56. *Id.*
57. Crain, *supra* note 53, at 93. *See also* Joint Conferences, *supra* note 52 at 20–39.
58. Price Cobb, a black psychologist, as quoted in the San Francisco Examiner, April 8, 1965, at 3.
59. San Francisco Chronicle, August 6, 1965, at 2.

supported desegregation.[60] More direct pressure was also brough to bear: 100 pickets, members of the Committee on Direct Action, marched outside the school district office for two days; over 500 persons attended the August 2, 1965 board meeting to hear the NAACP accuse the board of "subtle, sophisticated lying, trickery and deceit," and demand an immediate racial count.[61] The short-lived honeymoon was over. The board capitulated in the face of these tactics. It reconstituted its ad hoc committee, and agreed to authorize the long-sought racial census. It announced that it would collaborate with the newly created San Francisco Human Rights Committee in holding community forums about segregation.[62]

The racial data, which were published days after the meeting, proved anticlimactic. They revealed what everyone already knew, that there existed predominantly one-race schools in the city; more interestingly, they depicted San Francisco as substantially more integrated than most northern cities. The eight San Francisco high schools had black enrollments ranging from 8 to 34 percent. Of the fifteen junior highs, only two were more than half black. All ninety-five elementary schools had some white students and only one had no blacks: just seventeen were 90 percent or more white, and twenty-four were more than half black. Fifteen percent of the students in the exclusive Grant School were black.[63] If one regards a school with at least a 10 percent minority as desegregated, 76 percent of San Francisco's elementary school students—as compared with 14 percent in St. Louis and 20 percent in Baltimore—were enrolled in desegregated schools.[64]

There are, of course, a variety of ways in which these figures could be read, but the response of civil rights leaders indicated that they would not be used against the District. "It's too bad it took direct action to elicit the figures and the Board wouldn't respond to reasonable requests over a long period of time."[65] Spears hoped that the survey "will help clear the air." He reiterated his long-held view that the data had no value, that "the number of whites in a school has no bearing on the quality of education."[66]

The release of the survey did not substantially alter what had become an adversial relationship between the school administration and the civil rights community. The racial count offered a tempting target and an empty victory. Although the superintendent was obliged to reverse his position, no changes in the manage-

---

60. Interview with Ruth Kadish, who organized the council, *supra* note 19. Earl Raab, director of the Jewish Community Relations Council, member of the Human Rights Commission, and long-time participant in San Francisco civil rights issues, termed the council's support for desegregation "a mile wide and an inch deep." Interview with Earl Raab, in San Francisco, March 14, 1975.

61. San Francisco Chronicle, August 3, 1965, at 1.

62. *Id.*

63. *Id.*, August 5, 1965, at 1.

64. Crain *supra* note 53, at 93.

65. San Francisco Chronicle, August 5, 1965, at 1.

66. *Id.* at 20.

ment of the schools followed. Even the board's assurances that it would take race into account in assigning pupils now seemed merely rhetorical, for the practical consequences of that change had been minimal. Spears's position—that efficiency of operation and sound educational standards, not racial politics, should determine district behavior—had prevailed after all.

Shortly after the release of the census, Spears announced his retirement, effective in July 1967. While the maneuver left him a lame-duck leader for two years, it also forced the civil rights groups to concentrate their assault on the board. For the next two years, the administration conducted business as usual, scarcely perturbed by the commotion over segregation which swirled around the board; the board in turn sought desparately to diminish the expectations of its outsider antagonists.

The School Board as Reluctant Leader.   The school board had for so long deferred to the views of its superintendent that, when effectively obliged to lead, it did not know quite what to do. Searching for a new source of legitimacy, it sought community consensus "through a cooperative exploration of ways to achieve a better racial balance."[67] But the tactic failed. The NAACP and CORE boycotted the community meetings, demanding that the board immediately declare that "ghetto schools are educationally indefensible"; were such a statement not forthcoming, the organizations promised a student boycott in the fall of 1965.[68]

The conferences themselves accomplished little. Spokespersons various community groups rebuked the board for its failure to lead;[69] for their part the board and the superintendent criticized the range of ideas presented—including Princeton plans for pairing predominantly white and black schools and the closing of all black ghetto schools—as either impractical or ineffective.[70] Even as the two conferences were being held, the board of supervisors had failed to recommend Francois's proposal for an elected school board, and that fact may have lessened the board's felt need for community support.[71] The only suggestion that did secure agreement was the request that an outside agency assess the San Francisco situation and make comprehensive recommendations to reduce racial imbalance. Spears and his staff were obviously able to undercut the casually advanced suggestion of community members; only a more authoritative source, it was felt, could overcome administrative recalcitrance.

The school board's gesture toward community involvement in the summer of 1965 satisfied its sense of responsibility.   Commissioner Claire Lilienthal con-

---

67. Commissioner Claire Lilienthal, quoted in the San Francisco Examiner, August 17, 1965, at 22.

68. *Id.* Lois Barnes, NAACP Education Committee chairperson, spoke for the groups.

69. 1 Joint Conferences, *supra* note 52, at 49–50, 65, 75, 92.

70. *Id.* at 25, 29, 33, 46.

71. San Francisco Examiner, August 24, 1965, at 13. Mayor John Shelley had opposed the move as "retrogression, not progression." San Francisco Examiner, August 7, 1965, at 6.

cluded: "I believe that the Ad Hoc Committee certainly has an idea now of the varying points of view that represent the community."[72] No longer threatened by a charter amendment which would force them to run for election, the board reverted to its traditional regime, holding formal public meetings and ratifying the policy recommendations of the administration. The search for a new kind of political legitimacy through community consensus turned out to be remarkably short-lived.

Studies in Lieu of Decisions. In 1966, studies—undertaken both inside and outside the school district—were the order of the day. The State Fair Employment Practices Commission and the San Francisco Human Rights Commission had, in response to NAACP and CORE requests, undertaken to examine the district's employment practices. The findings were mixed: while the teaching and administrative staff was only 5 percent black (as compared with 11.8 percent of the citywide population), there was evident progress being made in hiring blacks at all levels.[73] To Spears, the investigation demonstrated "no trace of discrimination."[74] Yet the board, still cognizant of the possibility of an NAACP-initiated student boycott and made aware by Spears of the possibility of federal intervention, adopted a resolution calling on the administration to develop feasible plans for eliminating racial imbalance in employment, utilizaing if necessary the resources of the State Commission on Equal Opportunity in Education.[75]

The board also decided to act on the suggestion made at the community conferences that an outside agency be called upon to study segregation in the San Francisco schools. In April 1966—eight months after the last conference session—the board contracted with the Stanford Research Institute (SRI) to conduct a preliminary study which would form the basis of a master plan for desegregation. The board was seeking to buy time by commissioning a study; it also felt a desperate need for wisdom offered from the vantagepoint of detachment. The first objective, at least, was achieved: SRI did not produce its report until the waning days of Spears's administration, and the board postponed its response until Spears's successor had had the opportunity to study and react to the document.

The NAACP was unwilling to await the outcome of the SRI study. Ten members of that organization's Education Committee met with NAACP general counsel Robert Carter in May 1966, and heard him urge the filing of another lawsuit. "Elimination of de facto segregation is the most important task facing Negroes in the North. Housing and job opportunities are important, but we are

---

72. 2 Joint Conferences, *supra* note 52, at 48.
73. San Francisco Chronicle, August 7, 1965, at 6.
74. San Francisco Examiner, August 27, 1965, at 11.
75. *Id.,* September 8, 1965, at 1. *See also id.,* August 17, 1965, at 22 (Spears described the public schools as "sitting ducks" for groups anxious for quick solutions to complex social problems).

unlikely to achieve full equality until we have equal education."[76] Carter, whose acquaintanceship with San Francisco was limited, thought that desegregation could be accomplished simply through re-zoning neighborhoods.[77] The more knowledgeable local committee realized the limited utility of such an approach, if one's intention was to undo all racial isolation; and, by 1966, that goal was indeed what the more radical NAACP members had in mind. The Education Committee agreed to raise $15,000 for a lawsuit, but its primary interest lay in the possibility of creating a network of educational parks that would draw students from the entire city. It continued to see the threat of a lawsuit as a weapon to force a host of policy changes.[78]

For the next several years the NAACP Education Committee turned from sit-ins to statistics, functioning as a school research organization. Its members undertook the thankless task of obtaining and pulling together previously unnoticed data on school expenditures, in order to establish a correlation between low expenditures for teachers in predominantly black schools and low achievement test scores of students in those schools.[79] Those data, intended to embarrass the school board into decisive action, were eventually utilized in the 1970 *Johnson* case.

End of an Era. The last years of the Spears era were a deceptively quiet time. There were no particular disputes to focus controversy between civil rights groups, the administration, and the board. When Spears departed, his traditional school administrator's vision of the educational purpose of the schools remained largely unimpaired, his conviction that as superintendent it was his task, not that of political outsiders, to impart a misson to the school organization was unaltered.

It was only a cease-fire, not a lasting peace, that had been fashioned. The civil rights organizations, especially the NAACP, had turned from showy tactics to ultimately more consequential research; the SRI report, when ultimately released, would have the effect of a political time bomb. There existed other perceptible changes in San Francisco. Two communities within the city, one residentially desegregated and the other preponderantly black, had begun to focus their energies on the preservation of their own neighborhood schools. Three new members joined the school board in 1966 and 1967, and they were decidedly different from, more desegregation-minded than, their predecessors: Alan Nichols had long been associated with the Council of Civic Unity: Laurel Glass was an NAACP member, endorsed by that organization and by the Committee for Direct Action;[80] the traditional black position was filled by Zuretti

76. San Francisco Chronicle, May 22, 1966, at 4.
77. *Id.*
78. Interview with Lois Barnes, chairman of NAACP Education Committee, 1964–1967, in Berkeley, March 21, 1975.
79. *Id.* Also interview with Ann Bloomfield, chairman of NAACP Education Committee, 1967–1970, in San Francisco, March 14, 1975.
80. For a revealing account of how this Glide Memorial Church-sponsored organization

Goosby, who believed that educational opportunities for black children would be vastly improved in achievement-oriented middle-class schools, and strongly supported system-wide desegregation.[81]

Too Little, Too Late: 1967–1970

In July 1967 a "nationwide search" for a person of "vision, youth, experience, sensitivity and ability to communicate before taking action"[82]—in short, an educational politician—led to the appointment of Robert Jenkins to succeed Spears as Superintendent. Jenkins had survived ten years in Pasadena, California, presiding over what was reportedly the orderly desegregation of that system's schools. He was a man chosen for his talents both at innovating and involving citizens' groups in his administration.[83] To a board which had become increasingly supportive of desegregation, Jenskins appeared to be the man who would lead San Francisco into the new era. That was not to be the case. Three years later, "more tired than I've ever been in my life,"[84] Jenkins abruptly resigned in the face of mounting political turmoil over what was by any standards a modest approach to integration; his retirement coincided almost precisely with the filing of the *Johnson* suit.

The Emergence of Communitarianism. Throughout Superintendent Jenkins's tenure, desegregation was the most publicly visible question to confront the schools. Less noticed, but of substantial importance nonetheless, was a demonstrable shift in the concern of San Francisco communities. In two sections of the city, the southwestern corner (comprising the Ocean View, Merced Heights, and Ingleside neighborhoods) known as OMI and Hunter's Point, local groups organized to address the problems of their schools.

OMI—a racial microcosm of the city—obtained HEW funding in 1966 to attack housing and school problems which local groups had identified as causes of neighborhood deterioration and white flight.[85] Funds from the HEW grant

---

went about procuring the nomination of Glass, see Kuhn, How to Get Things Done in the City (Glide Urban Center 1969).

81. Interview with Zuretti Goosby, School Commissioner, 1967–1972 and 1974–present, in San Francisco, April 16, 1975. Stratten, Goosby's black predecessor, had never been considered a representative of the pro-integration black community, and when he was appointed by Governor Ronald Reagan to the California Youth Authority, Supervisor Terry Francois arranged a conflict-of-interest ruling by City Attorney Thomas O'Connor, forcing Stratten to resign his board seat. Interview with Terry Francois, plaintiffs' attorney in *Brock*, NAACP Board member and member Board of Supervisors, in San Francisco, March 28, 1975.

82. San Francisco Chronicle, May 22, 1966, at 2.

83. Report of the 1967 Grand Jury of the City and County of San Francisco 127.

84. Interview with Robert Jenkins, in Redlands, California (telephone), April 18, 1975.

85. The discussion of OMI is based on interviews with Laurel Glass, school commissioner, 1967–1972, in San Francisco, April 4, 1975; Donald Kuhn, in San Francisco, April 1, 1975; and Charlotte Berk, secretary of OMI, March 20, 1975. For data on the ethnic composition of the OMI community, *see* San Francisco Fair Housing Planning Committee for the Racial, Ethnic and Economic Integration of Residential Neighborhoods in San Francisco, One City or Two? 6 (October 1973) (using 1970 census data).

were distributed to the five elementary schools in the OMI area, and each school chose projects it deemed most needed. The overall objective was to enhance the schools' effectiveness and entice middle-class whites into remaining in the area.[86] From 1966 until 1970, this community organization struggled to make the school administration aware of OMI's existence. They were a mild-mannered and eminently respectable group, criticized by Saul Alinsky for failing to identify their "enemies" and pursue them more relentlessly. The organization envisioned a future in which desegregated schools would be the natural by-product of a genuinely desegregated residential area.

A second grassroots organization was emerging in the Hunter's Point–Bayview District, the depressed and isolated southeastern corner of the city.[87] In the wake of riots during September 1966, a community education committee began meeting regularly, trying to develop new programs to improve the prospects of youth in the area. Six years earlier, the neighborhood had been 50 percent white; by 1966 fewer than 10 percent of the 37,000 residents were white.[88] This demographic change, as well as the political notoriety which the neighborhood suddenly enjoyed, stimulated members of the committee to dream of new kinds of schools where ghetto students would be welcomed, where they would have the newest materials and the best-trained teachers, where they could become respected (not feared) citizens. Desegregation was not a part of this dream. Lack of proximity to white neighborhoods and white unease rendered that idea infeasible.[89] Instead, the committee sought to improve the schools it already had. As Beatrice Dunbar, chairwoman of that committee, stated:

> When we saw that our children were not achieving, we asked the Board of Education, administration and teachers to get involved with us. . . . We saw a need for more black principals and teachers because our children need an image of blacks. . . . We have parents come in to our meetings, relating some of the things that's happening to their children. . . . We try to help to solve some of these problems.[90]

Out of this dream grew SEED (Southeast Educational Development), a federally funded project concentrating on reforming the primary school program, utilizing community aids and operating under parent-teacher councils at each school site. The central administration had little interest, and less involvement, in the enterprise.[91]

86. *1965–1975: OMI Schools Ten Years Later,* 6 OMI News 4–5 (March 1975).

87. *See generally* Hippler, *The Game of Black and White at Hunter's Point,* in Culture and Civility in San Francisco 53 (1971).

88. SEED, Third Year Narrative Report (San Francisco Unified School District 1969).

89. *See* statement of Rev. Charles Lee, director of SEED, in 9A Hearings of the Senate Select Subcommittee on Equal Educational Opportunity 4277–78 (1971) [hereinafter cited as Senate Hearings].

90. *Id.* at 4282.

91. Interview with Robert Fisher, formerly education director of SEED, and now principal of Fremond School, San Francisco Unified School District, in San Francisco, March 31, 1975.

For the first time the Spanish-speaking population began to make itself visible. That community, concentrated in the Mission District, was politically fragmented into more than 200 small groups. But an Alinsky-style group, the Mission Coalition Organization, had begun to give residents some feeling of independent power, a belief that they could—were entitled to—influence conditions in their own schools.[92] Spokespersons went before the board of education in March 1967 seeking "a completely bilingual educational program from preschool through the adult level." Robert Gonzalez, representing the Mexican-American Political Alliance, addressed the board in Spanish, demanding "action, not talk."[93] These people were articulating the growing frustration of San Francisco's Latinos, whose youngsters had the highest drop-out rates in the city. The riot in Hunter's Point had produced a remarkable increase in programs for blacks, and while the Latinos were not threatening violence, a number of leaders were now willing to speak more forcefully on behalf of their constituents.[94]

The timing of these appeals was unfortunate, for they coincided with the release, in May of 1967, of the Stanford Research Institute's eight-volume, $205,000 study of the San Francisco schools, and its proposals for achieving a better racial balance.[95] Although the original contract contemplated community reviews of the alternative recommendations, conducted by SRI,[96] this provision was deleted in order to permit the new superintendent to choose his own format for community review. Responding to the SRI report consumed Jenkins's energies. Little attention was paid to these community-based movements, most of which did not concern themselves with desegregation, until the framing and implementation of the district court's remedy in *Johnson*.

The SRI Report and Jenkins's Response. The SRI study, released in the last days of the Spears administration, provided a critical test for the new superintendent. The report, entitled *Improving Racial Balance in the San Francisco Schools,* sought to show both the educational importance and the feasibility of just such an improvement; it offered a dozen alternative ways the district could go about the task of desegregation. The school board gave Superintendent Jenkins six months to study the SRI report and independently review the issue before presenting his recommendations. Liberals hoped that Jenkins would confirm his reputation as an integration-minded leader; the report afforded him the opportunity to act decisively. Conservatives were anxious. As long as Harold Spears had been in charge, they knew the administration would withstand pressures to alter the neighborhood school policy; would Jenkins react with similar

92. See Wirt, *supra* note 6, at 245–50.
93. San Francisco Examiner, March 10, 1967, at 1.
94. Interviews with Sal Cordova, Citizens' Advisory Committee member, currently director of Children's Bilingual Television, in Oakland; and Robert Lopez, Bilingual Task Force member, March 25, 1975.
95. Stanford Research Institute, Improving Racial Balance in the San Francisco Schools (1967).
96. *Id.,* Research Memo #8, at 1.

firmness? Both groups found themselves disappointed by the superintendent's reaction.

SRI's study had focused on desegregation. Jenkins's response, submitted on December 19, 1967, altered that focus. Its stress was "educational equality/quality,"[97] a phrase which was to recur in San Francisco's planning efforts during the next three years. The shift was more than semantic. SRI had been concerned about such mundane matters as school feeder patterns, the logistics of transportation, and the like; those issues, Jenkins suggested, reflected what was "typical" about San Francisco, but not what was "unique."[98] What San Francisco needed, Jenkins argued, were "ways to achieve a better racial and ethnic balance in the schools, ways that are consistent with the maintenance and extension of high educational standards for all students."[99]

Educational Quality/Equality, Jenkins's report, gave perfunctory attention to the SRI alternatives. Jenkins's aspirations were, however, broader than mere redistricting. He suggested, among other options, an "All-Year Outdoor Education Program."[100] an "Outdoor Science Resource Center . . . located in one of the rustic outdoor areas of the city itself . . . ,"[101] and an "Educational Park . . . a bold and dramatic approach in the pursuit of excellence for uban areas."[102]

The motivation behind these suggestions may well have been laudable—who would deny a new superintendent his educational visions? Their effect was simply to cloud the issue. The state and federal agencies that Jenkins had sought to co-opt into his planning were unpersuaded that the superintendent had any real interest in desegregation; they viewed the report as intended to bury the SRI proposals, not to reshape them into a form more fit for San Francisco. In a remarkably forthright evaluation, the California Department of Education's Bureau of Intergroup Relations, which had financed the writing of the Jenkins report, declared:

> The SRI alternatives . . . at least confronted the facts of [de facto segregation] and dealt with the reduction of imbalance. . . . It seems that the administration is unwilling to recommend any of the SRI alternatives. At the the same time, it seems unwilling to propose any definite plan of its own.[103]

That memorandum went on to point out that there existed plausible and polit-

97. Educational Equality/Quality Report #1: Program Alternatives (Stanford Research Institute, December 1967).

98. *Id.* at 9.

99. *Id.* at 14.

100. *Id.* at 28.

101. *Id.* at 29.

102. *Id.* at 36.

103. California State Department of Education, Bureau of Intergroup Relations, San Francisco's Report #1: Education Equality/Quality 1 (February 6, 1968).

ically feasible *"pilot or first-base programs of pairing, grade reorganization, school closing, and school enlargement. . . . This partial approach . . . would prove that the district means business in the matter of integration."*[104]

Jenkins had labeled his response "Report #1." He did not propose that the board adopt it, but rather that it be treated as a series of suggestions to which the "community" might react at a series of public forums.[105] Thus began San Francisco's second experiment in resolving the dilemma of desegregation through the vehicle of participatory democracy. Like the attempt two years earlier, this one proved a disaster.

The community meetings, which Jenkins had hoped would bring legitimacy, produced only conflict. Citizens' opinions about the schools' responsibility for reducing racial imbalance still ranged from the militant pro-desegregation position to support of neighborhood (and "naturally desegregated") schools; there had also emerged a nascent movement for some kind of community-controlled system. The forums provided an opportunity for these views to be vented; and, because they were better organized than the moderates, those holding extreme positions were most loudly heard. At the meetings little was heard about outdoor recreational and science programs; attention was riveted on busing.[106]

Jenkins's tactic had given the long-quiescent middle-class white parents the occasion to make their position plain; in the wake of the meetings, it was clear that their concerns would have to be met in designing new school arrangements.[107] Civil rights leaders found themselves forced to contend both with the school administration and the aroused community. Frustrated at having lost the initiative, fearful that the political crisis would escalate, 500 persons jammed the March 5, 1968 board meeting to demand that immediate steps be taken to produce racial desegregation.[108] The Coordinating Council on Integrated Education —the umbrella group for the civil rights, civic, and religious organizations— accused Jenkins of confusing the volume of the response with its relevance, and warned him not to act "on the basis of who speaks loudest."[109] What the council meant, of course, was that it no longer represented the only outside voice to be heard on the issue. The council submitted a memorandum describing a variety of

104. *Id.* (emphasis in original). Bureau of Intergroup Relations officials Frederick Grunsky and Theodore Neff noted that Superintendent Jenkins was never "really interested" in integration. Interviews, in Sacramento, April 23, 1975.

105. EE/Q Report #1: Program Alternatives 8 (December 1967). Jenkins reported that the idea of holding public forums was "foisted" on him by the state and federal consultants. Interview with Robert Jenkins, *supra* note 84.

106. In an analysis of the questions and comments aired at the meetings, the Human Relations Office noted that roughly half touched on the topic of busing. Memo, Report on Questions at the Nine Public Forums (Feb. 6, 1968); Memo, Final Report on EE/Q Forums (March 4, 1968).

107. Interview with Robert Jenkins, *supra* note 84, who said: "The forum revealed that people were concerned about busing, and we knew we would have to minimize this concern."

108. San Francisco Chronicle, March 6, 1968, at 1.

109. *Id.*

approaches for accomplishing desegregation of the elementary schools. It, as well as the NAACP, urged "flexibility" as the key to responsible action.[110]

The Citizens' Advisory Committee: Deflecting the Issue. Neither the board nor the superintendent was prepared to take any decisive action. Instead, Jenkins appointed two committees, a task force of administrators and teachers, and a 32-member citizens' advisory committee to the task force, to study all the proposals and to submit recommendations.[111] The task force did relatively little, because its members had other responsibilities; the citizens committee was an extraordinarily active group.

The citizens committee had been carefully selected to embrace a cross-section of community sentiment. It included representation from the NAACP and the Mothers Support Neighborhood Schools, as well as representatives from Hunter's Point–Bayview, the Latino community, the Jewish Communtiy Relations Council, and the Chinese Six Companies, the traditional Chinatown political and social organization. The majority of the committee's membership favored some action to promote desegregation.

The committee set to work immediately to assess the SRI and superintendent's recommendations. It adopted a tentative timetable which contemplated implementing some aspects of a total desegregation plan as early as the following September. This news was leaked to the press; the headline announcing the committee's proposal read "Integration Plan for San Francisco Schools OK'd."[112] The article raised the spectre of imminent busing, and the response was predictable. The board was confronted with a well-organized protest, and postponed its scheduled adoption of a policy statement to guide the committee's work.[113] On June 10, 1968, a lengthy and highly qualified statement was adopted. The statement had been preceded by a memorandum from the district's long-time legal counsel, Irving G. Breyer, to the superintendent, which concluded that:

> It is the legal responsibility of this school board to take positive, affirmative steps to alleviate racial imbalance. . . . If proposals recommended by the Superintendent are found to be practical and feasible by the Board of Education then it would be the legal responsibility of the school board to implement by proper action such recommendations.[114]

The policy statement committed the board "to improvement of quality education through the orderly integration of its schools, with due regard for sound

110. Proposal Submitted by the Coordinating Council for Integrated Schools on Methods to Improve Racial Balance in the SFUSD, (March 1968).
111. Letter from Robert Jenkins to Board of Education (n.d.); and list of Committee members, May 20, 1968.
112. San Francisco Chronicle, May 28, 1968, at 5.
113. *Id.,* June 5, 1968, at 11.
114. Memorandum from Irving R. Breyer to Robert E. Jenkins, Legal Responsibility of School District to Alleviate Racial Imbalance (May 13, 1968).

educational approaches and the unique problems of San Francisco." The statement was further hedged by the qualification, borrowed in part from Breyer's
memorandum, that only "practical plans that are reasonably feasible and
acceptable" would warrant board consideration. Lest anyone fear that sudden
dislocation of students was anticipated, the board set aside the 1968/69 school
year for initial planning, with intermediate and long-range plans to follow.[115]
No date for implementation was fixed. The board's statement, while stronger
than any previously put forward, also provided the board with a host of escape
hatches; not without accident had the drafting been done by a lawyer.

The committee's report, submitted in February 1969, was not unanimous.
The dissenters charged that the committee was "an effrontery to the citizens
of San Francisco . . . a tool of Dr. Jenkins . . . to implement his report despite
the mandate of the majority of this city as presented at the nine public forums."[116] The report did embrace desegregation, but in a markedly limited sense.
It focused its attention on the possibility of creating school clusters or "complexes" in the two western middle-class sections of the city, Richmond and
Park South.[117]

> The Committee urges the SFUSD to give the recommendations . . . top
> priority for implementation; in particular, the proposals for elementary
> school complexes. The recent separatist trend in San Francisco reflects,
> in part, a skepticism of the School District's willingness to move toward
> meaningful integration, but we are convinced that the school reorganiza-
> tion of the type we are recommending still has more than adequate sup-
> port among large segments of the San Francisco community, including its
> black community. However, every additional day of delay will only
> further reduce what faith remains in the School District's willingness to
> move ahead.[118]

Jenkins's response was predictable and, under the circumstances, proper. He
proposed that this report be studied by the parents, teachers, and administrators
in the 20 elementary schools of Richmond and Park South that would be affected
by the proposals. The superintendent had learned something from the earlier
fiasco of the public forums; this time, it was decided, there would be no large
meetings. Those involved at each school site would study and react independently to the report.

Yet even the device of fragmenting discussion could not contain the opposi-

---

115. Board of Education Policy Statement, June 10, 1968. Presaging the protest to
come, a resolution was submitted to the board by teamster official Jim O'Rourke of Local
85, claiming to represent 75,000 members, warning the district not to "deprive parents of
rights to send children to schools of their choices." San Francisco Chronicle, June 11, 1968,
at 11.

116. EE/Q Report No. 2, February 1969, at 49.

117. *Id.* at 7-11, 21, 37.

118. *Id.* at 3.

tion. The dissenting report had raised the possibility of imminent busing, and that red flag provoked vociferous—and, for the first time, violent—public response. At the March 18, 1968 board meeting, "intimidating squads of beefy goons" circulated and "administered brutal beatings to several members of the audience."[119] The violence was universally deplored, but the strength of the antagonism which it reflected persisted. "We will resist to our last breath the busing of our children far from their homes into other sections of the city," a spokesperson for the John Birch Society proclaimed.[120]

Planning the Complexes: The Almost-Peaceful Revolution. At the 20 Richmond and Park South school sites, discussion of the Complex proposal proceeded apace. Parents and teachers talked primarily about the effect of this new organizational structure on programs in the schools. "The idea of the Complex as we presented it," said Lucy Cannarozzi, who directed the process, "was really to improve educational quality through restructuring facilities, staff, and students."[121] One hundred thirty meetings during a four-month period elicited a myriad of ideas, including the assignment of a "resource teacher" to each school and the establishment of a "community council" which would afford parents some say in school decision-making. By May 1969, two years after the SRI study had been completed, Superintendent Jenkins announced that it was "Time For Action!"[122] He did not mean that the Complex concept would be implemented when school opened in the fall. Rather, he indicated that—in the aftermath of the Citizens Advisory Committee's report and the affected communities' reactions—the time had come to begin in earnest to plan and prepare for the proposed changes.

This delay dismayed the staunchest supporters of desegregation. Once again the NAACP discussed filing a lawsuit. Supervisor Francois, still a member of the NAACP board and by now clearly identified as a moderate, demurred, urging that the Complexes be given a chance to work;[123] Assemblyman Willie Brown, the Bay Area's most powerful black politician, also endorsed the Complex concept.[124] In the end, the NAACP voted unanimously not to proceed with litigation.

Prospects for success in the Complexes seemed remarkably good. There existed substantial support for the venture, both citywide and in the two areas whose schools would be reached. The board itself had become even more liberal, as conservative Commissioner Adolfo de Urioste was replaced by the younger, more dynamic David Sanchez; a majority of board members were now personal

119. San Francisco Chronicle, March 19, 1969, at 1.
120. *Id.* The speaker was Raymond Heaps.
121. Interview with Lucy Cannorazzi, formerly chairman, superintendent's Task Force on Educational Equality/Quality, currently Coordinator of Negotiations and Grievances for the district, in San Francisco, April 3, 1975.
122. EE/Q Report #3: Time for Action! May 20, 1969.
123. Interview with Terry Francois, *supra* note 81.
124. San Francisco Chronicle, June 4, 1969, at 1.

friends of, and continuing collaborators with, the civil rights movement. The Board voted to approve a schedule calling for the implementation of the Complexes in September 1970. Their approval was not, however, unqualified; it depended upon the availability of funding for the "quality" aspects of the program. Commissioner Colvin emphasized that the "plan must mean better education for the children involved."[125] To Laurel Glass, the board's action had brought the school system in line with the aspirations, if not the majority viewpoint, of the community. She urged: "Let's get out and really work together on this."[126]

A decade-long campaign by civil rights advocates had at last produced a tangible administrative response, a compromise tailored to the political realities of San Francisco, a victory for the NAACP in its ancient battle to secure desegregation. Many sections of the city remained unaffected by the proposal. OMI and SEED were progressing with their own plans for community renewal and control over their neighborhood schools. Few Spanish-speaking people were involved in the Complexes themselves, but by participating in the Citizens Advisory Committee, Hispanic community leaders had generated some support for the concept of bilingual education.[127] The Chinese Six Companies had also used the Citizens Advisory Committee as a forum to press for improvements in the instruction of Chinese immigrant children who were unable to speak English.[128] These communities continued to seek greater administrative responsiveness, and some regarded the Complexes as a hopeful sign, indicating new openness and willingness to embark on community-initiated ventures.

Only the white conservatives had suffered a serious setback in their efforts to maintain the status quo. The administration recognized this; its subsequent action was designed to overcome this lingering source of resistance, to press forward with the revivified concept of "equality/quality." The vehicle chosen for this purpose was the familiar one of community cooperation. Under the direction of Isadore Pivnick, Director of Innovative Planning, the process worked remarkably well. Pivnick set up Complex Advisory Councils in Richmond and Park South whose membership included principals, teachers, parents, and organizational representatives, meeting together in joint committees, designing the quality components that were to distinguish the Complexes and win public endorsement of the idea.[129]

Conceived by a clique of white liberals on the Citizens Advisory Committee, blessed by the Board of Education, the Complex idea assumed real form during

125. San Francisco Board of Education, Minutes, June 10, 1969, at 7. (During the 1960s, the Board ceased the practice of maintaining verbatim transcripts of its meetings.)

126. San Francisco Chronicle, June 11, 1969, at 1.

127. *See* note 116, *supra; see also* EE/Q Report #3: Time for Action!, May 20, 1969, at 13.

128. EE/Q Report #2, February 1969, at 25–31 (*Bilingual Programs for Language Handicapped Chinese*).

129. Interview with Isadore Pivnick, in San Francisco, April 13, 1975; also Complex Planning: A Preliminary Report, October 14, 1969, at 3–5.

the fall of 1969. Hundreds of persons gathered faithfully on Wednesday nights to work out the many administrative details of the plan: who would teach what, and where; what kinds of programs would be offered; what transportation arrangements were most suitable. Discussion and reports on these and other aspects of the new programs progressed rapidly, to meet the board's December deadline.

The superintendent's December 1969 progress report to the Board contained over 200 pages of details about the implementation of the Complexes, although specific pupil and teacher assignments, bus routes, and model curriculum components were not yet completed.[130] Shortly thereafter, the board endorsed the progress report by authorizing $1.2 million from the 1970/71 budget for the Complexes, contingent upon the superintendent's raising a comparable amount from outside sources.[131] "Promising possibilities" for such funds had already been identifed.[132]

At the beginning of 1970 it seemed that the peaceful revolution was at hand. San Francisco was going to desegregate some of its schools, not because it had been ordered to but because it saw that as the right thing to do. The planning process had been carefully designed to recruit the support—or at least quiet the opposition—of conservatives; it had also been structured to produce a plan that had a chance of accomplishing more than the mixing of racial groups. There even existed the hope that, if the Complexes worked, a variation of the same theme might be attempted in other, more ghettoized parts of the city. Yet six months later the situation was a shambles. Conservative opposition, sparked by the timely intervention of Mayor Joseph A. Alioto, grew increasingly vehement; the board wavered in the face of perceived resource inadequacies, and the NAACP, stung once too often by the politicization of the desegregation issue, filed suit in federal district court on June 24, 1970.

The Breakdown of Fragile Consensus. The fiscal and political crises arose almost simultaneously. By early spring it had become clear that the superintendent's early optimism about the availability of substantial outside funding was unfounded.[133]

The Economic "Necessity" of Compromise. The superintendent's final progress report was due on May 19. Board President Alan Nichols had been busily seeking public support for the Complexes, calling them "pilot programs: If they work, we can apply the idea elsewhere in San Francisco." But "to have them work requires more money," he noted.[134] The critical question remained: If

130. EE/Q: Schools for Living—An Adventure in Education, December 16, 1969 [hereinafter cited as Schools for Living].
131. San Francisco Board of Education, Minutes, January 6, 1970.
132. Schools for Living, *supra* note 151, at 10–11.
133. EE/Q Progress Report, March 30, 1970.
134. San Francisco Chronicle, February 12, 1970, at 1. Supervisor Diane Feinstein, a prospective mayoral candidate, had warned that if the complexes were impeded, the result

there was no more money, what would the school board do? In his May 19 Report, Jenkins suggested three alternatives:

Plan A: Implement both complexes, but reduce by half the number of participating schools.

Plan B: Implement one complex only.

Plan C: Implement both complexes and provide what quality components the limited budget allows.[135]

The superintendent recommended Plan C. The board felt otherwise; it decided against that plan on the basis of its prior commitment to the "equality/quality" concept of integration, and voted instead for the Solomonic Plan A.[136]

This solution pleased neither Richmond nor Park South. In a negotiating session involving representatives of both Complexes' Advisory Councils and the Teachers' Council, chaired by Board President Nichols, it was decided to request that the board reconsider its vote and instead approve Plan B, implementing the Richmond Complex, while providing some funds to permit the Park South group to continue its planning. Park South's representatives were not delighted with the outcome, but recognized that the Richmond organization was more socially and economically cohesive, and more politically influential with board members.[137] At its May 27 meeting, the board acceded to this position and approved Plan B.[138]

The Politics of Opposition. In 1970 the office of Mayor Joseph Alioto was a "fortress besieged."[139] Charges that the mayor had ties to the Mafia, though ultimately refuted, robbed him of any chance to run for the governorship in 1970 and forced him to focus his energies on reelection as mayor.[140] The desegregation issue was his vehicle for reestablishing political support. Alioto became, by choice, the focal point for political opposition to the Complex proposal.

This position was, to all appearances, a strange one. The mayor had built his reputation in good part on his capacity to work with the black community, particularly its younger leaders. "In his 1967 campaign, by his own account, Alioto forged an alliance with 'the black trade unionists, the young poverty workers,

might be the "massive upheaval" of a lawsuit. San Francisco Chronicle, February 12, 1970, at 1.

135. EE/Q Progress Report, May 19, 1970, at 4–7.

136. San Francisco Board of Education, Minutes, May 19, 1970, at 20.

137. Interviews with Nicki Salan, in San Francisco, March 2, 1975; Peter Mezey, in San Francisco, March 20, 1975; and Janet Benson, Richmond Teachers' Council Chairman, in San Francisco, March 25, 1975.

138. San Francisco Board of Education, Minutes, May 27, 1970. Chairman Nichols, however, refused to change his vote.

139. Interview with John De Luca, executive deputy to the mayor, in San Francisco, April 24, 1975.

140. Wirt, *The Politics of Hyperpluralism* in Culture and Civility in San Francisco 101, 118 (H. Becker ed. 1971); De Luca interview, *supra* note 139.

and the Baptists Ministers Union,' as well as with the women activists . . . against the active opposition of other and more established blacks. . . ."[141] He won a smashing election victory in Hunter's Point, and paid his debt with jobs and positions of community leadership. As John DeLuca, executive deputy to the mayor, put it: "Racial relations were, and are, this administration's top priority. We've created a whole new black middle class; 90 percent of those street sweepers who are earning $17,000 a year are black."[142]

Yet the position Alioto took was in fact consistent with views he had held since he defended the school board in the 1962 NAACP litigation. He favored desegregation, including voluntary busing of all students and obligatory busing of secondary school students, if necessary; he believed that school boundaries should be designed consciously to reduce racial isolation. He had appointed two liberals—Sanchez and Howard Nemerowski, a Great Society returnee—to the board of education. At mandatory elementary school busing, however, he drew the line. Six-year-olds were too young to have to ride a bus in order to affirm a principle. That was the position he carried to the community. It produced political shock-waves.[143]

The mayor plunged into the political thicket. He was in regular private contact with Superintendent Jenkins, urging him not to surrender to pressure.[144] At a meeting called in February by conservative parents in the Clarendon School, part of the proposed Park South Complex, Alioto made his position plain:

> Integration is a necessity and not just a legal necessity, but a moral necessity. But it ought not to be achieved by busing young children from their home environment. . . . The majority of parents don't favor this [Complex] plan, and neither do the majority of teachers and principals.[145]

The strongest response to Alioto came from Charles Belle, recently elected president of the San Francisco NAACP. Belle had earlier criticized Jenkin's plan because "it leaves out the most segregated sections of the city—Hunter's Point, Sunset [a white working-class neighborhood], and Chinatown," and proposed a "return to the militant activism" of the mid-sixties to counteract what he called a resurgence of "reaction and racism."[146] The mayor's intervention caused Belle to explode: "I am sick and tired and ashamed of the segregated

141. Wirt, *supra* note 6, at 266.

142. De Luca interview, *supra* note 139.

143. The foregoing account is based on interviews with John De Luca, *supra* note 139; Leroy Cannon, counsel to the board of education, in San Francisco, April 8, 1975; Terry Francois, *supra* note 81; Howard Nemerowski, member of the board of education, 1970-1972, in San Francisco, March 26, 1972; Earl Raab, *supra* note 60. Not surprisingly, the interpretations given to Alioto's actions varied markedly among the interviewees.

144. Interview with Robert Jenkins, *supra* note 84.

145. San Francisco Chronicle, February 4, 1970, at 1.

146. *Id.,* February 2, 1970, at 16.

school situation in San Francisco. We know white racists want to keep segregated white and black schools here."[147] On behalf of the NAACP, Belle threatened to file a lawsuit if the board did not respond to his demand that a plan for citywide integration be presented within 60 days.[148]

Into this controversy, materializing so suddenly after months of painstaking community amelioration, another divisive element was added. Supervisor John Barbagelata announced plans to present a policy statement to the voters in June, polling them on the question of mandatory busing.[149] School Board President Nichols was bitter about the deterioration of the board's attempt to do what it believed was prudent and right. "Alioto has created the polarization. . . Bringing politics and the judiciary into educational decision will damage them and undo the progress we are making."[150] That remark proved prophetic.

The high point in this drama was marked by Alioto's appearance on February 24 before the school board, as a "citizen," before a packed audience. He strongly argued for reconsideration of the board's December 1969 decision to fund the Complexes; Supervisor Barbagelata added the request that the board support his anti-busing ballot measure. To balance the political pressure, Assemblyman Willie Brown pleaded with the board to ignore these views and urged them to move forward rapidly, before the black community lost patience. A long list of speakers asked to be heard on both sides of the question. After listening to a representative sample, board members expressed their own views. Every member spoke out against the mayor's request. Most pointed out that the busing involved in the Complexes was minimal, and detailed the quality components of the Complex concept. Unanimously, they rejected the mayor's attempt to reverse their decision and criticized his interference with an independent governing body.[151]

Alioto and Barbagelata continued their campaign over the next several months, and in June the voters declared their support for Alioto's position. By nearly a three-to-one margin they asserted that the board of education should not be permitted to bus or reassign elementary school children to schools outside their neighborhoods without parental consent.[152] The referendum was merely a policy statement with no binding effect on the board, but it gave Alioto additional political credibility. The Mayor promised to do whatever he could to convince the school board members to abandon their plan for busing children in the Complex, and announced that he would recommend that a city charter amendment calling for an elected school board be placed on the ballot. Alioto recognized that he had lost this round of the political battle; he urged

147. *Id.,* February 4, 1970, at 1.
148. *Id.,* February 6, 1970, at 1.
149. *Id.,* February 4, 1970, at 1.
150. *Id.,* February 6, 1970, at 1.
151. San Francisco Examiner, February 25, 1970, at 1. *See also* San Francisco Board of Education, Minutes, February 24, 1970.
152. San Francisco Chronicle, June 4, 1970, at 1.

those who agreed with his position to file a lawsuit seeking to enjoin the Richmond Complex from being implemented.[153]

This suggestion was acted upon, and suit was duly filed in California Superior Court.[154] It was not, however, the most important case to be filed that month. Alioto's statements had persuaded NAACP President Belle that a desegregation suit could wait no longer. As he told Superintendent Jenkins: "I had hoped that we might avoid this, but the Mayor has turned desegregation into a political and emotional battleground. We'll get an instant solution in federal court."[155]

JOHNSON v. SAN FRANCISCO UNIFIED SCHOOL DISTRICT: THE UNPROSECUTED UNDEFENDED SUIT

The NAACP filed suit because, in the end, it had to. Alioto had raised the political ante to a point where some response was necessary. A lawsuit, always regarded as a vital tactic in the struggle to improve opportunities, had become the appropriate symbolic response to what was viewed as the white community's attempt to frustrate black aspirations. More pragmatically, the constitutional meaning of de jure segregation had expanded markedly since the NAACP filed its first complaint in 1962; a favorable court ruling, if not inevitable, could reasonably be expected.

The Initial Stages of the Lawsuit

The Plaintiffs' Case. It was one thing for San Francisco NAACP President Charles Belle to threaten a lawsuit, quite another for the organization actually to find a lawyer capable of the task and willing to do the work. The national organization, which had urged that a suit be brought, was heavily committed to the Detroit litigation,[156] and had neither lawyers nor resources to spare. The local chapter had lots of generals but few foot soldiers, at least among the ranks of its attorneys. James Herndon, a black lawyer associated with Charles Garry's San Francisco firm, volunteered to "coordinate" the effort, but he lacked the time to undertake the needed legal and factual research.[157] Ultimately it was Arthur Brunwasser, a young solo practitioner in San Francisco, who took on the case.

Brunwasser, the co-chairman of the American Jewish Congress Education Committee, was not—indeed, is not—a member of the NAACP, and had no pre-

153. *Id.* Also interview with Myra Berkowitz, who organized the meeting, in San Francisco, April 8, 1970.

154. Nelson v. San Francisco Unified School District, No. 618-463, San Francisco County Superior Court, June 15, 1970.

155. Interview with Robert Jenkins, *supra* note 84.

156. Milliken v. Bradley, 418 U.S. 714 (1974).

157. Interview with James Herndon, in San Francisco, April 8, 1975.

vious involvement in San Francisco's civil rights dispute. He had, however, grown enthusiastic about the Complex proposal (his daughter was to enter a school in the Complexes the next fall) and, like so many others, had been angered by Mayor Alioto's assault on the idea. Unlike the others, however, Brunwasser was interested in doing something; in the spring of 1970 he contacted James Herndon, offered his services, and found himself the chief attorney in the case.

"No one in the Bay Area had any experience with desegregation litigation,"[158] Brunwasser noted, and he was no exception. It was easy enough to identify a handful of black parents willing to sign on to a complaint. Putting together the factual case was a different proposition. The school expenditures-pupil performance data, which NAACP Education Committee Chairmen Lois Barnes and, later, Ann Bloomfield had developed, were marginally useful. But Brunwasser was obliged to do his own digging into the schools' records about building construction, school racial composition, and the like, in order to make out a case for illegal segregation. He got help in that endeavor not from the NAACP but from Nicki Salan, a parent who had been deeply involved in the Park South Complex planning. Between April and June, Brunwasser labored both to learn the relevant law and to apply it to the facts of San Francisco.

When the complaint was finally filed on June 24, 1970, it made page one news. It asked for "a preliminary and permanent injunction ordering the immediate and complete desegregation of the student bodies, faculties, and administrative personnel in the public elementary schools in San Francisco."[159] It also sought a temporary restraining order compelling the district to proceed with plans for the Richmond Complex; the board's wavering on that issue had left Brunwasser and the NAACP uneasy.

The scope of the suit was deliberately limited to the elementary schools. The NAACP felt that desegregation during the early years of schooling, before children's racial attitudes had had a chance to harden, was crucial; indeed, if primary school desegregation really worked, there might not be a need for court-ordered action for junior and senior high schools.[160] Time constraints also forced the limitation; the fact of segregation, as well as its ostensible causes, was more easily established for elementary than secondary schools.

The complaint in *Johnson* was consciously patterned after the recently concluded Pontiac litigation, which had stretched the bounds of de jure segregation farther than any previous federal court.[161] Inaction by a school board in the face of knowledge of segregation is tantamount to deliberate segregation, Judge Keith had held, and Brunwasser hoped to persuade the federal district court

158. Interview with Arthur Brunwasser, in San Francisco, March 24, 1975.

159. Civil Rights Action for Injunctive Relief, 1 Record 1, 6 (June 24, 1970) Johnson v. Unified School District, 339 F. Supp. 1315 (N.D. Calif. 1971) [hereinafter cited as Record].

160. Interviews with Lois Barnes, *supra* note 78, Ann Bloomfield, *supra* note 79, and Charles Belle, president of the NAACP, 1969–1971, in San Francisco, March 25, 1975.

161. Davis v. School District of City of Pontiac, 309 F. Supp. 734, *aff'd*, 443 F.2d 573 (6th Cir. 1971).

to apply the same standard. Brunwasser sought to demonstrate that San Francisco had sinned, both in what it had done and what it failed to do, and hence could be charged with de jure segregation.[162] To establish this, plaintiffs' case cited school district data which revealed increases in racial segregation between 1964/65 (the first year such figures had been published) and 1969/70. It reiterated the decade-long history of discussion and investigation of segregation in San Francisco's schools, placing particular emphasis on the SRI report and legal counsel Breyer's May 1968 memorandum to the board, in order to show the district's awareness of segregation, and the culpability which consequently could be attached to its subsequent inaction. Brunwasser identified a correlation—weak, but nonetheless real—between relatively low salary expenditures for teachers in primarily-black schools and student performance. He traced the maintenance of segregation to ten school construction projects which had been authorized or implemented during the past decade; among the new schools which allegedly had made San Francisco a more segregated district were several that were placed upon sites urged upon the board by the NAACP, which in 1964 was insisting upon the construction of neighborhood schools in Bayview-Hunter's Point as the price for its support of a school bond issue.[163] And he attacked OMI and SEED, not for their aspirations, but instead for their failure to reduce segregation.[164]

Two depositions were critical to this aspect of plaintiffs' case. William Cobb, the district's human relations officer, reluctantly admitted that he had advised the superintendent that several contemplated construction projects would increase racial imbalance. "I voiced opinions on practically all of these," Cobb stated, but they were not followed.[165] Cobb qualified his statement by noting that "[t]he controlling factor, whether you put a school here or whether you put an addition there, many times, doesn't rest on the effect of racial balance," a point which went wholly ignored.[166] Laurel Glass—professor at San Francisco State, NAACP member, and school board commissioner—proved to be Brunwasser's star witness. As she reported later, Glass was in a "touchy situation. I believed in the suit, but didn't want to incriminate the school system."[167] Her statements, although tinged with the caution that one would expect of an academic, were damaging to the district; they corroborated Brunwasser's assertions that little had been done to improve racial balance, and that the neighborhood school policy actively "discourages the achievement of racial integration."[168] Conspicuously absent from plaintiffs' case were some of the traditional

162. *See generally* Memorandum of Acts Constituting De Jure Segregation, 4 Record 711 (Sept. 17, 1970).
163. See text at note 57, *supra.*
164. See Deposition of Laurel Glass, 3 Record 322, 335–38 (July 20, 1970).
165. Deposition of William Cobb, 3 Record 304, 316 (July 14, 1970).
166. *Id.* at 318.
167. Interview with Laurel Glass, *supra* note 85.
168. Glass deposition, *supra* note 164, at 344.

elements of a de jure segregation case: detailed accounts of gerrymandering school boundaries in order to maintain racial separation, the busing of black children past white schools to attend predominantly black schools, or other more clearly segregatory conduct. Such evidence either was not available or had not been located.

The heart of plaintiff's case was not this recital of evil. Brunwasser attempted to show that segregation was harmful to black children.[169] He relied on the SRI report and the nationally known Coleman report as authoritative sources for the proposition (overstating the relevance of those findings). Laurel Glass was helpful also: "In my opinion, segregated education is an inferior education . . . [S]egregation within the context of societal attitudes reinforces for the black child that he is separate and inferior, and for the white child reinforces that he is separate and superior—both things are psychologically damaging, in my opinion."[170] The only witness Brunwasser called at the trial was Allan Wilson, professor of education at Berkeley, who testified: "There is substantial evidence that the longer a child exists in an inferior school, and most segregated schools are inferior, the worse his performance will be subsequently." A delay of one semester, Wilson argued, "would . . . cause irreparable educational harm to the black children in [a segregated] school."[171]

In short, plaintiffs' case combined a thinly argued claim that de jure segregation existed, placing strong emphasis on the hurtfulness of segregation itself; what sound policy should be, rather than what the Constitution requires in this instance, was stressed. As it turned out, plaintiffs did not have to do more, for the case was as weakly defended as it was argued.

San Francisco's Response. The board of education quietly welcomes the lawsuit.[172] It apparently favored desegregation, yet lacked the political will to implement it. In that context the lawsuit was a lifesaver. The court could resolve the board's dilemma by ordering it to do what the board felt was right, but which politically it could not undertake on its own.[173]

This attitude was reflected in the board's reliance on the city attorney's office to defend the suit. Although the city attorney handles almost all school litigation, the district had, in the past, sought outside counsel; indeed, when the NAACP filed its 1962 desegregation suit, it retained Joseph Alioto. At that time

169. Interview with Arthur Brunwasser, *supra* note 158. Brunwasser indicated that, if obliged to do so, he could have made a more substantial showing of intentional segregation.

170. Glass deposition, *supra* note 164, at 328–39.

171. Transcript, July 30, 1970 Hearing, 24–25 [hereinafter cited as transcript].

172. Interviews with Laurel Glass, *supra* note 85; Zuretti Goosby, *supra* note 81; Claire Lilienthal, member of the school board, 1958–1972, in San Francisco, March 14, 1975.

173. Only Alan Nichols, who shortly thereafter announced his resignation from the board, expressed reservations about the justice of a court order, given the failure of school authorities to resolve the deeply felt differences of opinion about desegregation. As he put it, "Reliance on the Court is not the best method for achieving what should be the common goal—fair and equal educational opportunity." San Francisco Chronicle, June 25, 1970, at 4.

446   Limits of Justice

the board had wanted to win (or at least achieve a favorable settlement of) the suit. This time, it wasn't so sure. George Krueger, the young deputy city attorney called upon to defend the case, had only recently begun to handle school litigation; most of his school-related work involved personal-injury suits.[174] The *Johnson* case was his first federal court appearance. But Krueger was a competent trial lawyer, who persuaded the board that he understood the record of the case, the law, and the particular problems confronting San Francisco.

Time was a handicap to Krueger Plaintiffs had been preparing their case for several months before it was filed; moreover, they could rely to some extent on years of earlier research. Krueger, with a dozen other cases on his calendar, had a month to respond. Ironically, one of those other cases involved defending the district in a suit seeking to block the implementation of the Richmond Complex.[175] "On Mondays and Wednesday, I'd wear my white hat, on Tuesday and Thursdays my black hat," he ruefully recalled.[176]

The district's case was straightforward. Krueger viewed plaintiffs as having to demonstrate specific acts of de jure segregation; he did not seek to show ways in which the district had *not* acted illegally, believing that to be an impossible and time-devouring task. The very vagueness of plaintiffs' accusations—a memorandum outlining asserted acts of deliberate segregation was not filed until September, by which time the case was under submission—made the defense more difficult. Krueger argued that the district had no duty to correct racial imbalance, and that "the best refutation of the *de jure* charge was the history of voluntary efforts to integrate."[177] Plaintiffs' evidence concerning the harm allegedly worked by segregation, whatever its cause, drew no response.

Thus, plaintiffs and defendants found themselves relying largely on the same record; the difference lay in its interpretation. To plaintiffs the record revealed a decade of evasion and delay; to defendants it demonstrated the good will of the district in trying to desegregate. Plaintiffs and defendants were not the only parties, or would-be parties, to the litigation. Holders of all the divergent points of view—the predominantly white, middle-class parents' groups, who now called themselves Concerned Parents; those blacks who preferred to run their own schools rather than be merged into unenthusiastic white neighborhood schools; and the Chinatown and Mission communities, reluctant to be drawn into the settlement of what was perceived as a black-white issue—sought an opportunity to be heard at some stage of the proceedings. The introduction of their cacophanous points of view introduced the court to the dimensions of this political issue.

174. Interview with George Krueger, Deputy City Attorney since 1965, in San Francisco, March 20, 1975.

175. *See* note 154, *supra.*

176. Interview with George Krueger, *supra* note 174.

177. *Id. See also* Memorandum in Opposition to Motion for Preliminary Injunction, 2 Record 16, July 20, 1970.

The Initial Intervenors. *Concerned Parents.* The conservative parents in Richmond had heeded Alioto's advice. On June 15 they filed suit charging that the adoption of the Richmond Complex plan violated federal and state constitutional and statutory rights.[178] A week later they found themselves upstaged by *Johnson,* a suit seeking far broader relief than they were resisting. On July 28 they filed a motion to intervene in the case.[179]

The intervenors included blacks, Chinese, Latinos, as well as whites. Their unhappiness lay not with "natural" desegregation, but with district efforts to uproot the neighborhood. The trial brief in the superior court suit, submitted with the motion to intervene, offered a ringing defense of the neighborhood school. "It is traditionally a local school, the Little Red Schoolhouse; an American tradition; a center of community life; and a pillar in the American conception of freedom."[180]

The intervenors' lawyer, Raymond Bright, was a local trial attorney, a sometime politician (self-described as a "Percy Republican"), who entered the case because his friends asked him to. He turned to a long-time solo practitioner, Julian Beek, to draft the needed documents.[181] Beek produced literally hundreds of pages of memoranda and motions, to little avail. The intervenors' primary concern was to stop the Richmond Complex, an issue of no interest to the court. Even when they sought to broaden their argument, the intervenors were permitted to play only a limited role at the factfinding stage of the inquiry.

The Brief Emergence of the Community-Control Issue. The NAACP had a particular interest in searching out black lawyers to carry the lawsuit. In Edward Bell they thought they had found their man. Bell had just graduated from Hastings Law School; a month earlier he had joined San Francisco's Neighborhood Legal Assistance Foundation. Although he was uninterested in desegregation, Bell agreed to work on the case because "that's where the action was." His real hope was to use the suit as a vehicle to further the prospects of community-controlled schools in San Francisco's black neighborhoods.[182]

A remark by Judge Weigel during the first day of the hearing gave Bell his opportunity. Weigel raised a number of questions he hoped the hearings would answer. "I [also] want you gentlemen to consider and provide me answers [to] . . . this question. . . . Assuming minority groups desire separate schools, and assuming they can show that such schools would not be inferior, should that desire, if it is manifested to this Court, be considered by the Court?" Weigel elaborated on his question. "[T]here's something new that's coming along. . . .

178. See note 154, *supra.*
179. Motion to Intervene, 3 Record 392, July 28, 1970.
180. Petitioners' Trial Brief on Federal and State Law, 3 Record 397, 439, July 28, 1970.
181. Interview with Raymond Bright, in San Francisco, March 24, 1975.
182. Interview with Edward Bell, in Oakland, April 7, 1975.

There [is] beginning to emerge a demand on the part of large segments of minority groups, particularly among the blacks, that they run their own schools and [that] they have black schools."[183]

Weigel wanted to know whether such desires were constitutionally relevant, and Bell undertook to draft a memorandum which responded affirmatively. His colleagues, Brunwasser and Herndon, were shocked. Bell talked privately with Weigel, and agreed to withdraw from the case. Although Bell sought subsequently to appear as *amicus,* and to require that individual notice be given to 14,000 black families,[184] his position—"that *Brown* says that it is unconstitutional to maintain schools that result in inferior education to black children. It is not unconstitutional for segregated schools to exist"[185] —was never again heard in the proceedings.

The Court as "Inquisitor"[186]

In the hands of a less firm judge, the multiplicity of positions advanced in *Johnson* could have led to anarchy in the courtroom. But Judge Stanley A. Weigel was able closely to control the proceedings—all too well, in the judgment of the intervenors and his outside critics.

Judge Weigel had sat on the federal bench since 1962, when President Kennedy rewarded the prominent Republican lawyer for his support in the 1960 election. Weigel had long been interested in civil liberties issues; in the early 1950s he defended 21 professors fired by the University of Claifornia for refusing to sign a loyalty oath.[187] The judge was no stranger to controversy on the bench. The previous April, in a suit brought to block construction of the Yerba Buena urban redevelopment project until residents of the area had been given replacement housing, Weigel issued the most sweeping injunction against an urban renewal project that had ever been seen. Eighteen months later, he would be asked by Peter Tamaras, a member of the San Francisco Board of Supervisors, to disqualify himself from both the Yerba Buena and the *Johnson* lawsuits on grounds of bias. "Judge Weigel is a wealthy man to whom many things have come easy," Tamaras said. "He lives in a penthouse on Russian Hill. He never had to look for a job. Maybe he has some sense of guilt for making a lot of money and sending his children to private schools. . . . He shouldn't get his therapy by halting the Yerba Buena Center and ordering crosstown busing."[188] Weigel

183. Transcript, July 30, 1970, at 15.
184. *Id.,* August 12, 1970, at 69–70.
185. *Id.,* August 5, 1970, at 67.
186. For a discussion of the "inquisitorial" mode of dispute resolution, see Thibault, Walker, LaTour & Holden, *Procedural Justice as Fairness,* 26 Stanford L. Rev. 1271, 1273–74 (1974).
187. San Francisco Chronicle, July 7, 1962, at 7.
188. San Francisco Examiner, January 25, 1972, at 7. For a discussion of the Yerba Buena case, *see generally* C. Hartman, Yerba Buena: Land Grab and Community Resistance in California (1974); Wirt, *supra* note 6, at 295–304.

survived the attack handsomely; his performance was vindicated by Chief District Court Judge Oliver J. Carter.[189]

This kind of experience breeds toughness, and Weigel demonstrated that quality early in the *Johnson* proceedings. He conducted the hearings vigorously, demanding—and getting—concise arguments from the lawyers.[190] The judge did not hesitate to inform the parties when, in his judgment, an issue was settled; remarks viewed as extraneous—particularly about the Richmond Complex— were quickly cut off. As a consequence the hearings were more truncated than either the district or the Concerned Parents intervenors had hoped for. Weigel's stated desire "to flush out every point of view" was not fully reflected in his actions. There was no trial in the case—only hearings on the motion for a preliminary injunction. A portion of one day was devoted to hearing plaintiffs' single witness, and a part of another day was given over to intervenors' witnesses.[191] The district's own data, the depositions, and the briefs: these were the bases upon which argument proceeded.

At the outset of the hearings, Weigel stated his view of the issues: although the board had not acted with "bad faith or malice" there nonetheless existed "substantial racial imbalance in many, many of the schools in this city," which meant that black children "do not have equal educational opportunity."[192] A critical question remained. As Weigel phrased it: "Does not a school board, which for ten years has known of the existence of serious racial imbalance, have a positive duty to do everything it can to act effectively in the interest of eliminating that imbalance?"[193] To the extent that the judge's question was intended to reflect positive law, as contrasted with moral obligations, it went well beyond prevailing doctrine; this matter, too, received cursory attention at the hearings.

Throughout the hearings Weigel sought settlement. As the proceedings ended, he declared:

> I still very much prefer—if this is a fertile seed, let it sprout—I would very much prefer to have the Board . . . by a certain date come up with a specific plan for the provision of equal educational opportunity, including meaningful correction of the racial imbalance, to be finished by a certain date, specifying the date when it is going to be completed.[194]

The judge made it clear that he would not wait indefinitely for such a resolu-

---

189. San Francisco Chronicle, February 8, 1972, at 1.

190. Because of the pendency of the *Johnson* litigation, Judge Weigel was unwilling to be interviewed. Analysis of the role he played is based primarily on the voluminous transcripts; secondarily on interviews with some of the lawyers who participated in the case.

191. Transcript, July 30, 1970, at 20–42; Transcript, August 6, 1970, at 25–36.

192. *Id.*, July 30, 1970, at 6, 7, 13.

193. *Id.*, August 6, 1970, at 8.

194. *Id.*, August 25, 1970, at 24.

tion: "Don't we have in pretty much everything we need to have for the definitive and final action of the Court?[195]

Judge Weigel had little doubt that desegregation in the "City That Knows How" would be more effective if embraced voluntarily than in the face of a court order. The then-pending *Swann*[196] case gave Weigel a chance to test whether his hopes for such a resolution were realistic. On September 11 he issued an "Order Setting Aside Submission" of the case until *Swann* was decided; at that time he stated that "this court should be able to act with greater certitude and, therefore, with greater fairness to all concerned."[197]

The September 22 order was also expressly cast as an invitation to the district to plan for eventual desegregation.

> This decision to postpone judgment should not be misinterpreted. Defendants should prepare themselves to be ready promptly to meet whatever requirements may be delineated by the Supreme Court. . . . [They] would do well promptly to develop plans calculated to meet the different contingencies which can reasonably be forecast. *If, for example, the Board of Education works out details for maximum changes based upon the assumption that the Supreme Court will require them, the Board will then be able to act effectively, in case of need, without causing confusion and with a minimum of unnecessary dislocation.*[198]

This invitation asked the district to undertake contingency plans, something that rational organizations are routinely supposed to do. Yet it was essentially ignored until April 1971, when *Swann* was decided and the court reached the remedial phase of the case. The problem was not that the message went unnoticed, but simply that the board of education was far too busy with immediate, pressing problems—including the breaking-in of a new superintendent —to act on the off-chance that it would forestall "unnecessary dislocation."

THE INTERREGNUM: SEPTEMBER 1970– APRIL 1971

Every year during the past decade has seen a crisis in American education. For San Francisco, the 1970/71 school term was worse than most. The school district, which hastily recruited a new superintendent, was faced with a bewildering assortment of problems, few of them directly linked with desegregation. The year included, among other events,[199] a protracted teachers' strike; a report that

195. *Id.,* August 12, 1970, at 77.
196. Swann v. Charlotte-Mecklenburg Board of Education, 402 U.S. 1 (1971).
197. Order Setting Aside Submission, September 22, 1970, at 4.
198. *Id.* at 5 (emphasis added).
199. This litany is drawn from Weiner, Educational Decisions in an Organized Anarchy 437–70 (unpublished Ph.D. dissertation, Stanford University, 1972) [hereinafter cited as Weiner] ; the items noted in the text are representative, not exhaustive.

62 schools were vulnerable to earthquake damage and would imminently have to be reconstructed or closed; the proposed "deselection" of white administrators and principals as a means of paring the central administrative staff while retaining newly hired minority professionals; student strikes over asserted administrative recalcitrance and demonstrably wretched conditions; a busing protest in the Richmond Complex; suits filed by the Chinese- and Mexican-American communities against the district which alleged that their children's educational needs had been ignored; a demand that a $500,000 black studies program be created in an inner-city high school; approval of a student-drafted bill of rights; and the district's first financial crisis—a reported $6.7 million deficit—in recent history. Small wonder, then, that Superintendent Shaheen would comment in April 1971, after barely nine months on the job, "I've never been so exhausted in all my life."[200] Small wonder also that planning for desegregation was perceived as an issue that could safely be ignored.

The Dilemma of Leadership

A New Superintendent and a Backlog of Bureaucratic Problems. Superintendent Spears had developed and trained a staff of administrators he could trust, during the long absences of his last years, to keep daily operations running efficiently; under Jenkins, that loyalty dissolved, staff members established fiefdoms, factions emerged, and Jenkins had trouble commanding performance.[201] Jenkins's sudden resignation left the board little time to search for a successor.

The board ignored the advice of the teachers' organizations, which proposed insider Milton Reiterman, head of personnel.[202] Instead they reached to Rockford, Illinois, to find Thomas Shaheen. Shaheen was not the board's first choice. But it was late in the hiring season, and Shaheen appeared strong, articulate, and a man of principle.[203] He convinced the board that he was totally committed to desegregated education, and that he saw no need to incorporate quality components to make the concept practicable. Shaheen had a reputation for aggressiveness, even ruthlessness, qualities which board members themselves lacked and which they saw as essential in coping with the prevailing, politically charged climate.

Shaheen styled himself a communicator. He organized encounter groups for top administrative staff as a device to encourage candor.[204] He filled his days

200. San Francisco Chronicle, April 9, 1971, at 1.

201. Interview with Albert Silverstein, director of planning under Superintendent Jenkins, in San Francisco, March 28, 1975.

202. San Francisco Examiner, August 21, 1970, at 1.

203. Interview with Laurel Glass, *supra* note 85, who—together with Commissioner Nemerowski—went to Rockford to interview Shaheen.

204. Interviews with Thomas Shaheen, superintendent from 1971–1973, in Valley Cottage, New York, March 23, 1975 (telephone interview); and Irving Breyer, legal advisor to the San Francisco Unified School District, 1933–1974, in San Francisco, April 18, 1975.

with school visits, talked before various social and political groups, and sessions with community leaders, bringing to all of them a vaguely messianic message of change. Shaheen was particularly interested in developing ties to minority communities; when he spoke to white liberal groups, the traditional supporters of the ideas he was advancing, he disquieted his audience. "Why should any high school student read Shakespeare?" he reportedly asked one largely Jewish community group, forgetting perhaps that Shakespeare was a symbol of the kind of academic excellence with which Jewish liberals identified.[205]

While Shaheen was communicating, Reiterman was effectively running the school district, consolidating the various central administrative factions. Instructional programs, the heart of Spears's concerns, were left to the discretion of site administrators and staff. What Spears had regarded as the substance of the schools—their educational mission—the central administration simply ignored. The result was a special kind of chaos known only to managers of school systems, prisons, and insane asylums.

The budget was particularly in a shambles. Jenkins had bought peace with the teachers' organizations by agreeing in 1968 to hire 900 additional teachers over a three-year period, despite steadily declining enrollments. As a result of this and other acts of largesse, per pupil expenditures had risen $221.70 in four years, reaching $725.44 per pupil in 1969/70. A consulting firm—hired for $45,000 at the instigation of the 1970 grand jury—concluded that the district would have to cut back. But where? With no one attempting to set priorities, building maintenance, curriculum, counseling and guidance, music and athletics—all the areas once delineated in a hierarchy of activities and services whose raison d'etre was pupil performance—could all claim shares of the education dollar. And who could argue that their claims were invalid?

In 1970 Howard Nemerowski joined the board of education. A personal friend of the mayor's, Nemerowski was critical of the school administration, which he viewed as topheavy, and sought a thorough house-cleaning; Nemerowski promised that he would personally chop his way through the tangle of vested interests which had grown up in the central administration.[206] Laurel Glass, who hoped that the appointment of a committed liberal superintendent would work a cure, came to realize that no administrator would relinquish what was regarded as personal turf.[207] The goal of organizational responsiveness remained ever-elusive as long as the bureaucracy was able to perpetuate and protect itself. The silent resistance and revealed incompetence of the central administrative staff was, in the end, to figure importantly in the halfhearted implementation of the *Johnson* decree.

205. Interview with Earl Raab, *supra* note 60.
206. Interview with Howard Nemerowski, *supra* note 143.
207. Interview with Laurel Glass, *supra* note 85.

Desegregation's Second Front: Administrative "Deselection." Shaheen thought he saw a way out: decentralize the administration of the San Francisco schools. In March 1971 he proposed a sweeping shakeup, involving over half of all administrative staff and all 90 persons employed in the central office. Fifty would be sent back to school positions, and 40 (the number Spears had found sufficient only a few years earlier) would be reassigned to three subdistrict offices.[208] The decentralization plan was immediately criticized by nearly everyone: Irving Breyer predicted a flood of litigation because "we've never demoted anyone before"; AFT President James Ballard, and Reynold Colvin, former board member and now counsel for the School Administrators' Association, offered sharp words.[209] Nor was the board impressed; it did, however, find one element of the proposal—the reduction of central office staff—appealing.

The board was also pleased that the percentage of minority administrators had climbed from 7 percent at the end of Spears's regime to nearly 21 percent in 1971.[210] But it realized that, if administrative layoffs were to be based on seniority, many newly minted minority administrators would find themselves back in the classroom. To avoid this it converted Shaheen's decentralization plan into a minority preference program; no minority administrators—only whites—would be demoted.

"Deselection" was not Shaheen's idea, but it became his policy.[211] When he presented the board with a list of 125 administrators who would be demoted, no minority person was included.[212] This action secured his standing with minority school administrators, but at the cost of dividing the bureaucracy into two decidedly unequal parts. The white administrators, many of whom had formed a local affiliate of the Teamsters' Union, successfully counterattacked: 121 of those slated for demotion demanded hearings; the group's attorney filed a charge of discrimination with HEW.[213] The hearings were briefly enjoined and, when they resumed, 26 names had mysteriously disappeared from the list of 125.[214] Attorneys for the administrators asserted that the ethnic data were inaccurate, that some of the persons scheduled for demotion were, in fact, members of minority groups.

The district lost badly at the hearings. In August the hearing officer ruled

208. Weiner, *supra* note 199, at 81–82; interviews with Thomas Shaheen, *supra* note 204, Claire Lilienthal, *supra* note 172, David Sanchez, School Commissioner, 1969–1974, in Washington, D.C., April 7, 1974 (telephone interview).
209. San Francisco Chronicle, March 3, 1971, at 1.
210. Anderson v. San Francisco Unified School District, 357 F. Supp. 248, 253 (N.D. Cal. 1972).
211. Interview with Thomas Shaheen, *supra* note 204. Shaheen noted that, a day after the board's action, he had privately expressed his misgivings; when board member Nemerowski heard about this, he cautioned Shaheen to hold his tongue.
212. San Francisco Chronicle, March 9, 1971, at 1.
213. *Id.,* March 23, 1971, at 4.
214. *Id.,* April 13, 1971, at 5; *id.,* May 7, 1971, at 2.

against it, and that decision was affirmed by a federal district court in 1972.[215] During the interim the board admitted defeat, voting to suspend all proceedings and reinstate all the demoted administrators. The attempt to increase the percentage of minority administrators through "reverse discrimination" at the administrative level had failed.

The consequences of this venture extended to desegregation. The two issues were not in fact linked—Shaheen personally favored desegregation; he had neither suggested nor enthusiastically embraced deselection—but the popular perception was otherwise. Deselection further eroded Shaheen's authority with his staff. It also made it more difficult for him to persuade hostile San Franciscans as to the virtues of citywide integration.

The Richmond Complex: Who Decides?

The Richmond Complex, San Francisco's attempt to wed quality with integration, was launched rather uneventfully in September. It provoked few of the crises predicted—the occasional walkouts by those insisting on reassignment to their neighborhood schools were, for instance, quietly resolved—but no dramatic educational innovations developed, either. The experiment was beset from the start with power struggles between teachers and the advisory council for internal control, and between the Complex and the district for autonomy.

The hope that teachers and parents could govern the Complex as partners was simply naive. The teachers had formed their own Richmond organization, the Teachers' Council. Once the Richmond Complex was approved, it maintained vigilant watch over the parents' actions.[216] An attempt by the parent council to exercise authority over teacher transfers was quickly beaten back by the Teachers' Council, who had made it plain that they were a third force to be reckoned with in any attempts to restructure the schools.[217]

The first year of the Richmond Complex was a time of testing for all parties, "winning some battles and losing more."[218] Fewer parents participated in the activities of the advisory council once the pleasure of planning gave way to the relative drudgery of implementation; the diminution of the council's powers and the prospect that additional funds would not continue to be supplied by the district also contributed to this diminished enthusiasm.[219] Enrollment was only 4

215. Anderson v. San Francisco Unified School Dist., 357 F. Supp. 248, 252 (N.D. Cal. 1972).

216. Interview with Janet Benson, *supra* note 137; Report on the Planning and Implementation of the Richmond Educational Complex, 1970/71 (n.d.) [hereinafter cited as Richmond Report].

217. *See* Miller, The Tenure of Tom Shaheen (AFT Pamphlet, January 15, 1972), for one teacher organization's critique of Shaheen. Miller is particularly distrustful of Shaheen's attempts to substitute encounter group methods for bargaining. Shaheen's attempts to win support for his positions among groups of teachers also did not help his relations with the organizations.

218. Richmond Report, *supra* note 216, at 69.

219. *Id.* at 46.

percent lower than had been predicted, indicating that the overwhelming majority of parents were willing to try the experiment at least for a year.[220] As the administration's efforts to win parental acceptance of desegregation were largely realized, prospects for a school-community partnership faded; both parents and teachers focused their energies not on the Complex but on individual school sites. Familiar patterns of relationship were restored, and the dreams of the Complex planners—community resource centers, special science and media laboratories, and the like—vanished.

The Complex did demonstrate that desegregation within a relatively homogeneous extended neighborhood could work; it also permitted teachers to try out new instructional styles and materials. Neither was a trivial accomplishment. It did not, however, live up to the expectations of its creators. The self-described "Adventure in Living" turned out to be all in a rather routine day's work.[221] Its fate, like that of so many of the new programs that had been initiated in previous years, depended in good part upon the financial and political resources it could muster. Like numerous other district programs, it could be described as an organizational prodigy, deserving of special attention. Yet just as with bilingual instruction, the SEED and OMI projects, all of which languished in the new regime, as well as the more mundane requests for additional building maintenance and repair, class size reduction, and the like, the district had no standards by which to assign priorities, no concensus about what constituted the district's essential obligations. As this central focus dissolved, all school district activities became marginal. In that context the aspirations of the Richmond Complex were soon forgotten. Self-maintenance was the only common concern in the struggle for survival.

The Nonresponse to the September Court Order

Committees and Computers. Not until December of 1970 did the school administration being to think about Judge Weigel's September order. With some prodding from the board, Superintendent Shaheen, faithfully emulating past practice, proposed that the task be handled by committees. But where Jenkins created only one committee at a time, Shaheen established three—the Certificated Staff Committee, composed of teachers and principals; the Staff Representative Committee, representing various divisions in the district; and the Citizen's Advisory Committee (CAC). Shaheen had little sense about what any of these committees would actually do or how they would relate to each other. He

---

220. *Id.* at 42.

221. See Council of Great City Schools, EE/Q in San Francisco Public Schools 58–59 (1972); Rittersbach, Change in an Urban School District (unpublished Ph.D. dissertation, Stanford University, 1972) (a report on the implementation of the Richmond Complex, which derives most of its data from the Richmond Report, *supra* note 216.

proposed only the most modest of budgetary commitments—the reassignment of a single district administrator—to assist in the process.[222]

The process of constituting these organizational inventions—determining who should be appointed and who should manage the enterprise—consumed over a month. Shaheen reached into the lower rungs of the administration to find his manager, Donald Johnson, who had worked under Isadore Pivnick on the Richmond and Park South Complex planning. But being handed a job does not guarantee its accomplishment.

Donald Johnson, who undertook the assignment, initially thought that the Citizens' Advisory Committee would advise while the Staff Representative Committee did the work. Things did not turn out that way. The Certified Staff Committee was drawn from middle-level management; only two of the district's eight assistant superintendents served.[223] And all of them had other things to do beside planning for a possible court order; only Johnson had full-time responsibilities for desegregation, and even he was enmeshed in Richmond Complex matters until early in the spring.[224] The staff committee met a dozen times between February and April, when Weigel issued his second order; those who attended heard a variety of schemes—intended, notably, to demonstrate that San Francisco's problems could all be solved by a computer—and did little.[225]

The Citizens' Advisory Committee was, at this stage of the planning venture, busily engaged in its own game of status politics. Almost the first thing that 46-member CAC did was to dissolve itself, in the face of accusations that its composition did not mirror the racial makeup of the school population.[226] The reconstituted committee, including all of the old members plus 22 new faces, devoted its four March and April meetings to determining who would lead it. Its members had so little trust in each other that, for a while, they adopted a scheme of rotating chairperson; and, as Johnson reported to Shaheen, some of its members "don't wish us success."[227]

One CAC member, Reverend Donald Kuhn, who earlier had engineered the appointment of Laurel Glass to the board of education, had great plans for the enterprise. Through his efforts, CAC was assigned primary responsibilities for planning. At the March 17 meeting of the Staff Representative Committee, Johnson confirmed the change: "School administrators, teachers, and staff" would be "working closely with the Citizens groups."[228] As things turned out,

222. San Francisco Board of Education, Minutes, December 17, 1970. See also Weiner, *supra* note 199, at 68.

223. *Id.* at 73.

224. Interview with Donald Johnson, currently superintendent of Sausalito Unified School District, in Sausalito, March 20, 1975.

225. Weiner, *supra* note 199, at 95–107.

226. San Francisco Chronicle, February 18, 1971, at 1; *id.,* February 22, 1971, at 1.

227. Weiner, *supra* note 199, at 133.

228. *Id.* at 104; interview with Donald Kuhn, *supra* note 85.

it was indeed the citizens—rather than the administrators—who decided what integration in San Francisco would look like.

Both the citizens' and staff committees were captivated by the idea of a rational solution to their task.[229] They looked to Len Hanlock, the district's recently hired manager of data processing, and David Branwell, a computer consultant retained by the district, for a neat way of doing the job. To Hanlock and Bradwell, desegregation presented an interesting technical problem: how could one produce a program that efficiently sorted students not only on the basis of race, but also on the basis of proximity, socioeconomic background (a particular concern of the superintendent), and classroom achievement? That task, they initially thought, involved the development of an ingenious computer program into which the district's data could be fed. As they soon learned, the district's antique record-keeping system was not up to the task: it possessed little if any relevant and reliable information. The district did not know where students lived (a sizeable number falsified their addresses in order to be admitted into a desirable school); which students had language or other handicaps; how well individual students were achieving; what their socioeconomic backgrounds were; it didn't even know the real capacity of its own school buildings. To Hanlock and Branwell, the hoped-for exercise in creative programming turned into a less appealing, and ultimately less successful, attempt to dig out needed and heretofore uncollected information. On April 21, almost six months after Hanlock and Branwell had begun working, Donald Johnson announced that essential data would not be available until June 1. He wistfully hoped "we'd have some models developed by the beginning of summer."[230]

The End of the Interregnum

Rationalism was not the order of the day in San Francisco. The district had too many problems, and too few good ways of handling them, to concern itself much with the prospect of an indefinite court order imposing indeterminate demands. Theodore Neff, a consultant with the California Education Department's Bureau of Intergroup Relations, met with the Staff Representative Committee in February on his own initiative; Shaheen wasn't interested in his help. Neff proposed a "systems model," complete with flow chart, to guide the district's planning effort,[231] little realizing how difficult it was to impose organizational order and discipline on San Francisco. Neff's recollection of the episode is clear: "No one in San Francisco really believed that the Court was for real, that something was going to happen after all those years. . . ."[232]

This reaction seems overly harsh. On January 29 the three associate super-

229. *See* Weiner *supra* Note 199, at 83–94. *See also* Council of Great City Schools, Equal Educational Opportunities Project, Data Processing Requirements for School Desegregation: A Case Study of the San Francisco Unified School District (1973).

230. San Francisco Chronicle, April 21, 1971, at 1.

231. Weiner, *supra* note 199, at 98.

232. Interview with Theodore Neff, *supra* note 104.

intendents had taken it upon themselves to send a memorandum to Superintendent Shaheen proposing desegregation of San Francisco's primary and secondary
schools in the fall of 1972; 18 months later. That task, they indicated, could be
accomplished with the same care that characterized the Richmond Complex
planning. September of 1971 was another story:

> . . . desegregation could be accomplished in Fall, 1971, at the cost of ex-
> cessively intensive effort and extended work hours of personnel and dis-
> regarding all the good practice we have learned about efforts toward orderly
> desegregation and proceeding to smoother integration.[233]

The luxury of "orderly desegregation" was not to be. On April 28, 1971,
shortly after the Supreme Court decided *Swann,* Judge Weigel issued an order
requiring that plans for school desegregation—to take place in the fall of 1971
—be filed.[234] The order produced panic in the school administration, consternation on the board, and substantial unease on the part of communities within the
city (notably the Chinese), who felt that they were about to be drawn into a
controversy they wanted no part of. Attention once again shifted, this time
decisively, to the court.

JOHNSON, ROUND TWO: "HOW CAN THERE BE A REMEDY WHEN THERE HAS BEEN NO WONG?"

> [T]here is no abatement of the need for thorough understanding of legal
> resources, skill in combining legitimacy and cognition, sophistication in
> identifying values and interests.[235]

The April Order

It was time, Judge Weigel concluded, to wrap up the San Francisco desegregation litigation. All of the arguments and rebuttals had been made eight months
ago; the judge had had ample opportunity to determine that a case for de jure
segregation had indeed been proved; what remained, as he viewed the matter,
was to shape a remedy. On April 20, hours after the Supreme Court had approved a truly massive busing scheme in *Swann,* Weigel held a press conference.
He announced that "in the near future" he would order the desegregation of
San Francisco's elementary schools for September 1971.[236] One week later, that
order was issued.

The April 28 order reminded the district of the court's September warning to
plan for a result that *Swann* had now legitimated. Its treatment of the legal and

233. Quoted in Weiner, *supra* note 199, at 77.

234. Johnson v. San Francisco Unified School Dist., 339 F. Supp. 1315, 1325 (N.D. Cal.
1971).

235. Selznick, *The Ethos of American Law* 13 (1974) (paper prepared for publication in
Politics and the Idea of Man) (I. Kristol & P. Weaver eds., forthcoming).

236. San Francisco Chronicle, April 21, 1971, at 1.

factual issues was confined to a footnote in which Weigel accepted every argument advanced by plaintiffs, even those for which evidence was at best scanty; inaction as well as action were the bases on which the court found de jure segregation.[237] A full recital of the district's wrongs did not appear until June 2.[238] Weigel's findings of wrongdoing were not fully satisfying even to himself. The judge noted, a week after the order was issued: *"regardless* of whether this is technically *de jure* or technically *de facto,* it is a situation of which no city should be proud...."[239] The task now, however, was to devise a remedy.

In that enterprise, Weigel enlisted the district and—to their surprise—the plaintiffs, ordering both to file "a comprehensive plan for the desegregation of all San Francisco public elementary schools to go into effect at the start of the school term in the fall of this year."[240] The judge realized the controversial nature of his order; but the law, he said, is clear, and "the law must be obeyed. . . . [D]isagreement with the law is no justification for violation."[241] He recognized, too, the practical difficulties his demand for a response within six weeks would create. But those problems were not, in his judgement, insurmountable.

A genuine will to meet and overcome then is the first requisite.
The stakes are surely high enough to generate that will. Respect for law in the education of the elementary school children of the city today can do much to reduce crime on the streets of the city of tomorrow.[242]

Tactical Maneuvers in the Face of the Inevitable

The School Board. The school board was in a quandary. The desegregation of San Francisco's elementary schools was not an unpleasant prospect. Indeed, the superintendent had told reporters immediately after the April order: "[T]his is an order which we have expected. The only thing we didn't know is when it would come. Now we have an order and it behooves us to comply with it.[243] But the board did not see quite how the job could be concluded by June. And

237. 339 F. Supp. 1315, 1326–27 n.3. (N.D. Cal. 1971).
238. *Id.* at 1329.
239. Transcript, May 6, 1971, at 36. *See also id.,* at 50:

I think this is de facto, but even if the Court—I think this is both de jure and de facto—but even if the Court is wrong in holding that it is de jure . . . you cannot support a continuation of that condition under the relevant law . . . regardless of whether it is de jure or de facto.

But compare Transcript, May 28, 1971, at 42:

This Court holds the view . . . that there has been by this School Board what is called de jure . . . segregation which cannot be continued.

At no other point in the nearly one-thousand-page transcript is such wavering by Weigel detectable.
240. 339 F. Supp. at 1327.
241. *Id.* at 1328.
242. *Id.* at 1329.
243. San Francisco Chronicle, April 29, 1971, at 1.

several of its members were offended by the implicit conclusion that the district had, in the past, acted wrongfully. "As a professional," board member Howard Nemerowski recalled, "I was appalled by the Judge's misreading and misinterpretations."[244] Those concerns led the board finally to fight Weigel's decision. It moved to stay the April 28 order, a motion denied on May 6;[245] and on May 20 the board, by a 4-3 vote, committed itself to appealing the decision.[246] The decisive voices were those of the lawyer, Nemerowski, and David Sanchez, who had come to fear the consequences of citywide desegregation for the Mission community he represented.[247]

The Intervenors Redux. The intervenors had no such dilemmas. In January the district had removed the intervenors' suit against the Richmond and Park South Complexes to federal district court,[248] and now they wanted to consolidate *Nelson* and *Johnson*. The intervenors had also changed their lawyers: three extraordinarily and diversely talented attorneys, Willis and Vivian Hannawalt and Quentin Kopp, had taken on the case,[249] and now sought to pursue it with considerable vigor.

On April 28, intervenors moved to reopen *Johnson* for purposes of taking new evidence; that, they argued, was necessary in light of the *Swann* decision. Were that motion denied, they stated, "a mistrial is warranted upon the basis of premature and publicly announced intent by this court to decide adversely to defendants and intervenors. . . ."[250]

The intervenors' lawyers eloquently—and, on occasion, amusingly—expressed their principled opposition to the court's conclusion that San Francisco had acted improperly with respect to race; the only misstep the district had taken, in the Hannawalt's eyes, was to undertake deliberate desegregation in the Richmond Complex. Their comments about the politics of desegregation were barbed:

"Affirmative action" has now become equated with "racial imbalance," and "racial balance" has become to some a means by which institutional failures can be hidden, to others an endeavor in which they can act out

244. Interview with Howard Nemerowski, *supra* note 143.

245. San Francisco Chronicle, May 2, 1971, at 1.

246. *Id.,* May 20, 1971, at 1.

247. Interviews with Howard Nemerowski, *supra* note 143, David Sanchez, *supra* note 208, and Claire Lilienthal, *supra* note 172.

248. Nelson v. San Francisco Unified School School Dist., No. C-71-116-SC (N.D. Cal., January 21, 1971).

249. The discussion of the motivations of—as distinguished from the papers filed by—the intervenors' lawyers is drawn from the transcripts (which reveal Kopp to be far less well-prepared than his colleagues); and interviews with Quentin Kopp, member of the board of supervisors and lawyer for the Chinese Intervenors, and Willis Hannawalt, lawyer for the original intervenors, both in San Francisco, March 19, 1975. Others—both parties to the litigation and astute observers of San Francisco politics—also offered their analyses.

250. Motion for Order to Reopen for the Taking of Evidence and to Consolidate Cases for Trial; or in the Alternative for an Order of Mistrial, April 28, 1971, 5 Record 757, 758.

roles more appropriate to the CIA, and to others a platform for political propaganda. . . .

"Racial imbalance" has enabled some to disguise the simple fact that the Negro community has succeeded where so many others have failed in stripping the emperor of garments never there: since children will teach children when the institution has been unable to do so, one might reasonably conclude that it is not the institution which has been doing much teaching of anybody. By virtue of disguising teaching failure behind "racial imbalance," the chief result of "affirmative action" has been to leave the rabbits in charge of the lettuce patch.[251]

When the Hannawalts spoke to the nonculpability of the district, they were equally trenchant:

There is nothing whatsoever in either *Brown* or *Swann* which requires that justice be blind to the effects of the institutional racism implicit in the notions that children are fungible commodities and that Negro children must be in the company of white children before they may improve their achievement.[252]

In their view, San Francisco's policies were indistinguishable from those of Springfield, Massachusetts,[253] which several years earlier had been exonerated by the Court of Appeals for the First Circuit. The substitution of the de jure for the de facto label did not make the difference, for "a camel is not qualified for a horse race by naming it Man-O-War."[254]

The intervenors and the district both sought suspension of Weigel's September 1971 integration deadline, pending the outcome of an appeal.[255] On June 4, after a cursory hearing, Weigel denied the motion; that action was consistent with how federal district court judges had been reacting to similar motions for much of the past decade. The case would go forward on schedule.

Planning for Desegregation. *The Citizens' Advisory Committee plans for the district.* Judge Weigel's April 28 order had been designed, in good part, to guide the district and the plaintiffs as each went about the task of producing a plan. If any aspect of that order was not clear, the judge had said, he would resolve the ambiguity. On May 6 the district posed two questions which needed clarification. What was meant by the "objective" of "[f]ull integration of all public elementary schools so that the ratio of black children to white children

---

251. Intervenor's First Objections to Plan Filed on June 10, 1971, June 14, 1971, 9 Record 979, 984–85 (hereinafter cited as First Objections).
252. *Id.* at 986.
253. Springfield School Comm. v. Barksdale, 348 F.2d. 261 (1st Cir. 1965).
254. First Objections, *supra* note 310, at 989.
255. Order Denying Defendant's and Intervenors' Motions to Suspend Order Pending Appeal, June 4, 1971, 5 Record 897.

will then be and thereafter continue to be substantially the same in each school"?[256] Was the district to equalize the distribution of all other minority groups, as well as blacks—notably the Asian and Spanish-speaking students, who between them comprised more than one-quarter of the student population? Did the requirement of "substantial" sameness permit (or require) the district to adhere to California guidelines, which defined a racially balanced school as one in which the proportion of students from a given ethnic group was no more than 15 percent above or below that group's proportion of the school-age population?[257]

These two questions were indeed critical to the district; clear answers were needed in order to make the planning task sensible. Clarity was not, however, forthcoming. "The answers to all of the requests . . . are to be found by careful consideration of the entire . . . memorandum and order itself."[258] Weigel's nonresponsiveness was deliberate. "I am not going to answer that question because that question invites the Court to do what the Board of Education ought to do;"[259] the "requirement" of "full integration" was, in fact, a "suggestion" and not itself an order.[260] The judge realized the limits of his authority: he could not order the desegregation of all minorities, because no evidence about discrimination practiced against minorities other than blacks had been submitted. Yet he asserted that "racism of any kind, whether it involves black children, or white children or yellow children or brown children, is a very bad thing,"[261] and hoped that in its planning the district would voluntarily embrace those issues as well. In short, Weigel could aspire to lead where legally he could not compel.

The district's plan was put together by the Citizens' Advisory Committee (CAC) almost by default: the board lacked the inclination, and the staff lacked the time, for the task. Someone else could do the work and take the political heat that would inevitably be generated by the process. CAC was willing. "We turned into a 'do business' outfit overnight," said Chairman Donald Kuhn.[262]

The schedule under which CAC operated left little time for educational dreaming. Gone was Superintendent Jenkins's hope for an educational park; funds for such an enterprise were nowhere to be found. CAC also dismissed the possibility of developing ad hoc solutions—involving, for example, minor boundary adjustments, preservation of already-desegregated schools, voluntary busing arrangements, and the like—both because these seemed unlikely to satisfy the court's mandate and, equally importantly, because the detailed evidence

256. 339 F. Supp. at 1328.
257. Transcript, May 6, 1971, at 2–4.
258. *Id.* at 5.
259. *Id.* at 9.
260. 339 F. Supp. at 1328. The wording of the order was complex enough to confuse lawyers for both plaintiffs and defendants.
261. Transcript, April 28, 1971, at 18.
262. Weiner, *supra* note 199, at 153.

that would have been needed to evaluate such schemes was not at hand. Instead, CAC sought standards by which to determine whether a given plan assured racial balance. It defined "racial balance" as the then-existing California guidelines did, permitting a given school to enroll 15 percent more or less of an ethnic group than that group's representation in the District.[263] Since, for example, 28.7 percent of San Francisco's elementary school children were black, a school which enrolled between 13.7 and 43.7 percent black children would be racially balanced with respect to blacks. There was no particular justification for this rule—which implied, for example, that while a 40 percent black school was "balanced" a 40 percent Latino school was not—but it had already received official sanction. Any other formula could be, and was, attacked as equally arbitrary. And it was a formula CAC was after.

Within this broad framework, debate focused on the wisdom of two different approaches, a "zone" approach and a "citywide" approach.[264] The zone approach—epitomized by Horseshoe, the plan ultimately adopted—sought to build upon the experience of the Complexes. It envisioned a city divided into numerous extended neighborhoods, permitting busing to be minimized. It tried to preserve "political integrity," by which was meant something akin to neighborhood schools, to minimize unhappiness and consequent white flight. To those who advocated a zone concept, the California guidelines represented the greatest amount of politically tolerable desegregation. By contrast, the citywide approach viewed the state guidelines as fixing the minimum of permissible desegregation. It was less concerned about white acceptance of the plans or the preservation of neighborhoods than with producing the greatest amount of economic and racial desegregation possible.

Members of CAC converted these broad notions into plans which could be put into effect the coming year. Data problems continued to haunt them—they did not, for instance, even know which schools would have to be closed in response to a report about possible earthquake hazards, and lacked block-by-block racial data on students until the end of May—but they persisted nonetheless. Room 31 of the central administration building was converted into a "round-the-clock" room, and citizens and the computer programmers did literally work around the clock for several weeks, trying out different arrangements on the computer.

It was the white women on the committee—notably Nicki Salan, Myra Kopf, and Naomi Lauter—who dominated this critical phase of the committee's work. Others, of course, had strong interest in the outcome. But they lacked the

263. Calif. Educ. Code, § § 5002-5003; Title 5, Ch. 14020-21, statutory provisions which—in effect—legitimated the Guidelines were themselves repealed by Stats. 1971, Ch. 1965, by initiative adopted at general elections, November 7, 1972. In Mullin v. Santa Barbara School Dist., Civ. No. LA 300, Jan. 15, 1975, the California Supreme Court upheld the repeal.

264. *See generally* Weiner, *supra* note 199, at 159-61; interview with Nicki Salan, *supra* note 137.

time, the competence, the extensive past experience with the district's schools, and the driving commitment to a particular kind of solution that these women possessed. As one Latino member of the committee remarked: "The whites had tremendous experience. It's one thing to know that there is a think tank, it is something else to see it in operation.[265]

On June 1, CAC made its recommendation to the board of education. Its preference was for Horseshoe, a Complex plan which divided the district into seven zones, left Richmond and Park South largely intact, placed the Latino and Chinese communities in a single zone, and barely satisfied the California 15 percent guidelines. Tri-Star, the leading citywide alternative, was ranked fourth among seven plans prepared by CAC while Sequoia—which made no effort to desegregate the Chinatown and Mission districts—was ranked third. A compromise which everyone on the committee could live with had been ratified.[266] On June 4 the board of education approved Horseshoe, and it was submitted to the court.[267]

A decade of public discussion and a court order had culminated in a hastily developed, formula-bound desegregation plan created by a small group of citizens and staff working far from public purview. The new superintendent, faced with innumerable daily dilemmas, could not devote time to the planning process or make it a part of the administration's overall concern. The board— worried about the budget, the schools' vulnerability to earthquakes, and the denouement of the deselection controversy—was happy to delegate responsibility to CAC and its small staff, and to accept their recommendation without serious quibble.[268]

The board similarly opted not to get involved in determining how to desegregate the teaching staff, another aspect of the court's order. The Citizens' Advisory Committee filed its report, and Assistant Superintendent for Personnel George Boisson filed his report; neither had consulted with the Negotiating Council, the group representing the teachers' organizations. Indeed, American Federation of Teachers' President James Ballard had proposed to Boisson a means of honoring teacher preference and securing desegregation, which Boisson ignored.[269] Rather than attempting to resolve this controversy, the board simply sent both reports along to Weigel and the Negotiating Council.[270]

The function of CAC was to deflect criticism from the board—and then disband. The final choice about remedy rested with the court.

265. Weiner, *supra* note 199, at 169.

266. *Id.,* at 199.

267. San Francisco Board of Education, Minutes, June 4, 1971. The Horseshoe plan is summarized in Weiner, *supra* note 199, at 371–75, 421–26.

268. Interviews with Laurel Glass, *supra* note 85, Donald Kuhn, *supra* note 85, and Thomas Shaheen, *supra* note 204.

269. Interview with James Ballard, president of the San Francisco Chapter of the American Federation of Teachers, in San Francisco, March 14, 1975.

270. San Francisco Board of Education, Minutes, June 17, 1971.

The NAACP's "Weekend Experts" Draft an Alternative.   Plans cost money, and that was one commodity the NAACP lacked. The order requiring plaintiffs to produce an alternative to the district's plan came as an unhappy surprise. "We thought that the system, not us, should be in the planning business," said Ann Bloomfield, head of the NAACP Education Committee.[271]

Bloomfield contacted the NAACP's national office; she got no money, but several suggestions about experts. Meryl Herman and J. Howard Munzer of Rhode Island College's School of Education, who had had some involvement in the Charlotte, North Carolina plan approved in *Swann,* were the only people on the NAACP experts list both willing to wait awhile for payment and able immediately to come to San Francisco. They were retained by the NAACP on May 21, flew out for a whirlwind 48 hours of meetings and city touring, then flew back and set to work. Three weeks later they had finished.

The plan they produced—the Freedom plan—resembled CAC's Tri-Star plan in many ways. It created six attendance areas, several of which were not contiguous; indeed, one of its zones contemplated busing some students from the northeast to the southwest corner of the city, a substantial distance even given the compactness of San Francisco. Boundaries were drawn to provide for socio-economic and achievement as well as racial mixture, insofar as the skimpy data available to the planners permitted such calculations. On teacher assignment, special programs, and the like, the Freedom plan was virtually silent; there just had not been time for serious consideration of anything apart from the placement of students.[272]

Resolution at Hand?   On June 10, both the NAACP and district plans were submitted to the court. In his "Statement in Open Court," Judge Weigel praised the response: "The defendants have vigorously defended the law suit. Indeed, they have filed an appeal but they show their respect for the law by complying with the order of the Court in now filing their plan for desegregation. The plaintiffs, too, have complied with the order of the Court. . ." Judge Weigel requested "all counsel—the Court emphasizes all—promptly to write to the Court offering their assistance . . . [about the plan] which will meet the requirement of the law with minimum inconvenience to the public and, especially, to the children and parents affected."[273]

Chinatown Tries to Intervene.[274]   In May 1971 the Chinatown community— more precisely the Chinese Six Companies, the traditional clan-based private

271. Interview with Ann Bloomfield, Chairwoman of NAACP Education Committee, 1967–1970, in San Francisco, March 4, 1975.
272. Weiner, *supra* note 199, at 401–20, reprints the Freedom Plan.
273. Statement in Open Court, June 10, 1971, 5 Record 984.
274. This section is drawn from a variety of sources, including V. Nee and B. Nee, Long-time Californ' (1972); Lyman, *Red Guard on Grant Avenue,* in Culture and Civility in San Francisco 20 (H. Becker ed. 1971); Wolfe, *Bok Gooi, Hok Gooi and T'ang Jen: or, Why*

political and social organization which has effectively, if unofficially, governed Chinatown since the first Chinese arrived in San Francisco to work on the railroads and gold mines in 1850—began to realize that what they had viewed as a squabble between blacks and whites might well disrupt their community-based public schools. The Six Companies do not speak for all of the Chinese population: increasingly, other voices—among them the Chinese-American Citizen's Alliance, a young professional group; a Chinatown Chamber of Commerce, with ties to the larger city community; and second- and third-generation Chinese who have left Chinatown for other parts of the city—compete for attention. But the Six Companies were, and remain, capable of putting on a show of strength. When 300 Chinese parents, organized by the Six Companies, railed at the Citizens' Advisory Committee plans at a May meeting,[275] who could say that this group was not "representative," or was less representative, than the committee itself?

To the Six Companies, desegregation was a disaster. It threatened their tenuous hold on the new immigrant population, some of whose younger members had already formed a defiant Red Guard group. It also constituted an assault on the Chinese people's ethnic identity. Chinatown families, who thought that a ten-block trip was a journey, would not be able to see their children at midday. The after-school Chinese culture schools could no longer count on the regular attendance of young students. What lay outside Chinatown—the *bok gooi* and *hok gooi* (respectively, the white and black devils); an academic environment less well-ordered and less concerned about achievement than their own—was unpromising. The Six Companies played up these fears in a stream of articles appearing in Chinatown's Chinese-language newspaper.

The protest to the Citizens' Advisory Committee stunned that group, but otherwise had no effect. Neither did the appearance, at the June 3 board meeting, of 600 "booing, footstomping . . . shouting . . . Chinese-American parents—half the audience."[276] The Horseshoe plan, which CAC and the board approved, kept most of Chinatown in a single zone, but required the busing of sizeable numbers of students into and out of Chinatown. The Six Companies decided to intervene directly in the litigation to ward off this possibility. They turned to Quentin Kopp, already an attorney for the original intervenors, and asked him to represent them.[277] Kopp accepted the assignment, leaving the original intervenors to

There Is No National Association for the Advancement of Chinese Americans? New York, September 21, 1971, at 36 [hereinafter cited as Wolfe] ; Senate Hearings, *supra* note 89, at 4223–28; and interviews with Philip Lum, principal in the San Francisco Unified School District and author of a forthcoming Ph.D. dissertation on the Chinatown schools in San Francisco, March 21, 1971;

Citizens Complaint Officer Al Cheng, San Francisco Unified School District, in San Francisco, April 7, 1975; and Ronald Wong, attorney with the San Francisco Neighborhood Legal Assistance Foundation's Chinatown office, in San Francisco, March 17, 1975.

275. San Francisco Chronicle, May 26, 1971, at 10.
276. San Francisco Examiner, June 4, 1971, at 1.
277. Interview with Quentin Kopp, *supra* note 249.

the Hannawalts, and tried to bring this new group into the case literally days before a final decision about a desegregation remedy was anticipated.

Kopp's "complaint of plaintiffs in intervention" and supporting memorandum, filed on June 18, were explosive documents.[278] The Chinese have an independent right to be heard, Kopp claimed. Although no one represented their interests, they were to be unwitting parties to court-ordered relief. Kopp attacked the suit as collusive: "the findings of fact and conclusions of law," he charged, "were obtained by negligence, acts of omission and obvious failure to present material evidence."[279] The Chinese community, Kopp concluded, "should not without hearing be subjected to a 'cure' they neither need nor want, for to do so merely perpetuates the invidious racial discrimination exemplified by the notorious treatment of the Japanese in California only a few short years ago."[280]

No judge likes to be accused of participating in a collusive lawsuit or imposing a remedy akin to the wartime internment of the Japanese; Weigel was certainly no exception. But he was unwilling to let this last distraction interfere with the conclusion of the case. On June 30 the motion to intervene was denied, each of its arguments curtly dismissed. Kopp was by no means finished: he filed a motion for a stay of the court's order, reargued the issue before Weigel in August, and appeared before the Court of Appeals for the Ninth Circuit when the case was heard on appeal. In the interim, he had launched an ultimately successful campaign for a position on the board of supervisors from the steps of Chinatown's Commodore Stockton School. However the case itself was ultimately resolved, Kopp would emerge a winner.

The Court's Dilemma: Maximum Desegregation or Institutional Legitimacy?

Judge Weigel's choices of remedy were difficult ones, which had not wholly been resolved by *Swann*. He treated essentially pedagogical issues as beyond his competence; reflecting then-uniform judicial practice, his concern focused on the degree of racial mixing that could properly be ordered. But in that realm, should he adopt the NAACP plan (more accurately, the skeleton of a plan), which promised substantially more racial mixing of students? Or should he adopt the board's proposal, a document which could be described, with only limited distortion, as embodying the wishes of a community whose choices were constitutionally constrained? Weigel sought additional advice before making that decision. Chairman Donal Kuhn of the Citizens' Advisory Committee informed Weigel's clerk that the judge had not received all of the committee's reports,

278. Complaint of Plaintiffs in Intervention, 6 Record 1208, June 18, 1971; Memorandum of Points of Authorities in Support of Motion to Intervene, *id.* at 1197.
279. Complaint of Plaintiffs in Intervention, 6 Record 1208.
280. Memorandum of Points and Authorities in Support of Motion to Intervene, 6 Record 1197, 1203.

and after that conversation Weigel obtained from the district the three alternative desegregation plans recommended by CAC to the board.[281] Weigel tried to reach John Finger, chief author of the Charlotte, North Carolinia plan, only to learn that he was on sabbatical in Europe.[282] On June 21 he scheduled an informal session, in chambers, "to help the court to fully understand the plans which [have] been submitted" and get the "unguarded cooperation" of all concerned.[283] This day-long conference was the prelude to two days of open hearings on the plans; in the annals of desegregation cases it was an extraordinary event.

Weigel had several puzzling problems to deal with. The first centered on the original intervenors who, true to their principles, had argued that—if the court found de jure segregation to exist in San Francisco—the only permissible plan was one such as the NAACP's, which wholly desegregated the schools; the Horseshoe plan, they declared, imposed selective burdens in the name of political compromise, and that they viewed as a fatal defect.

The intervenors still believed that San Francisco's segregation did not violate the Constitution. But if they were wrong, they were greatly concerned that the district's proposed remedy would only result in divisive annual petitions for further relief. It was better, they thought, to resolve these issues once and for all time. The intervenors could not make their position plain. The judge may have suspected that the intervenors' apparent turnabout was a clever trap, a maneuvever designed to lead Weigel into choosing an untenable remedy, thus affording yet another basis for appeal. Judge Weigel recognized this possibility: "I really don't think I want your assistance, Mr. Hannawalt," he commented at the conference. "What I want to do is to avoid excluding you. . . ."[284] There existed a lingering feeling that Weigel viewed these new-found allies as a continuing headache:

> *The Court*: . . . I guess we have to clear away the brush here.
> *Mrs. Hannawalt*: [I] don't like to be referred to as the "brush."
> *The Court*: Mrs. Hannawalt, I wasn't referring to you as the brush. . . .
> You certainly are so attractive and charming that I would not think of referring to you, nor even to your husband, who is not quite so attractive, as "brush."[285]

In fact the Hannawalts proved themselves enormously helpful in the process of eliciting information at the conference. Yet because the judge ruled that they had no standing with respect to remedy, they declined to participate in the open hearings. They were convinced, and probably quite rightly, that their position remained a mystery and their role was perceived as a special kind of threat.[286]

281. Weiner, *supra* note 199, at 312.
282. Transcript, June 3, 1971, at 73.
283. *Id.,* June 21, 1971, at 5.
284. *Id.* at 16.
285. *Id.* at 18.
286. *But see id.* at 46, suggesting that the judge understood but could not accept intervenors' position.

Most of the day was devoted to a detailed review of the two plans which had been submitted. Weigel expressed his unhappiness with the board "for having done very little until, on, or after April 28 . . . to get ready for the various contingencies that were . . . plainly foreseeable last September;"[287] he perceived the board as engaging in dilatory tactics, a point he had made earlier. At a hearing held on June 2, the district's lawyer, George Kreuger, had tried to demonstrate that several factors—among them the uncertain structural safety of San Francisco's schools, the difficulty of obtaining bus contracts, the multiracial population of its students, and an impending budgetary crisis—made it impossible to comply with the court's deadline for filing a plan. Weigel dealt ruthlessly with each point; the discussion of the structural safety problem is typical:

> *The Court*: . . . Is it the position of the defendants that because there is some question . . . as to the structural safety of several school buildings that therefore, if it be a constitutional right, the Board is under no duty to eliminate segregation in the San Francisco schools?
>   Is that their position?
>   . . . Well, is it your concept that the Court has ordered the production of a plan which would be so inflexible that emergencies and unforeseen contingencies could not be taken care of? . . .
>   Because if so, the Court now states that the understanding is one hundred and eighty degrees wrong.
>   *Mr. Kreuger*: I think I would definitely say, Your Honor, that is not my understanding of what the Court had ordered.
>   *The Court*: Okay. Then it seems to me that this disposes of this sort of red herring. . . .
>   *Mr. Krueger*: I don't think that it is a red herring when considered in light of the other four reasons why—
>   *The Court*: Then you think that while it has no independent relevance that other things give it relevance. Go ahead.[288]

Krueger was, of course, trying to make a broader argument: ". . . when you are attempting to come up with a plan for the integration of all the public elementary schools in San Francisco, you have to know what you are working with. . . . The district here faces . . . a lack of knowledge. . . ."[289] The Judge was unsympathetic to this position and, from his point of view, the fact that other matters had been occupying the board's attention since September was irrelevant.

Judge Weigel made it clear that he could not undo deficiences in the district's planning. "I feel a sense of harrassment by the tremendous number of problems on which I feel I have no grasp or expertise."[290] He was, however, willing to

287. *Id.* at 192.
288. *Id.,* June 2, 1971, at 12–13.
289. *Id.* at 19.
290. *Id.,* June 21, 1971, at 152. It is clear from the transcripts of this and the two-day public hearing which followed that Weigel's grasp of the nuances of planning for desegregation was extraordinary.

prod the district into reshaping Horseshoe, so that racial and ethnic deviations would be reduced to 10 percent if at all possible. Can this be done without "convulsive effort"? the judge asked Len Hanlock, the computer manager. "I would say that was highly unlikely with seven zones—or with multiple zones," Hanlock replied.[291] The judge persisted:

> *The Court*: Supposing the Court were to approve Horsehoe, are there possibilities for improving the racial balance in [two of the zones] . . . .
> *Mr. Hanlock*: There are possibilities.
> *The Court*: There are possibilities. Okay.
> *Mr. Hanlock*: There are possibilities, as you well know.[292]

The pressure placed on the district was felt; shortly after the hearing, the boundaries of several zones were slightly altered in an effort to improve the chances of Horsehoe's acceptance.[293]

Substantially less time was devoted to discussion of the NAACP's Freedom plan. That plan had certain undoubted advantages: it provided for significantly more socioeconomic and racial desegregation, and it kept the OMI community intact. To the NAACP, the fact that it had been drafted "by complete outsiders, who have no particular axes to grind," was also an advantage; the board had "been just too interested in community participation. . . . You go ahead and do it [desegregate], and then you start—and don't worry about selling it to the community."[294]

The court thought otherwise. In its view the fatal—if unavoidable—defect of the NAACP's Freedom plan was the absence of substantial community involvement of the sort which characterized Horsehoe's formulation.[295] Weigel had before him two plans, either of which he could order adopted. The NAACP's did a better job of reducing segregation, a point clearly apparent to the judge;[296] but, *because* it was the NAACP's plan and not the board of education's, it was less likely to gain community acceptance.

That difference was vital to a judge who recognized the controversial nature of any system-wide desegregation order, and the importance of securing acquiescence in, if not support for, his actions. For this phase of the task it was essential that he have some backing from the board of education. During the open hearing on the competing desegregation plans, NAACP witness Meryl Herman suggested that the court should give the school district "help from the prestige of the Judge's position."[297] Weigel found the suggestion congenial: "I . . . wouldn't be

291. *Id.* at 42.
292. *Id.* at 107.
293. Weiner, *supra* note 199, at 319.
294. Transcript, June 21, 1971, at 182, 187, 191.
295. *See e.g., id.* at 29–30.
296. *Id.,* June 24, 1971, at 582.
297. *Id.* at 772.

hesitant to pioneer—to develop all the community acceptance I know how."[298]
The primacy of that objective resolved the court's dilemma. On July 9, 1971,
Judge Weigel announced his decision: *both* plans were approved.

> It is left to the choice of the school authorities to implement either one.
> Since the school authorities themselves submitted Horseshoe, it is antic-
> ipated that they will elect to carry out that plan. . . .
>   While evidence of community sentiment or public feelings. . . . cannot
> be the measure of compliance with the law, if both plans do qualify under
> the law—and both do—it is hardly ill-advised to permit implementation of
> that which the competent school authorities themselves have brought
> forward after extensive public hearings. . . .
>   [I]t is essential to have the good willed, open minded and genuine co-
> operation of school administrators, teachers, other school personnel,
> parents and the community at large.[299]

Judge Weigel was speaking quite self-consciously to his real audience, the citizenry
of San Francisco.

The Protracted Appeal Process

The Chinese intervenors acted on the historical Mr. Dooley's wise precept: "I
care not who makes the law in a nation if I can get out an injunction." In July
and August they attempted to halt the proceedings and for a brief moment were
successful. A panel of Ninth Circuit Court judges stayed Weigel's order until the
court of appeals had heard the case. In its July 26 decision, handed down without a hearing having been held, the panel noted that it "would be interested as
to why Chinese pupils are mixed into a black-white problem and whether Irish
and Italian pupils, for example, are also included."[300] Arthur Brunwasser, the
plaintiffs' attorney, was understandably frantic; things like this didn't happen in
desegregation cases. Brunwasser contacted the New York NAACP office for
advice; he worked constantly for days, seeking reconsideration and reversal of
the panel's order. "I was afraid the whole thing would go down the drain,"
Brunwasser said.[301] On August 2 the order was vacated, the panel admitting
that it had not known about previous attempts to secure a stay. The intervenors'
brief moment of glory was over.

  At a hearing before Judge Weigel on August 2, another request for a stay was
predictably denied. Weigel took advantage of the occasion to attempt to allay
the fears of the sizable Chinese contingent which appeared in the courtroom:
"The whole purpose of the order of the Court is to provide for a better educa-

298. *Id.* at 773.
299. 339 F. Supp. 1315, 1321 (N.D. Cal. 1971).
300. Guey Heung Lee v. David Johnson and San Francisco Unified School District and
Robert Nelson *et al.,* No. 71-2105 (C.C.A. 9th Cir. 1971) Order, July 28, 1971.
301. Interview with Arthur Brunwasser, *supra* note 158.

tion for the Chinese children, and for all children. . . ."[302] The court of appeals upheld Weigel this time,[303] and shortly thereafter the effort to postpone the inevitable was finally at an end; Supreme Court Justice William Douglas rejected Kopp's last appeal for a stay:

> *Brown* . . . was not written for Blacks alone. It rests on the equal protection clause of the Fourteenth Amendment, one of the first beneficiaries of which were the Chinese people of San Francisco . . . The theme of our school desegregation cases extends to all racial minorities treated invidiously by a State or any of its agencies. . . .
>
> So far as the overrriding questions of law are concerned, the decision of the District Court seems well within bounds. It will take some intervening event or some novel question of law to induce me as Circuit Justice to overrule the considered action of my brethren on the Ninth Circuit. Petition denied.[304]

It would be almost three years before the circuit court decided *Johnson*. In the interval, Brunwasser pressed the district court to modify its order to assure that the mistakes made during the first year of system-wide desegregation were not repeated. A year after the district court decision, Brunwasser sought "further and supplemental relief," including an order desegregating the junior high schools.[305] The original intervenors criticized Brunwasser's reliance on affidavits, upon which his request was based, rather than "evidence tested by cross-examination and by other normal means by which critical and disputed facts are customery tested judicially."[306] Weigel's only response was to order the school district to report "within 20 days after the end of the school year in reasonable detail all action taken to comply with the judgment, and to show plans for implementation in compliance with the letter and spirit of the decision."[307] The judge's order signalled his unwillingness to take any further action until the court of appeals had reviewed the July 1971 decision. He confirmed that position by denying without opinion, on December 8, 1972, a motion to consolidate the still-pending *Johnson* case with *O'Neill v. San Francisco Unified School District,* a suit brought by the NAACP to desegregate San Francisco's junior and senior high schools.[308]

On June 22, 1974, the Court of Appeals for the Ninth Circuit finally delivered a *per curiam* opinion in *Johnson.*[309] In 1973 the Supreme Court in *Keyes* had

302. Transcript, August 2, 1971, at 35–36.
303. Order, August 21, 1971, *supra* note 300.
304. 404 U.S. 1215, 1216–17, 1218 (1971).
305. Motion for Further and Supplemental Relief, July 24, 1972, 7 Record 1502.
306. Intervenors' Motion in Opposition, 10, August 9, 1972, 7 Record 1640, 1650.
307. Order, August 19, 1972, 7 Record 1679.
308. No. C-72-808-RFP (N.D. Cal., May 5, 1972).
309. *Johnson V. San Francisco Unified School Dist.,* 339 F. Supp. 1315 (1971) *vacated and remanded,* 500 F.2d 349 (1974).

set forth the standards by which judicial inquiry in northern desegregation cases was to be guided. *Keyes,* the circuit court held, required a finding of "segregatory *intent*" which the district court in *Johnson* had not made, and hence "[t]he case must be remanded to afford an opportunity to re-examine the record on the issue of intent."[310] The court also ordered the Chinese intervenors to be heard when the case was remanded, rejecting Weigel's argument that the school district and the original intervenors adequately represented [p]arents of elementary school children of Chinese ancestry. . . ."[311]

The appellate court's intent requirement imposed a harder burden on plaintiffs than have subsequent opinions in other circuits. Had its opinion been issued with greater dispatch, it might well have proven consequential. The original intervenors were prepared with a host of discovery demands which, in their judgment, would have served as the basis for demolishing the conclusion that San Francisco had practiced de jure segregation; if they had had their way, the case might have received the full argument it deserved.[312]

By 1974, however, neither the Hannawalts nor the district had much taste for reopening what seemed to be a stale issue. The district did not want to examine the question with "microscopic attentiveness."[313] For their part the Hannawalts did not believe that "the pre-*Johnson* world could be restored. Many of the same reasons which made it proper not to upset a social organization in 1971 apply today; they argue for not upsetting the present. What's done is done."[314] Both sides, George Krueger commented, "want to see the court order work; no one is much inclined to flame the issue unnecessarily."[315] Settlement of the dispute, ratified by a consent decree, was in everyone's best interest.

Well, almost everyone. During the sporadic negotiations which have taken place since the fall of 1974, the Chinese intervenors have resisted approving any agreement which ratifies the status quo. Their opposition to desegregation has diminished, but they have "gotten used to it" rather than becoming happy about it.[316] These intervenors may press for an agreement which leaves Chinatown outside the embrace of Horseshoe. If they do, and if the NAACP finds that demand unpalatable, there may yet be another round of *Johnson* litigation.

The more interesting aspects of the post-1971 San Francisco desegregation story have occurred outside the courtroom. Horseshoe is generally intact. But

310. 500 F.2d. at 352.

311. 500 F.2d. at 352.

312. Interview with Willis Hannawalt, *supra* note 249. *See also* Response of Intervenors Robert Nelson, *el al.,* to Order Dated November 26, 1974, as Amended by Orders Extending Time Dated December 18 and 30, 1974, filed January 29, 1975.

313. Interview with George Krueger, *supra* note 174. For his part, Arthur Brunwasser indicated no desire to continue pushing the district to repair the Horseshoe Plan's defect. Interview with Arthur Brunwasser, *supra* note 158.

314. Interview with Willis Hannawalt, *supra* note 249.

315. Interview with George Krueger, *supra* note 174.

316. Interview with Quentin Kopp, *supra* note 249. *See also* Response to Intervenors Guey Heung Lee, *et. al.,* to Order Dated November 26, 1974, as Amended by Orders Extending Time Dated December 18 and 30, 1974, January 10, 1975.

desegregation has not been an unqualified success story in San Francisco. Administrative incompetence made its implementation awkward at best. White families continued steadily to move to the suburbs, as they had since the mid-1960s. The third-world communities—notably the Mission and Chinatown, but also the Filipinos and Japanese—began to press hard for bilingual programs that would effectively remove them from the desegregated schools. A host of other school lawsuits consumed district energy. The school board, finally changed into an elected body in the aftermath of *Johnson,* spent most of its time politicking, and devoted little attention to policy; by 1974 the administration of San Francisco's schools, at both the board and administrative levels, was in such a sorry state that the Public Schools Commission had been established, under the auspices of State Superintendent of Public Instruction Wilson Riles, to sort through the mess. And the hardy band of ideologues from the NAACP who had forced a final resolution of the desegregation issue in the courts lost interest in the question. They had left the schools behind in their search for new problems to solve.

THE AFTERMATH: THE POLITICS OF DESEGREGATION, 1971-1975

The Erosion of the Horseshoe Plan

The First Days of Desegregation. *Peace.* By and large the actual desegregation of San Francisco's elementary schools in September 1971 was a peaceful process. There were pockets of resistance in the white community—notably among navy families stationed on Treasure Island, who for the first time realized that they were part of the city—and, more dramatically, in Chinatown. There was, however, no violence, a fact which only in retrospect seems noteworthy.

The character of San Francisco itself affords one explanation for this relative tranquility: the city perceives itself to be a civilized place, not given to rock-throwing and bus-burning. And Mayor Alioto, who had spoken out against citywide desegregation, set out to keep the peace.[317] The mayor urged unhappy whites to "take their frustrations out on the court and in the ballot box"—a proposition calling for the creation of a popularly elected school board was on the November 1971 ballot—but not "in the streets." He was in constant communication with Assistant Superintendent Reiterman (by now, Alioto and Shaheen were not speaking), and the police, tracking down any incidents in the making; his staff talked daily with the anti-busing groups around the city. Alioto, a man repeatedly described by NAACP officials as "no different than Mississippi's

---

317. Interview with John DeLuca, *supra* note 139. Interviews with Earl Raab, *supra* note 60. Leroy Cannon, *supra* note 143, and Thomas Shaheen, *supra* note 204 confirm this account.

racists" and dubbed "Bilbo by the Bay" by mayoral opponent Diane Feinstein,[318] managed in September to keep the lid on.

Resistance. Peace did not, however, mean smoothly-managed integration.

Administrative incompetence. The district's planning left much to be desired. Administrators, who were supposed to be planning, instead "disappeared" for the crucial month of July. They had, as Shaheen reported, "no great enthusiasm" for desegregation.[319] Teachers didn't learn what school they would be assigned to until days before classes began. The process of distributing teachers in a way which equalized "competence"—the hopelessly vague phrase in the *Johnson* order which the district, following the lead of the NAACP, equated with salary and seniority—was done by hand, because the administrator responsible for the job had neither experience with nor trust of computers.[320] Student assignments and bus routings were not prepared until the last minute, a fact that galled many parents. Small segments within San Francisco also staged quiet rebellions.

White opposition. White parents in the Park South–Sunset districts of the city hastily formed a new organization, WALK (We All Love Kids), and scheduled an anti-busing rally the day before school opened. Alioto successfully prevailed upon them to cancel the rally, and work instead on the elected school board measure as a way of showing their disapproval of the board. WALK did stage one brief demonstration.[321] It also served as clearinghouse for parents interested in alternative schools, and claimed to have received 1500 inquiries by early September.[322] The organization did not, however, persist in its efforts; like their predecessors in Richmond, parents in this group were quite capable of either finding private alternatives to the public schools, working within the system to make private arrangements, or falsifying their addresses and sending their children to neighboring Daly City schools.

The naval base on Treasure Island was also resistant. The navy families living on government property had asked to be excluded from the desegregation plan; the secretary of the navy intervened to support this request.[323] Nonetheless, Treasure Island children were assigned to Zone 2, which included the largely black Western Addition. They joined forces with WALK, and refused to send their children to the assigned schools until finally ordered to do so by an embarrassed secretary of the navy, who reversed his position under considerable political pressure.[324] Like the Park South–Sunset parents, the navy families worked closely with certain elementary school principals, and were able to have

318. Interview with John DeLuca, *supra* note 139.
319. Interview with Thomas Shaheen, *supra* note 204.
320. Interview with James Ballard, *supra* note 269.
321. San Francisco Chronicle, September 9, 1971, at 9.
322. *Id.,* September 14, 1971, at 2.
323. *Id.,* September 9, 1971, at 9.
324. *Id.,* September 29, 1971.

their children concentrated in several predominantly white schools. By December 1971, Treasure Island school was 54 percent white, 20 percent less than in the previous year but highly discrepant from the white student population envisioned by Horseshoe.[325]

Boycott in Chinatown.[326]   The most substantial and sustained opposition to Horseshoe centered in Chinatown. That resistance was organized by the Big Six Companies, the traditionally conservative force in the community. The historic control of the Six Companies over Chinatown was maintained by keeping people—especially the new immigrants—dependent on the employment, housing, social, and educational services it provided. With the coming of federally funded social programs, such as the community action program, in the 1960s, that dependency declined. In addition, the Six Companies, alarmed by the recent tilt in American foreign policy toward the People's Republic of China, were desperate to maintain the loyalty of the American Chinese toward Taiwan. In October 1971 the Six Companies staged a demonstration in support of the Taiwan government, and it was rumored that marchers were promised money for Chinese alternative schools in return for a public display of loyalty to Taiwan.

Not that Chinatown needed to be bribed. When the public schools opened, the administration's plan called for 720 Chinese children to assemble in front of one of the Chinatown schools, to be bused elsewhere in the city. On the first day, 29 children showed up; on the second day, the group grew to 33. On both days almost twice as many Chinese adults were on hand, officially "to observe the busing procedures," unofficially to see "who did and who didn't boycott the buses."[327] This social pressure encouraged most Chinatown families to send their children either to private or parochial schools, or to "Freedom Schools," ironically enough named for the black schools set up in the South as part of the fight for desegregation.

Several Freedom Schools operated in Chinatown during the first year of desegregation. The largest such enterprise, Telesis, enrolled an estimated 800 children in four sites; the enterprise, organized by the Chinese-American Citizens' Alliance, was bankrolled by the Six Companies. Telesis recruited a number of teachers, (ironically including some Berkeley students interested in imparting a Maoist philosophy to the youngsters). The Six Comapnies also ran what was called the Nob Hill system, which enrolled about 500 children. A third school, the North Beach system, instructed an additional 150 children. All three systems were managed by a central committee, the Chinese Parents for Quality Education, which represented the various conservative Chinatown organizations.

The strength of the Chinese resistance to desegregation surprised the district. Just before school opened, Superintendent Shaheen engaged Al Cheng, a former Chinatown youth worker familiar with the community, to assist the district in

325. *Id.*, December 7, 1971, at 26.
326. *See* note 274, *supra.*
327. Wolfe, *supra* note 274, at 41.

obtaining compliance. For the first time a representative of the school system came in to speak with parents in Chinatown, trying to allay the prevalent suspicions. "We will accept nothing less than an end to busing" was the overwhelmming response.[328] Nor did Mayor Alioto discourage the Freedom Schools; indeed, he praised them as "preserving the Chinese culture."[329]

Over time the Six Companies became less willing to finance the Telsis schools. The schools were forced to fire their Maoist teachers, and then given insufficient funds to replace them. At one point Telesis approached the district with a proposal to establish a federally funded alternative school. Instead the district offered to expand its bilingual program, provide additional resources, and institute a free lunch program. At this writing the Freedom Schools enroll only an estimated 215 students. The rest rejoined the public school system; they did so only after the district intimated, in 1972, its willingness to compromise. By the fall of 1972 more than half of Chinatown's students were in the public schools, and that proportion has continued to increase. But the Chinese persist in their objections to busing, and of late have been seeking a vastly expanded bilingual-bicultural educational program.

Nonexistent "Balance" and No Educational Program. The Horseshoe plan approved by the court promised to "balance" racially all of San Francisco's elementary schools. On paper that objective could be accomplished. Yet even the plan's architects knew that the balance was delicate, and that certain zones would likely become imbalanced before the school year began: Zones 3, 4, and 5, for example, which encompassed Chinatown, the Mission district, and much of Hunter's Point, were barely within stage guidelines at the outset. No one could confidently gauge the depth of community resistance, or know how that resistance would be revealed.

By December 1971 it was clear that the elementary schools were substantially more desegregated, by any criterion, than they had previously been. It was also clear that Horseshoe would not produce the promised racial balance: 38 of the 99 elementary schools were, in one respect of another, imbalanced.[330] The outcome was not wholly attributable to that fabled phenomenon, white flight: although the white elementary school population declined from 34.5 to 30.1 percent,[331] this represented only a more rapid rate of departure than had been witnessed in previous years, not a new event. The departure rate has reverted to a level below that of the 1965–1970 period, and it appears that the *Johnson* order simply hastened an ongoing change in the ethnic composition of the student body by about two and a half years. No did the parochial schools absorb substantial numbers of new students: enrollment in that system actually

328. Fay Fong, Chairman of the Chinese Parents Committee, as quoted in the San Francisco Chronicle, September 14, 1971, at 4.
329. Interview with John DeLuca, *supra* note 139.
330. San Francisco Chronicle, December 7, 1971, at 26.
331. Status Report, *supra* note 8, at 90.

declined slightly between 1970 and 1971, and has continued to do so in the subsequent years.[332] Much of the fault lay with the zone lines themselves: zones which were nearly imbalanced in July were in fact imbalanced by September; the comings and goings of a relative handful of students guaranteed that result. These problems have persisted.

The difficulty with Horseshoe was attributable in part to its educational program—or, rather, lack of one. The zone boundaries recognized no ongoing educational enterprises, except the Richmond and Park South Complexes. The OMI Community Educational Project was divided between zones, with most of the white children assigned to schools in the Hunter's Point section of Zone 5, and the blacks placed in the Sunset schools in Zone 6. While the black families adjusted well to the new situation, many white families deserted the public schools for private academies, defeating the original intentions of the OMI project.[333]

SEED lost its educational program, as the Hunter's Point-Bayview community was split into two zones. Even as the Hunter's Point children were being sent to older schools in the Mission District, a new school, which had been fought for by the community, was being completed in Bayview. Many parents who had been involved in choosing an architect and helping to design the new Bayview school would not be allowed, because of Horseshoe, to send their children to it. The pride and involvement in the schools so carefully nurtured by SEED was evaporating, and parents were once again beginning to complain about the school system's callousness.[334]

The Mission Coalition berated the board of education for cutbacks in the bilingual education program budget, which had been made just prior to the opening of school in order to keep the district's fiscal ledger balanced. The Latino community was not unhappy about the idea of desegregation but objected to the fact that its children were being sent to schools where no special services for non-English-speaking Latinos were available. "The Court order should not have been allowed to disrupt the school program," said coalition representative Sal Cordova.[335]

The district's educational "lighthouse school," Frederick Burk, collapsed in the wake of desegregation. The school had previously been operated as a laboratory school, staffed by teachers and students from San Francisco State College; it drew a racially mixed student body from the entire city. Under Horseshoe, the school became a part of Zone 6, with regular district staff and whatever materials it could manage to acquire in the general redistribution that occurred in 1971. As a consequence the school became no worse—and no better—than the average

332. Interview with Sister Bernadette Giles, Office of the Roman Catholic Archdiocese of San Francisco, in San Francisco, March 26, 1975.

333. Interview with Charlotte Berk, formerly secretary of OMI, currently president of the Lowell High School Parents' and Teachers' Association, in San Francisco, March 20, 1975.

334. Interview with Robert Fisher, *supra* note 91.

335. Interview with Sal Cordova, *supra* note 94.

school in the district. San Francisco has subsequently shown no interest in exemplary programs of any kind, save in Park South, where the local parents' group was able to obtain outside funding for such a venture.[336] There are, of course, San Francisco schools which—either by reputation or in terms of students' achievement test scores—are "good." But the district itself can take little credit for encouraging this kind of excellence. Some of these are small "public alternatives," set up at parental instigation; in the others, a competent principal and a cadre of superb teachers of varying pedagogical persuasions have produced good results in the face of central office indifference.[337]

The Supreintendent and the "Liberal" Board Become the Targets. Someone had to take the blame for this situation. Just as baseball team owners fire the managers of mediocre teams, hoping that a new manager will produce more victories, San Francisco turned on Superintendent Shaheen. Shaheen had hoped to use the advent of desegregation as the vehicle for shaking up the administration—drastically cutting back Breyer's and Reiterman's power, decentralizing the structure, substituting a "philosophy of education" for the pragmatics of survival[338]—but at that he failed badly. Not that Shaheen was wholly blameless. He saw himself as a "facilitator," but gave even staff loyalists little support. He embraced too many new ideas at once, and consequently gave all of them short shrift. His distrust of San Francisco's old-line administrators was almost paranoid, and that exacerbated tensions in the central office. He preferred encounter groups and public meetings to face-to-face bargaining, a tactic that alienated the teachers' organizations.[339] Shaheen upset the board by his seeming nonchalance: during the first two weeks of school he proposed taking a European vacation.[340]

Superintendent Shaheen, the self-styled stalking horse for desegregation, became the focus of animosity. "Shaheenigans" were an issue in the mayoralty campaign that fall. Both Alioto and his Republican opponent, Harold Dobbs, urged Shaheen's replacement, and both endorsed Proposition S, the elected school board measure.[341] The voters approved the charter amendment in November, and Diane Feinstein, the only mayoral candidate to speak out for desegregation and Shaheen, received fewer votes than either Alioto or Dobbs. The Mayor won a smashing victory, and Quentin Kopp, lawyer for the Chinatown intervenors, was elected to the board of supervisors.[342]

The 1971 grand jury report also blasted Shaheen. The grand jury periodically

336. Interviews with staff of the Teacher Learning Center, in San Francisco, March 31, 1975; and Nicki Salan, *supra* note 137. Salan's Short History of the Park South Council (n.d., unpublished) also discussed this project.

337. Personal notes taken at presentation by James Kramer, executive director of the Classroom Teachers' Association, to the Riles Commission, in San Francisco, April 2, 1975.

338. Interview with Thomas Shaheen, *supra* note 204.

339. Interviews with James Ballard, *supra* note 269, Earl Raab, *supra* note 60, Irving Breyer, *supra* note 204, David Sanchez, *supra* note 208.

340. San Francisco Examiner, September 3, 1971, at 1.

341. San Francisco Chronicle, October 6, 1971, at 1.

342. *Id.,* November 12, 1971, at 1.

inquires into school matters; this time it emerged with a stinging indictment. Whereas a year earlier the jury had welcomed Shaheen, and reacted favorably to his attempted revision of the schools' administrative structure, the 1971 jury decried increased vandalism and truancy, the district's notoriously low achievement-test scores, and the lack of specific academic requirements for awarding high school diplomas. They criticized the zones as simply another layer of administrative bureaucracy, and suggested instead direct decentralization of authority.[343]

Two new board of education members, George Chinn, the first Chinese member of the board, and Eugene Hopp, former education chairman of the elite Commonwealth Club, were installed in January 1972. The appointed board, due to be dissolved following the June election, was now divided on the issue of school desegregation, and yet had to do something. An obvious move was to ease the superintendent out. Deprived of board support and alienated from his central administrative staff, Shaheen struggled to build a political base where he could.[344] He enlisted the minority administrators, who continued to view him as their hero and protector, and tried to elicit community and zone council support. At that effort his success was mixed. In February the intrepid superintendent visited Chinatown. Two hundred fifty angry Chinese people chased him from the area, pelting his car with rocks; millions of Americans watched the televised recounting of Shaheen escaping from a side door and sprinting for safety, barely ahead of a mob of irate Chinese.[345] Shaheen's efforts to win outside allies ultimately failed, and the superintendent concentrated his energies on negotiating a satisfactory settlement for the remainder of his contract.

By August 1972, Thomas Shaheen was gone. His resignation statement urged San Franciscans to "insist that your next superintendent be both an outsider and a philosopher."[346] Shaheen never realized that what San Francisco most needed, at this time, was a practical politician who knew something about managing a school system.

Thirty-four potential candidates campaigned for positions on the board of education, the first time an election had been held for these offices since 1897. The desegregation order and Shaheen were the major issues. Claire Lilienthal, Zuretti Goosby, and Howard Nemerowski, members of the board in 1970 when the *Johnson* suit was filed, declined to run. George Chinn and Eugene Hopp welcomed the chance for public endorsement of their anti-busing position. David Sanchez, who had shifted from his earlier unqualified support for citywide desegregation,[347] and labor's representative, John Kidder, who stated that while

343. Report of the 1971 Grand Jury of the City and County of San Francisco.
344. Interviews with Donald Johnson, *supra* note 224, and Al Cheng, *supra* note 274.
345. The incident is recounted in Wall Street Journal, June 2, 1972, at 1.
346. Statement by Thomas A. Shaheen, Superintendent of Schools, August 25, 1972, at 5.
347. Interview with David Sanchez, *supra* note 208. In voting against a proposal to desegregate the junior high schools, Sanchez expressed his doubts about the value of integration unaccompanied by specific programs to help minority students. San Francisco Chronicle, March 17, 1972.

he believed in desegregation "we have to be realistic about busing," also sought election.[348]

The four incumbents were easily reelected, with George Chinn drawing the largest number of votes and becoming thereby the president of the board. The three other candidates elected included two strong supporters of desegregation, Charlie May Haynes, widow of a black minister, and Lucille Abrahamson, president of the Education Auxiliary, successor to Claire Lilenthal as the board's Jewish liberal. The *Chronicle* summed up the election: "Anti-busing voters were angry with the liberal-dominated Board because they felt that it didn't fight hard enough against the Federal District Court Order to use forced busing to desegregate the elementary schools."[349]

The Routinization of Desegregation. *The Office of Integration.* Organizational innovations persist long after the reason for their initiation has disappeared. William Cobb remained the community relations officer of the San Francisco School District until his retirement in 1974, even though he no longer had a detectable community with whom he could relate. The functional successor to that job, the Office of Integration, has continued to operate under three different directors. Its initial task, the development of a desegregation plan to comply with Weigel's order, was followed by others, involving the implementation of *Johnson* and planning for integration of the junior and senior high schools. Desegregation has become routinized in San Francisco.

The several directors of the Office of Integration have all been committed to desegregation, but have lacked the bureaucratic clout to translate these beliefs into working policy. Donald Johnson, the office's first director, was unable to police the traffic on requests for transfer filed by Chinese students when they returned to the district in 1972. Despite the fact that many of these requests, ostensibly based on medical reasons, were signed by one or two well-known Chinese doctors, it was impolitic to dispute their legitimacy.[350]

The district also sought to maintain the level of white enrollment by dramatically increasing programs for gifted students. Prior to the desegregation order, gifted children had been offered a variety of enrichment activities, which varied generally with the school principal's ingenuity in scheduling time, space, and personnel. Starting in 1971, about 40 "total impact" classes—approximately one for every two elementary schools in the district—were established, and continue to operate. Judge Weigel's order had specifically noted that "gifted children . . . may be given special preferences or attention or handling in any manner which does not involve or promote racial segregation."[351] But the gifted classes have

348. San Francisco Examiner, May 22, 1972.
349. San Francisco Chronicle, June 7, 1972, at 1.
350. Interview with Donald Johnson, *supra* note 224; letter from Benjamin Criswell, president of the NAACP, to the San Francisco Medical Society, March 27, 1973 (noting "what appears to be a concerted effort by two doctors in Chinatown to encourage further violations of the law").
351. 339 F. Supp. 1322 (N.D. Cal. 1972).

produced a new kind of segregation. In 1974/75, whites, who constituted 24.9 percent of the elementary school population, accounted for 46 percent of gifted class enrollment; only half the proportion of blacks and Spanish-speaking students in the district were represented in those classes.[352] The reverse phenomenon occurred in classes for the educable mentally retarded, traditionally a dumping ground program both for difficult-to-manage and for slow-learning pupils; the proportion of blacks assigned to those classes was twice as high as the district-wide proportion.[353] There was nothing that Johnson could have done about either the gifted or educable retarded programs; they were outside his jurisdiction. So in many schools desegregation stopped at the schoolhouse doors. Inside the schools, blacks and whites had as little contact with each other as they had had prior to the implementation of Horseshoe.

At the end of 1973 a discouraged Donald Johnson left the district. He had managed to persuade the district not to abandon the Horseshoe plan in favor of one that achieved less racial mixing; he had not been able to render the larger aspiration of the court order a reality. Desegregation efforts persist. The enterprise is now managed by the Office of Integration, which spends much of its time attempting to resolve the daily dilemmas that continue to appear.[354] The office is also in the data-collection business. Its current report notes that about half of San Francisco's elementary schools are imbalanced, a worse situation than existed in the fall of 1971. Yet it lacks authority to address either of these issues or to attempt the creation of programs that might help something educationally good to emerge from Horseshoe. Even control over federal desegregation dollars has been taken from the office. The district's priorities are clearly elsewhere.

Desegregating the Secondary Schools: Does Anyone Still Care? The Citizens' Advisory Committee had originally set out to devise a system-wide desegregation plan in the spring of 1971. The pressure of responding to the court's order obliged it to concentrate on the primary schools. During the fall of 1971, members of that committee resumed their meetings, focusing on the secondary schools.[355] In March of 1972 the lame-duck board voted, four to three, to begin planning for secondary desegregation, with implementation to occur, not in the fall of 1972, but two years later. The intervening years were to be used to develop

352. Status Report, *supra* note 10 at 9; Status Report Prepared by the San Francisco Human Rights Commission, Programs for the Gifted, February 27, 1975, at 3.

353. Larry P.v. Riles, 343 F. Supp. 1306 (N.D. Cal. 1972).

354. Interview with Margery Levy, director of the Office of Integration from 1974 to the present, in San Francisco, April 10, 1975. Levy noted that "a few parents and principals constantly engage in efforts to test the limits and effectiveness of the Court order and District policy." One incident, which occurred the day of the interview, is illustrative: a staff member discovered that 95 pupils, who had been assigned elsewhere, were attending school on Treasure Island.

355. Citizens' Advisory Council, Minutes, September 21, 1971—a typical meeting—note that only 15 members were present.

"the most desirable educational program."[356] The newly elected board disbanded the Citizens' Advisory Committee, and turned the job over to the administrative staff.

Although in May 1972 the NAACP filed suit demanding the immediate desegregation of the secondary schools,[357] the board felt no pressure to make a quick response. The lawyer handling the case, Ben James, did not push for an early hearing. James is a solo practitioner. "Here I am," he said, "handling a divorce today, a drunk driving case tomorrow, and in between a major civil rights case."[358] He allowed the case to slip by, and the administration planned at its leisure.[359] Carlos Cornejo, who succeeded Johnson as acting director of the Office of Integration, attempted to create a totally desegregated system, one which also took into account the needs of the Chinese and Latino communities for special programs.[360] The obstacles were immense. The district was compelled by the *Johnson* decision to utilize the Horseshoe plan, but the location and size of the secondary schools made it impossible to maintain continuity between primary and secondary schools while at the same time assuring racial balance. If the Horseshoe zone scheme was the determining factor in designing a secondary school plan, the plan was bound to have similar problems with its feasibility in certain areas of the city and its inappropriateness in others. The alternative—to scrap Horseshoe and begin on a new plan—would reopen the controversy all over again; Cornejo could generate no enthusiasm for this alternative.

A progress report was presented to the board in Janyary 1974.[361] The board was beginning to feel some pressure from the federal government; it would get no additional desegregation funds unless it did something about the secondary schools by the fall.[362] Cornejo aimed for a bold design, but now it was the board that invoked Horseshoe to prevent a more imaginative and equitable solution to the problem at the secondary level.[363] Again, areas of the city with

356. San Francisco Chronicle, March 17, 1972, at 1.

357. O'Neill v. San Francisco Unified School Dist., No. C-72-808 RFP (N.D. Cal. May 5, 1972).

358. Interview with Ben James, lawyer for plaintiffs in *O'Neill,* in San Francisco, April 15, 1975. For an account of the "traditional" solo practioner, *see* J. Carlin, Lawyers on Their Own (1962).

359. Ex-superintendent Shaheen, who has worked with the NAACP on the *O'Neill* case, expressed his unhappiness at the long delay. Interview with Thomas Shaheen, *supra* note 204.

360. Interview with Carlos Cornejo, acting director of the Office of Integration, 1973/74, who resigned to become principal of Francisco Junior High School, in San Francisco, March 31, 1975. One administrative official described Cornejo's brief central office career: "The system ate Cornejo up."

361. Office of Integration, Progress for Planning of Student Assignments, (January 1974).

362. San Francisco currently receives $3,738,218 in Emergency School Aid Act (ESAA) funds; $1,038,651 of that amount is for the secondary schools. Status Report, *supra* note 8, at 108.

363. Interviews with Carlos Cornejo, *supra* note 360, Al Cheng, *supra* note 274, and Robert Lopez, *supra* note 94.

close ties to the board were able to preserve their advantages—minimum transportation and better plant facilities—while those in the outlying areas were obliged to travel longer distances and lose their special programs. It was obvious to Cornejo that, just as nonblack children were rarely in evidence in the Hunter's Point elementary schools, so, too, would white families resist a similarly designed secondary reassignment plan. The board preferred to overlook these discrepancies between the Horseshoe plan and attendance realities.

The administration's plan was "modified and modified and modified."[364] In the end, no plan was formally approved, but secondary school desegregation went into effect anyway.[365] In July the board responded to parental objections by adopting a "temporary attendance permit" transfer policy so loose as to permit anyone to attend the school of his or her choice. In effect, that action represented the adoption of a city wide voucher scheme, an idea the board had several years earlier considered and narrowly rejected. But none of the appealing elements of a voucher scheme—the creation of varied programs, the publication of information—accompanied the open-transfer policy.

Cornejo, who had worked hundreds of hours trying to implement secondary school desegregation, called the revised plan a "farce."[366] By September 1974, more secondary school students had received transfers than were originally scheduled to be bused in order to achieve racial balance.[367] Disgusted, Cornejo quit. "The provisos made the job impossible."[368]

The district's January 1975 data reveal that students did indeed use their temporary attendance permits to transfer into and out of schools for racial reasons. At the junior high school level, for instance, 130 white pupils transferred out of Pelton, none applied to be admitted; as a result, the school opened with 21 whites, 3.4 percent of the total enrollment.[369] By contrast, 158 whites shifted into Herbert Hoover, while only 38 transferred out; the school opened 41.5 percent white.[370] At the senior high school level, similar patterns emerged. Forty-one whites transferred out of (and just 1 into) Woodrow Wilson, while 78 whites transferred into, and 22 out of, McAteer. The Chinese also used their permits to switch schools; they left Mission and Woodrow Wilson in favor of

364. Deposition of Carlos Cornejo, in O'Neill v. San Francisco Unified School District, No. C-72-808-RFP, October 15, 1974, at 28.
365. *Id.* at 25–26.
366. San Francisco Chronicle, July 31, 1974.
367. *Id.,* September 20, 1974. A Chinatown group has brought suit against the district, challenging the board's secondary school desegregation plan on the ground that, because more Chinese students are bused out of Chinatown than non-Chinese are bused in, the Chinatown community bears an excessive portion of the burden of desegregation. Jung v. Morena, Civ. No. C-74-1811 (N.D. Cal., August 28, 1974); interview with Ronald Wong, plaintiffs' lawyer, *supra* note 274.
368. Interview with Carlos Cornejo, *supra* note 360.
369. Status Report, *supra* note 8, at 67, 104.
370. *Id.* at 67, 103.

Galileo and George Washington, two schools closer to home. In January 1975, Wilson had only 9.4 percent whites—rather than the anticipated 15.6 percent— and 71.4 percent blacks.[371]

Yet if pupils changed schools for apparently racial reasons, they shifted for other reasons, as well. In some instances as many whites (or blacks or Chinese) moved into a school as moved out of it. Overall, the secondary schools were more desegregated after "Operation Integrate" than before: every school was more racially balanced, in each of the racial categories, than it had been the previous year. Even Woodrow Wilson and Pelton, two almost all-black schools, had a few more whites than they had had before.[372]

The secondary school desegregation suit has dragged on. In 1975/76, the district tightened transfer standards somewhat; and both parties supported the dismissal of the case.

The more startling development is that, although the management of desegregation has been routinized in San Francisco, no one outside of the Office of Integration cares very much about the issue of desegregation any longer. The administration will do whatever is expedient. The board is paralyzed by the prospect of doing anything. The NAACP has become a substantially weaker organization than in 1970. San Francisco's public school enrollment continues to decline—from 82,033 in 1970/71, the year before the *Johnson* order, to 68,862 in 1975/76. Whites now make up only one-quarter[373] of the school-age population, and Third World groups are pressing for their own programs. Soon there won't be anyone left for blacks to be desegregated with.

Other Agendas

Blacks and Whites. Desegregation's limited success is traceable, in part, to the incapacity or unwillingness of school administrators and the board of education to make it work. Sustained indifference accomplished what outright defiance had been unable to bring about. But the appeal of desegregation has also dwindled among those blacks and white liberals initially most enthusiastic about it; other ethnic groups have been busily promoting their own agenda for school reform.

Sometime between the filing of the *Johnson* complaint and the present, many white civil rights workers lost their taste for desegregation, and moved on to other issues.[374] Blacks had never been directly involved, in substantial numbers, in the litigation. Looking back on the case, NAACP lawyer James Herndon realized that this had been a serious tactical error. "Unless an organization is

371. *Id.* at 86–87.
372. *Id.* at 81-87.
373. *Id.* at 6.
374. Interviews with Earl Raab, *supra* note 60; Nicki Salan, *supra* note 137; Ann Bloomfield, *supra* note 271; Lois Barnes, *supra* note 78; and Arthur Brunwasser, *supra* note 158.

prepared to do battle on all fronts relevant to a political litigation—and *Johnson* was a political litigation—it's best not to fight at all."[375]

The black community, of course, has had to live with a decision which, in important respects, did not improve their children's lives. A survey of pupil and teacher attitudes conducted in 1973 suggested the depth of the problem. In the argot of that study, black and Spanish-speaking children remain negative in their self-concepts and in their attitudes toward school, and score higher on measures of school anxiety than their white or Asian counterparts. Desegregation has improved neither their motivation nor their achievement. Blacks and whites have little to do with one another while at school. While teachers' attitudes toward multi-ethnic schools are generally positive, their expectations for Asian and white children are higher than for black and Spanish-speaking students.[376]

In more objective terms, black students have also fared badly. They continue to be statistically underrepresented in the gifted programs, overrepresented in classes for the mildly handicapped.[377] They also are suspended substantially more often their white counterparts. In 1973/74, 55.6 percent of the 1,775 junior high school suspended students and over two-thirds of the 1,150 senior high suspended students were black.[378] There is some evidence that elementary school desegregation increased both the number of suspensions and proportion of blacks receiving them: in 1970/71, 71 percent of all suspensions had almost doubled, to 795, and it was black children who were being suspended in three-quarters of the cases.[379]

This kind of evidence has prompted even those blacks who had been enthusiastic about desegregation to question its value as a means of improving educational opportunities for black students.[380] Many middle-class black families who supported the idea of desegregation have been less than delighted with its effects on their youngsters. Previously, these children attended school with middle-class white students; today, they have been joined by many poor black and Latino children, and their parents perceive the classroom environment as consequently less conducive to educational achievement. In recent years, middle-class black families have begun to follow the whites out of the city into the suburbs.[381] The

375. Interview with James Herndon, lawyer for plaintiffs in *Johnson,* in San Francisco, April 8, 1975.

376. Mercer, Evaluating Integrated Elementary Education, September 1973 (unpublished report delivered to the San Francisco Unified School District, part of a larger project on integration in California. *See, e.g.,* Wegner & Mercer, *Dynamics of the Desegregation Process: Politics, Policies, and Community Characteristics as Factors in Change,* in The Polity of the School: Political Perspectives on Education (F. Wirt ed., forthcoming).

377. See pages 481–82, *supra.*

378. San Francisco Human Rights Commission, Report on Suspensions, November 7, 1974, at 6.

379. San Francisco Unified School District, ESEA Proposal, May 1973, §2, at 23.

380. Interview with Zuretti Goosby, *supra* note 81.

381. Interviews with Zuretti Goosby, *supra* note 81, and Robert Nelson, a named intervenor in *Johnson* and head of Concerned Parents in San Francisco, April 2, 1975. Nelson claims that a number of middle-class black Richmond families moved to the suburbs rather

Hunter's Point–Bayview community, whose members lack the resources to move out, is similarly unhappy. Black families there have requested that their children be reassigned to the neighborhood schools from which desegregation had promised an escape.[382]

One does not hear much talk in San Francisco about desegregation—or, for that matter, community control—in the black community. Education is seemingly not an exciting issue anymore. For the time being, at least, the blacks have quietly given up.

The Other Ethnic Groups. In the other ethnic communities, notably Asian and Latino, there has been a renascence of interest in the public schools. Chinese, Latino, Filipino, and Japanese organizations have been consistently gaining strength, as their relative proportion of the school population has steadily grown during the past five years. (By 1978, blacks and whites together will be a minority of the school population.) In a way the desegregation order triggered their concern for equality of opportunity with the district's two predominant groups, the blacks and whites. A turning-point was the U.S. Supreme Court's 1974 decision in *Lau v. Nichols*,[383] which specifically ordered San Francisco to provide Chinese students who did not speak English a "meaningful opportunity to participate in the public educational program."[384] The *Lau* decision studiously avoided defining what kind of instruction would be "meaningful"; presumably, if the district had the wit to defend it, a Berlitz-type total immersion in English offering would have been approved. But to the newer foreign-language communities in San Francisco, *Lau* was an invitation to renew and sharpen their demands for bilingual-bicultural education.

Following *Lau*, Superintendent Morena (who has succeeded Shaheen) appointed the Citizens' Bilingual Task Force, a group which represented the most radical elements of the Latino and Asian communities. Whereas the NAACP Education Committee during the 1960s equated equal opportunity with a redistribution of black and white students, assuming that that remedy would bring with it equalization of educational resources[385] and would help to overcome the psychological harm of racial isolation, the Citizens' Bilingual Task Force took a decidedly different view:

The Master Plan must seek to rectify existing inequalities in the treatment and educational outcomes between English-speaking, and limited English-

---

than permit their children to be bused to the lower-class black Fillmore and Western Addition areas; Goosby stated that black families living in middle-class, predominantly black Bayview had moved slightly south, to Pacifica. Overall, black enrollment in the San Francisco elementary schools declined by 1 percent between 1971 and 1974. Status Report, *supra* note 8, at 19.

382. Interview with Robert Fisher, *supra* note 91; Status Report, *supra* note 8, at 93-94.
383. 414 U.S. 563 (1974).
384. *Id.* at 566.
385. See page 428, *supra.*

speaking children in a way that is compatible with the general and culture-specific goals and aspirations of various groups within the San Francisco community. . . .

The burden should be on the school to adapt its educational approach so that the *culture, language and learning style* of all children in the school (not just those of Anglo middle-class background) are accepted and valued. *Children should not be penalized for culture and linguistic differences, nor should they bear a burden to conform to a school-sanctioned culture by abandoning their own.* [386]

Those assumptions led the committee to recommend a full kindergarten-through-grade-12 bilingual-bicultural program which employed the child's native language as the primary language, utilizing English as the second language. It estimated that almost one out of every eight San Francisco students would enroll in the program. [387]

Although the committee contemplated that one-third of each class would be composed of English-speaking youngsters to preserve the bilingual aspect of the program and promote integration, it put forward that recommendation half-heartedly; it seemed difficult enough to find teachers fluent in Tagalog (the Filipino language) and English to teach the ever-expanding Filipino population, without trying to track down English-speaking students interested in studying Tagalog for 12 years. The task force report clearly implied a new kind of segregation. It also would cost a substantial amount of money to implement. Both factors led to considerable and sharply expressed opposition.

The Human Rights Commission [388] and Superintendent Morena [389] opposed the report, and called instead for bilingual instruction as a continuing component of the district's compensatory education program. Supporters of desegregation, like School Commissioner Goosby, found themselves for once aligned with opponents, like Commissioner Hopp, in objecting to the report and urging instead an expanded "English as a Second Language (ESL)" program for all limited English-speaking children. [390]

Behind the public expressions of opposition lay stronger feelings. Opponents

386. Report of the Citizens' Task Force for Bilingual Education. January 21, 1975, at iv. 7.
387. *Id.*
388.

The Human Rights Commission today called on the Board of Education to approach its consideration of a proper bilingual-bicultural master plan in such way as will emphasize helping non or limited-English speaking students to become competent in English and then return to the regular school classes.

San Francisco Human Rights Commission, Position Paper, March 24, 1975.
389. San Francisco Chronicle, March 19, 1975, at 18.
390. Goosby is quoted by the San Francisco Progress, March 22, 1975, at 8, 15, as stating that "every child who needs language help should be in an [English as a second language] program." Hopp is quoted in the same article as saying that "the goal should be to provide competence in English for every child who needs help."

of the bilingual-bicultural approach doubted its pedagogical worth. They saw it as "the ultimate insanity," the final politicization of the San Francisco public schools. They realized that, if adopted, the task force report would inevitably bring about the demise of even the vestige of desegregation.

Little of substance has happened since the task force report. Bilingual advocates continue to push for an expanded bilingual program, but the District lacks the resources and perhaps the taste for such an effort.[391]

The emergency of this Third-World group may well be the most significant unintended consequence of the *Johnson* decision. The Chinese, Latinos, and Filipinos have become full participants in the struggle for political deference in the schools. Ultimately they may have their way. As one thoughtful member of the school board said: "I used to know what was right and what was wrong. I just don't know anymore."[392]

IN RETROSPECT: SOME TENTATIVE OBSERVATIONS

Symbolic Politics and the Community

Critical to the drive for desegregation was a desire to secure official recognition that blacks and whites were formally equal, an end which, it was felt, only color-consciousness in pupil assignment could bring about. "The enactment of civil rights laws and the proclamation of egalitarian public policies are symbols that [blacks] can expect equal treatment and that policymakers view them as deserving equal treatment."[393]

The realities of segregation—the sizable proportion of blacks in integrated schools prior to *Johnson,* or the efforts of the district to move students from overcrowded black schools into nearby white schools, for instance—were only of limited importance in this struggle. What mattered most was the unwillingness of powerful white officials—Superintendent Spears and, later, Mayor Alioto—to defer to the wishes of the civil rights groups, and the felt need to change those positions. Once the symbolic victory had been secured, through the *Johnson* decision, most civil rights activists lost their interest in what happened.

"The symbolic elements in life," Alfred North Whitehead once commented, "have a tendency to run wild, like the vegetation in a tropical forest."[394] That is particularly the case when the symbol is as elusive and ever-changing as racial equality.

---

391. *Id.* Board President Lucille Abrahamson believes that the district will utlimately move in the direction of the *Task Force Report,* but will not be able to accommodate the report's demands for minority hiring, if only because of budgetary problems. Interview with School Board Commissioner Lucille Abrahamson, in San Francisco, April 7, 1975.

392. Interview with Zuretti Goosby, *supra* note 81.

393. M. Edelman, Politics as Symbolic Action 19 (1961).

394. A. Whitehead, Symbolism: Its Meaning and Effect 61 (1927).

In the field of race relations the talk. . . . is in terms of liberty and equality on one side and in terms of the prevention of social disorder . . . on the other side. Neither of these ostensible goals . . . specifies a condition that is objectively definable in the sense that there can be a consensus that it has been achieved. . . . [These goals] evoke political support and opposition; and their semantic ambiguity. . . . is precisely what makes them potent . . . symbols.[395]

If it were tangible equality, not deference, that was the primary objeçtive, the consequences of symbolism could properly be minimized; or, if the whole issue were a side-show, irrelevant to the ongoing institutional life of the schools, they could be dismissed. Neither is the case. The kind of education that San Francisco's children receive is shaped, in part, by the reality of court-ordered desegregation. The groups that worked so hard to bring about this policy change have either been disabled from involving themselves, or have not cared to concern themselves, with the immensely more complicated business of providing an intelligent and humane educational program is racially and socioeconomically heterogeneous schools. Meanwhile, for the black community the gap between public policies which create a belief in their right to equal treatment and daily experiences which reveal an absence of progress to that goal has steadily increased. For the black community, at least, the symbolisim of integration is no longer thrilling; it is now the Third-World groups' turn to discover whether they can do any better at the same game.

The Schoolmaster Court
There is no ideal way for a court to "manage" a conflict as complicated, and as multidimensional, as school desegregation. One tempting response might be to treat a desegregation case as a routine litigation, to be decided by applying legal standards to the relevant facts, ignoring both less-readily assimilable evidence and the larger political consequences of the court's decision. The appeal of this approach is its familiarity; it calls upon the court to do only what it is used to, and competent at, doing.

Yet that alternative seems unduly narrow and crabbed, too unresponsive to the dimensions of the problems inevitably presented and resolved—if only by silence—in the court's decision. As Justice White has pointed out, dissenting in *Bradley v. Milliken:*

The [district court's] task is not to devise a system of pains and penalties to punish constitutional violations brought to light. Rather, it is to desegregate an *educational* system in which the races have been kept apart,

395. Edelman, *supra* note 393, at 16.

without, at the same time, losing sight of the central *educational* function of the schools.[396]

This is the role that Judge Weigel attempted to play in the *Johnson* litigation. It is easy to point out places where Weigel's judgment was arguably wrong: for instance, in not eliciting a full airing of the factual bases for a finding of de jure segregation and refusing to hear the Chinese intervenors, thus encouraging the parties to appeal; in giving the district insufficient time to produce a thoughful plan for desegregation; in not appointing a master who would produce a more "expert" plan. Yet those second-guesses themselves are of debatable validity. Given the political pressure which the board felt, would it not have been compelled to seek and appeal, however substantial the case for de jure segregation? And given the school system's difficulty in seriously planning for the future, would a few months more or less have made a decisive difference? If the desegregation plan which San Francisco produced appears far from ideal it is no worse—indeed, it is probably better—than those adopted by a great many other school districts.

In short, the problems that have accompanied desegregation in San Francisco cannot readily be attributed to anything Judge Weigel either did or failed to do. They inhere in the issue itself, and in the dynamics of implementation. The San Francisco desegregation story suggests that the aspirations of a court order can, in important ways, fail to be realized not only because of overt defiance but also because of more subtle factors—administrative incapacities, shifting political agendas, and the like. Weigel's exhortations to do good were masterful. But they were just exhortations. A court cannot hope to do more.

There is an unhappy lesson for advocate lawyers in this school desegregation history. Litigation represents an end-run around the political process of dispute resolution. That is both its strength, from the advocates' viewpoint, and its limitation. The very system by-passed by bringing an issue to court will bear the responsibility for converting the court's decision into policy and practice.[397] It is possible for a judge to do more than Weigel did in supervising this process; it is not possible for any judge to substitute himself for the implementation process. Unless there exists a constituency eager to take advantage of its newly announced rights, to badger the system into responsiveness, the tangible benefits of a court decision (save as measured in terms of the lawyer's own reputation)

---

396. 418 U.S. 717, 94 S.Ct. 3112, 3136-37 (1974) (White, J. dissenting).

397. There is evidence that the lesson has been acted upon. The federally funded Youth Law Center, which has been responsible for much of the school litigation, spends rather more time negotiating with the district's lawyers for settlements than actually litigating. "If the problem was out in the schools," attorney Suzanne Martinez reports, "I can usually get it resolved; but if it's central office policy that's at issue, there's no way short of a lawsuit to change their minds." Interview with Suzanne Martinez, attorney, Youth Law Center, in San Francisco, March 25, 1975.

may be meager. The point is not that social litigation is necessarily wasteful, or that its promise of reform is invariably deceptive. Yet such litigation can be, and often is, both wasteful and deceptive in its effects unless the "classes" that bring class-action suits can function as political constituencies, and unless the partici-pants in such litigation worry at least as much about the consequences of victory as about how to engineer that victory in the rationalistic environment of a courtroom.

The Role of the Judiciary in the Desegregation of the Winston-Salem/ Forsyth County Schools, 1968–1975

Henry C. Lauerman

Measured by public acceptance, the desegregation of the Winston-Salem/Forsyth County, North Carolina school system was a success. But this study, prepared by Henry C. Lauerman, a professor of Law at Wake Forest University Law School, suggests that the litigation was characterized by persistent failures of the judicial system to clarify applicable substantive and remedial principles. —Eds.

THE SETTING OF THE LAWSUIT

This is Forsyth County

Forsyth County, rectangular in shape, about 26 miles in length east to west and 20 miles wide north to south, comprising 424 square miles, is in north-central North Carolina, somewhat off the main lines of interstate commerce, somewhat removed from metropolis.

Winston-Salem, the principal city and county seat of Forsyth County, is in the south-central part of the county. The principal industries and businesses in Forsyth County are located within the city limits. The industries manufacture consumer goods, mainly—tobacco products, textiles, furniture, electronics and communication equipment, and air-conditioning equipment. Winston-Salem ranks third in the Southeast in dollar volume of goods sold, exceeded by Atlanta and Richmond. Winston-Salem also is the home of Wachovia Bank and Trust Company, then the largest bank in North Carolina, and presently the nation's thirtieth largest general bank.[1] In 1961 an interstate highway, I-40, was built, traversing the county from east to west and bisecting Winston-Salem. Suburban residential development was stimulated by the highway but had not caused

1. Fortune (May 1975), at 75.

major employers to locate or relocate their plants close to the highway and beyond the city limits. Thus, the city of Winston-Salem was the major trading and the only industrial area in Forsyth County when the issue of school desegregation was being resolved in the courts.

Winston-Salem has been described as the "culturopolis" of the Southeast. Wake Forest University, Winston-Salem State University, and Salem College campuses lie within the city limits, along with the state-supported North Carolina School of the Arts, which has gained nationwide recognition as a training center for the performing and fine arts. The Bowman Gray School of Medicine and its teaching hospital, the N.C. Baptist Hospital, make Winston-Salem a medical treatment center. Winston-Salem was the first city in the United States to organize an arts council. Its symphony orchestra is enthusiastically supported.

An obvious concomitant of the concentration of business, financial, cultural, educational, and professional activities in Winston-Salem is the presence of large numbers of highly educated, knowledgeable citizens. Although political and social philosophies vary widely, the so-called "liberal tradition" of this century probably pervades Winston-Salem/Forsyth County to a greater extent than one might expect in a realtively self-contained community of its size.

The population had been increasing at an annual rate of 25 percent in Forsyth County during the sixties. Much of the recent population growth in the county apparently has occurred within the city limits. While the county as a whole grew in population from 189,428 in 1960 to 214,348 in 1970—an increase of 24,920—the city itself grew from 111, 135 to 132,913, an increase of 21,778. While the apparent increase in the population of Forsyth County beyond the city limits during this period was only 3,000, during 1960–1970 the city annexed several areas of high population density, thereby reducing the area and population beyond the city limits. The table below summarizes the population distribution by race in Forsyth County in late 1969 as reported in the 1970 Census.

	White	Percent	Black & Others	Percent	Total[2]	Percent
In Winston-Salem	87,054	65.7%	45,859	34.3%	132,913	100%
Beyond Winston-Salem	79,025	97.0	2,410	3.0	81,435	100
	166,079	77.5	48,269	22.5	214,349	100

Ninety-five percent of the blacks in Forsyth County live in Winston-Salem. Moreover, they live in only one section of the city, the east quadrant. In 1974, the Council on Municipal Performance labeled Winston-Salem the most residentially segregated city of its size in the country.[3]

The average income for Winston-Salem households in 1970 was $12,600. The national average for cities of 150,000 population was $12,624.[4] Within the city,

2. Economic Development Department, Winston-Salem, N.C. Chamber of Commerce, Pocket Library (1972) at 38, 39.

3. Council on Municipal Performance, University of Wisconsin (1974).

4. Sales Management (July 1974), at A39, B3, B4.

income distribution correlates with racial residential patterns. Prior to 1965, several black ghettoes touched the downtown area. But now they are almost gone because of urban renewal projects.

The county beyond the city limits is residential and largely white. The population, both black and white, probably is somewhat better educated and more affluent than the population of other cities in the South of comparable size. The races in Winston-Salem live apart. The black community is not as affluent as the white but, within its ranks, the socioeconomic status of individuals may vary as widely as it does in the white community. In a word, Winston-Salem has a comparatively progressive black community within a similar but large white community.

Voluntary School Desegregation in Forsyth County (1954–1970)

School Desegregation in Forsyth County, N.C., 1954–1963. During the nine years immediately following *Brown v. Topeka Board of Education,*[5] from 1954 to 1963, the Forsyth County Board of Education operated public schools beyond the city limits and the Winston-Salem Board of Education operated the schools within.

Desegregation of the County Schools. In 1953, one year before *Brown I,* a new union school, Carver School, opened its doors to *all* of the 1,500 black children of school age in Forsyth County who lived in the 400 square miles beyond the limits of Winston-Salem.[6] Prior to that time these children had attended several de jure segregated elementary and high schools scattered about the county. The new Carver School was acclaimed by the white and black communities as a model plant, not only equal to but better than many of the white schools. According to Lillian Lewis, a black member of the county board of education from 1960 to 1970, the principal objection of the black community to segregated schools was not separateness as such, but an awareness that the physical facilities and the tangibles of schooling provided for blacks were in fact not equal to those provided for the whites. Little wonder that the county board of education in 1953 was justifiably proud of its new union school for blacks.[7]

Years later, many young black adults of Forsyth County recalled in 1971 and 1972, when the court first ordered busing for white children,[8] that they, as young children, had been bused from the farthest reaches of Forsyth County to Carver School every day of their public school lives from 1953 to 1964—the latter year was the year when pupil assignments to Carver began to be made on the basis of

5. 347 U.S. 483 (1954) (Brown I); and 349 U.S. 294 (1955) (Brown II).
6. Winston-Salem, N.C. Chamber of Commerce, Data on School Consolidation (1962).
7. Interview with Lilian Lewis, member, Forsyth County Board of Education, 1960–1970, May 1, 1975.
8. Scott v. Board of Education, Civ. No. C-174-WS-68 (M.D.N.C.), Order, Aug. 17, 1970.

attendance zones after the city and county schools had been consolidated. However, when Carver School was opened, most blacks and their parents rejoiced because they could attend a new school facility equal to, or better than, the schools that white children were attending. No one thought of complaining in 1953 of the long bus ride to Carver School. Most children in the county, white and black, rode a bus anyway because they were not within walking distance (one and a half miles) of school. The somewhat lengthened ride to the new Carver School for blacks was not, at the time, considered an unjustified or unbearable burden.[9]

Following *Brown,* the county board of education was not supposed to assign black students to Carver Union solely on the basis of race. During 1955–1962 the county schools served about 20,500 students, of whom only 1,500 were black.[10] Moreover, most of the 1,500 county school black students lived just beyond the eastern limit of the city, in close proximity to Carver School. With respect to these students, the mandate of *Brown I,* as generally construed in the South during the two years following *Brown II,* would not necessarily have required them to attend school with white children, assuming that there were no white children living within the vicinity of Carver School.

There were, however, as many as 12,700 black children who resided in predominantly white neighborhoods throughout the county beyond the city limits.[11] The parents of these students were never proffered an election whereby they could choose for their child either Carver School or the school nearest their residence. The report of the Institute of Government had stated that such an election "would certainly seem valid, as a transitional measure. And quite possibly it might be valid as a permanent measure."[12] However, none of the black parents whose children were attending Carver sought a white school for their children. After *Brown,* they acquiesced, perhaps reluctantly in some cases, in having their children bused to the new Carver School.[13]

Brown had no visible effect on the county schools from 1954 to 1963. Those few white families who lived closer to Carver than any other school continued to attend the more distant white schools to which they had always been assigned. Carver School remained all black. Because no black parents who lived farther from Carver than from a white school elected to send their children to the nearer white county school, other schools in the county system remained all white.

Desegregation of the City Schools. In the two years immediately following *Brown II,* no black student attended school with white students in Winston-

9. Interview with Lilian Lewis, note 7 *supra.*

10. Winston-Salem, N.C. Chamber of Commerce, Data on School Consolidation (1962).

11. Interview with Assoc. Superintendent Raymond Saurbaugh, Winston-Salem/Forsyth County Schools, June 3, 1975.

12. J. Paul & A. Coates, The School Desegregation Decision, (Institute of Government, University of North Carolina 1954), at 99.

13. Interview with Raymond Saurbaugh, note 11 *supra.*

Salem, or elsewhere in North Carolina. In Charlotte, N.C., 80 miles southwest, and in Greensboro, N.C., 30 miles east—cities of comparable size—mixing of white and black students was also nil. However, during the summer of 1957 the civic leaders of the three cities coordinated their first steps toward desegregation in the public schools. In each of the three cities, one black high school student was permitted to attend a white high school located nearer to his or her home than the black high school to which that student would normally have been assigned. For the first time since public schools had started in North Carolina under the law of 1839, a black child attended public school with white children. In 1958 three black elementary pupils were admitted to a previously all-white school.

Each year thereafter another handful of venturesome black parents elected to send their high-school-age children to a white high school which was *nearer* to their homes than the black high school to which the children were otherwise regularly assigned according to the feeder plan. The number of black students attending formerly all-white city high schools in the ensuing years were as follows: 1958/59, 4; 1959/60, 8; 1960/61, 10; 1961/62, 18; 1962/63, 44.[14] Most of these were senior high school transfers. With one or two exceptions, elementary and junior high schools in Winston-Salem remained totally segregated by attendance zones.[15]

Thus, during the period of 1954-1963, all county public schools were either all white or all black. City *elementary* schools were either all white or all black. City *high* schools were all black, all white, or white with a very light sprinkling of blacks. But few persons believed that race was a basis, much less the sole basis, of assignment to schools. Racially identifiable schools resulted because of residential patterns and because, generally speaking, black parents apparently preferred to have their children attend school with black children and white parents preferred to have their children attend school with white children.[16]

School Desegregation Measures in Forsyth County, 1963-1970. *Consolidation of the City and County School Systems in 1963.* Consolidation of city and county schools in Forsyth County had been formally discussed by community leaders and government officials from time to time since 1947. The basic conflicts for resolution prior to consolidation concerned economy of operations, equitable distribution of expense between the city and county, and the effect of consolidation on the quality of education.[17] According to Marvin Ward, the present superintendent of Winston-Salem/Forsyth County Schools, during the years immediately following *Brown,* but preceding consolidation, no

14. Scott v. Board of Education, 317 F. Supp. 453, 468 (M.D.N.C. 1970) [hereinafter cited as Scott].
15. *Id.* at 469.
16. Interview with Marvin Ward, superintendent, Winston-Salem/Forsyth County Schools, April 23, 1975.
17. *Id.*

one, white or black, apparently foresaw that the creation of a countywide school system in a white county with a large, dense black core would set the stage for an educational experiment virtually unique.[18]

Legislation enabling the city and county to consolidate schools in Forsyth County was enacted by the General Assembly of North Carolina in 1961.[19] A plan for consolidation was approved by referendum ballot in May of 1962, to become operationally effective in the 1963/64 school year. The die was cast. For better or worse, county school problems were now city school problems and vice versa.

Among the impediments to consolidation had been the adoption by the city in the late 1950s of the elementary/junior high/senior high school unit structure (6-3-3), in lieu of the elementary/high school structure (8-4). During 1961 and 1962, the county also adopted a 6-3-3 school unit structure for *white* children where facilities permitted, but all black children living beyond the city limits continued to attend Carver Union School. By 1963 both the city and county operated with the 6-3-3 structure, except at Carver. This was the prevailing structure until the 1971/72 school year.[20]

The Winston-Salem/Forsyth County schools are administered by an eight-member elected board of education actiong through the school superintendent. The state has provided most of the funding for the public schools in North Carolina since the Act of the N.C. General Assembly of 1825, which created the Literary Fund for Common Schools with dividends arising from bank stock owned by the state and miscellaneous revenues.[21] Today the basic instructional and operational expense of the public schools is funded by the state on the basis of the number of students enrolled in each school system. However, most of the urban systems supplement the state funds with local funds. In 1974/75, for example, $48.9 million was the total operating cost for the Winston-Salem/Forsyth County schools. Of this sum, $27.8 million was supplied by the state, $16.9 million by Forsyth County, and $4.2 million by the federal government.[22] The board of education has no taxing authority and must conform its expenditures of county funds to those objects funded in the annual budget as approved by the county commissioners, of state funds in accordance with the regulations of the North Carolina Board of Education, and of federal funds in accordance with HEW directives.

Pupil Assignments.   "Beginning in 1963, the idea prevailed that desegregated school systems should no longer keep official records."[23] Hence for school years

18. *Id.*
19. Ch. 112, N.C. Session Laws (1961), at 210.
20. Interview with Raymond Saurbaugh, note 11 *supra.*
21. N.C.G.S., § 115-108 (1955).
22. Official Budget, Winston-Salem/Forsyth County Schools, 1975/76, at 5.
23. J. Paul and A. Coates, The School Desegregation Decision (Institute of Government, University of North Carolina 1954) at 8.

Winston-Salem/Forsyth County Schools Pupil Assignment 1969–70[26]

Elementary Schools		*Schools*	*No.*	*Blacks (Percent)*
All Black	[100% Black]	9	5,479	100
Black	[0–5% White]	2	1,432	99
Predominantly Black	[5–50% White]	0	0	0
Predominantly White	[5–50% Black]	9	669	11
White	[0–5% Black	17	183	1.5
All White	[100% White]	5	0	0
Total: 27,066 Students		42	7,763	28

Junior High Schools		*Schools*	*No.*	*Blacks (Percent)*
All Black	[100% Black]	3	1,309	100
Black	[0–5% White]	2	1,542	99.1
Predominantly Black	[5–50% White]	0	0	0
Predominantly White	[5–50% Black]	4	176	6
White	[0–5% Black]	6	93	1.9
All White	[100% White]	2	0	0
Total: 12,090 Students		17	3,120	24.2

Senior High Schools		*Schools*	*No.*	*Blacks (Percent)*
All Black	[100% Black]	3	1,777	100
Black	[0–5% White]	0	0	0
Predominantly Black	[5–50% White]	0	0	0
Predominantly White	[5–50% Black]	2	560	16.1
White	[0–5% Black]	4	150	2.8
All White	[100% White]	0	0	0
Total: 10,616 Students		9	2,487	23.5

1963/64 and 1964/65, immediately after consolidation of the city and county schools, no data exist on the race of students assigned to the schools. For the 1965/66 school year, Carver Union School became a neighborhood school serving a specific nonoverlapping attendance zone. Busing of black children from other parts of the county to Carver School was discontinued; however, it continued to be a grade one through grade twelve school.[24]

Some of the black children beyond the city limits thus deprived of transportation to Carver Union School were in elementary and junior high schools. Some of them had no choice but to attend the white school to which transportation was provided. Hence, not later than the 1965/66 school year, some mixing of black and white children in the public schools had taken place at all grade levels, but not in every school in Forsyth County by any means. As a result of the

24. Interview with Marvin Ward, note 16 *supra.*

changes in the Carver attendance plan and additional elections of blacks to attend white schools, the number of blacks attending predominantly white schools increased more than tenfold, from 44 for the school year 1962/63 to 509 for the school year 1965/66. During the next four years, principally because of changes in the feeder patterns into the senior high schools, black attendance at predominantly white schools was as follows: 1966/67, 1,246; 1967/68, 1,486; 1968/69, 2,155; 1969/70, 2,016.[25] However, by 1968/69 only 29 white students were attending schools that were otherwise black, not including 175 whites who were attending two special schools with 239 blacks.

During the first six years of consolidated city-county school operations, pupil assignment in the Winston-Salem/Forsyth County schools was strictly in accordance with a geographical attendance-zone plan. A child could attend a standard school other than that serving his or her attendance zone because of hardship or might, upon request, transfer to a school nearer to home if the nearer school had a vacancy in that student's grade. No other exemptions to the attendance-zone assignment were permitted.

The table above shows that 852 black children in the elementary grades (1–6) were attending predominantly white schools, whereas 6,911 were attending schools in which 99–100 percent of the students were black; 269 black junior high students were attending predominantly white schools; 2,851 students were attending schools in which 99–100 percent of the students were black. In the senior high schools 710 black students were attending predominantly white schools, whereas 1,777 were attending schools that were 100 percent black. Seventeen years after *Brown,* desegregation in the public schools of Forsyth County had occurred to the extent that 1,831 black students in all grades were attending predominantly white schools and 11,539 were attending schools in which from 99 to 100 percent of the students were black. In other words, about one black student in seven was attending a school with a substantial number of white students.

Faculty Assignments. Until consolidation, no white teacher was assigned to a predominantly black school and no black teacher was assigned to a white school. After consolidation, beginning in 1964, the board of education assigned teachers on a voluntary basis to teach across racial lines. Each year the number of teachers so assigned increased as follows: 1964, 8; 1965, 12; 1966, 107; 1967, 199; 1969, 333.[27]

For the school year 1969/70, 656 (26 percent) of the 2,100 teachers employed were black. This percentage of black teachers corresponds closely with the 22.5 percent black population of the county.

25. Scott at 460.
26. Scott v. Board of Education, Civ. No. C-174-WS-68 (M.D.N.C.), Order, May 25, 1970.
27. Scott at 460.

If it is assumed that there were approximately 460 teaching stations in black schools and that only 26 percent of the teachers therein should have been black if the teachers had been assigned purely at random, then about 340 white teachers (460 × 0.74) should have been assigned to black schools and 340 black teachers to white schools. In other words, a total of about 680 teachers should have been teaching across racial lines if assignments had been made at random. In fact, 333 were so teaching during the school year 1969/70. The system had arrived at the half-way point of total faculty integration through random assignment.

Equalization of Facilities. Until World War II there is little doubt that the physical facilities in black schools were not equal to those provided for white students. However, beginning in the postwar years an effort was made to insure that black and whites were equally treated.[28] By 1968/69 the chief difference in facilities between white and black schools was in the size of the school premises.[29]

JUDICIAL INTERVENTION IN THE OPERATION OF FORSYTH COUNTY SCHOOLS (1970/71)

When the U.S. Supreme Court decided *Green v. County School Board of New Kent County, Va.*[30] on May 27, 1968, the Winston-Salem/Forsyth County Schools had not yet become involved in desegregation litigation. Several factors may have forestalled litigation. For example, Forsyth County school authorities had made a conscious effort to improve schools attended mostly by blacks during the 1950s and 1960s, beginning with the building of Carver Union School in 1950. Of the sixteen schools in the Forsyth County system which were predominantly black in 1968, eight had been built between 1950 and 1963. The remaining eight black schools were at least 35 years old.[31] However, of these eight old schools, three had been predominantly white schools when they were built and had remained so for many years thereafter.[32] Of the fifty white schools in the system, eighteen were at least 35 years old. There were only seven "historically" black schools, that is, schools built for blacks prior to *Brown.* Only two of the historically black schools, Carver Union and Diggs Elementary, built in 1953, met modern standards. The other five historically black schools

28. Interview with Marvin Ward, note 16 *supra.*
29. For the pupil assignment plan, see Scott at 492–507.
30. 391 U.S. 430 (1968) [hereinafter cited as Green].
31. Scott at 460–62.
32. *Id.*, nn. 5, 6, 7. The three schools were North Elementary, built in 1923, which was predominantly white until 1964; Skyland Elementary, built in 1923, which was white until the 1940s; and Hanes Junior High, built in 1930, which was white until 1965. The changes in the racial characteristics of these schools resulted from the changing characteristics of the neighborhoods they served; however, the transition from white to black was accelerated by white transfers out under freedom-of-transfer plans.

had smaller classrooms than white schools, inadequate facilities, little playground room, and were 35 years old or older.

The quality of instruction at predominantly black schools improved markedly beginning in 1965 because ESEA money for remedial education was targeted into the black neighborhoods[33] and because an increasing number of white teachers were assigned to teach in black schools.[34] More than 2,000 black pupils were attending predominantly white schools.[35]

In addition to the lack of widespread and intense dissatisfaction with the educational opportunity for blacks in Winston-Salem/Forsyth County to motivate desegregation litigation, the law of the Fourth Circuit prior to the *1968 Trilogy,*[36] as laid down in *Swann v. Charlotte-Mecklenburg Board of Education*[37] in 1966, virtually precluded racial desegregation of the Forsyth County schools by decree. The Charlotte-Mecklenburg system closely resembled the Forsyth County system in three important aspects: (1) a city centrally located within a county; (2) segregated residential patterns within the city; and (3) recent *city-county consolidation* of the school system.[38] The pupil assignment plan in Charlotte-Mecklenburg, which had been approved in 1966 by the Fourth Circuit Court of Appeals, was based upon compact, contiguous attendance zones, established in good faith, and based upon criteria other than the racial composition of the neighborhoods. Many all-white and all-black schools remained in operation in Mechlenburg County. Freedom of transfer, without transportation provided, was a means for both white and black pupils, rich and poor, to transfer to a school outisde their regular attendance zone if there was a vacancy.[39] Because of its similarity to the Charlotte-Mecklenburg system, there was small likelihood of successful desegregation litigation in Forsyth County unless the Forsyth County Board of Education was proved to have gerrymandered the attendance zones to preserve segregated schools.

So the prior decisional law and the obvious efforts on the part of school officials to improve black educational opportunities in Forsyth County apparently led the NAACP Legal and Defense Fund (LDF) and other black interest groups to think that little was to be gained by initiating desegregation litigation in Forsyth County prior to 1968. That is to say, these groups believed that, until the *1968 Trilogy,* Forsyth County was in compliance with the school desegregation law as it existed in the Fourth Circuit. Furthermore, HEW had declared that Forsyth County was in compliance with its guidelines.[40]

33. Federal funding of school functions was as follows: 1964/65–$217,058; 1965/66–$607,393; 1966/67–$1,387,884; 1967/68–$1,421,180; 1968/69–$1,491,531. Interview with Director of Federal Programs, W-S/FC Schools.
34. Scott at 468.
35. *Id.* at 460–61.
36. Green, *supra* note 30; Raney v. Board of Education, 391 U.S. 443 (1968); Monroe v. Board of Commissioners, 391 U.S. 450 (1968), *all decided* May 27, 1968.
37. Swann v. Board of Education, 369 F.2d 29 (4th Cir. 1966).
38. *See* Swann v. Board of Education, 300 F. Supp. 1358, 1364 (W.D.N.C. 1969).
39. *Id.* at 1364–65.
40. Scott at 460.

For a long time Forsyth County had escaped the agonies of school desegregation litigation, but time ran out at last.

Litigation Begins in Forsyth County, N.C.

The Lighting of the Fuse—The Atkins Case. On February 28, 1968, the Winston-Salem/Forsyth County Board of Education adopted a six-year capital improvements program.[41] To fund the program, $24.8 million of bonds were authorized to be issued by a referendum ballot conducted on March 12, 1969. Included in the "first phase" of the program was an allocation of funds to expand East Forsyth High School, Walkertown Junior High School, and Parkland High School, three predominantly white high schools. The purpose of these expansions was to permit the transfer of black students from all-black senior and junior high schools; namely, from Carver Union and from Anderson Junior and Senior High.[42] A third all-black senior high school, Paisley, was also to be closed and its students disbursed along three other senior high schools, two of which— Reynolds and North—were predominantly white, and the third—Atkins—was all black.[43] If these changes had been made and the buildings expanded as planned, 1,475 black junior and senior high school students would have been transferred from black to predominantely white schools by school year 1970/71 at the latest.[44] In each case the physical facilities at the new school would have bettered those of the black school from which the students were to be transferred. Finally, deviations from the prevailing 6–3–3 grade structure would have been eliminated.[45]

The building program proved unpopular with the black community in spite of the fact that, on its face, the directly affected black junior and senior high school students were to have a better opportunity to get an education at new, predominantly white schools.[46] According to the program, one all-black senior high school, Atkins, was to remain in operation. It was "historically" black, built in 1930, and allegedly was "the worst senior high school plant in any senior high school in the system."[47] Not one dime was allocated to the improvement of Atkins in the six-year plan. Apparently, 1,000-plus black high school students were to be assigned to inferior school facilities indefinitely.[48] Secondly, the "best all-around school plant ever built for blacks in Forsyth County or Win-

41. Twin City Sentinel, Feb. 29, 1968, at 2.
42. *Id.,* March 1, 1968, at 1.
43. *Id.,* Feb. 29, 1968, at 2. The expansion of East was intended to accommodate 200 black high school students attending Carver Union, the expansion of Walkertown to accommodate 200 black junior high school students from Carver Union School. Anderson Junior-Senior High School housed 400 high school students. These were to be reassigned to white Parkland High School and replaced by additional junior high students.
44. Scott at 461.
45. *Id.*
46. Interview with Marvin Ward, note 16 *supra.*
47. Interview with J. Alston Atkins, plaintiff in Atkins case, July 5, 1975.
48. Atkins v. State Board of Education of N.C., Civ. No. 79-WS-68, Complaint, at 8.

ston-Salem,"[49] Carver Union School, apparently was to operate with half of its junior and all of its senior high classrooms vacant because a million dollars was to be spent to expand white junior and senior high schools to house black students attending Carver. Blacks asked whether it would not be better to save the million dollars by assigning white students to Carver as replacements for the black students who were to be transferred out. Finally, the smaller elementary schools apparently were to remain neighborhood schools, reflecting as always the racially segregated pattern of the residential areas.

To the black community, the building program signified a continuance of segregated schooling for elementary children; partial integration of black junior and senior high school students by transfer to white schools; no displacement or disturbance of any white pupils; the continuance of Atkins Senior High as a second-rate, segregated high school; and very little improvement in schools in black neighborhoods.[50]

One man resolve to act. A black attorney, J. Alston Atkins, filed a complaint *pro se* on June 10, 1969, in the district court. When he filed his complaint he had not received a copy of the opinion of the U.S. Supreme Court in the *Trilogy;* however, he was aware of their general import from newspaper accounts.[51] In his prayer for relief, he requested that the school authorities be enjoined from taking further action with respect to the issuance or sale of bonds authorized by the March 12 referendum.[52] In so doing he effectively blocked for the time being the issuance of the bonds, the implementation of the building program, and changes in pupil assignments dependent thereon.

Scott v. Winston-Salem/Forsyth County Board of Education.   On September 6, 1968, plaintiffs in the school desegregation case of *Swann v. Charlotte-Mecklenburg Board of Education*—the case in which the Court of Appeals for the Fourth Circuit in 1966 had approved a pupil assignment plan for the Mecklenburg County schools—filed a motion for further relief in district court based on *Green v. County School Board* and its companion cases.[53] Plaintiffs in *Swann* were represented by the National NAACP *Legal and Defense Fund* (LDF). LDF was involved in a score of desegregation lawsuits in North Carolina at this time.[54] A few days later, on October 2, 1968, counsel in *Swann* filed the complaint in *Scott et al v. Winston-Salem/Forsyth County Board of Education, et al.,* an action brought by thirty school children, by their parents and next friends, on

49. On Dec. 19, 1969, 1,135 black students attended Atkins. Scott at 459.
50. The six-year plan called for only one new school, a sixteen-room elementary school to be built in a black neighborhood. This was a "third phase" item. Its estimated cost was $800,000
51. Interview with J. Alston Atkins, note 47 *supra.*
52. Atkins v. State Board of Education of N.C., Civ. No. 79-WS-68, Complaint, at 13.
53. Note 36 *supra.*
54. *Cf.* counsel in Swann were C.O. Pearson of Durham, N.C.; Julius L. Chambers, James E. Ferguson, and James E. Lanning of Charlotte, N.C.; and Jack Greenburg and Robert Belton of New York City.

behalf of others similarly situated, alleging that, by several means, the board of education "has refused and proposed to continue refusing to adopt programs and practices which would insure to plaintiffs and members of their class an education free from racial discrimination and educational opportunities in Forsyth County."[55] All defendants allegedly had maintained and were maintaining "inferior schools, programs and facilities" for black pupils.[56] But the gravamen of the complaint consisted of nineteen specific allegations of anti-black discriminatory conduct by the board of education.[57] The plaintiffs prayed that the board be ordered to completely desegregate all schools and to eliminate the free-transfer plan, to completely desegregate all teachers and school personnel, to cease planning and commencing any school construction and to make no changes in school building utilization except with court approval, and to eliminate all disparities in physical facilities and curricula.[58]

The plaintiffs' motion for further relief in *Swann v. Charlotte-Mecklenburg* and the initiation of the *Scott* action against the Forsyth County Board of Education under the auspices of the NAACP Legal Defense Fund obviously were in part a reaction to the Supreme Court's 1968 mandate given boards of education in the South to disestablish dual systems everywhere, "root and branch." However, the dissatisfaction of many blacks with the failure of the boards of education in Mecklenburg and Forsyth counties to place a fair portion of the burden of integration on white pupils—except when a white pupil invoked freedom of transfer to escape a predominantly black school or one with a substantial number of black students—provided additional incentive for seeking judicial relief even though considerable progress in desegregation in both school systems had been made. For example, in commenting on the filing of the *Scott* case, one of plaintiffs' counsel, Julius L. Chambers, said that the "Carver issue" was a *major* reason for the new suit, though not the only one. According to an account in the Winston-Salem *Journal*, citizens of the Carver community had wanted the school made an area high school for both races and had called the board's decision to transfer Carver's high school students to East Forsyth High School a "moral compromise."[59]

Unquestionably, the Carver School issue symbolized the basic conflict in For-

55. In addition to counsel named in note 54 *supra*, Adam Stern of Charlotte, N.C. represented plaintiffs Scott *et al.*, and signed the complaint.
56. Scott v. Board of Education, Civ. No. 174-WS-68 (M.D.N.C.), Complaint, at 8.
57. *Id.* at 9.
58. *Id.* at 9–11. The board was charged with gerrymandering attendance zones; scheduling and routing buses to maintain segregation; failing to desegregate faculty and students; discriminating against black pupils in regard to school lunches and textbooks; using mobile units to provide additional space for whites transferring out of black schools; operation of special schools and vocational schools in a manner unfavorable to black students; creating disparities between black and white curricula; programming such desegregation as there was in a way burdensome to blacks but not to whites; permitting historically black schools to continue; favoring white neighborhoods with new construction; and discriminatory ability grouping.
59. *Id.* at 13.

syth County between the black and white communities. "We have to let you in our schools," said the whites to the blacks, "but we don't have to attend yours. You come to us; we won't come to you." Quality of education, educational opportunity, equal facilities, and other "rational" bases for the black demand to integrate the Winston-Salem schools probably were of less importance than black resentment of the condescending attitude of the white community toward the blacks as reflected in the Carver School issue. As a practical political matter, the elected board of education dared not bend to the blacks on the Carver School issue by reassigning white junior and senior high students to replace blacks that were to be transferred from Carver to predominantly white schools. Furthermore, as long as freedom of transfer was possible, modification of attendance zones to place whites in Carver would have been an exercise in futility.

The Winston-Salem chapter of the NAACP had urged the state and national headquarters and the NAACP Legal Defense Fund to help Atkins in his one-man fight to rectify the Carver School slander.[60] LDF obliged by filing the *Scott* action, charging the board of education with discriminating generally against black students and with maintaining a dual school system. Had it not been for the emotion-packed Carver School issue, the NAACP and LDF probably would not have supported the litigation in Winston-Salem until *Swann v. Charlotte-Mecklenburg* had finally been resolved.

The *Scott* Case

First-Year Proceedings and Collateral Developments. *Initial Proceedings.* On December 31, 1968, the district court dismissed the *Atkins* case.[61] Affirmance of this dismissal on appeal might have untied the school bonds. Accordingly, on January 13, 1969, plaintiffs in the *Scott* case moved the court to amend their complaint by adding a prayer to preliminary and permanently enjoin all expenditures of funds from bonds or other sources for capital improvements unless and until a comprehensive construction plan was approved by the court.[62] Seven months later, after a hearing, the court in its order of August 5, 1969, denied the plaintiffs' anti-construction motion. After observing that one of the purposes for which the school construction bonds were voted was to build an administration building, the court said that to completely tie up the bond authorization was unnecessary in view of the fact that the plaintiffs were not without a remedy should the board of education attempt some construction which violated plaintiffs' rights.[63]

60. Winston-Salem Journal, Oct. 3, 1968, at 1, 16.
61. Atkins v. State Board of Education of N.C., Civ. No. 79-WS-68 (W.D.N.C.), Memorandum and Order, December 31, 1968. The principal grounds for the dismissal of Atkins' *pro se* complaint was the plaintiff's lack of standing to sue because he had no children eligible to attend any public school in Forsyth County.
62. Scott v. Board of Education, Civ. No. C-174-WS-68, Plaintiff's Motion to Amend Complaint, January 13, 1969.
63. Scott v. Board of Education, Order of August 5, 1969, at 2, 3.

The order of August 5 was the only significant action by the trial court in the *Scott* case in 1969.[64] Public school operations in Forsyth County in the school year 1969/70 followed the same pattern as they had in 1968/69. Integration of pupils remained at about the level of the previous year.[65] Substantially more teachers were teaching across racial lines, however.[66] The school attorneys and the board of education had reason to believe that the trial judge, because of his order of August 5, was not disposed to permit the desegregation litigation to disturb or interrupt the operation of the school system except when such disturbance appeared unavoidably necessary to protect plaintiffs' rights. They expected the court of appeals to deny the appeal of plaintiff in the *Atkins* case. Then the school system could proceed with at least the noncontroversial items in its construction program. Finally, they believed that, on the merits, plaintiffs in *Scott* had much less than an even chance of forcing significant additional pupil integration on the school system because of the fact that the segregation in the schools was caused by segregated residential patterns, that is, by de facto, rather than de jure, segregation.[67]

Actions by the Forsyth County Board of Education. In November 1968 four white Republican candidates were elected to the Winston-Salem/Forsyth County Board of Education, replacing four Democratic members, including one black. At the December meeting the board consisted of five white Republican members, and three Democrats, one of whom was black. The Republican majority elected a Republican attorney as chairman. The victorious candidate had campaigned generally on quality education for all, the neighborhood school, and better communications between the community and the board of education. Although many whites and blacks viewed the "voluntary" integration process in the public schools with little enthusiasm, the steps taken by the board of education up to this point to comply with the "law of the land" had been accepted by the community. However, as the numbers of blacks assigned to predominantly white senior high schools increased, racial tensions mounted.

During its first six months in office the new school board had to deal with two racially oriented disturbances, one in each of the two predominantly white senior high schools with the largest number of black pupils enrolled.[68] At a third

64. By the end of October 1969, most of the many interrogatories had been answered, motions to dismiss had been denied, and the depositions of the superintendent of schools and the chairman of the board of education had been taken. Scott v. Board of Education, Civil No. 174-WS-68 (M.D.N.C.) Docket, at 1–6.

65. Scott at 460. During the school year 1968/69, 2155 black pupils attended predominantly white schools. During 1969/70, 2016 did so.

66. *Id.* at 468. During the school year 1968/69, 199 teachers taught across racial lines. During 1969/70, 296 did so.

67. Statements of the chairman of the board of education appearing in the Winston-Salem Journal, Dec. 26, 1969, at 1, and on Jan. 1, 1970, at 1.

68. Winston-Salem Journal, Dec. 12, 1968, at 1; *id.*, May 12, 1969, at 1. The first incident occurred at North High School and was caused by racial tension arising from the election of a white Homecoming Queen in Dec. 1968. The second incident occurred on May 7,

white senior high school, the black minority also had voiced its dissatisfaction with the administration of the school.[69]

Incidents of this kind prompted the board of education to take steps to minimize racially motivated disturbances.[70] Additional funds were sought from HEW under the Educational Emergency Aid Act of 1964, enacted to provide federal funds to assist schools in the South with their desegregation problems.[71] By the beginning of the 1969/70 school year the board of education had implemented an extensive program to facilitate the integration of black pupils into predominantly white schools.[72]

Summing up the First Year of Litigation.   As the first year of litigation drew to a close and the new school year of 1969/70 began, the neighborhood school concept continued to be the basis of pupil assignment in Forsyth County public schools, but freedom to transfer to schools more distant from a pupil's home than his or her assigned school was permitted for the first time, particularly if a black pupil wished to transfer to a white school. Substantial integration had taken place, but many racially identifiable schools remained. Of the 65 nonspecailized schools in the system, 13 were all black—9 elementary, 1 junior high, and 3 senior high schools—and 7 were all white—5 elementary and 2 junior high schools. In the 47 schools in which there was some racial mix, 4 were predominantly black and 43 were predominantly white. Only 15 white children in elementary schools were attending predominantly black schools, but 892—about 11 percent—of the black children in the elementary grades were attending predominantly white schools.[73]

Only 14 white children in junior high schools were attending predominantly black schools; whereas 269—about 8 percent—of the black children in junior

---

1969, when several black students at Reynolds High protested the selection of all-white cheerleaders for the next year's cheerleading squad. In the North incident the school was closed for 4 days; Reynolds was closed for 2 days.

69. On April 24, 1969, 11 white cheerleaders were elected at Parkland High School, where 90 blacks in a total student body of 1,490 were in attendance. Although the panel of candidates included a black girl, she was not elected. Tensions ran high. The principal was "accosted" as he arrived at his office by several black students who said they wanted to talk to him. After three hours of discussion they returned to their classes.

70. On April 7, 1969, the board of education adopted a seventeen-point program. Minutes of the Winston-Salem/Forsyth County Board of Education meeting on April 7, 1969.

71. Educational Agencies Financial Aid Act, 79 Stat. 1109, 20 U.S.C. § 237 (1970).

72. As a result of racial tension arising from an election of a Homecoming Queen, the school board closed North High School for four days, and posted law-enforcement officers in the buildings for one month after reopening. The board petitioned the city for a statute prohibiting the carrying of weapons on school grounds (which was passed immediately). The board established a human relations staff which went to each school having racial difficulties and presented prepared workshops in race relations for both students and faculty. Interview with James Dew, Winston-Salem Forsyth County School Administration, July 31, 1975.

73. Scott at 461.

high schools were attending predominantly white schools. No white children attended the three black senior high schools; whereas 710—about 29 percent—of the black pupils in senior high school were attending predominantly white schools. One predominantly white high school had 17 percent black pupils, another had 15 percent, the others had less than 5 percent.[74]

Black teachers were being encouraged to teach in predominantly white schools, and white teachers in predominantly black schools. Teachers who objected to teaching across racial lines were not being employed, but no previously assigned teacher had been required to teach across racial lines if the teacher objected to such an assignment. As the 1969/70 school year began, 296 teachers were teaching across racial lines.[75]

During the 1968/69 school year, racially motivated incidents had occurred in the three predominantly white senior high schools with the largest number of black pupils assigned. Many white parents felt the physical security of their children was threatened by desegregation taking place in the public schools. Desegregation litigation had tied up school construction in spite of the continuing increase in the number of black children attending white schools and the number of teachers teaching across racial lines.

A predominantly white board of education had pledged to preserve the neighborhood school. It had taken several measures to minimize interracial friction in the 1969/70 school year. It had not modified the attendance plan to increase the number of black pupils attending predominantly white schools; however, the public was aware that the School Study Commission was preparing a desegregation plan that in all likelihood would call for further assignments of black pupils to predominantly white schools at all grade levels. Probably most of the white population of Forsyth County believed that the board of education was doing all that could be reasonably required under law. On the other hand, the blacks in Forsyth County viewed the six-year building program and school utilization plans as an affront to them. The white-dominanted school board, they believed, was pledged to preserve white schools in white suburbs and black in black neighborhoods, and so deprive black children of "rights" which the Constitution guaranteed.

Physical school facilities for blacks were not quite equal to those of the whites; therefore, black people argued, public education for many black children was still separate and unequal. Furthermore, when black pupils were assigned to white schools, they were denied equal access to many extracurricula activities. The system remained permeated with discrimination solely on the basis of race. Such were the opinions of many blacks and a small number of whites in Forsyth County, including the editors of the daily newspapers.

No one could state with assurance as the 1969/70 school year began whether the faculty and pupil assignment systems then in effect in the Forsyth County

74. *Id.* at 457–59.
75. *Id.* at 468.

schools satisfied the right of every pupil to the equal protection of law. The chairman of the school board declared that rulings on desegregation by the appellate courts had caused confusion, frustration, and "total befuddlement" to lower courts and the public.[76]

The Second Year. *The McGuffey Desegregation Plan.* In late October 1969, a school consultant group from George Peabody College submitted its report of the study it had made of the Forsyth County schools to the School Study Commission. The Urban Coalition of Winston-Salem, which had agreed to finance the Peabody College study, expressed its displeasure with the Peabody Report because it contained no comprehensive recommendations for desegregation of the public schools, recommendations which the Urban Coalition had expected would be an integral part of any study of the problems of Forsyth County schools. During November and December 1969 the School Study Commission undertook to draft an integration plan for the Forsyth County schools with the assistance of one of the Peabody researchers, C.W. McGuffey. However, the black leaders in the Urban Coalition expressed little confidence in the work of the School Study Commission.[77] Recognizing that the Urban Coalition would not pay for McGuffey's desegregation plan, at its meeting on November 10[78] the board of education voted to request that the county commissioners appropriate $6,850 to defray the fee and expenses of McGuffey. The Commissioners did so, and McGuffey completed his plan in late December.

The McGuffey Plan was entitled "Short Range Plan for Integrating More Pupils Within the *Existing Unitary System*" (emphasis added). Of course, the black leadership in Forsyth County could not accept a study premised upon the proposition that the existing pupil assignment plan of the Forsyth County schools was "unitary" and therefore constitutional. On the other hand, the white majority in the county would not accept the substantially greater desegregation that McGuffey recommended if the system was already a "unitary" one as McGuffey had found. Instead of improving relations between whites and blacks, the Peabody Report and the McGuffey Desegregation Plan deepened the cleavage between the two races. The principal significance of the plan lies in the fact that community leaders, in trying to work out a viable plan for increasing the number of blacks attending white schools, had spent almost $50,000 for a study which had only heightened the tensions between blacks and whites.

76. Winston-Salem Journal, December 9, 1969, at 1.
77. Winston-Salem Journal, November 11, 1969, at 1. The School Study Commission consisted of 12 local business and community leaders appointed by the Urban Coalition, a group of 32 white and black civic leaders, whose basic mission was to minimize interracial tensions in the city. The commission had contracted in May of 1969 with the George Peabody College of Nashville, Tenn. to survey all aspects of the Winston-Salem/Forsyth County Schools.
78. *Id.* The Urban Coalition had paid $42,500 to the Peabody group.

HEW Demands Action. Until November 1969, HEW had excused school boards involved in desegregation litigation from submitting desegregation plans for approval by the commissioner of education. This policy was changed in November 1969, and on November 17, 1969, the Forsyth County and other southern school systems received a demand from HEW that a desegregation plan for schools be filed with the commission within 30 days.[79] The plan had to provide for the "complete desegregation of the schools" by December 31, 1969. Systems failing to comply would be subject to a delay in the processing of their requests for federal funds for the 1970/71 school year. HEW was declaring that the time for "all deliberate speed" was up for schools that were not yet completely desegregated but were still receiving federal funds.

The reaction of the chairman of the Winston-Salem/Forsyth County Board of Education to the HEW demand was nonchalant. There was "nothing to the letter" which could cause the school system to change its present plans. He noted that the School Study Commission was then preparing a pupil assignment plan and that this plan would be that which woul be given to HEW in response to its demand of November 17.[80]

The Atkins Case Revives. On November 25, 1969, the Fourth Circuit Court of Appeals reversed the dismissal of the original *Atkins* case and remanded it to Judge Gordon's court with instructions to permit the daughter of Mr. Atkins, and Mrs. Allen and her husband—who were parents of children in the public schools of Forsyth County—to intervene as parties plaintiff with standing to sue. The Allens had so requested when the appeal of the *Atkins* case was being heard by the court of appeals. The court of appeals authorized Judge Gordon, at his discretion, to consolidate the *Allen-Atkins* case with the pending "action brought by other parents," that is, the *Scott* case. In its *per curiam* opinion the court recognized that intervention such as that requested by the Allens must be timely, but that timeliness is not an absolute. The delay of the Allens in seeking to intervene in the *Atkins* case until the hearing on the appeal of the trial court's dismissal order was justified in this case.[81]

Atkins was the case which had initiated desegregation litigation in Forsyth County and which was delaying the school construction bonds and building program. When, on August 5, 1969, the trial court had denied the motion of the

79. Winston-Salem Journal, November 18, 1969, at 1.
80. *Id.*
81. Atkins v. State Board of Education, 418 F.2d 874 (4th Cir. 1969). In its *per curiam* opinion the court recognized that intervention must be timely but that timeliness is not an absolute. The delay of the Allens in seeking to intervene in the Atkins case until the hearing on the appeal of the trial court's dismissal order was justified in this case because Atkins, a Texas attorney who had not been admitted to practice in North Carolina, had no funds to employ counsel when he filed his complaint, *pro se*, and hence he could not obtain counsel to represent his daughter.

plaintiffs in the *Scott* case to amend their complaint by adding a prayer for an injunction of all school construction after the *Atkins* case had been dismissed,[82] the board of education hoped that at least those elements of the building program not related to desegregation litigation, such as a school administration building, could be started during the pendency of the *Scott* case. When the court of appeals revived the *Allen (Atkins)* action, it dashed the hopes of the board of education. School construction and the school bonds were now totally tied up pending the final resolution by the courts of the desegregation issue unless plaintiffs in the *Allen (Atkins)* case could be induced to modify or withdraw their prayer to enjoin school construction. In fact, negotiations toward this end had been initiated by defendants as early as May 1969,[83] and continued intermittently through 1970. They came to nought.[84]

Total Faculty Desegregation. The Nesbit Mandate. On November 29, 1969, the U.S. Supreme Court in *Alexander v. Holmes County Board of Education*[85] ordered the termination of dual school systems "at once." It reversed an order of the Court of Appeals for the Fifth Circuit, which had granted additional time to defendant to implement an effective desegregation plan, and ordered the court of appeals to give priority to the enforcement of the judgment. This decision prompted the Court of Appeals for the Fourth Circuit, in *Nesbit v. Statesville City Board of Education,*[86] to act summarily on December 2, 1969 on five segregation cases then on appeal, requiring in each case immediate formulation and implementation of an effective desegregation plan. "*All plans,*" the Fourth Circuit Court said, "*must include provisions for the integration of the faculty so that the ration of Negro and white faculty members of each school shall be approximately the same as the ratio throughout the system.*" (Emphasis added.)[87] For those schools in the systems subject to the *Nesbit* mandate and

82. Scott v. Board of Education, Civ. No. C-174-WS-68 (M.D.N.C.), Order of August 5, 1969, at 2, 3.

83. At the hearing of May 3, 1969, in the *Scott* case, Judge Gordon ordered counsel for both parties to meet in a good-faith effort to resolve the school construction tieup and to inform him of their progress within 30 days. The children, he said, were suffering from the dispute more than the adults fighting it. Winston-Salem Journal, May 3, 1969, at 1.

84. In a letter to plaintiffs' counsel in the Allen (Atkins) case, dated November 11, 1970, defendants' counsel made a final attempt to arrive at an agreement. Plaintiff rejected the proposal. Construction costs and interest rates were rising dramatically. School officials estimated that the delay in the school construction program cost the taxpayers of Forsyth County $2 million each year construction was delayed because of increased costs of construction and borrowing. The white community at large was well aware of the pecuniary harm being inflicted on the county because of the apparent intransigence of the plaintiffs in the *Allen* case. On the other hand, many leaders of the black community saw the six-year building program as another instance of neglect of schools in black neighborhoods which should be forestalled and drastically revamped in order to give the black community their due share of new construction. *See* Scott at 460.

85. 369 U.S. 19 (1969).

86. 418 F.2d 1040 (4th Cir. 1969).

87. *Id.* at 1042.

not operating on a semester basis, total desegregation was to become effective after the Christmas break; for other schools, at the beginning of the second semester.[88]

The Forsyth County Board of Education Reacts. On December 17, 1969, in the wake of the *Alexander* and *Nesbit* decisions ordering "at once" desegregation, plaintiffs in *Scott v. Winston-Salem/Forsyth County* filed a motion for a preliminary injunction ordering the defendants to present to the court for approval and to implement no later than February 1, 1970, a plan for complete desegregation, including but not limited to, faculty and pupils.[89]

The Winston-Salem/Forsyth County Board of Education now found itself in a dilemma. The board was deeply committed to improving the quality of education in Forsyth County. The new majority owed their election largely to the white voters, particularly to those living beyond the city limits. The board of education and its counsel had kept abreast of pertinent developments in desegregation litigation during 1969. They were fully aware that the Charlotte-Mecklenburg litigation and the orders of Judge McMillan in *Swann,* if upheld, might radically affect the outcome in the *Scott* case.[90] They were aware that time had run out and that the school districts in the Fourth Circuit would be required to desegregate at once if they were found to be operating dual systems and in *Nesbit* the Fourth Circuit Court of Appeals had ordered faculty desegregation to be part of the desegregation plan of five school districts. Perhaps total faculty desegregation in the Forsyth County schools was "just around the corner" if, indeed, the corner had not already been turned.

But their constituency was not as well informed. The white majority of Forsyth County knew that the board of education was being sued. Most of them believed that the local chapter of the NAACP was in control of the litigation. However, as elsewhere in North Carolina, the litigation was in the hands of the Legal and Defense Fund (LDF) of the NAACP, a legal entity separate from the NAACP itself, although both organizations cooperated closely. The white majority knew that this lawsuit had tied up urgently needed school construction. They knew that morning and evening newspapers clamored for capitulation to the demands of the plaintiffs for widespread desegregation after Judge McMillan's order in the *Swann* case of April 23, 1969.[91] They also believed that the

88. *Id.*

89. Scott v. Board of Education, Civ. No. C-174-WS-68 (M.D.N.C.), Order of January 19, 1970, at 1.

90. Winston-Salem Journal, May 9, 1969, at 1. In commentary on Judge McMillan's order of April 23, 1969 in the *Swann* case, the chairman of the Forsyth County Board of Education acknowledged that in many cases the decision in one district court may be persuasive in another.

91. For example, in an editorial in the *Winston-Salem Journal* on May 15, 1969, the following statements were made:

Whether our officials like it or not, the schools they preside over will have to measure up to the Fourteenth Amendment, and the Supreme Court has clearly ruled that school boards cannot hide behind "freedom of choice" and "free transfer" plans if

chairman of the board of education, an attorney and an outspoken critic of Judge McMillan's orders especially, and of desegregation in general, and the other board members, except the lone black member, would defend the neighborhood school.[92] Since the first faltering step in 1957, the Forsyth County schools had integrated more black pupils and black teachers each year into white schools, but had retained a geographical attendance-zone system of pupil assignment. No child was denied permission to attend any school he or she wished to attend if, at the same time, space was available, and generally it was.[93] The white man-in-the-street most probably thought blacks had come a long way in Forsyth County schools since 1954. Many thought that white-dominated school boards perhaps had gone too far in response to the several pressures for desegregation, and that certainly no black child in Forsyth County was being denied an equal opportunity for education at public expense. If he had read the newspapers carefully on certain days, he was aware that a federal judge in Charlotte had been causing turmoil by his rulings in a desegregation suit there,[94] but Charlotte was not Winston-Salem. Almost certainly he had never heard of the recent opinion of the U.S. Supreme Court in *Alexander v. Holmes County Board of Education* or that of the Fourth Circuit Court of Appeals in *Nesbitt v. Statesville City Board of Education* as he and his family unwrapped gifts on Christmas Day, 1969.

Few residents of Forsyth County were aware that on Tuesday, December 23, 1968, the board of education had been briefed by its attorneys on the two most recent cases, *Holmes* and *Nesbit,* in the desegregation series and on the trail blazing opinions of Judge McMillan in Charlotte during the past few months. The Supreme Court had not expressly outlawed racially identifiable neighbor-

---

these devices do not successfully dismantle the segregated school system that was so carefully set up by the old law. It is hard to believe that the Charlotte decision—which says they cannot hide behind the "neighborhood school" concept either—will not prevail.

The courts do not seem to forget that we used one stratagem after another, including busing and pupil placement, to maintain a segregated system, and they have made it clear that dismantling only a fraction of that system will not suffice.

So, how stands the majesty of the law here?

Not so majestic, we are afraid.

It is wrongly described, obeyed with careful selectivity but little deliberate speed, and it is persistently evaded in those instances when obedience seems unpleasant and unpopular.

The fact that our disobedience is subtle and nonviolent does not make us paragons of lawfulness that young people on campuses and in the streets should look up to. The difference, in behavior, both morally and legally, is only a matter of degree.

92. In its editorial of May 15, 1969, note 91 *supra,* the views of the school board chairman, in opposition to Judge McMillan's order of April 23, 1969, are set forth in some detail. The white members of the board generally concurred in those views, although some were less adamant than others.

93. Scott at 469.

94. *E.g.,* the April 23 order of Judge McMillan in *Swann* was reported in the Winston-Salem Journal, May 8, 1969, at 1, under the caption, "Mecklenburg School Order Likely to Affect Winston."

hood schools. If assignment to them was based upon nonracial criteria, if the present residential patterns were not caused in whole or in part by former de jure segregation, and if access to a white school was denied no black pupil, racially identifiable schools might be permissible. However, in *Nesbit*, the Fourth Circuit Court, by prescribing that *all* desegregation plans then on appeal contain a provision for immediate total desegregation of faculty, apparently had held that any racial imbalance in faculty in any school of a formerly de jure segregated system was presumptively an effect of such de jure segregation and had to be corrected at once. In any event, the board had to decide if they should desegregate their faculty according to the *Nesbit* formula before the trial court ruled on the plaintiffs' motion for a preliminary injunction which plaintiffs had filed ten days earlier. If the board did not do so, the court might feel constrained to order immediate, total faculty desegregation *sua sponte* just before or in the course of the second semester of the 1969/70 school year.

Presumably the board realized that a massive transfer of faculty after the second semester had begun might cause serious dislocations in instruction. They were also aware that, in many desegregation cases, good faith, or lack of it, on the part of a school board had been an important factor in shaping the final opinion and order of the court. If total desegregation of faculty was required by the law of the Fourth Circuit whenever a system had formerly operated as a dual system, then it might be well to order total faculty desegregation in Forsyth County without waiting for the court to order it done in the near future. Such a demonstration of "good faith" by voluntary compliance with the law would enhance the probability of having the "neighborhood school" pupil attendance plan accepted by the court.

The board decided to instruct the superintendent to draft a plan for total faculty desegregation prior to the second semester, which was to begin on January 23, 1960.[95] The heads of the teachers' associations were advised of the decision on Friday morning, December 26, and the public announcement of the decision[96] to prepare the plan was made by the chairman of the board of education that afternoon. In making his announcement, he said that the county would have a "unitary system" after faculties are completely desegregated by the start of the second semester. *"We feel we have a unitary system now as far as students are concerned."*[97] (Emphasis added.)

Initial reaction by the teachers' associations to the board's decision to totally integrate faculty so that approximately one black teacher would be assigned to each school for each three white teachers assigned was one of acceptance of the inevitable and a willingness to work out problems as they arose.[98] Reaction from parents was somewhat more guarded at first.[99]

95. *Id.,* December 30, 1969, at 5.
96. *Id.,* December 26, 1969, at 1.
97. *Id.*
98. *Id.* at 19.
99. *Id.* at 1.

One of the chief concerns of the new board of education was public involvement in education. The new Citizens' Advisory Council had not yet organized itself,[100] although it had been appointed a month before the decision to desegregate the faculty had been made. The details of the teacher reassignment plan were being hurriedly prepared by an 18-member committee comprised of school administrators and faculty, without public participation.[101] Public and press felt excluded.[102]

Public reaction to the transfer began to mount. Some blacks believed that black teachers would be harassed when teaching in a predominantly white school.[103] Many white parents likewise were convinced that black teachers would not be as effective as white teachers in white classrooms. Furthermore, a number of white teachers disliked the prospect of teaching black children whose culture and background were so unlike their own.

The board of education at first thought it would act on the faculty desegregation plan on January 5, 1971.[104] Then it was advised that the U.S. Supreme Court was about to act on several petitions for writs of *certiorari* to the Court of Appeals of the Fifth Circuit in desegregation cases in which that court, subsequent to *Alexander v. Holmes County Board of Education,* had permitted a school sytem to delay desegregation of the student bodies until not later than September 1970.[105] The board decided to postpone action on the teacher desegregation plan in the hope that the Supreme Court would relax its "desegregate now" mandate as enunciated in *Alexander.* The latest practicable date for final board action on faculty desegregation prior to the second semester was January 19, 1970. A public meeting of the school board was set for that date in a school auditorium.

During the interim, public opposition to the move intensified. On January 19, citizens groups were calling for resignation of the members of the board of education and feelings ran high.

On January 14 the Supreme Court granted *certiorari* in the cases from the Fifth Circuit, and in a *per curiam* opinion on the same date reversed the Fifth Circuit Court, thereby reaffirming its "desegregate now" mandate of November 29, 1969 in *Alexander v. Holmes County Board of Education.*[106] Thus, when the Winston-Salem/Forsyth County Board of Education met on the evening of January 19, a majority of its members and their attorney believed that the deseg-

100. *Id.,* December 30, 1969.
101. *Id.*
102. *Id.,* December 31, 1969, at 3.
103. *Id.,* Decmeber 30, 1969, at 3.
104. *Id.*
105. Hall v. St. Helena Parish School, 417 F.2d 801 (5th Cir. 1970).
106. The appeals court opinion was in Carter v. West Feliciana Parish School Board, 396 U.S. 290 (1970); the "desegregate now" mandate was expressed in *Holmes,* 369 U.S. 19 (1969).

regation of teachers by court order as required in *Nesbit* was unavoidable and imminent.[107]

About 2,000 parents, teachers, and others who attended the meeting argued, shouted and even prayed that the board reverse its decision to desegregate the faculty. The crowd asked that the board not act until it was ordered to, and perhaps not even then.[108] But the board voted for total faculty desegregation, 4–2, notwithstanding the pressure exerted by the crowd. A few days later, 425 teachers, most of whom were black, were served notices that they were to teach in schools, beginning January 23, 1970, where most of their pupils would be white.[109]

Several protest groups—such as the Concerned Citizens for Common Sense in Education, NBOC (No Busing our Children), and the Silent Majority—met, organized, and raised funds to be used to fight busing in the schools. Teacher desegregation at mid-year had driven home the fact that desegregation by court order in Forsyth County schools might be just around the corner, too.

Judge Eugene A. Gordon, the trial judge in the *Scott* case, took an unusual step to relieve the pressure on the board of education and to forestall reported plans by citizens groups to bring suit in the state courts to enjoin the board from implementing the teacher-transfer plan. After a hearing on the plaintiffs' motion of December 17 for a preliminary injunction in the *Scott* case, in an order of court, Judge Gordon said on January 19, 1970, that it appeared from exhibits then on file in the *Scott* case that further faculty desegregation had been immediately necessary to achieve a ratio of black and white faculty members in each school approximating the ratio throughout the system. If the board of education had not taken its action on January 14, 1970, he would have ordered it to do so by February 1 or shortly thereafter. He therefore now ordered the board of education to proceed with teacher desegregation.[110] Henceforth, the board could neither claim it had caused nor be accused of having caused the transfer of 425 teachers in January of 1970. The transfer was by Court Order of January 19, 1970.

Preliminary Injunction Denied in Scott. After six days of hearings, the district court, on February 17, 1970, denied plaintiffs' motion for a preliminary

107. Winston-Salem Journal, Jan. 15, 1970, at 1.
School board attorney, William F. Womble, repeated [at the meeting on January 14, 1970] a statement he had made to the board last month. He said, in his opinion, the board's only alternatives were to make the change now or make it at mid-semester.

108. *Id.* at 1, 3. One speaker urged parents to protest by taking their children from school, another suggested not paying taxes. A teacher complained that teachers "are being picked up like so many cattle to be led to the slaughter." The board was urged to defy orders "with every ounce of strength you have." "If you go to jail, we'll go with you," shouted some in the audience. The crowd shouted down one speaker who tried to speak in favor of the teacher-transfer plan and roundly cheered speakers with whom it agreed.

109. Scott at 469.

110. Scott v. Board of Education, Civ. No. C.-174-WS-68 (M.D.N.C.), Order, January 19, 1970.

injunction to completely desegregate the schools of Forsyth County.[111] The findings of fact on which District Judge Gordon acted deserve close scrutiny in view of subsequent developments.

Judge Gordon found that the faculties of the Forsyth County schools were desegregated "in accordance with the guidelines established in *Nesbit v. States-ville City Board of Education*"[112] as a result of the initiative of the board of education. He also pointed out that prior to the just-completed reassignment of teachers, the board had assigned more teachers each year from 1964 to 1970 to teach across racial lines.

He then reviewed the black-white pupil attendance patterns in the school system. *He found that these patterns were the result of an assignment system based upon geographic attendance zones with freedom of transfer to other schools having openings, and that substantially all black students who had requested transfer over the last several years had been permitted to do so. With respect to the actionsof the board of education since* Brown, *Judge Gordon found that, beginning in 1957, the board had made a good-faith effort to comply with* Brown, *that the number of children attending integrated schools had increased steadily through the years, and that the school system had consistently adhered to guidelines set up by HEW.*[113] With respect to the establishment of existing attendance zones, Judge Gordon said:

> *It has not been shown,* nor has it been contended that *the School Board's plan of geographic zoning was established in any way by reference to the race of the inhabitants of the various zones.* When the Board decided to discontinue Paisley Senior High School, new zone lines were deliberately drawn to increase integration at Reynolds and North High Schools. . . . [Emphasis added.] [114]

He further found that initial projects in the tied-up, six-year building plan, if completed, would have resulted in about 1,475 black students in black schools being reassigned to predominantly white schools.[115]

His findings concerning the residential racial patterns in Winston-Salem/Forsyth County are significant because of what he did not find as well as what he did find. He did *not* find that any action of the board of education caused the existing housing patterns. He observed that four schools had changed from white to black since they were opened, three of the shifts having occurred in the 1960s. He said:

> The population shifts show conclusively that black citizens have been able

111. *Id.,* Memorandum and Order of February 17, 1970.
112. *Id.* at 4.
113. *Id.* at 5, 6.
114. *Id.* at 7.
115. *Id.* at 9.

to acquire residences in those areas inhabited by white citizens, limited only by their economic ability and desire to do so.[116]

He did *not* find that *any* "state action" had caused the racially segregated housing patterns in Winston-Salem. He found that housing projects underwritten with federal funds were located in black neighborhoods "in response to the demand for housing *there*."[117] (Emphasis added.) Displaced black families had been re-housed at their request in the same locality as that in which they were living when they were required to move.[118]

In summing up, the court said that "affirmative action has been taken by those in authority since 1957 to desegregate the schools."[119] Nevertheless, the court, after the hearing on plaintiffs' motion for a preliminary injunction, did not conclude that the Forsyth County school system was operated either as a dual *or* as a unitary system.[120] It first must hear and analyze the entire evidence and the applicable law. Accordingly, the motion for the preliminary injunction was denied. Pending motions of some of the defendants for summary judgement were denied also, and the case was set for trial on the merits.[121]

The findings of fact by the district court in its order of February 17, 1970, after more than 16 months of pretrial during which the defendants had answered hundreds of interrogatories, after the depositions of the superintendent of schools had been twice taken, and after six days of hearings had been held, should have delighted the defendant borad of education. The gist of the findings was that no action by the board of education, other than colorblind geographical zoning, had caused the racial pattern in the Winston-Salem/Forsyth County schools. Furthermore, those historically black schools—that is, schools that were de jure black schools prior to *Brown*—would have been black prior to 1954, according to the district court's findings, if pupil assignments prior to *Brown* had been based on colorblind geographical attendance zones. Therefore, de jure segregation was not a *sine qua non* cause of the racial compoisiton of the student body of any school.

There was no finding that the board of education had consciously drawn any attendance zone or located any schools so as to perpetuate or create racially identifiable schools. Finally, in marked contrast to the findings of Judge McMillan in the *Swann* case,[122] the court attributed segregation in housing patterns in

116. *Id.* at 7.
117. *Id.* at 8.
118. *Id.* at 9.
119. *Id.* at 10.
120. *Id.* at 11, 12.
121. *Id.* at 12, 13.
122. Swann v. Board of Education, 306 F. Supp. 1299, 1304 (W.D.N.C. 1969). The court summarized its findings relating to the cause of racial imbalances in the Charlotte-Mecklenburg schools as follows:

Briefly summarized, these facts are that the present location of white schools in white areas and of black schools in black areas is the result of a varied group of

Winston-Salem either to the preference or poverty of blacks and not to any action by the board of education or any other government agency. Segregation in housing in Winston-Salem, therefore, was strictly de facto. Finally, the court found that since 1957 the school officials in Winston-Salem and Forsyth County had taken affirmative action to mitigate the effects of such de facto segregation by their free-transfer plan and, in recent years, by redrawing some school attendance zones so as to cause more desegregation.

The order of February 17, 1970, fairly construed, put the plaintiffs on notice that, *as of that date,* the district court had no factual basis upon which to order additional relief. The court's order vindicated the opinion of the chairman of the board of education, who had previously said, "We feel we have a unitary system now as far as students are concerned."[123] On the other hand, plaintiffs might have found some encouragement in the comments from the bench upon completion of the hearings on the preliminary injunction motion on January 28. The court emphatically said that *"present* laws" probably would require more desegregation of schools in Forsyth County, that there must be more desegregation, but that the court could not arbitrarily order the school board to submit plans for further desegregation until it had had an opportunity to study mountains of exhibits.[124]

Forsyth County Pupil Assignment for 1970/71, Plan No. 1.   The long-awaited Forsyth County pupil assignment plan for 1970/71 had been submitted to the court on February 16, the day before the court denied the plaintiff's motion for a preliminary injunction.[125] The plan, if implemented, would have reduced the 13 all- and almost-all-black schools to 9 by discontinuing one elementary and two senior black high schools and by converting an all-black junior high school into a predominantly white junior high. This additional desegregation was to be accomplished by the usual tactic of redrafting attendance-zone boundaries. Implementation of the plan would have caused overcrowding at two predominantly white senior high schools, but it would have permitted 1,615 more black

elements of public and private action all deriving their basic strength originally from public law or state or local governmental action. These elements include among others the legal separation of the races in schools, school busses, public accommodations and housing; racial restrictions in deeds to land; zoning ordinances; city planning; urban renewal; location of public low rent housing; and the actions of the present School Board and others, before and since 1954, in locating and controlling the capacity of schools so that there would usually be black schools handy to black neighborhoods and white schools for white neighborhoods. There is so much state action embedded in and shaping these events that the resulting segregation is not innocent or "de facto" and the resulting schools are not "unitary" or desegregated.

The court also found that freedom of choice had tended to perpetuate segregation by allowing minority-to-majority transfers.

123. Winston-Salem Sentinel, Dec. 26, 1969, at 1.
124. Winston-Salem Journal, Jan. 29, 1970, at 1.
125. Scott at 467.

students to attend predominantly white schools. These changes in the pupil assignment plan were in fact similar to those contemplated by the 1968 six-year building program.[126] The overcrowding at the two senior high schools was to be remedied by the construction of additional classrooms.

The board's first pupil-assignment plan for the 1970/71 school year continued the previous year's freedom of choice, but with modifications. The new plan gave priority to requests for majority-to-minority transfers if the school to which several students had requested transfers lacked space to accommodate all. Majority-to-minority requests would be honored first, until the overcrowding of a school as a result of such requests exceeded 10 percent. Furthermore, bus transportation would be provided for majority-to-minority transferees if they lived more than one and one-half miles from the school to which they transferred. Transportation would not be provided for minority-to-majority transferees.

After full weight was given to the innovative elements, the truth was that there were no startling innovations in the 1970/71 pupil assignment plan. The board of education sincerely believed that no child would be "effectively excluded from any school because of color or race under the plan" and that, therefore, the system under the 1970/71 pupil assignment plan was a unitary system. The faculty of each school was not racially identifiable, transportation was not furnished on a racially discriminatory basis, there apparently was no discrimination between the facilities or opportunities available to white and black children.[127] The board believed that they had fully complied with the mandates of the Supreme Court in *Brown* and in the *1968 Trilogy*. They had taken affirmative action to insure that all Winston-Salem/Forsyth County schools were realistically and effectively open to all children without regard to race or color and that the faculty and facilities at each school was equal to that at every other within the limits of possibility.

The First Desegregation Order in Scott. It will be recalled that in *Scott v. Winston-Salem/Forsyth County Board of Education,* the district court had denied plaintiffs' motion for a preliminary injunction on February 17, 1970,[128] shortly after Judge McMillan, in Charlotte, had decreed the integration of all schools in Charlotte on February 5, 1970.[129] The Supreme Court decided *Northcross v. Board of Education of Memphis, Tennessee City Schools*[130] on March 9, 1970, about the time that the district court began hearings on the merits in the *Scott* case. The hearings on the merits were completed on April 30, 1970. The Circuit Court of Appeals for the Fourth Circuit decision in *Swann v. Charlotte-*

126. Scott at 460–62. *See* pages 502–04 and notes 40–50 *supra.*
127. *See* note 29 *supra.*
128. Scott v. Board of Education, Civ. No. C-174-WS-68 (M.D.N.C.), Memorandum and Order of Feb. 17, 1970.
129. Swann v. Board of Education, 311 F. Supp. 265 (W.D.N.C. 1970).
130. 397 U.S. 232 (1970).

Mecklenburg[131] was rendered on May 5, 1970. The district court, in *Scott,* issued its first desegregation order on June 25, 1970.[132] The court disapproved the pupil assignment plan which had been proposed by the Winston-Salem/ Forsyth County Board of Education for the school year 1970/71,[133] although it affirmed the findings of fact previously made in its order of February 17, 1970.[134] The earlier findings, as previously summarized herein,[135] were equivalent to findings that state action had not caused segregated housing patterns and that the school board had not consciously assigned students on the basis of race, except to *increase* desegregation. The district court had not attributed present school segregation to past de jure segregation. The earlier findings led to the conclusion that the Winston-Salem/Forsyth County School System was not a "dual system" as defined in *Green* and *Northcross.*

The new findings of fact included a review of the consolidation of the city and county systems in 1963, general geographical and statistical data on Forsyth County and Winston-Salem, a description of the "racial make-up" of each school in the system, a history of pupil assignments since 1954, including a finding that HEW had regularly approved the system's desegregation plans until litigation had begun, a detailed description of the predominantly black schools, their attendance zones and population trends in these neighborhoods, and a less detailed description of the predominantly white schools.[136] The district court concluded its description of the predominantly black and white schools in Forsyth County with this observation:

> . . . A complete redrawing of the geographic attendance zones would not enhance the situation substantially because of the peculiar situation involved. This system encompasses highly urbanized and industrialized areas, suburban areas and rural and completely undeveloped areas. The vast majority of the black students in the system live generally in the northern and eastern parts of the city. Without substantial cross-busing there would be no way in which to cause any great degree of racial mixing.[137]

The district court continued its findings of fact with a summary of the provisions and probable effects of a pupil assignment plan proposed by plaintiffs' witness, the Larsen Plan,[138] and the plan of the board of education. He then found that the faculty had been totally desegregated[139] and that school curri-

131. 431 F.2d 138 (4th Cir. 1970).
132. Scott.
133. *Id.* at 460–62.
134. Memorandum and Order, note 128 *supra.*
135. *See* pages 518–20 and notes 113–24 *supra.*
136. Scott at 456–65.
137. *Id.* at 465.
138. The plaintiffs' expert witness, Jack L. Larsen of Rhode Island College, had testified in other N.C. desegregation litigation, especially in the Durham, N.C. case.
139. Scott at 468–69.

cula, transportation, athletics and other activities were administered in a racially, nondiscriminatory manner.[140] Finally, he found as he had before, that governmental action had little if any influence on racial residential patterns.[141] In all of his new findings of fact, not one tended to prove that the Winston-Salem/ Forsyth County Board of Education since *Brown* was maintaining a dual system, unless the mere existence of some schools with an imbalance of black and white pupils in a formerly de jure segregated system is proof of the existence of a "dual system." Nothing in *Green* or in any decision of the Supreme Court had so held. Judge Gordon expressly found that the board of education had not drawn school attendance zones so as to foster segregation.[142] In effect, none of the nineteen specific allegations of the complaint was found proved;[143] the only question left on July 25, 1970, was the question of student composition which he found not to be the result of governmental action.[144]

Yet, after virtually eliminating all factual bases for inferring that the Forsyth system was a dual system and immediatley following its expression of doubt that black children in the system believed that a dual system was in operation, the court plunged headlong into a discussion of the "plethora of decisions pertaining to the disestablishment of a *dual system*."[145] (Emphasis added.) The discussion was irrelevant and clearly erroneous in the absence of any finding of fact from which the existence of a dual system in Forsyth County as defined by the Supreme Court in the *1968 Trilogy*—as recently elucidated by the Fourth Circuit Court in *Swann*—could be inferred. The test of "reasonableness . . . must be followed in arriving at a decision in this case," the *district* court said, citing the Fourth Circuit Court's opinion in *Swann*.[146] It then concluded:

Though as set forth in the finding of facts herein, there are natural boundaries which tend to support the [attendance] zones for . . . [three black elementary schools], it is the opinion of the Court that by redrawing the zone lines, pairing, clustering or using other methods available to the

140. *Id.* at 469–70.
141. *Id.* at 471.
142. *Id.* at 475; Judge Gordon, said:

In any event, where de jure segregation has been eliminated and de facto segregation remains, there surely must come a time when the stigma of de jure segregation is removed, certainly so in this situation, particularly in those areas once populated by whites and now all-black or predominantly black.

In a school system where so many black pupils attend school with white pupils, where in each school black and white teachers work hand-in-hand and where athletes, black and white, make up the teams in the majority of the schools, it is difficult to believe that a Negro child, seeing this, as he must, would believe that a dual system of schools is being operated.

143. *Id.* In effect, none of the 19 specific allegations of the complaint (see page 505 and notes 55–57 *supra*) was found proved.
144. *Id.* at 473.
145. *Id.* at 476.
146. *Id.*

Board, that a reasonable *integration* could be accomplished in each of these schools.[147]

Furthermore, because of the large black residential areas in the city of Winston-Salem, some all-black and all-white schools would remain because they could not "reasonably" be integrated by court order.

In addition to ordering the change in the racial composition of the three elementary schools, the district court ordered that minority-to-majority transfers not be allowed generally. He also said:

> ... *To further refine its unitary system,* the Board should forthwith proceed to plan for the construction of two high schools, one in the northeast quadrant of the administrative unit and one in the southeast quadrant. [Emphasis added.] [148]

The relatively mild order of the district court undoubtedly reflected both its conviction that a dual system did not exist in Forsyth County and its fear that outright dismissal of the action would probably be reversed on appeal in view of *Northcross.*

Plaintiffs filed notice of appeal of the district court's order of June 25 on July 8,[149] and in their brief subsequently filed requested the court of appeals to order desegregation in every school and to require staffing in each school and at administration headquarters in accordance with the racial ratio of pupils throughout the system; and for other relief, including filing by the board of education of periodic reports with the Courts.[150] But the board of education delayed its appeal in the hope that it might persuade the district court to delete that portion of its order of June 24, 1970 requiring the integration of the three black elementary schools.

On July 14, 1970, with school opening but seven weeks away, the board filed with the court a report, ostensibly in compliance with the court's order of June 25, 1970. The report contained a new pupil assignment policy that forbade minority-to-majority transfers as the court had directed but it did not provide for the integration of the three black elementary schools which the court had ordered on June 25. Instead the board moved the court to reconsider and vacate the three-school mandate, arguing that the integration of these schools could not reasonably be achieved. The report of the board also contained a resolution of the board to build two high schools—one in the northeast and one in the southeast quadrant of the county—as the court had directed on June 25.

---

147. *Id.*
148. *Id.* at 477.
149. Scott v. Board of Education, Civ. No. C-174-WS-68 (M.D.N.C.), Docket Entries, at 4.
150. *Id.*, Plaintiff's Brief, §v.
151. *Id.,* Order of July 17, 1970, at 1.

And, finally, the report contained a summary of innovative programs in effect or proposed to increase contact between the races. This, too, had been ordered by the court.[151]

The court responded to the report and motion with alacrity by an order dated July 17, 1970. In that order, the court denied the board's motion to vacate the court's prior order to reasonably integrate the three black elementary schools. The court then directed the board of education to integrate the three black elementary schools named in its order of June 25, 1970 by means of clustering their attendance zones with the attendance zones of five designated white elementary schools in such a way that one of the black schools would be clustered with three white schools. He further directed that the black-to-white pupil ratio in each of the schools in the three-school cluster be 39 to 61, and that in the five-school cluster it be 39 to 66, with a 5 percent leeway in either direction. No transfers were to be permitted either into or out of any of the eight clustered elementary schools except for special education programs of special hardship.[152]

The court also struck down the proposed pupil-transfer policy that would have permitted a student to transfer from a school in which his race was in the majority to another school in which his or her race also was in the majority if the school to which he requested transfer had a lesser percentage of pupils of his or her race than the school from which he or she was being transferred. In other words under the board's proposal a white pupil in a school that was 75 percent white and 25 percent black could have transferred to a school that was 70 percent white and 30 percent black, but not vice versa, under the board's proposal. Also, a black pupil in a school that was 30 percent black and 70 percent white could have transferred to a school that was 25 percent black and 75 percent white, but not vice versa. The court gave no reason for prohibiting such majority-to-majority and minority-to-minority transfers.[153]

The board of education filed its notice of appeal from the orders of June 25 and July 17 on July 22. Only those portions of the orders requiring reasonable integration of the three black elementary schools and prohibiting all but majority-to-minority pupil transfers were appealed.[154]

In his order of June 25, Judge Gordon had dismissed the action as to the board of education's co-defendants: the Board of Commissioners of Forsyth County, the North Carolina State Board of Education, and State Superintendent of Public Instruction, because the court had found that the schools of Forsyth County were exclusively administered and controlled by the board of education.[155] After the court had ordered clustering of black and white elementary schools in its order of July 17, the board of commissioners voted to transfer

152. *Id.*, Order at 2.
153. *Id.*, Order at 3.
154. *Id.*, Notice of Appeal, July 22, 1970.
155. Scott at 478.

$196,340 previously earmarked for the purchase of new school buses to the county general fund and ordered the board of education to check with them before buying any buses. A majority of the commissioners vowed that they would go to jail rather than appropriate money for cross-busing. The great majority of the residents of the county supported the commissioners' action, seeing in the cluster order a threat to the neighborhood school and a promise of additional cross-busing in the future to achieve school desegregation.[156]

On August 3, 1970, with the opening of school only three weeks off, the board of education submitted a detailed plan for clustering the attendance zones of the eight elementary schools as directed by Judge Gordon in his order of July 17.[157] The plan required 27 additional buses to transport about 1,971 students out of their neighborhood attendance zones to other schools.[158] Fortunately, the additional transportation expense of these city children would be partially borne by the state because of the decision of the state officials on June 30 in the wake of *Sparrow v. Gill*[159] to provide transportation to children within corporate limits on the same basis that transportation was provided to those living outside of incorporated cities and towns.[160]

156. Winston-Salem Sentinel, August 12, 1970, at 1.
157. Scott v. Board of Education, Civ. No. C-17-WS-68, Docket Entries, at 3. Accompanying the clustering plan was another resolution by the board of education expressing the board's "strong opposition" to the plan on four grounds and authorizing its counsel to submit the plan, but also instructing him as follows:

> . . . to move the Court not to order the implementation of this or any plan for clustering the schools involved, to move to stay any order for the implementation of the plan, . . . and to pursue the appeal of any Order directing implementation of the plan.

The grounds for the board's opposition were as follows: (1) that the clustering was not constitutionally required and would require extensive transfer of materials, including mobile classrooms, at great expense, would disrupt transportation schedules, and interfere with established educational and extracurricular activities; (2) the plan would violate the existing nondiscriminatory neighborhood school system of pupil assignment which the board believed to be in the best interests of the children; (3) 2,081 pupils would be cross-bused at great cost; and (4) the system was spending $240,000 through Title I of the Elementary and Secondary Education Act each year in the three black schools to help eligible pupils overcome their learning handicaps. The programs would be greatly diluted by the dispersal of the students by clustering.
158. Winston-Salem Sentinel, August 17, 1970, at 1.
159. 304 F. Supp. 86 (M.D.N.C. 1969).
160. The Court held in *Sparrow* that the public school transportation statute of North Carolina unconstitutionally deprived some urban children of equal protection of law because of a provision in the statute which authorized public school transportation for pupils living within the corporate limits of a city or town; provided that the area in which they were living had been annexed after February 6, 1957. The Court ruled that the state could grant or deny public school transportation as it deemed right and proper but its action must not be arbitrary. The cutoff date of February 6, 1957, the Court held, was arbitrary in that it was wholly unrelated to the end sought to be achieved: the allocation of limited transportation funds for the benefit of those students most needing transportation. In June 1970, state officials decided to provide transportation for all school children, rural and urban, residing more than one and one-half miles from school. From the day of the decision in *Sparrow v. Gill*, the defendant board of education in the *Scott* case could no longer

A hearing on the board's motion to delay implementation of the clustering plan was held on August 12, 1970. The district court expressed concern that the opening of school was less than two weeks away, yet the board of education had done nothing to obtain the school buses necessary to implement his order of July 17. Counsel for the board of education attributed the board's inaction to the earlier action of the board of commissioners in withdrawing funds for the purchase of new buses. He also complained, "It is a physical impossibility to implement the order as it now stands," and argued that so drastic an order should not be implemented until its constitutionality had been tested in higher courts. To this the plaintiffs' counsel responded:

> I think these black kids have been denied their constitutional rights for 16 years already. I wouldn't want to be the one to say that these rights could be denied them for four more months.[161]

On August 17 the district court ordered the clustering plan implemented for the school year beginning on August 25, and denied the board's motion for a stay pending appeal.[162] The court also ordered the reinstatement of the board of commissioners and the state superintendent of education as parties defendant, particularly because of the commissioners' failure to cooperate with the board of education in obtaining transportation to implement the clustering plan.

The following day the board of education applied to Judge Craven of the Court of Appeals for the Fourth Circuit for a stay of Judge Gordon's order pending appeal. On August 19, 1970, Judge Craven denied the application.[163] By then, school officials had obtained the use of 66 school buses and were preparing to implement the cluster plan, moving furniture and supplies among the clustered schools, and preparing notices of new school assignments to 2,700 elementary pupils whose school assignments would be changed.[164] The question before the board now was whether to delay opening of all schools and the implementation of the clustering plan until Chief Justice Burger would act on an application to stay implementation of the cluster plan pending appeal.

On August 21 the attorney for the board of education flew to Washington and applied for a stay of implementation of the cluster plan pending action by

---

say with certainty that state law would require local governments to bear the entire cost of transportation of central-city pupils to peripheral schools when arguing against pupil assignment plans calling for extensive busing of pupils to and from the central city. *Sparrow* made urban busing for desegregation more practicable.

161. Winston-Salem Sentinel, August 12, 1970, at 1.
162. Scott v. Board of Education, Civ. No. C-174-WS-68, Order of August 17, 1970.
163. Winston-Salem Journal, August 20, 1970, at 1. Judge Craven denied the request for a stay because of the prior decisions of the Supreme Court, particularly *Alexander v. Holmes County.* He said: "The import of these cases is clear. Plans effectuated by district courts must be first implemented then litigated."
164. *Id.*

the Supreme Court on a writ of *certiorari* in the *Swann* case. At a meeting at noon of the same day the board of education decided to delay the opening of schools for two weeks, after it appeared that, at best, several days' delay in the opening of the clustered schools would be necessary in any case to implement the cluster plan.[165]

The decision to delay the opening of the Forsyth County schools paralleled the decision by the Charlotte-Mecklenburg School Board to delay the opening of their schools until Justice Burger might act on their request of August 20 to stay the implementation of Judge McMillan's order.[166] On August 31, Justice Burger denied both the Winston-Salem/Forsyth County and Charlotte-Mecklenburg applications for a stay.[167] And so, on September 9, 1970, the Winston-Salem/Forsyth County schools opened. Approximately 1,900 elementary school children rode school buses, in obedience to a court order.[168]

The second year of desegregation litigation drew to a close. The plaintiffs, the defendants and the public were all unhappy. Approximately 3,000 white and 1,500 black elementary pupils in the eight clustered schools within the city limits were bearing the brunt of the court's decrees. The other 40,000 pupils remained relatively unaffected by the court's action. Even the judge was unhappy. He would not have done what he did if he had not been under "a solemn obligation to follow appellate court decisions."[169]

Critique of the Court's Clustering Order. The ruling and substantive case law pertaining to pupil assignment in public schools when the court ordered the clustering of eight of the elementary schools in Winston-Salem to achieve school desegregation consisted basically of the *1968 Trilogy,*[170] *Northcross v. Memphis City Schools* (1970),[171] decided by the Supreme Court,[172] and *Swann v. Charlotte-Mecklenburg,*[173] decided by the Fourth Circuit Court on May 26, 1970, one month before the first desegregation order in *Scott.* The opinion of the Supreme Court in *Alexander v. Holmes County*[174] in 1969 added little to the law of pupil assignment except that dual pupil assignment systems must be eliminated "at once." The opinion of the Fourth Circuit Court in *Nesbit v. Statesville City,*[175] decided shortly after *Alexander,* echoed the note of urgency

165. Winston-Salem Sentinel, August 21, 1970, at 1, 12.
166. *Id.*
167. *Id.,* Sept. 1, 1970, at 1.
168. Winston-Salem Journal, Sept. 10, 1970, at 1.
169. Order, note 162 *supra.*
170. *See* note 36, *supra.*
171. 397 U.S. 232 (1970).
172. *Brown* is not included because, for twenty years, no school board has operated the kind of de jure, segregated system like those operated by defendants in *Brown* and the cases consolidated with it. The principles of *Brown* were adequately restated and reaffirmed in the *1968 Trilogy.*
173. Swann v. Board of Education, 431 F.2d 138 (4th Cir. 1970).
174. *See* page 512 and note 85 *supra.*
175. *See* pages 512-13 and notes 86-88 *supra.*

sounded in the latter case. Hence, the propriety of the memoranda and orders of court in *Scott* of June 25, July 17, and August 17, 1970, insofar as they dealt with the question of pupil assignment, purportedly in compliance with the opinions of higher courts,[176] must be gauged by the Supreme Court opinions in *1968 Trilogy* and *Northcross* and by the Fourth Circuit Court opinion in *Swann*. However, the facts in *Scott* differed significantly from those in the precedents by which the court in *Scott* was guided.

Nothing in the *Trilogy* weakened the rule that, absent a *present* constitutional violation, there is no basis for judicially ordering assignment of students on a racial basis. The present constitutional violation by school authorities in the *1968 Trilogy* was their continuing failure to eliminate lingering effects of former de jure segregation in the system involved.[177]

Nothing the Court said in *Northcross* expanded the duty imposed on school boards by the *1968 Trilogy*. The decision in *Northcross* merely cautioned the court of appeal not to set aside findings of fact unless they are clearly erroneous.[178] For example, the Supreme Court in *Northcross* held that the court of appeals had erred in setting aside a finding by the trial court that a dual system existed in *Memphis*.[179] Unquestionably the Supreme Court and the court of appeals believed that the existence of a dual system was a crucial finding if remedial action by the school board was to be ordered. They differed only on the question at what weight should be given the trial court's finding that a dual system was in existence.

In *Swann v. Charlotte-Mecklenburg*,[180] decided by the Court of Appeals for the Fourth Circuit on May 26, 1970, the court—with the fresh *Northcross* opinion before it—hardly pausing to consider whether the evidence of record was sufficient to sustain a finding that a dual system existed in Charlotte and Mecklenburg County, found specifically and expressly that the Charlotte-Mecklenburg Board of Education was operating a dual system.[181]

There was, to this point, no evidence that the Winston-Salem/Forsyth County school system was a "dual system" as "dual system" was defined by the Supreme

176. *e.g.,* Order, note 162 *supra.*
177. *See also* Swann v. Board of Education, 402 U.S. 1 at 3, 7, 9, 10 (1971). The Court reiterated that the objective of school desegregation litigation was to eliminate "all vestiges of state-imposed segregation."
178. *Cf.* Fed.R. Civ. P., Rule 52(c).
179. 397 U.S. 232, 235–37, (1970).
180. 431 F.2d 138 (4th Cir. 1970). The facts, as stated by the court of appeals, which might be considered as evidence of racially motivated decisions of school authorities resulting in racially identifiable schools, were: (1) nonintegrated racially identifiable staffing; (2) a free-transfer plan which tended to perpetuate segregation; (3) "other [unspecified] administrative practices" which tended to perpetuate segregation; (4) decisions of the school board to locate schools in black residential areas of such size that they would accommodate the needs only of the immediate neighborhood. The court recognized that these latter decisions were similar to those of school boards throughout the nation in response to residential segregation. *Id.* at 140.
181. *Id.* at 141.

Court in the *1968 Trilogy*.[182] The district court in *Scott* drew no such inference in its memorandum and order of February 17, 1970, denying plaintiffs' motion for a preliminary injunction.[183] The *Scott* case in Winston-Salem and the *Swann* case in Charlotte clearly are distinguishable on their facts. In *Swann,* Judge McMillan had found some evidence indicative of gerrymandering by the school board to perpetuate segregation in a few areas. In *Scott* there was no such finding. In *Swann,* the court attributed segregation in residential patterns to state action in substantial part; in *Scott,* it did not. Whether these findings of fact were supported by the evidence in either *Swann* or *Scott* is irrelevant. They were not found unsupported by an appellate court and therefore must be accepted as correct.

Scott also is clearly distinguishable on its facts from the *1968 Trilogy* and from *Northcross*. In the *Trilogy* and in *Northcross* the defendant school boards were found to be operating dual school systems. In *Scott,* no such finding was made.

In fact, although it was unaware of doing so, the court in *Scott was* writing on "the proverbial 'clean slate,'" in that its findings of fact attributed racial patterns in the Forsyth County Schools solely to factors other than governmental action. The racial imbalance in the Forsyth County schools was, therefore, de facto in the strict sense of the word. In no reported case had a southern trial judge ordered a school board to transfer children from their neighborhood schools to achieve desegregation when no act or acts of school or other officials had been found to have caused the schools to be racially identifiable.

One may fairly say that the court's order to cluster the eight elementary schools violated one of the canons of the judicial process; to wit, a remedy may not be ordered until a legal wrong is found or threatened. The findings of fact apparently exonerated all officials past and present from unconstitutional racially discriminatory behavior. Nevertheless, on September 9, 1970, about 2,000 elementary school children in Winston-Salem, pursuant to a court order, were bused out of their neighborhoods to attend schools more distant from their homes and away from many of their friends.

One final comment needs to be made. In its order of July 17, 1970, the court directed the board of education "to further refine its unitary system" by planning for the construction of two new high schools in the eastern part of the county. Obviously, if the board were operating a "unitary system" the court had no authority whatsoever to order refinements. The court's authority to intervene in the operation of the schools was ended when a dual system had been converted to a unitary system—refined or otherwise.

182. In *Green* the Court had defined a dual system as one in which either prior school segregation laws or racially motivated decisions by school authorities had caused one or more schools to be presently racially identifiable as "white" schools or "black" schools in every facet of school operations. 391 U.S. at 237.

183. See text at notes 113–22 *supra.*

The orders of the court of June 25 and July 17, 1970, in *Scott v. Winston-Salem/Forsyth County Schools,* were unsupported by the findings of the trial judge. He should not have issued them.

The Third Year. On October 6, 1970, the U.S. Supreme Court granted the defendants' petition for writ of *certiorari* to the Court of Appeals for the Fourth Circuit in *Swann v. Charlotte Mecklenburg Board of Education.*[184] On November 10, 1970, the Winston-Salem/Forsyth Couny Board of Education moved to stay argument in the appeals Court of its appeal in *Scott,* and the motion was granted by the court two days later.[185]

Meanwhile, the integration of the three black and five white elementary schools in Forsyth County since the beginning of the 1970/71 school year and the assignment of faculty to each school in the system in a ratio of white to black approximately equal to the ratio of white to black teachers throughout the system had not caused any serious disruption or interference with the functioning of the school system. Most of the parents and others concerned with the operation of the schools apparently believed that the crisis point of desegregation had passed and that the court was at last satisfied that the Forsyth County systems was a "unitary system." They based this belief on the fact that the court had concluded as a matter of law that except in the area of pupil composition, the board's first plan had created a unitary system.[186] They thought that the court ordered integration of the three black elementary schools necessarily had corrected the only nonunitary feature—that of pupil assignment. Whether the court and board had been required by the appellate court rulings to cluster the three black with the five white elementary schools remained debatable, but inasmuch as the clustering had now taken place, most citizens believed that the Forsyth County system necessarily had fulfilled all judicial requirements of a unitary system. The constitutional crisis had been met. The neighborhood school system survived, except in the eight clustered schools.

Remand of June 10, 1971. On April 20, 1971, the Supreme Court released opinions in *Swann v. Charlotte-Mecklenburg Board of Education*[187] and *Davis v. Board of School Commissioners of Mobile County.*[188] The Court of Appeals for the Fourth Circuit then had pending before it integration cases involving school systems in Orangeburg County, South Carolina; Roanoke, Virginia; and Norfolk, Virginia; as well as Winston-Salem/Forsyth County. The court of appeals asked counsel in these cases to brief the questions presented in the light of

184. Swann v. Board of Education, 400 U.S. 805 (1970).
185. Scott v. Board of Education, Civ. No. C-174-WS-68 (M.D.N.C.), Order of Nov. 12, 1971.
186. Scott at 477.
187. Swann v. Board of Education, 402 U.S. 1 (1971).
188. Davis v. Board of School Commissioners, 402 U.S. 33 (1971).

Swann and *Davis* and set the appeals in *all* of the cases for argument on June 7. *All* of the arguments were heard on June 7. The court of appeals, in a short *per curiam* opinion of June 10, 1971,[189] vacated in whole or in part each of the judgments and remanded each case to its respective district court because the respective district judges did not have the benefit of the Supreme Court mandates in *Swann* and *Davis* that adequate consideration be given to the possible use of bus transportation, split zoning, and other methods of maximizing desegregation of student bodies.[190] Apparently the court of appeals confined its review to the purely remedial aspect of the cases. In its haste to integrate schools, the appeals court ignored the palpable error of the district court in the *Scott* case wherein a remedy had been ordered without a finding of a constitutional violation.

Defendant Winston-Salem/Forsyth County Board of Education in the *Scott* case, in its brief filed with the court of appeals, had called attention to the lack of findings by the district court that the board of education had engaged in discriminatory, unconstitutional activity which had proximately caused existing, segregated pupil assignments in the following words:

> . . . that all of the Court's substantive findings support the conclusion that the board was operating a unitary system in which no pupil of a racial minority was excluded from any school, directly or indirectly on account of race; that in view of its other findings, no constitutional violation was shown, and therefore, there was no basis for judicially ordering the reassignments of [the three black elementary schools'] pupils on a racial basis.[191]

It seems that the district court's opinion,[192] the record on appeal, and defendant-appellant's brief in *Scott* clearly raised the crucial issue of whether there was sufficient evidence and finding of wrongdoing by defendant Forsyth County school officials to warrant a remedial decree. But defendant-appellant's plea fell on deaf ears.

In its mass remand of June 10, the court of appeals stated:

> It is now clear, we think, that in *school systems that have previously been operated separately as to the races by reason of state action,* the district judge or school authorities should make every effort to achieve the great-

189. Adams v. School District Number 5, Orangeburg County, South Carolina; Green v. School Board of the City of Roanoke; Brewer v. the School Board of the City of Norfolk; and Scott v. Winston-Salem/Forsyth County Board of Education, 444 F.2d 99 (4th Cir. 1971).

190. *Id.* at 101.

191. Brief for Appellant Winston-Salem/Forsyth County Board of Education, at 60, Scott v. Board of Education, 444 F.2d 99 (4th Cir. 1971).

192. Scott at 474–76. In fact the district court found that the board had "gerrymandered attendance zones to promote desegregation." *See also* note 142 *supra.*

est possible degree of actual desegregation taking into account the practicalities of the situation. *Davis, supra.*[193] [Emphasis added.]

"Previous" state action includes any action prior to *Brown I* as well later. By stating that "in school systems that have previously been operated separately as to the races by reason of *state* action" the duty exists to desegregate to the greatest degree practicable, the court of appeals intentionally or inadvertently made it unnecessary for a trial court to find that any part of *present* segregation in southern schools is proximately caused by past or present discriminatory action by school officials. No matter what the causes of existing residential and school segregation patterns, no matter how slight or localized the lingering effects of pre-*Brown* segregation may be, all school systems in the Fourth Circuit south of the Mason-Dixon Line are bound to desegregate to the maximum degree possible, "taking into account the practicalities of the situation" as the "practicalities are illustratively defined and delimited as practicable" in *Swann* and *Davis*. In other words, the Court of Appeals for the Fourth Circuit *conclusively presumed*, apparently, that all *present* segregation in public schools of the South could be attributed to former de jure segregation and no evidence to the contrary is relevant or admissible to prove otherwise.

If this is not what the court of appeals meant to say or imply, then the district court in *Scott* misconstrued the remand order of the court of appeals, because the district court in a subsequent order, dated June 22, 1971, stated:

> These opinions and orders [of the Supreme Court and court of appeals] make it clear that *because the State of North Carolina had state enforced dual systems prior to Brown,* the pupil assignment plan of the Winston-Salem/Forsyth County Board of Education must be substantially revised to achieve the greatest possible degree of desegregation.[194] [Emphasis added.]

The district court had at last articulated a reason why the Forsyth County school system had to be modified by decree of court. It was "because the State of North Carolina had state enforced dual systems prior to Brown."

Although the district court had previously said, "There surely must come a time when the stigma of *de jure* segregation is removed, certainly so in this case,"[195] after the remand and order of the court of appeals, the district court thought that the court of appeals required remedial action by district courts without a prior finding that the school authorities *now* were violating constitutional rights either: (1) by presently engaging in racially discriminatory conduct; or (2) by permitting the effects of such conduct in the past to persist in

193. Scott v. Board of Education, 444 F.2d 99, 100 (4th Cir. 1971).
194. Scott v. Board of Education, Civ. No. C-174-WS-68 (M.D.N.C.), Memorandum Order of June 22, 1971, at 1.
195. Scott at 475.

the system. Nothing in the prior case law warranted such a relaxation of the requirement that a present constitutional violation—the operation of a dual system—must be the basis for the relief decreed.

The Mandate of the Fourth Circuit Court of Appeals in the Scott Case. The remedial action required by the Supreme Court in *Swann* and *Davis,* after a constitutional violation had been found, was to "make every effort to achieve the greatest possible degree of racial desegregation, taking into account the practicalities of the situation."[196] The court of appeals in its remand of June 10, 1971, was more specific. It ordered each of the four defendant school boards to submit a "new" plan for desegregation,[197] thereby inferentially, if not expressly, disapproving the plans on appeal from Forsyth County and the three other school systems without explaining why any or all of the plans were inadequate. Specifically, district courts were ordered to submit findings of facts that were thought to make impracticable the achieving of a greater degree of desegregation in the event they approved plans in which one or more one-race or predominantly one-race schools were permitted when an alternate plan would have eliminated such schools.[198]

Obviously the court of appeals had construed the term "greatest possible degree of desegregation" as employed by the Supreme Court in *Davis* to mean, at least, the elimination of all one-race or predominantly one-race schools, black and white, throughout a school system. However, the court of appeals went on to state:

> In Winston-Salem/Forsyth County the school board may fashion its plan on the Larsen Plan with necessary modifications, or adopt a plan of its choice which will meet the requirements of *Swann* and *Davis.*[199]

The Larsen Plan to which the court of appeals referred was a pupil assignment plan that would have placed black pupils in every school in Forsyth County so that the percentage of black pupils would have ranged from about 20 to 43 percent in the 67 schools in the system as contrasted with a system-wide percentage of black pupils of 27.5 percent.[200] The district court had ruled previously that the Larsen Plan would impose an undue burden "not only upon the School Board, but vastly more important, upon the students, both black and white."[201]

The Larsen Plan in the *Scott* case, like the Finger Plan in the *Swann* case,

196. Davis v. Board of School Commissioners, 402 U.S. 33, 38 (1971).
197. Scott v. Board of Education, 444 F.2d 99, 101 (4th Cir. 1971).
198. *Id.*
199. *Id.* at 102.
200. The plan was devised by Jack L. Larsen, a professor at Rhode Island College during the winter and spring of 1970. He testified for the plaintiffs in the *Scott* case. The full plan was appended to the district court's order in the *Scott* case. Scott at 478, 492.
201. *Id.* at 426.

attempted to eliminate "racially identifiable" schools to the greatest degree practicable. Theoretically a school has an absolutely "racially unidentifiable" student if the pupils assigned to each classroom in the system have a black-to-white ratio equal to the black-to-white ratio in each *grade* throughout the system. Thus, if the ratio of black to white first graders throughout a system is 30–70, every first-grade classroom in the system will have 30 percent black pupils. The Larsen Plan did not attempt to achieve grade-by-grade racial unidentifiability. It attempted merely to achieve racially unidentifiable school units wherein the black-to-white ratio in each school would approach as closely as practicable the black-to-white ratio of all pupils, recognizing that this probably was as far as a system should go to achieve a racial unidentifiability. The district court and the Forsyth County Board of Education thus had received from the court of appeals two directives: (1) to eliminate as practicable all one-race or predominantly one-race schools; and (2) to adopt a plan which would achieve racially unidentifiable school units to the greatest degree possible (the Larsen Plan, for example), or to adopt any other plan that would satisfy the requirements of *Swann* and *Davis*.

School Board Reaction to the Remand. When the court of appeals on June 10, 1971 directed the Winston-Salem/Forsyth County Board of Education to "submit a new plan to comply with *Swann* and *Davis* on or before July 1, 1971," the board and the school administration set to work at once.

Some members of the board believed that the cluster plan, which the court of appeals had remanded, yet might be acceptable because, before *Swann* and *Davis* had been decided by the Supreme Court, the district court had said that the Larsen Plan was too burdensome to be practical and had clearly implied that, with the implementation of the cluster plan in the 1970/71 school year, the Forsyth County school system would be a unitary one. Several passages of the Supreme Court's opinion in *Swann* could be construed as admonitions to the courts of appeals to exercise restraint in modifying the desegregation orders of the district courts. Those favoring the resubmission of the cluster plan in compliance with court of appeals remand of June 10 could argue that the court of appeals did not really intend to require "new" plans but only the reconsideration of the plans then before it on appeal to insure that they complied with the mandates of *Swann* and *Davis*. Other members of the board of education apparently believed that a new plan similar to the Larsen Plan was necessary. Again, with the opening of a new school year just two months away, no one knew for sure what was required of the Forsyth County Board of Education to bring their pupil assignment plan into compliance with the mandates of the court of appeals and the Supreme Court. So the board of education directed the school administration to prepare four different pupil assignment plans: the first being substantially the cluster plan which had been in effect during the 1970/71 school year and which had been remanded by the court of appeals; the fourth being a plan, similar to the Larsen Plan, which provided for substantial desegregation in each of the schools throughout the system; and the second and third plans being plans which achieved intermediate degrees of school desegregation.

Neither the court of appeals nor any federal appellate court had yet explained what a "predominantly one-race school" was. If pupils would be assigned to each school in Forsyth County in the ratio of 27.5 percent black to 72.5 percent white—the ideal balance sought in the Larsen Plan—it could be argued that every school in the system would be a predominantly white school —a predominantly one-race school—and that the system would be nonunitary. However, the fact that the Supreme Court in *Swann* had approved a plan which, if implemented, would have scattered black pupils among the 106 schools of Mecklenburg County in percentages ranging from 9 to 38 percent[202] would rebut such an argument. The most reasonable conclusion to be drawn, therefore, from the several mandates, instructions, and suggestions of the Supreme Court and the court of appeals to the U.S. district court and the Forsyth County Board of Education was that a school in which neither race was "predominant" was a school in which the ratio of the races was equal or nearly equal to the ratio of the races comprising the whole pupil population. In other words, the court of appeals really meant "racially identifiable schools" when it used the term "predominantly one-race schools" in its remand order of June 10, 1971. So construed, *the mandate of Swann and Davis to southern school districts was to eliminate racially identifiable student bodies,* "taking into account the practicalities of the situation."

With reference to the "practicalities of the situation," the district court in *Scott* had both the *Swann* and *Davis* cases to guide it. In *Swann,* the Supreme Court had approved a plan which involved busing of 19,285 additional pupils in a student body numbering 84,500 pupils; 23,600 were being bused prior to the implementation of the plan. Thus, the plan approved in *Swann* increased the percentage of the total pupils in the system being bused from 27.8 to 50.8 percent, and increased the number of pupils bused in the preceding year by 81.8 percent.[203] The average length of the bus rides by a prior plan in Charlotte was 15 miles one way, requiring about one hour. The Supreme Court, therefore, thought that an average bus ride for elementary school pupils of 7 miles was not unreasonable.[204] The additional bus operating costs, before the gasoline price rise, were estimated to be almost $600,000.[205] In *Davis,*[206] the Supreme Court, consistently with *Swann,* rejected a desegregation plan for the elementary schools in Moblile, Alabama. The district court and the court of appeals in their

202. *See* Swann v. Board of Education, 420 U.S. 1, 10, 11, (1971).
203. Swann v. Board of Education 431 F.2d 138, 144–45 (4th Cir. 1970).
204. Swann v. Board of Education 402 U.S. 1, 31 (1971).
205. Swann v. Board of Education, 431 F.2d 138, 143 (4th Cir. 1970).
206. David v. Board of School Commissioners, 402 U.S. 33 (1971).

approved plans had treated the eastern part of the city, where most of the blacks lived, in isolation from the rest of the school system on the other side of a major north-south highway. The failure of the plans approved by the courts below to devise interlocking east-west zones straddling the highway with transportation across was held by the Supreme Court to be in violation of the mandate to achieve the greatest possible degree of desegregation "taking into account the practicalities of the situation."[207] Apparently the "practicalities of the situation" in Charlotte and Mobile, and presumably elsewhere in the South, could be invoked as an excuse to avoid all-school racial unidentifiability only to forestall extreme or manifest hardship in the implementation of a school desegregation plan.

The Decree of June 22, 1971. The district court in the *Scott* case was aware of the voluminous findings reported in the *Swann* case. It knew, too, in a general way, the amount of additional busing estimated to be necessary to implement a plan providing for substantial desegregation in every school in Forsyth County because it had considered and rejected the Larsen Plan. It knew that a plan to eliminate all racially identifiable schools in Forsyth County had to be implemented in order to comply with the mandates of the Supreme Court and the Fourth Circuit because *Swann* and *Davis* taught that only extreme hardship would justify any lesser measure of desegregation. The district court in the *Scott* case on June 22, 1971, therefore concluded:

. . . It is apparent that it is as "practicable" to desegregate all of the public schools in Winston-Salem/Forsyth County as in the Charlotte-Mecklenburg system and that the appellate courts will accept no less.[208]

The mandates of the appellate courts lacked a crystal's clarity. Construed they had to be. Did the district court in *Scott* construe them correctly? None can say with certainty because no appeal of the district court's order of June 17, 1971 was taken to the circuit court. However, the district court's construction was a reasonable one. If it was contrary to the intent of the appellate courts, the ambiguities of their orders and opinions are to blame.

The Neighborhood School in Forsyth County: R.I.P. The Total Desegregation Plan for 1971/72 and Implementing Order. The order of the district court of June 22, 1971, declaring that the appellate courts—and, inferentially, the district court—would accept no less pupil desegregation than that ordered in Charlotte-Mecklenburg, left the Forsyth County Board of Education with no alternative but to submit a new plan to the court which would provide for comparable

207. *Id.* at 36–39.
208. Scott v. Board of Education, Civ. No. C-174-WS-68 (M.D.N.C.), Memorandum Order of June 22, 1971, at 3.

student body desegregation in the public schools of Forsyth County. The new pupil assignment plan was submitted to the district court on June 19, 1971,[209] two days before the deadline of July 1, set by the court of appeals in its remand order of June 10.[210] In a unanimously approved resolution accompanying the new plan, the board of education said:

> . . . [T] he Board feels compelled to advise the Court that even though this is the least expensive, least disruptive, least burdensome, and most equitable plan the Board has been able to devise and still accomplish the required objective of racial balance in the public schools of Forsyth County which will be acceptable to the Court, it is not a sound or desirable plan, and should not be required because . . . [the accomplishment of the objective is] impossible without massive and expensive busing which imposes an otherwise unnecessary financial burden on the public and a tremendous burden of inconvenience and time consumption on pupils and parents and traffic hazards on pupils.[211]

In a hearing on July 16, the district court said that it would accept "the massive school desegregation drawn up by the City-County school board."[212] By memorandum order dated July 26, 1971, the district court ordered the plan implemented for the 1971/72 school year. In the order, the court observed that the plan submitted was "strikingly similar in essential aspects to the Larsen Plan."[213] It quoted the board's resolution accompanying the new plan in full and then said that, notwithstanding the findings and conclusions set out in its memorandum and order of June 25, 1970, and its order of August 17, 1970, pertaining to pupil assignment and the impracticalities of the Larsen Plan, it must comply with the June 10 mandate of the court of appeals and direct implementation of the plan. The board was given "plenary power" to make minor changes in the new plan in the course of implementation so long as the changes did not affect the racial ratio in any school more than 5 percent from that reflected by Chart 7 of the plan.[214]

The Effects of the Massive Desegregation Order. The plan, which the Winston-Salem/Forsyth County Board of Education submitted to the court and which the court ordered implemented for the school year 1971/72, provided for the conversion of the elementary/junior high/senior high school (6-3-3) system into an elementary/intermediate/junior high/high/senior high (4-2-2-2-2) system of schools in order to facilitate achievement of the greatest degree of desegregation.[215] Feeder patterns set out in the plan enabled a student to know

209. *Id.,* Memorandum Order of July 26, 1971, at 1.
210. Adams v. School District 5, 444 F.2d 99, 101 (4th Cir. 1971).
211. Scott v. Board of Education, *supra* note 109, at 2, 3.
212. Winston-Salem Journal, August 17, 1971, at 1.
213. Scott v. Board of Education, *supra* note 209, at 2.
214. *Id.* at 3–4.
215. *Id.* at 1.

with assurance which schools he or she would attend from the first through the twelfth grade. The plan also provided that those who were assigned to the same elementary school under the plan would be assigned as a group to the same schools at the various grade levels through all twelve grades, provided their residences remained within the attendance zone for that first school.[216]

The implementation of the plan had innumerable direct and indirect effects on the lives of the pupils, their families, and their teachers which are beyond the scope of this study. However, the plan achieved a degree of integration of student bodies in the 67 schools comprising the system which is believed to be unique in a system as large as the Winston-Salem/Forsyth County system. According to data submitted to the court shortly after the 1971/72 school year began, desegregation in the schools was such that it could be said that, with two exceptions, no school was racially identifiable. The following table supports this statement:[217]

School Units (Grades)	System Wide Black Enrollment	Range of Black Enrollment Among School Units
Elementary Intermediate (1–6)	29%	20–41%
Junior High (7–8)	28%	20–37%
High (9–10)	27%	19–34%
Senior High (11–12)	24%	19–30%
All Schools (1–12)[a]	27.5%	19–41%

[a]Two special and optional education centers were excluded. About 414 pupils were attending those schools of which about 239 were black.

The table shows that all black pupils except those in special educational centers were attending schools where white pupils were in the majority, yet in no school did blacks comprise less than 19 percent of the pupils. Under the plan, approximately 8,000 additional black students were brought into contact with a predominantly white in-school culture. This was more than two and one-half times the number of black pupils so assigned in the preceding school years.[218]

To achieve this degree of desegregation, approximately two-thirds of the black pupils and one-third of the white were required to attend schools outside of their prior neighborhood attendance zones. In sum, 20,500 students in all grades out of a total of 48,000 attended schools other than those they would have attended under the neighborhood assignment plan which had been proposed by the board for the 1970/71 school year.[219] The "neighborhood school" had been replaced by biracial grade groups which retained their identity while

216. *See* id. at 1–5.
217. *See* Scott v. Board of Education, Civ. No. C-174-WS-68 (M.D.N.C.), Memorandum of December 3, 1971, at 4–5.
218. *Id.* at 6.
219. *Id.* at 7.

moving from school to school as they progressed through the 4-2-2-2-2 system. As each of the 17 elementary biracial grade groups left the sixth grade to enter one of the 11 junior high schools, then went on into one of the 8 high schools, and finally into one of the 5 senior high schools, it would come in contact with other biracial elementary grade groups in increasing numbers, but members of each elementary group might preserve their in-school relationships to whatever degree they desired throughout their years in the public schools.

The Busing Burden. In order to achieve racially unidentifiable schools, busing mileage for the school year more than doubled, from 1.5 million in 1969/70 to 3.3 million in 1971/72. The number of school buses regularly operated by the city-county schools increased from 216 in 1969/70, to 276 in 1970/71, to 351 in 1971/72. While the total pupil enrollment declined from 50,455 in 1969 to 48,087 in 1971, the number of pupils transported almost doubled from 17,876 to 32,220.[220] Finally, if a pupil allowed ten minutes to get to the bus stop from home, waited ten minutes for school to begin after debarking, and waited ten minutes for the bus to leave after school, then of the 32,200 children being transported, each child was spending six hours at school and an average time of two hours in transportation to and from school. Round trips, *including waiting times,* ranged from about one hour to *three and one-half hours.*[221]

The increases in the transportation statistics would have been much greater except for the fact that the school opening times were staggered so that one bus, for example, could make a trip from the inner city to the outer parts of the county with a load of black children, drop them at their assigned school, and transport a load of white children from the county to the inner city. Obviously this could not be done without excessive lost time if the outer and inner schools opened and closed at the same time.[222]

Public Reaction to the Demise of the Neighborhood School. Reaction to the massive school reorganization and desegregation plan submitted to the court and made public on June 29 and its implementation pursuant to the order of the district court dated July 26 was surprisingly restrained and undemonstrative, although the great majority of white *and* black parents and pupils and teachers

220. *Id.*
221. *Id.* at 11.
222. The court found:

   . . . the staggered starting times and bus schedules create hardships among the parents, especially in those families where both parents work, and among the children involved . . . and family life has been disrupted both in the morning and in the afternoon because of the varying schedules of pupils.

   . . . .

   Long bus rides have shortened the day of pupils in the system. After-school activities have been disrupted and pupils have less time for play and family activities.

Id. at 9, 10.

opposed the far-reaching changes in school operations that implementation of the plan entailed. Anti-busing groups such as the white Silent Majority met, fulminated, and passed resolutions urging the board of education not to open schools until the Supreme Court had reviewed the district court's order. Most of the black community objected to the plan, mainly for two reasons. First, Atkins High School, the only senior high school situated in a black neighborhood, was to be converted into a high school (grades 9 and 10). Second, the plan called for grades 1-4 to be housed in schools located in white neighborhoods and grades 5-6 in schools in black neighborhoods.[223] Black parents were opposed to putting their young children on school buses. They believed that the young, black children would be carrying most of the burden of the desegregation order.[224]

Parents and pupils of both races believed that the novel 4-2-2-2-2 grade plan might be an educational disaster. Among older students the belief that athletic programs, extracurricular activities, and school morale generally would be adversely affected was widespread. Only a few thought that the plan was basically good. The board of education was widely criticized for having gone too far, even by those who had believed that contacts between black and white pupils in the public schools ought to have been increased.

Although, as one reporter wrote, "Many parents greeted the city-county busing program with about the same enthusiasm as they would a leprosy epidemic,"[225] no significant street demonstrations and no acts of violence occurred. The relatively passive acceptance of this drastic desegregation plan is attributable to many factors. First, the leadership of the county had urged parents of children who were being cross-bused under the cluster plan of the preceding year to "do what is right—obey the law, help your children in school, help your principal and teachers and school administration to provide the best quality education."[226] During the preceding school year, the Chamber of Commerce had sponsored a "Project CommUNITY" to improve interracial relations in all phases of community life, especially in the public schools. A director of intergroup relations was appointed by the school officials to supervise the handling of problems which arise when children with widely differing backgrounds are to be taught in the same classroom. As a result of these efforts, the eight-school "cluster plan" in 1970/71 with cross-busing had not caused serious disruption of the education of the 2,400 elementary pupils involved in that program during the preceding school year.

The court-decreed pupil assignment plan for 1971/72 imposed burdens on *all* students in the system similar to those which had been imposed upon the 2,400 elementary pupils in the attendance zones of the clustered schools in 1970/71. In order to forestall any serious dislocations, the board of educa-

223. Winston-Salem Journal, June 30, 1971, at 1, 14.
224. *Id.*
225. Winston-Salem Sunday Journal-Sentinel, August 8, 1971, at 25.
226. Winston-Salem Sentinel, September 1, 1970, at 1.

tion advanced registration one day to August 25, 1971, so that students, teachers, and bus drivers could test the new pupil assignment plan and bus transportation. On registration day some children missed buses, some buses were late, some broke down, one driver got lost, but when registration was completed, school officials believed that no unsolvable problems had surfaced. The foreman at the school bus garage said, "If we can do it today, we can do it any day."[227] Although many adjustments in schedules would have to be made, the plan would work; racially identifiable schools could and would be eliminated in Forsyth County. Indeed, the desegregation issue was "almost overlooked in the hectic rush to make the new plan work."[228]

The final enrollment for the school year 1971/72 totaled 48,087, a decrease of only 900 from the preceding year. The citizens of Forsyth County were not deserting their public schools in droves, despite their general displeasure with the "four-two-two-two-two" plan. Thus, on the Monday following the registration day, classes began. For the first time, no racially identifiable schools were in operation in Forsyth County. The percentage of black teachers among the 67 schools in the system varied from a maximum of 35 percent in one elementary school to a minimum of 21 percent in one high school. And, as previously stated, the percentage of black pupils varied from 19 percent to 41 percent. Surely, now, the Winston-Salem/Forsyth County school system was a unitary system.[229]

Chief Justice Burger's Memorandum of August 31, 1971. When the district court had ordered implementation of the Larsen-like plan on July 26, 1971, the board of education had not yet filed a petition for a writ of *certiorari* for review of the court of appeals's remand of June 10, 1971, wherein the court of appeals had, in effect, ruled in favor of the plaintiffs-appellants by ordering a new plan submitted in the light of *Swann* and *Davis,* thereby implying that the modest cluster plan which the district court had approved for the 1970/71 school year was inadequate as the plaintiffs-appellants had maintained. The remand by the court of appeals also, in effect, denied the cross-appeal which the board of education had taken, primarily on the ground that there was no finding that the board of education or other school official had acted so as to violate any pupil's constitutional rights.[230] The board had delayed filing for *certiorari* because it had hoped that the district judge might no require implementation of the school desegregation plan which the board had prepared and submitted to the court on June 29, 1971. This hope was not dashed until July 16, when the district judge, after a hearing on the plan submitted in response to his June 26,

227. Winston-Salem Journal, August 26, 1971, at 1.
228. *Id.*
229. *Cf.* note 142 *supra.*
230. Brief for Petitioner, Winston-Salem/Forsyth County School Board v. Scott, Petition No. 71-274 (M.D.N.C.) filed August 20, 1971, at 6–10.

1971, order, said that he would accept the plan. At once the board was faced with a decision to make: Should the implementation order, when it was finally rendered, be appealed to the Court of Appeals for the Fourth Circuit? Meanwhile, the petition to the Supreme Court for *certiorari*, to review the June 10 order of the court of appeals remanding the cluster plan of the preceding year, was held in abeyance. At a meeting on August 2, 1971, one week after the district court had docketed its order of July 26, ordering the new plan implemented, the board of education decided that no purpose would be served by appealing or requesting a stay of the latest orders of the district court of June 22 and July 26, 1971, directing that the new desegregation plan be prepared and implemented in 1971/72.[231] Instead the board directed its counsel to attach a copy of these latter orders, a copy of the new plan and a copy of the board's resolution in opposition to the new plan to the as yet unfiled petition for *certiorari* to the Supreme Court to review the court of appeals's action of June 10, 1971, on the board's appeal of the district court's action in the prior year. Counsel completed preparation of this petition for *certiorari* and addressed a request for a stay of the district court's order of July 26, 1971, to the Chief Justice. The petition for *certiorari* and the request for a stay were mailed on August 20, 1971, but did not reach the Chief Justice until August 23, 1971, seven days before school was to begin.[232] Thus, the Chief Justice had thrust upon him a request to stay at once a comprehensive integration plan approved by the district court for the 1971/72 school year until the Supreme Court acted on a petition for *certiorari* to review an order implementing a modest cluster plan for 1970/71 which the court of appeals had ordered re-done. The fact that the application for the stay did not reach the Chief Justice until Augsut 23 probably predisposed him to refuse to grant it. He said:

> To begin with, no reasons appear why this application was not presented to met at an earlier date, assuming that we accept the explanation tendered for failure to present it to the Court of Appeals. The time available between receipt of the application and response and the opening of the school term August 30 was not sufficient to deal with the complex issues presented. . . .[233]

On the record before him the Chief Justice and author of the majority opinion in *Swann* said that he could not "conclude with any assurance" that the district court in its order dated July 26, 1971, and the court of appeals in its remand dated June 10, 1971, did or did not correctly read this Court's holding in *Swann* and particularly of the explicit language as to a requirement of fixed

231. Winston-Salem Journal, August 3, 1971, at 1.
232. See Winston-Salem/Forsyth County Board of Education v. Scott, 404 U.S. 1221, 1223 (1971).
233. *Id.* at 1227.

mathematical ratios or racial quotas and the limits suggested as to transportation of students. Inasmuch as the heavy burden of proof of error was on the board of education, the Chief Justice was unwilling to disturb the order of the district court which implemented a pupil assignment plan in Forsyth County,[234] a plan that was strikingly similar in essential aspects to the Larsen Plan which the plaintiffs had asked the district court and the court of appeals to order implemented.[235]

In his memorandum denying the stay, the Chief Justice noted that the finding of the district court on June 26, 1970 that residential segregation in Forsyth County was not caused by public or private discrimination or state action but by economic facts and the desire of the blacks to live in their own neighborhoods rather than in predominantly white neighborhoods, had not been reviewed.[236] The Chief Justice also noted, *without comment,* that the district court had found that the "School Board had acted consistently in good faith" and that the district court "was of the view that 'good faith' is a vital element in properly evaluating local judgment in devising compliance plans."[237]

The findings to which the Chief Justice referred tended to prove that a "dual system" was not in operation in Forsyth County in 1970/71. They had not been reviewed, said the Chief Justice, by the Fourth Circuit Court of Appeals.[238] As a matter of record, however, the circuit court had, on June 10, 1971, effectively but not expressly, ruled that Forsyth County *was* operating a dual school system, because it had denied a cross-appeal of the board of education from the district court's order of June 26, 1970.[239] The basis of the board's appeal to the circuit court had been that "all of the District Court's substantive findings supported a conclusion that the Board was operating a unitary system and that in view of its other findings no constitutional violation was shown."[240]

The Chief Justice apparently realized that there might be substantial error in the *Scott* record. Later in his memorandum of August 31, he again referred to the obscurity of the findings:

> This case is further complicated by what seems to me some confusion respecting the standards employed and the findings made by the District Court and the terms of the remand order of the Court of Appeals. Under *Swann* and related cases of April 20, 1971, as in earlier cases, judicial power can be invoked only on a showing of discrimination violative of the constitutional standards declared in *Brown v. Board of Education.* The Court of Appeals in its remand following the decision in *Swann* did not

234. *Id.* at 1232.
235. *See* note 213 *supra.*
236. 404 U.S. 1227 at 1224.
237. *Id.*
238. *Id.*
239. Scott v. Board of Education, 444 F.2d 99 (4th Cir. 1971). *See* notes 189–95 *supra.*
240. Brief for Appellee, Scott v. Board of Education, 444 F.2d 99 (4th Cir. 1971).

reverse the District Court's findings, but rather directed reconsideration in the light of *Swann*. In view of the circumstances that was an appropriate step. The present status of the findings is not clear to me. . . .[241]

The Chief Justice' s rationale of approval of the court of appeals's remand may be faulted for two reasons. First, the Supreme Court in *Swann* had not dealt with the question of what constitutes "a showing of discrimination violative of constitutional standards." It had accepted the finding of the district court, as affirmed by the court of appeals, that Charlotte-Mecklenburg was in fact a dual system.[242] Therefore, the court of appeals had erred *if* it had directed the district court to reconsider its findings about the presence of a violation of constitutional standards for equal educational opportunity in the light of *Swann*, because there was no "light" from *Swann* cast on this issue. Moreover, the court of appeals, in remanding the *Scott* case, had not in fact directed "reconsideration of the findings" by the district court as the Chief Justice apparently believed. In its remand of June 10, 1971, it had ordered that new plans be submitted by the school board "to comply with *Swann* and *Davis*."[243] The only findings that the district court and the school board were to reconsider on remand were findings that cross-busing and other desegregation measures were unreasonably burdensome.[244]

It is fair to say that the Chief Justice probably believed that there was error in the record before him, but the applicant had failed to pinpoint it. A petition for *certiorari* had been filed. If there was substantial error it would be found in due course. Meanwhile, the process of desegregation should go forward. Indeed, it had already taken place with the opening of school the day before he denied the petition for a stay. No purpose would be served by a stay at this date, and so the Chief Justice denied it.

Reaction to the Memorandum of the Chief Justice. Meanwhile, in Forsyth County, North Carolina, the massive school desegregation plan was in operation, it was working, and all schools were open and functioning without widespread protest because the leadership of the county had convinced most parents that the Supreme Court required the elimination of all racially identifiable schools. Unfortunately, the Chief Justice in his memorandum of August 31 had expressed concern because the Winston-Salem/Forsyth County School Board had stated in its resolution of June 26, 1971, that the plan it was submitting under protest was

241. 404 U.S. at 1231.
242. Swann v. Board of Education, 402 U.S. 1, 8 (1971).
243. Scott v. Board of Education, 414 F.2d 99, 101 (4th Cir. 1971).
244. The court of appeals said:

We remand these cases because the respective district judges did not have the benefit of the Supreme Court mandate that adequate consideration be given to the possible use of bus transportation and split zoning.

414 F.2d 99, 101.

based on its understanding that the Supreme Court required a "fixed 'racial balance.'"[245]

The board had not said that a *fixed* racial balance in each school was required. It has said that it was required to achieve "*a* racial balance in the public schools of Forsyth County."[246] The plan that it had submitted provided for percentages of blacks in the regular schools of the system ranging from 18 to 36 percent black because it had been required to achieve the maximum degree of desegregation possible taking into account the practicalities of the situation. Obviously the board did not believe that it had to achieve the *same* racial balance, a "*fixed*" racial balance, in each school. However, the board believed that it was required by court mandates to assign a racial mix of pupils to each school as nearly equal to the racial mix existing throughout the system as the practicalities of the situation permitted. If this construction of the mandate to achieve "the greatest possible degree of desegregation taking into account the practicalities of the situation" was erroneous, the error was attributable to the suggestion of the court of appeals that the Larsen Plan might be adopted, and the declaration by the district court that it would accept no less integration than that which had been ordered in Charlotte.

In any event, the Chief Justice's memorandum of August 31 aroused hope that the Supreme Court might be willing to grant the board's request "to review the case on its own merits,"[247] a review the board of education believed the court of appeals had not undertaken on June 10, 1971 when it had acted almost summarily in remanding the *Scott* case and three others to the district courts with orders to prepare new plans. Several of the board members were concerned because the Chief Justice's memorandum had made it appear that the board had not requested the stay as quickly as it should have, had not prepared its motion for a stay as well as it might have, and therefore had not done all that it could to get a delay. To this criticism the superintendent of schools said: "A copy of the whole fool plan went with [the stay application]."[248] The public now began to doubt that the board of education should have eliminated all racially identifiable schools in view of the Chief Justice's comment that the Supreme Court did not require "fixed" racial balances. The local newspaper ran an editorial entitled, "Once More Into Chaos."[249]

At its next meeting the Winston-Salem/Forsyth County Board of Education directed its attorney to file a motion in the district court to vacate the court's desegregation order of July 26. Meanwhile, the schools would not be closed as several citizen groups recommended after the Chief Justice had intimated that

245. Winston-Salem/Forsyth County Board of Education v. Scott, 404 U.S. 1221, 1228 (1971).

246. *Id.* at 1227.

247. Winston-Salem Sentinel, September 1, 1971, at 1.

248. Winston-Salem Journal, September 1, 1971, at 1.

249. Winston-Salem Journal, September 2, 1971, at 8. The press was convinced that the Chief Justice "could hardly have done a greater disservice to the people of this county."

the district court and the board of education had done more than they were legally required to do to create a unitary system.[250] Accordingly, a motion to vacate its order of July 26, 1971 was filed with the district court on September 9, 1971.[251]

During the month of September, Forsyth County school officials were accused of "covering up" the seriousness of busing problems.[252] On September 20, about 85 junior high and high school students marched about a mile to reinforce their demands to be assigned to their neighborhood schools. No parents accompanied the marchers.[253] But generally, as September wore on, the burdens on parents, pupils, teachers, and taxpayers of eliminating racially identifiable schools proved to be bearable. With each passing day the argument that the implementation of the plan ordered by the district court would be impracticable became less tenable because implementation had taken place, and public education in Forsyth County went on.

Certiorari *Denied.*   The complaint in the *Scott* case had been filed on October 7, 1968. Three years later, each of the 67 nonspecialized schools in Forsyth County had, by court order, become racially unidentifiable in regard to faculty and student body composition. The neighborhood school was no more. In view of the statements of the Chief Justice, many believed that the Supreme Court would modify the burdensome, total integration decree of the district court of July 26, 1971.

However, that decree, and that of June 22, 1971 to the Court of Appeals for the Fourth Circuit had not been appealed. The board of education had appealed only for a writ of *certiorari* to review the decision of the court of appeals of June 10, 1971, wherein that court, in a *per curiam* opinion, remanded the *Scott* case *and* three other school desegregation cases to the respective district courts with an order to each of the school boards to submit new desegregation plans to comply with *Swann* and *Davis.*

Apparently the Supreme Court was of the opinion that nothing in the order of the court of appeals of June 10, 1971, was substantially at variance with what the Supreme Court had held in *Swann, Davis,* and earlier cases. This is merely a surmise and remains so because the Supreme Court refused to review the court of appeals's June 10 remand order in the *Scott* case when it denied the petition of the Winston-Salem/Forsyth County Board of Education for a writ of *certiorari* on October 26, 1971.[254]

The third year of litigation to desegregate the Winston-Salem/Forsyth County

250. Winston-Salem Journal, September 8, 1971.
251. The motion was denied on December 3, 1971. Scott v. Winston-Salem/Forsyth County Board of Education, Civ. No. C-174-WS-68 (M.D.N.C.), Memorandum Order of December 3, 1971.
252. Winston-Salem Journal, September 8, 1971, at 3.
253. Winston-Salem Sentinel, September 20, 1971, at 17.
254. 404 U.S. 912 (1971).

schools was over. The right to appeal the orders of June 22 and July 26, 1971 had expired. All 67 schools were desegregated—totally.

The Fourth Year. *Did the District Court Revise Its School Desegregation Guidelines?* When the third year of litigation to desegregate the Winston-Salem/Forsyth County schools ended on October 26, 1971, with the denial of the board's petition for *certiorari,* the only unfinished business in the *Scott* case was the motion of September 9, 1971 by the board of education requesting the district court to vacate its order, dated July 26, 1971, under which the schools had been totally desegregated. The motion had been made largely on the strength of Chief Justice Burger's memorandum of August 31, 1971.[255]

Although the public schools of Forsyth County were in full operation, the district court shared the concern of many parents of elementary school children whose children were required to spend many hours traveling between homes in the outer area of the county and schools in the central city and vice versa. After a hearing on the motion to vacate, the court found that the average daily mileage per bus increased from 37 in 1970/71 to 51.2 miles in 1971/72. The buses traveled while loaded a total of 1,114 miles per day in 65-mile-per-hour zones on interstate highways, at a maximum school bus speed of 35 miles per hour.[256] Not only was "cross-busing" time-consuming, inconvenient, and expensive, but it exposed children to greater risks of harm because of the use of the expressways to facilitate the long hauls necessitated by the court's desegregation order. In a letter to plaintiffs' and defendants' counsel dated October 5, 1971, the court expressed its anxiety.[257]

However, neither the fears of the court for the safety of the children on the expressways nor the puzzling memorandum of the Chief Justice of August 31, 1971, were of sufficient weight to cause the district court to vacate its order of July 26. Instead, the district court, by memorandum order dated December 3, 1971, reserved judgment on the board's motion to vacate its July 26 order and authorized, but did not direct, the board of education to submit revisions to the pupil assignment plan for implementation in the 1972/73 school year.[258]

255. Defendant's Motion, Scott v. Winston-Salem/Forsyth County Board of Education, Civ. No. C-174-WS-68 (M.D.N.C.), dated September 7, 1971, at 4. In support of the motion, defendant argued:

> It appears clear from the Chief Justice's opinion denying an application for a stay in this case that he does not believe that the Board of Education was required to achieve the results decreed by this Court's orders of June 22 and July 26, 1971. It would therefore be appropriate for this Court to reconsider and vacate its orders. . . .

256. Scott v. Board of Education, Civ. No. C-174-WS-68 (M.D.N.C.), Memorandum Order dated December 3, 1971, at 8.

257. In his letter, the trial judge requested:

> that the school board at the hearing present a plan to take all children in grades one through six off the Interstate. Hopefully, a plan in this respect can be presented that will result in substantial integration of grades one through six over that which existed in the 1970–71 school year.

258. Scott v. Board of Education, Civ. No. C-174-WS-68 (M.D.N.C.), Memorandum Order dated December 3, 1971, at 18.

In the course of its memorandum order of December 3, 1971, the district court quoted extensively from the memorandum of the Chief Justice, and concluded:

> It appears clear from the opinion of the Chief Justice denying application for a stay in this case that he does not believe the Board of Education was required to achieve the results decreed by this Court's orders of June 22 and July 26, 1971.[259]

Earlier, in its memorandum order of December 3, the district court had said that the board of education had not done more than they were required to do by order of the district court when they had submitted, under protest, the massive desegregation plan, which had been implemented by the July 26 order of the district court.[260] In thus absolving the board of education from being over-zealous in its school desegregation efforts, the district court accepted full blame for any misrepresentation of the mandates of the appellate courts. The board of education had done only what it had been ordered to do and no more. Because the Chief Justice was apparently of the opinion that the district court had gone too far, the district court in its memorandum order of December 3 took pains to explain that it had never construed *Swann* to require any particular degree of racial balance or mixing. *Swann* only required the elimination from the public schools of "all vestiges of state-imposed segregation."[261]

The crucial question, said the district court, was: *"Does the equal protection clause of the Fourteenth Amendment to the Constitution under the facts of this case require the continuation of the present practices?"*[262] In other words, was the massive cross-busing to achieve a racial mix in every school of Forsyth County, as the district court had ordered, constitutionally required?

After stating the question and then construing *Swann* anew, the court concluded that, prior to any court order, the board of education had taken numerous steps to eliminate its former dual school system; that the board of education had fully complied with the court's order of July 17, 1970, to cluster eight schools, and with the desegregation orders of June 22 and July 26, 1971; and that, whether or not the board had done so previously, it is clear, by any standards, "that the Board is now operating a unitary school system."[263] The court also said:

> . . . To accomplish this has necessitated the massive "cross-busing" of about 11,000 pupils who would not require any busing under a neighborhood plan and has required about 8,000 pupils, who even already bused [*sic*] to be bused greater distances over more heavily traveled highways. *The achievement of this result imposes hazards, time consuming burdens*

259. *Id.* at 12.
260. *Id.* at 2.
261. *Id.* at 15.
262. *Id.* at 13.
263. *Id.* at 16, 17.

and inconveniences which ought not to be required on a continuing basis. [264] [Emphasis added.]

The court then authorized the board of education to submit revisions of the pupil assignment plan to be effective for the 1971/72 school year. The court reminded the board that in drafting its revisions the board should bear in mind:

1. The cluster plan under which the schools operated during the 1970/71 year was not accepted on appeal.
2. A racially neutral plan of geographic attendance zones may be inadequate if it failed to counteract the continuing effects of "discriminatory location of school sites or distortion of school size in order to achieve or maintain an artificial racial separation."
3. If the revised plan called for any predominantly one-race schools, "the Board would have the burden of proving that their racial composition was not the result of present or past discrimination." [265]

Such was the court's answer to what it had said was the crucial question: Did the Constitution, under the facts of this case, require continuation of its decreed plan for the assignment of pupils? The memorandum order of December 3, 1971, stated that the hazards, time-consuming burdens, and inconveniences caused by the court's orders ought not to be required on a *continuing* basis, the inference being that the burdens were justified *pro tempore* as a remedial measure. The gist of this memorandum order was that the district court had not erred up to this point, the board of education, if it wished to do so, had now only to submit revisions of the plan to ease the burdens which "ought not to be required on a *continuing* basis." (Emphasis added.)

The guidelines to be observed by the board in the event it elected to submit revisions to the pupil assignment plan presumably recapitulated the mandates of the appellate courts about pupil assignment as construed by the district court. The second guideline is irrelevant to the *Scott* case because the record is barren of any finding that the Forsyth Board of Education had ever engaged in any of the discriminatory school-zoning practices adverted to in the second guildeline. Thus, the law and guidelines the district court set out for the enlightenment of the board of education in its memorandum order of December 3 were more illusory than real.

The court said, in effect, that the Forsyth County school system now was *a unitary* system, and that the burdens of the present plan were not constitutionally required on a *continuing* basis. At some future date they should be reduced. The board could elect to submit revisions to the plan for the 1971/72 school year. Such revisions must provide more school desegregation than the 1970/71

264. *Id.*
265. *Id.* at 18.

cluster plan which the court of appeals had rejected. Finally, if the revisions included predominantly one-race schools, the burden of proof would be on the school authorities to prove that their racial composition was not the result of present or past discrimination.

The last guideline bears close scrutiny in the light of the court's prior finding of facts. The only discriminatory state action chargeable to the Winston-Salem/ Forsyth County school authorities or other officials, according to the findings of the district court, was the action of the state and local school officials in operating separate schools for black and white children pursuant to Article IV, Section 2 of the Constitution of North Carolina until *Brown v. Topeka Board of Education* was decided in 1954. Hence, the board of education could only conclude that, if they could prove that the racial composition of a particular, predominantly one-race school today was not attributable to de jure segregation prior to 1954, then the court would not reject the school's inclusion in a pupil assignment plan, assuming always, of course, that the board had been colorblind in drawing the boundaries of the attendance zones of such predominantly one-race schools. This latter assumption had already been found true by the district court, months earlier, in its findings of fact in its memorandum orders of February 17 and June 25, 1970, wherein it had found in effect that *voluntary* segregated housing was the proximate cause of predominantly one-race schools in Forsyth County at least since 1954, and that the pattern of voluntary segregated housing outdated *Brown* by many years.[266] On the basis of these facts, the only rational inference was that schools in Forsyth County, constructed *after* 1954, and which had been predominantly white or black since that time, and schools constructed *prior* to 1954 and which changed their basic racial composition since 1954, could not be directly or indirectly causally related to prior de jure segregation or racially discriminatory action by school officials. Therefore, such predominantly one-race schools could be considered neither vestiges of a dual system nor schools whose racial composition was the result of present or past discrimination. Apparently the third guideline applied principally, if not solely, to the eight "historically" black schools still in operation in the 1972/73 school year.

Thus construed, the district court in its memorandum order of December 3, 1971, had considerably relaxed the rules it had prescribed in its order of June 22, 1971, in which it had said that the appellate courts would accept no less school desegregation in Forsyth County than had been required in Mecklenburg County, where the court there had ordered a racial mix in each school ranging from 9 to 38 percent black.[267]

The Board of Education Guesses Wrong. The board of education obviously could not decline the invitation to make revisions to the pupil assignment plan

266. See notes 113–22, 133–42 *supra.*
267. Note 202 *supra.*

which would ease the "hazards, time-consuming burdens, and inconveniences" caused parents, pupils and teachers, and the public by the desegregation order of July 26, and which would also comply with the guidelines of the court order of December 3, 1971. The court had requested suggestions to alleviate the hardships it had created. The board had a duty to the public to respond to the court's plea for help.

The board of education decided to submit a complete revision of the elementary school pupil assignment plan whereby elementary children would return to neighborhood schools and all elementary schools would house grades 1-6, instead of grades 1-4 and 5-6 the so-called "4-2" grade structure placed in effect by the court's order of July 26. The thirty-seven elementary schools would feed into junior high, high, and senior high schools in patterns similar to those under the 1971/72 plan so that the racial ratios in those higher schools would be basically unchanged. According to estimated enrollment data for 1972/73 the racial mix in the thirty-seven elementary schools would have been as follows if the plan[268] had been implemented:[269]

	Proposed Plan for 1972-1973		As Assigned in 1971-1972		As Assigned in 1969-1970	
	Schools	Blacks	Schools	Blacks	Schools	Blacks
All Black (100% black)	8	4,718			9	5,479
Black (0–5% white)	1	308			2	1,432
Predominantly black (5–50% white)	0	0			0	0
Predominantly white (5–50% black)	13	1,667	37	7,095	9	669
White (0–5% black)	7	124			6	93
All White (100% white)	8	0			5	0
	37	6,817	37	7,095	31	7,673

Under the board's proposal for 1972/73 the number of black elementary school children in predominantly white schools would have been more than double the number so situated in 1969/70, the year preceding the court-ordered cluster plan. However, the plan would have decreased the number of black elementary children so situated in the coming year, 1972/73, to less than one-fourth of the number so situated in 1971/72, under the massive desegregation order. Under the board's proposal for 1972/73, therefore, 5,428 fewer black children would have been in a predominantly white school environment in the first six grades of school.

Justification for depriving 5,428 young black children of the benefits of pre-

268. See Scott v. Board of Education, Civ. No. C-174-WS-68 (M.D.N.C.), Memorandum Order dated July 21, 1972, at 3, 4, where a brief summary of the plan appears.
269. Data for this table were supplied by the director of research, Winston-Salem/Forsyth County schools.

dominantly white schools in the elementary grades was a reduction in the busing burden of some 9,000 elementary pupils, of whom about 4,000 would be able to walk to school.[270]

In addition, the board of education, in reliance upon the district court's finding that the board had operated a unitary system in 1971/72, argued in support of its proposed 1972/73 pupil assignment plan that, even if the remedial power of the federal courts permitted the ordering of the 1971/72 plan as a remedial measure, "such power does not continue after the vestiges of a dual system have been eliminated."[271] Therefore, the board of education argued, it should be allowed to discontinue racial assignments to achieve a racial balance in each school at least at the elementary level.

If the board of education guessed that the district court might approve the return to neighborhood schools for the elementary school children of Forsyth County and would so quickly cease to oversee the assignment of pupils by school officials, the board had guessed wrong.

After a hearing on May 17, 1972, on the motion of the board of education for permission to implement the proposed revision to the pupil assignment plan which had been in effect for the 1971/72 school year, the court, in a memorandum order of July 21, 1972, denied the board's motion of September 9, 1971 to vacate the implementation order of July 26, 1971.[272] This was the motion on which the court had reserved judgment in its order of December 3, 1971. In its July 21, 1972 order, the court also denied the board's motion to implement the board's proposed revisions to the pupil assignment plan for the 1972/73 school year. Therefore, pupil assignments for the 1972/73 school year again would be in accordance with the order of July 26, 1971, and the "hazards, time-consuming burdens, and inconveniences," which ought not to have been required "on a continuing basis," were required to be continued another year, at least, unless an appellate court directed otherwise or unless the board submitted revisions to the pupil assignment plan which were acceptable to the court, revisions which the court would consider but no longer invited.[273]

After three years of litigation, after sifting through mountains of evidence and pondering innumerable decisions of appellate courts, the law of school desegregation as applied by the presiding judge in the *Scott* case boiled down to

270. Scott v. Board of Education, note 268 *supra.*
271. Scott v. Board of Education, Civ. No. C-174-WS-68 (M.D.N.C.), Defendant's Motion, dated March 15, 1972, at 4.
272. Scott v. Board of Education, note 268 *supra.*
273. In its memorandum order denying the board's motions, the district court said that time had not served to allay its apprehension for the safety and welfare of the elementary school children expressed in its letter to counsel of October 4, 1971. However, it then said:

It is apparent from the decision in Swann that there may be situations where one-race schools are constitutionally acceptable. . . . But this Court cannot in good faith find that the number of one-race schools proposed by the Board complies with *Swann.*

Id. at 5, 11.

this: *If a school system was de jure segregated by state law prior to* Brown *the school officials have a duty to take whatever remedial steps are necessary to disestablish racially identifiable schools, taking into account the practicalities of the situation.* Furthermore, in discharging its duty to disestablish all racially identifiable schools in Forsyth County, some one-race schools might be maintained if "the practicalities of the situation required." However, inasmuch as no one-race school was in operation in Forsyth County during the 1971/72 school year, and inasmuch as the longest bus ride, one way, was one hour and ten minutes, not including waiting times, and the earliest pickup time was 6:40 A.M. and the last bus stop in the evening was 5:00 P.M.,[274] the practicalities of the situation in Forsyth County did not require any one-race schools to be maintained in Forsyth County.

In a nutshell, the district county declared on July 21, 1972 that it had been required by law to disestablish all racially identifiable schools in Forsyth County because the North Carolina Constitution had required separate education of the races in the public schools prior to *Brown.* Having done so, the court further declared that *it would retain indefinitely control* over all changes in pupil assignment plans that would affect the planned racial ratio in any school by more than 5 percent.[275]

The Board Loses Another Appeal and Pays the Price. The defendant board of education appealed the order of the district court dated July 21, 1972. On March 5, 1973, the Court of Appeals for the Fourth Circuit heard arguments, and, on April 30, 1973, the circuit court affirmed the district court's order of July 21, 1972, in a brief, unpublished opinion.[276] In its opinion the court of appeals noted that the district court indicated plainly that it had no desire to impose on the school district any more busing than was constitutionally required under the circumstances. However, the district court had properly rejected the board's revision, which "would have meant a resegregation of a substantial portion of the school system."[277]

The court of appeals did not have before it the order of the district court, dated December 31, 1971, wherein the district court had said that the busing

274. *Id.* at 8.
275. *Id.* at 11, 12. The court said: "[T]he Court reiterates and confirms that the Board has plenary power to make amendments as provided in the July 26, 1971 order." In its July 26, 1971 Order, the Court previously had said:

[R]ealizing time is of the essence and problems concerning pupil assignments will likely arise when the Board attempts to actually implement the Plan, the Board had plenary power to make minor changes in the Plan so long as the changes do not affect the racial ratio in any school by more than 5 percent from that reflected in Chart 7 of the Plan.

Memorandum Order, note 209 *supra,* at 4.
276. Scott v. Board of Education, 475 F.2d 1400 (4th Cir. 1973).
277. Scott v. Board of Education, No. 72-2162, Court of Appeals for the Fourth Circuit, Decision dated April 30, 1973, at 2.

burdens of the court-approved plan ought not to be required on a continuing basis. The tenor of the court of appeals opinion was that the burdens would continue until the board of education could devise an alternative "which within constitutional limits, might reduce the extent of busing required."[278]

Thus, the board of education had thrust upon it by the district court the duty of eliminating racially identifiable schools by desegregation in schools in *approximately* the same ratio as the ratio of black to white pupils throughout the system. This was done. By affirming the order of July 21, the court of appeals *tacitly* concurred in the district court's opinion that this drastic *remedial* measure was required solely because the state of North Carolina operated dual systems prior to *Brown*. The court of appeals had gone somewhat further. It had, if effect, approved the plan, as implemented in 1971/72, as a continuing modus operandi of the Winston-Salem/Forsyth County schools, subject to such revisions as the board may care to make, provided that any of such revisions does not affect the planned pupil racial ratio in any school by more than 5 percent.[279] Changes by school board action of greater magnitude were to be henceforth subject to the approval of the district court to ensure that racial mixing was not reduced beyond constitutional limits.

In addition, the court of appeals directed that plaintiffs' counsel be allowed reasonable attorney's fees for all services rendered by them in the *Scott* litigation subsequent to June 30, 1972, the effective date of Section 718 of the Emergency School Aid Act of 1972. Henceforth, the board of education would risk having to bear the total cost of any desegregation litigation in which it did not prevail.

Untying the School Construction Bonds. On April 3, 1972, the district court ruled that the principal objective sought by the plaintiffs in the *Allen* (formerly *Atkins*) action—namely, the desegregation of the schools of Forsyth County—had been achieved when the board of education had implemented the 4-2-2-2-2 plan in compliance with the court's order in the *Scott* case of July 26, 1971. There no longer existed within Winston-Salem and Forsyth County "Negro schools, schools identified or identifiable as Negro schools, or schools with a majority of Negro students or with a disproportionate minority of Negro students."[280] The plaintiffs in the *Allen* case had sought to promote the integration of the public schools in Forsyth County through the means of purposeful expenditive of construction and repair funds, particularly the $24.8 million of authorized but

---

278. *Id.*

279. 86 Stat. 369, 20 U.S.C. § 1617 (1972).

280. According to the *Tenth Day School Enrollment Report* statistics for the 1975/76 school year prepared by the director of research, Winston-Salem/Forsyth County Schools, in only 13 schools are the ratios of black-to-white pupils within 5 percent of that shown in Chart 7 of the 1971/72 Plan. In the remaining 48 schools, the ratios of black-to-white pupils now differ in excess of 5 percent from that shown on Chart 7. These changes are not the result of pupil assignment revisions. They are attributable to slight errors in the 1971/72 estimates and to subsequent shifts in housing patterns.

unissued school construction bonds. Now that integration had been accomplished, although by different means, the plaintiffs had no further claim for relief, and the district court dismissed the *Allen* action. On January 10, 1973, the Court of Appeals for the Fourth Circuit affirmed the district court's dismissal.[281] Appellants did not petition for *certiorari*.

In its unpublished decision, the court of appeals said that it appeared from the record that the question of future location and improvement of public schools was a "live question" in a companion case, *Scott v. Board of Education,* then on appeal before the court.[282] Thus, when the court of appeals decided the *Scott* case on April 30, 1973, and a petition for *certiorari* was not filed, the bond attorneys for the board of education issued a no-litigation certificate on July 15, 1973, and the school construction bonds which had been authorized by the referendum of March 16, 1968, could now be issued and the construction could go forward.

During the five years of litigation from 1968 to 1973, construction costs had risen. The assistant superintendent for business affairs of Forsyth County schools estimated that construction costs had increased by 30 percent during the period. The *Scott-Allen* litigation cost the county approximately $7.5 million.

CONCLUSIONS

The Appellate Courts Failed to Detect Palpable Error
In not a single instance did the court find that the Winston-Salem/Forsyth County Board of Education had located a specific school or drawn an attendance zone with an intent to segregate blacks and whites.[283] The court characterized the racial composition of the pupil population of the Forsyth County public schools as "de facto" segregation.[284] The court found that the number of children attending integrated schools had steadily increased through the years,[285] and that the board of education had closed one senior high school and had gerrymandered one senior high school and had gerrymandered zone lines to promote desegregation.[286] Finally, the court found that the faculty, staff, transportation, extracurricular activities, and facilities were desegregated.[287] How, then, did the district court in the *Scott* case assume authority, in the first instance, to intervene in the operation of the Winston-Salem/Forsyth County schools by ordering the board of education to cross-bus several thousand elementary school pupils in the 1970/71 school year?

First, the district court ordered the board to change its freedom-of-transfer

281. Allen v. Winston-Salem/Forsyth County Board of Education, No. 72-1722 (4th Cir. 1973), Per Curiam Opinion of January 10, 1973.
282. *Id.* at 2.
283. 317 F. Supp. 453, 475 (M.D.N.C. 1970).
284. 317 F. Supp. at 475.
285. *Id.* at 473.
286. *Id.*
287. *Id.*

policy so as to limit nonhardship transfers to cases in which the transferee would be transferring from a school in which he or she was in the majority to a school in which he or she would be in the minority. The court ordered this change because the continuation of the free-transfer policy might be "expected to encourage resegregation."[288] In evaluating the propriety of this mandate when there was no finding of prior constitutional violation, it should be remembered that a school transfer policy that either resulted in substantial pupil segregation or was intended to have that effect, in a system that otherwise had been a unitary system, probably would, and fairly could, be deemed to be a forbidden discriminatory policy.

Whether such a policy, absent a discriminatory purpose, would be unconstitutional solely because the trial judge believed that de facto racial ratios in the schools comprising a unitary system *might* be adversely affected is another question. Under the circumstances a high probability of marked change in racial ratios might be justification for relief *quia timet,* restricting freedom of transfer to cases of majority-to-minority transfers only. In the *Scott* case, therefore, the court's order to limit freedom of transfer to majority or minority transfers was not necessarily improper relief *quia timet,* even though the court had found no prior constitutional violation and no discriminatory intent on the part of the board of education in having permitted minority-to-majority transfers.

However, the district court ordered further relief on the assumption that it was duty bound to decide if the board of education "had done enough" to overcome the many problems pertaining to the integration of the schools.[289] The court also ordered the clustering of five white with three black elementary schools. The court overlooked the crucial fact that it had said: (1) that, in all aspects except pupil composition, the public schools of Forsyth County were racially unidentifiable; and (2) that the racial identifiability of student bodies was solely the result of de facto segregation of housing and the racially neutral action of the board of education "of locating the schools where the children were located."[290] Although the court found that there were "natural attendance zone boundaries" which tended to support the then existent pupil assignments to the three black elementary schools that were to be clustered with the five white schools, the court thought that "a reasonable integration in each of these schools *could* be accomplished"[291] (emphasis added) and proceeded to decree it.

It is generally held that, in the absence of a finding that some vestiges either (1) of former segregation of pupils by law, or (2) of discriminatory official action still persist in a school district, a district court is without authority to intervene.[292] If this is good law the error of the district court was palpable, substantial, and prejudicial.

288. *Id.* at 474.
289. *Id.*
290. *Id.*
291. *Id.* at 476.
292. In Bradley v. School Board of City of Richmond, 462 F.2d 1058, 1069 (4th Cir.

Months later, the district court in the *Scott* case said that it had based its remedial decrees on the fact that the constitution of the State of North Carolina required racial segregation in public schools prior to *Brown*.[293] There may be some dicta in *Swann* that would have permitted a court to presume in the beginning that racially identifiable schools in a former de jure segregated system are in fact vestiges of state-enforced segregation.[294] However, as de jure segregation receded into history, such a presumption became less tenable. The fact that a former de jure segregated system had, in 1970, one or more racially identifiable schools should have created at most only a rebuttable presumption that the racial compositions of these schools were vestiges of the former de jure segregation[295] or present or past discriminatory action of state officials or the school board.[296]

In the light of the findings in the *Scott* case, any presumption that racially identifiable schools in a formerly de jure segregated system are vestiges of such segregation or of official discrimination would appear to have been conclusively rebutted. What further evidence could have been adduced and what other findings made to rebut a presumption that state-imposed school segregation laws prior to 1954 caused racially identifiable school populations in 1970? Hence it is unreasonable to infer that, when the district judge in *Scott* said that racially identifiable schools must be disestablished "in those systems that have previously operated separately as to the races because of state action,"[297] the court was referring only to systems where *vestiges* of such pre-*Brown* segregation still were present. He meant exactly what he said—that all southern public school districts had a duty to "disestablish" racially identifiable schools because at one time they had been segregated by law.

The alleged lack of any finding by the district court in *Scott* that some vestiges of former de jure segregation or of discriminatory action by school

---

1972), the Fourth Circuit Court of Appeals quoted from the Supreme Court's opinion in *Swann*:

> Remedial judicial authority does not put judges automatically in the shoes of school authorities whose powers are plenary. Judicial authority enters when local authority defaults.

The Fourth Circuit Court of Appeals then observed that in Spencer v. Kugler, 326 F. Supp. 1235 (D.N.J. 1971):

> [A] three-judge court had held: ". . . de facto segregation, defined as racial imbalance that exists through no discriminatory action of State authorities, to be beyond the ambit of the Fourteenth Amendment." 462 F.2d at 1070. See also Washington v. Davis, 91 S. Ct. 2040, 2048 (1976) where the Supreme Court said that the differentiating factor between de jure and de facto school segregation "is purpose or intent to segregate."

293. See note 273 *supra*.
294. *See* Swann v. Board of Education, 402 U.S. 1, at 6–7 (1970).
295. Newburg Area Council v. Board of Education, 489 F.2d 925, 930 (6th Cir. 1973).
296. Swann v. Board of Education, 402 U.S. 1, 27 (1970).
297. See note 273 *supra*.

officials still persisted in Forsyth County schools was one of the bases for the appeal to the Court of Appeals for the Fourth Circuit.[298] But the court of appeals—under the lash of the Supreme Court to achieve the greatest possible degree of desegregation of dual school systems at once in accordance with the Supreme Court's opinions in *Alexander v. Holmes County Board of Education, Swann,* and *Davis*—apparently either overlooked the error, deliberately shut its eyes to it, or, like the district court, believed that the mere fact that a school system had been at one time segregated by state law was ample warrant to invoke the full range of remedies available to federal courts to desegregate, that is disestablishment of all racially identifiable schools in such systems at once, bearing in mind the practicalities of the situation.[299]

Whatever the reason, the Court of Appeals for the Fourth Circuit deigned not to address itself to the absence of any finding by the district court in the *Scott* case of any constitutional violation that would justify the exercise of the court's remedial powers. Then, when the board of education addressed a request for a stay in the enforcement of the remand of the court of appeals pending action by the Supreme Court on the Board's petition for *certiorari,* the Chief Justice adverted to the fact that the record in *Scott* indicated some confusion about the standards employed and the findings made by the district court and the terms of the remand order of the court of appeals.[300] But, nevertheless, the stay was not granted and *certiorari* was denied; whatever confusion and error there might have been remains imbedded, apparently forever, in the record of the *Scott* case.

Today thousands of children are required to ride school buses in Forsyth County because of the court's decree. If the basis for that decree was the existence of *vestiges* of state-imposed school segregation prior to *Brown,* the decree is unsupported by the findings of fact. Alternatively, if the basis for the decree is the single fact that the Winston-Salem/Forsyth County schools were segregated *de jure* prior to *Brown,* regardless of the actual causes of the racial composition at the schools when the desegregation order issued, the order is essentially punitive rather than corrective. In either event the judicial process miscarried.[301]

Unwarranted Faculty Reassignment

One of the most traumatic measures taken to achieve desegregation of the Winston-Salem/Forsyth County schools proved to be the midyear reassignment of faculty in January 1970[302] in order to bring the school system into compliance

298. See note 230 *supra.*
299. See note 193 *supra.*
300. See note 241 *supra.*
301. It may well be that plaintiffs in Scott had not adduced all of the evidence available to prove that vestiges of past segregation existed in the Forsyth County schools when the Court issued its first desegregation order. If so "justice" may have been done although the "judicial process" miscarried. However, the judicial process is no process at all if the judgment rests on unproved or unstated findings or on an unrecognized rule of law.
302. See notes 99–110 *supra.*

with the mandate of the Court of Appeals for the Fourth Circuit as stated in *Nesbit v. Statesville City Board of Education* and the four companion cases wherein the court had decreed that in each case the desegregation plan "must include provisions for the integration of faculty so that the ratio of Negro and white faculty members of each school shall be approximately the same as the ratio throughout the system."[303] The Winston-Salem/Forsyth County Board of Education and the U.S. District Court for the Middle District of North Carolina and other federal district courts in the Fourth Circuit construed *Nesbit* as requiring that a faculty assignment policy not in accordance with the *Nesbit* mandate would be deemed to be a hallmark of a nonunitary school system by the Fourth Circuit.[304]

Prior to *Nesbit*, the Supreme Court had dealt with the question of faculty assignment in southern school districts in several cases. In 1965 the Supreme Court had said in *Bradley v. School Board of City of Richmond* that faculty assignments were a relevant issue in desegregation litigation and that a desegregation order should include provisions relating to the assignment of faculty.[305] In 1969, shortly before the Court of Appeals for the Fourth Circuit decided *Nesbit,* the Supreme Court had reversed a ruling of the Court of Appeals for the Fifth Circuit whereby that court had struck down an order of a district court to a school district requiring that teachers be assigned to each school in accordance with the ratio of black to white teachers system wide.[306] But nowhere had the Supreme Court declared that apportionment of faculty as ordered in *Nesbit* was a *sine qua non* of a unitary school system.

The faculty-assignment rule in school desegregation cases handed down by the Court of Appeals for the Fourth Circuit has never been reviewed by the Supreme Court. No other circuit court of appeals has adopted it. It stands out in sharp contrast to the holding of the Supreme Court in *Swann* that a district court has "broad power to fashion a remedy that will assure a unitary school system."[307]

It would appear that, once a unitary system has been achieved in other respects, considerable latitude should be allowed school authorities in assignment of black and white faculty; provided, of course, no assignment violates any teacher's rights under the Constitution and state and federal fair employment acts. Absent a conscious intent to discriminate in schools where black children were in the majority, sound educational reasons might justify the appointment of a higher percentage of well-qualified black teachers to such a school than would be appointed to a school where a majority of the pupils were white.

303. See note 87 *supra.*
304. See note 302 *supra.*; Bechet v. School Board, 308 F. Supp. 1274 (E.D. Va. 1969); Bradley v. School Board, 325 F. Supp. 828 (E.D. Va. 1971); Swann v. Board of Education, 311 F. Supp. 265 (M.D.N.C. 1969).
305. 382 U.S. 103, 104 (1965).
306. United States v. Montgomery County Board of Education, 395 U.S. 231 (1969).
307. 402 U.S. 1, 17 (1970).

The *Nesbit* mandate has no redeeming virtues but those of uniformity and ease of enforcement. The rule caused needless travail in the Winston-Salem/ Forsyth County system. It may be an appropriate measure in some desegregation cases, but there seems to be little need for a policy in the Fourth Circuit that in every system in the circuit teachers shall be assigned to each school in approximately the same ratio of black to white as the ratio prevailing system wide. The *Nesbit* mandate therefore is an unwarranted intrusion of the federal judiciary into the operation of the schools of the Fourth Circuit in general and of Forsyth County in particular.

The Costs of Court-Ordered Busing

The desegregation by court order of the public schools of Forsyth County has been costly. The *bus-to-pupil* ratio has doubled since court ordered desegregation began,[308] and the busing mileage per year has more than doubled. Thousands of children ride buses who would walk to school if desegregation had not been ordered. Other thousands ride longer because of the court's orders. Extracurricular activities have suffered. School loyalties, for better or worse, have been weakened.[309]

Debate continues over the merits and demerits of racial mixing in classrooms.[310] Even the courts profess some doubt as to the educational benefits to be derived from desegregation by cross-busing. For example, the Court of Appeals for the Fourth Circuit, in reversing a district judge's order to consolidate a predominantly black, large city school district with several predominantly white suburban districts for the purpose of obtaining a "viable" racial mix in the schools said:

> We think it is fair to say that the only "educational reason" offered by the numerous school experts in support of the consolidation was the egalitarian concept that it is good for children of diverse economic, racial and social backgrounds to associate together more than would be possible within the Richmond School District.[311]

The Supreme Court in *Brown* merely said that no child may be effectively excluded from any school by state action solely on the basis of race. The Court also said that the effective exclusion of black children from some schools solely because of their race generated "a feeling of inferiority in Negro children and

308. According to data supplied by the director of transportation, Winston-Salem/ Forsyth County Schools on August 13, 1975, 401 school buses were in operation in 1975/76, compared with 216 in 1969/70. Total school enrollment in 1975/76 is 45,040; in 1969/70 it was 50,455.

309. *See* Scott v. Board of Education, Civ. No. C-174-WS-68 (M.D.N.C.), Memorandum Order of December 3, 1971, at 8–11.

310. *See, e.g.,* Mills, The Great School Bus Controversy (1973).

311. Bradley v. Board of Education, 462 F.2d 1058, 1068, (4th Cir. 1972).

retards mental and educational development."[312] The Court in *Brown* and in subsequent cases did not balance the benefits to be gained by removing the feeling of inferiority in black children against potential educational detriments that might result from mandatory desegregation of the magnitude of that ordered in the Winston-Salem/Forsyth County schools. And no such evaluation will be attempted here. All that can be said for certain is that the data available at present conclusively prove neither the educational and behavioral wisdom nor the folly of massive public school desegregation measures, including "fixed-ratio" faculty assignment.

The school authorities in Forsyth County were found by the district court to have acted in good faith in administering the schools of Forsyth County prior to the first desegregation order; that is, they were attempting to comply with the law as they understood it.[313] Over their strong objections they have complied with the court's desegregation orders to the letter. But to what avail?

Under the pupil assignment plan now in effect in Forsyth County there is no practical way for a child to avoid busing or other transportation for at least two of his or her six years of elementary school. If the pupil is black, he or she will probably be bused for four years. However, many elementary school children rode buses prior to the desegregation order, particularly in rural areas. Most junior high and high school students rode buses to school prior to desegregation. It is true that the bus rides are longer now, but probably the busing burden is not the principal adverse effect of the present pupil assignment plan.

Of greater significance is a growing awareness that the pupil assignment plan is to be a dominant factor in school operations for the indefinite future.

The Pupil Assignment Plan Resists Modification

The present pupil assignment plan provided for a range of percentages of black students in each school from 18 to 36 percent.[314] It was to be "equally unfair" for all students. During the five-year period in which the plan has been in effect, some of the chains of schools feeding into the senior high schools established under the court-approved 4-2-2-2-2 plan have become significantly more white than others because of changing residential patterns. During the 1975/76 school year, the "most-white" school chain in the plan consisted of schools where whites outnumber blacks 4 to 1; whereas the "least-white" chain consisted of schools wherein whites outnumbered blacks only 4 to 3 on the average and, in some schools in the chain, the ratio was 2 to 3.[315]

312. Brown v. Board of Education, 347 U.S. 483, 494 (1954).
313. Scott v. Board of Education, 317 F. Supp. 453, 473–76 (M.D.N.C. 1970).
314. *See* Scott v. Board of Education, *supra* note 209, Chart 7.
315. If, for example, Johnny enrolls at *A* elementary school (grades 1–4), proceeds to *B* intermediate school (grades 5–6), then *C* junior high (grades 7–8), into *D* high (grades 9–10), and finally into *E* senior high (grades 11–12), he will attend schools where whites outnumber blacks 4 to 1. On the other hand, if Mary enrolls in *U* elementary school, and then successively into *V, W, X, Y,* and *Z* schools, she will attend schools where blacks outnumber

If one accepts the proposition that there is a minimally viable white-black ratio in a school, such as 3 to 2, which, if not maintained, tends to cause white students to disappear from the school entirely,[316] Forsyth County schools may be dangerously close to that point today with respect to its "least white" school feeder chains. Some members of the board of education, therefore, feel some compulsion to reduce, at least, the racial ratio disparities among the several school feeder chains.[317]

All of the board members agree that the overcrowding at some schools and the vacant seats in others which have been caused by changes in residential patterns over the past five years should be corrected if it is practicable to do so. They also agree that the busing burden should be reduced, particularly for the younger children.

But the board has been unable to devise modifications to the pupil assignment plan which are acceptable to a majority of its members ever since the court's rejection of the modification proposed for the 1972/73 school year. The lack of unanimity among board members seems to reflect an unwillingness of most members to accept the concept of either periodic or ad hoc adjustment or "fine tuning" of the pupil assignment plans to correct developing racial imbalances. The board has no legal obligation to do so once it has created a unitary school system.[318] Furthermore, the public was assured by the board of education when the present 4-2-2-2-2 plan was submitted to the court that the pupils assigned to the same school in the first grade would, under the plan, be assigned to the same schools at various grade levels, through all twelve grades.

Parents and children alike prefer a stable to an unstable school attendance plan. Parents will accept changes in the plan if they are convinced that the education of their children will be enhanced, but not otherwise. Obviously, if the board of education fine tunes the racial composition of the schools in each chain from time to time, no child will have assurance of his or her school assignment from one year to the next. Not only will the children necessarily attend at least five different schools during their public school careers and spend countless hours

---

whites in schools *U, V, W,* and *X,* and constitute 42 percent and 35 percent of the student population of schools *Y* and *Z.* Data derived from the 10th Day Enrollment Data, 1975/76.

316. One district court in the Fourth Circuit has so found. See Bradley v. Board of Education, 338 F. Supp. 67, 128 (E.D. Va. 1971).

317. This comment and those on the following pages pertaining to school board and parental views are inferences drawn by the writer from his participation in the meetings on the board of education during the past three years.

318. In *Swann* the Supreme Court in 1971 said:

Neither school authorities nor district courts are constitutionally required to make year-by-year adjustments of the racial composition of student bodies. . . . [I]n the absence of a showing that either the school authorities or some other agency of the State has deliberately attempted to fix or alter demographic patterns to affect the racial composition of schools, further intervention by a district court should not be necessary.

402 U.S. at 32–33. In 1976 the Court again so held. *See* Pasadena City Board of Education v. Spangler, 44 I.W. 5114 (June 28, 1976).

in transit, but they would have no assurance of whom their schoolmates might be from one year to the next. This instability and rootlessness of school assignment in Forsyth County would coincide with instability in many homes because the family itself is fighting for survival.

Some members of the board of education are therefore reluctant to make any adjustments in the pupil assignment pattern unless compelled to do so because of virtually unbearable overcrowding of school facilities. Furthermore, these members discourage making any adjustments which arguably could have either desegregation or segregation as one of the objections. Inasmuch as most assignment changes may be viewed either as increasing or diminishing desegregation, these members are "do-nothings" who prefer to let the "fool plan" run its course on the theory that this stand-pat attitude allows the individual parent, black and white, the greatest freedom of choice and yet complies with the law. In the absence of convincing data about the educational value of racially unidentifiable schools, they prefer to let the sense of the community determine the racial composition of the schools. As long as the board of education does nothing, it does not expose itself to litigation by integration or to criticism from those who yearn for a return to the 6-3-3 system, with its neighborhood elementary schools.

But meanwhile the most-white school chains grow whiter and the most-black school chains grow blacker. Resegregation is occurring to some degree. The day may be coming when Forsyth County school children will be bused to schools where their own race predominates to about the same degree as it would predominate if they attended a neighborhood school. If that day comes, school integration by court order will have failed. Yet we may hope that during the next five years the races will finally bury old animosities and be mutually convinced more *by valid data* than by untested faith that black and white children mutually benefit by going to the same schools.

Intervention by the Courts in School Operations in Forsyth County Will Continue

The Winston-Salem/Forsyth County Board of Education again finds itself an active litigant, as defendant, in the *Scott* case. Plaintiffs and their successors in interest filed an additional claim on November 6, 1974, which has survived defendant's motion to dismiss and for summary judgment,[319] and is now pending, pretrial discovery having been completed. The plaintiffs ask further relief because the board of education is continuing to segregate or is about to resegregate pupils according to race because of in-school ability groupings.

The board of education has responded with pages of documentation on the methods relied upon to justify their ability groupings. Nevertheless, the court thought that there was more than a scintilla of evidence to support plaintiffs'

319. Scott v. Board of Education, Civ. No. C-174-WS-68 (M.D.N.C.), Order dated April 29, 1975.

charges when it denied defendants' motion. At issue are the methods used to assign pupils to remedial instructional and academically talented classes, the assignment of faculty to such classes, and the methods used to evaluate achievement of pupil in them and the procedures for returning students to the main stream of instruction.

The resumption of litigation probably is attributable in some measure to a dispute with HEW in the summer of 1974 in which HEW threatened to cut off aid to be granted under the Emergency School Assistance Act unless the board of education complied with a number of directives of HEW which the latter alleged, on the basis of an inspection of the Forsyth County system by its representatives, were being violated in the course of the operations of the schools. Among the directives being violated were some pertaining to ability groupings.[320]

Whatever the merits of the plaintiffs' motion for further relief, the district court finds itself embroiled in a pedagogical controversy about the merits of educational programs in the public schools because of their potential effect on the racial composition of instructional classes. The Court of Appeals for the Fifth Circuit recently said:

The Board Has Lost Some of the Public's Confidence

If ability grouping does cause segregation, whether in classrooms or in schools, ability grouping may, nevertheless, be permitted in an otherwise unitary system *if the school district can demonstrate that its assignment is not based on the present results of past segregation* or will remedy such results through better educational opportunities. [Emphasis added.] [321]

The law of the Fifth Circuit, if applied in Forsyth County, apparently would create two classes of students for purposes of special-education grouping: those pupils who were in the public schools before the desegregation of 1971/72 and those who began school later. The burden of proof created by the ruling above would apply only to those students who had been exposed to a dual system. The others presumably could be assigned on any rational, nonracial criteria based on ability and achievement.

But no one knows what the rule is in the Fourth Circuit. No one knows what tests should be administered or what criteria should be used to determine if ability grouping for slow learners is justified because of the accelerated progress, if any, slow learners are experiencing in special groupings. Within the school system itself, sharp differences of opinion exist about the merits of ability grouping without regard to the resegregation potential inherent in ability grouping.

If any dispute is not appropriate for judges to decide, this one appears to be.

---

320. *See* letter of Regional Director of Civil Rights Div., Region IV, August 12, 1974, to Superintendent, Winston-Salem/Forsyth County Schools.
321. McNeal v. Tate County School District, 508 F.2d 1017, 1020 (4th Cir. 1975).

The Board Has Lost Some of the Public's Confidence

The principal effect of school integration in Forsyth County by the federal judiciary has been to deprive the school system of the enthusiastic support of the white middle class. The lower middle class feels trapped. Many of the upper middle class have left the system unless their children are eligible for academically talented classes. Generally, the white pupils remaining in the system tend toward neighborhoods or class groupings in school which afford an education with as few blacks as possible. Of course there are exceptions to this tendency. In the main, black parents continue to be somewhat more apathetic toward public school affairs. Indeed, the loss of all-black and predominantly black schools may have enhanced their apathy. However, most adult blacks and many whites believe that interracial understanding has improved greatly since total desegregation began.

All in all, local public confidence in the overall effectiveness of the public schools to educate probably has waned during the past four years, although such data as there are do not show any sharp drop in the achievement scores with reference to the national norm. The loss of public support and confidence is not irremediable. The public schools retain much public good will. However, there seems to be a growing awareness that local schools are no longer under local control in many areas of administration. If the board of education is powerless to act, then to petition the board is futile.

The role played by the federal judiciary in the desegregation litigation has been an important, if not the principal, factor in the undermining of the board of education as an effective school administration agency during the past five years. Perhaps the time has come for more centralized school administration along the lines of other industrialized nations. A matter as important as the education of the nation's youth cannot be left either to the caprice of law declared by disinterested judges or to the vagaries of local school officials who are uncertain about how to proceed. If such centralization should occur because of popular dissatisfaction with local administration, desegregation litigation must rank high among the factors contributing to the dissatisfaction.

The Balance Is Yet to Be Struck

The effects of the desegregation litigation will be a force in the political, social, and economic life of Forsyth County for a long time. Unquestionably, our youth have deeper insights into the attitudes and culture of another race than did the preceding generations of whites and blacks who attended essentially one-race schools, but opinions vary concerning the degree of interracial understanding to tolerance which school integration is attaining. Similarly, little agreement exists about the effects of integration on academic achievement.

Whatever progress in race relations that has been made because of school integration has entailed considerable direct and indirect costs. No one knows now if court-ordered school integragation is worth the price. The balancing of benefits gained against detriments suffered must await some future historian's genius. Meanwhile, the integrated public schools of Forsyth County, like schools everywhere, strive to educate our youth for the challenging and promising world of tomorrow.

Serving Two Masters: Integration Ideals and Client Interests in School Desegregation Litigation

Derrick A. Bell, Jr.

One of the difficult and controversial issues in any litigation brought in behalf of a class is the degree to which representations made by lawyers reflect an informed consensus of the class. While lawyers privately debate this matter, little appears in print about it.

The following essay was prepared by Derrick Bell, a professor of law at the Harvard Law School, at the request of the IJA Project on Judicial Administration of School Desegregation Litigation. It was published in the Yale Law Journal. *It was responded to by Nathanial Jones, general counsel of the National Association for the Advancement of Colored People, in a letter to the editors of the* Yale Law Journal; *Professor Bell replied to that letter. We are reproducing here, as a basis for further thought, the entire exchange.—Eds.*

In the name of equity, we . . . seek dramatic improvement in the quality of the education available to our children. Any steps to achieve desegregation must be reviewed in light of the black community's interest in improved pupil performance as the primary characteristic of educational equity. We define educational equity as the absence of discriminatory pupil placement and improved performance for all children who have been the objects of discrimination. We think it neither necessary, nor proper to endure the dislocations of desegregation without reasonable assurances that our children will instructionally profit.—*Coalition of black community groups in Boston*[1]

Reprinted by permission of the Yale Law Journal Company and Fred B. Rothman & Company from *The Yale Law Journal* 85 (1976): 470-516.

Pamela Federman, Susan Mentser, and Margaret Stark Roberts assisted in researching and preparing this article.

1. Freedom House Institute on Schools and Education, Critique of the Boston School

The espousal of educational improvement as the appropriate goal of school desegregation efforts is out of phase with the current state of the law. Largely through the efforts of civil rights lawyers, most courts have come to construe *Brown v. Board of Education*[2] as mandating "equal educational opportunities" through school desegregation plans aimed at achieving racial balance, whether or not those plans will improve the education received by the children affected. To the extent that "instructional profit" accurately defines the school priorities of black parents in Boston and elsewhere, questions of professional responsibility are raised that can no longer be ignored:

How should the term "client" be defined in school desegregation cases that are litigated for decades, determine critically important constitutional rights for thousands of minority children, and usually involve major restructuring of a public school system? How should civil rights attorneys represent the often diverse interests of clients and class in school suits? Do they owe any special obligation to class members who emphasize educational quality and who probably cannot obtain counsel to advocate their divergent views? Do the political, organizational, and even philosophical complexities of school desegregation litigation justify a higher standard of professional responsibility on the part of civil rights lawyers to their clients, or more diligent oversight of the lawyer-client relationship by the bench and bar?

As is so often the case, a crisis of events motivates this long overdue inquiry.

Committee Plan, 1975, at 2 (emphasis added) (on file with *Yale Law Journal*). This 15-page document was prepared, signed, and submitted in February 1975, directly to federal judge W. Arthur Garrity by almost two dozen of Boston's black community leaders. The statement was a critique of a desegregation plan filed by the Boston School Committee in the Boston school case: Morgan v. Hennigan, 379 F. Supp. 410 (D. Mass.), *aff'd sub nom.* Morgan v. Kerrigan, 509 F.2d. 580 (1st Cir. 1974), *cert. denied*, 421 U.S. 963 (1975); Morgan v. Kerrigan, 388 F. Supp. 581 (D. Mass.), *aff'd,* 509 F.2d 599 (1st Cir. 1975); Morgan v. Kerrigan, 401 F. Supp. 216 (D. Mass. 1975), *aff'd,* 530 F.2d 401 (1st Cir. 1976). It was written during two all-day sessions sponsored by the Freedom House Institute, a community house in Boston's black Roxbury area. Judge Garrity had solicited comments on the school committee's plan from community groups. Those who prepared this statement did so on behalf of the Coordinated Social Services Council, a confederation of 46 public and private agencies serving minority groups in the Boston area. The cover letter was signed by Otto and Muriel Snowden, co-directors of Freedom House, Inc. and two of the most respected leaders in the Roxbury community. They advised Judge Garrity that the statement "represents the thinking of a sizable number of knowledgeable people in the Black community, and we respectfully urge your serious consideration of the points raised." Letter from Otto and Muriel Snowden to Judge W. Arthur Garrity, Feb. 4, 1975 (on file with *Yale Law Journal*).

Plaintiffs' counsel in the Boston school case, *supra,* expressed sympathy with the black community leaders' emphasis on educational improvement, but contended that the law required giving priority to the desegregation process. Few of the group's concerns were reflected in the plaintiffs' proposed desegregation plan rejected by the court. *See* Morgan v. Kerrigan, 401 F. Supp. 216, 229 (D. Mass. 1975), *aff'd,* 530 F.2d 401 (1st Cir 1976).

2. 347 U.S. 483 (1954).

The great crusade to desegregate the public schools has faltered. There is increasing opposition to desegregation at both local and national levels (not all of which can now be simply condemned as "racist"), while the once vigorous support of federal courts is on the decline. New barriers have arisen—inflation makes the attainment of racial balance more expensive, the growth of black populations in urban areas renders it more difficult, an increasing number of social science studies question the validity of its educational assumptions.

Civil rights lawyers dismiss these new obstacles as legally irrelevant. Having achieved so much by courageous persistence, they have not waivered in their determination to implement *Brown* using racial balance measures developed in the hard-fought legal battles of the last two decades. This stance involves great risk for clients whose educational interests may no longer accord with the integration ideals of their attorneys. Indeed, muffled but increasing criticism of "unconditional integration" policies by vocal minorities in black communities is not limited to Boston. Now that traditional racial-balance remedies are becoming increasingly difficult to achieve or maintian, there is tardy concern that racial balance may not be the relief actually desired by the victims of segregated schools.

This article will review the development of school desegregation litigation and the unique lawyer-client relationship that has evolved out of it. It will not be the first such inquiry. During the era of "massive resistance," southern states charged that this relationship violated professional canons of conduct. A majority of the Supreme Court rejected those challenges,[3] creating in the process constitutional protection for conduct that, under other circumstances, would contravene basic precepts of professional behavior. The potential for ethical problems in these constitutionally protected lawyer-client relationships was recognized by the American Bar Association *Code of Professional Responsibility,* but it is difficult to provide standards for the attorney and protection for the client where the source of the conflict is the attorney's ideals. The magnitude of the difficulty is more accurately gauged in a much older code that warns: "No servant can serve two masters: for either he will hate the one, and love the other; or else he will hold to one, and despise the other."[4]

3. This strategy was effectively defeated in one decision, NAACP v. Button, 371 U.S. 415 (1963). *See* pp. 591–602 *infra.*

4. *Luke* 16:13 (King James). At the outset it should be made clear that the problems growing out of the lawyer-client relationship in civil rights cases are not limited to the public interest field. James Lorenz, who founded the California Rural Legal Assistance Program (CRLA), has suggested that the latitude enjoyed by public interest lawyers in determining litigation strategy is often available to private practitioners. He notes that lawyers in big firms may undertake litigation or sponsor legislation on behalf of a whole industry. *See* Comment, *The New Public Interest Lawyers,* 79 Yale L.J. 1069, 1123 n.87 (1970). The authors correctly point out that clients of big firms are less vulnerable to manipulation by the lawyer and that the "latitude" exercised by the private lawyer is to further his client's interest. *Id.*

SCHOOL LITIGATION:
A BEHIND-THE-SCENES VIEW[5]

The Strategy

Although *Brown* was not a test case with a result determined in advance, the legal decisions that undermined and finally swept away the "separate-but-equal" doctrine of *Plessy v. Ferguson*[6] were far from fortuitous. Their genesis can be found in the volumes of reported cases stretching back to the mid-nineteenth century, cases in which every conceivable aspect of segregated schools was challenged.[7] By the early 1930s, the NAACP, with the support of a foundation grant, had organized a concerted program of legal attacks on racial segregation.[8] In October 1934, Vice-Dean Charles H. Houston of the Howard Univerity Law School was retained by the NAACP to direct this campaign.[9] According to the NAACP Annual Report for 1934, "the campaign [was] a carefully planned one to secure decisions, rulings and public opinion on the broad principle instead of being devoted to merely miscellaneous cases."[10] These strategies were intended to eliminate racial segregation, not merely in the public schools, but throughout the society. The public schools were chosen because they presented a far more compelling symbol of the evils of segregation and a far more vulnerable target than segregated railroad cars, restaurants, or restrooms. Initially, the NAACP's school litigation was aimed at the most blatant inequalities in facilities and teacher salaries.[11] The next target was the obvious inequality in higher education evidenced by the almost total absence of public graduate and professional schools for blacks in the South.[12]

Thurgood Marshall succeeded Houston in 1938 and became director-counsel of the NAACP Legal Defense and Educational Fund (LDF) when it became a

5. The author was a staff attorney specializing in school desegregation cases with the NAACP Legal Defense Fund from 1960 to 1966. From 1966 to 1968 he was Deputy Director, Office For Civil Rights, U.S. Department of Health, Education and Welfare,

6. 163 U.S. 537 (1896).

7. For a detailed list of cases attacking a wide range of inequalities involving physical facilities and equipment, richness of curriculum, and salary, number, and qualifications of teachers, see Leflar & Davis, *Segregation in the Public Schools—1953,* 67 Harv. L. Rev. 377, 430-35 (1954), *See also* Larson, *The New Law of Race Relations,* 1969 Wis. L. Rev. 470, 482-83 & n.27.

8. J. Greenberg, Race Relations and American Law, 34-35 (1959). For an account of the development of the NAACP's legal program, see Rabin, *Lawyers for Social Change: Perspectives on Public Interest Law,* 28 Stan. L. Rev. 207, 214-18 (1976).

9. J. Greenberg, *supra* note 8, at 35. Houston's work as the early architect of test cases that led eventually to the *Brown* decision is reviewed in McNeil, *Charles Hamilton Houston,* 3 Black L.J. 122 (1974).

10. J. Greenberg, *supra* note 8, at 35, quoting from 1934 NAACP Annual Report 22.

11. *See* note 7 *supra.*

12. *See, e.g.,* Missouri *ex. rel.* Gaines v. Canada, 305 U.S. 337 (1938); Sipuel v. Board of Regents, 332 U.S. 631 (1948) (examined further in Fisher v. Hurst, 333 U.S. 147 [1948]); Sweatt v. Painter, 339 U.S. 629 (1950); McLaurin v. Oklahoma State Regents for Higher Educ., 339 U.S. 637 (1950).

separate entity in 1939.[13] Jack Greenburg, who succeeded Marshall in 1961, recalled that the legal program "built precedent," treating each case in a context of jurisprudential development rather than as an isolated private law suit.[14] Of course, it was not possible to plan the program with precision: "How and when plaintiffs sought relief and the often unpredictable course of litigation were frequently as influential as any blueprint in determining the sequence of cases, the precise issues they posed, and their outcome."[15] But a lawyer-publisher Loren Miller observed of *Brown* and the four other school cases decided with it, "There was more to this carefully stage-managed selection of cases for review than meets the naked eye."[16]

In 1955, the Supreme Court rejected the NAACP request for a general order requiring desegregation in all school districts, issued the famous "all deliberate speed" mandate, and returned the matter to the district courts.[17] It quickly became apparent that most school districts would not comply with *Brown*

---

13. *See* J. Greenberg, *supra* note 8, at 37. The NAACP continued its legal program under its General Counsel, Robert L. Carter, who was succeeded in 1969 by Nathaniel Jones, the current General Counsel.

14. *Id.* at 39.

15. *Id.* Greenberg recently wrote about the early school cases:

The lawyers who brought the cases had adequate financial resources and an organizational base which could produce cases which presented the issues they wanted decided, where and when they wanted them. But this was far from automatic and not subject to tight control. Applicants had to appear and desire to go to the schools in question, but this sometimes could be encouraged, and, more important, unpropitious cases could be turned down. No one, other than the NAACP and the NAACP Legal Defense Fund, was then interested in or financially able to bring such suits. In essence, there was a large measure of control, a substantial ability to influence the development and sequence of cases, which does not exist with many other efforts to make law in the courts today. . . .

Greenberg, *Litigation for Social Change: Methods, Limits and Role in Democracy,* 29 Record of N.Y.C.B.A. 320, 331 (1974).

16. L. Miller, The Petitioners: The Story of the Supreme Court of the United States and the Negro 334 (1966). Miller noted:

The state cases all presented the issue of the application of the equal-protection-of-law clause of the Fourteenth Amendment, and the Court could have reached and decided that question in any one of them, but the wide geographical range gave the anticipated decision a national flavor and would blunt any claim that the South was being made a whipping boy. Moreover, the combination of cases included Kansas with its permissive statute, while other cases concerned state constitutional provisions as well as statutes with mandatory segregation requirements. Grade-school students were involved in the Kansas case; high-school students in the Virginia case, and all elementary and secondary students in the Delaware and South Carolina cases. The District of Columbia case [Bolling v. Sharpe, 347 U.S. 497 (1954)] drew due process of law into the cases as an issue, in distinction to the equal-protection-of-law clause, and also presented an opportunity for inquiry into the congressional power to impose racial segregation. The NAACP had touched all bases.

Id. at 345.

17. Brown v. Board of Educ., 349 U.S. 294 (1955) (*Brown II*).

voluntarily. Rather, they retained counsel and determined to resist compliance as long as possible.[18]

By the late 1950s, the realization by black parents and local branchers of the NAACP that litigation would be required, together with the snail's pace at which most of the school cases progressed, brought about a steady growth in the size

18. Issues concerning the professional behavior of attorneys who assisted school boards in resisting compliance by using every imaginable dilatory tactic and spurious argument are beyond the scope of this article. A review of materials discussing the refusal of virtually all laywers in the Deep South to represent civil rights clients until the late 1960s is found in V. Countryman & T. Finman, The Lawyer in Modern Society 579-89 (1966). *See also* Frankel, *The Alabama Lawyer, 1954-1964; Has the Official Organ Atrophied?,* 64 Colum. L. Rev. 1243 (1964). The failings of civil rights lawyers due to overcommitment to their ideals, with which this article is concerned, pale beside the conduct of many lawyers representing school boards and state agencies.

Former NAACP General Counsel (now Judge) Robert L. Carter, like most commentators, places responsibility for resistance to *Brown* on Southern officials. Carter, *An Evaluation of Past and Current Legal Approaches to Vindication of the Fourteenth Amendment's Guarantee of Equal Educational Opportunity,* 1972 Wash. U. L.Q. 479, 486. But of course those officials were fully represented by lawyers. A telling manifestation of the misconduct of school board lawyers is the line of decisions that depart from the American rule denying attorneys' fees to successful litigants. In Bell v. School Bd., 321 F.2d 494 (4th Cir. 1963), the court justified its departure from the general rule:

> Here we must take into account the long continued pattern of evasion and obstruction which included not only the defendants' unyielding refusal to take any initiative, thus casting a heavy burden on the children and their parents, but their interposing a variety of administrative obstacles to thwart the valid wishes of the plaintiffs for a desgregated education. To put it plainly, such tactics would in any other context be instantly recognized as discreditable. The equitable remedy would be far from complete, and justice would not be attained, if reasonable counsel fees were not awarded in a case so extreme.

Id. at 500. The *Bell* decision was followed in Felder v. Harnett County Bd. of Educ., 409 F.2d 1070 1075-76 (4th Cir. 1969) (Sobeloff, J., dissenting); Bradley v. School Bd., 345 F.2d 310 (4th Cir.), *vacated and remanded on other grounds,* 382 U.S. 103 (1965); Kelly v. Altheimer, 297 F. Supp. 753 (E.D. Ark. 1969); Pettaway v. County School Bd., 230 F. Supp. 480 (E.D. Va. 1964). For a general discussion, see Note, *Awarding of Attorney's Fees in School Desegregation Cases: Demise of the Bad-Faith Standard,* 39 Brooklyn L. Rev. 371-402 (1972).

Congress viewed these awards as sufficiently appropriate to include a provision for such awards in §718 of the Emergency School Aid Act of 1972, U.S.C. §1617 (Supp. IV 1974). The Supreme Court interpreted this provision in Northcross v. Board of Educ., 412 U.S. 427 (1973), as entitling prevailing parties in school desegregation litigation to a reasonable attorney's fee as part of the cost, absent special circumstances rendering such an award unjust. The provision was given a degree of retroactivity in Bradley v. School Bd., 416 U.S. 696 (1974). There the Court held that §718 can be applied to attorney's services that were rendered before that provision was enacted, if the propriety of the fee award was pending resolution on appeal when the statute became law. Lower courts have also interpreted the provision liberally. *See* Thompson v. Madison County Bd. of Educ., 496 F.2d 682, 689 (5th Cir. 1974) (rejecting defenses based on employment of plaintiffs' counsel by a civil rights organization and on the fact that plaintiffs incurred no obligation for legal fees); Henry v. Clarksdale Municipal Separate School Dist., 480 F.2d 583 (5th Cir. 1973); Davis v. School Dist. of the City of Pontiac, Inc., 374 F. Supp. 141 (E.D. Mich. 1974). *But see* Thompson v. School Bd., 363 F. Supp. 458, 466 (E.D. Va. 1973), *aff'd* 498 F.2d 195 (4th Cir. 1974).

Many school board lawyers would probably defend their actions on the theory that *Brown* did not automatically become the "law of the land," and that, as one Alabama

of school desegregation dockets. Because of their limited resources, the NAACP and LDF adopted the following general pattern for initiating school suits. A local attorney would respond to the request of a NAACP branch to address its members concerning their rights under the *Brown* decision. Those interested in joining a suit as named plaintiffs would sign retainers authorizing the local attorney and members of the NAACP staff to represent them in a school desegregation class action. Subsequently, depending on the facts of the case and the availability of counsel to prepare the papers, a suit would be filed. In most instances, the actual complaint was drafted or at least approved by a member of the national legal staff. With few exceptions, local attorneys were not considered expert in school desegregation litigation and served mainly as a liaison between the national staff lawyers and the local community.[19]

Named plaintiffs, of course, retained the right to drop out of the case at any time. They did not seek to exercise "control" over the litigation, and during the early years there was no reason for them to do so. Suits were filed, school boards resisted the suits, and civil rights attorneys tried to overcome the resistance. Obtaining compliance with *Brown* as soon as possible was the goal of both clients and attorneys. But in most cases, that goal would not be realized before the named plaintiffs had graduated or left the school system.[20]

---

lawyer put it, "[n]o federal or state court of record in America has ever held that a decision of the Supreme Court of the United States or that of any other federal court is 'the law of the land' or 'the law of the Union.' Such decision is never anything more than the *law of the case* actually decided by the court and binding only upon the parties to the case and no others." Pittman, *The Federal Invasion of Arkansas in the Light of the Constitution,* 19 Ala. Law, 168, 169–70 (1950), *quoted* in Frankel, *supra* at 1249. Responding to this position, Professor (now Judge) Marvin Frankel suggested that orderly processes would come to a halt if this "law of the case" theory were followed generally in other areas of the law. He took exception to the advice given Southern school officials that they should "ignore Brown until or unless they are specifically sued," suggesting that such advice nourished "a kind of lawlessness at all levels of society." Frankel, *supra* at 1249-50.

19. Local attorneys filed papers and gathered information; they usually played a subordinate role in hearings and seldom made or even suggested major tactical decisions in the litigation. This is not to minimize the important role that local attorneys played. Without their assistance, particularly in the early days, many school desegregation cases could not have been filed. Local counsel often made the preparations for hearings and generally moved the admission, for the purposes of the case, of national staff lawyers who were not usually admitted to practice before the courts where the litigation was pending. They were on the scene to meet with the plaintiffs and members of the class, explain the progress of the case, and provide the national office staff with information and factual data. As they gained expertise, some local attorneys did much more and, in a few instances, handled every aspect of the case both at the district court level and on appeal. The latter situation was less frequent during the late 1950s and early 1960s than it is today. *See* Rabin, *supra* note 8, at 217 ("key factor in the recent development of the LDF has been the new role assumed by cooperating [local] attorneys").

20. For example, in Spangler v. Pasadena City Bd. of Educ., 519 F.2d 430 (9th Cir. 1975), the graduation of the named plaintiffs provided the basis of the school board's claim in the Supreme Court that the desegregation suit (which was not certified as a class action) was moot. Brief for Petitioner at 24-25, *vacated and remanded,* 96 S. Ct. 2697 (1976). The court agreed the case was moot as to the named parties, but retained jurisdiction because of the intervention of the United States pursuant to 42 U.S.C. §2000h-2.

The civil rights lawyers would not settle for anything less than a desegregated system. While the situation did not arise in the early years, it was generally made clear to potential plaintiffs that the NAACP was not interested in settling the litigation in return for school board promises to provide better segregated schools.[21] Black parents generally felt that the victory in *Brown* entitled the civil rights lawyers to determine the basis of compliance. There was no doubt that perpetuating segregated schools was unacceptable, and the civil rights lawyers' strong opposition to such schools had the full support of both the named plaintiffs and the class they represented. Charges to the contrary initiated by several southern states were malevolent in intent and premature in time.[22]

The Theory

The rights vindicated in school litigation literally did not exist prior to 1954. Despite hundreds of judicial opinions, these rights have yet to be clearly defined. This is not surprising. Desegregation efforts aimed at lunchrooms, beaches, transportation, and other public facilities were designed merely to gain access to

21. I can recall a personal instance. While working on the James Meredith litigation in Jackson, Mississippi, in 1961, at a time when the very idea of school desegregation in Mississippi was dismissed as "foolishness" even by some civil rights lawyers, I was visited by a small group of parents and leaders of the black community in rural Leake County, Mississippi. They explained that they needed legal help because the school board had closed the black elementary school in their area even though the school had been built during the 1930s with private funds and was maintained, in part, by the efforts of the black community. Closing of the school necessitated busing black children across the county to another black school. In addition, the community had lost the benefit of the school for a meeting place and community center. The group wanted to sue the school board to have their school reopened. I recall informing the group that both LDF and NAACP had abandoned efforts to make separate schools equal, but if they wished to desegregate the whole school system, we could probably provide legal assistance. The group recognized as well as I did that there were only a few black attorneys in Mississippi who would represent the group, and that those attorneys would represent them only if a civil rights organization provided financial support. Sometime later, the group contacted me and indicated they were ready to go ahead with a school desegregation suit. It was filed in 1963, one of the first in the state.

The Leake County incident was unusual at that time because, in most instances, civil rights lawyers advised black parents of their rights under *Brown* in situations where there was little or no discussion of alternatives to integration. I did not consider my advice to the Leake County representatives anything more or less than the best and most accurate legal counsel I could provide. My view then was that a federal suit designed simply to repoen a segregated black school, even if successful, would constitute far less than the full realization of rights to which these parents were entitled under *Brown.* Following my detailed exposition of what their rights were, it was hardly surprising that the black parents did not reject them. To put it kindly, they had not been exposed to an adversary discussion on the subject.

This NAACP insistence on integration even preceded *Brown. Davis v. County School Board,* which reached the Supreme Court as a companion case to *Brown* originated with a request by blacks to the NAACP for legal help following an unsuccessful year-long effort to obtain a new high school. According to one commentator, "[t]wo attorneys did come; but they explained that, in view of the new policy of the N.A.A.C.P., they could not help with litigation unless a suit was filed to abolish school segregation." Wilkerson, *The Negro School Movement in Virginia: From "Equalization" to "Integration,"* in II The Making of Black America 259, 269 (A. Meier & E. Rudwick eds. 1969).

22. *See* p. 592 *infra.*

those facilities. Any actual racial "mixing" has been essentially fortuitous; it was hardly part of the rights protected (to eat, travel, or swim on a nonracial basis). The strategy of school desegregation is much different. The actual presence of white children is said to be essential to the right in both its philosophical and pragmatic dimensions. In essence the arguments are that blacks must gain access to white schools because "equal educational opportunity" means integrated schools, and because only school integration will make certain that black children will receive the same education as white children. This theory of school desegregation, however, fails to encompass the complexity of achieving equal educational opportunity for children to whom it so long has been denied.

The NAACP and the LDF, responsible for virtually all school desegregation suits, usually seek to establish a racial population at each school that (within a range of 10 to 15 percent) reflects the percentage of whites and blacks in the district. But in a growing number of the largest urban districts, the school system is predominantly black.[23] The resistance of most white parents to sending their children to a predominantly black school and the accessibility of a suburban residence or a private school to all but the poorest renders implementation of such plans extremely difficult.[24] Although many whites undoubtedly perceive

23. "About half of the Nation's black students, 3.4 million, are located in the 100 largest school districts." Staff of Senate Select Comm. on Equal Educ. Opportunity, 92d Cong., 2d Sess., Report: Toward Equal Educational Opportunity 114 (Comm. Print 1972).

More recent figures are even more depressing. It now appears that over two million black children attend schools in the nation's 20 largest urban school districts. An average of 60 percent of the school populations in these districts are minority-group students, and 90 percent of them attend schools that are predominantly nonwhite. In the nation's five largest urban districts, the percentages of minority students are: New York 66 percent; Los Angeles, 56 percent; Chicago, 71 percent; Philadelphia, 66 percent; and Detroit, 72 percent. In the next five largest districts (Houston, Baltimore, Dallas, Cleveland, and the District of Columbia). the minority school population averages 68 percent. Over 1.5 million minority children reside in these 10 districts. HEW, Office for Civil Rights, Fall 1972 and Fall 1973 Elementary and Secondary School Survey Press Release Format Reports for 95 of the 100 Largest (1972) School Districts. (1975).

24. Whether because of school desegregation or not, there has been a sharp decline in the number of white children in many urban public school districts. While the national decline in white enrollment between 1968 and 1973 was about 1 percent annually, white pupil totals during the five-year period fell by 62 percent in Atlanta, 41 percent in San Francisco, 32 percent in Houston, 21 percent in Denver, 40 percent in New Orleans, and 26 percent in New York. Boston lost 40 percent of its white pupils, or about 5,000 per year, from 1970 to 1975. Ravitch, *Busing: The Solution That Has Failed to Solve*, N.Y. Times, Dec. 21, 1975, §4, at E3, col. 1.

Dr. James Coleman, the nationally known education expert whose studies furthered the school desegregation effort, *see, e.g.,* HEW, Equality of Educational Opportunity (1966), sparked an ongoing debate with a new study suggesting that school desegregation orders in large cities significantly encourage the exodus of whites from cities to suburbs. *See Integration, Yes; Busing, No* (Interview with Dr. James Coleman), N.Y. Times, Aug. 24, 1975 §6 (Magazine), at 10. In a symposium called to evaluate Dr. Coleman's findings, our social scientist reported that although a statistical analysis of population changes in 125 school systems over a five year period revealed that a majority lost white students, there was no "significant" statistical link between the rate of desegregation and the level of immigration. Farley, *School Integration and White Flight,* in Symposium on School Desegregation and White Flight 2 (Center for Nat'l Policy Rev., Catholic Univ. & Center for Civil Rights, Notre Dame, G. Orfield ed. Aug. 1975).

a majority black school as ipso facto a poor school, the schools can be improved and white attitudes changed.[25] All too little attention has been given to making black schools educationally effective. Furthermore, the disinclination of white parents to send their children to black schools has not been lessened by charges made over a long period of time by civil rights groups that black schools are educationally bankrupt and unconstitutional per se.[26] NAACP policies nevertheless call for maximizing racial balance within the district as an immediate goal while supporting litigation that will eventually require the consolidation of predominantly white surrounding districts.[27]

The basic civil rights position that *Brown* requires maximum feasible desegregation has been accepted by the courts and successfully implemented in smaller school districts throughout the country.[28] The major resistance to further

25. *See, e.g.,* D. Bell, Race, Racism and American Law 579–83 (1973); Black Manifesto for Education (J. Haskins ed. 1973); J. Comer & A. Poussaint, Black Child Care 217–18 (1975); A. Davis, Racial Crisis in Public Education: A Quest For Social Order (1975). Quality schooling was available in some black schools even prior to *Brown. See, e.g.,* Sowell, *Black Excellence–The Case of Dunbar High School,* 35 Pub. Interest 3 (1974). A recent study has uncovered 71 public schools in the Northeast which are effective in teaching basic skills to poor children. Thirty-four of these schools serve student populations that are 50 percent or more black, Sixteen of the schools have black percentages greater than 75 percent. Letter from Ron Edmonds, Director, Center for Urban Studies, Harvard University Graduate School of Education, to author, Feb. 11, 1976 (on file with *Yale Law Journal*).

26. L. Fein, The Ecology of the Public Schools: An Inquiry Into Community Control 6 (1971):

> In effect, the liberal community, both black and white, was caught up in a wrenching dilemma. The only way, it appeared, to move a sluggish nation toward massive amelioration of the Negro condition was to show how terrifyingly debilitating were the effects of discrimination and bigotry. The more lurid the detail, the more guilt it would evoke, and the more guilt, the more readiness to act. Yet the same lurid detail that did, in the event, prompt large-scale federal programs, also reinforced white convictions that Negroes were undesirable objects of interaction.

27. Significantly, LDF does not share NAACP's thirst for bringing more metropolitan school cases. James Nabrit reported that "in our litigation program at the Legal Defense Fund, at least for the short-run future, we have no plans to pursue requests for interdistrict relief in the courts. I take the *Milliken* case to send us a broad signal that such cases are unlikely to succeed." Conference Before the United States Commission on Civil Rights, Milliken v. Bradley: The Implications For Metropolitan Desegregation 21 (Gov't Printing Off. Nov. 9, 1974).

28. The standards are contained in Swann v. Charlotte-Mecklenburg Bd. of Educ., 402 U.S. 1 (1971), and Keyes v. School Dist. No. 1, 413 U.S. 189 (1973). In a companion case to *Swann,* lower courts were directed to make "every effort to achieve the greatest possible degree of actual desegregation, taking into account the practicalities of the situation." Davis v. Board of School Comm'rs, 402 U.S. 33, 37 (1971). Except where problems of distance and majority black percentages intervene, most courts continue to order plans patterned after the directives in *Swann, Keyes* and *Davis.* But increasingly the Supreme Court seems to be applying stricter standards of school board liability. *See e.g.,* Spangler v. Pasadena City Bd. of Educ., 519 F.2d 430 (9th Cir. 1975), *vacated and remanded,* 96 S. Ct. 2697 (1976). *See also,* United States v. Texas Educ. Agency (Austin), 532 F.2d 380 (5th Cir. 1976), *vacated and remanded,* Austin Indpt. Sch. Dist. v. United States, 45 U.S.L.W. 3409 (Dec. 7, 1976); Dayton Bd. of Educ. v. Brinkman, 518 F.2d 853 (6th Cir. 1976), *cert. granted,* 45 U.S.L.W. 3485 (Jan. 18, 1977).

progress has occurred in the large urban areas of both South and North where racially isolated neighborhoods make school integration impossible without major commitments to the transportation of students, often over long distances. The use of the school bus is not a new phenomenon in American education,[29] but the transportation of students over long distances to schools where their parents do not believe they will receive a good education has predictably created strong opposition in white and even black communities.[30]

The busing issue has served to make concrete what many parents long have sensed and what new research has suggested:[31] court orders mandating racial balance may be (depending on the circumstances) educationally advantageous, irrelevant, or even *disadvantageous.* Nevertheless, civil rights lawyers continue to argue that black children are entitled to integrated schools without regard to the educational effect of such assignments.[32] That position might well have shocked

29. Of the more than 256,000 buses that traveled over 2.2 billion miles in 1971-1972, only a small percentage were used to achieve school desegregation. NAACP Legal Defense and Educational Fund, *It's Not the Distance, "It's the Niggers,"* in The Great School Bus Controversy 322 (N. Mills ed. 1973).

30. *See* pp. 581–85 *infra;* note 1 *supra.*

31. As one author summarized the situation, "During the past 20 years considerable racial mixing has taken place in schools, but research has produced little evidence of dramatic gains for children and some evidence of genuine stress for them." N. St. John School Desegregation Outcomes for Children 136 (1975). Some writers are more hopeful, *e.g.,* Weinberg, *The Relationship Between School Desegregation and Academic Achievement: A Review of the Research,* 39 Law & Contemp. Prob. 241 (1975); others are more cautious, *e.g.,* Cohen, *The Effects of Desegregation on Race Relations,* 39 Law & Contemp. Prob. 271 (1975); Epps, *The Impact of School Desegregation on Aspirations, Self-Concepts and Other Aspects of Personality,* 39 Law & Contemp. Prob. 300 (1975).

32. NAACP General Counsel Nathaniel R. Jones cites frequent statements by Chief Justice Earl Warren to support his organization's position that "the *Brown* decision was not an educational decision resting in educational considerations. Rather, it was a decision regarding human rights." Denying that the quality of segregated schools is a major priority in NAACP school suits, he writes, "When we bring desegregation suits on behalf of black and white children, we do so because state-imposed school segregation is a living insult, in that it perpetuates that condition which the 14th Amendment proscribes." Comments of Nathaniel R. Jones at Harvard Law School, May 2, 3, 1974, at 1-2, 5 (on file with *Yale Law Journal*).

Civil Rights lawyer J. Harold Flannery, counsel in the Boston school desegregation case, asserts:

> The constitutional objective is, and has always been, to rid this public institution completely of official segregation and discrimination, and comprehensively desegregated schools, i.e., each a microcosm of the district as a whole, is the central indicium of compliance—wholly without regard to educational consequences.

Letter from J. Harold Flannery to author, Aug. 25, 1975, at 4 (on file with *Yale Law Journal*). *See* note 38 *infra.*

Rhetoric irretrievably linking the relief under *Brown* to integration does not alter the educational decision made when racial balance remedies are advocated and obtained. Professor Alexander Bickel recognized as much:

> Inevitably the Suprreme Court [in *Swann* and its companion cases] imposes a choice of educational policy, for the time being at least, when it orders maximum integration, a choice committing moral, political and material resources to the exclusion of alternate attempts to improve the educational process, and I don't think we can be sure that the choice is the right one everywhere.

many of the Justices who decided *Brown,* and hardly encourages those judges asked to undertake the destruction and resurrection of school systems in our large cities which this reading of *Brown* has come to require.

Troubled by the resistance and disruptions caused by busing over long distances, those judges have increasingly rejected such an interpretation of *Brown.* They have established new standards which limit relief across district lines[33] and which reject busing for intradistrict desegregation "when the time or dis-

---

Bickel, *Education in a Democracy: The Legal and Practical Problems of School Busing,* 3 Human Rights 53, 54 (1973). In the same article, Professor Bickel suggested that, given the paucity of alternative suggestions by either plaintiffs or school board counsel, racial balance remedies are adopted "because there is not much else that a court can do that will have an impact." *Id.* at 59-60.

Of course, the NAACP position that integration is required regardless of its educational effect allows it to ignore the social science studies pointing to disappointing minority group academic achievement in desegregated schools. *See* note 31 *supra.*

33. In Milliken v. Bradley, 418 U.S. 717, 745 (1974), the Supreme Court held (5-4) that desegregation remedies must stop at the boundary of the school district unless it can be shown that deliberately segregative actions were "a substantial cause of interdistrict segregation.":

> Before the boundaries of separate and autonomous school districts may be set aside by consolidating the separate units for remedial purposes or by imposing a cross-district remedy, it must first be shown that there has been a constitutional violation within one district that produces a significant segregative effect in another district.

Id. at 744-45. The Court so held despite the fact that the only effective desegregation plan was a metropolitan area plan. The majority opinion severely criticized by the dissenting Justices, has also been attacked by legal writers. *See e.g.,* Symposium, *Milliken v. Bradley and the Future of Urban School Desegregation,* 21 Wayne L. Rev. 751 (1975); Amaker, Milliken v. Bradley: *The Meaning of the Constitution in School Desegregation Cases,* 2 Hastings Con. L.Q. 349 (1975); Comment, Milliken v. Bradley, *Roadblock or Guide Post?: New Standards For Multi-District School Desegregation,* 48 Temp. L.Q. 966 (1975).

The *Milliken* standard was followed in United States v. Board of School Comm'rs. 503 F.2d 68 (7th Cir. 1974), *cert. denied,* 421 U.S. 929 (1975). The district court deemed its interdistrict order necessary because requiring what it termed a massive "fruit basket" scrambling of schools within the city would simply lead to a white exodus from what would become substantially black schools. The court of appeals reversed all orders relating to a metropolitan remedy, but found "white flight" an unacceptable reason for failing to desegregate the city schools. A subsequent ruling approving a limited interdistrict remedy based on the state's failure to make school district boundaries coextensive with consolidated countywide government was vacated by the Supreme Court. 45 U.S.L.W. 3500 (Jan. 25, 1977). *But see* Newburg Area Council, Inc. v. Board of Educ., 510 F.2d 1358 (6th Cir. 1974), *cert. denied,* 421 U.S. 931 (1975), approving in the light of *Milliken* standards a pre-*Milliken* order requiring consolidation of city and county school districts on findings that neither had fully complied with the *Brown* desegregation mandate. After remand of the case, the Jefferson County and Louisville school districts merged under the provisions of state law. The court of appeals subsequently granted plaintiffs a writ of mandamus directing the district court to approve a desegregation plan for the newly created district to take effect for the 1975-1976 school year. Newburg Area Council, Inc. v. Gordon, 521 F.2d 578 (6th Cir. 1975). A countywide desegregation plan that would leave no school with a black majority was approved, although black pupils would be bused eight or nine years, to one or two years for whites. Cunningham v. Grayson, 541 F.2d 538 (6th Cir. 1976), *cert. denied,* 45 U.S.L.W. 3503 (Jan. 25, 1977). For similar cases, see Evans v. Buchanan, 393 F. Supp. 428 (D. Del.) *aff'd,* 96 S. Ct. 381 (1975); United States v. Missouri, 515 F.2d 1365 (8th Cir. 1975), *cert denied,* 44 U.S.L.W. 3280 (U.S. 1975).

tance of travel is so great as to either risk the health of children or significantly impinge on the educational process."[34] Litigation in the large cities has dragged on for years and often culminated in decisions that approve the continued assignment of large numbers of black children to predominantly black schools.[35]

LAWYER-CLIENT CONFLICTS: SOURCES AND RATIONALE

Civil Right Rigidity Surveyed

Having convinced themselves that *Brown* stands for desegregation and not education, the established civil rights organizations steadfastly refuse to recognize reverses in the school desegregation campaign—reverses which, to some extent, have been precipitated by their rigidity. They seem to be reluctant to evaluate objectively the high risks inherent in a continuation of current policies.

The Boston Case. The Boston school litigation[36] provides an instructive example of what, I fear, is a widespread situation. Early in 1975, I was invited by representatives of Boston's black community groups to meet with them and NAACP lawyers over plans for Phase II of Boston's desegregation effort. Implementation of the 1974 plan had met with violent resistance that received nationwide attention. Even in the lulls between the violent incidents, it is unlikely that much in the way of effective instruction was occurring at many of the schools. NAACP lawyers had retained experts whose proposals for the 1975/76 school year would have required even more busing between black and lower-class white communities. The black representatives were ambivalent about the busing plans. They did not wish to back away after years of effort to desegregate Boston's schools, but they wished to place greater emphasis on upgrading the schools' educational quality, to maintain existing assignments at schools which were already integrated, and to minimize busing to the poorest and most violent white districts. In response to a proposal filed by the Boston School Committee, they sent a lengthy statement of their position directly to District Judge W. Arthur Garrity.[37]

34. Swann v. Charlotte-Mecklenberg Bd. of Educ., 402 U.S. 1, 30-31 (1971). *See also* Davis v. Board of School Comm'rs, 402 U.S. 33, 37 (1971) (requiring "every effort to achieve the greatest possible degree of actual desegregation taking into account the practicalities of the situation").

35. For limitations on busing notwithstanding a substantial reduction in the potential for desegregation, see Mapp v. Board of Educ., 525 F.2d 169 (6th Cir. 1975); Northcross v. Board of Educ., 489 F.2d 15 (6th Cir. 1973), *cert. denied,* 416 U.S. 962 (1974); Goss v. Board of Educ. 482 F.2d 1044 (6th Cir. 1973), *cert. denied,* 414 U.S. 1171 (1974); Mapp v. Board of Educ., 477 F.2d 851 (6th Cir.), *cert. denied,* 414 U.S. 1022 (1973); Carr v. Montgomery County Bd. of Ed., 377 F. Supp. 1123 (M.D. Ala. 1974), *aff'd per curiam,* 511 F.2d 1374 (5th Cir.), *cert. denied,* 96 S. Ct. 394 (1975).

36. Morgan v. Hennigan, 379 F. Supp. 410 (D. Mass.), *aff'd sub nom.* Morgan v. Kerrigan, 509 F.2d 580 (1st Cir. 1974), *cert. denied,* 421 U.S. 963 (1975); related decisions cited in note 1, *supra.*

37. *See* note 1 *supra.*

At the meeting I attended, black representatives hoped to convince the lawyers to incorporate their educational priorities into the plaintiffs' Phase II desegregation plan. The lawyers assigned to the Boston case by the NAACP listened respectfully to the views of the black community group, but made clear that a long line of court decisions would limit the degree to which those educational priorities could be incorporated into the desegregation plan the lawyers were preparing to file.[38] That plan contained far more busing to balance the racial populations of the schools than was eventually approved by the federal ourt. Acting on the recommendations of appointed masters,[39] Judge Garrity adopted several provisions designed to improve the quality of the notoriously poor Boston schools.[40] But as in the Detroit and Atalanta cases discussed below, these provisions were more the product of judicial initiative than of civil rights advoacy.[41]

38. The court appointed a panel of four masters who held hearings on all plans submitted, adopted portions of each, and, with some additions, filed them with the court. Morgan v. Kerrigan, 401 F. Supp. 216, 227 (D. Mass. 1975), *aff'd*, No. 75-1184 (1st Cir. Jan. 14, 1976). At one of the masters' hearings, plaintiffs' attorney J. Harold Flannery presented a closing argument that emphasized the need to proceed immediately with full desegregation:

> Educational innovation and school desegregation, I would hope, are complementary or not opposed or competing. But it seems to us an irreducible minimum that we must begin with assignments and then look to program, because that's the constitutional mandate. School desegregation, not educational innovation, that's not the Brown case. It is a race case, may it please the Court, not so much [an] education case.

Transcript of Masters' Hearings at 1809. *See* note 32 *supra.*

39. The plan filed by the masters, 401 F. Supp. at 227, included educational components at the expense of maximum racial balance. In their report, the masters found plaintiffs' plan "unsatisfactory" in several respects, despite its achievement of thorough numerical desegregation. In their view, "a plan should assure not just proper assignment of students, but also educational programs appropriate to the special needs of students who have been victimized by segregation." Report of the Masters in Tallulah Morgan, et al. Versus John Kerrigan, et al. Mar. 31, 1975, at 18 (on file with *Yale Law Journal*).

40. Dividing the system into eight community districts, the court established parent advisory councils at the citywide and community district levels and "racial-ethnic councils" at each school. Councils at the school level will participate in evaluating schools and school programs. The racial-ethnic councils, which will be composed of representatives from each racial and ethnic group, will investigate minority-group problems, propose solutions, and follow up with implementation activities. In addition, they will also work with parents, teachers, and administrators to further a sense of common purpose for improved schools. The advisory councils at the community district and citywide levels will communicate problems to the community district superintendents and the school committee. The court also initiated contractual relationships between the public schools and 20 colleges and universities in the Greater Boston area to upgrade and equalize educational opportunities. Twenty businesses have been paired with schools, and 110 other institutions, members of the Metropolitan Cultural Alliance, are pledged to provide innovative and enriching programs for students. Morgan v. Kerrigan, 401 F. Supp, 216, 248-53, 259-60, 265-68 (D. Mass. 1975), *aff'd*, No. 75-1184 (1st Cir., Jan. 14, 1976).

41. In the course of the San Francisco school litigation, Johnson v. San Francisco Unified School Dist., 500 F.2d 349 (9th Cir. 1974), District Judge Weigel asked counsel: "Assuming minority groups desire separate schools, and assuming they can show that such schools would not be inferior, should that desire, if it is manifested to this Court, be con-

The Detroit Case. The determination of NAACP officials to achieve racial balance was also tested in the Detroit school case. Having failed in efforts to obtain an interdistrict metropolitan remedy in Detroit,[42] the NAACP set out to achieve a unitary system in a school district that was over 70 percent black. The district court rejected an NAACP plan designed to require every school to reflect (within a range of 15 percent in either direction) the ratio of whites to blacks in the school district as a whole, and approved a desegregation plan that emphasized educational reform rather than racial balance.[43] The NAACP general counsel, Nathaniel R. Jones, reportedly called the decision "an abomination" and "a rape of the constitutional rights of black children," and indicated his intention to appeal immediately.[44]

The Atlanta Case. Prior to Detroit, the most open confrontation between NAACP views of school integration and those of local blacks who favored plans

sidered by the Court." Seeking to clarify his question, Judge Weigel explained, "[T]here's something new that's coming along. . . . There [is] beginning to emerge a demand on the part of large segments of minoirty groups, particularly among the blacks, that they run their own schools and they have black schools." D. Kirp. "Multitudes in the Valley of In-decision": The Desegregation of San Francisco's Public Schools, 1975, at 60 (unpublished paper prepared for the Institute of Judicial Administration project on judicial roles in deseg-regation of education litigation) (on file with *Yale Law Journal*) [see San Francisco Case *supra*—Eds.]. When a young black attorney recruited for the case by the NAACP sought to prepare a memorandum with an affirmative response to Judge Weigel's question, his col-leagues on the case were shocked. Subsequently, the young attorney agreed to withdraw from the case, and his position was not asserted in any subsequent proceeding. *Id.* at 60-61.

42. *See* Milliken v. Bradley, 418 U.S. 717 (1974).

43. Bradley v. Milliken, 402 F. Supp. 1096 (E.D. Mich. 1975). The Court pointed out that under the plaintiffs' definition.

any school whose racial composition varies more than 15 percent in either direction from the Detroit system-wide ratio is racially identifiable. Accordingly, an ele-mentary school with 57.3 percent - 87.3 percent black enrollment, a junior high school with 58.0 percent - 88.0 percent black enrollment and a senior high school with 51.9 percent - 81.9 percent black enrollment are desegregated schools. Carrying . . . [the] plan a step further, an elementary school that is 56 percent black is a racially identifiable white school and an elementary school that is 85 percent black is a desegregated non-racially identifiable school.

Id. at 1112. The court also noted that plaintiff's plan would involve the transportation of thousands of black students from one predominantly black school to another and expressed concern that "rigid and inflexible desegregation plans too often neglect to treat school children as individuals, instead treating them as pigmented pawns to be shuffled about and counted solely to achieve an abstraction called 'racial mix.'" *Id.* at 1101. The court adopted a desegregation plan using a 50-50 enrollment as a starting point, but requiring only that no school be less than 30 percent black. *Id.* at 1133, 1135. In addition, lengthy provisions were included regarding faculty assignments, reading and communications skills, in-service training, vocational education, testing, students' rights and responsibilities, school-commu-nity relations, counseling and career guidance, co-curricular activities, bilingual and ethnic studies, and monitoring by citizens' groups. *Id.* at 1132-45. The decision was affirmed, Bradley v. Milliken, 540 F.2d 229 (6th Cir. 1976), *cert. granted,* 97 S. Ct. 380 (1976).

44. *Judge in Detroit Bars Busing Plans,* N.Y. Times, Aug. 17, 1975 at 1, col. 1; Detroit Free Press, Aug. 17, 1975, at 8A, col. 1. A local NAACP official was no less outspoken, referring to the decision as "a traditional calamity [that] takes us back to the days of Dred

oriented toward improving educational quality occurred in Atlanta. There, a group of plaintiffs became discouraged by the difficulty of achieving meaningful desegregation in a district which had gone from 32 percent black in 1952 to 82 percent black in 1974. Lawyers for the local NAACP branch, who had gained control of the litigation, worked out a compromise plan with the Atlanta School Board that called for full faculty and employee desegregation but for only limited pupil desegregation. In exchange, the school board promised to hire a number of blacks in top administrative positions, including a black superintendent of schools.

The federal court approved the plan.[45] The court's approval was apparently influenced by petitions favoring the plan's adoption signed by several thousand members of the plaintiffs' class.[46] Nevertheless the national NAACP office and LDF lawyers were horrified by the compromise. The NAACP ousted the Atlanta branch president who had supported the compromise.[47] Then, acting on behalf of some local blacks who shared their views, LDF lawyers filed an appeal in the Atlanta case. The appeal also raised a number of procedural issues concerning the lack of notice and the refusal of the district court to grant hearings on the Compromise Plan. These issues gave the Fifth Circuit an opportunity to remand the case to the district court without reaching the merits of the settlement

Scott," and asserting that "[t]he NAACP will not allow this kind of traversty of justice to exist without being challenged. . . . The NAACP . . . is deeply angered. . . .'" *Busing Foes Laud De Mascio Ruling, id.* at 1A, col. 7. Apparently the comments of neither official were tempered by the realization that the mayor of Detroit, Coleman Young, and the president of its school board, C.L. Golightly, both of whom are black, had favored a plan that would emphasize improving school quality. Both had opposed the NAACP's racial balance plan, and both praised the court's opinion for rejecting the idea that busing is a magic formula and for addressing itself to the improvement of Detroit's school system. *Id.* Roy Wilkins sent the mayor a telegram calling the statement "of a piece with those uttered by the most vicious Southern racists." Wentworth, *Detroit Blacks Divided,* Wash. Post. Sept. 2, 1975, at 1, col 6. For a detailed review of decentralization and desegregation efforts in Detroit, see Pindur, *Professional Comment: Legislative and Judicial Roles in the Detroit School Decentralization Controversy,* 50 J. Urb. L. 53 (1972).

45. Calhoun v. Cook 362 F. Supp. 1249 (N.D. Ga. 1973). The plan included provisions that there would not be less than 20 percent blacks in already integrated "stabilized" schools nor less than 30 percent in other schools. The district court found that plan reasonable "considering the small percentage of white children (21 percent) now remaining in the system. . . ." *Id.* at 1251 & n.7.

46. *See id.* at 1251 n.5.

47. Trillin, *U.S. Journal: Atlanta Settlement,* New Yorker, Mar. 17, 1973, at 101, 102. In an article attacking the Atlanta compromise, Dr. Buell G. Gallagher, vice chairman of the NAACP National Board of Directors, expressed the general view that any compromise with segregation would be a disaster.

> Of one thing we may be sure: the system of racial caste will never be weakened or eradicated by blacks who cooperate with it. Every instance of the acceptance of segregation, whether voluntary or coerced, forges the chains of inequality more firmly. Segregation will not be eradicated by those who abandon integration as a goal, no matter what tortuous logic or euphemistic language may be used to rationalize the expedient compromise.

Gallagher. *Integrated Schools in the Black Cities?,* 42 J. Negro Educ. 336, 348 (1973).

agreement.[48] Undaunted, LDF lawyers again attacked the plan for failing to require busing of whites into the predominantly black schools in which a majority of the students in the system were enrolled. But the district court's finding that the system had achieved unitary status was upheld by the same Fifth Circuit panel.[49]

As in Detroit, NAACP opposition to the Atlanta Compromise Plan was not deterred by the fact that local leaders, including black school board members, supported the settlement. Defending the Compromise Plan, Benjamine E. Mays, one of the most respected black educators in the country, stated:

> We have never argued that the Atlanta Compromise Plan is the best plan, nor have we encouraged any other school system to adopt it. This plan is the most viable plan for Atlanta—a city school system that is 82 percent Black and 18 percent white and is continuing to lose whites each year to five counties that are more than 90 percent white.
>
> . . . .
>
> More importantly, Black people must not resign themselves to the pessimistic view that a non-integrated school cannot provide Black children with an excellent educational setting. Instead, Black people, while working to implement *Brown,* should recognize that integration alone does not provide a quality education, and that much of the substance of quality education can be provided to Black children in the interim.[50]

The NAACP also opposed the more recent compromise settlement of the St. Louis school litigation. The consent order, as in Atlanta, focuses on minimal percentages of teachers and staff positions. Liddell v. Board of Educ. No. 72-C-100(1) (E.D. Mo., Dec. 24, 1975) (consent order). The order commits the board to reducing racial separation in the high schools, establishing magnet schools at the elementary level and specialized schools at the high school level, and undertaking a study of curriculum improvement. Following issuance of the consent judgment, the NAACP sought to intervene, but the motion was denied.

48. Calhoun v. Cook, 487 F.2d 680 (5th Cir. 1973). *See* note 130 *infra.* Significantly, the court permitted the Compromise Plan to take effect pending further hearings. *Id.* at 683-84. The Fifth Circuit noted that blacks occupied a majority of school board posts, two-thirds of the school administration and staff posts, and over 60 percent of the faculty positions. In addition, "the numerous nonappealing black plaintiffs who agreed to and support the present plan attest the district's lack of discrimination against black students as well as its freedom from the effects of past race-based practices." *Id.* at 719.

49. Calhoun v. Cook, 522 F.2d 717 (5th Cir. 1975). In a per curiam opinion denying appellant's petition for rehearing and petitions for rehearing *en banc,* the court denied that their decision conflicted with earlier Fifth Circuit decisions and Supreme Court rulings requiring every effort to achieve the greatest possible degree of actual desegregation. "It would blink reality and authority . . . to hold the Atlanta School System to be nonunitary because further racial integration is theoretically possible and we expressly decline to do so." Calhoun v. Cook, 525 F.2d 1203 (5th Cir. 1975).

50. Mays, *Comment: Atlanta—Living with* Brown *Twenty Years Later,* 3 Black L.J. 184, 190, 191-92 (1974). For similar views, see Hamilton. *The Nationalist vs. the Integrationist,* in The Great School Bus Controversy 297 (N. Mills ed. 1973); Haskins, *A Black Perspective on Community Control,* Inequality in Educ., Nov. 173, at 23; Sizemore, *Is There A Case For Separate Schools,* 53 Phi Delta Kappan 281 (1972); Sizemore, *Education for Liberation,* 81 School Rev. 389 (1973); Young & Bress, *A New Educational Decision: Is Detroit the End of the School Bus Line?,* 56 Phi Delta Kappan 515 (1975).

Alternatives to the Rigidity of Racial Balance

Dr. May's thoughtful statement belies the claim that *Brown* can be implemented only by the immediate racial balancing of school populations. But civil rights groups refuse to recognize what courts in Boston, Detroit, and Atlanta have now made obvious: where racial balance is not feasible because of population concenterations, political boundaries, or even educational considerations, there is adequate legal precedent for court-ordered remedies that emphasize educational improvement rather than racial balance.[51]

The plans adopted in these cases were formulated without the support and often over the objection of the NAACP and other civil rights groups. They are intended to upgrade educational quality, and like racial balance, they may have that effect. But neither the NAACP nor the court-fashioned remedies are sufficiently directed at the real evil of pre-*Brown* public schools: the state-supported subordination of blacks in every aspect of the educational process. Racial separation is only the most obvious manifestation of this subordination. Providing unequal and inadequate school resources and excluding black parents from meaningful participation in school policy-making are at least as damaging to black children as enforced separation.

Whether based on racial balance precedents or compensatory education theories, remedies that fail to attack all policies of racial subordination almost guarantee that the basic evil of segregated schools will survive and flourish, even in those systems where racially balanced schools can be achieved. Low academic performance and large numbers of disciplinary and expulsion cases are only two of the predictable outcomes in integrated schools where the racial subordination of blacks is reasserted in, if anything, a more damaging form.[52]

---

51. Despite emphasis of plaintiffs' counsel on racial balance, the court in the Boston and Detroit cases approved plans that contained several education-oriented provisions. *See* notes 40, 43 *supra.* For a similar case, see Hart v. Community School Bd. of Educ., 512 F.2d 37 (2d Cir. 1975) (approving use of predominantly minority junior high as a "magnet" school rather than requiring racial balance in all junior high schools as sought by plaintiffs).

It is true that the Supreme Court has evidenced considerable resistance to requests that "educational quality" be brought within the guarantees of the Constitution. *See* San Antonio Independent School Dist. v. Rodriguez, 411 U.S. 1 (1973). And predictably, some lower courts interpret *Rodriguez* as a bar to ordering school districts to adopt specific educational plans as a remedy for unconstitutional segregation. *See* Keyes v. School Dist. No. 1, 521 F.2d 465 (10th Cir. 1975), *cert. denied,* 96 S. Ct. 806 (1976) (holding district court lacked authority to impose detailed program of bilingual and multicultural education). But in *Keyes* the court agreed that the board was obligated to help "Hispano school children to reach the proficiency in English necessary to learn other basic subjects." 521 F.2d at 482. Moreover, were the Denver court not already committed to a major desegregation effort on the racial balance model, it might have been more willing to impose education-oriented remedies.

52. See generally Hawkins v. Coleman, 376 F. Supp. 1330 (N.D. Tex. 1974) (disproportionately high discipline and suspension rates for black students in the Dallas school system found to be the results of "white institutional racism"). During the 1972-1973 school year, black students were suspended at more than twice the rate of any other racial or ethnic group. Children's Defense Fund, School Suspensions: Are They Helping Children? 12 (1975). The report suggests the figure is due in large part to the result of racial discrimina-

The literature in both law and education discusses the merits and availability of educational remedies in detail.[53] The purpose here has been simply to illustrate that alternative approaches to "equal educational opportunity" are possible and have been inadequately explored by civil rights attorneys. Although some of the remedies fashioned by the courts themselves have been responsive to the problem of racial subordination, plaintiffs and courts seeking to implement such remedies are not assisted by counsel representing plaintiff classes. Much more effective remedies for racial subordination in the schools could be obtained if the creative energies of the civil rights litigation groups could be brought into line with the needs and desires of their clients.

The Organization and Its Ideals

Civil rights lawyers have long experience, unquestioned commitment, and the ability to organize programs that have helped bring about profound changes in the last two decades. Why, one might ask, have they been so unwilling to recognize the increasing futility of "total desegregation," and, more important, the increasing number of defections within the black community? A few major factors that underlie this unwillingness can be identified.

Racial Balance as a Symbol. For many civil rights workers, success in obtaining racially balanced schools seems to have become a symbol of the nation's commitment to equal opportunity—not only in education, but in housing, employment, and other fields where the effects of racial discrimination are still present. As Dean Ernest Campbell has observed. "[T]he busing issue has acquired meanings that seem to have little relevance for the education of children in any direct sense."[54] In his view, proponents of racial balance fear that the failure to establish busing as a major tool for desegregation will signify the end of an era of expanding civil rights. For them the busing debate symbolizes a major test of the country's continued commitment to civil rights progress. Any retreat on busing will be construed as an abandonment of this commitment and a return to segregation. Indeed, Campbell has suggested that some leaders see busing as a major test of black political strength. Under a kind of domestic domino theory, these leaders fear that failure on the busing issue would trigger a string of defeats, ending a long line of "major judicial and administrative decisions that substantially expanded the civil rights and personal opportunities of blacks in the post-World War II period."[55]

---

tion, insensitivity, and ignorance as well as to "a pervasive intolerance by school officials for all students who are *different* in any number of wasy." *Id.* at 9. *See also* Green, *Separate and Unequal Again,* Inequality in Educ., July 1973, at 14.

53. For a collection of sources, see Bell, *Waiting on the Promise of* Brown, 39 Law & Contemp. Prob. 341, 352-66 & nn. 49-119 (1975).

54. Campbell, *Defining and Attaining, Equal Educational Opportunity in a Pluralistic Society,* 26 Vand. L. Rev. 461, 478 (1973).

55. *Id.* The author also suggests that

busing serves as a symbolic safeguard against white duplicity. Although some may

Clients and Contributors. The hard-line position of established civil rights groups on school desegregation is explained in part by pragmatic considerations. These organizations are supported by middle-class blacks and whites who believe fervently in integration. At their socioeconomic level, integration has worked well, and they are certain that once whites and blacks at lower economic levels are successfully mixed in the schools, integration also will work well at those levels. Many of these supporters either reject or fail to understand suggestions that alternatives to integrated schools should be considered, particularly in majority-black districts. They will be understandably reluctant to provide financial support for policies which they think unsound, possibly illegal, and certainly disquieting. The rise and decline of the Congress of Racial Equality (CORE) provides a stark reminder of the fate of civil rights organizations relying on white support while espousing black self-reliance.[56]

Jack Greenberg, LDF director-counsel, acknowledges that fund-raising concerns may play a small role in the selection of cases. Even though civil rights lawyers often obtain the clients, Greenberg reports, "there may be financial contributors to reckon with who may ask that certain cases be brought and others not."[57] He hastens to add that within broad limits lawyers "seem to be free to pursue their own ideas of right, . . . affected little or not at all by contributors."[58] The reassurance is double-edged. The lawyers' freedom to pursue their own ideas of right may pose no problems as long as both clients and contributors share a common social outlook. But when the views of some or all the clients change, a delayed recognition and response by the lawyers is predictable.[59]

---

argue that the "separate but equal" standard was impossible to realize only because of black political impotence, and that the current existence and continued growth of black political power means that segregation today need not, and would not, result in resource inequality, the suspicion remains that somehow the whites will connive to bring extra educational benefits and resources to white children. Busing, then, symbolizes the opportunity for blacks to discover what it is that whites have in their schools and to share fully in it—whatever "it" is.

Id. at 479.

56. *See* A. Meier & E. Rudwick, CORE: A Study in the Civil Rights Movement 1942-1968 (1973).

57. Greenberg, *supra* note 15, at 349.

58. *Id.*

59. Professor Leroy Clark, a former LDF lawyer, is more critical than his former boss about the role of financial contributors in setting civil rights policy:

[T]here are two "clients" the civil rights lawyer must satisfy: (1) the immediate litigants (usually black), and (2) those liberals (usually white) who make financial contributions. An apt criticism of the traditional civil rights lawyer is that too often the litigation undertaken was modulated by that which was "salable" to the paying clientele who, in the radical view, had interests threatened by true social change. Attorneys may not make conscious decisions to refuse specific litigation because it is too "controversial" and hard to translate to the public, but no organization dependent on a large number of contributors can ignore the fact that the "appeal" of the program affects fund-raising. Some of the pressure to have a "winning" record may come from the need to show contributors that their money is accomplishing something socially valuable.

School expert Ron Edmonds contends that civil rights attorneys often do not represent their clients' best interests in desegregation litigation because "they answer to a miniscule constituency while serving a massive clientele."[60] Edmonds distinguishes the clients of civil rights attorneys (the persons on whose behalf suit is filed) from their "constituents" (those to whom the attorney must answer for his actions).[61] He suggests that in class-action school-desegregation cases the mass of lower-class black parents and children are merely clients. To define constituents, Edmonds asks, "[To] what class of Americans does the civil rights attorney feel he must answer for his professional conduct?"[62] The answer can be determined by identifying those with whom the civil rights attorney confers as he defines the goals of the litigation. He concludes that those who currently have access to the civil rights attorney are whites and middle-class blacks who advocate integration and categorically oppose majority-black schools.

Edmonds suggests that, more than other professionals, the civil rights attorney labors in a closed setting isolated from most of his or her clients. No matter how numerous, the attorney's clients cannot become constituents unless they have access to him before or during the legal process. The result is the pursuit of metropolitan desegregation without sufficient regard for the probable instructional consequences for black children. In sum, he charges, "A class action suit serving only those who pay the attorney fee has the effect of permitting the fee paying minority to impose its will on the majority of the class on whose behalf suit is presumably brought."[63]

Clark, *The Lawyer in the Civil Rights Movement—Catalytic Agent or Counter-Revolutionary?* 19 Kan. L. Rev. 459, 469 (1971).

The litigation decisions made under the pressure of so many nonlegal considerations are not always unanimous. A few years ago, LDF decided not to represent the militant black communist, Angela Davis, LDF officials justified their refusal on grounds that the criminal charges brought against Davis did not present "civil rights" issues. The decision, viewed by staff lawyers as an unconscionable surrender to conservative contributors, caused a serious split in LDF ranks. A few lawyers resigned because of the dispute, and others remained disaffected for a long period.

60. Edmonds, *Advocating Inequity: A Critique of the Civil Rights Attorney in Class Action Desegregation Suits,* 3 Black L.J. 176, 178 (1974). Edmonds is director of the Center for Urban Studies, Harvard Graduate School of Education.

61. *Id.*

62. *Id.* at 179.

63. *Id.* Poverty law lawyers have recognized a smiliar problem. As one group of student commentators have put it:

Many public interest lawyers, while representing specific clients in most of their legal work, see themselves as advocates for a much more loosely defined constituency or community. The lawyer's relationship to that constituency affects his independence in handling specific cases and, more importantly, in setting priorities as to the matters he will handle.

. . . Where the named plaintiffs in a class action control the law suit, there may be a tension between their desires and the interest of the larger class. It is often true, however, that the named plaintiffs are nominal only. Even so, this does not mean that the "larger class" controls the legal action. The lawyer's relationship to the class on whose behalf he brings the suit is likely to be extremely limited. In class actions, of

It goes without saying that civil rights lawyers take the strongest exception to Edmonds's position. NAACP General Counsel Nathaniel Jones denies that school suits are brought only at the behest of middle-class blacks, and points out what he considers to be the absurdity of attempting to poll the views of every black before a school desegregation suit is filed. But at the same time he states that his responsibility is to square NAACP litigation with his interpretation of what Supreme Court decisions require.[64]

Client Counsel Merger. The position of the established civil rights groups obviates any need to determine whether a continued policy of maximum racial balance conforms with the wishes of even a minority of the class. This position

---

course, courts are charged with determining whether the class is adequately represented, but it is important to realize the extent to which the lawyer is independent of the "class" client in determining the positions he takes.

Comment, *supra* note 4, at 1124-25. Another commentator writes:

By definition, the public interest law firm begins with a concept of the public interest and fashions its clients around that. This reverses the traditional process where attorneys begin with clients and then fashion a concept of the public interest to correspond to the interests of their clients.

Hegland, *Beyond Enthusiasm and Commitment,* 13 Ariz. L. Rev. 805, 811 (1971). Edgar and Jean Cahn, two of the most respected experts in the field of law reform, also have voiced their concern about the lack of accountability to clients and the willingness of too many lawyers to operate without consulting the client because the lawyer "knows best." Cahn & Cahn, *Power to the People or the Profession?—The Public Interest in Public Interest Law,* 79 Yale L.J. 1005, 1042 (1970).

64. Letter from Nathaniel R. Jones to author, July 31, 1975:

It would be absurd to expect that each and every black person should be polled before a lawsuit is filed, or a plan of desegregation is proposed. Certainly, school boards, who resist these suits, do not poll their patrons on their views before shaping a position.

The responsibility I, as chief litigation officer of the NAACP have, is to insure that each plan the NAACP submits to a court, or any plan upon which a court is expected to act, and the overall legal theory relied upon must square with the legal standards pronounced by the Supreme Court as necessary to effectively vindicate constitutional rights, and bring into being a unitary system.

It seems to use that the Edmonds thesis could have the effect of trading off constitutional rights in favor of expedient, short-term objectives that would result in perpetuating the evil proscribed by law. This constitutes a form of plea bargaining by school systems caught with their hands in the constitutional cookie jar of black children.

Racism, which we have demonstrated in the school cases, from Little Rock to Boston, to be the basic cause of segregation of pupils, is systematic in nature. It poisons the well, so to speak, thus affecting housing, jobs and other areas in which blacks must function. The only effective way of uprooting it is to pull it out systematically and fundamentally. This is not easy nor is it painless. But we have never found the fight against racism to be so.

Jones presented views similar to those contained in his letter at a May 1974 Harvard Law School symposium featuring the Edmonds view. He emphasized that potential clients requested that school desegregation suits be filed on their behalf. Co-panelists responding to Edmonds with Jones were LDF President Julius Chambers and Jack Greenberg, LDF Director-Counsel. Both were sharply critical of Edmonds's position, but declined invitations to amplify their views for inclusion in this article.

represents an extraordinary view of the lawyer's role. Not only does it assume a perpetual retainer authorizing a lifelong effort to obtain racially balanced schools. It also fails to reflect any significant change in representational policy from a decade ago, when virtually all blacks assumed that integration was the best means of achieving a quality education for black children, to the present time, when many black parents are disenchanted with the educational results of integration. Again, Jones would differ sharply with my evaluation of black parents' educational priorities, but his statement indicates that it would make no difference if I were correct. The Supreme Court has spoken in response to issues raised in litigation begun and diligently pursued by his agency. The interpretation of the Court's response by him and other officials has tehn determined NAACP litigation policies.[65]

The malady may afflict many idealistic lawyers who seek, through the class-action device, to bring about judicial intervention affecting large segments of the community. The class action provides the vehicle for bringing about a major advance toward an idealistic goal. At the same time, prosecuting and winning the big case provides strong reinforcement of the attorney's sense of his or her abilities and professionalism. Andrew Watson has suggested that "[c]lass actions . . . have the capacity to provide large sources of narcissistic gratification and this may be one of the reasons why they are such a popular form of litigation in legal aid and poverty law clinics."[66] The psychological motivations which influence the lawyer in taking on "a fiercer dragon"[67] through the class action may also underlie the tendency to direct the suit toward the goals of the lawyer rather than the client.

CIVIL RIGHTS LITIGATION AND THE REGULATION OF PROFESSIONAL ETHICS

NAACP v. Button

The questions of legal ethics raised by the lawyer-client relationship in civil rights litigation are not new. The Supreme Court's 1963 treatment of these

65. A bizarre illustration of the lengths to which this reasoning can take the lawyer motivated by his own ideals is presented in a recent (and perhaps final) chapter of the East Baton Rouge school case, which was originally filed in 1956. *See* Davis v. East Baton Rouge Parish School Bd., 398 F. Supp. 1013 (M.D. La. 1975). A motion for "supplemental relief" was filed by an attorney without authorization by any plaintiff. Referring to counsel as an "attorney-intervenor," Judge E. Gordon West interpreted the motion as seeking "'more integration' . . . sought solely for sociological reasons rather than for the purpose of improved educational opportunity for children." *Id.* at 1015. Nevertheless, the court appointed a state educational expert to investigate the East Baton Rouge school system to determine its compliance with the Constitution and prior court orders. A few of the expert's education-oriented recommendations were adopted, and the court then declared the board was operating a unitary school system and dismissed the suit. *Id.* at 1019-20.

66. Council on Legal Education for Professional Responsibility, Inc., Lawyers, Clients & Ethics 101 (M. Bloom ed. 1974).

67. *Id.*

questions in *NAACP v. Button*,[68] however, needs to be examined in light of the emergence of lawyer-client conflicts which are far more serious than the premature speculations of a segregationist legislature.

The Challenge. As the implementation of *Brown* began, southern officials looking for every possible means to eliminate the threat of integrated schools soon realized that the NAACP's procedure for obtaining clients for litigation resembled the traditionally unethical practices of barratry and running and capping.[69] Attempting to exploit this resemblance, a majority of southern states[70] enacted laws defining NAACP litigation practices as unlawful. In Virginia, though unethical and unprofessional conduct by attorneys had been regulated by statute since 1849,[71] NAACP legal activities had been carried on openly for many years. No attempt was made to use these regulations to proscribe NAACP activities until 1956. In that year, during an extra session "called to resist school integration,"[72] the Virginia legislature amended its criminal statutes barring running and capping to forbid the solicitation of legal business by "an agent for an individual or organization which retains a lawyer in connection with an action to which it is not a party and in which it has no pecuniary right or liability."[73] An attorney accepting employment from such an organization was subject to disbarment.[74] The NAACP sued to restrain enforcement of these new provisions, claiming that the statute was unconstitutional. The Virginia Supreme Court of Appeals found that the statute's purpose "was to strengthen the existing statutes to further control the evils of solicitation of legal business."[75] The court held that the statute's expanded definition of improper solicitation of legal business did not violate the Constitution in proscribing many of the legal activities of civil rights groups such as the NAACP.[76]

68. 371 U.S. 415 (1963).

69. Barratry is "the offence of frequently exciting and stirring up suits and quarrels . . . either at law or otherwise." 4 W. Blackstone, Commentaries *133. Cappers and runners are persons engaged to solicit business on behalf of an attorney or other professional. *See* People v. Dubin, 367, Ill. 229, 233, 10 N.E.2d 809, 811 (1931) (capper employed by dentist); *In re* Mitgang, 385 Ill. 311, 332, 52 N.E.2d 807, 816 (1944) (runner employed by attorney).

70. The states were Arkansas, Florida, Georgia, Mississippi, South Carolina, Tennessee, and Virginia. NAACP v. Button, 371 U.S. 415, 445 (1963) (Douglas, J., concurring).

71. *Id.* at 423.

72. 31 U.S.L.W. 3123 (Oct. 16, 1962).

73. NAACP v. Button, 371 U.S. 415, 423 (1963) (summarizing ch. 33 [1956] Acts of Gen. Assembly of Va., Extra Sess. 33).

74. 371 U.S. at 434-35.

75. NAACP v. Harrison, 202 Va. 142, 154, 116 S.E.2d 55, 65 (1960).

76. *Id.* at 159-60; 116 S.E.2d at 69: The Virginia Supreme Court also found that the NAACP's civil rights activities violated Canons 35 and 47 of the American Bar Association's *Cannons of Professional Ethics*, which the court had adopted in 1938. *Id.* at 156; 116 S.E. 2d at 67. Canon 35 provided:

The professional services of a lawyer should not be controlled or exploited by any lay agency, personal or corporate, which intervenes between client and lawyer. A lawyer's responsibilities and qualifications are individual. He should avoid all relations which

The Supreme Court Response. The Supreme Court reversed, holding that the state statute as construed and applied abridged the First Amendment rights of NAACP members. Justice Brennan, writing for the majority, reasoned that "the activities of the NAACP, its affiliates and legal staff shown on this record are modes of expression and association protected by the First and Fourteenth Amendments which Virginia may not prohibit, under its power to regulate the legal profession, as improper solicitation of legal business. . . ."[77] Justice Brennan placed great weight on the importance of litigation to the NAACP's civil rights program. He noted (with obvious approval) that blacks rely on the courts to gain objectives which are not available through the ballot box and said:

> We cannot close our eyes to the fact that the militant Negro civil rights movement has engendered the intense resentment and opposition of the politically dominant white community of Virginia; litigation assisted by the NAACP has been bitterly fought.[78]

The Court deemed NAACP's litigation activities "a form of political expression" protected by the First Amendment.[79] Justice Brennan conceded that Virginia had a valid interest in regulating the traditionally illegal practices of barratry, maintenance, and champerty,[80] but noted that the malicious intent which constituted the essence of these common law offenses was absent here. He

---

direct the duties by or in the interest of such intermediary. A lawyer's relation to his client should be personal, and the responsibility should be direct to the client. Charitable societies rendering aid to the indigents are not deemed such intermediaries.

Cannon 47 provided:

No lawyer shall permit his professional services, or his name, to be used in aid of, or to make possible, the unauthorized practice of law by any lay agency, personal or corporate.

The canons were intended to set the standards of professional conduct for the commercial rather than the civil rights or poverty law practitioner. The danger that they would be applied to the latter group remained sufficiently serious three years after the *Button* decision that Attorney General Nicholas deB. Katzenbach urged the legal profession to meet the needs of the poor by relaxing its rules against lawyers soliciting clients. Speaking to a national conference on law and poverty, he said that the "historic strictures" of the canons of ethics should not be permitted to stand between poor people and legal help. He pointed out the anomaly of lawyers "reduced to inaction by ethical prohibitions against profiteering when the client may well be penniless," and urged the American Bar Association "to draft cannons of ethics that would allow solicitation of poor clients but continue to forbid it when done for profit." N.Y. Times, June 25, 1975, at 15, col. 1, *quoted in* V. Countryman & T. Finman, *supra* note 18, at 575-76.

77. 371 U.S. at 428-29.

78. *Id.* at 435 (footnotes omitted).

79. *Id.* at 429.

80. Maintenance is "an officious intermeddling in a suit that no way belongs to one, by maintaining or assisting either party with money or otherwise, to prosecute or defend it." 4 W. Blackstone, Commentaries ★134. Champerty is "a species of maintenance . . . being a bargain with a plaintiff or defendant . . . to divide the land or other matters sued for between them, if they prevail at law; whereupon the champertor is to carry on the party's suit at his own expense." *Id.* at ★134-35.

also reasoned that because the NAACP's efforts served the public rather than a private interest, and because no monetary stakes were involved, "there is no danger that the attorney will desert or subvert the paramount interests of his client to enrich himself or an outside sponsor. And the aims and interests of NAACP have not been shown to conflict with those of its members and non-member Negro litigants. . . ."[81]

To meet Virginia's criticism that the Court was creating a special law to protect the NAACP,[82] the majority found the NAACP's activities "constitutionally irrelevant to the ground of our decision."[83] Even so, Justice Douglas noted in a concurring opinion that the Virginia law prohibiting activities by lay groups was aimed directly at NAACP activities as part "of the general plan of massive resistance to the integration of the schools."[84]

Although the issue was raised by the state,[85] the majority did not decide whether Virginia could constitutionally prohibit the NAACP from controlling the course of the litigation sponsored, perhaps because the NAACP consistently denied that it exercised such control.[86] Justice White, concurring in part and dissenting in part, cautioned:

81. 371 U.S. at 443.
82.

For this Court to reverse [the Virginia Supreme Court of Appeal's ruling that NAACP activities amounted to improper solicitation of legal business], it must disregard many court decisions that hold that solicitation is not proper. It is saying that Negroes have one set of ethics and we have another.

31 U.S.L.W. 3135 (Oct. 16, 1962) (*quoting* closing argument before Supreme Court of Henry T. Wickham, counsel for the State of Virginia).
83. 371 U.S. at 444-45.
84. *Id.* at 445.
85. "In reply to Mr. Justice White's question of what factors are necessary for violation of the statute, Mr. Wickham [counsel for the State of Virginia] stated that control is the key." 31 U.S.L.W. 3125 (Oct. 16, 1962). The Virginia Supreme Court had found: "The absence of the usual contact between many of the litigants and the attorneys instituting proceedings is indicative of the control of the litigation by the NAACP and the Conference." NAACP v. Harrison, 202 Va. 142, 155, 116 S.E.2d 55, 65-66 (1960). *See* note 76 *supra.*
86. In its brief, the NAACP argued:

While [the NAACP] only underwrites litigation aimed at the elimination of racial segregation, *per se,* once legal action is begun, the organization exercises no further control. When the lawyer-client relationship is established between the litigant and counsel, all action thereafter is taken with the client's consent.

Brief for Petitioners at 8, NAACP v. Button, 371 U.S. 415 (1963). At trial, counsel for the State of Virginia elicited the following testimony from NAACP officials:

Q. [Mr. Mays] [D]o you not insist that the case be conducted exactly in the way the Conference directs?
A. [Mr. Banks, Executive Secretary of the Virginia State Conference of Branches of the NAACP] That, sir, is a situation that would be between the attorney and the client.
Q. You leave the entire matter of litigation to the attorney and the plaintiff himself?
A. . . . [Y]es. There are certain broad principles that the Association has . . . and it would certainly have to fall within those broad limits.

If we had before us, which we do not, a narrowly drawn statute proscribing only the actual day-to-day management and dictation of the tactics, strategy and conduct of litigation by a lay entity such as the NAACP, the issue would be considerably different, at least for me; for in my opinion neither the practice of law by such an organization nor its management of the litigation of its members or others is constitutionally protected.[87]

Justice White feared that the majority opinion would also strike down such a narrowly drawn statute.

Justice Harlan's Dissent. Joined by Justices Clark and Stewart, Justice Harlan expressed the view that the Virginia statute was valid. In support of his conclusion, Harlan carefully reviewed the record and found that NAACP policy required what he considered serious departures from ethical professional conduct. First, NAACP attorneys were required to follow policy directives promulgated by the National Board of Directors or lose their right to compensation.[88] Second, these

---

Q. But, within those limitations you leave it entirely to the litigant and the attorney as to the manner in which the litigation is conducted?
A. That is correct.
Q. And the Conference does not interfere?
A. The Conference has nothing to do with the attorney and the litigant.
Transcript of Record at 262-63.

A. [Mr. Wilkins, Executive Secertary of the NAACP] Well, I have heard our lawyers say many times that they cannot do anything that the plaintiff does not want done. I have heard them stop in the middle of a case, after they had reached a certain stage, and I have sat in on these conferences that took place on strategy, in which they ... have said, "Well, before we can go further, we will have to find out what the plaintiff wants to do."
Q. [Mr. Mays] Have you run into any instances where the plaintiff wanted to do something different from the lawyer?
. . . .
A. I know of no such specific case.
Id. at 302-03.
87. 371 U.S. at 447.
88. The NAACP Board of Directors had passed a resolution requiring that:

Pleadings in all educational cases—the prayer in the pleading and proof be aimed at obtaining education on a non-segregated basis and that no relief other than that will be acceptable as such.
Further, that all lawyers operating under such rule will urge their client and the branches of the Association involved to insist on this final relief.
Transcript of Record at 246. This requirement was brought out at trial:

Q. [My Mays, attorney for State of Virginia] Well, as you understand it then, ... the Conference would not pay the lawyers unless they followed NAACP policy?
A. [Mr. Hill, attorney for NAACP, as witness] That is true.
Q. And, of course, the policy, the main policy was to go for desegregation in the schools [rather than separate-but-equal schools]?
. . . .
A. There isn't any question about it.
Q. So that in those cases, if the plaintiffs decided on some other courses of action,

directives to staff lawyers covered many subjects related to the form and substance of litigation. Third, the NAACP not only advocated litigation and waited for prospective litigants to come forward; in several instances and particularly in school cases, "specific directions were given as to the types of prospective plaintiffs to be sought, and staff lawyers brought blank forms to meetings for the purpose of obtaining signatures authorizing the prosecution of litigation in the name of the signer."[89] Fourth, the retainer forms signed by prospective litigants sometimes did not contain the names of the attorneys retained, and often when the

---

> of course counsel could not follow the plaintiff's direction and expect compensation from the Conference?
>
> A. Not and expect compensation from the Conference no.

Id. at 94.

89. 371 U.S. at 450. For example, as a preliminary step to filing a school desegregation suit, NAACP branches circulated petitions to be presented to local school officials demanding compliance with *Brown*. Parents signing such petitions often became plaintiffs when the school board rejected their demands. One NAACP directive to local affiliates stated:

> 5. Signatures should be secured from parents or guardians in all sections of the county or city. Special attention should be given to persons living in *mixed neighborhoods*, or near *formerly white schools*.
>
> 6. The signing of the petition of a parent or guardian may well be only the first step to an extended court fight. Therefore, discretion and care should be exercised to secure petitioners who will—if need be—go all the way.

Transcript of Record at 218.

But the NAACP denied that it solicited plaintiffs for litigation. Mr. Wilkins, Executive Secretary of the NAACP, stated:

> We do not go out into the general population and solicit a man by saying, "Don't you want to challenge such and such a law?" or "Don't you want to go to court on this or that point?" I think it is fair, however, and it is a matter of record, that we have said publicly, on many occasions, that such and such a law we believe to be unconstitutional and unfair and we believe that Negro citizens are deprived of their rights by this statute, or this practice, and that we believe it ought to be challenged in the courts, which is the proper place to challenge such legislation, and that we urge colored people to challenge these laws and that if any one of them steps forward and says he wishes to challenge such a law, we will agree to assist him, providing the case passes all of the requirements. But for actually going out and buttonholing people and saying, "Will you come in and help us test this?" we don't do that either.

Id. at 295. Lester Banks, Executive Secretary of the Virginia State Conference of Branches of the NAACP, testified at trial:

> Q. [Mr. Mays, attorney for State of Virginia] Does the Conference instigate or attempt to instigate a person or persons to institute a lawsuit by offering to pay the expenses of litigation?
>
> A. [Mr. Banks] No. sir, the Conference does not.
>
> Q. It never looks for plaintiffs?
>
> A. The Conference never looks for plaintiffs.
>
> Q. And always it is an instance where the prospective plaintiff comes to the Conference and asks for help?
>
> A. That is correct.
>
> Q. There are no exceptions in your experience?
>
> A. I can think of no exceptions.

Id. at 260-61.

forms specified certain attorneys as counsel, additional attorneys were brought into the action without the plaintiff's consent. Justice Harlan observed that several named plaintiffs had testified that they had no personal dealings with the lawyers handling their cases and were not aware until long after the event that suits had been filed in their names.[90] Taken together, Harlan felt these incidents justified the corrective measures taken by the state of Virginia.

Justice Harlan was not impressed by the fact that the suits were not brought for pecuniary gain. The NAACP attorneys did not donate their services, and the litigating activities did not fall into the accepted category of aid to indigents. But he deemed more important than the avoidance of improper pecuniary gain the concern shared by the profession, courts, and legislatures that ourside influences not interfere with the uniquely personal relationship between lawyer and client. In Justice Harlan's view, when an attorney is employed by an association or corporation to represent a client, two problems arise:

> The lawyer becomes subject to the control of a body that is not itself a litigant and that, unlike the lawyers it employs, is not subject to strict professional discipline as an officer of the court. In addition, the lawyer necessarily finds himself with a divided allegiance—to his employer and to his client—which may prevent full compliance with his basic professional obligations.[91]

He conceded that "[t]he NAACP may be no more than the sum of the efforts and views infused in it by its members," but added a prophetic warning that "the totality of the separate interests of the members and others whose causes the petitioner champions, even in the field of race relations, may far exceed in scope and variety that body's views of policy, as embodied in litigating strategy and tactics."[92]

Justice Harlan recognized that it might be in the association's interest to maintain an all-out, frontal attack on segregation, even sacrificing small points in some cases for the major points that might win other cases. But, he foresaw that

> it is not impossible that after authorizing action in his behalf, a Negro parent, concerned that a continued frontal attack could result in schools closed for years, might prefer to wait with his fellows a longer time for good-faith efforts by the local school board than is permitted by the centrally determined policy of the NAACP. Or he might see a greater prospect of success through discussions with local school authorities than through

90. Some clients did not know the names of their lawyers, and many others stated they had had no contact whatsoever with counsel since they signed the authorization form. *E.g.,* 371 U.S. at 442n.6; Transcript of Record at 119-20, 124, 151-52, 171.
91. 371 U.S. at 460.
92. *Id.* at 462.

the litigation deemed necessary by the Association. The parent, of course, is free to withdraw his authorization, but is his lawyer, retained and paid by petitioner and subject to its directions on matters of policy, able to advise the parent with that undivided allegiance that is the hallmark of the attorney-client relation? I am afraid not.[93]

NAACP v. Button *in Retrospect*. The characterizations of the facts in *Button* by both majority and the dissenters contain much that is accurate. As the majority found, the NAACP did not "solicit" litigants but rather systematically advised black parents of their rights under *Brown* and collected retainer signatures of those willing to join the proposed suits. The litigation was designed to serve the public interest rather than to enrich the litigators. Not all the plaintiffs were indigent, but few could afford to finance litigation intended to change the deep-seated racial policies of public school systems.

On the other hand, Justice Harlan was certainly correct in suggesting that the retainer process was often performed in a perfunctory manner and that plaintiffs had little contact with their attorneys. Plaintiffs frequently learned that suit had been filed and kept abreast of its progress through the public media. Although a plaintiff could withdraw from the suit at any time, he could not influence the primary goals of the litigation. Except in rare instances, policy decisions were made by the attorneys, often in conjunction with the organizational leadership and without consultation with the client.

The *Button* majority obviously felt that the potential for abuse of clients' rights in this procedure was overshadowed by the fact that Virginia enacted the statute to protect the citadel of segregation rather than the sanctity of the lawyer-client relationship. As the majority pointed out, litigation was the only means by which blacks throughout the South could effectuate the school desegregation mandate of *Brown*.[94] The theoretical possibility of abuse of client rights seemed a rather slender risk when compared with the real threat to integration posed by this most dangerous weapon in Virginia's arsenal of "massive resistance."

Most legal commentators reacted favorably to the majority's decision for precisely this reason.[95] Justice Harlan was criticized by these writers for refusing to recognize the motivation for Virginia's sudden interest in the procedures by which the NAACP obtained and represented school desegregation plaintiffs. Professor Harry Kalven saw Harlan as driven "by an almost heroic desire to neutralize litigation on race issues."[96] In Kalven's view, Harlan's analysis of the

93. *Id.*
94. *Id.* at 429-30.
95. *E.g.,* Birkby & Murphy, *Interest Group Conflict in the Judicial Arena: The First Amendment and Group Access to the Courts,* 42 Texas L. Rev. 1018 (1964); 12 Am. U.L. Rev. 184 (1963); 32 U. Cin. L. Rev. 550 (1963); 1963 U.Ill. L.F. 97.
96. H. Kalven, The Negro and The First Amendment 90 (Phoenix 1966).

possible conflict of interest between the NAACP lawyer and his client "verge[d] on the absurd":

> It in effect tells the Negro that Virginia can curtail seriously the activities of the NAACP because of Virginia's benign interest in protecting Negro clients from the conflicts of interest that may arise when they are represented by NAACP lawyers in civil rights cases without financial cost to themselves.[97]

Nevertheless, a few contemporary commentators found cause for sober reflection in Harlan's dissent.[98] And even those writers who viewed the decision as necessary to protect the NAACP conceded that the majority had paid too little attention to Justice Harlan's conflict-of-interest concerns. As one writer noted, Justice Brennan's response—quoting from Justice Harlan's opinion in *NAACP v. Alabama* ex rel. *Patterson*[99] to the effect that NAACP interests were identical with those of its members—was inadequate.[100] In the Alabama case the NAACP was attempting to protect the secrecy of its membership; the Court ruled that the organization had standing to defend the privacy and freedom of association of its members because they could not come forward without revealing their names and sacrificing the very rights at stake. But in school cases, as Justice Harlan observed in *Button,* an individual plaintiff might prefer a compromise which would frustrate attainment of the goals of the sponsoring groups. "[F]requently occasions might arise in which the choice between an immediate small gain and possible later achievement of a larger aim should at least be put to the plaintiff in whose name the suit was being brought, not decided for him by third parties."[101] It is no answer that the plaintiff is always at liberty to withdraw his name from the case, because "if the plaintiff does not know how—or if—his case is being conducted, he is not likely to be able to ascertain with any precision where his interests lie. Furthermore, the issue may be so complex that the litigant needs professional advice before the alternatives become clear to him."[102]

The ABA Response

Button's recognition of First Amendment rights in the conduct of litigation led to subsequent decisions[103] broadening the rights of other lay groups to ob-

97. *Id.* at 89-90.
98. *E.g., The Supreme Court, 1962 Term,* 77 Harv. L. Rev. 62, 122-24 (1963); 29 Brooklyn L. Rev. 318 (1963); 15 S.C. L. Rev. 845 (1963).
99. 357 U.S. 449 (1958).
100. Birkby & Murphy, *supra* note 95, at 1036.
101. *Id.* at 1036-37.
102. *Id.* at 1037.
103. *E.g.,* Brotherhood of Ry. Trainmen v. Virginia *ex rel.* Virginia State Bar, 377 U.S. 1 (1964) (state restrictions on the practice of law voided to the extent that they impinged upon the right of a labor union to maintain a legal staff to give advice respecting prospective litigation and to recommend attorneys for investigation of claims under the Federal Em-

tain legal representation for their members.[104] In so doing, these decisions posed new problems for the organized bar. The American Bar Association, faced with the reality of group practice which it had long resisted, has attempted to adopt guidelines for practitioners; but the applicable provisions of its new *Code of Professional Responsibility* provide only broad and uncertain guidance on the issues of control of litigation and conflict of interest as they affect civil rights lawyers.[105]

The *Code of Professional Responsibility* again and again admonishes the law-

---

ployees Liability Act); United Transp. Union v. State Bar, 401 U.S. 576 (1971) (protecting the union's right to handle members' claims under the Federal Employees Liability Act); United Mine Workers of America, Dist. 12 v. Illinois State Bar Ass'n, 389 U.S. 217 (1967) (labor union entitled to hire attorneys on a salary basis to assist members in processing workmen's compensation claims).

104. *Cf.* Freund, *Civil Rights and the Limits of the Law,* 14 Buffalo L. Rev. 199, 207 (1964) (referring specifically to the genesis of the libel case, New York Times Co. v. Sullivan, 376 U.S. 254 (1964), in the reporting of civil rights protests in Alabama).

105. *The Code of Professional Responsibility* took effect in 1970 and was amended in 1970, 1974 and 1975. It consists of nine canons which broadly state the standards of professional conduct. There are two explanatory sections under each canon: Ethical Considerations (EC), which are "aspirational in character" and for purposes of guidance describe more particularly the principles set out in the canons; and Disciplinary Rules (DR), which "state the minimum level of conduct below which no lawyer can fall without being subjected to disciplinary action." ABA, Code of Professional Responsibility and Code of Judicial Conduct 1 (1975) (Preliminary Statement) [hereinafter cited by provision only]. The DR's are the only part of the *Code* which are mandatory and applicable to all lawyers "regardless of the nature of their professional activities." *Id.*

The key section for public interest lawyers is Canon 2, the outgrowth of *Button* and its progeny. Canon 2 provides that "A Lawyer Should Assist the Legal Profession in Fulfilling Its Duty to Make Legal Counsel Available." This Canon has created great controversy; as one writer observed,

> the new Canon must prohibit individual champerty, maintenance, barratry, solicitation of legal business, and advertising, while encouraging similarly-directed group activities. Inasmuch as any group can act only through its members, a fine line is then drawn between conduct of a lawyer that furthers his own interest or that furthers the common good. Particularly is this true when individual benefits are produced by permissible "professional" activities.

Smith, *Canon 2: "A Lawyer Should Assist the Legal Profession in Fulfilling Its Duty to Make Legal Counsel Available,"* 48 Texas L. Rev. 285, 287 (1970). *See* Elson *Canon 2–The Bright and Dark Face of the Legal Profession,* 12 San Diego L. Rev. 306 (1975); Nahstall, *Limitations on Group Legal Services Arrangements Under the Code of Professional Responsibility, DR 2-103 (D) (5): Stale Wine in New Bottles,* 48 Texas L. Rev. 344 (1970).

The ABA's recognition of group services has been grudging. In what has been called "a lateral pass to the Supreme Court," group legal services by nonprofit organizations were initially permitted "only in those instances and to the extent that controlling constitutional interpretation at the time of the rendition of the services requires the allowance of such legal service activities." DR 2-103(D)(5); Sutton, *The American Bar Association Code of Professional Responsibility: An Introduction,* 48 Texas L. Rev. 255, 262 (1970). Subsequent amendments have liberalized the range of permissible professional activity in the areas of legal services and group practice. *See, e.g.,* EC 2-33 (Feb. 1975), which reminds lawyers of their professional obligations to individual clients and cautions against situations where there may be interference by lay officials or where, because of economic considerations, competence and quality of service may suffer.

yer "to disregard the desires of others that might impair his free judgment."[106] But the suggestions assume the classical commercial conflict or a third-party intermediary clearly hostile to the client. Even when the *Code* seems to recognize more subtle "economic, political or social pressures," the protection needed by civil rights clients is not provided, and the suggested remedy—withdrawal from representation of the client—is hardly desirable if the client has no available alternatives.[107]

The market-system mentality of the drafters of the *Code* surfaces in another provision suggesting that problems of control are less likely to exist where the lawyer "is compensated directly by his client."[108] But solving the problem of control by relying on the elimination of compensation from a source other than the client was rejected in *Button*. All that remains is the warning that a person or group furnishing lawyers "may be far more concerned with establishment or extension of legal principles than in the immediate protection of the rights of the lawyer's individual client."[109]

The *Code* approach, urging the lawyer to "constantly guard against erosion of his professional freedom"[110] and requiring that individual lawyers "decline to accept direction of his professional judgment from any layman,"[111] is simply the wrong answer to the right question in civil rights offices where basic organizational policies such as the goals of school desegregation are often designed by lawyers and then adopted by the board or other leadership group. The NAACP's reliance on litigation requires that lawyers play a major role in basic policy decisions. Admonitions that the lawyer make no important decisions without consulting the client[112] and that the client be fully informed of all relevant con-

---

106. EC 5-21 Cannon 5 provides: "A Lawyer Should Exercise Independent Professional Judgment on Behalf of a Client." And EC 5-1 reminds the lawyer of his or her duty to remain "free of compromising influences and loyalties."

107. EC 5-21 provides:

> The obligation of a lawyer to exercise professional judgment solely on behalf of his client requires that he disregard the desires of others that might impair his free judgment. The desires of a third person will seldom adversely affect a lawyer unless that person is in a position to exert strong economic, political, or social pressures upon the lawyer. These influences are often subtle, and a lawyer must be alert to their existence. A lawyer subjected to outside pressures should make full disclosure of them to his client; and if he or his client believes that the effectiveness of his representation has been or will be impaired thereby, the lawyer should take proper steps to withdraw from representation of his client.

108. EC 5-22 provides:

> Economic, political, or social pressures by third persons are less likely to impinge upon the independent judgment of a lawyer in a matter in which he is compensated directly by his client and his professional work is exclusively with his client. On the other hand, if a lawyer is compensated from a source other than his client, he may feel a sense of responsibility to someone other than his client.

109. EC 5-23.
110. *Id.*
111. EC 5-24.
112. EC 7-7.

siderations[113] are, of course, appropriate. But they are difficult to enforce in the context of complex, long-term school desegregation litigation where the original plaintiffs may have left the system and the members of the class whose interests are at stake are numerous, generally uninformed, and, if aware of the issues, divided in their views.

Current ABA standards thus appear to conform with *Button* and its progeny in permitting the representation typically provided by civil rights groups. They are a serious attempt to come to grips with and provide specific guidance on the issues of outside influence and client primacy that so concerned Justice Harlan. But they provide little help where, as in school desegregation litigation, the influence of attorney and organization are mutually supportive, and both are so committed to what they perceive as the long-range good of their clients that they do not sense the growing conflict between those goals and the client's current interests. Given the cries of protest and the charges of racially motivated persecution that would probably greet any ABA effort to address this problem more specifically, it is not surprising that the conflict—which in any event will neither embarrass the profession ethically nor threaten it economically—has not received a high priority for further attention.

Idealism, though perhaps rarer than greed, is harder to control. Justice Harlan accurately prophesied the excesses of derailed benevolence, but a retreat from the group representational concepts set out in *Button* would be a disaster, not an improvement. State legislatures are less likely than the ABA to draft standards that effectively guide practitioners and protect clients. Even well-intentioned and carefully drawn standards might hinder rather than facilitate the always difficult task of achieving social change through legal action. And too stringent rules could encourage officials in some states to institute groundless disciplinary proceedings against lawyers in school cases, which in many areas are hardly more popular today than they were during the massive resistance era.

Client involvement in school litigation is more likely to increase if civil rights lawyers themselves come to realize that the special status accorded them by the courts and the bar demands in return an extraordinary display of ethical sensitivity and self-restraint. The "divided allegiance" between client and employer which Justice Harlan feared would interfere with the civil rights lawyer's "full compliance with his basic professional obligation"[114] has developed in a far more idealistic and thus a far more dangerous form. For it is more the civil rights lawyers' commitment to an integrated society than any policy directives or pressures from their employers which leads to their assumptions of client acceptance and their condemnations of all dissent.

---

113. EC 7-8.
114. NAACP v. Button 371 U.S. 415, 460-62 (1963) (Harlan, J., Dissenting).

THE CLASS-ACTION BARRIER TO
EXPRESSION OF DISSENT

Even if civil rights lawyers were highly responsive to the wishes of the named plaintiffs in school desegregation suits, a major source of lawyer-client conflict would remain. In most such suits, the plaintiffs bring a class action on behalf of all similarly situated black students and parents; the final judgment will be binding on all members of the class.[115] As black disenchantment with racial-balance remedies grows, the strongest opposition to civil rights litigation strategy may come from unnamed class members. But even when black groups opposed to racial-balance remedies overcome their ambivalence and obtain counsel willing to advocate their position in court, judicial interpretations of the federal class-action rule make it difficult for dissident members of the class to gain a hearing in pending school litigation.

Ironically, the interpretations of Rule 23 which now hinder dissent derive from early school desegregation cases in which the courts sought to further plaintiffs' efforts to gain compliance with *Brown*. Typical of the early solicitude for plaintiffs in school desegregation cases was *Potts v. Flax*.[116] Defendants maintained at trial that the suit was not a class action because the two plaintiffs had not affirmatively indicated that they sought class relief.[117] The district court found first that the suit properly presented the question of constitutionality of defendant's dual school system. The court then determined that although the

---

115. The school desegregation cases that led to the decision in *Brown* and virtually every school suit since then have been filed as class actions under the *Federal Rules of Civil Procedure*. Fed. R. Civ. P. 23(a) sets forth the prerequisites to a class action:

> One or more members of a class may sue or be sued as representative parties on behalf of all only if (1) the class is so numerous that joinder of all members is impracticable, (2) there are questions of law or fact common to the class, (3) the claims or defenses of the representative parties are typical of the claims or defenses of the class, and (4) the representative parties will fairly and adequately protect the interests of the class.

It is clear from the Notes of the Advisory Committee on Rules, Fed. R. Civ. P. 23, 28 U.S.C. app., at 7766 (1970), that under the 1966 revision of Fed. R. Civ. P. 23, subdivision (b)(2) was intended to cover civil rights cases including school desegregation litigation, "where a party is charged with discriminating unlawfully against a class, usually one whose members are incapable of specific enumeration." 7A C. Wright & A. Miller, Federal Practice and Procedure §1776 (1972). Fed. R. Civ. P. 23(b)(2) provides:

> An action may be maintained as a class action if the prerequisites of subdivision (a) are satisfied, and in addition . . . (2) the party opposing the class has acted or refused to act on grounds generally applicable to the class, thereby making appropriate final injunctive relief or corresponding declaratory relief with respect to the class as a whole. . . .

116. 313 F.2d 284 (5th Cir. 1963).

117. One parent testified that he was bringing suit for his own children and not for all other Negro children. The other parent was not questioned on this issue. *Id.* at 288.

suit was instituted only by individuals, the right sued upon was a class right—the right to a termination of the system-side policy of racial segregation in the schools—and thus affected every black child in the school district.[118] The Fifth Circuit, approving the lower court's reasoning, doubted that relief formally confined to specific black children either could be granted or could be so limited in its effect. Viewing the suit as basically an attack on the unconstitutional practice of racial discrimination, the court held that the appropriate relief was an order that it be discontinued. Moreover, the court suggested, "to require a school system to admit the specific successful plaintiff Negro child while others, having no such protection, were required to attend schools in a racially segregated system, would be for the court to contribute actively to the *class* discrimination."[119]

At one time, expressions of disinterest and even disapproval of civil rights litigation by portions of the class may have been motivated by fear and by threats of physical and economic intimidation. But events in Atlanta, Detroit, and Boston provide the basis for judicial notice that many black parents oppose total reliance on racial-balance remedies to cure the effects of school segregation. As one federal court of appeals judge has put it: "Almost predictably, changing circumstances during those years of litigation have dissolved the initial unity of the plaintiffs' position."[120] Black parents who prefer alternative remedies are

118. Flax v. Potts, 204 F. Supp. 458, 463-66 (N.D. Tex. 1962).

119. 313 F.2d at 289. The Fifth Circuit had earlier suggested the importance of class-wide relief in school desegregation cases in Bush v. Orleans Parish School Bd., 308 F.2d 491, 499 (5th Cir. 1962). *Potts* was followed in Bailey v. Patterson, 323 F.2d 201, 206 (5th Cir. 1963), a suit to desegregate public facilities. *See also* Gantt v. Clemson Agricultural College, 320 F.2d 611 (4th Cir. 1963).

The Advisory Committee Notes to the 1966 revision of Rules 23 cited *Potts* to illustrate its view that Rule 23(b)(2) authorized class actions in civil rights cases. *Potts* has been cited frequently in subsequent civil rights cases. *E.g.,* Jenkins v. United Gas Corp., 400 F.2d 28, 34 (5th Cir. 1968); United States v. Jefferson County Bd. of Educ., 372 F.2d 836 869-70 (5th Cir. 1966), *aff'd en banc,* 380 F.2d 385 (5th Cir.), *cert denied,* 389 U.S. 840 (1967).

The *Potts* principle has been applied even in situations where members of the class are alleged to oppose the action or are antagonistic toward plaintiffs. In Moss v. Lane Co., 50 F.R.D. 122 (W.D. Va. 1970), *remanded on other grounds,* 471 F.2d 853 (4th Cir. 1973), the court certified as a class action an employment discrimination suit brought by a discharged black employee on behalf of all black employees, even though the defendant employer argued that plaintiff did not have the consent of other class members to represent them. The employer supported its position with affidavits of all its black employees disclaiming any authority from them to commence ths suit. The trial court reasoned that if the plaintiff prevailed, an injunction requiring an end to discriminatory practices would benefit all in the class, and noted further that some class members might have been afraid to join plaintiff for fear of placing their jobs in jeopardy. 50 F.R.D. at 125.

Similarly, satisfaction of the plaintiff's individual claim does not render an employment discrimination suit moot as to the class. Jenkins v. United Gas Corp., 400 F.2d 28 (5th Cir. 1968). Problems may arise in employment discrimination suits where the main relief sought is damages in the form of back pay. The appropriateness of class actions in such suits is discussed in Comment, *Class Actions and Title VII of the Civil Rights Act of 1964: The Proper Class Representative and the Class Remedy,* 47 Tul. L. Rev. 1005, 1015-16 (1973).

120. Calhoun v. Cook, 522 F.2d 717, 718 (5th Cir. 1975)(Clark, J.).

poorly served by the routine approval of plaintiffs' requests for class status in school desegregation litigation.[121]

Basic principles of equity require courts to develop greater sensitivity to the growing disagreement in black communities over the nature of school relief. Existing class-action rules provide ample authority for broadening representation in school cases to reflect the fact that views in the black community are no longer monolithic. One aspect of class-action status requiring closer scrutiny is whether the representation provided by plaintiffs will "fairly and adequately protect the interests of the class."[122] Because every person is entitled to be adequately represented when his or her rights and duties are being adjudicated, it is incumbent upon the courts to ensure the fairness of proceedings that will bind absent class members. The failure to exercise such care may violate due process rights guaranteed by the Fifth and Fourteenth Amendments.[123]

These problems can be avoided if, instead of routinely assuming that school desegregation plaintiffs adequately represent the class, courts will apply carefully the standard tests for determining the validity of class-action allegations and the standard procedures for protecting the interests of unnamed class members.[124] Where objecting members of the class seek to intervene, their conflicting

---

121. "It is undoubtedly true that many federal district judges have been careless in their dealings with class actions, and have failed to comply carefully with the technical requirements of Rule 23." Board of School Comm'rs v. Jacobs, 420 U.S. 128, 133 (1975) (Douglas, J., dissenting).

122. Fed. R. Civ. P. 23(a)(4). The issue of adequacy of representation is of critical importance in school desegregation cases where all members of the class are bound by the decrees entered. C. Wright & A. Miller, *supra* note 115, §§1765, 1771, *See* Note, *Class Actions: Defining The Typical and Representative Plaintiff Under Subsections (a)(3) and (4) of Federal Rule 23,* 53 B.U. L. Rev. 406 (1973) (arguing for a more vigorous application of the prerequisites for class action status).

123. Cf. Hansberry v. Lee, 311 U.S. 32 (1940). At the least, the Fifth Circuit has held that the res judicata effect of a 23(b)(2) class action is not binding on the class when the class representative has failed to appeal from a trial court's judgment which granted the individual full relief but provided only partial relief to the rest of the class. Gonzales v. Cassidy, 474 F.2d 67 (5th Cir. 1973). The court found that the failure to appeal from the individual full relief but provided relief to the class (such appeal not being patently meritless or frivolous) was itself evidence of inadequate representation.

124. Several steps might be taken to protect class interests:

1. *Determination of class action.* Courts should take seriously their independent obligation under Rule 23(c)(1) to decide Rule 23 issues "as soon as practicable after the commencement of an action brought as a class action," even if neither of the parties move for a ruling. C. Wright & A. Miller, *supra* note 115, § 1785. The rationale of Potts v. Flax, 313 F.2d 284 (5th Cir. 1963), now incorporated into subdivision (b)(2) cases, does not lessen the need for diligent judicial scrutiny of subdivision (a)(4) standards.

2. *Notice to class.* Individual notice to known members of the class is required by Rule 23 (c)(2) in Rule 23(b)(3) actions. Eisen v. Carlisle & Jacquelin, 417 U.S. 156 (1974). Individual notice might prove unnecessarily burdensome to plaintiffs in Rule 23(b)(2) civil rights suits and is not required. C. Wright & A. Miller, *supra* note 115, § 1793. But some effective means of advising the class of the existence of the suit, the type of relief to be sought, and the binding nature of the judgment should be considered by the court. *See*

interests can be recognized under the provisions of Rule 23(d)(2).[125] In this regard, the class-action intervention provisions are in harmony with those contained in Rule 24.[126]

Even with the exercise of great care, the adequacy of representation may be difficult to determine, particularly at the outset of the litigation. For this reason, Professor Owen Fiss has suggested that the standard for adequacy of representation for certifying a class action should differ from that used in allowing intervention.[127] If the standards are the same, he reasons, the logical result will be that no member of the class will be allowed to intervene in a class-action suit as a matter of right once it is determined that the representation is adequate as to the class. In some instances, although the representation by the named party is adequate as to a class, unnamed class members will have interests deserving of independent representation but not sufficiently important or conflicting to re-

---

Fed. R. Civ. P. 23(d)(2). Local newspapers usually report the filing of school suits, but provide little information about the significance of the class action nature of the litigation. Notice prepared by plaintiffs might, at the court's direction, be distributed to each minority child in the school system. Predecent exists for providing each parent with a letter and questionnaire advising the parent of the pending action and inquiring whether the parent wished to be represented by the plaintiffs and their counsel. Knight v. Board of Educ., 48 F.R.D. 108 (E.D.N.Y. 1969). An individual notice procedure would provide several advantages. It would:

(a) Enable a fairly accurate determination to be made as to class support for the suit and for the form of relief sought by plaintiffs;

(b) Provide the court with indications regarding the possible need for special steps that might be taken to protect the interests of the class;

(c) Provide class members with an opportunity to provide information through the questionnaire as to individual instances of discrimination they have experienced;

(d) Provide class members with an opportunity to challenge class certification; and

(e) Provide objecting class members an opportunity to intervene. (Specific provision for intervention in class is provided in subdivision (d)(2).)

3. *Preliminary hearing on class action issue.* In those instances where members of the class raise objections to the adequacy of plaintiffs' representation or the character of relief sought, courts may hold a hearing before deciding under subdivision (c)(1) whether to allow a class action. Challenges will seldom be made at the outset of school desegregation litigation. Subdivision (c)(1) orders are, of course, not irreversible and may be altered amended at a later date. C. Wright & A. Miller, *supra* note 115, § 1785.

4. *Partial class actions and subclasses.* Rule 23(c)(4) enables the court to authorize the class action as to only particular issues and to divide a class into appropriate subclasses. In school litigation, members of plaintiffs' class may differ substantially, but could rather easily be encompassed within the motion and hearing process normal to school litigation. *Cf.* Carr v. Conoco Plastics, Inc., 423 F.2d 57 (5th Cir.), *cert. denied,* 400 U.S. 951 (1970); Johnson v. ITT—Thompson Indus., Inc., 323 F. Supp. 1258 (N.D. Miss. 1971).

125. Fed. R. Civ. P. 23(d)(2) provides:

In the conduct of actions to which this rule applies, the court may make appropriate orders . . . (2) requiring, for the protection of the members of the class or otherwise for the fair conduct of the action, that notice be given . . . to some or all members of any step in the action, . . . to intervene and present claims or defenses, or otherwise to come into the action. . . .

126. C. Wright & A. Miller, *supra* note 115, § 1799.

127. O. Fiss, Injunctions 560-61 (1972).

quire that the class action be dismissed, the class representative replaced, or the class redefined to exclude the intervenors. The denial of intervention as of right whenever representation is adequate as to the class is particularly unacceptable to Fiss because the class representative is self-selected.[128]

In *Norwalk CORE v. Norwalk Board of Education*,[129] groups seeking integration more extensive than that sought by the named plaintiffs became ensnared in the traditional reading of the class-action rule. The district court denied a motion to intervene as of right under Rule 24(a)(2) by a group purportedly representing blacks and Puerto Ricans in the community. CORE, which represented a class similarly defined, had challenged the method of school desegregation (the closing of facilities in the black and Puerto Rican communities and the transporting of minority children to predominantly white outlying schools) rather than the objective of desegregation itself. It sought reopening of the school facilities in the minority communities. The proposed intervenors asserted that this would hamper the board's efforts to integrate the schools. In denying the motion to intervene, the court reasoned that since neither group opposed school integration and both sought integrated schools, the question was simply whether the original plaintiff had standing to bring the suit. However, the district court in effect satisfied the intervenors' request by refusing the two-way busing sought by the original plaintiffs.[130]

Courts have been more sensitive to the differing interests of persons of varied racial, ethnic, and national backgrounds. While efforts of white parents to intervene as defendants in order to make arguments similar to those being made by school boards generally have not been successful,[131] courts have allowed inter-

128. *Id.* Professor Fiss notes that in an injunction suit where damages are not sought, the defendant is unlikely to challenge the class allegations—particularly if the plaintiff's case is viewed as weak and his counsel incompetent. *Id.* at 514. Challengers to the self-appointed class representative are not likely to be organized or to have counsel. Because the motion to intervene may be filed months and even years after the suit is initiated (although still only a short period after the conflict in interests and goals becomes apparent), courts are generally reluctant to grant intervention petitions.

129. 298 F. Supp. 208 (D. Conn. 1968), *aff'd*, 423 F.2d 121 (2d Cir. 1970).

130. Intervenors fared somewhat better in the Atlanta school case. There, the Fifth Circuit held that the district court improperly denied intervention petitions filed by both CORE (seeking a community control plan) and the NAACP (seeking a full integration plan). It ruled that the lower court's approval of an integration-limiting compromise plan formulated by the defendant school board and the plaintiffs should have been preceded by a plenary hearing to obtain the views and objections of other persons purporting to represent members of the class. Calhoun v. Cook, 487 F.2d 680, 683 (5th Cir. 1973). Even as to the more radical CORE petition, the Fifth Circuit stated that CORE might have been able to justify its position if given the opportunity. *Id.* (It should be noted that this decision was rendered in the context of Rule 23(e), which requires approval of the court for the settlement of any class action; the court may have been more willing to allow intervention in this situation than in ongoing litigation).

131. *See, e.g.,* United States v. Board of School Comm'rs, 466 F.2d 573 (7th Cir. 1972), *cert. denied*, 410 U.S. 909 (1973); Spangler v. Pasadena City Bd. of Educ., 427 F.2d 1352 (9th Cir. 1970), *cert. denied*, 402 U.S. 943 (1971); Hatton v. County Bd. of Educ., 422 F.2d 457 (6th Cir. 1970); Augustus v. School Bd., 299 F. Supp. 1067 (N.D. Fla. 1969). *But see*

vention in recognition of the distinct interests of Mexican-[132] and Chinese-Americans.[133] The disagreements among blacks as to whether racial-balance remedies are the most appropriate relief for segregated schools, particularly in large urban districts, reflect interests as divergent as those which courts have recognized at the request of other ethnic minorities.

The failure to carefully monitor class status in accordance with the class-action rules can frustrate the purposes of those rules and intensify the danger of attorney-client conflict inherent in class action litigation.[134] To a measurable degree, the conflict can be traced to the civil rights lawyer's idealism and commitment to school integration. Such motivations do not become "unprofessional" because subjected to psychological scrutiny.[135] They help explain the drive that enables the civil rights lawyer to survive discouragement and defeat and renew the challenge for change. But when challenges are made on behalf of large classes unable to speak effectively for themselves, courts should not refrain from making those inquiries under the Federal Rules that cannot fail, when properly

---

Smuck v. Hobson, 408 F.2d 175 (D.C. Cir. 1969). The *Smuck* court held that white parents could intervene in order to appeal a school desegregation decision after a majority of the board had determined not to appeal. The court found the requisite interest in the parents' legitimate concern for their children's education and also found potential harm if the petition were denied. The court stated that the desegregation decision presented "substantial and unsettled questions of law" which could be the basis of an appeal. *Id.* at 180.

132. *E.g.,* United States v. Texas Educ. Agency, 467 F.2d 848, 853 n.5 (5th Cir. 1972).

133. Johnson v. San Francisco Unified School Dist., 500 F.2d 349, 352-54 (9th Cir. 1974).

134. Dam, *Class Actions: Efficiency, Compensation, Deterrents and Conflict of Interest,* 4 *J. Legal Stud.* 47, 49 (1975):

> Two different *conflicts of interest* should be considered. The first involves the representative party, who is a volunteer not normally chosen by the class members to act on their behalf. The representative plaintiff may have interests that are not in all ways congruent with those of the members of the class. The second, and for the analysis here more significant, conflict is faced by counsel representing the class. In particular, his decision calculus as to settlement versus continued litigation may be sharply different from that of the class.

A former legal services staff person has viewed the potential for lawyer-client conflict in class actions as even more serious when such actions are brought by law reform lawyers. Brill, *The Uses and Abuses of Legal Assistance,* 31 Pub. Interest 38 (1973). He charges that in the San Francisco legal services program, lawyers had a "one-track" commitment to class action strategy even though the results of this commitment were "minimal or even harmful." *Id.* at 41, 44. Class action suits were pursued when the legislative route might have been more effective and even when their use "jeopardized the specific goals and the autonomy of the community organizations [the lawyers] presumed to serve." *Id.* at 45. Even successful suits were sometimes counter-productive; the defeat of the one-year residency requirement for welfare recipients, for example, resulted in austerity measures and new restrictions resulting in a decrease in the total number of welfare recipients. *Id.* at 43-44. Subsequently, the director of the legal services office issued a strong denial of the charges, stating that the lawyers did serve their clients well and that class action suits were quite successful. Carlin, *The Poverty Lawyers,* 33 Pub. Interest 128 (1973). In an earlier article, however, Carlin presented a less rosy view of his office. He noted, *inter alia,* the division between militant white lawyers in the office and more conservative black professionals and neighborhood leaders. Carlin, *Storefront Lawyers in San Francisco,* Transaction, Apr. 1970, at 64. 74.

135. *See* p. 591 *supra.*

undertaken, to strengthen the position of the class, the representative, and the counsel who serve them both.

THE RESOLUTION OF
LAWYER-CLIENT CONFLICTS

There is nothing revolutionary in any of the suggestions in this article. They are controversial only to the extent they suggest that some civil rights lawyers, like their more candid poverty law colleagues, are making decisions, setting priorities, and undertaking responsibilities that should be determined by their clients and shaped by the community. It is essential that lawyers "lawyer" and not attempt to lead clients and class. Commitment renders restraint more, not less, difficult, and the inability of black clients to pay handsome fees for legal services can cause their lawyers, unconsciously perhaps, to adopt an attitude of "we know what's best" in determining legal strategy. Unfortunately, clients are all too willing to turn everything over to the lawyers. In school cases, perhaps more than in any other civil rights field, the attorney must be more than a litigator. The willingness to innovate, organize, and negotiate—and the ability to perform each with skill and persistence—are of crucial importance. In this process of over-all representation, the apparent—and sometimes real—conflicts of interest between lawyer and client can be resolved.

Finally, commitment to an integrated society should not be allowed to interfere with the ability to represent effectively parents who favor education-oriented remedies. Those civil rights lawyers, regardless of race, whose commitment to integration is buoyed by doubts about the effectiveness of predominantly black schools should reconsider seriously the propriety of representing blacks, at least in those school cases involving heavily minority districts.

This seemingly harsh suggestion is dictated by practical as well as professional considerations. Lacking more viable alternatives, the black community has turned to the courts. After several decades of frustration, the legal system, for a number of complex reasons, responded. Law and lawyers have received perhaps too much credit for that response.[136] The quest for symbolic manifestations of new rights and the search for new legal theories have too often failed to

---

136. Blacks lost in Plessy v. Ferguson, 163 U.S. 537 (1896), in part because the timing was not right. The Supreme Court and the nation has become reactionary on the issue of race. As LDF Director-Counsel Greenberg has acknowledged:

[Plaintiff's attorney in *Plessy*, Albion W.] Tourgée recognized [that the tide of history was against him] and spoke of an effort to overcome its effect by influencing public opinion. But this, too, was beyond his control. All the lawyer can realistically do is marshall the evidence of what the claims of history may be and present them to the court. But no matter how skillful the presentation, *Plessy and Brown* had dynamics of their own. Tourgée would have won with *Plessy* in 1954. The lawyers who brought *Brown* would have lost in 1896.

Greenberg, *supra* note 15, at 334.

prompt an assessment of the economic and political condition that so influence the progress and outcome of any social reform improvement.[137]

In school desegregation blacks have a just cause, but the cause can be undermined as well as furthered by litigation. A test case can be an important means of calling attention to perceived injustice; more important, school litigation presents opportunities for improving the weak economic and political position which renders the black community vulnerable to the specific injustices the litigation is intended to correct. Litigation can and should serve lawyer and client as a community-organizing tool, an educational forum, a means of obtaining data, a method of exercising political leverage, and a rallying point for public support.

But even when directed by the most resourceful attorneys, civil rights litigation remains an unpredictable vehicle for gaining benefits, such as quality schooling, which a great many whites do not enjoy. The risks involved in such efforts increase dramatically when civil rights attorneys, for idealistic or other reasons, fail to consider continually the limits imposed by the social and political circumstances under which clients must function even if the case is won. In the closest of lawyer-client relationships this continual reexamination can be difficult; it becomes much harder where much of the representation takes place hundreds of miles from the site of the litigation.[138]

Professor Leroy Clark has written that the black community's belief in the efficacy of litigation inhibited the development of techniques involving popular participation and control that might have advanced school desegregation in the South.[139] He feels that civil rights lawyers were partly responsible for this unwise reliance on the law. They had studied "cases" in which the conflict involved

137. Several commentators have noted the tendency of law reform advocates to delude themselves with what one writer calls a "myth of rights," defined as "a social perspective which perceives and explains human interaction largely in terms of rules and of the rights and obligations inherent in rules." S. Scheingold, The Politics of Rights: Lawyers, Public Policy, and Political Change 13 (1974) (footnote omitted). *See* Mayer, *The Idea of Justice and the Poor,* 8 Pub. Interest 96 (1967).

138. Marian Wright Edelman, a former LDF staff lawyer who lived and practiced in Missisippi before moving to Washington, has spoken of her concern about the distance between her and her clients. She stated:

"We are up here filing desegregation suits, but something else is going on in the black community. I sensed it before I left Mississippi. We hear more about nondesegregation, about 'our' schools, about money to build up black schools. I'm not sure we are doing the right thing in the long run. We automatically assume that what we need to do is close lousy black schools. But desegregation is taking the best black teachers out of the black schools and putting lousy white teachers in black schools. It has become a very complex thing."

Comment, *supra* note 4, at 1129 (interview). The passage of time has left Ms. Edelman less uneasy. In 1975, she wrote, "School desegregation is a necessary, viable and important national goal." Acknowledging that the middle class can escape to the suburbs or private schools and that black children in desegregated schools are often classified as retarded or disciplined disproportionately, she nevertheless urged desegregation because "[t]he Constitution requires it. Minority children will never achieve equal educational opportunity without it. And our children will never learn to live together if they do not begin to learn together now." N.Y. Times, Sept. 22, 1975, at 33, col. 2.

139. Clark, *supra* note 59, at 470.

easily identifiable adversaries, a limited number of variables, and issues which courts could resolve in a manageable way. A lawyer seeking social change. Clark advises, must "make clear that the major social and economic obstacles are not easily amenable to the legal process and that vigilance and continued activity by the disadvantaged are the crucial elements in social change."[140] For reasons quite similar to those which enabled blacks to win in *Brown* in 1954 and caused them to lose in *Plessy* in 1896,[141] even successful school litigation will bring little meaningful change unless there is continuing pressure for implementation from the black community. The problem of unjust laws, as Professor Gary Bellow has noted, is almost invariably a problem of distribution of political and economic power. The rules merely reflect a series of choices by the society made in response to those distributions. "'[R]ule' change, without a political base to support it, just doesn't produce any substantial result because rules are not self-executing: they require an enforcement mechanism."[142]

In the last analysis, blacks must provide an enforcement mechanism that will give educational content to the constitutional right recognized in *Brown*. Simply placing black children in "white" schools will seldom suffice. Lawyers in school cases who fail to obtain judicial relief that reasonably promises to improve the education of black children serve poorly both their clients and their cause.

In 1935, W. E. B. DuBois, in the course of a national debate over the education of blacks which has not been significantly altered by *Brown,* expressed simply but eloquently the message of the coalition of black community groups in Boston with which this article began:

[T]he Negro needs neither segregated schools nor mixed schools. What he needs is Education. What he must remember is that there is no magic, either in mixed schools or in segregated schools. A mixed school with poor and unsympathetic teachers, with hostile public opinion, and no teaching of truth concerning black folk, is bad. A segregated school with ignorant placeholders, inadequate equipment, poor salaries, and wretched housing, is equally bad. Other things being equal, the mixed school is the broader,

140. *Id.*

141. *See* note 136 *supra.*

142. Comment, *supra* note 4, at 1077 (interview with Professor Bellow). Expressing serious reservations about NAACP's test-case strategy, Professor Bellow felt law suits should be treated as "vehicles for setting in motion other political processes and for building coalitions and alliances." For example, Bellow suggests that a suit against a public agency (*e.g.,* a school board) "may be far more important for the discovery of the agency's practices and records which it affords than for the legal rule or court order it generates." Such discovery may provide the detailed documentation that can spur movements for real political change. *Id.* at 1087. Bellow would also frame injunctive relief requests narrowly—so as to obtain quick relief that will encourage clients by accomplishing some change—rather than set out after all-encompassing orders that take years to litigate and may end in defeat or unenforceable rulings. *Id.* at 1088. Similar suggestions are made in Bell, *School Litigation Strategies for the 1970s: New Phases in the Continuing Quest for Quality Schools,* 1970 Wis L. Rev. 257, 276-79. And for a step-by-step account of how one attorney assisted her clients in obtaining a bilingual education program without resorting to any litigation, see Waserstein, *Organizing for Bilingual Education: One Community's Experience,* Inequality in Educ., Feb. 1975, at 23.

more natural basis for the education of all youth. It gives wider contacts; it inspires greater self-confidence; and suppresses the inferiority complex. But other things seldom are equal, and in that case, Sympathy, Knowledge, and the Truth, outweigh all that the mixed school can offer.[143]

DuBois spoke neither for the integrationist nor the separatist, but for poor black parents unable to choose, as can the well-to-do of both races, which schools will educate their children. Effective representation of these parents and their children presents a still unmet challenge for all lawyers committed to civil rights.

CONCLUSION

The tactics that worked for civil rights lawyers in the first decade of school desegregation—the careful selection and filing of class action suits seeking standardized relief in accordance with set, uncompromising national goals—are no longer unfailingly effective. In recent years, the relief sought and obtained in these suits has helped to precipitate a rise in militant white opposition and has seriously eroded carefully cultivated judical support. Opposition of any civil rights program can be expected, but the hoped-for improvement in schooling for black children that might have justified the sacrifice and risk has proved minimal at best. It has been virtually nonexistent for the great mass of urban black children locked in all-black schools, many of which are today as separate and unequal as they were before 1954.

Political, economic, and social conditions have contributed to the loss of school desegregation momentum; but to the extent that civil rights lawyers have not recognized the shift of black parental priorities, they have sacrificed opportunities to negotiate with school boards and petition courts for the judicially enforceable educational improvements which all parents seek. The time has come for civil rights lawyers to end their single-minded commitment to racial balance, a goal which, standing alone, is increasingly inaccessible and all too often educationally impotent.

EDITORS' POSTSCRIPT

In January 1976, Professor Kalodner received a number of letters highly critical of the foregoing essay which had been presented at a conference sponsored by the Institute of Judicial Administration in December 1975. In the interest of fairness, excerpts from two of these are set out below.—Eds.

Letter from William L. Taylor, Director of the Center for National Policy Review, Washington, D.C.:

. . . I came away troubled about the future course of your project and the potential impact it may have on efforts to vindicate constitutional rights in

143. DuBois, *Does the Negro Need Separate Schools?*, 4 J. Negro Educ. 328, 335 (1935).

the courts and in other forums. Naturally, much of my concern centers on Derrick Bell's paper, "Serving Two Masters." If the paper is properly viewed as an indictment of lawyers for plaintiffs, I think it would be fair to conclude after the day's discussion that not only was it "not proved," but was seriously challenged.

Derrick made almost no effort to respond to factual and conceptual points that went to the heart of his thesis. For example, he had no answer to my suggestion that leaving aside the question of representing a class, a lawyer has an obligation to seek on behalf of an *individual* client the full relief he is entitled to under law and that such relief frequently entails desegregation of an entire school system. In other words, the problem being discussed stems not so much from efforts to represent a class but from the fact that the relief sought necessarily impinges on the interests of many people both white and black. When I raised this, the discussion quickly turned to the obverse question—What are the duties of a lawyer whose client seeks *less* than the relief to which he is entitled and whose settlement may adversely affect members of the class who wish more? This is certainly an important question but quite different from the one I posed. And it is one not just for plaintiffs' lawyers to answer but for Derrick since he is the advocate of trading off constitutional rights for other, unspecified, gains.

Nor was there an answer to many of the other questions raised—what are the other "educational" interests that could be asserted? Why are they not capable of being asserted either through intervention or the bringing of separate lawsuits? Isn't it true, contrary to the implication of the article, that the prime examples of anti-integration interests asserted by blacks were those of middle or upper income black citizens, not low income people, and that there is no apparent reason why they could not have obtained representation? Further, there was no rebuttal to specific repudiations by Nate Jones [Nathaniel Jones, General Counsel, NAACP] and others of the innuendo throughout the article that plaintiffs' lawyers were insensitive to the interests of their clients and that they failed to consult with them.

Many other questions no doubt could have been raised. Being something of an ancient mariner in this business, I have first or second-hand knowledge of a good many of the past events discussed and to put it conservatively, my understanding does not comport in many places with the selective descriptions and interpretations in the Bell paper.

Letter from Norman J. Chachkin, formerly with the Legal Defense Fund and presently Co-director of the Federal Education Project of the Lawyers' Committee for Civil Rights Under Law, Washington, D.C.,

> *Chachkin wrote, in criticism of the failure to present a paper describing school board counsel's conduct, that such an essay "could easily have been written" accusing*

*"school board counsel of leading their clients' actions for their own finan-
cial or political gain, of advising and implementing unconscionable delays
in the provision of constitutional rights, of blatant and repeated factual
and legal misrepresentations to trial and appellate courts which are characteristic of school desegregation cases." Chachkin continued:* School board
counsel were not called upon in that conference meeting to defend themselves against charges of unethical conduct, and especially charges framed
in the vague and elusive way in which Derrick's paper discusses the subject.
(When you come right down to it, you either accept Derrick's view of reality and reject all others, or his paper loses any substance whatsoever.) In
sum, I think Nate [Nathaniel Jones, General Counsel, NAACP] was right
in being highly offended at the background and structure of the conference, although I thought your handling of the session itself was scrupu-
lously fair.

And the thesis that IJA is just "studying" the subject, "let the chips fall
where they may," is also not a good enough answer. Any lawyer knows
that the response is largely determined by the form of the question. It
should have been evident by the end of the meeting on Friday that Derrick
was speculating from a position of great ignorance about the variety of
tactics and situations which have arisen in school desegregation cases.

Letter from Nathaniel R. Jones, NAACP General Counsel, to the Editors of the *Yale Law Journal*, December 8, 1976.

The three-dimensional article of Professor Derrick Bell, Jr., . . . which appeared
in the March [1976] issue of the *Yale Law Journal*, prompts this letter of response. I discern the three dimensions to be legal, ethical and political.

The political dimension was not lost upon any who have been "in the trenches"
of school desegregation litigation, for it has conditioned virtually all that has
happened in the last few years with respect to efforts to eliminate school segregation. Bell's discussion is vulnerable on a number of counts, and I think it
terribly important for them to be spelled out in the same periodical in which
they appeared.

The political issue was raised as Professor Bell discussed the justification for
reexamining what we are doing about school desegregation. That basic justification is negative public reaction to the desegregation process. There are many
answers to that argument. One is that constitutional issues are, under our form
of government, not resolved by public opinion polls or plebiscites. Another
answer was stated by Louis E. Martin, who heads the 10-member Sengstacke
chain of black newspapers. Since Professor Bell was writing about black interests,
the views of Mr. Martin, who is also black and who also has respectable credentials in the black community, are entitled to great weight. He recently wrote:

What is happening in and about the schools seems to have no relation to
the actual situation, but represents a manipulation of the truth—a sort of

cynical, political and academic sleight of hand aimed at deceiving people about the possibility for change. The result is unnecessary anger, frustration and disillusionment with the schools, with government and with the courts.

The Bell article totally ignores the political conditions described by Mr. Martin as well as the factors that have created this negative public climate. His prescription is to switch rather than fight.

The legal and ethical dimensions of Professor Bell's article are premised on the assertion that civil rights lawyers have "convinced themselves that *Brown* stands for desegregation and not education." From this ground, Bell develops the thesis that civil rights lawyers have failed adequately to represent the interests of children in segregated schools, and thus violated their ethical responsibilities to their clients. (The article is strangely silent on the ethical obligation of school board lawyers, paid by public funds, to consider taxpaying black Americans and their constitutional claims.) The Bell indictment of civil rights lawyers (and the NAACP) fails on several counts, most conspicuously for the simple reason that there is *no* cause of action for educational quality per se. The Supreme Court in *Rodriguez v. San Antonio Independent School District* refused to extend the equal protection clause to encompass issues of educational inequality which are not caused by purposeful racial discrimination. The only constitutional violation, therefore, for which judicial remedies will lie, is racial segregation. When segregation is proved to exist—the violation of the Fourteenth Amendment—federal jurisdiction may be invoked, but only to correct that violation. *To the extent that educational deficiencies are traceable to that unlawful history, the remedy may go further.*

For example, courts have included educational adjuncts and components to desegregation plans when necessary to repair the effects of past discrimination, assure a successful desegregation effort, and minimize the possibility of resegregation. This was done in *United States v. Jefferson County Board of Education;*[1] *Morgan v. Kerrigan;*[2] *United States v. State of Texas;*[3] *Alexander v. Holmes;* and *United States v. Hinds County.*[4]

Professor Bell's evidence for the existence of a legal cause of action for education quality, presented in note 51, proves no more than that *educational quality can be considered in remedies for de jure segregation.* It is thus not civil rights lawyers who have "convinced themselves that *Brown* stands for desegregation and not education," but the courts.[5] The courts up until now have evidently under-

1. 380 F.2d 385, 394 (5th Cir. 1967) (remedial programs).
2. 401 F. Supp. 216, 246, 264 (D. Mass. 1976), *affirmed,* 530 F.2d 401, 428 (1st Cir. 1976), *cert. denied,* 44 U.S.L.W. 3717 (June 14, 1976) (state-financial assistance).
3. 342 F. Supp. 24 (E.D. Tex. 1971), *affirmed,* 466 F.2d 518 (5th Cir. 1972) (staff training, counselling, special education).
4. 396 U.S. 19; 432 F.2d 1264.
5. The United States Supreme Court, on December 15, 1976, granted *certiorari* in

stood, as Professor Bell apparently has not, that segregation is itself the deepest educational harm because it is the result of institutional racism and a condition of state-imposed racial caste. Desegregation would in fact go a long way toward eliminating the educational damages with which Professor Bell is concerned. With integrated schools it is much more difficult to subordinate blacks as a group through unequal or inadequate school resources. Blacks have learned that "green follows white." With desegregation—and white children being reassigned to previously black schools, also comes new resources.

Professor Bell's argument, moreover, curiously seems to blame civil rights lawyers for a "decline" in the "great crusade to desegregate the public schools." It is true that in academic circles, to say nothing of the political realm, the merits of busing have been much questioned of late, but in those cities and towns where integration has occurred with the support of local public officials or school board members, the transitions have been successful. Professor Bell's reliance upon "evidence" from James Coleman is surprising in view of the criticism heaped upon him by his academic peers. In any event, it is clear, despite Bell's assertion to the contrary, that federal courts have been as strong as ever in their support for integration.[6]

If, on the other hand, Professor Bell means to claim that black support for desegregation has declined, this is a more serious charge. Professor Bell correctly points to cases in Atlanta, Boston, and Detroit. However, Professor Bell fails to specify any factual evidence of the extent of those "increasing number of defections within the black community." What is even more disappointing is that Professor Bell has apparently closed his eyes (and his ears) to the ranting and raving of mobs agitated by anti-busing statements and code words from no less an officer of government than the President of the United States. The overwhelming number of blacks favor desegregation and oppose segregation as an affront to their humanity. That some blacks question the desegregation process must be attributed to this shameful demogoguery.[7] With respect to Atlanta, he

---

Milliken v. Bradley. It agreed to hear an appeal of the state of Michigan of a district court order requiring the state to participate in underwriting costs of educational programs. The state argued that the remedy is exceeding the violation. The NAACP is and has been strongly supporting the Detroit board and vigorously opposing the state position.

6. For a detailed list of the numerous northern school desegregation decisions, which stand in bold refutation of Professor Bell's assertions that the courts are backing away on school desegregation, *see* United States v. School District of Omaha, 521 F.2d 530, 535 n.7 (8th Cir. 1975), *cert. denied,* 96 Sup. Ct. 361. To this should be added a July 26, 1976 decision of the Sixth Circuit, *Brinkman v. Dayton Board. See also,* NAACP v. Lansing Bd. of Educ., No. G-305-72-C.A. (W.D. Mich. 1975); Amos v. Milwaukee Bd. of Educ., No. 65-C-173 (E.D. Wisc., Jan. 19, 1976; Arthur v. Nyquist, Civ. No. 1972-325 (W.D.N.Y. 1976); Evans v. Buchanan, Civ. No. 1816-1822 (D. Del. 1975); Reed v. Rhodes (N.D. Ohio, July 31, 1976).

7. The fierce reaction of major black and civil rights organizations last May when the Justice Department considered filing a brief in the Supreme Court on behalf of Boston school officials, refuted Professor Bell's contention that desegregation lacks widespread support.

failed to note that the record reveals a sad history of trial court resistance to mandates from the court of appeals. And he also failed to discuss the "deals" that were cut with the chief victims being lower-income black families. Yet he presents absolutely no support beyond the bland assertions of Ron Edmonds that civil rights lawyers represent only the interests of middle-class blacks. Given the history of widespread black support for and white opposition to integration, the burden is certainly on Professor Bell to come forth with proof of extensive black disaffection.

In light of this discussion, Professor Bell's allegation that civil rights lawyers do not ethically represent the interests of the black community can scarcely stand. In the first place, the legal avenues toward educational quality which he claims we are ignoring simply do not exist. Second, even if disagreement exists within the black community, Professor Bell presents no evidence to support his claim that counsel cannot be obtained "to advocate . . . divergent views." To the extent that those views do not square with the Constitution, they should be and are rejected by courts. Edmonds, while assistant superintendent for public instruction for Michigan, had an opportunity to submit his views for judicial scrutiny. He did and they were rejected.

Professor Bell quotes with approval Edmonds' allegation that the importance of middle-class contributors has determined the fact that civil rights lawyers support desegregation. For one thing this betrays gross unfamiliarity with the way NAACP policy is formulated. Not only is that untrue, it is about as logical as arguing that because a black man is paid by a "white" university his opposition to busing is predictable. Such vulgar economic determinism scarcely deserves comment.

The most important defect of the Bell article is encapsulated in the observation that:

> Those civil rights lawyers, regardless of race, whose commitment to integration is buoyed by doubts about the effectiveness of predominantly black schools should reconsider seriously the propriety of representing blacks, at least in those school cases involving heavily minority districts.

Here is the ultimate fiat behind Bell's article: no one who disagrees with Bell's analysis can ethically represent black plaintiffs. In short, he is inviting the one organization that has led the fight, the NAACP, to step aside. That is not a likely prospect.

Bell, here, also raises a straw man and then dashes him to the ground. No civil rights lawyers who represent the NAACP have "doubts about the effectiveness of predominately black schools." Why does Professor Bell think suits were filed in Detroit and Cleveland? Our view is that a desegregated school or district can be a "majority" black school or district provided there is reflected in the school or district assignment schemes that indicate no state-imposed pattern of disparity.

Emphatically, a desegregated school need not be majority white. What Bell's article ultimately lacks, therefore, is not only analytical and factual precision, and comprehensiveness, but the recognition that lawyers are reaching judgments of feasibility and effectiveness based upon established judicial precedents, which are apparently at variance with Bell's views. This they do without breaching their ethical responsibilities to their clients. To the contrary, they are keeping faith with their clients and the Constitution.

Response by Derrick Bell to December 8, 1976, Letter by Nathaniel R. Jones, NAACP General Counsel

Despite its critical tone, and its quite predictable defense of NAACP litigation policies, Mr. Jones' letter is a document of positive potential. It signals his and, one must assume, his organization's recognition that educationally oriented remedies may be sought appropriately in school desegregation cases. This policy shift will be welcome news for the many legal scholars, black community leaders, and parents who have reported to me their agreement with the positions taken in the "Serving Two Masters" article.

I reviewed there several factors that might explain the rigid reliance by civil rights lawyers on racial balance and busing remedies in school cases. I then suggested (as I have been doing first privately and then publicly since 1968) that for the large and growing percentage of black children living in predominantly black, urban school districts, the *Brown* promise of "equal educational opportunity" might be pursued more effectively through remedies intended to reform those aspects of the segregated system that denied adequate and appropriate school resources to black children, and excluded black parents from meaningful participation in the educational process.

At one point, Mr. Jones reiterates his often expressed fear that relief aimed at educational improvement is not feasible because the courts have refused to recognize a right of "educational quality per se." But happily, he then acknowledges that where racial separation is caused by school board action, it is virtually certain that the responsibility for the inferior schooling provided blacks can be attributed to the same officials. Mr. Jones writes, "To the extent that educational deficiencies are traceable to that unlawful history, the remedy may go further."

He supports this statement by citing several cases in which "courts have included adjuncts and components to desegregation plans." The NAACP's current posture in the Detroit school case is most gratifying of all. There, the state of Michigan has obtained Supreme Court review of an order, urged by the Detoit board, to require educational programs subsidized by the state.[1] Mr. Jones

1. Milliken v. Bradley, 540 F.2d 229 (6th Cir. 1976), *cert. granted,* 45 U.S.L.W. 3363 (Nov. 11, 1976).

reports, "The NAACP is and has been strongly supporting the Detroit Board and vigorously opposing the state's position."[2]

This recognition and support reverses as earlier total commitment to racial balance in Detroit,[3] and should provide a much-needed new thrust to school desegregation litigation in that city and elsewhere. I do not disagree that there is educational benefit as well as constitutional entitlement to racial mixed schools. But the experience of the last decade belies Mr. Jones' assertion that "[w]ith integrated schools it is much more difficult to subordinate blacks as a group through unequal or inadequate school resources."[4] Assigning white children to previously black schools will bring new resources to those schools because, Mr. Jones assures us, "green follows white." But slogans offer little protection against the harsh realities of racism. And the truth is—as the high levels of disciplinary action against black children and their continued low achievement records show—racism as well as money can descend on the desegregated school.

Mr. Jones may reject the studies showing that black children are not making educational progress in desegregated schools. But he can hardly ignore the Supreme Court decisions in Detroit,[5] Pasadena,[6] and more recently in Austin, Texas[7] that will render effective desegregation, particularly in large urban areas, increasingly difficult.

2. In the Cleveland, Ohio school case, the NAACP is seeking educationally oriented relief, as granted in Detroit, as well as racial balance of pupils and faculty. *See* Plaintiffs' Proposed Order Concerning Guidelines For the Desegregation Plan, filed Sep. 20, 1976, in Reed v. Rhodes, Civ. No. C73-1300 (N.D. Ohio).

3. 85 Yale L.J. at 480 n.32, 484 n.38 [p. 579 *supra*].

4. *See*, in addition to 85 Yale L.J. at 480 n.31 [p. 579 *supra*]. Kirp, *Race, Politics, and the Courts: School Desegregation in San Francisco*, 46 Harv. Educ. Rev. 572 (1976); and Miller and Gerard *How Busing Failed in Riverside*, Psychology Today 66 (June 1976).

5. Milliken v. Bradley, 418 U.S. 717 (1974).

6. Pasadena City Board of Educ. v. Spangler, 427 U.S. 424, 96 S. Ct. 2697 (1976).

7. Austin Indept. School Dist. v. United States, 45 U.S.L.W. 3409 (Dec. 7, 1976), *vacating* 532 F.2d 380 (5th Cir. 1976). The *Austin* decision is particularly ominous. The Fifth Circuit had condemned the school board's neighborhood school policy which, because of segregated residential patterns, resulted in the assignment of 45 percent of the system's Mexican-American students to predominantly minority schools.

In a *per curiam* decision, the Court remanded the case for reconsideration in light of Washington v. Davis, 426 U.S. 229 (1976). The relevance of the *Davis* case is apparently its elevation of standards for proving discriminatory intent. Upsetting a lengthly list of lower court decisions, the Court in *Davis* held that the use of an unvalidated employment test that excluded a disproportionately high number of black applicants did not require its invalidation under constitutional standards. It was not, the Court said, a purposely discriminatory device, if intended to upgrade communicative abilities of employees in jobs where such ability was important.

It requires only a meager imagination to predict how the new *Austin* standard of segregatory intent will be interpreted by some members of the Supreme Court in future cases. Indeed, while concurring in the *Austin* result, Justice Powell, joined by Chief Justice Burger and Justice Rehnquist, urged inclusion of the issue of remedy in the remand order because, in his view, extensive busing plans ordered by lower courts are exceeding the constitutional violation they are intended to remedy.

A possibly unfavorable judicial response to a civil rights position is no reason to repress rather than espouse it. But the thrust of my article was that a substantial percentage of black parents have become disenchanted with the results of relief relying on racial balance and busing, and thus politics and professional ethics dictate reassessment of that policy. My article documents and Mr. Jones acknowledges black disenchantment in Boston, Detroit, and Atlanta. But he rejects the conclusion that these examples typify attitudes of blacks across the country.[8]

There may be communities where racial balance remedies continue to enjoy substantial support, but most black and white parents, as W. E. B. Du Bois asserted, are more concerned with the quality of their children's education than with either integration or separation.[9]

Mr. Jones need not accept my assessment of black parental priorities, and his letter makes clear his belief that my criticism is unwarranted. But to the extent that his statement reflects a new recognition of the importance of educationally oriented remedies, the interests of those he represents will be better served, and the conflict between integration ideals and client interests will be headed toward resolution.

Such strict standards of proof, combined with closely circumscribed views on remedy, could undermine chances for racial balance and educationally oriented remedies in future cases. In this less favorable judicial climate, it is essential that civil rights lawyers communicate more closely with clients and class about both harm alleged and remedies sought.

8. I have been working closely with one of several black community groups who are concerned about the educational value of racial balance and busing remedies obtained in their behalf by civil rights lawyers in school desegregation cases. This group, called BUILD, is located in Buffalo, New York. In 1968 this group obtained control over an all-black elementary school, BUILD Academy. This school remains predominantly black although it is open to children throughout the district. In recent years, levels of academic achievement at the school have risen dramatically, and moral of students, parents, and teachers is remarkably high.

Responding to a desegregation plan proposed by plaintiffs' experts that would involve large-scale busing and the closing of BUILD Academy, the group published a statement containing the following language:

> Our primary concern is quality education. We view Desegregation/Intergration or "racial balance" as one means to that end. We do not equate racial balance and a quality education as absolutely one and the same.
> . . . .
> Since integration (racial balance) has not always proven to be a panacea for quality education in other northern cities where it has been implemented, we believe that the Buffalo Board of Education should incorporate an alternative approach into their desegregation/integration plan. Thus, if racial balance fails to produce the desired and expected gains in reading levels and general mastery of educational skills which will enhance the ability of black youngsters to compete in the academic and economic marketplace . . . we strongly recommend that the concept of community involvement in decision making concerning curriculum, governance, and personnnel as was well as general school programs and operations (similar to BUILD Academy) be expanded to include pre-K through twelfth grades.

BUILD's Recommendation about Buffalo's Desegregation/Integration Plan, Buffalo Challenger, August 11, 1976 (copy of statement on file at Yale Law Journal).

9. 85 Yale L.J. at 515 (p. 611–12 *supra*).

COMMENTARY

The Professional Educator in the Desegregation Suit

Forbes Bottomly

A critical relationship in the implementation of a desegregation decree is that between the trial judge and the educational planner. Situated between an often hostile educational system and the legalistic approach of the court, the educational planner finds himself in a difficult and insecure position. Forbes Bottomly, a former superintendent of schools in Seattle Washington, examines the problems of communication between the court and the educator, offers suggestions for resolving these problems, discusses guidance a court might give educational planners, and outlines the variables with which planners usually focus on in implementing a comprehensive desegregation plan. Forbes Bottomly is chairman of the Department of Educational Administration at Georgia State University. —Eds.

In a desegregation case, the relationship between the trial judge and the educational planner—the defendant superintendent of schools or the person designated to head the desegregation planning process—is often complex and frustrating. Yet in the dynamics of desegregation the mutual understanding and rapport these two are able to attain may determine how well the desegregation order is implemented. Those professionals caught up in desegregation litigation and the planning for remediation—specifically, the trial judge, the attorneys, the educational planners—may serve that cause by working to improve communications among themselves.

This is easier said than done. The glare of publicity which attends desegregation cases often works against efforts to improve communications. Litigants are sometimes seduced into making public statements from which retreat or compromise is difficult. Then, too, the parties are usually in court because the plaintiffs have exhausted administrative remedies, an exercise which in itself tends to leave a disputative and querulous residue. As Shoemaker and others have found, the administrative routine is sometimes so elaborate, so slow and complex as to indefinitely delay access to the courts or even to hide the real reason for denial.[1] Therefore, the trial judge in accordance with his or her style may end up helping litigants to save face, pouring oil on troubled waters, or perhaps sternly laying down the law.

In exploring this relationship, I will first examine some of the most difficult problems of communications, and second, attempt to provide suggestions for resolving them. Third, I will dwell briefly on the guidance a judge might give to the planners of desegregation designs. The last section will outline the variables with which planners ordinarily must deal in developing a comprehensive desegregation program.

PROBLEMS OF COMMUNICATION

The very nature of desegregation provides a deep-seated source of tension.[2] School officials have often known that their systems were in violation of the law, yet because of local, state, and—more recently—national political pressures, they have felt unable to take the appropriate affirmative action to desegregate without coercion.[3] These may be people of good will who are liberal in their racial outlook. When the Seattle School Board set in motion its own affirmative action desegregation effort, as superintendent I was often asked by colleagues and patrons why the board did not wait until ordered to do so by the courts. Their argument, in effect, was: Let the court take the heat. My reply was that, "while laying it on the judge" may be the easiest route to follow, it nevertheless depreciated the legislative function of the board. Where a judge is forced to take on legislative functions whenever a board shrinks from its responsibility, or is obliged to assume administrative functions in working out and implementing a remedy when the professional school staff retreats, communications are certainly not enhanced, nor is the judicial system strengthened. Such use of the court places unwarranted encumbrances on the court calendar. It also saddles the judge as an individual with the burden of public anger and hostility over a highly emotional issue. Besides, one might ask, What kind of an example does the board set for the students of a school system when teachers are attempting to instruct in theories of political science and respect for the law?

While some of this attitude on the part of school people may be due to an understandable desire to keep the school board free of controversy, or to a wish

1. D. Shoemaker, *et al.,* With All Deliberate Speed, 13 (1957).

2. A re-study of the Report of the National Advisory Commission on Civil Disorders (1968) reveals the depth and complexity of the problems of racial division and their consequences.

3. Report of the United States Commission on Civil Rights, Federal Enforcement of School Desegregation (September 1969); *see also* Martin, *Getting Desegregation Done* 8 Integrated Educ. (September 1970), at 41–46.

to avoid being involved in difficult decisions, or maybe to plain perversity, much of it is also due to a lack of understanding of the growing manner in which people are using the courts to seek social and personal justice. The legal process has reached into the system and structure of the schools to touch the lives of individual children and teachers not only in the matter of desegregation, but also in areas of citizenship rights, discipline, and even curriculum.

Because of this intrusion, I suggest a workshop on the role of the courts for all school administrative personnel. Working on the theory that understanding is good preventative medicine, Seattle attorney Gary Little from time to time conducts a series of such workshops for local school board members and administrators. The results appear to be a reduced reliance upon the courts to resolve problems and a greater effort to use responsive administrative means to do so. Such workshops, while carefully avoiding allusions to any pending or immediate litigation, show how relief is sought by those who believe that their rights have been violated. For example, an imaginary plaintiff who asks for a declaratory judgment establishing his or her right to attend a desegregated school, and to restrain defendant school officials from depriving that right, is followed through the process as a case study. A school official often plays the role of the plaintiff, walking, as it were, "a mile in the other person's moccasins."

It may be revealing to an educator to examine other available legal actions such as mandamus, taxpayers suits; even the growing possibilities which lie in suits for damages against school officials personally for harm purportedly done by past violations of rights. The parents' actions in the Topeka case[4] would be an excellent lesson. There, nothing was done to desegregate some schools until the plaintiffs filed a suit against the local school board, the state board of education, and the Department of Health, Education and Welfare asking for damages in the amount of $200 million for children who had attended inferior segregated schools during a ten-year period. In addition, the workshop might profitably review the procedures which govern the court and their importance to the judge not only in arriving at a finding, but also in the search for a remedy.

At the point of seeking a remedy, the relationship between the trial judge and the litigants changes. It is one thing for a judge to wade through the facts to arrive at findings; it is another to develop a desegregation order that will satisfy the litigants and also be constitutionally sound enough to withstand an almost certain appeal should it not satisfy them. The judge's purpose now becomes one of finding a workable solution, and the need for clear communication becomes paramount. The judge must set forth a procedure for arriving at the proper order, then weigh the conflicting arguments in terms of law and precedent. The educational planner, on the other hand, now released from the legal battlefield of guilt or innocence, is nevertheless often under the political pressures. The pressures make it difficult to develop a plan, or optional plans, based upon sound data,

4. Johnson v. Whittier, Civ. No. T-5430 (D.Ky., September 10, 1973).

and which will provide the necessary relief and the maximum in educational benefits. Under these conditions, the importance of understanding of one another's role in the process cannot be overemphasized.

As a minimum in such an effort is the use of plain language. The reduction of the esoteric professional lingo of the educator and the technical usage of the lawyer to unassuming, everyday terminology would go a long way toward reducing blocks to communications. Circuit Judge J. Skelly Wright observed that after hearing arguments and re-arguments for a full year, and listening to "expert" witnesses, the real issue was so hidden in an overgrown garden of numbers and charts and jargon that he was finally compelled to make his judgment on the basis of "straightforward moral and constitutional arithmetic."[5]

In a Seattle case[6] I spent a number of hours on the stand explaining a plan to integrate the Seattle junior high schools by converting them to middle schools and instituting such educational reforms as continuous progress, individualized learning, enquiry pedagogy, spiral curriculum, team teaching, and media centers. The plaintiffs were seeking an injunction in a state district court against the school board and the superintendent to prevent implementation of the integration plan. From time to time the judge would interrogate me, and from the nature of his questions it was apparent that he was having difficulties in squaring my terminology with his ideas of schooling. We were enjoined both in our efforts to desegregate and to institute the accompanying educational reforms.[7] Only after special pleading by Seattle school counsel, Gary Little, who was able to translate my pedagogical verbiage into ordinary language did the judge recant sufficiently to allow us to continue with the reforms, albeit without the integration.

Equally important as plain language is the need for educators to understand that the solution requires the use of carefully prescribed legal procedures. Senior Judge Frank A. Hooper, who patiently guided desegregation in the U.S. District Court of North Georgia for a period of fourteen years, reflecting upon his need to keep legal procedures intact, has said, "because I was a Southerner, I was determined to avoid any semblance of impropriety."[8] The emotionalism attendant upon the desegregation efforts in some southern states along with the intense political reactions by governors and legislators[9] stressed the need to operate within very narrow procedures. "A judge must keep the legal requirements foremost; social aspects should be kept apart," Judge Hooper emphasized. It was, perhaps, this emphasis on adherence to procedure which brought en-

5. Hobson v. Hansen, 327 F. Supp. 844 (D.D.C. 1971).

6. Citizens Against Mandatory Busing v. Palmason, 80 Wash.2d 121, 492 P.2d 536 (1971).

7. An action later sternly reversed by the Washington State Supreme Court in C.A.M.B. v. Palmason, 80 Wash.2d 445, 495 P.2d 657 (1972) (*en banc*).

8. Interview with Senior Judge Frank A. Hooper.

9. Southern Regional Council, Inc., The South and Her Children: School Desegregation 11 (1971).

forcement of *Brown* throughout the South, while in the North the issue has become increasingly politicized at the state and national levels.[10]

But educators have found themselves impatient with the procedures. Under pressure from parents, school board members, employees, and politicians, they view the scene from a social-political-educational position. They often have strong feelings about what constitutes sound education and believe that they have an understanding of the social dynamics of their communities. They are afraid that legal precedents developed under the exigencies of other cases in other parts of the nation might be uncritically applied as solutions in their school districts.

A veteran of desegregation planning, as superintendent of schools in Chattanooga and in Atlanta, John W. Letson, accepts the judgment of the court as a legal mandate; but believes that the remedy is not a legal matter so much as one of social engineering. "The remedy oftentimes does not, and should not, require the narrow point-of-law approach. A legal precedent doggedly pursued without regard to local social or educational consequences may lead to the defeat of the very end which the remedy seeks."[11] He is concerned that the requirements of cross-busing along with judicial application of prescribed ratios of black and white students and teachers may aggravate the white flight to the suburbs with the consequence of central-city resegregation. His views have been reinforced by recent statements by sociologist James Coleman, who sees the school district boundaries arising as new instruments of segregation.[12] Judge J. Skelly Wright has warned, "In our metropolitan cities we are setting up two geographically, politically and equally distinct civilizations . . . whites have taken the city limits as their protective shield against integration."[13]

A classic example of the dynamics of white flight is Richmond, Virginia. According to Sam Sentelle:

> The Richmond city schools sustained a loss of approximately 1,000 white students each year from 1965 through 1969. In 1969, the student population ratio by race was 70.5% black and 29.5% white. With implementation of a new desegregation plan in 1970, the city showed a loss of 3,900 whites. From 1970 to 1971, nearly 4,000 white students left the city schools making a total loss of more than 7,800 whites over a two-year period.[14]

10. Farrell, *School Integration Fight Hardens in Shift North,* 4 J. Law & Educ. 194, 196–97 (1975).

11. Interview with John W. Letson, now dean, School of Ed., Valdosta State College.

12. *See* Coleman, *Recent Trends in School Integration,* 12 Educ. Researcher 3 (1975), and countervailing views by Jackson, *Some Limitations in Coleman's Recent Segregation Research,* 57 Phi Delta Kappan 274–75 (1975).

13. Reported in 13 Integrated Educ. 24 (March-April 1975).

14. Sentelle, *Racial Mixing by Consolidation in Richmond, Virginia,* 101 Intellect 164 (December 1972).

Cullen states that "In Memphis, the public schools have lost 38,000 white pupils since 1971. Private schools, almost all white, have gained 23,000 students. The black-white ratio has gone from nearly even to more than seventy per cent black."[15]

The next logical step, of course, would be to pursue relief by crossing the city boundaries to include the suburbs in desegregation efforts. This was attempted in Richmond. The Federal Court for the Eastern District of Virginia in its January 10, 1972[16] ruling said that any effort by the central city alone would be doomed to failure. Gordon Foster suggests that there is a lesson to be learned from the desegregation experiences in those areas where city and suburbs have been consolidated, such as Nashville, St. Petersburg, Charlotte, and the county units of Florida. "There is simply no suburb to which one can flee, since no school in the total metropolitan area is racially identifiable."[17]

But for the children isolated in most city school systems there appears to be no such relief. Until legislative action provides a metropolitan solution which, despite the recent Louisville experience,[18] appears unlikely to have wide appeal, or until the Supreme Court finds that school district boundaries have been used to deprive plaintiffs of their constitutional rights, further relief appears foreclosed.

I have dwelt on the white flight not to make value judgments here about all-black cities surrounded by all-white suburbs. Examining and speculating about the consequences of the human ecology which is bringing that about would make a significant study for social and political scientists. The point is that a decision by a trial judge, however heedfully he or she might separate social issues from legal procedures, will have powerful long-term social consequences.

Educators want these possible consequences to be considered by the court before its determination of a desegregation order. They are apt to point out that in *Brown,* "the [Supreme] Court, departing from conventional dependence on judicial precedence, based its judgment . . . largely on what was referred to as the authority of modern psychological knowledge."[19] If the Supreme Court can make such a departure, then a federal district court can also, they argue. And they might turn the Court's statement in *Swann* to their own meaning: "once a right and a violation have been shown, the scope of a district court's equitable powers to remedy past wrongs is broad, for breadth and flexibility are inherent in equitable remedies."[20]

15. Bradley v. School Board of City of Richmond, Virginia, 338 F. Supp. 67 (E.D. Va. 1972).

16. Cullen, *White Flight Plagues South,* Atlanta Journal and Constitution, Sunday, May 18, 1975, at 16B.

17. Foster, *Desegregating Urban Schools,* 43 Harv. Educ. Rev. 33 (1973).

18. *See* Weher, *School Merger: It's A Family Affair,* Louisville, 46–55 (June 1975).

19. Smith, *An Analysis of Court Ordered Desegregation,* 57 Nat'l Ass'n Secondary School Principals Bull. 34 (April 1973).

20. Swann v. Charlotte-Mecklenburg Board of Education, 402 U.S. 1, at 15 (1971).

"What I would like to see," reflected John Letson, "is the possibility for school people to discuss these racial and educational ramifications with the trial judge outside the confines of the adversary situation which legal procedures seem to require."

While educators may be concerned about legal procedures, the trial judge may upon occasion be impatient with reluctant educators. "[I]n any school desegregation case where violation of the Fourteenth Amendment has been found," writes Noel Fox, "the responsibility for providing a remedy lies with the school authorities."[21] This may be somewhat akin to the ancient admonition about putting the fox in charge of the henhouse. For Baratz has indicated, in her study of the Washington, D.C. case of *Hobson v. Hansen,* that those who resisted change are the ones responsible for rectifying the wrongs. Unless there are great punishments or rewards it is unlikely that they will seek to make the plaintiffs' ideas work.[22]

But "remedial judicial authority does not put judges automatically in the shoes of school authorities whose powers are plenary. Judicial authority enters only when local authority defaults."[23] The judge cannot continually supervise the schools no matter how derelict the school officials might seem. Therefore, unless the school officials themselves help plan as well as carry out the desegregation orders, there will probably be persistent tension between the court and the educators.

Another source of tension has been the problem of extracting needed data from school systems. While the history of desegregation is partly a history of courage on the part of school people who have risked their jobs, or even life and limb, to accomplish affirmative action and to insist on obedience to the law,[24] it is also partly a narrative of footdragging, procrastination, excuses, resistance, and failure of nerve.[25] A paralysis often seems to set in when administrators feel themselves in the vice between the hostility of parents and school boards and the requirements of the court, a paralysis that makes the compiling of even simple data a monumental task.

The result is an institutional tendency to exaggerate the problems of budging a school bureaucracy and the difficulty in obtaining such accurate statistical information as is required in planning a remedy. A recent evaluation by Baratz of the District of Columbia's implementation of the 1971 decree "revealed that 60% of the schools studied in 1974 were out of compliance, mainly because of poor management, and lack of information."[26] The District's projections were

21. Fox, *The Kalamazoo School Decision,* 11 Integrated Educ. 81 (May-June 1973).
22. Baratz, *Court Decisions and Educational Change: A Case History of the D.C. Schools, 1954-1974,* 4 J. Law & Educ. 78-79 (January 1975) [hereinafter cited as Baratz].
23. In *Swann* (402 U.S. at 15), the Court expresses impatience at the deliberate resistance to court mandates, and at dilatory tactics.
24. Affirmative School Integration (Hill & Feeley, eds., 1968).
25. Swann v. Board of Educ., 402 U.S. 1 (1971).
26. Baratz, *supra* note 22, at 77.

off and its records did not even have the right number of buildings. In Boston the court-appointed masters found that "the system projected an enrollment for Fall, 1974 of over 93,000 students, yet *no* day since September, have more than 71,000 students materialized. The typical day has shown attendance of less than 70,000.[27] In Jacksonville, Florida, the school system used excuses to thwart the court's efforts to secure vital information on pupil residence. According to Entin, such information translated to dot maps "would have allowed the use of affirmative gerrymandering as a more effective and less costly alternative to the massive degree of busing finally required. . . ."[28]

Another dilatory tactic school officials have used is the offering of proposals such as "freedom-of-choice," "open-enrollment," "magnet schools," "resource centers," and "third-site" programs, all of which allow parental choice and which have been declared insufficient by the courts. The persistence with which defendant school officials present such plans knowing that they are not acceptable must at times test the court's patience. Yet another method is to design a proposal so elaborate and so costly as to appear infeasible.

To a school person, the desegregation case is a once-in-a-lifetime event. To a judge it is one of an endless chain of plaintiffs and defendants. It is difficult for school officials to understand that working out remedies is a burden on judicial time; that the judge usually has a backlog of cases, large and small, all of which carry a great obligation for seeing justice done.

IMPROVING COMMUNICATIONS

These areas of tension speak of misunderstanding about not only expected outcomes, but also how those outcomes will be achieved. Granted that the trial judge has broad powers to order compliance with the law, it seems to me that the effectiveness with which the order is carried out may be enhanced through face-to-face efforts to understand the part each plays in the whole drama.

The history of desegregation is marked with strong and courageous court orders, some of which have been carried out with diligence, others in disturbing numbers have been given only a surface semblance of compliance. Iron-clad rules have been more form than substance. For, as Baratz has indicated, while a court can "successfully order a school system to rectify specific, 'objectively measurable' disparities, be they distribution of children, teacher services, dollars, or textbooks, it cannot successfully decree reform."[29]

Dean Letson believes that an educational planner would welcome an opportunity, temporarily away from the formal adversary procedure, to relate to the

27. Report of the Masters in Morgan v. Hennigan, 379 F. Supp. 410 (D. Mass. 1974), March 31, 1975, Appendix E, at 2.

28. Entin, *The Black Burden in Jacksonville Desegregation,* 10 Integrated Educ. 8 (July-August 1972).

29. Baratz, *supra* note 22, at 78.

judge his concerns, apprehensions and hopes for reform in the educational system and accommodation within the community. And the judge, judicial propriety aside, may appreciate the opportunity to educate the educator in the legal process, its workings and limits, its protections and its history. My own anxieties about the judicial process have been eased by such discussion—indeed, as my knowledge has increased as to the role of procedure in the pursuit of justice so has my feeling of confidence in the system.

As a beginning, the educator should understand the constraints placed on a federal district judge. With all its potential powers, the district court is bound by directions from the appellate courts. If such directions may be at variance with the district court's views of the law, they must nevertheless be honored. Knowing the importance of this internal discipline of the court system may help planners understand why the judges behave the way they do.

Educators, along with the general public, lacking adequate understanding of the court's role in the total system, have been inclined to fault a judge's actions. And in the past, not recognizing the need for positive public information, judges have often parroted or rephrased the language of the Supreme Court without giving an explanation of the factual basis of the decision.[30] More recently under mounting criticism, the courts along with school people have become more public relations conscious. If school officials are at all constructive community opinion-makers, as they have been historically,[31] they will surely use whatever knowledge about the judicial process they acquire in a positive way, helping to allay the fears of the public. As Gaston has reported in his study, such positive leadership has been associated with progress in integration:

> In those schools where whites and blacks have created successful integration, one common crucial factor has been intelligent community leadership. In districts where desegregation has been a failure—where true integration never had a chance—community leadership ranged from good-intentioned mindlessness to outrageous intransigence.[32]

To help with the understanding, I recommend a retreat, in the judges chambers, of the professional parties to the suit where an exchange such as this might take place. It would be off the record. Chronologically it would be after the verdict has been reached, but before the desegregation order has been issued. In this way it will not influence the finding of fact and the verdict, yet be early enough to allow the judge to consider the input in developing the order for remedial action. A nonadversary climate of open expression would prevail, a climate enhanced by an agreement that the attorneys for the litigants, although

---

30. Blaustein & Ferguson, Desegregation and the Law 221 (1962).
31. McCloskey, Education and Public Understanding 24 (1967).
32. Gaston, *The South: Goals Still Distant But Many Schools Go Well,* South Today 3 (December 1970).

present, would not speak. The purpose of the retreat would be simply an exchange of views between the judge and educators. I know that some judges would consider such a meeting as improper, and should such a meeting take place that attorneys might feel very uncomfortable as the school problems were elaborated, but it may well yield a determination on the part of the participants to search for a reasonable and lawful solution, a solution which, once found, could be implemented with mutual support.

JUDGE'S GUIDELINES

How the court proceeds with a desegregation order guides the approach which the educational planner takes. The judge may make a sweeping injunction leaving the local school administrator to grapple with the day-to-day details. If this is done out of knowledge of the resources available to carry out the order it may be the kind of strong leadership needed with an obstinate community. But if it is done out of the judge's exasperation over footdragging, or because of his burdened calendar, or perhaps worse, out of his lack of understanding of the complexity of the process of desegregation, a lack which leads him to oversimplification, there may be trouble ahead in enforcement. A fear hardly based on experience that a judge may order massive busing for the next school year when buses are not available and planning time is inadequate haunts educational administrators.[33] In such a situation the school system's attorney may be back in court time and again asking the judge for clarification of this or that, pleading for a delay, and protesting that adequate resources are not available. In addition, the plaintiff's attorney will surely be asking that the judge set aside time to hear complaints about noncompliance. The judge may be deluged with a large number of pieces, large and small, of the complex educational patterns which make up a desegregation plan.

United States District Judge Albert A. Henderson, Jr., of the Northern District of Georgia, believes that the judge should avoid getting mired down in the minute details of desegregation planning. If the judge issues a broad order which clearly sets forth the legal requirements, the planners will have room to develop the details. He prefers to have the planners bring in several options from which he might choose, modify, combine, or use as a reference in developing a remedy which is adequate. The judge would be wise to require in the order that the planner provide a justification for each recommendation presented in the plan or plans.[34]

As part of its effort to facilitate compromise the court may seek the help of

33. Much of this type of dread may be based upon misperceptions arising out of national publicity given to such actions as that of the Charlotte, North Carolina School Board, which voted to postpone opening of school in the fall of 1970 because, it claimed, the U.S. district judge's order would require 526 new buses that would cost over $5 million.

34. Interview with Judge Henderson.

a third party. Judge Hooper appointed a biracial committee of ten prominent persons, five black and five white. He asked for fifteen nominations from the white and fifteen from the black communities before appointing the ten. There was no objection from either on the makeup of the committee. He met with this committee from time to time, always on the record, to receive progress reports and to help prevent impasses. While such a procedure required of the judge considerable time away from other pressing duties, he believed that the dynamics of desegregation cases required a unique relationship among the participants. He saw the judge's role as that of "pouring oil on troubled waters" and the judge's demeanor that of exercising great patience.[35]

Another model is that of the court hiring an outside consultant to develop a plan. This is often done when a defendant school district is unable to provide the expertise for doing so, or where the district is intractable, or where conflict rages over several plans developed by different constituencies. An example of this model is that developed by United States District Judge W. Arthur Garrity, Jr. Faced with an explosive desegregation situation in Boston that had become entangled for years in state litigation and political furor, Judge Garrity appointed a panel of masters whose eminence and prestige was beyond question. The panel was presided over by Jacob J. Spiegel, former Justice of the Massachusetts Supreme Judicial Court. The other members were Francis Keppel, chairman of General Learning, Inc. and former U.S. Commissioner of Education; Edward J. McCormack, Jr., former state attorney general; and Charles V. Willie, respected Harvard University professor. In making the appointment Judge Garrity wrote:

> The Court has before it several voluminous proposals for school desegregation. Because of the complexity of the various plans that have been filed, the need for speedy determination of a plan to go into effect in September, 1975, and the value of expertise in a number of fields relevant to such determinations, the court is appointing a panel of masters to conduct hearings and make recommendations to the court.[36]

The masters were charged with examining the various proposals and plans which had been developed and with making recommendations for the desegregation of the Boston public schools. "The masters are to be guided in evaluating . . . the plans by the remedial guidelines set forth in the court's opinion of June 21, 1974, in the court's order of October 31, 1974, other relevant rulings in this case, and by the constitutional and legal standards set forth in applicable cases and statutes, including *Swann v. Charlotte Mecklenburg Board of Education,* 1971, 402 U.S. 1; *Green v. County School Board,* 1968, 391 U.S. 430; *Keyes v.*

35. Interview with Senior Judge Frank A. Hooper.
36. Order of Appointment and Reference to Masters, Morgan v. Kerrigan, E.D. Mass. Feb 7, 1975 (Garrity, J). It should be noted that none of the appointees was particularly experienced in desegregation planning. Staff under the direction of Dean Robert Dentler of Boston University provided the expertise.

School District No. 1, Denver, Colorado, 1974, 380 F. Supp. 673, and the Equal Educational Opportunities Act of 1974, 20 U.S.C. §§ 1701-58."[37]

The order asked that provisions be made for the desegregation of vocational schools, athletic programs, and that consideration be taken of bilingual education, special education, including advanced work classes, and others. It allowed the panel to recommend magnet schools and metropolitan options, provided they helped bring about prompt system-wide desegregation.

It also described the procedure which the masters would follow, their compensation and directions for reporting their recommendations. The guidelines were broad, yet specific enough to satisfy the judge's constitutional requirements. The references to citations, however sufficient for legally knowledgeable planners, may not provide enough specifics for the educational planners. For example, what is meant by desegregation in terms of student ratios, teacher ratios, busing times, and what kinds of variations would be allowed?

The Planner's Adjustment

The professional school staff of a defendant school district has probably gone through several desegregation planning phases before the court order calls for "a plan that promises to realistically work, and promises realistically to work now."[38] The first phase was a defensive one. As school officials become aware that segregation existed and foresaw possible court action, they devoted themselves to gathering data to defend the school board against charges of de jure segregation. Later, the planners—under growing pressure from black parents and civil rights leaders—came to admit that de facto segregation at least existed, by recommending to the school board open-enrollment types of opportunities for student attendance. These voluntary transfer programs, as token desegregation efforts, usually began with parents paying their students' transportation; later the school district provided the transportation costs. The next step usually was the closing of some black schools and transporting children to white schools. Then, to counteract the charge that one-way busing laid the burden exclusively on black children, the idea of magnet schools, third-site programs, resource centers, and other attractive names for enriched educational sites come into vogue.[39]

During this time the educational planners carefully watched the evolution of constitutional law on the subject. As lay people they were often perplexed by the apparent conflicts within the judicial system as the meaning of desegregation emerged in various courtrooms. Each new case tended to approach a definition and provide a precedent. Some judges began to accept the plaintiff's view that a

37. *Id.*

38. In Green v. County School Board, 391 U.S. 430 (1968), the U.S. Supreme Court expresses impatience at the delays in carrying out constitutional requirements.

39. For an excellent description of the stages of desegregation, *see* Mercer, *et al., Racial/ Ethnic Segregation and Desegregation in American Public Education,* National Society for the Study of Education Yearbook 292 (1973).

ratio of black and white students in each school—indeed, in each classroom—was the only remedy that would meet their requirements. But Judge Hooper disagreed with this view. He pointed out that the United States Supreme Court on more than one occasion ruled that busing should not be ordered solely for the purpose of attaining a uniform ratio of students throughout any school system. But despite such ruling, he observed, many district judges and circuit courts of appeal have not observed the statements of the Supreme Court.[40]

The planners were also confused by what appeared to be the politically reactive, on-again-off-again enforcement tactics of the Department of Health, Education and Welfare civil rights officials.[41]

These uncertainties, when added to the need to respond sensitively to their local school board's political position on the matter, often placed the school system's educational planners in a defensive mode. It is a large adjustment to move from a position of defensiveness to a positive one requiring affirmative planning for remediation and compliance after the court makes it findings.

The Judge's Law

In addition to the retreat suggested above, the court may facilitate the planning process by laying out rather explicit criteria. It may not be enough for the court to refer to *Swann, Green, Keyes, Milliken,* and applicable federal laws and leave it up to the planners and their lawyers to make the appropriate interpretations. As an educational planner I would appreciate having a clear definition of adequacy in at least the following areas:

1. The tenable limits within which students may be assigned to schools to achieve constitutionally acceptable desegregation.
2. The degree to which optional attendance zones, neutral sites, magnet schools, and alternative programs fit the law.
3. The variance, if any, from the tenable limits which will be allowable for special education for the handicapped, for the gifted, for kindergarten children, for athletic and other extracurricular programs.
4. The definition of desegregation within a school as well as within a school system, such as prohibition against tracking ability grouping and other segregative assignments.[42]

40. Interview with Senior Judge Frank A. Hooper.
41. The HEW enforcement officers of the Civil Rights Act who were so energetic in aiding the courts in southern desegregation, after the inauguration of President Nixon found themselves in a crossfire from Capitol Hill and the White House. After Leon Panetta, who headed the enforcement effort, was fired, HEW enforcers began asking for delays.
42. In Hobson v. Hansen, 269 F. Supp. 401 (D.D.C. 1967), Judge J. Skelley Wright ordered the D.C. school authorities to do away with ability grouping, an action which outraged many school people who saw the judge's action as an invasion of pedagogical prerogatives.

5. A definition, with tenable limits, of a desegregated staff, including teachers, administrators, and nonteaching employees.
6. A guide for the equitable distribution of resources among the schools, including the use of Elementary and Secondary Act Title I funds.
7. A meaning of "burden"—that is, the measure to which desegregation may be achieved through the burdening of minority students and minority communities with school closures, one-way assignments, busing distances and other inconveniences more than the majority pupils and communities.
8. A definition of "reasonable" transportation times and distances.
9. The extent to which metropolitization may be considered in a remedial plan.
10. Other instructions such as a timetable for submission of the plan or plans; target date, at least, for implementation; a description for an appeal procedure for hardship cases; and a process for monitoring the plan, once implemented.

If the judge's order is inadequate, if it demands too much too soon, or is too vague in defining the legal requirements as the judge sees them or, indeed, if he or she leaves constitutional requirements to be defined through compromise between the defendant and plaintiff, the way is opened for delay and ambiguity in the planning process and the implementation.

In addition to these ten points I suggest that the judge make some statement about the need for quality education. If this cannot be done appropriately in the order, it may be done in other ways. The Boston masters, for example, footnoted a quote Judge Garrity made in a district court hearing to the effect that a desegregation plan must not be simply a physical reshuffling of students. There should in addition be a deep concern for educational dimensions, and the necessity of considering the quality of education.[43] The masters drew upon this in their narrative: "[W]e believe . . . that a plan should assure not just proper assignment of students, but also educational programs appropriate to the special needs of students who have been victimized by segregation."[44]

THE PLANNER'S RESPONSE

The same may be said for the educational planner. If one does an inadequate job of gathering and interpreting data to support a definition of what constitutes good education, or if one fails to point strongly to the implications of possible judicial actions upon education, one is opening the door to serious educational and sociological problems.

After receiving the judge's criteria, the educational planner may deal with the variables that go into the mapping of a desegregation plan. These ordinarily are:

43. Report of the Masters, *supra* note 27, at 19.
44. *Id.* at 18.

- Student population identified by domicile, race, and socioeconomic characteristics.
- Racial composition of the student populations of each school.
- Socioeconomic and educational characteristics of the total district population by residence.
- Total population and enrollment projections.
- Number, capacity, condition, and location of educational facilities.
- Organization of the educational system by grade level.
- Staffing patterns, assignments, and racial composition.
- Transportation available and projected needs.
- Financial needs, with budgeting practices and procedures.
- Description and location of special programs, alternative schools, and kindergartens.
- Applicable state laws, rules, and regulations governing the schools.
- Accrediting agency requirements.
- Public information needs and public involvement.
- Resources outside the schools, such as private schools, higher education, businesses, and associations.
- Curricular and instructional methods, materials, and needs.
- Multiethnic rights and needs, with concern for cultural identity and pluralism.
- Staff, parents, and student human-relations training requirements.
- Options for hardship cases.
- Time limitations and deadlines for implementation.

This list is not all-inclusive, but reveals the complexity of the enterprise. If the school system is fortunate enough to have a conscientious planning staff, it will try to develop a plan that incorporates essential educational reform along with lawful desegregation. If not, the most a judge might expect is superficial compliance. Baratz has pessimistically observed that the professional reservoir of ideas is low and that "the professional resources necessary to effecting change are not available."[45] I am more optimistic. What the planners do not want to do is to develop a plan that will fail because it demands too much of a system and its people. They want to avoid what Baratz reported in the D.C. case: the court-developed plan actually created more crises for the school structure and its people and offered an opportunity for them to act out their struggles on one another.[46]

A Planning Process

The first step is for the planners to look carefully at the characteristics of the entire school district and its neighboring areas. Topographical maps are excellent

45. Baratz, *supra* note 22, at 79.
46. *Id.* at 78.

for this purpose, with schools plotted and notated by capacity and level. Map overlays of clear acetate sheets upon which is shown information related to family incomes, educational levels, employment, property value, transportation routes, home ownership, and the percent of the tax dollar spent on education may be helpful. This information is available from state agencies, city and regional planning offices, and U.S. Census Bureau. When one lays over this a dot map showing domiciliary areas by race, a pattern begins to emerge. After careful study of this configuration the planners with a marking pencil may begin to outline areas of desegregation that would bring about the most promising kind of integration—namely, the integration which includes socioeconomic factors, occupational and educational consideration, as well as racial balance.[47] As Stuart Smith has pointed out, the "indiscriminant mixing of social classes will result in educational and social chaos and not in integration."[48] The areas outlined, insofar as possible, should take into consideration traditional areas of political and social service such as ward, precincts, and other service areas. These may be valuable in communicating and resolving problems as the program is implemented.

Besides, the idea is to maximize the feeling of community within the areas and minimize the sense of disruption. In a large urban district such areas of desegregation, besides providing a better community feeling, may set the stage of a decentralized administration of the program. The whole process is closer to the people, more community-oriented, and thus easier to manage. Care must be taken, however, to assure that student desegregation in each area meets the guidelines set by the judge for the entire district.

At the same time, this preliminary inspection would show the most feasible transportation routes. Overlays developed from the statistics of the metropolitan transportation engineers show streets by peak traffic use as well as pinpointing safety problems. The importance of projections of population growth and decline, and of land-use information, cannot be overemphasized. As one can readily see, the planning staff would be well served by the expertise of an urban planner.[49]

Every school district will have significant information about the student population. This information will usually be computerized and easily retrieved in various combinations. The Seattle School District pioneered the computer technique of geocoding pupil data.[50] By this process all students were identified, on a finely gridded map of the city, as to place of residence and by race, age, grade, and other significant educational planning data. This gave the planners

47. *See* Jackson *et al., Perspectives on Inequality: A Reassessment of the Effect of Family and Schooling in America.* 43 Harv. Educ. Rev. 37–164 (1973).

48. Smith, *supra* note 19, at 42.

49. This is the approach taken by the staff of the Metropolitan Planning Project in developing the desegregation plan, Metro Ways to Understanding (MASBO Corp., Winchester, Mass., 1974).

50. Report of the Superintendent's Task Force on Desegregation Planning (Seattle Public Schools, February 1972).

the capacity to quickly develop simulations to test alternative desegregation plans, with the additional aid of computer print-out maps. By 1977 such a system is available to major metropolitan school districts.

Student enrollment projections by grade, by individual school, and by race are needed. Because of the rapidly changing population characteristics of American cities, these should be carefully developed and tenable limits set forth within which future enrollments would probably fall. The weighing of factors that relate to living quality, such as the growing energy shortages and pollution problems, in relation to their possible effect upon future residential patterns ought to be explored. Educational planning no longer can afford to go it alone unconcerned with other forces in the environment, for to a large degree it has been those factors which brought the present problems of racial isolation to the schools.[51] Educational planning and comprehensive urban planning are part of the same process.

Based upon population projections and an assessment of the capacity and usability of buildings, the planners will, perhaps, run a series of simulations within each desegregation area, as defined above, to determine various methods for reaching the legal racial composition set forth by the judge. While these simulations would try various approaches,[52] I would suggest that there be some that run across school district boundaries into the suburbs. The projection of student enrollment in many cities of America will show a future time when the black population is of such size as to prohibit in-city desegregation. Many cities have already passed that mark. Such information may be of value to a judge if one wishes to consider at all the social consequences of various plans and continue to weigh the possibilities of relief through metropolitan approaches.

The simulation runs provide the planners with the means for working out optional transportation routes. With geocoding the computer is able to map them relatively easily. However, before accepting any such plan it is recommended that someone with a stop-watch and a school bus actually make the runs under live conditions. No amount of careful map-reading will reveal all the realities of time, distance, and safety on the streets. Given the emotionalism surrounding busing, one may predict a challenge on these points. The number of buses required and the unit cost per mile of providing transportation under the various options will have to be calculated. In this regard it would be well to have comparative data with other similar cities and other districts in the state. The political and economic purpose is to achieve the legal requirements with the least possible busing.

Students with special needs must be given special consideration. In the Seattle plan, "those students will not be reassigned who require special facilities, pro-

51. United States Commission on Civil Rights, Equal Opportunity in Suburbia (July 1974).

52. *See* Flannery, *School Desegregation Law: Recent Developments,* 10 Integrated Educ. 11–19 (May-June 1972).

grams, staff, or other special treatments that are impractical to provide in a regular school setting. This exclusion would apply to special education programs; certain alternative programs, such as Project Interchange, Title VIII programs, and certain experimental programs, except where comparable education may be offered."[53] The Boston masters believe that special needs override the desegregation requirements, but call for integrating of handicapped children into each area's schools.[54] Inclusion in the plans of provisions for the education of the talented, those needing bilingual instruction, extracurricular programs, kindergarten, and preschooling will prevent later problems.

Any integration plan today will also include consideration of the identity needs of minority children. To promote this, a strong component of curriculum development assuring due recognition of the part minority cultures and minority persons have played and do play in America should be included as a part of the program of all children. And those symbols which are the relics of slavery and second-class citizenship—songs, flags, epithets, dress codes—and which have to do with intimidation, need to be eliminated in a desegregated school.[55]

An essential part of desegregation is that of staff assignment. The court will usually decree the desegregation of the teaching staff. And if past hiring practices have been shown to be discriminatory, it may also order the development of an employment plan that will compensate for such discrimination.

Many court-ordered plans of the past have thrown black and white children together with little attempt to help prepare the way. The results have been chaotic. Well before the first bus runs, training sessions for teachers, parents, and student leaders will set the scene for a smooth opening. Indeed, superintendents, principals, secretaries and custodians need such training, too, because they all help to set the school climate. To help with this a district may call upon experts from the U.S. Office of Education or from colleges and universities where experts are available. Seattle, which at first used the services of those proficient in Thomas Gordon's *Effectiveness Training* programs, later developed its own team of trainers.[56]

The inclusion of outside resources in the plan makes considerable sense. As I have said, the schools cannot go it alone. Help from the institutions of higher learning, from business and industry, from other governmental units and agencies provides a broad base of support as well as increased educational options. The Boston master's plan has not only detailed such possibilities, it has provided for the original contacts with such resources and the obtaining of preliminary commitments.[57]

53. Report of the Superintendent's Task Force on Desegregation Planning, *supra* note 50, at 55.

54. Report of the Masters, *supra* note 27.

55. Henderson, *Is It Worth It?* 4 J. Law & Educ. 43–62 (1975).

56. *Staff Development . . . Human Relations Training,* In Touch [Citizens Committee for Quality Integrated Education Publication] (July 22, 1971).

57. Report of the Masters, *supra* note 27, at 44–50.

Of all the aspects of the plan, none is more important than public information. Very careful and detailed methods for keeping the public informed as to how the plan, if accepted, is to be implemented will prevent chaos and the resulting anger and frustration. The wise planner will develop very clear messages to parents and students telling them exactly how the program will work, informing them specifically where to go and what to do. Messages worded with reassurance will help to ease the anxieties always felt in desegregation cases.

Also at this juncture a means for parental involvement in specific school activities might be solicited. Descriptions of parent committees and boards for school support would help parents in their desire to get involved. As a matter of effective administration, the educational leader would take advantage of the restructuring required to relate the schools more closely to the real needs of the community. Here may be a chance with parental help of making progress in career education. Continuous progress, individualized learning, and the development of school resource centers may be enhanced because of parental concern. Advances in the basic skills of reading, writing, speaking, and arithmetic can be made. It has been my experience that educational improvement is more closely related to parental involvement than any other single variable the schools are able to affect.

The judge will look closely at cost factors. Program budgeting and cost estimates for all aspects of each plan are valuable parts of the report. The use of a program planning budgeting format will help the planners demonstrate the relationship between projected expenditures and outcomes.

Planning is a technical process, and the use of the computer will speed up the handling of complex data. Yet it must be remembered that desegregation is a human activity. The planner is not a master chess player moving people here and there as in a game. The dynamics of integration, while it includes legal requirements, educational considerations, social science, and technical knowhow, is fundamentally a sharing of responsibility. The process has graduated from the stage of condescending white planners manipulating black students to achieve desegregation with as little discomfort to the white population as possible. An understanding on the part of the educational planner that majority and minority power is to be shared equitably in the process will go a long way in establishing healthy relationships not only in the desegregation process itself but in the climate of the schools later on.

The judge and the planner are dependent upon each other. Where there is clear communication, an understanding of one another's roles, and well-defined legal requirements, the planning process stands to go well. If the judge is assured that optional plans presented are carefully designed, workable, educationally sound, and sensitive to community needs, he will have confidence after weighing them against the criteria of constitutionality and feasibility in selecting one for his order. And who knows, perhaps out of this relationship and understanding may come a finer definition of what the Constitution really requires in our search for racial justice.

Index